Ed Wood,
Mad Genius

ALSO BY ROB CRAIG

The Films of Larry Buchanan:
A Critical Examination (McFarland, 2007)

Ed Wood, Mad Genius

A Critical Study of the Films

ROB CRAIG

McFarland & Company, Inc., Publishers
Jefferson, North Carolina, and London

LIBRARY OF CONGRESS CATALOGUING-IN-PUBLICATION DATA

Craig, Rob, 1954–
Ed Wood, mad genius : a critical study of
the films / Rob Craig.
p.   cm.
Includes bibliographical references and index.

ISBN 978-0-7864-3955-3
softcover : 50# alkaline paper ∞

1. Wood, Edward D. (Edward Davis), 1924–1978 —
Criticism and interpretation.   I. Title.
PN1998.3.W66C73   2009   791.4302'33092 — dc22   2009017911

British Library cataloguing data are available

On the cover: (foreground) Ed Wood, Jr., circa 1950s (Photofest);
(background) "Flying Saucer Resurrection"
(Digital illustration by Curt Pardee)

Manufactured in the United States of America

*McFarland & Company, Inc., Publishers
Box 611, Jefferson, North Carolina 28640
www.mcfarlandpub.com*

For Mom and Dad

Acknowledgments

Film lovers in general, and Ed Wood fans in particular, owe a great debt of thanks to Wade Williams, the super-collector who almost single-handedly rescued the films of Edward D. Wood, Jr., from certain oblivion. His Herculean efforts at preserving and remastering these films, and offering them for new generations to enjoy through exemplary VHS and DVD releases, are largely responsible for the contemporary cult of Ed Wood. Indeed, films such as *Night of the Ghouls* would never have seen the light of day were it not for Williams' dedication to preserve the legacy of Ed Wood. It goes without saying that without Williams' passion for making Wood's films available, book projects such as this could not exist, and the author is eternally grateful. The author would also like to extend sincere thanks to the following people, without whom this work would have been impossible: Doyle Greene, for invaluable comments and suggestions; Kalynn Campbell, for his singular insight into the artistic process; Ian Sundahl, for procuring rare screening materials; Rylan Bachman, for sharing his encyclopedic knowledge of the dancers from *Orgy of the Dead*; Scott Mitchell, for supplying rare Wood short fiction; Greg Woods, for his enthusiasm in preserving the legacy of underappreciated films and filmmakers; Greg Luce and Mike Vraney, for continuing to discover and preserve forgotten films; and my wife Elisa, for her unflagging support of creative effort.

Table of Contents

Preface

I first encountered the films of Edward D. Wood, Jr., one sunny afternoon circa 1980, when a revival house screened Wood's *Plan 9 from Outer Space*. Even with the fuzzy focus, tinny sound and catcalls of the inebriated audience, the remarkable splendor of Wood's vision came shining through, and by film's end I was a bonafide Wood devotee. Afterwards, the Medved Brothers, authors of a book called *The Golden Turkey Awards*, the first to introduce Wood to a mainstream audience, held court in the theatre lobby, surrounded by doting fans, and pontificating on *Plan 9*'s lamentable ineptness, giving as evidence such anecdotal nonsense as hubcaps used as flying saucers, a claim which anyone paying attention could instantly deny. I spoke with a smaller group in the corner of the lobby. We breathlessly discussed what we knew to be true — that Wood was a daring and utterly unique outsider film artist, a wildly creative producer of bizarre personal art, and a filmmaker of sublime stature.

Unfortunately, the condescending view posited by the Medveds and others took hold, and Wood became legend not as a film artist of note, but as a freak of nature, a literary clown, an alcoholic buffoon of fringe Hollywood, a filmmaker so awkward and unfocused that he had inadvertently created, with *Plan 9 from Outer Space*, "the worst film of all time." Discarding the patent absurdity of such a claim, Wood's films are in fact neither bad, nor good — they are art; astounding, bizarre film-poems with many, many flaws, and many more hypnotic charms.

This book is not a biography of Wood the man, nor is it a history of his career as filmmaker, nor a chronicle of his prodigious literary output (volumes all waiting to be written, it would appear). It is simply a meditation on his films, along with some thoughts as to themes, motifs and passions which recur with notable regularity. To my mind, the canon of Edward D. Wood, Jr., is an august one, a rare treasure of 20th century independent film, a group of films most extraordinary, deserving contemplation and reflection. It is hoped that this modest volume will add to a discussion of these films on their own merits, and give Wood his long-awaited due as a modern film artist of note.

Introduction

Edward D. Wood, Jr., is one of the most famous filmmakers of all time. This is as it should be. However, the reason for his fame is ironic, misleading, and highly suspect. Wood's infamous films, such as *Glen or Glenda?** (1953), *Bride of the Monster* (1956) and *Plan 9 from Outer Space* (1959), have acquired reputations as some of the worst motion pictures ever made, and Wood thusly dubbed as "the worst director of all time." Dismissing the patent absurdity of such a quantifiably unverifiable claim, still the notion of this filmmaker creating such wretched output bears scrutiny. What exactly, makes Wood's films so fascinating, yet repugnant, to so many?

Certainly, Wood's films are low-budget, and boast an undeniable primitivism. Yet many other films, and their filmmakers, might easily fit the same description. Film, above all, is an economically based art form; one can only spend on a motion picture what one has secured from backers. Especially in the exploitation film genre, a field Wood was intimately familiar with, threadbare productions were ubiquitous, and there is many an exploitation film far shoddier than anything Wood ever attempted.

Also, Wood made films which, although shot on the lowest possible budgets, tackled subjects and landscapes perhaps beyond the films' potential scope, resulting in peculiar mini-epics, which in some cases seriously overshot their marks by stretching their meager budgets too thin. As well, Wood cast his films with an eclectic combination of fading stars from a previous generation, and peers from the Hollywood area who could only be called "fringe" or "outsider"; folks who were either marginalized actors or else not actors at all, pulled into service to enact roles for which they may have been ill-equipped.

Finally, Wood primarily functioned throughout his career as a writer, and it is his bizarre hyperbolic prose which graces his films with their singular iconoclastic charms. Wood's prose haunts his films in two ways. Firstly, the lurid, overreaching dialogue conveys a hyper-dramatic world not even remotely resembling actual speech or situation. Secondly, Wood's tumultuous exposition and wild structural experimentation assure that his films will follow an unpredictable narrative track unlike similar films of the era, or the melodramatic tradition in general.

The end result of these aesthetic quirks are films which overstep the boundaries of normal narrative cinema at every turn, and often look more like experimental cinema, or avant-garde theatre, than commercial film product. Under-rehearsed non-actors spout Wood's fastidious prose in overwrought ecstasy; plots meander, stall and take violent turns from accepted expositional theory; the story hatches within a dingy, dime-store universe where the threads of the actors' costumes, the cardboard props, and the makeshift interiors are at times

---

**The original film was released without the question mark but later versions added the question mark and it has become part of standard use.*

3

painfully obvious. One might even be tempted to call Wood's films "amateur," so obvious is the hand of the artist. Yet these same films, several of which saw major mainstream theatrical releases, are undeniably entertaining, have a striking if insular logic, and ultimately share an aesthetic allure and philosophic integrity which is undeniable. They are, in short, the work of an artist.

Although they adhere ostensibly to B-movie genre formula, Wood's films have as much in common with the artistic avant-garde as with conventional Hollywood tradition. Intentionally or not, they also share a good deal with the Absurdist theatrical tradition. Additionally, Wood's writings have many of the qualities of avant-garde poetry, and it is these factors intermingled which make Wood's films so much more than, indeed anything *but*, "the worst motion pictures of all times."

As many film buffs (and authors such as Susan Sontag and Annalee Newits) have gleefully attested, much of filmdom's scruffier and more ungainly product may be readily consigned to the status of "camp" or "cheese." These ironic, yet derisive terms earmark the films as having entertainment value only when their audiences disparage the texts for those very flaws and shortcomings which purportedly entertain. Although the "camp" and "cheese" movements differ on nitpicking points regarding the films' origins and desire to intentionally entertain through either designed or inadvertent incompetence, both camps invariably label the texts as inferior products, worthy only of ridicule from a supposedly superior audience.

Aside from the snide presumption and intellectual snobbishness in this position, there is the question of intent. Can a film (or any cultural text) which was created as straightforward entertainment thus engage an audience in ways not originally intended by its maker, and be noted as such? More significantly, can films whose shortcomings, or differences from traditional cinematic fare, are undeniable, be appreciated as legitimate films texts? Certainly, the bounty of "trash cinema" yields many rough treasures, exciting and confounding texts which delight even as they baffle. Film scholar Doyle Greene has astutely stated of that august canon, "so-called bad films through their strange and unconventional aesthetics achieve avant-garde, confrontational qualities—as unintentional as that effect may be."[1] Wood's entire *oeuvre* may well fall into that category.

The notion of low-budget narrative film, lovingly dubbed by both fans and detractors as "trash cinema," serving as something more than meaningless ephemera and worthy of adoration if not study, has gained credence of late, thanks to writers like Jeffrey Sconce who, in his seminal 1995 essay "Trashing the Academy: Taste, Excess, and an Emerging Politics of Cinematic Style," coined the term "paracinema" in an attempt to codify various genre of film which had heretofore been considered throwaway commercial product, unworthy of reverence or serious study.[2] Sconce and others have proposed, quite effectively, that throwaway cinema product (primarily exploitation and genre B-movies, but also including films foreign to a native culture) significantly reflect not only the prejudices and passions of their maker(s), but profound social issues of the culture and time period whence they sprang. An examination of these films offers as much about their prevailing cultural environment as their maker(s), and are worthy cultural documents, brimming with historical and aesthetic artifact. Again, Greene suggests, "many films consigned to camp or cheese status may in fact represent a form of alternative and even experimental cinema through their very disregard of conventional form, coherent narratives, and cinematic realism."[3]

Wood's films are an innovative if awkward stitching of conventional Hollywood syntax with a wildly personal "counter-syntax," via Wood's idiosyncratic writing and threadbare production values. Primarily, Wood was influenced by the American B-movie mythos in toto:

Legendary independent filmmaker Ed Wood contemplates his good fortune as he kneels before his idol, mentor and "cash cow," horror icon Bela Lugosi, during rehearsals for Wood's inaugural feature, *Glen or Glenda?* (1953).

the crime thriller, the western adventure, the pulp fiction nightmare, the exploitation potboiler. There is an emphasis on melodrama, and often occasions of shocking structural detours, strange plot twists, and hyperbolic dialogue carried to uncanny limits. Wood borrowed from, as often as he departed from, some honored conventions of classical Hollywood cinema, yet his meager budgets and idiosyncratic authorship skills assured that his screenplays would come to life as anything but bland, predictable Hollywood fare. And the notion of classical Hollywood cinema being a "fixed" genre with immutable rules is itself a notion undergoing increased scrutiny, as stated succinctly by Greene: "Hollywood genres themselves become exhausted, evolving from their classical innovative state to a period of self-reflexivity and internal critique to an all-out conscious parody of the genre itself."[4]

Perhaps too much has been made about Wood's childhood in Poughkeepsie, New York, and his mother's habit of periodically draping him in little girl's dresses.[5] While several accounts verify that this occurred, the extent to which this ritual was performed is unknown. And while it most certainly had an impact on the young boy Wood, this practice was not all that uncommon.[6] The reasons for parents performing this apparently eccentric act on their offspring are complex and obscure, and cannot be analyzed sufficiently here. At an unconscious level, it might appear that the parent was attempting, through this highly symbolic, virtually alchemical act, to integrate the child's psyche by balancing both genders equally, and undertaking an experimental merging of Jungian anima and animus archetypes into one integral, potentially well-adjusted whole.

On the conscious level, the parent's motivations for this masking of the child's true gender may have been much more petty, crude, even cruel. In addition to signaling an infantile wish on the part of the parent that the child were, in fact, the opposite sex, the (presumably involuntary) forcing of foreign clothing onto the child assuredly had the chilling effects of humiliation and emasculation on the usually male subject. As such, it acted as a brutal, but highly effective, power play over the child, reducing him to a powerless "clown," replete with absurd and shameful costume.

Regarding Wood, one can never know how this behavior affected his psychology. That he appeared to embrace this ritual of wearing female clothing well into adult life, and even championed the phenomenon in his films and writings, does not necessarily mean that he endorsed or celebrated the practice, although such would be his apparent agenda in several cases. It is equally likely that the donning of female clothing was still, in adulthood, a self-inflicted punishment, a psychologically triggered act of shame that was, conceivably, compulsive and out of his control. If this were the case, it would suggest that the parents' thoughtless act in childhood had a far more damaging, far-reaching effect on Wood's psyche than even they, in their self-absorbed righteousness, might care to acknowledge. This occurrence, for better or worse, likely went far to make Wood the iconoclastic creative outsider he subsequently became.

Regardless, the obscuring or "masking" of one's gender, one's true self, through symbolic coverings would become a major theme in Wood's art, most overtly in his surrealist autobiography *Glen or Glenda?*, but also in other films and writings. This symbolic act of hiding one's self with an emblem such as a sweater or mask signals moral rebirth in *Jail Bait*, untamed "bestial" lust in *The Bride and the Beast*, and sullied innocence in *Night of the Ghouls*. Thus, this sad and obscure psychological quirk in Wood makes for a most engaging and enduring thematic template in his art. Should one finally thank the parents, or merely forgive them? After all, in Wood's own words, "They didn't know what the hell they were doing to me."[7]

Crafting his films in the viciously competitive environment of low-budget 1950s independent cinema, Wood managed to forge a series of wildly innovative features under virtually impossible financial, economic and one might daresay psychological conditions. Working completely and utterly alone, an indefatigable outsider even in his own Hollywood community, Wood toiled endlessly to bring his strange vision of the world to an audience, an audience which barely noticed him at first. Wood's audience came later, and in droves, and this posthumous adoration is the acid test of the visionary artist. The irony is that although Wood might be considered a flop as a mainstream commercial filmmaker, as an outsider film artist he may yet become a sort of god. It seems likely that the legend of Wood as an exemplary outsider artist will last far longer than his ersatz reputation as a mere "bad" director.

Ed Wood's films undeniably reflect the political and cultural environment of postwar America. The fixation on religion which haunts all of Wood's films suggest a troubled but powerful spiritualism, a creative and morally centered mind struggling to deal with the many cursed ethical issues of the day. Wood's films are filled to the brim with sacred rituals, the dead coming to life, spiritual battle in the very heavens, and always at root, puny man's horrible freedom of will, to choose to do good, or evil, a freedom which causes him no end of mischief and despair. In the end, Wood shows his audience how to achieve personal salvation through unconditional love for one's self and for all others. Wood was also intrigued with the social roles of men and women, the shifting roles of gender in postwar America, and he champions throughout his films a joining of forces between men and women, between Jung's anima and animus, between Freud's Eros and Thanatos, before all hope for the world is lost. This notion is expressed most succinctly in Wood's recurring suburban couple, a male/female dyad which represents a dystopian heterosexual coupling always on the verge of collapse, yet always with the promise of radical personal and societal evolution.

One might finally consider Wood a clever agent-provocateur who used his meager films as a soapbox upon which to preach his message of love, peace and tolerance for all creatures, for unconditional acceptance of the outsider, the eccentric and the rebel in a society which seems bent on ostracizing and/or destroying same. As such, some see Wood as a spiritual leader, a remarkable poet-philosopher, a veritable messiah of mass culture. Wood fashioned a parody Christmas card in the early 1950s in which he dressed himself up as Jesus Christ, apparently a role model for this spiritual seeker, and adorned the photograph with the words, "Lo, I Am with You Always." Thanks to the films, his "sacred texts," Wood's uncanny prophecy has come true, probably until culture itself implodes.

1

Selected Short Subjects

During his days as a U.S. Marine in the Second World War, possibly in the Battle of Tarawa, Edward D. Wood, Jr., by his own account, stabbed a Japanese guerrilla numerous times, momentarily entranced in a murderous frenzy, virtually hacking the man to pieces with his bayonet even after the soldier was presumably dead.[1]

How this explosion of wanton bloodlust, and the subsequent trauma it produced in Wood, affected his later adult life, and most importantly his art, can only be intuited. Yet this singular event likely helped shape his nihilistic view of life, and the concurrent obsession with death and resurrection, which occurs in virtually all of his works. The fixation with the resurrected and vindicated spirit of the deceased which propels most of his films could be said to be a function of guilt, of in some way wishing back to life a soul which the author had dispatched with uncharacteristic violence. By all accounts a sensitive and compassionate man, Wood must have been horrified at being put in a situation such as that which occurred in the Pacific Rim, and even more horrified at the passion with which he took to killing this foreign soul conveniently designated as "the enemy."

Granted, the war created very real and easily identifiable enemies, and in fact the Japanese soldier had attacked Wood as well, knocking out most of his front teeth with either a bayonet or rifle butt,[2] so the killing was ostensibly a regrettable but understandable act of self-preservation in a combat setting. Still, to a life-loving man such as Wood, the event must have caused him great grief, perhaps even torment. It was a life-changing encounter which undoubtedly haunted Wood the rest of his days. We can see the spirit of the slain Japanese soldier in his very first film, *Crossroads of Laredo*. It reappears in the recreated thug in *Jail Bait*, in the resurrected police lieutenant in *Plan 9 from Outer Space*, in the various goblins which prowl the earth in *Night of the Ghouls*, even perhaps in the guiding demon-spirit of Criswell in *Plan 9*, *Ghouls* and *Orgy of the Dead*. It is the spirit of someone trying to reenter the living world, attempting to have his prematurely stifled voice heard, and make perhaps a change for the better before passing, once and for all, into the fathomless ether of time.

Wood was one of many artists who excelled at the short form (TV commercials, short subjects, television pilots, etc.). In both writing and film, Wood's genius came to life most gloriously in short bursts of prosaic ecstasy, vignettes and set pieces which may or may not have benefited from trying to string them together in longer sets of narrative collusion. Wood's feature films absolutely benefit from these rapturous sketches full of hyperbolic prose and surreal incident; it is what gives his features their episodic, always-surprising structure. Yet it is unfortunate that many if not most of his shorter works are elusive and unavailable for review, for perhaps it is here that Wood's creative genius was at its most pure and distilled.

Wood's first film, a half-hour Western called *Streets of Laredo* (circa 1948), remained unfinished for decades until Brett Thompson, C.J. Thomas, and Dolores Fuller took the extant silent footage and added narration, cobbling together a reasonable facsimile of what Wood likely intended with the piece, certainly a forerunner to his later, extant short Western, *The Crossroad Avenger* (1953); the restored *Streets of Laredo* (retitled *Crossroads of Laredo*) is included as an extra in the DVD release *The Haunted World of Edward D. Wood, Jr.* (2005).

Thanks to Greg Luce, the tireless film archivist at Sinister Cinema, two more of Wood's earliest film ventures are also available to enjoy. The first, (*Trick Shooting with*) *Kenne Duncan* (1952), is a promotional film commissioned by Remington Firearms, and *Crossroad Avenger* (1953) is a western-themed television pilot film. In each, we can see Wood excelling in the short film form, and each has surprises in store, hints of future themes and settings.

Crossroads of Laredo (circa 1948)

Crossroads of Laredo, the reconstructed version of Edward D. Wood, Jr.'s first film project *Streets of Laredo*, showcases the neophyte director at his most awkward and enthusiastic, yet prophecies some of Wood's future obsessions in uncanny ways. The 16mm film was originally shot in 1948. Wood's first business partner, and co-producer of the film, John Crawford-Thomas, saved the footage from oblivion and, with Wood collaborator Dolores Fuller, digitally restored the film in 2005. The resultant video, clocking in at 23 minutes, is included in Bret Thompson's excellent documentary *The Haunted World of Edward D. Wood, Jr.* (2005, Image Entertainment).

Understandably primitive, shot silent and with sound added only in the video restoration, *Crossroads of Laredo* comes across as primarily an example not of modern, postwar cinema, but of the silent-era Western film, a genre Wood grew up with and loved dearly. *Crossroads* can thus be seen not only as an unwitting homage to silent cinema, but also as a most important landmark in Wood's career, representing Wood's own personal "silent era."

While the newly composed score by Ben Weisman and Dolores Fuller is pleasant, and additional narration by Cliff Stone does effectively patch numerous glaring plotholes in the ambiguous scenario, it is probably best to watch *Crossroads* as a silent film, as the film footage is what clings closest to Wood's original conception. Also, by focussing on the visual, one can see Wood's early attempts at crafting charming, if primitive, visual tableaus with small casts and meager resources, a writer's talent which would reach marvelous evocation in later feature projects, and which boasts some memorable scenes even in this virtually amateur production.

In *Crossroads*, Wood plays a pivotal character who is killed off briskly at the film's opening. This shocking murder of a sympathetic character, a sacrifice of spiritual import which leads a troubled community to a convulsive but ultimately healing metamorphosis, is a plot point which occurs with unerring frequency in the balance of Wood's films, and may be his most prevalent recurring theme. It is thus quite significant that Wood himself plays this archetype in his very first film. One can certainly see subsequent manifestations of this character in many Wood films, from Zeke in *Crossroad Avenger* to Glenda in *Glen or Glenda?* to police lieutenant Daniel Clay in *Plan 9 from Outer Space*.

This recurrent template may well represent various colorful masks for Wood himself, their deaths the author's symbolic death as he endures, artistically and personally, the painful yet immortalizing apotheosis of martyrdom, resurrection and finally sainthood which represents the fate of the suffering, starving artist who goes unappreciated in his time. As well, this persistent figure may well be the ghost of the Japanese soldier Wood killed during his military career, his continual resurrection an attempt by Wood to address his grief over the apparently unavoidable, yet undeniably traumatic event. At the least, Wood's sacrificing of himself in the first minutes of his very first film project is a significant moment, certainly suggesting some sort of ritualistic atonement of guilt towards an horrendous, life-altering act which, occurring just a few years previously, was certainly still fresh in the perpetrator's mind.

The film opens with several close-up shots of a hand holding a six-gun in its holster, presumably insert shots meant to be used elsewhere in the finished film, but which effectively illustrates the most recognizable icon in Western cinema, the cowboy's gun, and underscores the film's allegorical phallocentrism. The narrator offers the following by way of sketching the main narrative: "As our story opens, a handsome young cowboy has sold his herd of cattle in San Antonio, for top dollar, and is just riding through a little crossroads town near Laredo. He aims to look up an old friend, and repay him for loaning him his stake." The scene switches to show the young cowboy (Wood) riding towards town on horseback. Another cowboy, Tex (Don Nagel), who has been made aware of the young cowboy's good fortune, lays in wait for him. Both men ride off from the local general store, in an opening scene repeated almost verbatim in Wood's television pilot, *Crossroad Avenger* (1953).

Following is an impressive shot of the two cowboys riding down a dusty trail, with farm dogs yelping behind them, a fairly sophisticated bit of alluring *mise-en-scène* in the threadbare production. Tex catches up with the young cowboy on the outskirts of town and forces him to drop his weapons. In a most felicitous bit of unrehearsed hyper-realism, the young cowboy's horse keeps walking in front of him, as if sensing the danger his friend is in and trying to protect him. Tex shoots the young cowboy in cold blood, a reckless plot point which nonetheless sets up the subsequent scenario and tellingly, if awkwardly reflects the soul-crushing violence of the just-ended world war. As mentioned, this highly ceremonial death also specifically addresses Wood's self-loathing over the traumatic killing of the Japanese soldier, a symbolic act of self-destruction which likely meant much to the sensitive young author.

A collage of confusing shots follow, with wildly varying points of view, which the narrator tries to clarify. Most interesting here is a tracking shot of the trail, from the supposed perspective of Tex, a crude yet effective point-of-view shot which looks like it could have been snipped out of a chase scene from one of D.W. Griffith's Biograph films.

Tex arrives back in town, and chats briefly with the sheriff (Chuck LaBerge) and the parson (Christopher Longshadow). A dance hall girl sneaks up behind Tex and surprises him, leading the haunted killer to draw his gun on the poor woman, a crude visual depiction of guilty conscience which again employs common silent film syntax. The dance hall girl offers herself to Tex, who kisses the woman passionately, until another dance hall girl joins them and suggests they all retire to the saloon. An awkward unraveling of the film's plot by the narrator introduces the film's two main characters, Lem (Duke Moore) and Barbara (Ruth McCabe). During this exposition, there is an impressive exterior scene in front of the saloon which features a good number of players, including cowboys, drunks, prostitutes, etc., an interesting attempt by Wood to insert as much production value as possible into this tiny film.

Lem goes to Barbara's nearby bungalow, a ramshackle structure which distinctly evokes the mythos of the postwar suburb, the new frontier. As the two old friends walk together back towards town, Tex, exiting the saloon, sees the mystery man chatting with the community's rarest, most valuable asset, a good woman, a prize he immediately covets. Lem enters the saloon while Tex makes time with Barbara. Lem subsequently sees Tex and the fickle Barbara making out, but decides against intervening. Under a spreading chestnut tree, the wily Tex propositions the presumably lonely and vulnerable woman. According to the narrator, "Tex has had a lot of women, and knows just what to say. He tells Barbara that he's loaded, and that the parson's right over there. Let's get hitched! He sweeps her off her feet, and she happily agrees." The parson walks off arm in arm with the happy couple, perhaps a sly comment by Wood on the blindness of religion towards corrupt, potentially disastrous partnerships, or worse, suggesting complicity in their formation and sanction.

Time passes. Barbara stands at her front door, visibly unhappy and with bags under her eyes, suggesting weariness and/or spousal abuse. The narrator confirms this impression: "Now a whole year has gone by, and Barbara is starting to find that being married to Tex is not all it's cracked up to be. Tex spends all his time at the Crossroad Saloon, floozing with the girls, and maybe more. But Barbara loves Tex, and tries to make the best of things." The next shot shows Tex sitting against a tree, cleaning his gun and smoking a cigarette, a perfect illustration of the sullen, lonely male citizen of phallocentric culture, a pathetic, real-life Marlboro Man, isolated from his loved ones, his very environment, an infantile male animal completely rejecting his anima. Barbara walks out of the house carrying a baby which is wrapped in a blanket. This quirky image is yet another throwback to the era of silent melodrama, where long-suffering women and their ill-fated offspring were a ubiquitous icon of vulnerability in a hostile environment, an elemental visual token of fragile civilization in the silent western's primeval jungle of deadly conflict.

Barbara walks up to Tex, who rebuffs both wife and child with a crude hand gesture, reinforcing in elemental form the patriarchal male's self-absorbed, infantile agenda. Tex's visual posture of phallocentric selfishness is underscored by the attending narration, presumably intended to be dubbed-in dialogue as witness the actor's simultaneous mouthing of the words: "I don't need you, or your squalling brat! All I need is my gun, and the money it gets me! I'm outta here!" This cruel, puerile confession confirms that Tex is indeed the archetypal wayward son of patriarchal culture. The further allusion to his phallic surrogate as being key in his attainment of fortune pegs him clearly as a latter-day entrepreneur-capitalist, a specific emblem of postwar America. As the villain in Wood's makeshift microcosmic universe, Tex becomes a symbol of pretty much everything that was wrong with late-model capitalism, in a scruffy if charismatic nutshell.

Having rejected wife and child, and spurning adult responsibility, Tex rides into town, where he hopes to escape his domestic imprisonment and enjoy the perks of ill-gotten capitalistic enterprise, those generic adolescent thrills available to anyone with appropriate coin. Tex's horse could be seen as a surrogate for transportation in general, the modern automobile specifically, that almost-magical machine which would become mass man's cherished, fetishized means of escaping an oppressive home environment and its attendant responsibilities. As Tex rides off into the proverbial sunset, there is a sublime shot of Barbara and baby, poignant and well-composed, another quick sketch by Wood which evokes silent film's singular visual language. Barbara finally sits on the dirt, forlorn and defeated, a beautiful image of the exploited and abandoned breeder of men's babies, left to fend for herself, both economically and emotionally. Tex and Barbara are clearly drawn here as Wood's prototypical dystopian suburban couple, a troubled yet powerful domestic dyad which will be invoked in virtually every subsequent Wood effort as a most interesting revision of the traditional heterosexual social construct.

Tex arrives in town and is immediately surrounded by the dance hall girls, who entice the capitalist to spend his ill-gotten fortune for their proscribed pleasures. Disgusted with Tex's reckless treachery, nice guy Lem heads off on horseback to see Barbara, whom he still fancies. By now Lem seems to be poised by Wood to be not only the hero of the piece, but an interesting counterpoint to phallocentric breeder-industrialist Tex. Lem arrives at Tex's house and informs the sad Barbara about her philandering husband's cheating with the saloon girls as well as his suspicion that Tex killed a man for his money. Lem confesses his love for Barbara and promises to take care of her, another intimation of his avowedly humane agenda. More importantly, Lem vows to kill Tex for his treachery, and thus declares himself an enemy of patriarchal capitalist culture. A splendid close-up of the forlorn Barbara reveals that she honors this new agent of decency.

Lem returns to town and orders a saloon girl to fetch Tex. Tex exits the saloon and a clumsily executed gunfight ensues, with Tex finally falling to the ground, wounded; progressive politics has felled greedy capitalism. The noise of gunfire summons the townspeople, who gather around the limp body. In one of the biggest shots in the film, in which Wood interestingly takes some unusual liberties with his silent western template, about a dozen people run from all corners of the western backlot to assemble in the middle of Main Street, an odd aggregation which includes two small boys and a young girl dressed inexplicably as a cowgirl, decidedly a postwar archetype and a person one would never find in a small frontier hamlet still on the verge of lawlessness. This is where Wood most clearly sketches his Wild West as a microcosm of the modern postwar suburb, containing a variety of adults with diverse careers, as well as well-fed and presumably spoiled children.

Lem climbs on his horse and attempts to get away, as the sheriff follows. The parson sees that Tex needs medical attention, so he orders two men to take him to the local medico. The men place Tex on a door, a ritualistic act that signals the beginning of the undeniably Woodian third act, the centerpiece of *Crossroads* and virtually all of Wood's subsequent work: the funeral of an ambivalent anti-hero, and its multitudinous impact on a grieving community.

The act of placing Tex on the door signals his demise, as the narrator underscores: "The girls gather 'round, but it is too late — Tex's soul has left his body." A touching scene follows, wherein the four whores, who owed their economic survival to the felled anti-hero, swoon with remorse, truly fallen angels who have lost their capitalist savior. The subsequent funeral procession, lovingly recorded by Wood from various angles and peppered with a plethora of close-ups, clarifies that this is the pivotal moment in the scenario for the author. The entire town turns out to follow Tex's dingy cardboard coffin to its final resting place, resulting in a quaint parade of humanity, headed by Tex's male peers, with all the women he touched following behind, and children and dogs taking up the rear, an exquisite microcosmic sketch of postwar civilization mourning the death of capitalism, and fearing the ascension of its as-yet unnamed replacement.

Central to this scene is the crude wooden cross placed as the tombstone on Tex's grave, a symbol of redemption which Wood used again, verbatim, in *Crossroad Avenger*. The Judeo-Christian icon for ethereal compensation meant so much to the deeply spiritual Wood that in his masterpiece *Plan 9 from Outer Space* (1959), when the fake marble cross in the graveyard set wobbled implausibly, Wood made sure to retain the faulty take, so as to catch the audience's attention and be noted as the crucial symbol it was.

The widow Barbara brings Tex's gun and holster to the service and places the now impotent symbols of violent phallocentrism on Tex's redemptive cross, nullifying forever their power to cause harm. As the parson reads from the Bible and sprinkles ashes over Tex's grave, Lem bursts through the gathered and approaches the grave, both to pay his final respects and to accept his fate at the hands of the community. The service ends, and Lem surrenders his weapon to the sheriff, underscoring his disdain for violent analogs of phallocentrism. As the male posse prepares to carry Lem off for trial and execution, he gives a glance back to Barbara, who still mourns at the grave. He seeks her forgiveness, but it is not immediately forthcoming. The parson exits, leaving Barbara alone with her sorrows.

As the sheriff and his men escort Lem to jail, the funeral attendees follow angrily, having turned quickly from a somber group of respectful mourners to an angry lynch mob. Remorse over loss turns to hate towards the cause, and the sheriff does seems ready to hang Lem without a trial, so powerful is the passionate if misguided energy of the crowd against the fragile vicissitudes of frontier justice. Lem stoically accepts his fate as the noose is strung around his neck. To the shock of onlookers, however, Barbara pushes her way through the crowd, walks up to Lem and gives him a passionate, not unerotic kiss. Woman has thus forgiven, and simultaneously redeemed Man, as the anima heals animus, another cherished Wood theme, sketched most profoundly in *Glen or Glenda?* (1953). This pivotal visual moment is confirmed as Barbara informs the crowd, via an overstated voiceover, that Lem is innocent, and furthermore, that she loves him!

In an extraordinary closing shot, Barbara walks slowly, silently away from the camera, further and further away from the community which exploited her, and towards the vast, promising expanse of the endless Western plains. Soon, Lem runs up, embraces and kisses her. The two stand, rather diminutive in a long shot backdropped by the mountains beyond, a primal sketch of Wood's revisionist Adam and Eve ready to enter a recreant yet hopeful postwar Eden. The two walk, arm and arm, into the distance, fearless warriors of the future. *Crossroads* thus sketches in minimalist form the treacherous journey ahead for the postwar suburban couple, along with the addressed hope for an emergent heterosexual dyad of progressive, courageous, and most importantly post-phallic and post-capitalist citizens, potential architects of an emancipatory post-holocaust culture.

There is a definite, and predictable, gender binary in *Crossroads*. In Wood's elemental Wild West sketch, men are men and women are women, or more specifically, men are *male* and women are *female*. There is no room for progressive gender rumination in this most simplistic of historical tableaus. What is curious, however, is the *preeminence* of women in *Crossroads*. For a tiny suburban outpost, miles away from the major urban center of Laredo, there seems to be an abundance, even an overabundance, of female personages. From the few shots which attempt to depict the community in toto, one might even surmise that there is at least one woman for every man here, a fantastic demographic which would not reflect the actual, brutal frontier town of the time period, nor the typical B-Western feature of the day, which invariably boasted a token female in an overwhelmingly male environment. Wood thus seems to be prophesying the advancing dominion of women in the subsequent decade, or even more provocatively, the necessity of a vibrant, ascendant female principle to balance any male-dominated culture which wished to outgrow the cataclysmic devastation so recently unleashed in a horrible war of nations.

As for the role of the male in *Crossroads*, it is significant that the film devotes such a great deal of time and energy to Tex, the villain of the piece. In Wood's emphasis on the prominent position played by evil in his little microcosmic America, he prophecies a most important postwar trend, the emergence of the anti-hero in popular culture, the almost obsessive fascination with evil and its human operatives that would blossom forth in the subsequent decade in films such as *The Wild One* (1954, d: Laslo Benedek) and *Rebel Without a Cause* (1955, d: Nicholas Ray). This sinister yet charismatic figure would occur with greater frequency in film and literature in an increasingly self-searching and morally ambivalent time period. Concurrently, Wood seems to be invoking the symbolic death of capitalism in his killing of Tex, a notion reinforced by the film's preoccupation with Tex's funeral and its undeniably positive aftereffects. This assuredly political act shows Wood at his most confrontational, and presages his delving into controversial political territory with increasing fervor in his upcoming features work.

(*Trick Shooting with*) *Kenne Duncan* (1952)

In this most unusual promotional film, well-known B-movie cowboy star Kenne Duncan performs various "trick" shooting stunts at targets in a strange little shooting booth which is emblazoned with advertising for Remington Arms, as well as a banner which boasts, "Kenne Duncan, the Notorious Movie and Tele-Villain."

The targets include Necco wafers and clay pipes which Ruth, an attractive woman dressed as a cowgirl, sets up for him. Judging from close-ups of the woman's hand bearing a wedding ring, it may be assumed this was Duncan's wife at the time.

Shilling for his sponsor, Duncan proudly announces his use of the new "Remington 552, auto-loading 22-caliber rifle," and later, "the beautiful Remington Nylon 566, which is also auto-loading. This model is called the Apache Black, with adjustments for both windage and elevation. It is very accurate and lightweight."

Duncan's stunts, while impressive skill-wise, are strictly of the carnival variety, an observation reinforced by various inserted shots of posters and advertisements depicting Duncan performing at state fairs and nightclubs, indicating that Duncan traveled widely with his sharp-shooter act during this time period. The film's only onscreen title is "Kenne Duncan ... THE FACE That Is Known To Millions of TV and Western Movie Fans." Producer-director Wood was apparently both exploiting the regional fame of Duncan, as well as honoring a bonafide cowboy star, with this short subject, as well as tapping into a long history of western sharp-shooter acts which toured the United States, often in conjunction with travelling carnivals, from the latter days of the 1800s, well into the 20th century.

Duncan's numerous trick shots continue, intercut with photographs from some of his movie roles, including *Cheyenne Wildcat, Texas Renegade, Powder River Gunfire, Colorado Kid, Outlaw Queen, California Gold Rush* and *Natchez Trace*. While giving director Wood an editorial excuse to cut away from what is essentially a sequence of similarly framed static shots, these crude inserts also serve a salient subtextual purpose, as Duncan appears to be shooting at his former triumphs, either to chase away old ghosts of earlier success, or to prove to himself and the audience, through his shooting acuity, that he has not yet lost his viril-

Popular B-movie villain Kenne Duncan displayed an expert gun hand in *Trick Shooting with Kenne Duncan,* a promotional film shot for Remington Arms by neophyte filmmakers Wood and Ronnie Ashcroft.

ity. The difficult shots Duncan performs with the classically phallic rifles are rather overt metaphors for sexual prowess, not a little ironic in that Duncan was known in Hollywood circles as both well-endowed and sexually voracious. This crude metaphor is reinforced by the dynamic between Duncan and Ruth, who sets up her man's targets and then stands obediently to one side, just out of harm's way but not out of sight, a crude visual homage to phallocentric culture.

As narrator, Duncan comes across as stiff and disengaged; his stilted attempts at comic banter fall especially flat. His stone-like visage suggests a humorless personality, which is reinforced every time he attempts to smile at the camera, efforts which result in strained, awkward grimaces. Yet his infamy seems legitimate: One fascinating sequence opens with posters for Duncan's appearances in Japan, and then segues into newsreel footage of Duncan's visits there. The huge crowds which greet this imported American cowboy are impressive, and suggest how important (or at least, omnipresent) Western culture was, even in war-torn Japan.

The film ends with Duncan and his wife standing next to the shooting booth, waiting for off-screen applause, as the camera zooms into a Remington firearms poster. This short subject is an alternately engaging and depressing document of a fading Western star and what he has taken to doing in order to survive (personal appearances in "modern" postwar culture with more than a whiff of desperate carny ballyhoo to it). His fate could certainly also be assigned to Western culture in general, which by the atomic age was entirely anachronistic, more of a novel curiosity than a vital or important phenomenon. Perhaps the operative word in this sad treatise is "trick"; Duncan performs his "tricks" like an obsolete freak or trained animal to a jaded and increasingly sophisticated audience. For Wood, and co-producer Ronnie Ashcroft (*The Astounding She-Monster*, 1958), the film was certainly a creative exercise in homaging a fading star and dying culture, as well as a showcase of low-budget, corporate-sponsored independent cinema at its most perfunctory.

Crossroad Avenger (1953)

Crossroad Avenger is a fascinating early effort by Wood, not only in its tempt to create a viable storyline for a proposed television series, but also in introducing some themes which occur in much of Wood's subsequent work. It is in many ways a remake of Wood's inaugural film *Crossroads of Laredo,* in color and with slightly improved production values, and certain elements in the earlier film crop up, almost verbatim, in *Crossroad Avenger.*

Shot on an attractive western back lot location, *Crossroad Avenger* looks quite similar to other TV Westerns of the time period, as well as the B-movie Westerns which were quickly fading from the big-movie screen thanks to the television revolution. The pilot film stars Tom Keene, a popular cowboy star of the 1930s and 1940s,[3] as "the Tucson Kid," an insurance investigator who is sent from town to town in order to verify the legitimacy of insurance claims. While the hero's occupation may strike some as completely lacking in excitement or romance, it does give the proposed series a framework from which the hero can hop from location to location, and thus from story to story, in a vaguely anthological framework, creating the potential for unlimited storylines.

Unfortunately, Keene as the hero is somewhat of an anachronism, as he is paunchy and all too obviously well past middle age, the very emblem of a "fading" cowboy star. He lacks the requisite charisma of a bonafide TV "star" such as Clayton Moore, who revolutionized the TV Western as the Lone Ranger. This miscasting is also true of Ed, the deputy, played by another famous cowboy star, Tom Tyler.[4] Tyler seems even older, and less fit, than Keene, and his delivery of dialogue is quite stilted. Wood was an avowed fan of the B-Western genre, and likely saw these cowboy icons not only as exploitable properties, but as bonafide celebrities, so he may have cast a blind eye to their lack of drawing power and screen presence. Perhaps Wood felt that the name of Tom Keene might help sell the series, which never did find a buyer. Still, Keene's character is of interest as it suggests a prototype of a character occurring in much of Wood's art: He is a progressive, an outsider and a loner, sent to a corrupt community to cleanse it of evil, and heal spiritual wounds, in an attempt to bring justice to a land not yet tamed.

As the film opens, the insurance company investigator (Keene) arrives in a small town named Crossroads to see why the beneficiary of a burned saloon wants his insurance payment in cash. Meanwhile, in Crossroads, the local entrepreneur and bad guy, Bart Miller (Lyle Talbot), and his band of thugs, Dance (Don Nagle), Lefty (Kenne Duncan) and Max (Bud Osborne),[5] discuss their nefarious deeds, which includes the recent murder of Jim Hawks, the sheriff, and the torching of a saloon

Tom Keene was a popular star in low-budget Westerns from various studios including RKO and Monogram in the 1930s and the 1940s. By the time Wood starred the actor in his TV pilot *Crossroad Avenger*, the aging Keene had been reduced to playing bit parts in the smallest productions.

owned jointly by the sheriff and Bart. (This admission reveals a spurious commercial venture between business interests and the government, likely quite common during the era.) It is decided that Bart and Dance will head out of town, and frame the first stranger for the sheriff's killing. It is notable that the community to which the Tucson Kid will lend his help has recently lost its sheriff, its spiritual leader and head patriarch. It is a town in upheaval, vulnerable to evil.

The Tucson Kid, now using the alias "Duke Smith," approaching Crossroad, is ambushed by Bart and Dance, who inform him they intend to string him up for the murder of the sheriff. Soon Ed, the deputy (Tyler), arrives. The deputy petitions for a fair trial for "Duke," but Bart has soon bullied him into opting for an immediate hanging. Just when all hope for "Duke" seems lost, shots ring out from the brush and stop the hanging posse dead in its tracks. The shots were fired by Zeke (Harvey Dunn), an elderly man the group calls "an old desert rat." An extended argument between Zeke and the posse culminates with Zeke stating, "Pretty soon yer gonna find out I know plenty," suggesting he will prove to be a font of wisdom in an environment where truth seems rare. Zeke insists that this stranger be given a fair trial. "Duke" restates that he was in Broken Bow the night before, and could not have possibly killed the sheriff "or anyone else." The deputy finally relents and leaves "Duke" in Zeke's custody. Zeke invites "Duke" to stay with him until his name can be cleared.

Zeke is by far the most interesting character in the film. He is ostensibly sketched as comic relief, as witness a key shot: Zeke, grinning like an idiot, and his burro Alonzo slowly walk towards the camera, accompanied by comical music, in a scene which paints the old man as essentially ludicrous, perhaps a "divine idiot." Yet Zeke proves to be all-knowing and wise. He fulfills a pivotal role as the film's narrator, relating to the Tucson Kid, and the audience, this community's sordid past. He also functions as a Jungian "wise old man," a spirit of truth, stability and hope in a fallen society. He is an early sketch of an archetype that Wood would return to time and again, especially as Kelton the Cop, the "divine idiot" in a trinity of Wood films.

Meanwhile, back at the ranch, Bart and his gang discuss further ways of framing "Duke Smith" for the sheriff's murder. They decide to kill Zeke that very evening, and blame this new murder also on the unfortunate stranger. That evening, Zeke shares his camp with "Duke" and fills the stranger in on the entire sordid backstory of Crossroads. Jim, the sheriff, was shot in the back by an unknown assailant; Zeke believes the killer was Bart or one of his gang. Zeke also mentions the near-fatal fire at the saloon a month earlier, which also seemed suspicious. As it turns out, Zeke had been sleeping off a hangover in the saloon when the fire started and was able to rescue Jim, who had been locked in one of the store rooms. This odd plot turn seems almost a backhanded defense of alcoholism by Wood, a notion which is reinforced by Zeke's gleeful laughter as he describes his drunken behavior.

Zeke finally reveals that Jim and Bart were partners in the saloon, so after Jim's death, Bart became the sole owner and beneficiary. "Duke" decides to tell Zeke his true identity in gratitude for his honesty, and Zeke is thrilled to discover he has the famous "Tucson Kid" as a guest. Suddenly, shots ring out; Bart and his gang have surrounded the camp. In the ensuing gunfight, Lefty is wounded and Zeke is fatally shot. The dying Zeke warns the Tucson Kid, at length, to leave the area immediately, for the villains plan on pinning his death on the stranger.

The Tucson Kid buries Zeke in a makeshift grave with a wooden cross marking it. He states that he will not leave Crossroads until he finds out what nefarious doings are going on at Bart's mysterious "Double D" Ranch. As noted in *Crossroads of Laredo*, this specific emphasis on the funeral of a heroic and/or pivotal character is a Woodian quirk which would occur in virtually all of his subsequent works, and symbolized always by the phallic cross of Christendom. The next day, Bart and Dan arrive in Crossroads and tell the deputy that they noticed a grave near Zeke's camp. They relate that they dug up the grave, and "discovered" Zeke buried there. They try to convince the deputy that this proves that the stranger committed both killings. The deputy is uncertain, but rides off with the killers to see for himself.

Arriving at the camp, the deputy is disturbed to find that the thugs really have dug up Zeke's body. He insists they rebury him so that he may "rest in peace." It is most significant that Zeke is not merely killed, but that special emphasis is taken to convey that he was buried, and then dug up again. It is pivotal that it is Zeke's "resurrected" spirit which furthers the agenda of seeking justice, and leads to victory and the healing of the community. This peculiar "resurrection" or "raising of the dead" theme becomes a virtual obsession in several of Wood's subsequent films, most particularly *Plan 9 from Outer Space* (1959), *Night of the Ghouls* (circa 1959) and *Orgy of the Dead* (1965). As well, Zeke finds narrative recurrences in characters such as the Ghoul Girl (Vampira) in *Plan 9* and the Storyteller (Criswell) in *Night of the Ghouls* and *Orgy of the Dead*. In each case, these animated "undead" characters propel the narrative, and act as significant motivators to forwarding the plot to a satisfying conclusion. Wood is clearly borrowing here from a long history of religious resurrection parables, most notably the Christian myth of Jesus Christ, as the blueprint for these recurring "supernatural" characters who manifest great change during their lives "after death." As noted earlier, Wood introduced this career-long theme, using himself as the sacrificial martyr, in *Crossroads of Laredo*.

As the group prepares to re-bury Zeke, the Tucson Kid enters, guns at the ready, and insists that he will find his friend's real killer at all costs. Dance sneaks up behind him, and the deputy asks him to drop his guns. The Tucson Kid accuses Bart and his gang of both murders. Bart pleads his innocence, restating that he and Jim were partners in both the saloon and an oil site on the ranch. The deputy insists that regardless, the stranger this time will get a fair trial.

The Tucson Kid decides it is time to come clean with the deputy, so he hands him a paper he found when he went snoop-

Tom Tyler achieved fame as a movie star in the mid–1920s via a highly popular series of silent Westerns. Tyler had another brief career peak in 1941 when he played the lead in the popular Republic serial *Adventures of Captain Marvel*. By the early 1950s, failing health reduced the actor to infrequent appearances, including *Crossroad Avenger*, one of his last roles.

ing the night before at Bart's ranch. It states that Jim, the sheriff, was entitled to 85 percent of the profits realized from the new oil rig set up on the ranch. Bart and his gang realize that the jig is up, and they reach for their guns. In the ensuing gunfight, Bart's thugs are apparently killed, and Bart surrenders to the deputy. A wounded Dance makes one last attempt to shoot the deputy, but he misses and kills his boss instead. Back in Crossroads, the deputy thanks the Tucson Kid for his help in cleansing his town of evil. The Tucson Kid mounts Duke and rides back to the home office, towards his next adventure.

The somewhat threadbare production values notwithstanding, it is easy to see why *Crossroad Avenger* never found a distributor or made it to series. The increasingly insatiable maw of the television industry latched early onto the ubiquitous genre of the theatrical B-Western as a serial format with considerable potential for the small screen. During the early 1950s, when Wood was hawking his product to television syndicators, there were over thirty Western series already on the air; by the decade's end, there were well over 100 such programs. Considering his love of the genre, it is not surprising that Wood decided on a Western-format pilot film; it is less surprising that he found no backers, what with the glut of similar product on TV at the time. According to various sources including Rudolph Grey and Wood himself,[6] *Crossroad Avenger* and another half-hour Western film starring Keene, which may or may not be the elusive Wood film *Boots* (1953), were combined to make a short feature entitled *Adventures of the Tucson Kid* (circa 1954), which supposedly was syndicated to television in the mid–1950s.

It would be misleading to suggest that Wood intended *Crossroad Avenger* as an allegorical piece which depicted postwar Man at the crossroads between the memory of two world wars and the promise of an era of predicted peace, nor of "modern" man during his painful metamorphosis into "postmodern" man. Yet it is intriguing that this, one of Wood's earliest efforts, was set in "the old world" of a lawless American frontier long suppressed, whereas the bulk of his films take place in contemporary, even modern settings, which invariably emphasize progressive, even Utopian societies. Even more striking is Wood's utilization of an ensemble cast of older B-Western actors, popular stars who had made their name in previous decades. Wood's dragging of these older performers into the most decidedly postmodern medium of television may have been nothing more than a somewhat desperate act of opportunism, yet it also has the spirit of something akin to cultural alchemy, in which members of the old world are virtually forced into the new one, with potentially meaningful advantage for both.

* * *

Two of Wood's most intriguing short works remain lost. The two-reelers *The Final Curtain* and *The Night the Banshee Cried* (both purportedly shot in 1957) revel in the supernatural elements which Wood so loved to work with. They likely ruminate on the highly metaphoric occult netherworld seen in *Glen or Glenda?*, *Plan 9 from Outer Space*, *Night of the Ghouls* and *Orgy of the Dead*, and in a severely compromised form even in *Necromania* (1971). As first noted by Rudolph Grey, several scenes from *The Final Curtain* were used in *Night of the Ghouls*.[7] In his scattershot memoirs *Hollywood Rat Race*, written circa 1964–1965 but unpublished until 1998, Wood claimed that *The Final Curtain* was in production in early 1957, and that Bela Lugosi was intended to star. Wood even states that Lugosi was reading the script when he died, a revelation which adds a hyper-real quality to the film's mythic reputation.[8] Later in the book, Wood claims that *The Final Curtain* was "filmed for television," and starred "C.J. Moore." Of course, the footage from *The Final Curtain* which appears in *Night of the Ghouls* features Carl James "Duke" Moore as "the vampire actor"; these scenes are woven into the narrative of *Night of the Ghouls* via rewritten narration voiced by Criswell, and will be discussed further in the chapter on that film.[9] As for the genesis of *The Final Curtain*, Wood offers a tantalizing overview of the scenario in a chapter on writing, again from *Hollywood Rat Race*:

> *Final Curtain*, which was not only a half-hour television show but was later turned into my novel *Orgy of the Dead*, came to me while I was going to drama school in Washington, D.C. (Oh yes! I also went through the drama school bit.) I lived in an atticlike affair over a theatre, and there is nothing more spooky than a theatre after hours. Every sound is magnified hundreds of times. Picture yourself in a gigantic building, there is no one there but you, and it's very dark. I can guarantee the imagination will start to percolate with enough ideas for a lifetime.[10]

One can glean the general concept of the filmed *The Final Curtain* from the short story as it appears in Wood's *Orgy of the Dead* novelization, recently reprinted by Woodpile Press in *Suburbian Orgy*. A slightly altered version of *The Final Curtain* can be found in a reprint collection of Wood short stories, *The Horrors of Sex* (Ramble House, 2001). In the tale, a weary middle-aged Actor prowls a darkened theatre at night, after the final performance of a play. As he searches obsessively for something, he knows not what, the Actor is haunted by all sorts of terrifying sounds and visual phenomenon. At the stroke of midnight, the Actor is inexplicably drawn to a spiral staircase, which he climbs compulsively, even though the railings turn into slithering snakes. After reaching the third floor and inspecting twenty rooms, the Actor is mesmerized by the mannequin of a female vampire, and even ponders if he is in love with it. Finally reaching a "hidden" room, the Actor sees the object of his search — a coffin, his own coffin, as he realizes that he is destined to die this particular evening: "It is at this moment I know I am going to climb into this cushioned box and permit the lid to close over me."[11] This sophomoric yet amusing allegory of life and death might well have made a meandering yet atmospheric half-hour film if done properly; regardless, the unearthing of *The Final Curtain* would be cause for celebration.

Prolific B-movie character actor Lyle Talbot, who appeared in nearly 300 films and television programs, played the villainous Bart Miller in *Crossroad Avenger*, one of several roles Talbot essayed for Wood. Among Talbot's many show business achievements was co-founding the Screen Actors Guild.

Even less is known about *The Night the Banshee Cried*, which, like *The Final Curtain*, may have been intended as a prototype of a proposed television anthology series called *Portraits in Terror*. As a short story, *The Night the Banshee Cried* appeared in magazines as well as a chapter in Wood's novelization of *Orgy of the Dead*. In this extremely abstract, even expressionist story, a female protagonist, who appears to be stuck in a state of conscious, living death ("When I died, I cried"), haunts the fog-shrouded bog behind her former home. She is hounded by a beautiful female demon called "The Banshee" who unnerves her with endless, terrifying screams. The unlucky ghost-protagonist finally understands, in a flash of insight, that she has been brought back from mere "mortal" death to take over for the Banshee, who "has gone, gone forever." With a lump in her throat, she proclaims, "I *am* the banshee, now...."[12] *Banshee* is not dissimilar to *The Final Curtain* in its basic plot-line, wherein a lone commentator embarks on a terrifying yet mystically compelling journey towards a morbid, predestined fate; in each story, Wood mixes a child-like fascination with death, and what lies beyond, with world-weary observations on a life wasted and regretted. *The Night the Banshee Cried* has the additional draw of being written for a sexy young actress; one can easily picture either Maila Nurmi or Valda Hansen essaying the role effectively. Some sources claim the story was filmed, as was *The Final Curtain*, but Wood is mute on the subject in his memoirs, and elsewhere.

It is interesting that Wood saw the potential for a horror anthology TV series well before the concept burst on the scene in the late 1950s and early 1960s with programs such as *The Twilight Zone, One Step Beyond, Thriller, The Outer Limits,* and *Way Out*. Possibly encouraged by early genre TV anthologies such as *Lights Out* and *Tales of Tomorrow*, both presented live, Wood's *Portraits in Terror* project would have been amongst the first *filmed* series in the genre, and might well have had considerable success in syndication. One swoons at the notion of a Wood-produced horror anthology TV series along the lines of *The Twilight Zone*, perhaps even with Wood doing on-screen introductions!

After devoting the bulk of his life to writing screenplays for other producers, and producing a handful of his own feature films, Wood returned in 1975 to writing and directing a series of short films produced under the spurious banner of "Sex Education Correspondence School," and available by mail order via advertisements in men's magazines.[13] Although none of these films have surfaced thus far, it is likely that they are little more than short sex films, perhaps disguised as educational through the addition of on-screen explanatory titles. Still, it would be fascinating to see what Wood, a unique cross between libertine and prude, did with this most abused and ubiquitous film form.

2

Glen or Glenda? (1953)

Edward D. Wood, Jr.'s inaugural feature, *Glen or Glenda?*, is a remarkable production from several perspectives. Judging from his commercial television and short subjects work, one might have expected Wood to construct an entertaining, yet pedestrian and formulaic, western adventure or crime thriller. What Wood crafted instead was an extraordinary, deeply personal polemic which pleaded tolerance of difference while cannily addressing some salient social issues of the guilt-ridden, soul-searching postwar era. Surprisingly, this unique feature film documents, questions and dissembles the changing sex roles between men and women in the immediate era after World War II, forging a flawed yet provocative discussion of gender politics years before the subject became dynamic. Enhancing this most peculiar text are the film's baffling patchwork structure, eclectic narrative scenario and wild stylistic departures, making the resultant film appear more like the avant-garde underground cinema of Luis Bunuel or Maya Deren than the typical B-level grindhouse programmer of the period.

Breaking into the theatrical feature film market was no mean feat for Wood, even in the expansive 1950s, when independent film production soared due in large part to the landmark government decision in 1948 to wrest the major motion picture studios from their distribution networks and theatre chains. This enabled smaller, independent producer-distributors to release productions, something that, a decade earlier, would have been well nigh impossible.[1] Notably, these indie productions were no longer marginalized as the exploitation and black film genres, for instance, had been for years. Low-budget potboilers of every stripe ran alongside well-shined Hollywood product in theatres throughout the U.S. and elsewhere. In many ways, the 1950s was truly a renaissance of independent film. One of the hardiest independent film genres was the exploitation film, a theatrical sub-market which flourished primarily between 1934 and 1953, and to some degree beyond. A lucrative, if ghettoized, genre since the birth of cinema, the exploitation film took taboo or controversial social issues of the day, many if not most of a sexual nature, and mounted cheapjack productions which purported to educate the audience even as it served its primary purpose, to titillate that same audience with salacious sights and sounds of the topics discussed.

Although the basic template for the classical exploitation picture assured a certain uniformity amongst most product, certain films stand out in the canon as being exemplary in concept and execution. Many feel the champion in the field is *Mom and Dad* (1944; d: William Beaudine). Snuck into theatres amidst the turmoil of World War II, *Mom and Dad*, produced by roadshow legends J.S. Jossey and Kroger Babb, is considered by many to be the seminal exploitation picture, a cynical and grisly depiction of sexual America, as seen through the unblinking eye of pseudo-educational pretense. Veteran exploitation producers knew well that

23

One of several alternate release titles for *Glen or Glenda?* was *I Led 2 Lives.*

the audience which sought out these lurid exposés was not seeking enlightenment, but thrills, and the best of the exploitation pictures delivered this tried-and-true cinematic quotient in full measure. As *Mom and Dad* ostensibly discussed the scourge of venereal disease, audiences were treated to a veritable horror show. Producer George Weiss had success with several pictures of this same sensational nature, and his most successful film, *Test Tube Babies* (1953) is considered a classic in the field, on a par with the aforementioned *Mom and Dad*. Starring handsome Timothy Farrell, considered by many to be exploitation's "cut-rate Clark Gable,"[2] *Test Tube Babies* tells of a newlywed couple who, discovering they cannot conceive children, are introduced to the scientific wonders of artificial insemination. Farrell plays a kindly doctor who describes at length the mechanics of the new process, in a bland room with Venetian blinds, a setting which succinctly reflects the sterile, repressive sexual atmosphere of the era. Yet the primarily somber film manages to thrill via some provocative stock footage of female anatomy and most significantly, via a titillating catfight between two females, a departure from good taste and narrative reason as gratuitous to the film as it was ubiquitous to the genre.

Given his impressive track record with similar product, Weiss was likely interested when Ed Wood purportedly approached him with an idea for a film which would tell the real story of Christine Jorgensen (1926–1989), who had shocked the world late in 1952 by claiming to be the first recipient of a sex-change operation. Born George William Jorgensen, the millionaire photographer underwent extensive surgery in Denmark under Dr. Christian Hamburger to change from male to female. Although similar operations had been performed in Germany in the 1930s, Hamburger's revolutionary treatment incorporated the use of hormones to augment the desired gender transformation. The media frenzy which greeted Jorgensen upon her return to the United States in early 1953 could not have been lost on producer Weiss, who likely envisioned an exploitation-tinged documentary about the celebrity. According to several accounts, Weiss attempted to gain permission from Jorgensen to film her life story.[3] Jorgensen understandably had no desire to become the subject of a tawdry, sensational account of her recent travails, sensing correctly that Weiss and company would turn the event into fodder for cheap thrills on the new cinematic midway. However, Jorgensen would subsequently lend her name to several similar projects, including a 1970 biographical film and a best-selling autobiography. In addition, Jorgensen toured extensively throughout the 1970s and 1980s, lecturing about her experience.[4]

According to popular legend, Wood countered with an offer to make a fictionalized account of the Jorgensen story, with himself starring as a generic man/woman. While this account has some credibility, it is curious that Wood, himself an inveterate transvestite, would stumble onto such a scheme accidentally, a change of plans which would place him square in the middle of his first feature, in a most provocative and potentially unflattering light. Also, whereas the original concept for the film focused on real-life personage Jorgensen and on the new and baffling world of sex-change surgery, Wood's subsequent film jumped, almost willy-nilly, between two allied yet profoundly different subjects: the radical and relatively rare surgical sex-change operation, and the obviously less life-changing, socio-sexual proclivity of transvestitism. Superficial similarities aside, transvestitism, the wearing of clothing commonly associated with the opposite birth sex of the wearer, is an activity both harmless and relatively common, more akin to casual hobby than profound life decision. Sex-change surgery is a rarer, quantifiably dangerous procedure which radically alters the subject's life in myriad ways.

Although the two phenomena have the observable, desired effect of converting the subject into an alternate gender, this is where the similarities end. Wood was thus either being disingenuous or naïve in throwing the two concepts together, except where he succeeds in using both as metaphors for other themes, such as the elusive quality of personal identity, and the importance of expressing individuality in an increasingly regimented culture.

Transvestitism was recurrent in ancient mythology, folk tales, literature and theatre, a venerable tradition which evolved into the drag queen and female impersonator of modern times. Transvestitism's long history reaches far earlier than circa 1915 when sociologist Magnus Hirschfeld coined the term to describe persons who chronically donned clothing of the opposite sex. At this time, transvestitism was considered the expression of psycho-sexual neurosis, as opposed to sociological behavior, with a propensity towards fetishism, as well as a likely indicator of overt or suppressed homosexual inclinations. Today the term transvestitism is considered obsolete, replaced by such terms as transgender and cross-dressing, both of which signify attempts to rescue the activity from the punitive two-gender binary which the previous term tended to embody, even as it underscored the function of taboo in the behavior.

Cross-dressing now reflects as well as illustrates the widely accepted belief that gender is determined primarily by dress, behavior, performance, etc. (collectively called "signification"), rather than immutable biological or sexual factors. Authors such as Judith Butler have articulated this philosophy extensively; in her seminal gender studies tract *Gender Trouble: Feminism and the Subversion of Identity,* Butler notes:

> If one thinks that one sees a man dressed as a woman or a woman dressed as a man, then one takes the first term of each of those perceptions as the "reality" of gender: the gender that is introduced through the simile lacks "reality," and is taken to constitute an illusory appearance. In such perceptions in which an ostensible reality is coupled with an unreality, we think we know what that reality is, and take the secondary appearance of gender to be mere artifice, play, falsehood, and illusion. But what is the sense of "gender reality" that founds this perception in this way?[5]

As Wood was a self-proclaimed transvestite (and under-dresser as well, donning female undergarments over male clothing), could Wood have pitched the original Jorgensen concept to Weiss knowing all along that he would somehow insist himself in the eventual production, on a most personal level, or was this a fortuitous, after-the-fact decision? The world may never know, yet the resultant film certainly depicts Wood as a champion not only of sexual difference in general, and certain sociological quirks in specific, but more enduringly, as a fierce advocate of personal independence in a world turning increasingly regimented and conformist. As well, Wood's real-life transvestite alter-ego, "Shirley," depicted here as "Glenda," amusingly illustrates the female principle incarnate, a recurring motif in Wood's films.

To counter the inevitable comparison of the effeminate male, specifically one who publicly dons women's clothing, with the homosexual male, Wood emphatically states in *Glen or Glenda?* that "a transvestite is *not* a homosexual," and thusly draws a line in the sand to differentiate between the subjects of his film, including himself, and those who he considers, by implication, to be morally and psychologically corrupted. This is an odd note of disdain from a filmmaker who otherwise claims to be egalitarian and devoted to freedom of personal expression. Some observers have suggested that Wood "dost protest too much" in regards to his heterosexuality, and consider him to have been a closeted homosexual, a typically intolerant reaction to transvestite behavior at the time. More likely, however, is the assumption that Wood, knowing that he was treading precariously within overlapping areas of sexual identity by prancing around in female garb in order to state a specific instance of expression within a staunchly heterosexual lifestyle, also knew that in 1950s America, homosexuality was still a taboo subject, untouched even by the outwardly licentious yet inherently conservative exploitation film market. Although Wood was dealing in subjects which suggest homo-sexual fraternity, if not outright sympathy, he was very careful, perhaps even too careful, to distinguish between the two. This may have been as much an attempt not to alienate the almost exclusively heterosexual exploitation film audience as an attempt to divert any unwanted accusations or untoward personal assumptions. Significantly underscoring this combination of caution and guilt is the fact that Wood himself, the star character in his trea-tise on sexual acceptance, is unbilled in the main credits of *Glen or Glenda?*, the lone mys-tery figure in a cast of leading players otherwise identified.

From a marketing point of view, what likely put producer Weiss in favor of Wood's shaky project was the neophyte director's ability to get legendary horror star Bela Lugosi to par-ticipate. The Hungarian-born actor had made his name synonymous with horror upon his portrayal of Bram Stoker's literary vampire, Dracula, first in an acclaimed stage production and then in a wildly successful 1931 motion picture. By the late 1940s, however, Lugosi was in dire straits. Having been typecast early on as "the one and only" Dracula, and rarely con-sidered for more traditional roles, Lugosi had been forced to star in low-budget horror films. Lugosi appeared in many entertaining but low-rent "Poverty Row horrors" such as *Invisible Ghost* (1941), *The Ape Man* (1943) and *Scared to Death* (1947) for various independent pro-ducers. But by 1948, after his ever-so-brief return to the limelight via the horror-comedy clas-sic *Abbott and Costello Meet Frankenstein* (1948), even these paltry film jobs had diminished.

Never savvy in financial matters, Lugosi and his wife Lillian were nearing the poverty level themselves, and Lugosi resorted to returning to the stage in productions both legitimate and hoary, in the United States and Great Britain. This period of Lugosi's life is brought to life in a fascinating book, *Vampire Over London: Bela Lugosi in Britain* by Frank J. Dello Stritto and Andi Brooks, which covers in detail the exhausting, at times heartbreaking sojourn to the United Kingdom made by Lugosi during an increasingly desperate time in the actor's life, a time when a successful and appreciated Hollywood legend would be enjoying a happy and healthy retirement. Additionally, in 1953 Lugosi's twenty-year marriage came to an end, put-ting the actor into a depression from which some say he never fully recovered. Overlaying all of this was Lugosi's notorious battle with narcotic painkillers, an affliction which would lead to his dramatic, widely publicized entry into a drug rehabilitation program in 1955.

Enter Ed Wood. Wood's largely untold relationship with the aging actor is a volume waiting to be written by some intrepid biographer. Some see it as one of pure exploitation, and others of timely felicity. Some see Wood as an opportunist, using the ailing actor as a desperate, cynical way to class up and give box office appeal to his otherwise admittedly obscure movie productions. Others have painted Wood as a veritable savior, a dear friend who gave Lugosi not only much-needed employment in his chosen field during his final years, but companionship as well. The truth probably lies somewhere in between, but as Lugosi his-torian Frank Dello Stritto relates, Wood figures prominently in Lugosi's last years:

> Edward D. Wood, Jr.—sometimes sports promoter, sometimes manufacturer of 3-D Christ-mas cards, director, producer and writer of unforgettably bad films, and now a cult figure in his own right—is the pivotal figure in Lugosi's last years. Questionable as his cinematic talents may have been, he did succeed in getting Lugosi work when no-one else either could or would. He had been the guiding hand in San Bernadino and bringing Lugosi to St. Louis in *Arsenic and Old Lace.* Now, besides films, he was pushing a Bela Lugosi radio show and even a Bela Lugosi comic book.[6]

As for the specifics of the screen legends' original encounter, details are sketchy and con-tradictory, but filmmaker Fred Olen Ray offers some helpful insight via an interview he con-ducted with Wood shortly before Wood's death in 1978. In Wood's own words, "Alex Gordon and I had an apartment together. He knew Lugosi, I didn't. Lugosi turned me down at first, but Lillian, his wife at the time, turned him on to it. I paid him $1,000 a day ... he needed the money."[7] This claim is verified, and embellished, in an Ed Wood interview with Rudolph Grey in *Nightmare of Ecstasy: The Life and Art of Edward D. Wood Jr.*[8] According to Lugosi historian Richard Bojarski, the actor was paid $5,000 for his work on *Glen or Glenda?*, which covered five shooting days, a figure which correlates with Wood's assertion.[9]

Most sources agree that Lugosi, having accepted Wood's offer to appear in a low-budget exploitation film, took the assignment seriously and treated the project with the respect and integrity he would have given a big-budget Universal horror picture in his glory days. In Grey's book, producer George Weiss was especially effusive: "Lugosi was enjoying himself like a baby with a toy. There weren't four takes on anything. He went through like the trouper he was."[10]

In the film's opening credits, Wood credits himself with "Original Story, Written and Directed by," indicating that he was proud of this labor of love. The film opens with a disclaimer, a common conceit of the exploitation genre which served two main purposes. Firstly, on-screen explanatory text underscores the purportedly "educational" nature of the film in question, lending these notoriously spurious productions a sorely needed, if disingenuous air of legitimacy. As well, exploitation producers took every opportunity to pad a film's running time with cost-cutting measures such as inexpensive graphics work, stock footage and repeated scenes.

Glen or Glenda?'s disclaimer runs as follows: "In the making of this film, which deals with a strange and curious subject, no punches have been pulled — no easy way out has been taken. Many of the smaller parts are portrayed by persons who actually are, in real life, the character they portray on the screen. This is a picture of stark realism — taking no sides— but giving you the facts— All the facts— as they are today.... You are society — JUDGE YE NOT."

Again in traditional exploitation fashion, the scene is set thusly for a scenario which promises to be both titillating and informative. The somber proclamation also positions the audience as moral arbiter, a role likely not embraced by the average cinematic thrill-seeker of the day. *Glen or Glenda?* was an unwieldy cross between freak show, documentary, and social expose, and its audience (more likely drawn to it by morbid curiosity than social concern) could not be expected to be an objective or dispassionate party to the proceedings.

The first scene in *Glen or Glenda?* depicts Lugosi in a mad scientist's laboratory, reading an ancient volume, an evocative *mise-en-scène* which effortlessly alludes to Lugosi's long history as a horror film star, and sets the film's prevailing motif as fantastic, lurid melodrama. The lab is a veritable catalog of pulp melodrama icons and horror film clichés: skulls in symmetry, a hanging skeleton next to what appears to be a native corpse, various sundry science-lab artifacts, a sickle, a voodoo warrior's battle shield, dusty bookshelves. This random collection of leftovers from a Hollywood prop department creates a peculiar anthropological potpourri. *Glen or Glenda?* thus cleverly, almost subliminally, positions itself not as an exploitation picture of "stark realism," but as yet another in the legacy of Lugosi's long string of horror film hits, a most canny move on Wood's part. This specifically intended *mise-en-scène* is underscored by the horror film music played throughout the laboratory scenes.

This opening could have been lifted, virtually intact, from any number of the horror films Lugosi made for Poverty Row studios such as Monogram and Producers Releasing Corporation throughout the 1940s. The fact that this clever opening segment was consciously designed by Wood to evoke the atmosphere of Lugosi's horror films begs the question — did Wood intend this most unusual framing device for his "autobiographical documentary" as an homage or parody of the genre invoked? Other than for sorely needed star value, why feature Lugosi at all? Lugosi's position and purpose in *Glen or Glenda?* seems pivotal, yet ever-elusive. As well as the film's resident god-figure, Lugosi also acts as "host," an outsider to the film's actual events, who comments on the proceedings while speaking directly to the film audience. In essence, Lugosi is watching *Glen or Glenda?*, as is the audience, and then offering his own not-uncritical commentary. In this manner, Lugosi's character spookily prophecies a soon-common pop icon of 1950s and 1960s culture — the television horror-movie host. Local TV celebrities such as Zacherle, Vampira and Ghoulardi became all the rage in Baby boomer television beginning in the mid–1950s and lasting well into the subsequent decade, as "hosts" of televised horror, science-fiction and other genre films, usually commenting sardonically on the films presented. These hosts, in addition to providing amusing entertainment for the audience with their wildly theatrical antics, most importantly served a critical function, in effect judging the films as did the audience, and connecting film and audience into one cultural dyad which before TV had been well nigh impossible. In fact, the TV horror host's coaxing of their audience to participate in lambasting the films suggests a most elemental use of Brechtian philosophy, in which the audience is either seduced or shamed into participating in the action occurring "onstage."

As the prologue unfolds, Lugosi sits, rather slumped, in a wingtip chair, a ambiguous admixture of god-figure, teacher, wise elder and sad old man. He looks weary, and suggests

Horror star Bela Lugosi was resurrected from career oblivion by Wood, who placed the actor front and center in his first feature, *Glen or Glenda?* The aging thespian played a scowling puppet master of foolish mortals.

amongst other things an obsolete father figure, a symbol of patriarchy exhausted. As Lugosi begins to speak directly to the audience, spouting absurdist blank verse with his syrupy accent and lisping intonation, these visual allusions are reinforced, most especially the god-figure and daffy old man. Lugosi intones, "Man's constant groping of things unknown, drawing from the endless reaches of time, brings to light, many startling things! 'Startling' because they seem new, sudden! But most are not new! Designs of the ages!" This nonsensical-seeming declaration in fact sets the stage for *Glen or Glenda?*'s most interesting dialectic, that of overlapping traditional cultural notions with provocative new assertions and revelations, an attempt to stitch the innocent prewar world to the dangerous and obscure new one. At root a flowery restatement of the old adage, "Everything old is new again," the declaration underscores *Glen or Glenda?*'s recurrent assertion that progressive sociological and psychological developments have precedent in recorded history, and this dichotomy will reveal itself in remarkable ways as the main thesis unfolds.

Lugosi strikes the viewer familiar with the psychology of Carl Jung as a viable representation of the "wise old man," an archetypal figure which occurs in dreams and therapeutic sessions and can symbolize many things to the subject of these visions; as Jung noted, "The old man thus represents knowledge, reflection, insight, wisdom, cleverness and intuition on the one hand, and on the other, moral qualities such as goodwill and readiness to help, which makes his 'spiritual' character sufficiently plain." As Lugosi's scenes always appear outside of the main narrative thread of *Glen or Glenda?*, yet inevitably "interact" with these narrative segments by commenting on or manifesting change within the scenario, it will be helpful to view them as *Glen or Glenda?*'s own "dream sequences," highly metaphorical asides which have much in common with psychological dream theory.

Lugosi's bombastic declarations abruptly cut to a stock footage clip of a thunderstorm with lightning and a thunder clap, the first of such cuts which will represent different things at different points throughout the film. In this case, the abrupt violence of the scene reinforces something mystical, a cataclysm in the heavens, an angry god, a vengeful world spirit enraged by what is to be unveiled. The film returns to a different view of the laboratory, now revealing a living room table adorned with chemistry lab equipment (test tubes, beakers, mortar and pestle, etc.). Other props visible in this new angle include a globe, a tribal battle shield, a coyote skull, and various hardbound texts. Surrounded by these significant cultural symbols, Lugosi mixes various chemicals in a flask, an act which reinforces the notion that his character is in some sense a creator of life, either God himself or a man playing God, an allusion which suggests a common theme in horror films of the period, especially after the horrors of the atomic bomb, that of irresponsible Science. The Lugosi character also evokes the ancient spirit of the alchemist, a virtually supernatural being who had the power to transform beings into heroes or demons at will.

With a human skeleton in prominence, reminding the audience of the fragile mortality of humankind, Lugosi continues to mix various solutions until he creates a chemical cocktail which smokes profusely, reinforcing his presence as a modern-day alchemist. Lugosi smiles triumphantly, and gushes, "A life is begun!" This assertion reinforces the notion that Lugosi is playing a god or god-surrogate, in some fashion a creator of life. The abundant smoke present on the set during this scene gives an ethereal, otherworldly verisimilitude. Although the room appears at first glance to be the cluttered laboratory of a deranged scientist, it is now seen also as a universal, primordial space, a cosmic void of the heavens whence all life emanates.

The scene dissolves into stock footage of a teeming city, rife with pedestrians and rapidly moving motor vehicles, a familiar urban motif which quickly sketches modern civilization in all its glory and horror. With this all-important dissolve, which brings the film into semi-documentary territory for a brief period, the bright white human skull in the foreground of the laboratory set literally metamorphosizes into the teeming masses, a powerful visual allusion to human mortality. The scene dissolves back to Lugosi, who watches with undeniable disdain these generic scenes of civilization, now cleverly composited into the bottom half of the frame. The allusion here is that Lugosi is indeed God, watching his creation with a mixture of awe and disgust, passing a largely negative judgment on his wayward handiwork. After observing for a moment, Lugosi utters a wildly existential, somehow damning proclamation: "People! All going somewhere! All with their own thoughts, their own ideas! All with their own ... *personalities!* One is wrong, because he does right! One is right, because he does wrong! Pull the string! Dance to that which one is created for!"

The last two, infamous lines show Wood at his most prosaic, and solidify the notion that Lugosi is playing a god figure, one who sees human beings as mere puppets of cosmic forces, puppets whose destiny is set at birth and "dance" through life to a predetermined script, animated by the whims of a cosmic puppeteer. Wood thusly suggests that the unfortunate creatures whom he is about to bring to life (men who wear women's clothing) are in fact compelled to do so, slaves to impulses given them by their creator. This has been seen as an apologist stance by some observers, and yet it goes far to explain Wood's career-wide preoccupation with destiny as a driving force in man's life.

Lugosi laughs mockingly, and then sighs forlornly, as the scene dissolves back to the full frame of urban bustle. Lugosi looks away from his creation, up towards the direction of the sky, and mutters, "A new day is begun!" The sound of a baby's cry prompts Lugosi to whisper, reverentially, "A new life is begun!"

The scene dissolves into stock footage of a wailing ambulance racing down a suburban street, a crudely effective emotive signal of trouble in postwar paradise. This dissolves to a small apartment, where what appears to be a man, dressed as a woman, is lying still on a bed, presumably dead. In the background an effeminate man wearing work coveralls minces about, clearly agitated. Lugosi's face once again appears over the scene via superimposition, in ominous close-up, as he dictates his verdict: "A life is ended!" As the dour, prophetic god-head fades out, there is a knock on the door. The mincing man runs to answer it, and Wood now begins his narrative proper, while cleverly introducing the rather unorthodox subject matter of the film in a manner so sly as to be almost subliminal.

This "death of a transvestite" scene is a sublime, classical death scene tableau, a recurrent literary template, and well used here. The corpse lays in awkward, fey repose, like Sleeping Beauty; perhaps a kiss from a male will wake him up. The tension of the scene well illustrates the simultaneous power of attraction and revulsion "she-males" hold over heterosexual men.

Additionally, in a bold dramatic signature which would become pivotal in the films of Wood, *Glen or Glenda?*'s main narrative segment begins with a death and a wake; in essence, a funeral. Many of Wood's subsequent films and screenplays (and presumably novels as well) feature the death and/or funeral of a significant, oftimes sympathetic character, often in the first act. The preeminence and significance of death in Wood's metaphoric universe could not be clearer. More often than not, death itself is the *deus ex machina* in the cinema of Wood, a vengeful and cruel death whose tragedy ignites the ensuing melodrama. Thus, it is not by accident or laziness, but opportunistic design, that the home movie footage of Bela Lugosi, the last known footage of a man soon deceased, becomes the igniting element in Wood's masterwork *Plan 9 from Outer Space* (1959).

Glen or Glenda? proceeds to cleverly sketch male culture's ambivalent reaction towards sexual deviancy, via the behavior of the various men who enter and inhabit this poor soul's death chamber. A white-coated medico rushes in, almost passionately, and kneels before the corpse like a distraught lover, checking the suicide's heart with a stethoscope. It is he who has the only physical contact with the dead soul. The physician leans next to the bed in a position both compassionate and engaging, as if offering the corpse either a show of grief, or a declaration of love. One cannot help but think of Prince Charming and Sleeping Beauty in this whimsical set-up, in which a male virtually genuflects towards a fallen fellow (who may or not be of the gender at first perceived), and who seems all but set to resurrect the fallen soul with a reanimating kiss.

Meanwhile, two uniformed policemen cower in the corner of the room, next to the door, terrified of the horrifying "she-thing," attempting to stay as far as possible from the freak in its claustrophobic sepulcher. The behavior of the two cops is significant, as they represent patriarchal culture at its most blatantly phallocentric. They spend the entire scene as far removed from the corpse as possible, clearly terrified of this bizarre, sexually threatening freak of the atomic age. Certainly, the emasculation implied by this creature who has voluntarily eschewed his manhood would terrify one whose self-identity is solely centered on the phallus (and its techno-fetishist weaponry analogs), and whose abandonment would signal castration, impotence and, in phallocentric culture, certain death.

Yet Police Inspector Warren (Lyle Talbot) fearlessly approaches and stands somberly over the corpse and almost lovingly reads the suicide note, becoming the closest thing to a sympathetic figure seen in this impromptu wake. He comes across as a bemused but gracious father figure, not necessarily understanding this creature's tale of woe, but sympathizing nonetheless, as he ruminates on the sorry fate of this latest victim of the cruel postwar world.

Through voice-over, the corpse explains to the audience his reasons for choosing death: "The records will tell the story. I was put in jail recently. Why? Because I, a man, was caught on the street wearing women's clothing. This was my fourth arrest, for the same act. In life, I must continue wearing them. Therefore, it would only be a matter of time until my next arrest. This is the only way. Let my body rest in death in the things I cannot wear in life." A quick cutaway shot to a radiator as the deceased intones, "This is the only way," conveys, somewhat sketchily, that the man/woman ended his life by asphyxiation and/or ingestion of poison gas. As anticipated, the suicide note is a mournful, self-pitying tale of nonconformity, persecution, self-loathing, and finally tragic self-destruction. Yet the voice used for the suicide is a mocking, comic one, not unlike the proverbial henpecked husband seen in cartoons of the day, a weakling with a speech impediment, and yet another in a bottomless barrel of mixed messages offered by *Glen or Glenda?*.

As witness the nervous, fearful behavior of the assembled males, the queer death of this she-man bespeaks an upsetting, convulsive reflection on patriarchal culture. This obscure misfit's death, like Glenda's virtual death upcoming, are finally sacrifices, so that not just the man, but the male-dominated community itself may evolve. This sacrifice is underscored by the voice of the deceased, who still inhabits the scene via an overdubbed soliloquy, thus remaining an important character in the ensuing story. The dead who still speak, either through their legacy and/or physical or spiritual resurrection, are recurring archetypes in the films of Wood, with *Plan 9 from Outer Space* perhaps the definitive example.

Yet finally, perhaps, the pivotal ancillary figure in the death scene is the man (dressed in worker's coveralls and listed in the credits as "the janitor") who stands nervously in the room with the corpse at the scene's inception, and subsequently admits the assembled male multitude. The viewer may presume the character to be a landlord or building superintendent who stumbled upon the deceased in his rented room. Yet the man's behavior suggests something quite different; his highly emotional reactions give the definite impression that he may have been personally involved with the deceased. His pantomimic gestures, which include hand-wringing, pacing, and general mincing around, suggests to the first-time viewer something darker, that this clearly traumatized man was the suicide's lover. This shocking allusion, whether accidental or intentional, nonetheless evokes on an almost subliminal level a subject matter unaddressed consciously throughout most of *Glen or Glenda?*; that of the crossdressers' potential homosexuality. (It may also be significant, or merely felicitous, that this character was played by the film's producer, George Weiss.)

Set in a doctor's office, replete with large desk and massive library, the next scene serves to provide the almost obligatory educational lecture, a fixture of the exploitation picture genre, done as much to inform the audience as to kill screen time. What Wood does with this "boring" lecture portion of the film, however, is to use it as a springboard to expansive narrative threads as well as some provocative montage sequences, and it is within this setting that *Glen or Glenda?*'s profound psychological discussion ensues.

A nurse informs Dr. Alton (Timothy Farrell) that Inspector Warren has arrived to see him. As Warren thanks Alton for sharing his precious time, while unwrapping a cigar, the camera crawls in slowly to the two men, who seem poised to bond in a most intimate way. Yet as the cop and the doctor converse, they sit as far apart from each other as possible, ironically illustrating the real state of affairs between males in postwar America: connected intellectually, but distant emotionally.

Alton asks Warren, oddly, "Business or pleasure, inspector?" to which Warren replies, even more oddly, "In a way, business...." Coded double-entendres abound in the films of Wood, but this one is especially intriguing, as it suggests that both professionals have more than a professional interest in the strange new world of sexual perversions, and are not immune to its potential titillation quotient. In addition, this is a nice nod to the probably titillated audience, whose interest is most assuredly of a morbid and voyeuristic nature.

Warren and Alton continue this strange cat-and-mouse game, in which neither party directly addresses the subject at hand, an odd flirtation amongst same-sex participants. Warren reminisces on his twenty years of law enforcement, and then ruminates on the importance of learning. Finally, Warren offers this cryptic statement: "We only have one life to live. We throw that away, what's left?" as he tellingly lights his cigar, cleverly illustrating that all humans, in one way or another, "throw their life away," for how can anyone preserve it intact in a toxic, fallen culture?

The two professionals continue to hem and haw over the actual subject of the discussion with some wonderfully obtuse dialogue, a coy dance around the subject which finally frustrates the busy medical man, who insists: "Let's get our stories straight — you're referring to the suicide of the transvestite?" Warren indifferently replies, as if still not ready to commit himself to this most disturbing subject, "If that's the word you men of science use for a man who wears women's clothing, yes." Alton replies, in complete deadpan, "Yes, in cold, hard, medical language, that's the word, as unfriendly and as vicious as it may sound." Warren then offers, "Would an operation do any good? I understand you were quite prominent in a case that hit the headlines a few weeks ago" (an overt reference to the Christine Jorgensen case which was the impetus for this film).

Alton finally gives the corpse a proper name: Patrick, aka "Patricia." In an effort to educate the policeman, Alton proceeds to describe two cases, which provide the core narrative framework of *Glen or Glenda?*, a framework which is nonetheless distorted beyond recognition by Wood's eclectic, scattershot editorial structure. As Alton appears in tight close-up, he intones, in a manner quite similar to that of Lugosi, "Only the infinity of the depths of a man's mind can really tell the story," certainly an odd bit of poetic license from a man who obviously prides himself on being practical and non-emotional.

The film cuts to another of many stock footage shots of a stormy sky, this time presumably to illustrate the torturous workings of the "infinity of the depths of a man's mind...." Again we see a smirking Lugosi; God has returned, and now speaks the doctor's name, aware of every narrative thread occurring in this movie, which now boasts at least three. Speaking to the audience, Lugosi says, "Dr. Alton, a young man though he is, speaks the words of the all-wise. No one can really tell the story. Mistakes are made, but there are no mistaking the thoughts in a man's mind. The story is begun!"

Another thunder-and-lightning punctuation, and the film cuts to the filmmaker, Wood, walking down a Hollywood street in broad daylight and in full drag, a beautiful and haunting evocation of the exposed, tortured artist. Big-boned, handsome and very masculine, Wood prancing about in ridiculous thrift-store skirt and fuzzy sweater, in full makeup and sporting a gaudy blonde wig, appears the epitome of God's edict, "Mistakes are made!" Wood positions himself in this early shot as a pitiable freak of nature, a figure of scorn and ridicule, something fascinating yet loathsome. Feminist critic Judith Butler considered the phenomenon of drag to be a singular, potentially subversive, contradiction in the prevailing mythos of binary-obsessed sexual exclusivity: "[D]rag fully subverts the distinction between inner and outer psychic space and effectively mocks both the expressive model of gender and the notion of a true gender identity."[11] Wood's exhibition as "Glenda" in *Glen or Glenda?* surely qualifies as a drag performance, and clearly illustrates one of the act's key values: "The performance of drag plays upon the distinction between the anatomy of the performer and the gender that is being performed."[12] This bold conceit of *Glen or Glenda?* will be one its abiding charms throughout, and will illuminate much in the film's fitful gender-centric discourse.

Wood approaches and stops in front of a department store window, inside which a sexy female mannequin models some slinky lingerie. Wood compares himself to the mannequin, even trying to imitate it by putting his hands on his hips, and looks off in the distance. As Wood and the mannequin share this beautifully composed two-shot, Wood turns towards camera and stands, like the mannequin, in a stiff pose, with an ironic smile on his face, which one cannot help but note is a very sad smile. This is the image of a miserable, even tortured human being. Alton comments, "One might say, 'There, but for the grace of God, go I.' " This is a truly pitying remark to the tragic figure before the viewer, as Wood turns towards camera with a face not happy or content, but full of anguish. Wood-in-drag, courageous and nonconformist though he is, does not look to be a happy person. He looks less like someone expressing a daring freedom of choice, and more like a prisoner to bizarre neuroses he cannot control. This first glimpse at Wood suggests a rather harsh judgment, even self-loathing, on the part of the filmmaker. Underneath all the camp and wry wit and glamour of the artist, and the gleeful, joyful laughter of the audience, this one shot clearly signals what will reveal itself, in full, upon further examination: Ed Wood's cinema is a cinema of tragedy, of personal and collective shame, of unending guilt and grief, of a hellish lifetime haunted by unfulfilled and unfulfillable dreams. Psychological and existential pain beats at the heart of Wood's films.

With this scene, and the introduction proper of Glen-as-Glenda, Wood is perhaps sketching a salient reading (or possibly a sincere but naïve misreading) of psychologist Carl Jung's concepts of anima and animus, the unconscious inner personalities which inhabit both male and female. The anima harbors the more intuitive, creative and feminine potentials within the male, while in the animus resides the more logical, masculine aspects of the female; in each case, these traits are either expressed or repressed, according to the subject's psychological make-up and cultural environment. It may be thus helpful to view *Glen or Glenda?* through the eyes of classical Jungian psychology, inasmuch as Jung's famous theories regarding the anima and animus, that is, the powerful unconscious forces within man and woman, seem to apply so directly to much of what is going on in the film.

From this angle, Glenda may be seen as Wood's overt, almost comical emblem of anima manifest, with the feminine qualities buried inside the male most ostentatiously "expressed" in the glorious mask of Glen's "Glenda," a mask which all but threatens to take over and swallow up the male entity which hosts it.[13] Based on Jung's belief that the anima is energized via incorporated components of the subject's significant female others, the matriarch foremost, Glenda could thus be seen as a virtually conscious invocation of Glen's mother, a theory which will pan out profoundly as the film unspools.

Yet countering this main thrust will be an avowed ambivalence towards the very notion of gender as "essence," a recurring assertion that gender is largely determined by signifying outward symbols and affects, which feminist critics such as Butler frame thusly: "[G]ender is culturally constructed: hence, gender is neither the causal result of sex nor as seemingly fixed as sex."[14] This dialectic tension, woven throughout *Glen or Glenda?*, gives the film not merely its wavering focus and awkward thesis, but its very dynamic and ultimately modern declaration on the topic of gender studies, a discourse still in its infancy at the time.

This key scene dissolves into the first of *Glen or Glenda?*'s shrewd and revealing montages, which begins with two newspaper headlines: WORLD SHOCKED BY SEX CHANGE and "Man Nabbed Dressed as Girl." Over these paste-up declarations, Alton quips, "Why is the world shocked by this headline? Why? Once, not so very long ago, people of the world were saying...." A cartoon-like female voice takes over, saying, "Airplanes? Ha! Why, it's against the Creator's will. If the Creator wanted us to fly, He woulda given us wings!" This expressionistic bit of polemic is stated over a stock footage shot of a war plane dropping either bombs or supplies onto a field. The implication, however, is that the plane is defecating, in essence mocking the narrator's ignorant statement, in one of *Glen or Glenda?*'s frequent, clever uses of stock footage montage as socio-political commentary, and one of several instances in *Glen or Glenda?* where Wood dabbles in satire, a playful tinkering with narrative and genre which would reach astounding heights in *Plan 9 from Outer Space*.

Next, a comically dour farmer, chewing on wheatgrass, stands in front of a spare woodland backdrop, as the viewer hears his thoughts: "Automobiles? Bah! They scare the hosses! If the Creator had wanted us to roll around the countryside, we'd a been born with wheels!" Over attractive stock footage of modern highways at rush hour, vast urban cityscapes, and other impressive scenes of modernity in full flower, Alton responds, "Silly, certainly! We were not born with wings. We were not born with wheels. But in the modern world of today, it's an accepted fact we must have them. So we have corrected that which nature has not given us."

This intricate montage continues, restating its original thesis of ignorance and intolerance: "If the Creator had wanted us to fly, He would have given us wings" is shown over a close-up of a woman's face. "If the Creator had wanted us to be born boys, we certainly would have been born *boys*!" is shown, tellingly, over a tight close-up of a woman's ear, with dangling earring, the earring supposedly signifying gender. But in fact, the sex of the model in question is unknown, as a male could certainly be wearing the earring; the ear could even conceivably be Wood's. *Glen or Glenda?* here again muddies the waters of strict gender assignment by contrasting rigid and intolerant beliefs about "essential" sex roles with images which obscure, not clarify, easy gender identification, an obfuscation which again evokes the voice of Butler and others: "As a shifting and contextual phenomenon, gender does not denote a substantive being, but a relative point of convergence among culturally and historically specific sets of relations."[15]

Underscoring this sense of gender confusion which Wood has just astutely drawn, Alton quips, "Are we sure? Nature makes mistakes. It's proven every day." The scene now returns to shots of Wood in drag, walking by the department store window again, yet another cruel yet brilliant bit of cynical self-parody on the part of the filmmaker. Alton clarifies the strange image before the viewer: "This person is a transvestite, a man who is more comfortable wearing girl's clothes. The term 'transvestite' is the name given by medical science to those persons who wear the clothing of the opposite sex. Many a transvestite actually wishes to be the opposite sex." To be sure, a men dressed in flashy drag was not an unusual sight in postwar media; Milton Berle was enchanting the early national television audience with a similar exhibition during the exact period in which *Glen or Glenda?* was released. What Wood did with this trite entertainment was to raise it above the vulgar, misogynist vaudeville of Berle and others, and harness it as a powerful aesthetic and political tool. To clarify, Glen-as-Glenda is a transvestite, but *Wood*-as-Glenda is a *drag performer*, unleashing through *Glen or Glenda?* all the politically subversive elements which that public exhibition may entail: "[W]e see sex and gender denaturalized by means of a performance which avows their distinctness and dramatizes the cultural mechanism of their fabricated unity."[16]

In this sublime production still from *Glen or Glenda?*, newlyweds Glen and Barbara (Wood and Dolores Fuller) stand before the suburban hearth, the scene of much torment and betrayal in the films of Ed Wood.

The scene shifts to show Wood relaxing at home, still in wig and sweater, and reading a women's magazine, appearing very much the caricature of the postwar housewife, lounging about the house while waiting for the breadwinner (male) to return from work. Alton ironically states, "The title of this can only be labeled 'Behind Locked Doors.' Give this man satin undies, a dress, a sweater and a skirt, or even the lounging outfit he has on, and he's the happiest individual in the world. He can work better, think better, he can play better, and he can be more of a credit to his community and his government because he is happy. These things are his comfort. But why the wig and makeup?" Here, Wood is forcing his stated agenda, rather awkwardly, by insisting that letting men run around in women's clothing is good for not only his own circle of friends, but society at large. In a broad sense the statement is correct, as only by letting people be individuals, expressing themselves regardless of the conformist beliefs of the community, can they be both happy and productive.

The scene changes to show Wood, finally given his character's name, Glen. Alton informs the viewer that Glen is engaged to be married to Barbara, "a lovely, intelligent girl," a reckless attempt to create the impression that Glen is a "normal" heterosexual man, engaged to a "normal" heterosexual girl, involved in a "normal" heterosexual relationship. Yet this first scene between the archetypal "man and woman" in the piece portrays a sympathetic yet peculiar, almost mocking caricature of the idyllic postwar couple. It is interesting to note that in addition to feminizing his male protagonist, for obvious reasons, Wood also takes care to make the woman, his partner-to-be, an independent, high-achieving college graduate; if not exactly a feminist heroine, at least a step in the right direction. The two are first shown sitting at a table in a kitchen, holding hands, and talking over future plans, a generic scene which, but for its sketchy *mise-en-scène*, might have come from any number of television situation comedies of the day. The first thing Barbara notices, however, are Glen's fingernails, which she declares are almost as long as her own, challenging even then Glen's sexuality, and their relative gender "positioning." Barbara states coyly, "We'll have to paint them some time." The camera angle changes slightly to favor Glen, as he somewhat theatrically states, "We'll trim them?" Barbara replies, "That's for sure!" The palpable tension residing in this introductory scene signals that something is seriously wrong with Glen. Although a likable character, his unstable gender projection has already shocked the audience, and even confused his lover. Jung would likely observe that even while wearing his "masculine" persona, Glen's unruly, subversive anima attempts projection, demanding to be seen and heard via signifying gestures like long fingernails and slightly effeminate manners.

After this all-too-brief introduction of the main characters and a potential storyline, *Glen or Glenda?* abandons its ever-precarious narrative to indulge in yet another fascinating montage polemic, again frustrating the film's fitful attempts to tell a tale. With these exotic and iconoclastic editorial sequences, however, Wood is in full force both as agent provocateur and film satirist. And to again cite Jung, for whom dreams were always educational and instructional in nature, the omnipresent editorial detours in *Glen or Glenda?* may be most helpful if read as the dreams (both fantasy and nightmare) of the postwar collective unconscious. In addition, filmmaker Wood's own obsessions and prejudices, overlaid with his character Glen's specific dreams and nightmares, all serve essentially the same purpose as the fairy tale or the dream in psychological analysis, where everything is symbolic, universal, and potentially significant.

As an anonymous man carries a large black steamer trunk down a flight of basement stairs, Dr. Alton continues his treatise on the imbalance of postwar sex roles: "Modern man is a hard-working human. Throughout the day, his mind and his muscles are busy at building the modern world and its business administration. His clothing is rough, course, starched, according to the specifications of his accepted job." The scene changes to show a balding man attempting to rest at home in a sterile, nondescript living room set. As the man removes his shoes and awkwardly tries to get comfortable on a striped couch, Alton continues to deride the fashion shackles of the atomic age. The balding man is next seen standing next to a prop bus stop in front of a black backdrop, a strikingly artificial set which augments the universal banality of the iconic figure. He takes off his hat, which appears to bother him, as Alton verifies, "And get the hat! Better yet, get the receding hairline! Men's hats are so tight they cut off the blood flow to the head, thus, cutting off the growth of hair. Seven out of ten men wear a hat, so the advertisements say. Seven out of ten men are bald," leaving the viewer to conclude cause and effect from this most obtuse bit of circumstantial evidence. The scene changes to show three girls in hats, chatting outside a storefront, as Alton smoothly segues into, "But what about the ladies? Yes, modern woman is a hard-working individual also, but when modern women's day of work is done, that which is designed for her home comfort is comfort. Hats that give no obstruction to the blood flow. Hats that do not crush the hair. Interesting thought, isn't it?" One might rightly wonder why Wood seems to obsess on headwear as an almost-sacred arbiter of gender signification; might he be playfully suggesting that, in line with Jung's thinking, it is what goes on *under* the headwear, i.e., within man's mysterious, bottomless brain, that makes all the difference? Wood may also be cunningly referencing the omnipotence of signifying elements in determining gender over the fickle, unknowable fathoms of the neurotic mind, again foreshadowing the philosophy of Butler and others: "The effect of gender is produced through the stylization of the body and, hence, must be understood as the mundane way in which bodily gestures, movements, and styles of various kinds constitute the illusion of an abiding gendered self."[17]

In a baffling segue, the scene now changes to show what at first appears to be stock footage of a tribal dance ritual, presumably from some vintage jungle film. Upon closer inspection, one may assume that the oddly composed scene was created new for *Glen or Glenda?*. It shows Wood's canny virtuosity with spare prop elements, as the setting looks, at first blush, quite convincing. However, the peculiar iconic artifice of Wood can be clearly seen. Two male "natives" dance in a clearing next to a large oak tree. Both wear fairly realistic tribal masks. The war mask of the lead male, although ostensibly comical in appearance, does feature a cartoony "evil grimace," devilish horns and hostile, angry eyes, in an attempt to approximate both the visage of a raging bull and a horned demon, each of which can easily be seen as emblematic of the "savage" male libido, and presumably a mask for a devilish unconscious as well. One "native" beats a tom-tom, while the other shakes a spear. The truly Woodian element in the scene are the seven human skulls strewn rather casually about the tree and a makeshift wooden framework. Jung documented several functions of tree imagery in dreams, fantasies and fairy tales. In the structure of *Glen or Glenda?*, if one takes the liberty of calling these frequent editorial detours as the film's dream or fantasy sequences, one might readily apply it here by accepting that the tree signifies "the individuation process as it prepares itself in the unconscious and gradually enters consciousness."[18]

Glen is becoming ready to grow psychologically, by delving into the "prehistory" of his unconscious. Alton clarifies this possibly profound shift thusly: "Just for comparison, let's go native, back to the animal instinct. There, in the lesser civilized part of the world, it's the male who adorns himself with the fancy objects, such as paint, frills and masks. The true instinct. The animal instinct. In bird and animal life, is it not so that it is the male who is the fancy one? Could it be that the male was meant to attract the attention of the female? What's so wrong about that?" The scene concludes with the two male natives dancing with several comely young women natives, presumably to show how the adornment of fancy objects (the mask and the spear?) attracts the female to the male. Finally, one of the males picks up and carries off a female, "caveman-style."

The scene returns to the barren living room with the striped couch, where both the bald man and a sexy robed woman sit together, now presented as a most improbable couple in a stiflingly sterile environment. Alton intones, "Where is the animal instinct in modern civilization? The female has the fluff and the finery...." Over more stock footage of crowds walking a city street, Alton now turns sexist and preachy: "Little Miss Female, you should feel quite proud of the situation. You of course realize that it is predominantly men who design your clothes, your jewelry, your makeup, your hair styling, your perfume.... There is no law against wearing such apparel on the street, as long as it can be distinguished that man is man and woman is woman," a most revealing comment on strict gender roles in modern patriarchal culture.

The scene changes to show a person, wearing a dress, sitting in an easy chair, reading the morning paper, which obscures the person's face as it boasts the headline, WORLD SHOCKED BY SEX CHANGE. The person puts down the paper, revealing him to be male, as denoted by a full, bushy beard, as Alton says, "But what is it would happen if this individual would appear on the street? You're doing it now! You are laughing!" Here *Glen or Glenda?* calls its audience's bluff by forecasting their crude, sexist reaction to the subject at hand, underlined with this playful bit of serio-comic trickery. Yet *Glen or Glenda?*'s real subversion here is a double bluff, for what if the person reading the newspaper were in fact, a female, wearing a fake beard? This clever sketch illustrates the folly of carelessly ascribing gender via crude outward markings and symbols, as suggests Butler: "Genders can be neither true nor false, neither real nor apparent, neither original nor derived. As credible bearers of those attributes, however, genders can also be rendered thoroughly and radically *incredible*."[19]

The scene changes to show Wood as Glen, now dressed "sufficiently" as a male. Wearing a suit and smoking a cigarette, Glen is now the very picture of the postwar heterosexual male, dashing and cavalier. Glen walks down the same street and looks longingly at the same department store mannequins as his alter ego Glenda had previously. Yet Glen appears tormented as he gazes at women's brassieres while wringing his hands, so close to yet so far from his object(s) of desire. Alton now attempts vainly to resurrect the narrative thread of the picture: "Thus, the strange case of Glen, who is Glenda, one in the same person, not half-man, half-woman, but nevertheless, man and woman in the same body; even though by all outward appearances, Glen is fully and completely a man..." adding yet another somewhat insecure declaration of staunch heterosexuality on the part of the filmmaker towards his protagonist-self. Yet this attempt at clarification actually further obscures easy answers, blurring the gender line yet again, suggesting that "male is female is male," i.e., all genders branch from one multifarious sexual mystery. By emphasizing "Glen, *who is* Glenda," Wood may be suggesting that man *is* woman, just in different socio-cultural garb. This jarring cut from montage to narrative nicely reveals the soul of Wood as tortured artist, in two distinct incarnations. In effect, Wood has performed a successful gender transformation before the viewer's eyes. *Glen or Glenda?* is Wood's virtual sex change operation, a revealing to the world of his peculiar preferences, an act both of confession and atonement.

Again, this unfolding thesis of *Glen or Glenda?* shares much with Jung's notions of the unconscious forces within man, forces which exert themselves in each sex by attaching predominant qualities of the opposite sex to them. To cite Jung, "The inferior Eros in man I designate as anima, the inferior Logos in woman as animus."[20] Eros describes attributes of sensitivity, compassion, sensuality and relatedness, traditionally associated with women and seen as "feminine"; Logos describes qualities of logical thinking, discrimination and perceptiveness, traditionally associated with men and seen as "masculine."[21] In effect, Glenda may be seen as a bizarre outward manifestation of Glen as he is "stuck" in his unconscious, his anima, striving to escape the authoritarian power of his unconscious, and illustrated in *Glen or Glenda?* via a comical "projection" known as the transvestite Glenda. As Jung states, the addressing of the anima within man, and attempts to integrate it into the conscious psyche, is a traumatic yet essential project for anyone wishing to achieve a modicum of mental health and stability, a ritual of sorts that signals the subject's transformation from adolescent to adult. Glen's chronic metamorphosis into Glenda is thus a ritual action, as Jung might state, "a precipitating crisis" which will ultimately allow the integration of the whole personality.

After promising to return to the ever-fragile anchoring narrative, *Glen or Glenda?* leaves it again just as abruptly with another dizzying jumble of Woodian collage moments. The first depicts a white party dress hanging on a clothes form in an empty room, a primitive sketch of the pettiness inherent in depicting gender by outward symbols only, a sketch which illustrates well this observation by Butler: "Clearly there are cases in which the component parts of sex do not add up to the recognizable coherence of unity that is usually designated by the category of sex."[22]

This stunningly symbolic shot is accompanied by a narrated dialogue exchange between a man and a young boy, a revealing exchange which ends up being the very heart of a dense film with a claim to many hearts. The boy wants to wear his sister's dress to an upcoming Halloween party, but the father's voice sternly warns, "There are names for boys who go around wearing women's clothes...." A new voice, the saving voice of the mother, joins the warring duo to state, "You go ahead and wear your sister's dress, Glen. You always did look better as a girl than you do as a man." This simultaneously damning and nurturing edict from Glen's mother, which in effect castrates the young man even as it draws him to the family bosom, most certainly echoes the author's own mother, possibly even in her very words, in a shocking confession of childhood trauma, relating directly to Wood's own biographical admission of being chronically dressed up as a girl by his mother. The mother here is seen as enabler, if not outright architect, of Glen's (and Wood's) aberrant behavior, giving approval over the patriarch's objections and in so doing negating the power of the patriarch in the family dynamic, making the female the boss in this most diabolical nuclear family.[23]

While explaining Glen (and Wood's) subsequent lifestyle choice, this tiny yet pivotal scene also reinforces the role of gender dominance in the culture in general. With the emasculated young male first being coaxed, and later in life freely choosing, to "become" a woman in certain social settings, he does this not merely to acquiesce to a domineering mother figure, but to side with the winning team in this particular family power struggle. In short, Glen's (and Wood's) lesson is that "women" are the power figures in his world, and so he decides to "become" one. From a traditionally Oedipal perspective, Glenda may be seen as Glen's escape from identifying with a passive, ineffectual father figure, as emblem of the failed "male" gender, and an attempt to appease a dominating mother figure, as well as ally himself with the dominant "female" gender, victorious in this family at least. In this way, Glen-as-Glenda not only worships and appeases the omnipotent matriarchal power figure, but in effect becomes an iconic recurrence of her, reinforcing this family's experience of "the Mother as the Law."[24] The scene also solidifies Jung's declaration that the internalized experience of the mother forms a key component of the male's subsequent anima projection.

This key scene segues into a most appropriate coda which serves primarily as a comedic, self-loathing punchline to the previous confession. Over a shot of Wood, now happily primping in full drag, Alton sarcastically delivers a verdict even more damning: "Glen did wear the dress to the Halloween party; he even took first prize!" This suggests that society finally noticed, condoned, perhaps even applauded this freakish behavior, giving Glen (Wood) back-handed encouragement to follow this pursuit. Though it may be that he was embraced primarily as an object of ridicule, a clown to be mocked, useful to the culture as representing a form of "other" from which to base "normal" men against, it may also have made Glen (Wood) feel like he actually belonged in this strange new world, an obscure footnote to culture at large, but one at least acknowledged.

Glen or Glenda?'s mood next shifts profoundly into a self-loathing mode, as Alton intones, "Then one day, it wasn't Halloween any longer!" Wood sits in drag, reading a magazine, when a woman enters the room and becomes shocked and disgusted at the she-male's appearance. Considering Glenda to be Glen's projected, non-integrated anima, it makes sense that the clearly drawn female in the scene is repulsed, for as Jung states, "[A] man who lives his anima is shunned by all really womanly women."[25] The viewer will discover that the woman was Sheila, Glen's sister, but the scene also well represents the dynamic between the archetypal female and her reaction, understandably horrified, at a man who dares to question the arbitrary gender demarcation of the day, again using fashion as the primary means of codification and most overtly, and comically, encroaching on the female's clearly defined gender territory by brazenly appropriating the accepted fashions which then defined the psycho-social construct labeled "woman."

The scene shifts again, back to what appears to be a return to some sort of protagonist-driven narrative sequence, but by now the viewer knows better than to take anything for granted in this most circuitous "Chinese Puzzle" of a film. Glen, now dressed as a man, leafs through his clothes drawer, perhaps deciding which gender to appropriate, as Alton declares, "Glen is a transvestite, but he is *not* a homosexual," a somewhat emphatic and insecure statement which underlies the apparently staunch heterosexism which anchors *Glen or Glenda?*, a heterosexism which will eventually be undone by Wood's own, perhaps unwitting, machinations. Alton next offers a cold, pedestrian definition of transvestism: "Transvestism is the name given by medical science to those men desperate to wear the clothing of the opposite sex, yet whose sex life in all instances remains quite normal," ending in another rather insecure declaration of "normality" by the author. This recurrent reiteration of fierce normality by Wood may be an effort to appease the latent insecurities of the film's original, predominantly male audience, as much as to reassure himself that although weird, he wasn't "queer."

As if to undermine all the venerated sobriety which has just ensued, what follows is a hilarious, if disingenuous deceit, and another of *Glen or Glenda?*'s most subversive uses of stock footage for pure propaganda purposes. Over a stock footage shot which shows a laborer scrubbing down a railroad signal tower, itself an overt phallic symbol seen as being "worshipped" and serviced by an obedient male, Alton reveals, "Would you be surprised to learn that this rough, tough individual is wearing pink satin undies under his uniform? He *is*!" The chances of this being true are nil, but Wood breathtakingly reveals here the indelible truth that a man's secret desires and fetishes are indeed unknown to his fellow man. Everyone in the world, underneath their prescribed gender-centric "uniform," could in fact be wearing "pink satin undies," or any other permutation which belies and subverts culture's attempt to quantify and label gender through the most superficial, and easily corrupted, exterior codes such as dress, fashion, and personal grooming. The secrets of a man's soul are hidden within, under his uniform, his conscious mind, his poker face, the totality of the "mask" he offers society.

Following is another two-shot sequence which, as expected, undermines the previous one. The first shot, an exterior, depicts a milkman, shown from the back and thus anonymous and archetypal, carrying two bottles of milk towards a dwelling. The second shot, an interior, shows a woman, also from the back and thus also anonymous and archetypal, bent over and dusting a coffee table in what is presumably her home. The viewer's eye is immediately drawn towards the woman's extended and swaying buttocks, as Alton obliquely references a corny, ubiquitous dirty joke: "And then there is your friendly neighborhood milkman, who knows how to find *comfort* at home." Wood has again fooled the viewer, who logically thought that the milkman was another example of a cross-dresser (more accurately, an under-dresser), going about his service to phallocentrism while secretly worshipping its opposing gender. However, the male as depicted here is just a garden-variety adulterer, a poster-boy for reckless heterosexism. Yet significantly, he is also drawn as a potential enemy of the suburban moral code, in that the viewer assumes that he is about to approach the housewife for an anonymous sexual indiscretion. The notion of "the milkman boffed my wife!" was a universal joke, disguising paranoid insecurity of a postwar era in the early stages of changing from a primarily industrial to an increasingly service-oriented economy. What businessman of the era did not, even fleetingly, entertain the notion of a male in the service sector, as represented by the ubiquitous "milkman," sexually servicing his wife as he labored, thus corrupting and undermining the supposedly sacrosanct moral structure of postwar suburban "paradise"? *Glen or Glenda?* here seems to be suggesting that the postwar heterosexual social contract was not as airtight and invulnerable as its members might have wished it to be, in yet another devastating act of subversion on the part of this most diabolical agent provocateur. As well, the symbolic "pink satin undies" of the previous scene have moved, as they are presumably now being worn by the sexy housewife, who is also presumably about to lose them in acquiescence to the milkman. This subversive emblem of gender demarcation, and sexual power, has been miraculously switched by Wood from one sex to the other, in the artist's ongoing barrage of overlapping, self-contradictory clues which seem determined to obfuscate traditional gender demarcation lines. Here, *Glen or Glenda?* seems to be a coy philosophical burlesque on the age-old gender-centric query, "Who wears the pants in *this* family?"

Soon, the scene changes to show Glen's fiancée (also Wood's then-partner, Dolores Fuller) in a kittenish close-up. Alton identifies her thusly: "Glen is engaged to be married to Barbara, a lovely, intelligent girl." As this line is a repetition of one stated verbatim several minutes previous, one can see Wood's nascent insecurity bubbling over; he seems determined (over-determined?) to convey the fact that he, and thus cross-dressers in general, are "real men," despite their peculiar psycho-sexual appetites. As Alton continues, "The problem: Glenda, Glen's other self," the scene cuts to Wood, sitting in a chair, dressed in yet another woman's outfit, and looking absolutely miserable. Alton attempts to clarify, but instead further obscures understanding, with the cryptic remark, "The girl that he himself is; his other, individual personality." This self-contradictory remark suggests that Wood regarded his "Glenda" self not as a whimsical sexual fetish, but a traumatically imprinted psychological identity and (perhaps involuntary) gender aberration, in essence a postmodern redux of Nathaniel Hawthorne's Scarlet Letter, wherein society forced a visual code onto a member who had sinned sexually, thus politically, against it. As stated previously, this declaration of "Glen's other self" reinforces the assumption that Glenda may be seen as Glen's projected anima, stuck in a neurotic divination of those qualities, primarily but not exclusively feminine, which Glen has refused to address, likely due to traumatic childhood events. Glen's eventual acceptance and embracing of this queer "other self" is essential to his psychological well-being, for only the anima can transport a man into a conscious based on a fully aware, sensitive partaking of life.

The scene now dissolves into the same living room, later that evening. Through this alchemical dissolve, the "feminine" Glenda morphs into the masculine "Glen" before the viewer's eyes. Now Barbara sits by his side, wearing the same dress that Glen was just wearing. They have in effect swapped genders and switched personas, via a cheap but effective cinematic trick, in yet another marvelous bit of cinema alchemy by *Glen or Glenda?*; the "queer" couple just seen has now magically morphed into the accepted heterosexual archetype of the postwar era. This magical evocation of a male-female dyad, or syzygy, was for Jung an important although nonexclusive pairing of opposites which found its outlet in many cultural traditions, and it serves a pivotal and dynamic purpose in this scenario.[26]

Barbara hands Glen the newspaper, which features the headline WORLD SHOCKED BY SEX CHANGE. Barbara ruminates on "how some people's minds work." Glen calmly defends himself by explaining, "Some people aren't happy the way they are," not only *his* personal truth, but also a universal one. The conformist Barbara counters, "That's a pretty drastic step to take." Glen sighs, knowingly, "If it's the only way, I'm for it." Wood here shamelessly advocates for radical change in sexual politics, if only to ensure man's evolutionary happiness.

Barbara wonders out loud what she would do if she found herself in "the mental turmoil that person went through," or even worse, if she "suddenly realized that there was something mentally wrong with you," looking at Glen and making him visibly uncomfortable. Barbara shakes off this disturbing thought by stating, "It's hard to visualize. Here we are, *two perfectly normal people*, about to be married, and lead a normal life together. And there's this poor fellow, who couldn't be happy if it wasn't for modern medical science." Glen is visibly shaken by Barbara's emphatic statements, not only because of her harsh judgment against this type of behavior, but also his own cowardice in being unable to confess his sins to his loved one. Barbara ends her musings with, "Our Freud German psychology explains a lot of the facts, but I'm afraid the end of studies is the beginning of reality" (sic), which correctly intuits that only knowledge *plus* life experience equals wisdom. In addition to underscoring the predominance of the anima in Glen's largely defensive actions (and reactions), this scene is one of several which highlight Barbara's impressive capacity for "discrimination, judgment, insight," and shines a flattering light on her well-developed animus, suggesting that she may well be an important balancing force in Glen's life.[27]

The scene changes to show Glen, now alone on a sunny city street, dressed as a man, yet clearly emasculated by the previous encounter, in which he was proved weak and ineffectual ("girly"), not by his choice of clothing, but by his actions. He was unable to summon the courage to tell his fiancée the truth, and this act of moral cowardice on his part is far more damning than his harmless fetish. Glen walks towards and then past camera, grimacing and holding his head in an over-dramatized expression of anguish. As *Glen or Glenda?* has by now successfully erased the line between narrative and documentary, and by extension melodrama or autobiography, the viewer can easily see the scene also as a rare and poignant portrait of filmmaker Wood, an artist in sheer agony, and compulsively expressing this self-torture through his art.

As Jung often stated, the psychological wanderer's journey through the "ritual initiation" towards balancing his inner and outer selves and integrating his conscious and subconscious mind, is in many ways a "heroic deed" not unlike that of the fairy tale heroes of antiquity, who battled monsters within and without to achieve lasting peace and mental purity for himself and his community. As has been hinted at thus far, and will be revealed ultimately, the goal of this life task involves vanquishing the negative compulsions of childhood, the matriarch's deleterious impact foremost: "It is evident that the great deed really means overcoming the mother and thus winning immortality."[28] Jung insisted that the ritual integration of the anima or animus was, above all, an act of moral courage, and the subject of moral courage is a major theme in *Glen or Glenda?* (and by default a major theme in Wood's highly personal art), making Glen's journey from "Glen-Glenda" to Glen all the more significant as an analog of these basic Jungian precepts.[29] This scene functions extremely well as a portrait of the artist Wood in turmoil, and well mirrors the daring split between conscious and unconscious impulses which runs through *Glen or Glenda?*: Should Glen tell his beloved his terrible secret, just as Wood has confessed this same secret to the film audience?

The scene returns to Glen and Barbara in the same positions as before, but now Barbara is wearing a fluffy white sweater, which Glen fondles and obsesses on. *Glen or Glenda?* has effectively turned women's clothing, thus woman's very spirit, into cheap, easily coded fetish objects, which throws some light onto what Glen sees in the other world of Glenda's: softness and gentleness, an outer manifestation of the very anima of feminine principle which seemed elusive (and desired) to the psychologically rigid heterosexual male of the day. Obviously, Glen seeks a female counterpart to his tortured male psyche in an attempt to balance

In this scene of posed violence from *Glen or Glenda?* Wood threatens and attacks his real-life partner, Dolores Fuller, asserting a peculiar "manhood" as a she-male. Dolores seems more amused than terrified by his pathetic attempts to appropriate not just her garment, but her gender as well.

things— his projected anima, dubbed Glenda, is a neurotic attempt to achieve this— as Jung states, "As a rule, man needs the opposite of his actual condition to force him to find his place in the middle."[30]

Later, Barbara notices that something is bothering Glen, and asks what it is, but Glen has not the courage to tell of his horrible secret, which he fears will not only vilify him within the community, but estrange him forever from his object of desire, the cherished female. Barbara continues, gently coaxing Glen: "Who knows? Maybe I could help." Glen replies, not entirely with irony, "That's just it— you could." Barbara could certainly "help" Glen, not merely by sharing her coveted garmentalia, but by allowing Glen to unveil his long-repressed second self which, he might hope, Barbara could identify with and recognize, if not immediately embrace.

Barbara then asks, "Glen, is it another woman?" Glen is taken aback, speechless, for she has intuited his dark secret; the problem is, figuratively speaking, *another woman*, that woman being Glenda. This hilarious *bon mot* speaks volumes, for another woman *is* at fault for threatening Glen and Barbara's potential happiness, that "woman" being the anima-spirit known as Glenda. As Jung observed in many a therapeutic situation, "[T]he anima comes between them like a jealous mistress who tries to alienate the man from his family."[31]

This shock moment cuts abruptly to stock footage of a bison stampede, an incongruous juxtaposition that jolts the audience even as it cleverly evokes Glen's tortured mindset at this crucial juncture. Soon, God-figure Lugosi appears over the stampeding herd, shouting, "Pull the string! Pull the string!" The edict stated here may be seen to suggest either, "Tell the truth!," goading Glen into having the courage of his convictions, or perhaps "Open the curtain!," suggesting that Glen finally show Barbara the secret which lies dormant between them. Lugosi continues, "A mistake is made! A story must be told!" As Jung's "wise old man," Lugosi again intones that Glen's "story" (that is, his ritual initiation via his projected anima), must be revealed to Barbara, just as Wood's personal psychological struggle is being revealed to the film's audience. The revelation of this initiatory experience to all concerned parties is needed not only to save this personal relationship, but to balance the masculine and feminine forces of the universe.

The scene changes to show Glen in his bedroom, preparing to transform into Glenda. He removes a blond wig from a box and prepares to don his alter ego, as Alton intones, "It's always the same— Glen is afraid to tell her, but he must tell her soon! Should he tell her now, or hit her between the eyes after the wedding, when it might be too late for either of them?" The scene cuts to more stock footage of a highway at rush hour, as Alton ruminates existentially, "The world is a strange place to live in. All those cars, all going someplace, all carrying humans who are carrying out their lives." The scene cuts to the exterior of the Monica Apartments, as Alton continues: "The world is shocked by a person who changes his sex!," restating the film's original thesis yet another time, the phrase by now becoming *Glen or Glenda?*'s mantra. Glen is seen crossing the busy street, dodging presumably the very cars seen earlier, "all carrying humans who are carrying out their lives." Glen walks to a lingerie shop and looks longingly at the sexily dressed female mannequins. Alton confirms what the audience senses Glen is thinking: "There are so many problems in their situation. Glen and all the other 'Glens.' Perhaps the fear of the discovery of the underthings they wear under their regular clothing. Or that which they wear in their nightly visit to Morpheus, God of Sleep." Glen enters the shop, in which a lone female mannequin, dressed in slinky black bra and panties, dominates the frame, another striking symbolic specter of Glen's projected anima. As Glen approaches the sales counter, his shadow blends in with the shadow of the mannequin thrown against the back wall, creating a strange two-headed ghost, that ghost well expressing the dualist spirit of "Glen-Glenda," and presumably a foreshadowing of the anticipated merging of Glen's two "selves." This impressive, virtually subliminal visualization of the hoped-for integration of conscious and unconscious, aka "individuation," suggests that Glen is well on the way towards self-actualization, that elusive, lofty psychological prize won only through the torturous acknowledgment and redress of life errors, aka self-knowledge.

The female clerk asks Glen what he desires, and he casually, cigarette in hand, says, "Yeah, lemme see a nightie! Size 12. Black, very sheer...." The clerk produces the requested fetish-object, and Glen caresses it lovingly. As the clerk gives her sales pitch, and Alton smirks, "Perhaps he admires the material too long," Glen fondles the material obsessively, and the clerk's face soon changes from fake smile to sincere horror.

Cut to stock footage of another thunderstorm with angry, God-sent lightning, as Alton intones, "But Glen and all the other Glen and Glendas have an even bigger problem," and another extraordinary Wood montage begins. Over more stock footage of traffic, and a parking lot in front of an immense manufacturing plant, two "Regular Joes" begin a dialogue in voiceover about how they hate working, and hate even more the end of the weekend which brings Monday. The conversation soon veers inevitably to the horror of sex-change operations. Over stock footage of a gigantic vat of molten, bubbling metal, which places this found-footage collage as set in a steel mill, Joe #1 says, "Say, did you read about the guy who changed to a girl? Says he was perfectly normal, too!" Joe #2 replies with disgust, "How could a guy be normal and go do a thing like that to hisself?" As he says this, there is a shot of a white-hot steel rod plunging in and out of a steaming hole in a milling machine, a most crude yet vivid metaphor for the passionate, fiery, yet potentially damning fire of heterosexual intercourse. Joe #2 counters, "All the same, it must take a lot of guts to pull a stunt like that," over another shot of a vessel pouring molten steel into receptacles, suggesting that courageous, autonomous selves are invariably forged through the "white-hot fires" of self-loathing and societal estrangement. Joe #2 responds defensively, "That's a problem I don't ever intend to face," over a close-up of the previously seen white-hot rod plunging hastily into the steaming hole, in effect the phallus escaping to or hiding within the vagina, unwilling to consider any notion which may threaten the fragile, traditional heterosexual experience. Joe #1 continues, "Maybe that's a problem we should all face." Joe #2 tentatively queries, "I don't getcha...," as the molten steel phallus timidly peeks out of the safety of the steel vagina, inquisitive but afraid. Joe #1 continues, "Just think of the unhappy life, the miserable times this world of ours must have given this guy," over a shot of a sparkling vat of molten metals. Joe #2 ponders, "I still don't getcha," as the fearful molten phallus retreats yet again into its harboring vagina. Joe #1 attempts to clarify: "Now, here is a guy who wanted to be a girl. Now supposing there was no way to change this thing?" Joe #2 quips incredulously, "You sound as if you are really heat up on this thing!" as the white-hot phallus peeks out again, somewhat emboldened. Joe #1 states conclusively, "I guess I am," again over the backdrop of the forging fire of molten metal. Joe #2 pleads, "Do you realize what would happen if every man in the country that wanted to wear women's clothes, or felt like a woman, went to their doctors and said they wanted a sex change?" As he pleads against this incipient threat to his fragile manhood, there is a new shot, this time of a thin, very long, ribbon-like strip of white-hot steel, which is thrust into and quickly devoured by another vagina-like milling opening. Joe #2, threatened by the specter of this baffling new creature not male nor female but something wholly other, witnesses his thick, hard phallus transformed into something far thinner and more flexible, and most tellingly, far longer that his previous faux-penis; does this represent progress, or encroaching impotence, to the terrified heterosexual male? Joe #1 confidently concludes, "Of course. That's why I say perhaps society should be a little bit more lenient. Maybe society should try to understand them as human beings...." The scene changes to stock footage at the same highway with traffic seen earlier, only this time at night, a beautiful and somewhat somber scene. Joe #1 wearily concludes, "Another day done, thank goodness. See ya tomorrow, Jack!" This magnificent montage, which implies that these average Joes spent their entire day meditating about the poor Glen or Glendas of the world, as well as pondering their own places in this strange new world, ends with another thunder and lightning burst, another affirmation from the gods above that something profound (either emancipatory or diabolical) has just occurred. The blatant, simplistic, yet wholly effective symbology created by the stock footage, which stunningly illuminates the provocative discourse of the "Regular Joes" of the world, shows Wood at his peak as editorial poet.

This singular montage tumbles fitfully into another miniature narrative segment, in which a troubled Glen visits a fellow transvestite named Johnny, to share his dilemma over the impending marriage, and his torment over telling Barbara his dirty little "secret." The catastrophic incongruity between desire and compulsion which is the spirit of *Glen or Glenda?* is underscored perfectly in the following montage, which begins as Glen, as Glenda, strolls a city street at night, smoking a cigarette, and looking not unlike a streetwalker trolling for business. This virtually *noir* shot paints Glen-Glenda's plight as the dark, impressionistic wanderings of a tortured psyche. That the heroic Glen, trapped inside his projected anima, should be shown wandering the city night fits in perfectly with Jung's assessment of the mythological heroes of dream and fairytale analysis, and their symbolic import to the psychologically tortured: "[H]eroes are usually wanderers, and wandering is a symbol of longing, of the restless urge which never finds its object, of nostalgia for the lost mother."[32]

As inevitable counterpoint to this, Alton, the deadpan voice of reason, continues, and is now also shown onscreen, with the following edict: "Glen should seek the advice of a competent psychiatrist, but then very few transvestites wish to change their *strange* desires," an overtly judgmental statement which suggests that Glen and his brethren seek not mere assistance in embracing their behavior, but therapy in order to cure them of it.

Also, this early declaration of the potential healing nature of the psychiatric profession offers a clue to another one of Glen's ultimate goals: Glen's "Glenda" may be seen in some ways as a misguided attempt to seek a man's leadership, to locate a strong father figure to replace the ineffectual one he lacked in childhood. Ironically, Glen does eventually visit the psychiatrist Alton, who acts definitively as a father surrogate, guiding Glen towards his final, healing journey.

Alton continues, this time somewhat more compassionately, "This is their life; to take it away from them might do as much harm as taking away an arm or a leg, or life itself. Many even carry their transvestite desires to the grave with them." The scene clarifies this last statement by returning briefly to the suicide scene which started *Glen or Glenda?*'s dizzying journey through the tortured landscape of postwar sexual difference. This confession underscores the necessity of Glen's other self, and reveals a deeper truth: This other "person," the anima encoded in the text as the transvestite Glenda, represents an essential part of any healthy, integrated human being, albeit currently projected outward and therefore out of balance.

The scene shifts to a happier time, one year ago, when Glen and Barbara made their marriage vows. The couple fawn over each other like two kids in puppy love. Glen offers Barbara a ring, and Barbara gushes ecstatically, "Oh, I was beginning to think you'd never get around to it!" After setting the date, to coincide with Barbara's college graduation, Glen's mood awkwardly shifts from joy to despair, and Barbara notices: "Suddenly it seems like you're a thousand miles off!" Glen distracts Barbara from the inevitable by admiring her dress, and saying, "When I look at you, you tie me in knots," to which Barbara replies, "I love to tie you in knots," suggesting not only the clichéd sexual energy between heterosexual man and woman, a powerful energy which often results in tying the marriage "knot," but also to the confusing, unsettling questions and feelings about one's assigned gender which the loved one inflames in the lover. The scene ends in a most provocative editorial conceit: As Barbara continues to gush over Glen, the scene fades out. While we continue to hear Barbara's endless proclamations of love on the soundtrack, the scene now reveals Glenda, walking that dark street of night, alone again and tortured by the shame of an unbearable moral crime. The threat to a happy marriage which this specter of diabolical perversion represents could not be more starkly drawn, as well as again revealing this anima manifestation as a villain of sorts, that "jealous mistress who tries to alienate the man from his family."

Glenda enters his/her apartment, clearly disturbed, the time assumed to be the present. A clap of thunder is heard, and Glenda falls to the floor, stricken by the righteous anger of God; God-figure Lugosi now appears via superimposition, and utters the infamous, cryptic line, "Beware! Beware! Beware of the big, green dragon that sits on your doorstep! He eats little boys! Puppy dog tails and big, fat snails! Beware! Take care! Beware!"

In fairy tales and mythology, as well as dream analysis, the serpent or dragon is often observed to represent the incarnation of a diabolical mother figure, so Lugosi's mention of a dragon who "eats little boys" most assuredly references the troubled psyche's ongoing battles with untoward matriarchal influence forged in a distraught childhood, and this mantra, repeated throughout *Glen or Glenda?*, reinforces the notion that the projected anima is composed largely of psychological imprints of a dominating, corrupting mother, a figure who nonetheless has a strange, potentially fatal attraction to the suffering offspring. As Jung observed in his research, "The serpent symbolizes the mysterious numen of the "mother" (and of other daimonia) who kills, but who is at the same time man's only security against death, as she is the source of life."[33]

As Lugosi's face fades to black, *Glen or Glenda?*'s most profound and psychologically infused montage unspools, a baffling treasure trove of symbology strung together in a collage which depicts the unending nightmare of the self-loathing "sexual deviant's" tortured psyche. Glenda stands against a black void of a backdrop, in full drag, and gesturing to an off-screen presence to "come hither" (that is, to embrace and accept who "he" is). The reaction shots feature Barbara, reacting in anguish to the horrible revelation of Glen's "gender crime," and reminding the viewer that "a man who lives his anima is shunned by all really womanly women."

Barbara finally falls to the floor, weak from the devastating discovery. Next we see Barbara lying on the floor of the apartment, with a giant tree inexplicably fallen on top of her, pinning her down. Certainly, this shot crudely suggests the trapping power of the phallus, in terms of accepted gender demarcation; anyone who dares threaten this order will be "felled" by the brute phallocentric structure of man's psycho-sexual neurosis. In terms of dream and fantasy symbology, the tree often represents the "the still unconscious core of the personality. ... indicating a state of deep unconsciousness."[34] The deadly "state of deep unconsciousness" inherent in Glen while Glenda rules his psyche does threatens his loved one with a "crushing" death.

Glenda enters the scene, and the fuller shot now reveals the apartment in utter disarray, with fireplace, furniture, and even wall hangings all askew, as if hit by a tornado. The sanctity and security of the happy heterosexual marriage, depicted overtly in 1950s cinema and television by a well-ordered domicile, will be shattered and uprooted by this strange perversion called transvestitism, which will tear the happy homestead asunder as if hit by a psychological hurricane, just as the un-integrated anima will wreak havoc on an individual, and any relationship caught within.

What occurs next is even more psychologically potent. As Glenda attempts to lift the crushing tree off of Barbara, he disappears into thin air, leaving her to presumably die. A close-up of a horrified Glen, now dressed like a man "should be," looks on in terror as his beloved in imminent peril. Glen quickly rushes to his lover's aid and easily lifts the tree off her, rescuing her from certain phallocentric doom. The two embrace, as the viewer understands that clearly, the perverted Glenda, with her presumptuous frills and poisonous secrets, is too "weak" to save a heterosexual relationship; only a consciously declared and visually coded heterosexual male can rescue his woman (and women) from the phallic dangers of this new age. Here, *Glen or Glenda?* makes its most boldly heterosexist statement, that sexual deviancies are moral perversions, leading to weakness of character which sabotages its victims unto death; only staunch heterosexuality will survive the day and preserve the order of things. This stance is in direct contradiction to much which has preceded it, especially the progressive sexual politics which *Glen or Glenda?* posited in its opening reel, yet it is in keeping with Jungian psychology, in which only the erasure of the entrenched, projected anima called Glenda, and the emergence of the psychologically integrated Glen, will garner its subject the strength to save his lover, his alter ego, his very world from utter annihilation.

The enduring indecision of *Glen or Glenda?* is underscored brilliantly in the next segment, in which Glen and Barbara, now identifiably "man" and "woman," are married by a clergyman. The scene takes place in another cosmic void, without prop or artifact but for two lamps hanging suspended in mid-air, an attempt to set this void in some sort of expositional "space," but more importantly, a reinforcement of the heterosexual unit which *Glen or Glenda?*, at this moment at least, seems to be heartily pushing. Glen and Barbara have their backs to the camera, so one cannot see how they feel about this impending union. The viewer can, however, see the face of the clergyman, who appears somewhat dour. The scene is silent but for music, so as the agent of God speaks the vows, we cannot hear him. The viewer may assume that the sanctions he presumes to bestow on this couple have no power, and will be rendered impotent at some future time. This sense of impending doom is remarkably reinforced by the introduction of a fourth character into the sketch: the Devil. This most cartoonish depiction of man's eternal fear of malevolent evil is conveyed via a man with pointy beard, high eyebrows and big horns, grinning in a sinister way. That this emblem of diabolical discord also happens to be the couple's ring-bearer reinforces the notion that this union is both doomed *and* damned. As the Devil hovers over Glen's right shoulder, the viewer knows whence this evil influence comes — from Glen's alter ego, Glenda, who threatens to sabotage this union even as it attempts to coalesce. The clergyman silently pronounces the pair "man and wife," and the two turn towards camera and walk slowly out of frame, the Devil nodding his head in affirmation. The Devil has endorsed yet another failed union destined for the fires of eternity. Yet in many a fairy story and analyzed dream, the Devil, after transforming the protagonist in his own image, may find in the end that he has been deceived, and his diabolical project has backfired.[35]

God-figure Lugosi is next seen in close-up as he angrily sputters, "Tell me! Tell me, dragon! Do you eat little boys? Puppy dog tails and big, fat snails?" By now the viewer comprehends that the "dragon" which God speaks of is code for the demon-mother, who had such a negative impact on Glen's psyche, and is perhaps the mastermind behind the "animated" anima known as Glenda. Lugosi's face dissolves into Glen's, also in close-up, shivering as if in torment, with ethereal smoke engulfing him, as a little girl's voice is heard, mockingly stating, "Puppy dog tails! Puppy dog tails! Everything nice! Ha ha ha! Puppy dog tails!" It is significant that this most twisted use of the children's nursery rhyme which begins with "What are little boys and girls *made of?*" posing an existential question which is the secret of *Glen or Glenda?*: What "makes" a person one sex or another? As well, the recurring allusions to childhood remind the viewer that the trauma which creates a "freak" such as Glen's "Glenda" was most certainly forged in an abused childhood. The "wise old man's" references to Glen as a "little boy" underline the notion that a male who is possessed by his anima is psychologically immature, and "Glenda" in fact masks an overextended puberty.[36]

Glen or Glenda? now shifts into its most schizophrenic mode. The scenes which follow were purportedly added to the film later, by producer Weiss, for two reasons. Firstly, the added scenes extended the film's short running time to feature length. Also, these superficially peripheral scenes add some steaminess to the ironically "sexless" film which Wood produced. Even so, these peripheral scenes, which were likely not in Wood's original scenario, cannily underscore several elements of Wood's basic thesis, albeit in truncated form. Most importantly, these throwaway scenes reinforce the powerful yet elusive pull (that is, the dialectical tension) between the sexes. These shots also mimic Wood's footage in their baffling shuffling of the sexes, especially in terms of clichéd gender markers such as clothing, makeup and props, fetish objects which can be claimed by either sex for any purpose. As well, this blurring of the sexual boundaries has much to say in terms of power dynamics between persons, a theme hinted at, but primarily unexplored in *Glen or Glenda?*, but well-conveyed, inadvertently, in several upcoming sequences.

The first sequence shows a shirtless man whipping a woman on a couch. The most elemental yet brutal manifestation of the phallocentric order of things (man as "master," woman as "slave") is depicted succinctly in this blunt scene. As a deadpan Lugosi looks on in incongruous reaction shots, the viewer wonders whether this God-figure sees these cruel actions as the natural order of things, or a perverse aberration of the laws of the universe (even worse, perhaps a source of voyeuristic arousal). Alas, it is up to the viewer to decide what these scenes mean to them, as "God" reveals nothing with his poker face.

Following this are several striptease numbers, where attractive women flirt and partially disrobe for the camera and audience. This staple of grindhouse and exploitation film, which had reached its peak during the early to mid–1950s, seems harmless enough at first blush, but as Roland Barthes well described in his essay on the phenomenon, "*Striptease*,"[37] the act of stripping is essentially an act of power by male-dominated interests, wherein the woman, by removing her clothing, has completed an act of submission and degradation for the male collective. When the woman has finally removed all of her clothing, her submission and humiliation towards the male pack is complete. Thus, even in this tamer coded manifestation, striptease was as politically damning and sexually devastating as any debasing act of hardcore pornography, so soon to fatally infect mainstream culture.

As well, this parade of anonymous women may all be seen to reflect generic anima symbols, an allusion most striking when one notes the simultaneous elevation and debasement of these symbols in the text. Not surprisingly, Jung noted that "the anima has its historical precedent in the worship of women," a worship which, as seen, is a two-sided coin, balancing sincere adoration with exploitative objectification.[38] It is even more salient when one acknowledges that repressed erotic desires, such as those exploited in the striptease sequences and exploitation film in general, were observed by Jung to be inextricably connected to chronic anima projection.[39] Undoubtedly, the elusive anima, individually and collectively, may appear in many guises: "[L]ike the 'supraordinate personality,' the anima is bipolar and can therefore appear positive one moment and negative the next; now young, now old; now mother, now maiden; now a good fairy, now a witch, now a saint, now a whore."[40]

The first stripper coyly flirts with an off-screen figure, which by the reaction shots can be assumed to be Lugosi-as-God. In essence, this brazen woman is soliciting God for sexual relations, defying the very heavens with her haughty overtures. Lugosi, however, looks at the woman in utter disgust, and this rejection of the female by "God" is nicely accented in the next sequence, in which a second woman, who appears in torment as signaled by her histrionic hand gestures, finally rips off her dress in a violent act which suggests humiliation, self-loathing, even an invitation to rape. Quick inserted close-ups of a horrified Glen allude to his possible latent homosexuality, as he seems absolutely terrified of this near-naked woman who taunts him. But as the woman continues her striptease and public humiliation, her mood changes profoundly, and she coyly gestures towards the audience to come embrace her, even as Glen and Lugosi continue to express revulsion in cutaway shots. The woman finally begins to feel herself up, suggesting that this violent act of self-humiliation has managed to help her achieve erotic arousal, a not uncommon scrap of male sexual fantasy.

The next segment returns to the sadomasochistic motif of the first whipping scene. Another woman, whose arms are tied to a post in a blatant allusion to the crucifixion of Jesus Christ, is rescued by yet another woman, who frees her from her sexual bondage. Significantly, both women have tourniquets tied around their mouths, rendering them literally and metaphorically speechless, their voices mute in this cruel phallocentric hell-world. From a narrative point of view, the scene may even suggest that the women were prisoners of some (likely male) sexual fiend, and their narrow escape from further degradation, violence, and possibly even death was due to the two working in tandem, as sexual brethren. Yet metaphorically, the emancipation of these two women suggests much of what *Glen or Glenda?*, is awkwardly and haphazardly trying to suggest: a freedom from sexual tyranny by all sexes, and an egalitarian unity of the sexes to form a more progressive, healthful reinvention of the roles of both power dynamics and gender demarcation in modern society. To again cite Jung, the cross may well symbolize the self, specifically the wholeness of being, an exquisite symbol of the mighty tension of opposites struggling for harmony.[41]

Augmenting this notion is the next sequence, in which the women previously seen being whipped, now lies on the couch alone, in the throes of ecstasy. Having thrown off the shackles of her phallocentric tyranny, the woman can now writhe, unencumbered, to enjoy the thrill of auto-erotic sexuality. Of course, in this dizzyingly contradictory text, this erotic emancipation cannot be left unchallenged, so it is with a certain inevitability that another woman creeps up on the lounging female. The dominant woman, who looks so similar to the woman on the couch she could be taken as her exact double, ties up the lounging woman's hands and stuffs a gag in her mouth, in actions as violent as those of the whipping man seen earlier. The message here is clear: The tyranny of sexual domination may come from any gender, in any form, and apparently clear sexual markers mean little if anything. As well, the warring elements within humanity, with aggression constantly battling pacific tendencies, is cleverly illustrated in this bizarre set-piece in which it appears that a distraught and disturbed woman is literally battling *with herself*.

The scene cuts to a close-up of a bemused Lugosi, framed with one eye of an angry voodoo totem staring behind him, in yet another striking binary coupling. The scene cuts to show a sexy brunette primping in the mirror, enchanted with her mirror-stage self, and again the scene cuts back to scowling God-figure Lugosi, disgusted with "man's" fatal narcissism. The scene changes to show the brunette, now lounging alone on the ubiquitous couch, as she begins a session of auto-erotic stimulation. The woman masturbates herself to sleep to the accompaniment of emphatic orchestral music. As the satisfied female slumbers, she is joined by a male fop in a silk robe, sporting a pompadour and a goatee, a skid-row libertine who creeps up on the sleeping beauty only to assault her. As Lugosi looks on disapprovingly, the woman awakens and screams, as the predator paws and molests her. Soon, however, it appears that the "victim" seems resigned to her fate, as she wraps her legs around her would-be assailant in a gesture both resigned and inviting. The attack turns into a burlesque-tinged, highly theatrical semi-willing rape scene, a damning indictment of the male chauvinism of the filmmakers, and an essential element in any successful grindhouse exploitation film of the day. It may also metaphorically depict a most brutal attempt at integrating the violent, unconscious animus into a reluctant female.

Following this traumatic rape, which is all the more distressing as it had no narrative anchor, *Glen or Glenda?* stumbles back to the main narrative, as Glen sits in his destroyed honeymoon domicile, haunted by mocking voices and howling winds. He is clearly terrified of the bloodthirsty sexual orgy which has just transpired. The mocking girl-child heard before returns to taunt Glen once again, by underscoring the apparently obvious: "I'm a girl—*you are not!*" Cigarette in hand, Glen retreats, horrified, a dashing icon of pulp fiction reduced by a child's voice to a cowering animal, crushed not only by culture's harsh judgment but also by his own diabolical mental demons.

The scene cuts to show a door, against which hangs a crooked painting of three 18th-century fops playing cards, a telling emblem of traditional male bonding that suggests that this door, ever elusive to Glen, represents his only conceivable exit to a world of "normal" heterosexual fraternity. In front of the door there suddenly appears a stern, angry male figure—most likely a stand-in for Glen's father. Certainly, to Jung and others for whom psychology reigned paramount, the relationship of the subject to the father, with its inevitable masochistic and homosexual aspects, was of crucial importance in the individual's psyche, and its effects clearly apparent in much waking and dreaming behavior.[42] The figure may also represent the generic heterosexual male, revolted at Glen's betrayal of his sex, or perhaps even Glen's own, disowned and disinherited "normal" self.

Elsewhere in this ethereal house-scape, another specter appears, this time a woman, presumably Glen's domineering mother, overlaid again as a generic female archetype, who also sports a look of pure revulsion. As seen, Jung always returned to the primacy of the mother, and her significant contribution to the troubled males' psyche, as a crucial architect of the subject's subsequent mental development. As crucial as mother and father are to the troubled psyche, they are also obscure, and their exact influence and position in the troubled mind may never be completely intuited; as Jung stated, "[P]arents are also the least known of all human beings, and consequently that an unconscious reflection of the parental pair exists which is as unlike them, as utterly alien and incommensurable, as a man compared with a god."[43]

Suddenly, a standing schoolroom blackboard appears in the primordial homestead, with a series of cryptic messages scrawled in chalk. "SNIPS AND SNAILS" has a strange drawing underneath, which could easily be taken for a crude phallus with testicles. Next, "LITTLE GIRLS, " with "LITTLE" emphasized, is connected to "EVERY THING NICE" via a sketch of a long and winding road which leads to a blossoming deciduous tree and mountains in the distance. The mountain may suggest a paradise lost to the unrepentant sexual deviate, while in psychological syntax it often alludes to the journey from immaturity to the adult personality, and thus stands for the very essence of *self*.[44] Again, the tree may symbolize a state of deep unconsciousness, perhaps about to awaken or "blossom" into the conscious mind. Completing this occlusive hieroglyphic equation, a drawing of a steamship sails towards a station wagon, with a standard smiling stick figure completing the tableau. As the phallic steamship sails towards the possibly female stick figure, the station wagon stands between them, blocking the eventual meeting of these two sexual emblems; the automobile thus represents a "mystery element" which prevents Glen from successfully merging his male and female selves into one holistic, "normal" heterosexual man. Unlocking the key of the automobile's metaphorical definition will prove to be the secret of *Glen or Glenda?*, the secret of successfully merging all gender-centric elements within both individual and society.

Glen appears to understand the mystery of the automobile; he looks at this psychological encryption of his subconscious mind in sheer horror, as it succinctly reveals to him the foggy, circuitous mental processes which make him the twisted, failed "man" he is; Glen-as-Glenda stares directly into the frightening void which his twisted, projected anima has at long last revealed to him. More societal stereotypes materialize around him, all bearing looks of stern disapproval. Through an accelerating sequence of cuts, this damning jury of Glen's peers increases velocity, as the girl finishes her taunting: "Ha! Ha! Ha! Puppy dog tails!" As the girl mocks, "Ha ha ha!," each "ha" is nicely punctuated by a quick shot of one of the judging members of Glen's peers, reinforcing each mockery as judgment from the community. The "little judge girl" reiterates, "I'm a girl!" A similar voice, presumably that of a little boy, but sounding *exactly* like the girl, responds, "I'm not!," an aural vagueness which obscures matters even further. In psychological terms, chronic dreaming or fantasizing about being a child again, or in this case being forced to see himself as a child, reinforces the sense that Glen is still emotionally infantile. As Jung observed in a patient, "that he is definitely immature in certain respects is expressed in the dream by his being brought back to his boyhood."[45]

Finally, a broken Glen falls to the floor in sheer exhaustion from this harsh judgment, as the entire gaggle of judges point accusing fingers at him. The Devil rises from behind the sacred, betrayed "marriage couch" and menacingly approaches his newest victim. The Devil and the representatives of the community surround Glen, and back him into a corner of his wrecked domicile. The Devil makes one final gesture of triumph, and disappears into the ether. The community slowly backs away from Glen, who has miraculously turned into alter ego Glenda in full splendor, completely calm and self-assured, a handsome "woman" proud of who "she" is. It would appear that the forging fire of societal judgment has not crushed, but strengthened and reinforced, Glen's determination to define his personal gender as "he" sees fit. As Glenda emerges, the film's main music theme repeats, reaffirming the glorious transcendental quality of this hard-won apotheosis. This scene also brilliantly shows all the forces, internal and societal, which forge the problematic psychological creature known as the anima, come to life via the improbable but identifiable projection christened "Glenda." To again cite Jung, "Anima is the soul-image of a man, represented in dreams or fantasies by a feminine figure.... [I]f a man or a woman is unconscious of these inner forces, they appear in projection."[46]

Glen's victory, however, seems short-lived. He turns to view a door slowly open, and Barbara enters the room, her arms outstretched like a zombie or a somnambulist. Glen is about to embrace Barbara, who seems willing to finally accept "him" for who "he" is, when she changes abruptly into the Devil, who again mocks and taunts this twisted, misguided mortal. Glen's torment has no end, and he retreats, repulsed by his near-embrace of all that is Evil. An overturned love seat suddenly contains the specter of Barbara, rocking back and forth seductively and gesturing towards Glen with her arms outstretched, so close and yet so far from this tortured soul. Barbara's wardrobe changes three times in quick succession, the third get-up mimicking Glenda's uniform. Glenda approaches cautiously, the two figures looking ever more similar as they draw closer to each other, in an indelible shot which clearly shows the key parallelism of the two sexes when defined by outward symbols, i.e., signification, and brings up the question of what constitutes the essence of "a body." Butler ruminates, "Is 'the body' or 'the sexed body' the firm foundation on which gender and systems of compulsory sexuality operate? Or is 'the body' itself shaped by political forces with strategic inter-

In this perfect production still from Wood's signature feature *Glen or Glenda?*, real-life partners Dolores Fuller and Wood ponder their future together as the Devil (Captain DeZita) hovers over-head, a reminder of the overwhelming spiritual and psychological challenges which faced the postwar American couple.

ests in keeping that body bounded and constituted by the markers of sex?"[47] The scene also suggests the union of opposites, a binary or syzygy which for psychologists like Jung, formed the foundation for a healthy integrated individual, again restating Jung's observation that "man needs the opposite of his actual condition to force him to find his place in the middle."[48]

Suddenly, Barbara's advances turn to lewd mocking, and Glenda shrinks back in horror. Glenda kneels before his love and looks in astonishment at this vision before him, so desired, and yet so elusive, so familiar, and yet so foreign, and sees, in a visual epiphany, how remarkably similar he and his love are, draped in the haphazard, comical garb of a superficial, fetish-obsessed culture. This stunning shot also echoes the enduring mythos that two diametrically opposed, yet intrinsically similar souls reinforce the tension that a psychologically attuned mind is a creative, autonomous force continually balancing between sets of opposites.

Barbara rises to her feet, dragging Glenda along with her, and begins laughing at the strange man-freak, even pulling at his clothes in a playful approximation of physical attack. A close-up of a saddened Glenda is accented by an abundance of superimposed hands waggling, a silly yet profound moment which suggests in elemental cinematic shorthand the tortured ramblings of a man's bedeviled mind. The community figures seen previously gather once again to howl with laughter at Glen's naive bravado, each taking the opportunity to draw close to Glen to mock him, as the montage takes an ever-darker turn. Finally, the Devil, architect of all that is brutal in human affairs, appears in close-up, the triumph of crushing a human soul evident on his face. The Devil speaks, now appropriating the words first uttered by "God," and later echoed by the community: "Beware! Beware! Beware of the big green dragon that sits on your doorstep. He eats little boys! Puppy dog tails, and big fat snails! Beware! Take care! Beware!" Glenda falls to the floor, exhausted as ever. "She" is next seen looking in the bedroom mirror as before, but this time "she" sees nothing but a horrible, disgusting freak staring back, truly his morbid and revolting image-ideal. Glenda sees now what other people *really* see him like. Glen violently rips the comical wig from his head, and stares at the clownish face before him with a mixture of astonishment and pure disgust, seeing for the first time the freak that is Glenda, wondering what could have possibly twisted his mind to make him such a laughable atom-age mutation. Here, Jung's anima is finally revealed to its befuddled owner, a terrible shock to be sure, yet a key step to its eventual integration into the healthy psyche.

Dr. Alton returns, saying, "Glen (Glenda) has made the decision." The scene reverts, one hopes to presume, to the present day, as Glen sits across from Barbara, now ready to tell her the horrible secret which he can contain no longer; Glen has learned through torturous experience what Jung clearly observed: "[I]f one lives out the opposite sex in oneself one is living in one's own background, and one's real individuality suffers."[49] The scene proceeds in silence, as Alton clarifies: "Glen has decided to tell Barbara of his dual personality; to tell her of the nighties and the negligees, the sweaters and skirts, the robes and dresses, the stockings and the high heel shoes, the wig and the makeup. All that goes into *making Glen into Glenda.*" This notable remark underlines signification, that is, the superficial, exterior props used to create "man" and "woman" in modern society, as the sole arbiters of gender; yet, as *Glen or Glenda?* itself preaches, surely gender is formed by more than this? Butler poses the question thusly: "If the body is not a 'being' but a variable boundary, a surface whose permeability is politically regulated, a signifying practice within a cultural field of gender hierarchy and compulsory heterosexuality, then what language is left for understanding this corporeal enactment, gender, that constitutes its 'interior' signification on its surface?"[50]

As Glen speaks, he touches Barbara's angora sweater, trying to both connect emotionally with his love mate and also, by touching, become one with her, to change places with that sex he so defiantly prefers over his own. In so doing, Glen reinforces Alton's previous edict, that in the simplistic world of *Glen or Glenda?*, gender may indeed be defined merely by who wears "the pants" (or the fluffy sweater...). Barbara pulls back from Glen's creepy, lustful touch, distraught over this disturbing revelation, perhaps even seeing the specter of her own unresolved animus in this strange vision before her.

As the scene returns to sync sound, Glen pleads with Barbara for forgiveness, as Barbara listens, in mute shock. Barbara ponders dramatically over her response as the scene dissolves back to the heavens, where God-figure Lugosi now entertains Glen, who joins the deity in his chambers. Glen approaches his lord and master cautiously and genuflects at his feet. This touching scene has much of the autobiographical to it, as neophyte filmmaker Wood bows before a vaunted Hollywood icon, both in humble reverence to this cinema legend, and in apology for his part in reducing this former superstar to his current, sorry state of affairs. Lugosi here deftly fulfills the role of Jung's "wise old man," both to character Glen and to filmmaker Wood, perfectly encapsulating the "concentration of moral and physical forces that comes about spontaneously in the psychic space outside consciousness...."[51] Simply stated, Lugosi has helped, both as actor and archetype, to enable Wood's dream of exorcising his personal demons, literally through his creative efforts on Wood's behalf, and metaphorically as a vital character in Wood's highly cathartic, autobiographical screenplay.

However, this wise old "God" will not be appeased cheaply: With a dismissive wave of his hand, Lugosi makes Glen, this pitiful postwar buffoon, vanish into thin air. The scene dissolves back to show Barbara as last seen, still frozen in a gesture of painful indecision; the viewer may assume that the preceding moment was an illustration of Barbara's thought process, in which her god-self, her conscience, judged and dismissed her mate and his sorry tale of woe. Yet just as one expects Barbara to tell Glen to go to hell, she says, "Glen, I don't fully understand this, but maybe together we can work it out." Barbara removes her angora sweater in an ironic reference to the bawdy, gender-centric stripteases seen earlier in the film, and hands the garment to Glen, who accepts it humbly. Fade out.

Barbara has not only shown forgiveness and "bared" herself for her beloved, she has passed on gender signification of the female over to the male, allowing him to appropriate that which was formerly hers alone, and thus furthering the notion in *Glen or Glenda?* that signifying gender markers, both prevalent and cherished in previous societies, have completely lost their ability to confidently denote sex in the modern world. This is not to say that the heterosexual imperative will not go on unabated, only that it serves no intrinsic purpose, other than perhaps a socio-political one. Butler clarifies: "[T]here is no reason to divide up human bodies into male and female sexes except that such a division suits the economic needs of heterosexuality and lends a naturalistic gloss to the institution of heterosexuality."[52]

The main portion of the narrative now (finally) concluded, *Glen or Glenda?* lurches forward with yet another diversionary detour, as the scene returns to Dr. Alton's office. Warren listens in fascination to Alton's summation of Glen's unique tale, reminding the viewer that Glen's entire story was a flashback (and conceivably, even a fictional creation) emanating from Alton's fertile mind. Warren asks expectantly, as might the audience, "Is that the end of the story?" to which Alton replies, "Not quite...." Alton clarifies that Glen's case is a "less advanced type" case of sexual freakery, and teases Warren and the audience with the "extremely advanced" case he is about to unravel. Warren (and likely the restless audience) might be both excited and chagrined to learn there is more to come in this convoluted maze of a movie.

Alton's summation is revealing, however: "Glen's case was entirely of his own mind, brought about by the environment of his early youth," and he punctuates the Jungian inferences which have haunted the film thus far. The roots of the disturbed and projected anima of Glen (and Wood) are summed up succinctly in this stark statement, which reveals so much about origins and affects. The psychological "hero" must replace dependency upon the immature unconscious with an increasing diet of mature self-reliance, a journey which compels an awkward contest with unconscious forces, the shadow of the mother foremost. This ongoing battle was called by Jung a "ritual initiation," a symbolic label which describes the process through which a person traverses from one degree of being to another, a trek that must include a traumatic break with the binding influence of the matriarch. The unconscious influence of the mother is hardy and inexorable, however, and in many cases leads to an obstinate projection, called by Jung the anima, and symbolizing the unconscious prerogative which underlies conscious behavior. This archetype, often illustrated by a female closer in age to the man than his mother, becomes the "hero's" constant, if unwanted companion in the endeavor for psychological balance. From a certain perspective, this describes "Glenda" to perfection. The similarity between much of *Glen or Glenda?*'s bountiful symbology and the many rich symbols observed in Jung's psychoanalytic work is stunning and profound; Jung's description of the anima could almost have come from the pressbook of *Glen or Glenda?*: "The projection-making factor is the anima, or rather the unconscious as represented by the anima. Whenever she appears, in dreams, visions and fantasies, she takes on personified form, thus demonstrating that the factor she embodies possesses all the outstanding characteristics of a feminine being."[53]

Alton's succinct overview verifies several earlier scenes in *Glen or Glenda?* which suggested that as a boy, Glen not only liked to dress up in girl's clothing, but was encouraged in this act by a domineering mother and a deferential father. The importance of early childhood trauma in creating sexual deviants is clearly stated here, and one might readily assume that Wood knew whereof he spoke, and spoke of himself. When Warren soon asks, bluntly, why some men dress in women's clothing, Alton reaffirms, "It usually starts in early childhood, from one cause or another," also reaffirming the notion that Glen's (and Wood's) peculiar psycho-sexual lifestyle was decidedly forged by traumatic childhood experiences.

Perhaps inspired by Alton's clear-cut explanations, perhaps enlightened by the amazing tale just told, Warren next surprises the viewer, as well as Alton, by relating a clever, useful allegory which goes far to explain Glen's, and others,' strange behavior: "Then the way I get it, this Glen and the character he created, much as an author creates a character in a book, was invented as a love object, to take the place of the love he never received in his early youth, through lack of it from his parents. The character was created, and dressed, and lives the life the author designs for him to live, and dies only when the author wants him to die." This revelation again echoes Jung's observations about the projected, outlaw anima, and its owner's need, and ability, to extinguish (integrate) it whenever he is able and willing.[54]

Alton confirms Warren's insightful theory, and then proceeds to tell the second sexual history, this time of a man called Alan. The viewer first sees the extremely feminine Alan in character as "Ann," adorned fully as a woman and looking quite believable as such, a far cry from the overt masculinity of Glen/Wood. Alton continues, "Alan's mother wanted a little girl. Alan's father didn't care much one way or the other." From this very first revelation, it is immediately apparent that Alan's story is not going to be a different story from Wood's own, as filtered through Glen, but essentially a retelling or filtering of Wood's story, reinforcing certain elements while bringing in others not addressed fully in Glen's "fictional" scenario.

As the scene changes to footage of schoolboys romping in a school playground, Alton informs the viewer that Alan was a bright student, but did not participate in sports or other "boy" activities. It is amusing to see several of the boys in this footage staring directly at the camera in puzzlement and wonder — perhaps Wood shot this scene "on the fly," and caught the children acting in genuine surprise — but the scene does reinforce the notion of Alan as being a bonafide outsider, as witness the boys playing without him, but staring at him via the camera's eye, looking agog at the "queer" little boy who doesn't like to play with them (and who furthermore likes to take secret pictures of them!). Alton adds an odd bit of information: "Yet Alan did like sports, *girls'* sports, but was rejected by the girls just as he was rejected by the boys." As Alton states this bit of personal history, two little girls in topcoats walk across the frame in the foreground while staring directly at the camera, a startling moment which simultaneously reinforces the introduction of girls into the equation while illustrating the girls' rejection of Alan, another clever bit of editorial horseplay by Wood. Alton concludes his introduction of Alan's estrangement from his gender-centric peers thusly: "It seems he belonged to *neither* of them." Alan, like Glen, like Wood, are neither male nor female; they are *both*, and *none*, a third sex perhaps, or more excitingly, *beyond* sex. An outsider to both sexes Alan, like Glen before him, also underwent "initiation by anima," by submitting to painful experiences of rejection. Integrating this pain is a crucial element in eventual psychological integration, as Alan, Glen and Wood all discover.

The next scene shows Alan, dressed as the womanly "Ann," presumably during his teenage years, happily dusting books on a night table, as Alton cryptically states, "Alan was becoming a woman and he didn't know it. A woman in mind only, but *the mind rules!*" This emphatic declaration of the predominance of the mind in all matters sexual and psychological well reinforces the prevailing Jungian spirit in *Glen or Glenda?*, again alluding to the ascendancy of the psychological approach to life which was taking the Western world by storm at the time, in its declaration that the suffering which afflicts modern man was not principally coming from outside (i.e., "physical") forces, but from the interior battle between warring conscious and unconscious forces. And as "Glenda" had so vividly, if unwittingly shown previously, "[T]hose contents of the unconscious that are so near, so close that they are almost conscious, have a tendency to get exteriorized."[55] Excitingly, Wood's ongoing self-analysis, first through "Glenda" and now through "Ann," has shown exactly what Jung declared: "The ego, ostensibly the thing we know most about, is in fact a highly complex affair full of unfathomable obscurities. One could even define it as a *relatively constant personification of the unconscious itself*, or as the Schopenhauerian mirror in which the unconscious becomes aware of its own face."[56] And Butler might add, "In the place of an original identification which serves as a determining cause, gender identity might be reconceived as a personal/cultural history of received meanings subject to a set of imitative practices which refer laterally to other imitations and which, jointly, construct the illusion of a primary and interior gendered self or parody the mechanism of that construction."[57] This remark certainly echoes one of *Glen or Glenda?*'s prevalent themes, that gender identification emanates primarily, irrevocably, from one's individual cultural narrative, and this panoply of imprints, mostly internalized, eventually determines not only what a person *wants* to be, but more importantly what he *thinks* he is.

Alton continues, "Then came the fateful year of 1941. Alan was drafted. He was accepted." A briefly sketched, indelible montage follows, showing Wood's singular talent as editorial poet, as World War II is woven through Alan's (and Wood's) peculiar fetishistic journey of personal difference. As these primarily stock shots unspool, Alton explains that while in the service, Alan managed to maintain a secret alter ego, keeping a suitcase full of women's clothing nearby at all times, so that on the weekends, when he wasn't killing the enemy, he would lounge around in a rented room in women's garb. The subversive nature of Alan's second personality completely undermines the supposed affinity and solidarity of the U.S. Armed Forces, stating clearly that even amongst our own troops were dangerous "outsiders" who had secret lives. Wood's dizzying montage of man at war encapsulates history's most terrible global conflict in the space of approximately two minutes, a stunning feat for the artist, and likely a cathartic release for the embittered ex–Marine as well.

After concluding this traumatic global conflict, *Glen or Glenda?* scurries back to the sterile office of Dr. Alton, as he and Warren sit stiffly across from each other, discussing what to do with society's freaks. Alton: "It was in the hospital, while recovering from a wound, that Alan learned of foreign doctors who were performing new surgical sex change operations." This reference to a soldier lying wounded in hospital and fantasizing about the future of his "double life" is likely a reference to Wood's own military service, and his wounding by the Japanese soldier whom he subsequently killed.

Apparently, Alan eventually came to Dr. Alton for advice. At this revelation, Alton leaves his throne-like seat of authority for the first and last time in the film, to approach a conveniently placed medical anatomy chart which hangs on the wall. Ironically, on the opposite wall hangs the same picture of three fops at a card table which graced the door to Glen's fantasy domicile in the previous dream/nightmare sequences, connecting *Glen or Glenda?*'s dream world with the real world, and lending Alton's subsequent medical lecture a subliminal fantastic flavor. Alton explains that Alan was a pseudo-hermaphrodite, and clarifies: "A hermaphrodite is someone who has the organs of the male and female in plain sight. A pseudo-hermaphrodite is someone who has one perfectly formed organ of either sex, and one imperfectly formed one that's difficult to detect."

This somewhat disingenuous statement, designed ostensibly to once again distance the main character of the scenario, as well as its author, from some of the more overt sexual outcasts of society, alludes to more than intended. From a psychological point of view, the metaphor of the hermaphrodite expresses the role of dualist synergy in the balance of conscious and unconscious influences in both sexes, and the immense influence of contrary sexual forces in each. As Jung stated, "This inversion of roles is probably the chief psychological source for the alchemical concept of the hermaphrodite. In a man it is the lunar anima, in a woman the solar animus, that influences consciousness in the highest degree."[58]

Alton walks off set, and back to his authoritative chair next to Warren. Alton then declares, regarding Alan, "That which nature had given him was a mistake. Alan had to decide whether *he* wanted to become a *man*, or *she* wanted to become a *woman*," underscoring the prevailing notion in *Glen or Glenda?* that all creatures are, at least at root, both sexes, and conscious gender creation determines which predominates. "Small boned, fair of complexion, his hair thick, like a woman's, his body slim, hips slightly girlish...." As Alton thusly describes Alan to Warren, he looks wistfully at camera and rubs his pencil in an uncharacteristic close-up. One senses that Alton is either gaining some erotic stimulation from this description of his patient, or perhaps he is fondling this phallic substitute in an attempt to maintain a fragile connection to his heterosexual identity, which is endangered by the presence of the mysterious, and very feminine Alan-Ann.

Next, Alton drops a psychological *bon mot*, which may again be assumed to be part of Wood's personal history: "[I]n early childhood he was brought up to think that being a woman was the thing to be." This reference to the omniscience of matriarchy in childhood mirrors Glen's earlier revelations about a domineering mother who all but commanded her son to "become" female to assure a place of safety and honor in the disturbed family dynamic. As Glenda is a preconscious invocation of Glen's mother, so is Alan, most likely, a direct product of the emotional machinations of an all-powerful mother figure. In addition to explaining Alan (and Wood's) evolution into Ann, this scene yet again reinforces the role of gender dominance in culture. Wood's ideology, stated earlier and underscored via Alan's story, is that woman is clearly the power figure in the world of the child, and the child is father to the man. Certainly, the postwar nuclear family was by and large a solidified matriarchy, with the children, and often the father, beholden to the care-taking of the mother, and thus subject to her will. The mother was indeed "the law" in the average middle-class family of the day, and Wood is merely extrapolating what is essentially obvious, that the breeding ground of youth creates the emotionally charged fiction which is modern adulthood. What is imprinted by the matriarchal imperative during child-rearing will have resonating effect(s) on the subsequent maturity of the offspring, and this may include, as seen throughout *Glen or Glenda?*, bizarre "mutations" of personal self which struggle throughout adulthood for self-respect and societal acceptance.[59] Not so much an admonition to females in the audience (of whom there were probably few) to "be careful how you raise your sons," *Glen or Glenda?* is merely making a sociological observation, an observation fraught with emotional angst but one which also is essentially objective: Within the sweet tyranny of the middle-class matriarchy, a woman is "the thing to be." As Jung and many others have noted, "[T]he mother has from the outset a decidedly symbolic significance for a man, which probably accounts for his strong tendency to idealize her."[60] As Jung's work revealed, the man's internalization, and subsequent neurotic denial of, the "image of the mother" is what largely leads to the creation of the highly problematic yet potentially emancipatory anima: "The mother-imago, however, represents the unconscious, and it is as much a vital necessity for the unconscious to be joined to the conscious as it is for the latter not to lose contact with the unconscious."[61]

The next sequence depicts Alan's sex change, via another smart editorial montage, and annotated as always by Alton: "During the following two years, Alan would go through the tortures of the damned, but never was there a whimper from him because he knew that at the end of it all, he would at last be that which he had always dreamed." The montage begins with a somewhat ridiculous medium close-up of Alan having his pulse taken by an off-screen nurse. Alan is lounging on a loveseat, has a bandage wrapped around his head, and wears a feather boa. It appears he is in drag, but a subsequent showing of the same shot, post-surgery, will beg the question of how one can confidently spot gender via precarious outward signifiers. Regarding the phenomenon of drag, Butler astutely notes: "[T]he performance suggests a dissonance not only between sex and performance, but sex and gender, and gender and performance."[62]

As the operations ensue, Alton comments, "Still, the hormone shots continued, day after day, week after week, month after month," at one point over a close-up of a hypodermic needle penetrating flesh, a skin-crawling shot uncomfortable enough to presumably make anyone considering this operation think twice; even the horror film music used here punctuates the inherent pain of these ungodly "tortures of the damned." As Alton coos, "And then came the big day!" over a comical close-up of a pulsating anesthesia bag, looking very much like deflating testicles, the montage offers creepy surgical scenes depicting the series of operations needed to transform Alan to Ann, with Alan on the operating table, surrounded by a masked doctor and three masked assistants huddled around him. The masks on the medical personnel emphasize both the potentially sinister and anonymous quality of these technicians. Alton observes, "First, the breasts are brought out; the body of the woman begins to appear now," as the doctor applies forceps to the breast region.

At roughly the hour mark, *Glen or Glenda?*'s most shocking scene occurs, an extraordinary second or two which reveals Wood's more subversive nature. As Alton intones, "Then comes the major surgery, the removal of the man, and the formation of the woman...," this last shot in the surgery sequence depicts the masked, anonymous doctor, now finished with

2. Glen or Glenda? (1953)

modifying Alan's face and breasts, aggressively attacking Alan's genital region with a forceps, as the medical crew watches in complete deadpan (or shock?). The shot is book-ended on both sides by stock footage lightning shots, and the overt horror film feel of the scene, replete with dramatic, spooky music, evokes visions of sociopathic butchery, Nazi experimentation, and the creation of Frankensteinian monsters. This brief but indelible image likely served as a "painful" moment for the film's audience, at least those whom could empathize with the violent and painful procedure; Wood thus mischievously also castrates his audience here, a daring agent provocateur to the last.

Castration, both as a physical and figurative act, is one of the primary symbols for man's emasculation by the female principle, the mother foremost, and has much historical precedent. For explorers of psychology such as Jung, the act of castration, as it occurred in dreams and fantasies, symbolized a dominance of the neurotic mother-imago over the mind of the son: "[T]he effects of a mother-son complex on the son may be seen in the ideology of the Cybele and Attis type: self-castration, madness and early death."[63] Alan's specific castration in *Glen or Glenda?* may also symbolize an attempt to castrate (and thus disable) the mother, as noted again by Jung in dream analysis: "I was especially struck by the fact that a castration had obviously been performed on the mother, for in front of her gory genitals lay the cut-off male sexual organs."[64]

The scene shifts to God-figure Lugosi in his ersatz "heavenly laboratory." Alan, still dressed as an effeminate male, approaches his god quietly, reverently. Lugosi takes one look at his malformed creation, waves his hand, and Alan disappears into the ether. The scene jump-cuts to the same set in a minor gaffe of cheap optical trickery. Lugosi now looks to his left, and waves the new Ann into existence. Ann is now dressed as a woman, in an evening gown with sparkly jewelry. Lugosi looks none too thrilled with his "queer" new creation. Ann slowly turns and walks away from her master. Although the scene ostensibly suggests an evolutionary apotheosis, a successful personality transformation, the spirit of death hovers over the event as well; at least four human skulls, one human skeleton, and a giant animal skull are clearly visible throughout, and lend the scene an overtly morbid air. As throughout *Glen or Glenda?*, here Lugosi again functions as Jung's "wise old man" archetype, a figure who poses endless, obscure queries to his protégé in order to induce self-reflection and encourage moral judgment. Also, Lugosi waves his supernatural hand over his subject to transfer certain occult powers to them, giving them both motive and means to conquer their crushing mental burdens.[65]

The scene returns briefly to show the doctor modifying Alan's genitals, so one might surmise that the previous "emancipation" scene was Alan's drugged fever dream as he was violently being "relieved" of his manhood. The montage concludes by returning to its opening shot, in which a bandaged Alan/Ann lounges in her feather boa, grinning like an idiot. The viewer is now confused as to whether the creature seen here is the post-surgical Ann, replete with female body parts, or the pre-surgery, cross-dressing male called Alan. Through the astute use of relative juxtaposition, Wood as editorial poet further undermines the reliability of outward gender signifiers in determining sex, as the futile quest of clear gender definition takes yet another devastating hit. To again cite Butler, "In imitating gender, drag implicitly reveals the imitative structure of gender itself — as well as its contingency."[66]

Alton caps this traumatic montage with, "But in time, Alan is Ann, a happy, lovely young lady that modern medicine and science has created almost as a Frankenstein Monster!" This tongue-in-cheek statement clearly references the painful, violent surgery scenes just witnessed, and casts a prejudicial light on the creation of sexual "monsters" by modern medicine, again underscoring *Glen or Glenda?*'s militant stance for psychology over surgery, in essence for the triumph of mind over matter.

Back in the office, Alton adds a most interesting coda to Ann's story: "However, in this particular sex switch, it is not the end. *Acting* the woman and *being* the woman are two entirely different things," a line which again deftly underscores the essential difference between sex and gender. As the viewer sees Ann sitting in a chair, happily reading a book in her new persona, Alton preaches, "Ann must learn how to be a woman, do her own hair, how to make the correct styling for her facial contours. The proper walk must be adopted. A lady is a lady, whatever the case may be!" In this rigid culture, Ann seems to have merely traded signifying strictures from one sex to another, and may not escape the confines of prejudicial conformity even with her life-threatening surgical adventures. Here, *Glen or Glenda?* suggests that those who voluntarily "go through the tortures of the damned," in order to have their gender "junk" moved around, are perhaps suffering for nothing, and cannot after all escape their fate in a restrictive, conformist society.

Later, in Alton's office, the new Ann now sits across from Alton, as the two commence their psychoanalysis sessions. At one point, Alton offers Ann a cigarette, in what could be construed as an awkward gesture of flirtation. The two also sit much closer to each other than Alton did in proximity to his colleague Warren. Perhaps Alton wanted to create this new "she-man" to have a new plaything to toy with emotionally and/or sexually; one is reminded of Alton's wistful description of Alan/Ann to Warren earlier in the film, a description bursting with emotional energy. Perhaps Alton, and not medical science, is the real "Frankenstein" here? As Alton patiently explains to Ann "how to be a woman," the viewer realizes that he is explaining merely how to be submissive and sexually attractive to the male, and *Glen or Glenda?*'s sub-textual male chauvinism is clearly expressed here. As she coyly listens to her new role in massaging the collective male ego, Ann takes a puff of cigarette and exhales the smoke through her nose as she smiles, almost sinisterly. Ann can see that the real reason to shed Alan was to accrue some of the societal *power* he lacked as an effeminate man. Now Ann can conquer the sexual world as Alan never could. *Glen or Glenda?*'s chauvinist tack continues in the assumption that only as a female, can a weak or "queer" male be accepted by, and useful to, male society; Jung might add that Alan has now literally been *absorbed* by his anima![67]

Ann is next seen staring at fashions in a department store window, and seems pleased as a cad (Wood regular Conrad Brooks, in one of several bit parts) walks by, looks her up and down, and walks on. Several other pedestrians pass by, making this scene ironically one of *Glen or Glenda?*'s biggest. After Ann gazes at all the finery now legitimately available to her, she turns towards camera, smiles, looks at the sky and shakes her fists in a silly, "Gee whiz!" gesture of satisfaction. Through the scene, Ann is eerily counter-pointed by a large, phallic tree jutting out of the sidewalk, making the shot an unusual set-piece visually accentuating the underlying male/female binary of *Glen or Glenda?*, while recalling the phantasmic tree which almost killed Glen's love interest, Barbara, during one of his guilt-fueled nightmares. As well, the tree reminds the viewer of "the living contents of the unconscious," still bubbling under the problematic creature which is "Alan/Ann."[68]

Back at the office, Alton concludes, "This case had a happy ending due to the corrections of medical science," rudely contradicting the diabolical portrayal of medical science in the gruesome surgery montage. Alton then tells Warren that Glen and Barbara had a series of intense therapy sessions regarding Glen's problem, in an overt campaign for the science of psychotherapy, relatively new in the U.S. and a less bloody alternative to the surgical mutilation which creates sexual "Frankenstein Monsters." Alton relates the story of Alan/Ann to Glen and Barbara, and emphasizes how Glen's case is "completely different." Here Wood seems determined to distance himself and his alter ego from the truly "queer" sexual deviants, a slightly sexist prejudice, and one of *Glen or Glenda?*'s recurring flaws of faith. Yet one rather remarkable touch shows Wood's playfulness, even addressing such a serious subject matter: In the scene Glen sits, center frame, between Barbara and Dr. Alton, with Alton's telephone placed catty-cornered on the desk, so that it roughly mimics the shape and placement of Glen's "all-male" genitalia, sexual emblems which were likely threatened by the painful surgical story just told. Are Glen's genitals thus safe from torment, hidden as they are by the telecommunications icon-as-surrogate? Or does the phone represent Glen's bared, exposed genitals, entirely vulnerable to the "chopping block" of Alton's psychological edicts?

Alton informs Barbara, "Glen's body holds only one sex, that of the male," in one sense an obvious declaration. Yet in this "ancient" world where premarital sex was not ubiquitous amongst the middle class, this information might actually be new to Barbara, as she does seemed relieved to hear it. Alton then relates "these pertinent facts" about Glen, assisted by a revealing montage which may go to the very core of Wood's psyche as well. "Glen's father had no love for his son," Alton groans in a most damning declaration rendered even more poignant as it likely refers to Wood as well. This sobering statement is comically illustrated by a close-up of a mustachioed patriarch in what appears to be a bar, a sketch which paints Glen's (and Wood's?) father as a no-good, drunken bum. Alton confirms this: "His father wanted Glen to be a football hero, or a baseball player, so he could brag to his cronies down at the corner saloon, as his cronies bragged to him about their sons." This is a devastating critique of Old World machismo, painting a simplistic, likely accurate portrait of the somewhat one-dimensional, negative influence of an absent, indifferent patriarch upon an impressionable youngster. As Jung noted, the mother's influence has many aspects, whereas the father's represents a monolithic specter of oppressive hegemony.[69]

Alton continues the sad, even tragic story: "Thus, the ruse of Glen's fictitious character. He invented it when he could find no love from his mother, and no love from his father. His mother had hated her own father. Glen reminded her of her father. Therefore, she gave all her attention, love and affection to her daughter. Glen, then, also decided to became a 'daughter.'" This circuitous familial chronology reflects yet another psychological truth, that the influence of the mother and the father travels from generation to generation, and is not merely a response to the individual persons who inhabit those roles, but the accumulation of all that these symbolic roles historically represent. As Jung clearly articulates, "[B]ehind the father stands the archetype of the father, and in this pre-existent archetype lies the secret of the father's power, just as the power which forces the bird to migrate is not produced by the bird itself but derives from its ancestors."[70]

Alton turns towards Glen and states dramatically, "You can kill this fictitious character of yours any time you wish. For your happy ending, it's the only way." Glen ponders this confusing revelation, and proclaims, "Then you think I can kill this second character by transferring her qualities to Barbara?" Thus in a sense asking Alton permission to become "normal," Glen's "Glenda" could be seen as in some ways a misguided attempt to seek a man's leadership, to locate the strong and caring father figure which he lacked in childhood, and which he ironically does find when he consults psychiatrist Alton, a strong and wise father-surrogate who guides Glen on his healing journey.

Alton's "verdict" also restates one of *Glen or Glenda?*'s prevailing theses and a keynote to Jungian psychology, that of the function of the male-female syzygy, the efficacy of the union of opposites through integration, an enduring psychological principle which relates to the Eastern world's spiritual principles of yin and yang.[71] As Jung noted, the successful integration of the anima elements in the male often triggers an improvement in the quality of his relationships with the opposite sex.

Barbara, justifiably confused by the largely self-serving psychological mumbo-jumbo, asks sheepishly, "Should I continue to let him wear girls' clothing, or should I put my foot down?" Alton insists that if Barbara "puts her foot down," Glen would only go behind closed doors to continue his potentially divisive "second life." Alton then intones, somewhat mystically, "Love is the only answer!" Finally, Barbara poses a practical, and possibly selfish question: "Suppose Glen never gets over wearing girls' clothing?" Alton calls her bluff by asking, "Would it matter very much?" Realizing she has been cornered into playing "the good woman," Barbara smiles wanly and sighs, "I love Glen. I'll do everything I can to make him happy." The lovebirds hold hands and grin sheepishly at each other, as Barbara gladly acquiesces to male cultural edicts.

The scene cuts to a phallic church steeple, and the camera pans down to show Glen and Barbara walking alone out of the church. It is somewhat sad to observe that there were no guests or witnesses to this most sacred event, an absence which suggests that in the end, society at large still does not accept or forgive Glen for his transgressions. Still, the marriage completed, the heterosexual unit is safe and intact, under the approving stare of organized religion, that great oppressor of personal difference. The officially sanctioned newlyweds hop into Glen's spiffy new Nash convertible to begin their attempt at a "normal" domestic partnership, and the hieroglyphics previously seen on the chalkboard in Glen's waking nightmare now become clear. The automobile, the "mystery element" of the chalkboard symbology, is clearly Glen's Nash Rambler; the major obstacle to Glen's eventual happiness was his reluctance/refusal to court and marry Barbara posthaste, and thus project his tortured and projected anima onto the *real* object of his desire. The Nash thus symbolizing Glen and Barbara's love union, and their ensuing marital "journey," this hard-won union promises both parties long-sought emotional happiness and heretofore elusive psychological balance. As well, a steepled church in dream and therapeutic symbology often represents phallic authority, and automobiles often suggest a nurturing carriage, an ersatz womb, so one could also read the scene as Glen finally leaving the crippling structure of male-dominated neurosis and truly embracing the female aspects of both self *and* society. In *Glen or Glenda?*'s strict, punitive universe, one could cynically rephrase this revelation into, "Glen finally learned to grow up and be a man," but by accepting the female principle as embodied in another, Glen is taking significant steps towards shedding the crippling, catastrophic aspects of this "second self."

Later, Barbara sits at home in their cozy new love nest. Wood comes in through the primordial door of all knowledge, leaving forever the dark, deviant world of his adolescent past and entering the promising, bright world of heterosexual "normalcy." Alton observes, "Glenda begins to disappear forever from Glen," neglecting to note that this transformation is largely thanks to Barbara's long-suffering understanding and self-sacrifice, an omission which ignores the fact that it was often the female who undertook the bulk of the emotional work in the successful union of the day (and subliminally reinforcing the recurring anima referencing throughout *Glen or Glenda?*).

Finally, Alton blissfully coos, "Glen has found his mother, his little sister, his wife, and his Glenda, all in one lovely package," a remarkable observation which could have emanated almost verbatim from one of Jung's notebooks, as witness this comment: "This demon-woman of mythology is in truth the 'sister-wife-mother,' the woman in the man, who unexpectedly turns up during the second half of life and tries to effect a forcible change of personality."[72]

The two lovers nuzzle each other, and Glen can now begin the actual work of transferring his internalized female onto his externalized mate, embracing wholeheartedly the convoluted gender logic of the modern heterosexual duo. Glenda was, for all intents and purposes, Glen's "ritual initiation" into male adulthood. The end result/reward of this initiation is Glen's marriage to Barbara, leading to the long-sought possibility of finding "true love." As Barbara sits, waiting for her man, the viewer notes that she looks remarkably like Glenda. She has absorbed Glen's anima, and can now truly be Glen's "better half."

As marriage is considered by Jung and others to be primarily a psychological relationship, full of traps and pitfalls yet offering extraordinary opportunities for psychic growth to brave souls, this new journey which Glen and Barbara have finally agreed to take may well have significant treasures to offer both parties. The viewer may recall that *Glen or Glenda?* took special care to note that Barbara has finished college, whereas Glen's educational level remains unclear. This suggests that Barbara's intellectual level is higher than Glen's, and likely her psychological maturity as well, in keeping with general psychological observations of the sexes. Barbara may well be the life teacher that Glen so desperately needs.[73]

After this dramatic crescendo, one expects that this dizzying psychological treatise has finally exhausted itself, but the scene returns yet again to the cold, emotionless "dead space" of Alton's office, the viewer seemingly unable to escape *Glen or Glenda?*'s particular expositional hell. Alton restates the obvious to Warren, saying that these two entirely different cases had entirely different endings. Warren dourly asks in close-up, "But what of the hundreds of other less fortunate Glens the world over?" as he stares directly at the audience, in his role as Wood's mouthpiece, reaching out to others in the audience with similar problems, with a plea for acknowledgment and acceptance.

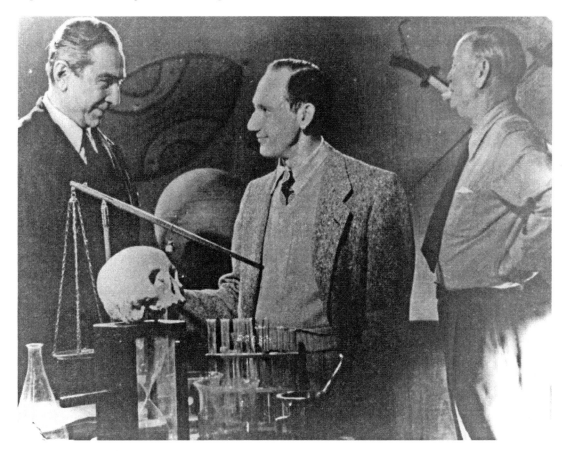

In this behind-the-scenes shot, Bela Lugosi (left) chats with *Glen or Glenda?* producer George Weiss and cinematographer William C. Thompson.

Glen or Glenda? ends with a swift three-shot montage: The film's resident newspaper, headlined WORLD SHOCKED BY SEX CHANGE, lays on a city sidewalk, as garbage falls over it; a black boot enters the frame and stomps on the newspaper, symbolizing perhaps the shadow of individuality-crushing fascism, or the intolerance of mass society towards radical sexual ideology. The scene dissolves back into Lugosi in his lab, as he opens his ancient book of knowledge. The camera approaches Lugosi via an impressive dolly shot, possibly the only one in *Glen or Glenda?*, as "God" whispers, "Yes! But what of the others, less fortunate Glens, the world over? (sic) Snips and snails and puppy dog tails!" Lugosi sighs, and pounds the good book in angry resignation. *Glen or Glenda?*'s parting shot depicts bustling highway traffic at night, a simple landscape of the dark night of teeming humanity. The "wise old man" has finished his work, having successfully aided both of *Glen or Glenda?*'s "heroes," who gained guidance and direction from his prudence and wisdom.[74]

The final cast listings reveal even more about this remarkable film. First listed is Bela Lugosi, not as god, philosopher or saint, but as "Scientist," a modern iconic label which reinforces his role both as alchemist and "wise old man." Lyle Talbot is listed not as a cop, but as "Inspector," that is, investigator of mysteries and seeker of profound truths. Timothy Farrell is listed, expectedly, as "Psychiatrist," underscoring the importance of that exalted figure as *character*, and alluding to *Glen or Glenda?*'s fitful attempts to incorporate the theories of Jung into its endearing but shaky thesis. The star of the show, Wood, is called "Glen-Glenda" in the credits, suggesting not two personas, but one character with dual aspects, in keeping with the main Jungian thread of the film. Again, Wood chooses a whimsical pseudonym to credit himself, which as postulated earlier may have several intriguing purposes.

As discussed, *Glen or Glenda?* can be read as a most intuitive and expansive illustration of Jung's theory of anima and animus, the feminine and masculine principles struggling for ascendancy within their opposite-sex "hosts." As the main protagonist(s) are male, the general argument is that of the feminine aspects of a masculine character struggling to emerge within individual personalities, and certainly in postwar culture collectively. Though this emergence takes overt, simplistic, even comical forms in *Glen or Glenda?* does not diminish the text's unwavering emphasis on spiritual and psychological balance in any organism attempting towards progressive development.

Glen or Glenda? takes a provocative stance regarding this assertion, wildly contradicting itself in spots, yet concluding with an odd convergence of two main points. Firstly, after describing how gender can be so easily manipulated and thus regarded as mute, *Glen or Glenda?* clarifies an elemental spiritual truth, that at heart, all humanity is one gender, and that male and female are notable, but not mutually exclusive subsets within this. Truthfully, there is much more to unite than separate the sexes, and our common humanity covers much more ground than our perceived or declared gender differences.

It is certainly remarkable that *Glen or Glenda?* shares such an affinity with Jungian philosophy, and can be read successfully as a metaphorical tale of the trials and tribulations of the anima and animus concepts. It would be fascinating to discover if Wood, a voracious reader, had stumbled across Jung's writings at some point, and had incorporated, even subconsciously, some of its basic outlines. In a sense even more fascinating is the notion that Wood dreamed up this wild scenario completely on his own, and intuitively mirrored those profound thoughts which Jung had formulated mere years before; a revelation which would add fuel to Jung's assertion of a collective unconscious, where an endless font of communal wisdom resides, available to all on an unconscious level, and extractable through creative intellectual effort.

As well, *Glen or Glenda?* takes great pains, through symbolism and narrative departure, to emphasize the omniscience of *death* within the fragile human equation. As witnessed by God-figure Lugosi, the creation of life is inextricably tied up with the inevitability of death. Wood, the artist, was obsessed with death throughout his career, and virtually all of his films feature death as an actual or symbolic character, but *Glen or Glenda?* launches this strange fascination in a most vivid way. To Wood, as to Jung, life's journey towards self-hood has personal apotheosis as its conscious goal, but both also delineate the finish line to this neurotic, never-completed race as the death of being. This inevitable demise of the person is ideally neither feared nor embraced, but merely accepted as an existential truth, a truth which, through psychological repression, may motivate its subjects in significant ways not consciously accredited.

Even *Glen or Glenda?*'s alternate release titles, *I Changed My Sex* and *I Led Two Lives*, reinforce the film's pervasive mission of radical gender roles reassessment. "I Changed My Sex" can obviously be read as the confession of a man who changes into a woman, but the phrase also clearly suggests that Wood, as author, was consciously trying to nudge his *entire* sex, that is *the male population in aggregate*, towards a progressive reworking of its traditional traits and roles, an act revolutionary and profound. "I Led Two Lives" also has myriad possible interpretations, and can easily be seen as a blanket statement of Wood as author again, suggesting that in *Glen or Glenda?* he saw himself functioning as both man and woman, poet and philosopher, lurid diarist and agent provocateur, political documentarian and traditional storyteller, et al.

This core idea of the film's discourse, cannily elucidated in code in the film's title, suggests that Wood knew exactly what he was doing in this extraordinary first effort. This distinctive binary revelation is even reinforced by the very film itself, whose structural dichotomy, vacillating between documentary and narrative (in effect a battle between the "cinema of prose" and "cinema of poetry"), clearly underscores the film's thematic polarity. It is almost as if Wood knew intuitively that the topic discussed here, in an ephemeral, obscure film buried in the independent film ghetto of the 1950s, would somehow prophecy and augment one of the most popular, and controversial debates of subsequent decades, and eventually become a significant part of that debate.

Yet the secret of secrets in *Glen or Glenda?* is the revelation that gender is a mercurial, fictive construct, comprised of masculine and feminine traits drawn equally from biology, environment and self-determination. Significantly, this construct emanates not from a fixed course of historical or physiological imperative, or with any prevailing rules or recipes, but is (at least ideally) a malleable and ever-changing thing, which the individual can, within certain predetermined anchors, modify to his/her own choosing, creating in the process a wholly unique being which reinforces certain gender-based eventualities even as it defies traditional gender expectations.

This emancipating, even radical notion is also in direct contradiction to most Western schools of philosophy and religion, the Judeo-Christian theology foremost amongst them, which states dogmatically that a male is a "man" due to his penis and largely active, dynamic role in society, and a female is a "woman" due to her vagina and primarily supportive or passive role in that same society. Any significant diversion from this strict formula is perverse, immoral and/or mentally incorrect. This rigid heterosexism has shaped, and still shapes, entire cultures, with it's unshakable edict that only the strict heterosexual social construct is moral, constructive and proper. Wood's radical thesis dares to rock this sacred cultural belief to its very core, one probable reason why *Glen or Glenda?* as text, and Wood as philosopher, is mocked, trivialized and ignored for serious study. Wood's glorious notion of an evolutionary, gender-dodging world of beings unidentifiable as traditionally male or female would subvert and annihilate many of modern culture's pivotal aesthetic, political and economic tenets, offering a blueprint for a new world where gender acts as creative force, not psycho-sexual dogma, a means and not an end.

Finally, perhaps the most important point to remember about this extraordinary tract is that *Glen or Glenda?* is, at root, a cinematic autobiography of a fledgling filmmaker. It is likely one of the first, and only, cinema autobiographies in history. Who else has made such a compelling, and hyper-critical, portrait of themselves, as an artist, in the celluloid medium? Which came first in *Glen or Glenda?*'s case, the exploitation film or the autobiography? Considering that the source of the film in this as most cases is the screenplay, one might intuit that from the writer's point of view at least, the project was first and foremost an autobiography, fashioned cleverly into an exploitation film. (Wood's indelible gender-bending character was invoked again in his 1963 novel *Killer in Drag*, which featured Glen, a criminally inclined transvestite who successfully dodged the law in the guise of "Glenda," his female "mask.")

It seems likely that in its first run, *Glen or Glenda?* fared no better than any other quick-buck exploitation product of the day, running its playdates in theatres across the nation to disinterested audiences, under several different titles, to then languish in the vaults of Screen Classics for years, until uncovered by some curiosity-seeking film collectors in the late 1970s, when the film turned up at midnight screenings at revival houses in New York and California, sparking the Ed Wood revival. One infamous run of *Glen or Glenda?* in 1978 at New York's Thalia theatre is supposedly where author Rudolph Grey first encountered the work of Ed Wood, and was thus inspired to write the seminal Ed Wood memoir, *Nightmare of Ecstasy*, which in turn led to Tim Burton's 1994 bio-pic *Ed Wood*, and thus to the Cult of Wood.[75] Less successful was Paramount Pictures' 1982 theatrical reissue of *Glen or Glenda?*, which played to nearly empty multiplex auditoriums. Yet over two decades later, *Glen or Glenda?* boasts a growing legion of loyal fans, many of whom have insightful thoughts on this most unusual and provocative film. In *Forbidden Fruit: The Golden Age of the Exploitation Film*, Felecia Feaster and Bret Wood honor the work in no uncertain terms:

> When he made *Glen or Glenda?* ... [Wood] invested in the film a great deal of his own feelings and opinions, resulting in a motion picture that is a true, unqualified original, his awkward visual styling aptly suited to the bold, hallowed pronouncements being voiced. A tortured plea for social acceptance, *Glen or Glenda?* addressed Wood's own penchant for cross-dressing in a wildly disorganized but deeply impassioned film.[76]

Glen or Glenda? is an insightful, courageous, glorious, at times brilliant film, so much more than its creator and original audience could have ever hoped for. It uncannily foreshadows the ascendancy of the volatile subject it ruminates on, awkwardly and with self-contradiction — the question of culturally annotated gender, versus the apparently immutable occurrence of biological sex. Wood's performance in *Glen or Glenda?*, as author and actor, and ultimately as symbol, goes far to illuminate some of the greatest truths, and even greater contradictions, of this eternal, perhaps unsolvable debate. Butler concludes her *Gender Trouble* with a query which Edward D. Wood, Jr., may have answered decades earlier, in the peerless analysis-as-performance known as *Glen or Glenda?*:

> What performance where will compel a radical rethinking of the psychological presuppositions of gender identity and sexuality? What performance where will compel a reconsideration of the *place* and stability of the masculine and the feminine? And what kind of gender performance will enact and reveal the performativity of gender itself in a way that destabilizes the naturalized categories of identity and desire?[77]

3

Jail Bait (1954)

After Ed Wood's auspicious and peculiar feature film debut, one could hardly guess what to expect from his next feature outing, and *Jail Bait* radically differs from *Glen or Glenda?*, although there are certain striking parallels and similarities, not the least of which are the use of similar cast members and sets. Firstly, *Jail Bait* is a relatively straightforward narrative melodrama. Also, it has a tight structure and coherent story-line, perhaps moreso than any other Wood feature, due perhaps to the participation of co-scenarist Alex Gordon. Still, within the somewhat pedestrian format of a crime thriller, Wood manages to imbue the scenario with all sorts of poetic touches, the most noticeable being the use of simplistic religious metaphors and symbols throughout, strewn about haphazardly and without any chronological focus, but significant to the proceedings as punctuation of plot and character. Wood's uncanny ability to radically alter an ostensibly mundane *mise-en-scène* is well-illustrated in *Jail Bait* which, for all its superficial familiarity, appears to take place in some alien cosmic void, not the sunny Southern California milieu in which the story is set. This otherworldly quality greatly augments the overlay of religious symbology which haunts *Jail Bait* from the first to last frame.

In addition to consistent reference to Judeo-Christian religious metaphor, much of *Jail Bait* lends itself to the mythology of the ancient Egyptian deity, Osiris. As chronicled primarily by Plutarch, Osiris was considered the king of Egyptian deities, associated with rescuing the Egyptian civilization from barbarism, and introducing them to moral law. Osiris is also revered for his introduction of fruits and grains into the formerly carnivorous Egyptian diet, and is associated with the growth of wheat and grains, and crops fertility in general. Osiris's sister, and subsequently his wife, Isis, was instrumental in Osiris's reign, taking over the government for him while he traveled the land, enlightening his people. However, Osiris's evil brother Set conspired against him, and finally drowned him in the Nile.

Isis eventually retrieved her brother's dismembered body and assembled all the pieces, wrapping them in linen bandages to create the first mummy, an effort to preserve the material body for the afterlife, and a practice which became widespread in Egyptian culture. The evil Set continued to hound Osiris's spirit, accusing him of crimes committed even after his death. These accusations resulted in a protracted trial which proved Osiris's innocence posthumously. Ceremonies to celebrate Osiris's fate, and his subsequent reign over the harvest, originally took place at Osiris's burial site in Seis, near a large lake. The festival, taking place at night, included a melancholy chant sung by mourners. A striking characteristic of the celebration was the "nocturnal illumination," in which celebrants kept their homes lit all night long by oil lamp. This festival eventually expanded to include not only the fallen Osiris, but

2 TNT
TORRID
TERRIFIC
THRILLERS

MR. EXHIBITOR:
They're Clean !
They're N E W !
They're $ $ $ $ $
FOR YOU !

GIRLS IN A
MAN'S WORLD!
INTRODUCING
PEACHES PAGE

"THE BLONDE PICK-UP"

SHE WAS ONLY '18'
AND EAGER FOR HER
'NEW' PROFESSION

WOMEN
GAMBLED
HONOR!
...MEN
PROMISED
LOVE!..GIRL
RIVALS MATCH WITS!

THE MOST EXCITING
BODY IN HOLLYWOOD

PLUS

THESE GIRLS ARE HOT!..
Stay away from them!..
They're "JAIL BAIT"

Released by AMERICAN FILM Co.

FOR IMMEDIATE BOOKINGS
AMERICAN FILM COMPANY
1329 VINE STREET
Phone: WAlnut 2-1800-01   PHILA. 7, PA.

This circa 1956 advertising herald positions Wood's *Jail Bait* at the bottom of a grindhouse double-bill with another exploitation feature, *The Blonde Pick-Up*, a retitling of *Racket Girls* (1951, d: Robert C. Derfano), a George Weiss potboiler about women wrestlers.

the beloved dead in general, evolving into the more recent "Night of All Souls."[1]

Significantly, *Jail Bait* takes place over the course of several weeks, but *always at night*; the film's characters seem to be constantly sleepwalking through a murky setting of eternal darkness. Given the overt religious nature of the scenario, one might call this setting a modern incarnation of the Biblical purgatory, a metaphor for the eternal prison of a sinful, fallen culture, most specifically suggesting the ancient Hebrew notion of Hell, known as Sheol, "a dim sort of pit where all the dead gathered and became sightless, soundless, and forgotten."[2] This striking narrative quirk also surely echoes the aforementioned "nocturnal illumination" of the ancient Osiris ritual, making the whole of *Jail Bait* a form of celluloid "Night of All Souls." This creepy otherworldly ambience in *Jail Bait* is greatly enhanced by the wildly inappropriate music score. This strange and beautiful music was composed by Hoyt Kurtain (aka Hoyt S. Curtin, soon to become the prolific composer for Hanna-Barbera animation studios) for an earlier film, *Mesa of Lost Women* (1953), for the same producers. The producers of *Jail Bait* merely lifted this earlier score and added it, rather haphazardly, to Wood's gritty crime thriller. The music consists of flamenco guitar and piano riffs, in vaguely free-form jazz cues which, although hauntingly beautiful, evoke no excitement or dramatic tension whatsoever. The mournful, almost avant-garde music emphasizes the alien texture of the film, and makes the most dramatic and tense scenes seem dreamy and unreal, in effect a modern incarnation of the "melancholy chants" used in the Osiris death ritual.

Wood produced *Jail Bait* for Louisiana-based producers C. Francis White and Joy N. Houck.[3] According to *Glen or Glenda?* producer George Weiss, Houck and White gave director-producer Wood a modest budget for making *Jail Bait*, and he shared none of the considerable proceeds from its subsequent distribution, a fate which was to haunt Wood his whole career. As Weiss stated in an interview with Rudolph Grey, "They really took him on *Jail Bait*."[4]

Jail Bait's opening titles roll as a Nash police cruiser prowls a busy Alhambra, California, street at night, while dreamy jazz music plays, setting the stage not for a gripping crime melodrama, but a weird spiritual tale in some modern purgatory. The credits sequence ends, and a different police car pulls up to a local police precinct, where the officers haul a noisy drunk into the station. The drunk, a peripheral character, serves as a sly stand-in and self-parody for alcoholic director Wood, and symbolizes the prominence of alcohol in the ensuing melodrama. Wood's problematic relationship with booze, alternately glorifying and demonizing it, is an essential part of many of his screenplays, with *Jail Bait* being perhaps the most prominent.

Inside, Miss Gregor (Wood's partner and muse at the time, Dolores Fuller) sits in the lobby, and is soon met by Inspector Johns (Lyle Talbot) and Detective Bob Lawrence (muscleman Steve Reeves, winner of the Mr. Universe title in 1950, and soon to achieve world fame as Hercules). Miss Gregor has posted the bail money for her brother, Don, who was recently arrested for carrying a gun. Johns scolds Miss Gregor: "Carrying a gun can be a dangerous business," to which the young woman cryptically replies, "So can building a skyscraper." A bedraggled Don Gregor (Clancy Malone, in his only film role) walks out of stir, collects his belongings, and requests his gun. Johns coyly quips, "I think we'll hold on to that for a little while." Don pouts, puts on his tie, and leaves with his long-suffering sister. Don and Sis get into her Nash automobile (likely the same one used as Glen and Barbara's "honeymoon car" in *Glen or Glenda?*) and drive home. Inside the police station, Johns and Lawrence discuss Don; Johns is sure he is mixed up with Vic Brady, a notorious local hood. John muses, "How can a great doctor have such a *jerk* for a son?" Lawrence queries, "Sins of the father?" the first of many religious references in *Jail Bait*.

Don and Sis return to their home and relax in the living room (the set here is similar to Glen and Barbara's living room in *Glen or Glenda?*, lending a strange continuity to the two films). Don immediately hits the booze, reinforcing the predominance of alcohol in the scenario, first signaled by the arrested drunkard. Don offers his sister a drink, but she refuses. Don drinks and pouts, fully expecting a lecture of reprimand from his sibling; he sputters defensively, "Listen, Sis. I'm over 21; I know what I'm doing." Sis mentions their father, and asks, "Do you know what it would do to him?" as she grabs Don's hand, making him drop his glass, which shatters loudly, nicely foreshadowing the father's heartbreak over the son's indiscretions. The evermore-guilty Don picks up the drink meant for Sis and swallows that as well, a completely self-centered and desperate act.

Returning to the Osiris analogy, Don's sister is remarkably set up as his "Isis"; he tellingly refers to her as "Sis" (as in Isis), and never calls her by her actual name. Her existence in the scenario is novel, as any number of other B-level crime thrillers of the era would have, as the protagonist's female counterpart, a lover or girlfriend or wife, some sort of romantic interest. As Don has only his sister to love and worry over him, there is no romantic tension whatsoever in the piece. In fact, Sis does act the role of Don's "wife" in many ways, from fretting and cajoling and offering advice and solace, to harboring and hiding him during periods of extreme danger. She is, in effect, Isis to his Osiris, *both* sister and wife.

Don removes a large volume from a bookshelf under the liquor cabinet and opens it. (Considering the religious nature of *Jail Bait*, the volume may well be the Holy Bible.) The pages have been carved out, and inside sits a small revolver which Don extracts; the errant son has gutted the sacred legacy of this family, replacing it with something violent and destructive. Sis protests Don's latest stupidity, stating, "You know that gun is *jail bait!*" This line, which references the film's title, is spoken softly and off-camera, making it an entirely peripheral notion. The gun isn't evil; the wayward son of Man is. Don ignores the warning, and wanders out into the California night. On his way out the door, Don meets his father (Gregor Herbert Rawlinson) coming in.[5] Sporting a white beard, he comes across as an educated man, likely involved in the sciences, evoking learned icons such as Sigmund Freud, i.e., a "wise man."

Gregor informs Sis that he is already aware of his son's pal, Vic Brady, the notorious hood. Sis fixes dad a drink as he tells her about a telephone conversation he had with Inspector Johns. Yet with all this ominous information, Gregor is eternally optimistic, or more likely in serious denial, as he feels that "everything will work itself out." Gregor confesses that he gave Don too much in his youth, and that "plus the lack of a mother's attention, God rest her dear soul," is probably the cause of his son's current rambling. This maudlin exchange introduces the notable absence of a loving mother figure in the main character's childhood, which echoes similar causal evidence in *Glen or Glenda?*, and also suggests that a postwar "nuclear family" without a vital and caring maternal presence is doomed to dysfunction and disaster.

Sis is certain that Vic Brady will lead Don into serious trouble, but as Gregor grabs his drink and hoists a healthy slug of booze, he mutters "perhaps, perhaps not." Obviously, alcohol is Gregor's escape from reality, his socially accepted means of denial, granting him a tenuous fatalism which avoids entirely the harsh realities of postwar child-rearing. Wood's treatment of alcohol in *Jail Bait*, although virtually obsessive, is problematic, and not without thoughtful conflict.

As if to admit his own guilt in the matter, albeit subconsciously, Gregor next knowingly walks over to the large book with the hole in the middle, from which Don has extracted the firearm. Gregor paws the empty space and looks up at the camera, grimacing. His sacred text has been defiled, he knows that his son is now headed for disaster, and that he is not guilt-free in the matter. More-

After an illustrious, decades-long career on stage, screen and radio, silent-film matinee idol Herbert Rawlinson appeared in Wood's *Jail Bait*, which would be his last performance; Rawlinson died shortly after production wrapped.

over, Gregor sees that sacred knowledge and moral wisdom, his "gods," have been vivisected by the nihilism of this evil new age, which has contaminated, perhaps fatally, his beloved offspring.

The scene changes to the Hunters Inn, a swanky bar and grill in nearby Temple City. Don meets up with his partner-in-crime, Vic Brady (Wood stalwart Timothy Farrell). Sitting at the bar and guzzling whiskey and sodas, the two wannabe thugs chat. Like a hurt child, Don whines about his recent arrest, and Brady placates him with his share of the money from the robbery they pulled before the film began. Even in this first scene, Brady is seen as the nihilistic surrogate father figure Don prefers over his old-fashioned biological patriarch (and considering the peer-oriented activity of drinking, an ill-advised *brother* figure, a Set to his Osiris). As the two talk, the main portion of the frame is taken up with rows of liquor bottles, again reinforcing the omnipresence of alcohol in this fallen postwar world (as in the entire Wood film universe).

A panicked Brady sees Inspector Johns and Detective Lawrence enter the bar, and quickly takes Don's revolver from him. The two cops surround the hoods by sitting on either side of them at the bar, making the crooks visibly uncomfortable. Johns taunts the hoods mercilessly, with jabs like, "Gee, I guess you don't care who you serve in this joint, do you?" Don and Brady tell them to lay off: "You cops, you're all alike!" Lawrence retorts, "Like crooks, *you're* all alike!" As the four men sit in a row at the bar, dressed in remarkably similar gray suits with dark ties, what is illuminated is a much more subversive truth, that cops and robbers are indeed very much alike, *very much like each other*, an essential and ubiquitous binary of the modern social contract, and a brilliant touch on Wood's part. (It may also by a sly statement on Wood's part about relative masculine virility that cops sip beer, while robbers guzzle hard liquor.)

Finally, Johns intones: "We're trying to keep you from gettin' to your grave too early," underscoring the spirit of death which obsessively hovers over the Woodian universe. Johns continues to taunt Don with, "Too bad your father's such a great man," which enrages Don, leading Johns to add, "You're really a pretty low character." The mercilessly teased youth knocks over the inspector's beer glass, giving the cops an excuse to frisk him. Finding no firearms, they release him. Johns tells the two hoods to vacate the premises, and they sheepishly slink out of the bar.

Outside, Brady chastises Don for his impulsiveness: "That's no way to talk to a cop, boy! You got a lot to learn!" Don vows revenge, but Brady calms him down by switching the subject to their next caper, stealing the payroll from the nearby Monterey Theatre chain. Don declares he doesn't want to continue this ill-advised life of crime, but Brady bullies him into compliance. During this scene, Don and Brady stand in front of the awning to the Hunters Inn, cropping the bar's name until just "The Hunt" appears, nicely echoing the composition inside, wherein cops and robbers are indistinguishable characters in an eternal game between predator and prey, hunter and hunted. This peculiar game, or dance, between eternal adversaries with essential similarities could truly be called "the hunt."

Back at the troubled Gregor household, Sis, wearing a sheer nightie, wakes up her father, who has passed out in a drunken stupor, and wonders out loud whether they should have contacted Inspector Johns about Don's latest activities. With his eyes half-closed, Gregor groggily states, "I just can't *see* Don doing anything wrong," a viciously ironic line as the man is literally *blind drunk*. Gregor morosely ponders, "Where have I failed?" Sis emphatically replies, "You haven't failed!" Gregor counters, "Words, my daughter! Words! The proof is in the *fact*!" Gregor is slowly awakening to the reality of his failed parenting skills, and the heavy burden of guilt he bears for both his child's sad fate, and society's affliction as recipient of that fate.

Jail Bait shifts radically here, to an anachronistic performance out of an earlier time and place. A theatre sign states, "5 Big Vaudeville Acts, featuring Minstrel Days with Cotton Watts and Chick," as an off-screen announcer declares, "That was Goody Dreams spending an evening in Maggie Murphy's home!" A remarkably strange stage act follows (purportedly filmed by Houck and company, without Wood's involvement), featuring a white man in black-face, trading hoary old jokes with his female partner, about lions and lion taming. A typical exchange goes as follows: "Why, the lion can't *hurt* you!" "Yeah, but he sure can make me *hurt myself!*" The sorry comedy relief ends with an equally archaic tap dance routine done in front of an on-stage orchestra. The tradition of black-face, an integral part of American vaudeville performance throughout the late 19th and early 20th centuries, and given perhaps its finest showcasing in Al Jolson's performance in the 1927 film *The Jazz Singer*, was all but obsolete after World War II, and given the emergent civil rights movement of the 1950s, this scene in *Jail Bait* could be considered sorely out of place and ill-advised, if not outright racist. One must assume that this sequence was filmed, either by Wood or other parties, to please the distributors, who released *Jail Bait* primarily in the rural Deep South, where such an act would be greeted with nostalgic acceptance. If *Jail Bait* were also released on the East and West Coasts, especially in the Los Angeles and New York metropolitan areas, it would not be surprising to learn that this segment had been excised from release prints shipped to these more "liberal" territories.

Petty thugs Don Gregor (Clancy Malone) and Vic Brady (Timothy Farrell) attack night watchman "Mac" (Bud Osborne) in a brutal scene from Wood's *Jail Bait*.

Returning to *Jail Bait*'s narrative thread, Don and Brady break into the flagship theatre of the Monterey Theatre Chain after closing. Presumably, the preceding act occurred there, although no continuity shots are offered. Don and Brady enter the backstage area, guns drawn, and surprise the night watchman, Paul "Mac" McKenna (familiar Wood player Bud Osborne). Brady bullies "Mac" to open the safe; in close-up, Brady speaks towards camera, telling the guard he does not value life at all, and doesn't care if he lives another day or not. This arresting shot offers an adroit profile of the modern sociopathic criminal mind. "Mac" reluctantly opens the safe and extracts the cash. Meanwhile, Miss Willis (Mona McKinnon, who appeared in several other Howco releases), the secretary to the theatre chain manager, returns unexpectedly and happens upon the crime scene. Don panics and shoots "Mac," while Brady trails the poor woman into the empty theatre lobby and shoots her in the back, a most cowardly and violent act committed in a most symbolic setting, the "theatre" of life.

Brady returns to the theatre office and carelessly stuffs his pockets full of the box office cash. (One can easily see Wood fantasizing about stealing the payroll of a lucrative theatre chain, considering the paltry production deals he made throughout his career with shady, unscrupulous distributors, Howco included.) Don, however, is paralyzed with fear and remorse over his killing, and Brady has to literally shake him to get Don to escape. The two run out of the death chamber amid the sound of police sirens approaching (with the cash that clearly dangled out of Brady's pockets inside the theatre conspicuously absent in the exterior shots). Brady and Don drive through the dark night, closely followed by cops. With the sublime jazz music on the soundtrack, the scene comes across as somewhat meditative, not thrilling or energetic, a decidedly tranquil moment which again reinforces the poetic synchronicity of cops and robbers, i.e., "the hunt." The cops begin shooting at the robber's car in the middle of the city (a reckless and unlikely event even then), but Brady ducks into a side street and loses their pursuers.

Back at the Monterey, two attendants place the injured Miss Willis on a couch. As the police doctor examines the woman, two cops discuss her condition, thus informing the audience that Willis was not fatally injured and will recover shortly. This scene of a woman draped in a white sheet, lying on a bed-like object, and surrounded by "grieving" and concerned males (replete with a caring doctor hovering over the victim and taking her hand), recalls the death scene tableau in *Glen or Glenda?*, as well as perhaps the earliest Wood death scene from *Crossroads of Laredo*.

Inspector Johns enters in an interesting shot wherein the man stands next to a stage light, emphasizing the overtly theatrical nature of Wood's lurid melodramatic universe. Johns inquires about the situation and receives the startling reply: "Robbery, attempted murder, and murder!" Inquiring about "Mac," the police doctor hilariously informs Johns, "Couldn't be any deader!" Back in the theatre office, Johns shoes away a snoopy newspaper woman (Regina Claire) and her photographer, Louie (Conrad Brooks). The newswoman tries to flirt with one of the cops, who replies, tongue-in-cheek, "Please, lady! I'm on duty!" Johns offers the others a sketchy eulogy to the night watchmen, who was a retired police officer of 30 years service, and took the theater job because he was bored. Hearing this, a cop exclaims, "That makes our boys *cop killers*!"

Soon, Brady and Don return to Brady's apartment, where Brady's moll Loretta (Theodora Thurman, an attractive and popular fashion model, in her only screen role) greets them in sexy, sheer lingerie, a signature Wood touch. Brady informs his mistress about recent events as he swigs several shots of Johnny Walker Red, in a nicely handled, dolly-driven two-shot. Don is off-screen during this exchange, and as the camera pulls back again, Loretta breathlessly announces that Don has left the building. Brady grabs his gun and runs out, ordering

In a *Jail Bait* scene eerily reminiscent of a similar segment in *Glen or Glenda?*, a group of men surround, and appear to mourn, a fallen female (Mona McKinnon; all others unidentified).

Loretta to stay put, an order to which the lingerie-clad gun moll theatrically replies, "'Stay here,' he says! Where does he suppose I'd go, dressed like this?"

Elsewhere, a terrified Don prowls the eternal city night, thinking of possible solutions to his dilemma. He ends up at his father's downtown office, which is oddly open at what must now be a very late hour. Gregor's nurse, Dorothy Lytell (La Vada Simmons, in her only screen role), sits in the lobby, awkwardly reading a book, when Don enters. It is worth noting that Gregor's office is exactly the same as Dr. Alton's office in *Glen or Glenda?*, even down to the painting on the wall, reinforcing the preeminence of Science in both films. Don confesses his sins to his father, a fully religious action which will begin Don's journey towards spiritual healing. Like the biblical Isaac, who eventually becomes aware of the pain his very existence has caused his father Abraham, and who changes from self-centered victim to other-directed healer, so too does Don at this late date see, in painful clarity, how his criminal actions have emotionally tortured his long-suffering patriarch. The suffering of both parties in this scene is tangible, as each realizes both their sins towards the other, and also their deep mutual love, until now woefully under-expressed.[6]

Don states that he wished he had changed his ways sooner, but as he tells his father, "It goes deeper now," not merely his untoward actions, but the pain and the contamination of his mortal soul. This vivid allusion to a cut or wound reminds one of the Old Testament tale of Abraham and Isaac, as told in the book of Genesis. The elder Abraham was admonished to sacrifice his son, Isaac, under direct orders from God, and was to "skillfully" use a sacrificial knife to do so. The "deep" cut, literally and metaphorically, which Abraham was assigned to make on this innocent was prevented at the last minute by the intervention of God Himself.[7]

Don next states, "I walked all last night, until tonight," suggesting that the scenario has entirely skipped the daylight hours, reinforcing the notion that the ever-present night of *Jail Bait* represents some sort of spiritually infused primordial nocturne of metaphoric import. Perhaps not coincidentally, Gregor, who reminded the viewer of a learned man of Science like Sigmund Freud in earlier scenes, in this confessional scene looks more like a character from the Old Testament, another sketch of the Genesis hero Abraham. Don admits to his father that he killed a man, and a stunned Gregor replies, "Why did you *kill*?" He is shocked above all that Don has broken one of the sacred Ten Commandments, "Thou shalt not kill." Don offers his father the sordid details, ending with the self-centered, "It was either him or me." Gregor somberly states, "Better it had been you," on oddly cold statement from a father to a son, unless it refers again to a spiritual point of view, wherein the father fears that his son's soul may now be threatened with eternal damnation.

Gregor solemnly states, "No matter what you've done, you're still my son, and if you'll turn yourself over to the police, I'll stand by you. But if you don't, I'll do everything in my power to see that you are apprehended." Referencing again the biblical fable of Abraham and Isaac, as Abraham almost sacrificed his son Isaac out of a sense of duty to God, here Gregor seems prepared to sacrifice his son out of fierce loyalty to his "gods," which are honesty, moral righteousness and, above all, *the law.* As punctuation to this sobering declaration, an off-screen doorbell rings. It is the police, and Don now knows "for whom the bell tolls." Johns, Lawrence and another detective, McCall (John Robert Martin), arrive to question Gregor. Don begs his father for time to surrender in his own way, and Gregor hides the youth, favoring him momentarily over his beloved "God." Gregor waxes philosophical to Inspector Johns, with more overt religious allusions: "Many things are not of our choosing, but we must face that which is ordained us. Destiny is a strange and mysterious thing, my dear inspector." Gregor promises the policemen that Don will turn himself in shortly. The cops leave, and Gregor retrieves his son, telling him to escape the back way, where "the darkness of the night shall hide you ... for awhile," an allusion which suggests that the eternal nighttime of *Jail Bait* is both prison *and* harbor. Don leaves, as Gregor hangs his head in sorrow and exhaustion, bearing the weight of the very heavens on his shoulders.

Outside, Don tries to escape through the back alley, but Brady is laying in wait for him, and escorts him at gunpoint back to his apartment. Loretta is lounging around in silk pajamas when Brady and Don enter. Brady chastises Don for his folly. Don confirms that he is going to give himself up, and Brady knows he means business when the radio conveniently reports the entire incident verbatim, and in great detail. The radio sits alone on a night table, and features a cross design on its speaker front, yet another symbolic icon denoting religious confession and atonement. The announcer (purportedly Wood himself)[8] clarifies that Don is "the son of the world-famous plastic surgeon, Boris Gregor," and for the first time the viewer knows why Gregor is so esteemed in his community. This revelation of the elder Gregor's occupation of surgeon, that is, one whose main instrument of healing is a *knife*, aligns him emphatically with his Old Testament counterpart, Abraham, whose sacrificial knife was the crucial element in the whole sordid tale.

Don continues his speech of repentance to Brady and Loretta, as he ponders why he did these evil things: "Maybe for thrills." Brady reminds Don that if he goes to the cops, "he'll burn," a none-too-subtle reference to biblical hellfire. Don even reinforces the religious allusion, saying "Sure, I'll burn," resigned to his spiritual fate. Don tries to leave, but Brady pulls a gun and shoots him once in the back and once in the front, as Loretta stares on, nonplussed. Don falls to the floor in front of the cross-bearing radio set, and this cruel death of a troubled but sympathetic protagonist marks *Jail Bait* indelibly as the cinema of Wood. Brady tells Loretta he is going to dump the corpse "in the river, where else?" in the first of two references to the saving baptism of a fallen soul, but for now he props the body in the kitchen closet, which significantly has not a door, but shiny curtains. When Don is placed in the kitchen closet, it's literally "curtains" for him, as well as "The Final Curtain." (The kitchen set is similar to the one occupied by Glen's cross-dressing pal Johnny in *Glen or Glenda?*.) Also, Vic Brady really comes to life here as the incarnation of Set, Osiris's evil brother. Not only has he been conspiring against the health and safety of Don, his "brother" and partner-in-crime, from the start of the film, but he has finally killed him, and moreover plans on dumping him in a river.

Loretta amusingly pouts, "I don't like dead men cluttering up my place," revealing her to be a hard, soulless being. As Brady fixes himself a much-needed drink, Loretta berates her mate like any shrewish, middle-class housewife might her long-suffering, henpecked husband, ending her tirade with, "You're no good!" Brady slaps her in the face, a physical insult to which Loretta replies, "That's it, Vic. Destroy everything and everybody. That's your style," restating the criminal's nihilistic agenda. The brave (or stupid) Loretta continues her tirade against Brady, finally declaring that she wants no part of his swift decline into disaster. Brady reminds Loretta where he found her (in the gutter, naturally), and insists she is going to stick with him until the bitter end. Loretta softens, embracing this monster without whom she realizes she would be nothing, clearly illustrating that low self-esteem is an essential ingredient of such toxic partnerships. Brady coyly declares, "Something will turn up; it always does," revealing him to be at heart, just a silly optimist-in-denial like Gregor. Brady sits and thinks, finally stating, "You hit the solution on the head —*my face!*"

Later that evening at the Gregor household, Sis arrives home and tells her father that she could not locate her brother. Gregor rightly intuits that something malefic has happened to Don, and further that if his son doesn't show up at police headquarters soon, he himself will be arrested as "an accessory after the fact." Yet Gregor courageously states, "My life means little to me now. It is Don that we must think of." Gregor soon receives a phone call from Brady, who lies and tells the distraught man he has his son in custody, and demands to see him for some unnamed operation. Gregor reluctantly agrees to the meeting, and hangs up the phone. Turning to his daughter, for the first time Gregor mentions her by name: "Marilyn, do you remember your nurse's training?" Gregor has intuited that Marilyn is no longer Don's sister, but the tragic patriarch's only remaining heir. The poignant tension of this scene again recalls the biblical Abraham and Isaac, with an ironic twist. Much of the pathos and tension of the Old Testament tale revolves around Abraham's knowledge of his doomed son's dire fate, versus the faithful Isaac's blissful ignorance. In *Jail Bait*, the tragedy of the elder Gregor's futile attempt to save his son lies in the audience's awareness of Don's secret murder, and the father's "blissful ignorance" of this dreadful fact.[9]

Three days pass. At the police station, Inspector Johns is looking over some police files when Detective Lawrence walks into the room, topless. (The handsome Reeves engages here in some gratuitous beefcake. According to Dolores Fuller, the awkward model-cum-actor had great difficulty in putting on his tie, and this scene required many takes.[10]) As the young policeman coyly dresses in front of his superior, Johns suggests that Lawrence make a run over to the Gregor home and see if anything new has developed regarding young Gregor, making the excuse that he could also "make some time" with Marilyn.

Lawrence soon arrives at the Gregor home, as always enveloped in an eternal twilight. Marilyn is extremely cold to Lawrence, blaming the cops for involving her father in this sordid mess with Don; she shuts the door in the cop's face. As Marilyn and Gregor prepare to go to Brady's lair, Marilyn puts a revolver into her purse. Gregor and daughter are soon driving through the unending urban night, and finally reach Brady's apartment complex. Loretta lets the pair into her pad, and Brady yells at Gregor for bringing Marilyn along. Gregor insists that he needs his daughter as assistant to the as-yet-unnamed medical procedure he must perform, and Loretta convinces Brady to let the girl stay. In this scene, Theodora Thurman stands in center frame, directly between Gregor and Brady, her hands on her hips, posing exactly as a fashion model would for a magazine cover shoot, showing off a particularly ugly blouse. This scene signals that Wood also considered *Jail Bait* a celluloid fashion show of sorts, as witness Thurman's frequent wardrobe change, plus the inordinate number of costuming credits.

Gregor orders Brady to remove his shirt and shoes, as power begins to shift radically in the protagonist's favor. As Brady undresses, he finally reveals his plan to the audience: "You're gonna give me a completely new face!" Gregor convinces Brady that he must undergo anesthesia in order to withstand the painful and delicate operation. Brady slumps on the couch, topless and flabby, the very picture of the impotent societal loser; he has no choice but to give up his power in order to embrace his delusional goals. Brady gives his gun to Loretta, with explicit orders to shoot both Gregors if there is any trouble. Loretta readily agrees, a cold-blooded killer at heart. Brady further reminds Gregor that his son's life hangs in the balance, a shameful trick that only works as Gregor still harbors vague hope that his son is still alive.

As Marilyn anesthetizes Brady, Gregor informs Loretta that he must retire to the kitchen to fetch hot water for the operation. Loretta protests, as she knows that Don's body is still in the closet, but Gregor manages to convince the gullible, debased female that the trip is essential. Luckily for the protagonists, as soon as Brady is comatose, his tawdry little kingdom falls apart, for the disciples of evil are ignorant, conscious only of the secondary, indigent moral truths. Gregor walks into the kitchen and searches for an appropriate vessel for the water. In the living room, Loretta and Marilyn bicker, defending their male heroes in Woodian dialogue alternately awkward and sublime. Gregor finally stumbles onto the closet and stares in utter shock as his beloved son's stiff corpse totters to the floor, a moment which seamlessly blends pathos, farce and satire as only Wood could.

A benumbed Gregor soon returns to the living room with a container of hot water, bravely keeping his grief in check. Loretta warns him to be careful, for the sake of his son's life, and Gregor repeats, meaningfully, "Yes. My son's *life.*" The viewer now knows that what Gregor cherishes, and must defend, is his son's spiritual fate, his *afterlife.* The operation begins as the scene fades out.

In the next scene, Brady's head is now covered in bandages, looking very much like a mummy, with clear allusions to the Osiris legend. Gregor and Marilyn are wearing white lab coats, making them look simultaneously sinister and angelic. A clearly unnerved Loretta groans, "I couldn't take much more of that! You made his face look like raw meat!" Gregor calls Loretta's bluff again, stating that he assumed Brady ordered her to kill the pair after the surgery was completed, yet warning her this would be a foolhardy move, as Gregor will be essential to Brady's full recovery, should complications develop. The dim-witted Loretta falls for this hackneyed power play, and lets the pair leave unharmed. Gregor tells Loretta to make sure Brady visits him in two weeks, at which time the bandages will be removed.

Two weeks pass. Johns and Lawrence ponder the Gregor case, which has been too quiet for their liking. On cue, Gregor calls Johns and requests their presence that very evening. Back at Loretta's apartment, Brady sits uncomfortably, chain smoking, and rambling that with his new face, he can forge a whole new life of crime. Soon, Brady and Loretta arrive at the Gregor home. Inexplicably, Brady's head is now covered in what appears to be a plaster cast, not the loosely draped gauze wrappings seen in the previous scene. The head looks now like an ancient, mummified death-mask, in one of Wood's highly symbolic "continuity errors," which may not be error at all: As Isis rescued her brother Osiris from the river, and preserved him as mummy, so "Sis" and her father have "resurrected" their lost Osiris, even though this is a fact the audience is not yet aware of.

Brady threatens Gregor with harm if he didn't do a good job with the plastic surgery, and Gregor confidently replies, "I *know* I did a good job," which suggests he believes he has performed not just an accomplished task, but a good moral act, and perhaps even a magical one. There is even a trace of haughtiness in Gregor's over-confidence, yet another allusion to his biblical counterpart, Abraham, whose intrinsic arrogance is humbled only by God's right-eous edicts. As soon as Brady sits down, the cops enter the scene. The masked Brady plays it cool, insisting he isn't the thug they are looking for. Inspector Johns asks Gregor who is behind those bandages, and Brady tellingly reiterates the question: "Yeah, doc, who *is* behind these bandages?," a question of great significance. Gregor somberly intones, "A doctor's duties sometimes must be shown in strange ways," an overt allusion to the biblical saying, "The Lord works in mysterious ways." Gregor continues, "First, he has his loyalty to his patients. Then, he has his loyalty to the law. And still another—loyalty to his own family!" Actually, Gregor's primary loyalty may be to *the law*: spiritual and moral law, that is.

Gregor slowly, dramatically, snips away at the bandages, the scene punctuated with close-ups of the assembled. Gregor removes the bandages, and the observers gasp in collective horror at a face still unseen by the audience. Gregor smiles and remarks, "There! It is done!" as if he is praying, "Thy will be done!" A shocked Inspector Johns responds, "You are right, doctor. It's *not* the man we expected!" Brady, still unaware of his strange destiny, dares the cops to identify him. Johns asks the theatre secretary, Miss Willis, to enter from another room, and she dutifully identifies the man sitting in the chair as the man who shot the night watch-man: Don Gregor! Johns hands a mirror to the unmasked man, as the audience sees his face for the first time. Gregor has fashioned the killer Brady into the likeness of his beloved, mur-dered son, Don. Forcing a killer to wear the face of the very man he killed is poetic justice of a very rare kind, and with this act, Gregor has managed both to momentarily resurrect his son from an untimely death, and also sacrifice him, as the biblical Abraham was prepared to do with Isaac, to fulfill his loyalty to "the law." As well, "Sis," as Isis has, according to the leg-end and with the help of her father, retrieved her brother from death, and created a spiritual resting place for Don/Osiris's reassembled material body, i.e., through his "mummification," and the tragic death and miraculous resurrection of a sympathetic character takes center stage once again in the cinema of Wood, this time with the help of myth-icon Isis, the great mother of creation.

As an unshaven Brady looks in horror at the face of the very man he killed, Gregor confirms, "This *is* my son—the man who killed the policeman." Brady/Don leaps from his chair and runs outside, with the police in close pursuit. As Gregor and Marilyn embrace, gun-shots are heard. In the Gregors' back patio, which boasts an immense swimming pool, the cops chase Brady/Don, who continues to shoot at them without conscience.[11] Johns runs out-side and shoots the bullet which finally fells Brady/Don, who falls down, convulsing in his death throes, eventually toppling over into the cleansing water of the pool, finally receiving the purifying baptism he so sorely needs for a serene immortality in paradise. As *Jail Bait* ends, so does its celebration of fallen mortals and their subsequent resurrection and glorification — overall a memorable postwar "Night of All Souls." Brady's conspiracy against Don Gregor has failed, as did Set's conspiracy against his brother Osiris, as do most evil conspiracies eventually, for although these plots may remove the physical targets from their mortal coils, the morally ignorant actions tend to elevate their targets' greater legacy, assuring that they will become "larger than life," in many instances iconic and mythological, with Osiris being a fine example.

With its exemplary use of religious metaphor and ancient mythology, *Jail Bait* can be seen as an allegorical tale of Man's fall from grace, and his torturous punishment in a bleak modern purgatory of eternal night, until he confesses, repents, atones, and accepts his fate, which is death, but a blessed and forgiven death, absolved from eternal damnation by a lucky, last-minute baptism. The tortured innocent, Don Gregor, is a fine example of fallen modern man, essentially a guiltless fellow but one with fatal flaws and proclivities, or as David C. Hayes noted, one of Wood's "Good Guy[s] with a Bad Habit."[12] Similar in spirit to its ancient counterpart, the tale of Abraham and Isaac, *Jail Bait* is essentially a tragedy, albeit one with important moral and dramatic rewards. In each somber tale, the stark absence of fortunate outcome, the cruel denial of familial reunion, even the doubtfulness of eventual spiritual concord leave both character and audience sadder but wiser, with many lessons learned but just as much forfeited. In each fable, the overconfident elder is humbled by extreme loss, and gains spiritual wisdom at great personal cost.[13]

Vic Brady's highly symbolic death nicely caps the other biblical analogies in the film, as he is assuredly a scapegoat of sorts. He stands for everything that is wrong with a fallen, sinful community, one obsessed with materialism and superficiality and nicely symbolized by the elder Gregor's well-intentioned yet ill-advised choice of occupation, which reinforces the cosmetic modification or *masking* of errant personality over inner development and moral evolution. Originally outlined in the Old Testament book of Leviticus, the scapegoat (or "escape goat") was an integral part of an atonement ritual which used a goat (or a person) as a sacrifice to purify a commonwealth of accumulated moral trespasses, a body of sins too great to be erased via individual confession and repentance. The sacrifice, invariably a public ceremony, was designed not to punish the sacrificial animal (although the "scapegoat" likely saw things differently), but to collectively remove incurred sin from the society in question, to rid it ritualistically of regretted transgressions. Vic Brady's shooting at the poolside, most significantly while in the mask of Don Gregor, who represents the repentant, grieving community, does qualify as a sacrificial killing. The "public" nature of the swimming pool, an emblematic societal gathering place, marks the killing not as a lone act of justice and revenge, but a community ritual with profound moral implications. In sum, Vic Brady in *Jail Bait* is a scapegoat for runaway capitalism and its obedient handmaidens, material accumulation and the worship of style over substance.

As well, the omnipresent use (abuse) of alcohol is one of the signature notes in any Wood film, and in *Jail Bait*, it is virtually a character in its own right, acting as catalyst to the heroes' mistakes, but also as salve to their spiritual wounds, certainly another sign of a decadent, fallen culture in need of sacrifice and redress. Not surprisingly, booze ends up in *Jail Bait* as a paradox of nectar and poison, savior and killer, as it served Wood.

Wood's notorious obsession with female apparel is well served in *Jail Bait*, as witness the aforementioned abundance of costuming credits, and the delightful Ms. Thurman's frequent wardrobe changes. As David C. Hayes observes in his excellent overview of Wood's literary output, *Muddled Mind: The Complete Works of Edward D. Wood, Jr.,* "No Wood book would be complete without a rant or two about the fashion of the day, " so too it is the rare Wood film which concludes without an ostentatious parade of current fashion trends, with *Glen or Glenda?* being the prototype.[14]

In sum, *Jail Bait* is a superlative instance of a creative filmmaker elevating a pedestrian genre melodrama by imbuing it with allegorical substance and unique aesthetic peculiarities, creating an engaging work which stands both as part of the intended genre, yet an unique exception to that genre. If there was any doubt after the decidedly iconoclastic *Glen or Glenda?*, with *Jail Bait* Wood proved that he could mount an entertaining genre thriller as well as any more well-heeled filmmaker of the day. One can assume that Wood was proud of this rare creation, as the end title of *Jail Bait* proudly boasts, "Made in Hollywood, U.S.A," in unabashed recognition of that apocryphal land of magic, myth and the mystery arts.

4

Bride of the Monster (1956)

With *Bride of the Monster* (henceforth referred to as *Bride*), Ed Wood took yet another quantum leap as a filmmaker of note, crafting with the slenderest of resources an engaging homage to Poverty Row horror films of a decade previous, and cannily imbuing the scenario with timely references to the disturbing implications of newly unleashed atomic weaponry, the ghastly specter of which was casting an ominous shadow over modern civilization. After using (some might say *misusing*, or even abusing) the great Bela Lugosi as a mysterious supernatural deity in *Glen or Glenda?*, Wood gave Lugosi a role for the ages in *Bride*, in which the maturing thespian returned for one last time to one of his great loves, the charismatic villain whose megalomania leads to downfall and destruction. Radically revising a perfunctory storyline from colleague Alex Gordon, Wood proved with *Bride* that, given a taut pulp screenplay, Lugosi could still act with the best of them; his performance in *Bride* is one of the actor's finest roles, not as stunning as his work in the inimitable *Dracula* (1931, d: Tod Browning), but easily on a par with other roles of the era such as *Mystery of the Mary Celeste* (1935, d: Denison Clift) and *The Black Cat* (1934, d: Edgar G. Ulmer). In fact, Lugosi hams it up admirably in *Bride*, lording over his pasteboard-and-found object kingdom with the gleeful energy of a man half his age. As he dutifully did with the obscure dialogue in *Glen or Glenda?*, in *Bride* Lugosi gives even the most hackneyed and trite Wood dialogue the austere, ever-professional reading it deserved, lending a helpful air of legitimacy to the film.

Bride's release title, *Bride of the Monster*, and its working title, *Bride of the Atom*, were both clearly meant to evoke memories of the horror film classic *Bride of Frankenstein* (1935, d: James Whale). Like many, if not all, of the standard horror pictures of the day, it uses modern trappings to retell the fairy tale "Beauty and the Beast," wherein relative inner beauty and ugliness are exposed, pitted together and eventually reconciled. Wood's original title for the film, *Bride of the Atom*, is a provocative and even politically charged one, and it is disappointing that this title was discarded. As the film unspools, it will be revealed that Wood's notion was that the "Bride" referred to was Mankind in harness to a technology-based, totalitarian government, specifically the then-expanding Military Industrial Complex of the United States, and its unholy and decidedly disastrous "marriage" to "the Atom," that is, the destructive and reckless aspects of Science. As any schoolchild knows, Science + Government = Totalitarianism, and *Bride* presents, in simplistic allegorical form, this diabolical wedding in archetypal terms easily perceived by an astute audience. As well, the ghosts of Sigmund Freud's notions of Eros, the life force, and Thanatos, the death instinct, hover over *Bride*, and when these two antithetical forces "wed" at film's finale, the result, as predicted by German philosopher Herbert Marcuse (1898–1979) and others, is certain catastrophe.[1]

In its basic scenario, *Bride* follows the general template of any number of horror films of the previous twenty years, and in particular borrows some plot points from films Lugosi did for Poverty Row producers such as Sam Katzman, for companies such as Monogram Pictures and Producers Releasing Corporation. It is known that Wood adored these films, and this is likely where Wood cemented his fondness for Lugosi. Although he was paid pitifully small amounts for his performances in these threadbare, throw-away programmers, Lugosi immensely enjoyed the majority of these roles, the last significant roles he would ever obtain in his career. He offered a professionalism to his portrayals in these "quickies" far in excess of what the producers, or audience, could realistically hope for, and many of the films have since become minor classics of their genre.

However, Wood cleverly uses this B-horror template in the service of mounting a postwar Cold War political thriller, with "The Atom" itself in many ways the villain; a comparison of the working title, *Bride of the Atom*, to the release title, *Bride of the Monster*, makes this quite clear. The title, with its emphasis on subject and object connected via a corrupt and ill-fated "marriage" of sorts, signals a binary which will pan out in interesting ways throughout the film, a coupling of innocence and baseness, passivity and aggression (with a nod to the master/slave dialectic of German philosopher Georg Wilhelm Friedrich Hegel (1770–1831), outlined in his seminal work, *Phenomenology of Spirit*, and as mentioned, creation and destruction as embodied in the symbols Eros and Thanatos.

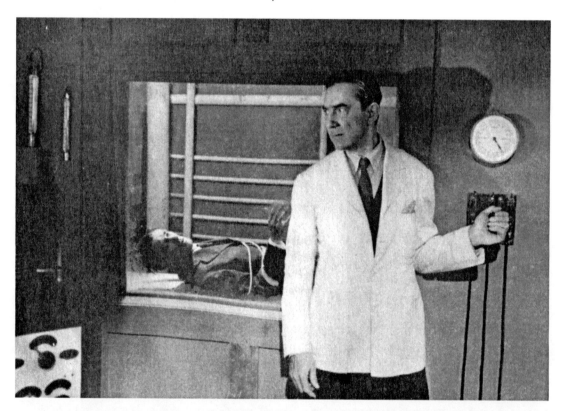

Return of the Ape Man (1944, d: Phil Rosen), one of many Poverty Row horror flicks that the iconic Bela Lugosi made for cheapjack producers in the 1940s, shares much with the similar motif of Wood's *Bride of the Monster*, showing that Wood was intimately familiar with the genre, and was consciously trying to evoke its spirit in his scenario for *Bride*. Lugosi's "freezing chamber" victim (left) is John Carradine.

In this extraordinary cast portrait from the B-horror sleeper *The Black Sleep* (1956, d: Reginald LeBorg), Tor Johnson (center) mugs with fellow cast members John Carradine (bearded), Lon Chaney, Jr., Sally Yarnell and George Sawaya. In the film, Johnson played a mute victim of evil science similar to Lobo, the character created for him by Ed Wood.

Ironically, it is not one country or another which is the victor and savior in *Bride*, but law enforcement which, alone, can stop evil from destroying the world. Cops are, in the Wood film universe, increasingly portrayed as the greater law, moral law, or simply, *"the law."* In any unholy alliance between Science and Government, the Law is an essential third party to guarantee that justice may be at least addressed, and perhaps served.

Bride shares much with its immediate predecessor, *Jail Bait*; both are, in part, plucky, tongue-in-cheek crime thrillers, with baffled, comical cops and sneaky yet equally comic villains trying to second-guess each other. *Bride* also borrows *Jail Bait*'s dreary, melancholy *mise-en-scène*, shocked into life only via the fantastic pulp fiction dialogue and plotting of Wood. *Bride* shows Wood as an absolute master of mixing genres and styles to fabricate something wholly unique and, in many cases, quite subversive, creating fantastic character-driven narratives that combine pulp fiction with fantasy in ways few other artists have done as well.

Bride is easily recognizable as a horror–science-fiction hybrid, one of the most prolific and popular film genres of the 1950s. This genre, which used as its basic narrative template stories of a fantastic, pulp fiction nature, was also cleverly utilized by many producers and studios as a mouthpiece for Cold War propaganda, wherein evil, decadent Old Europe (Communist Russians, Nazis, etc.) threatened righteous, disciplined New America, primarily with evil scientific monstrosities, all of which nicely symbolized the collective savage libido of the foreign villain, unleashed and out of control. Yet *Bride* also shares some notable plot elements with another most interesting genre of the immediate post–World War II era, the Cold War thriller, a genre which featured spies, soldiers of fortune and evil scientists as the villains in what were, at root, propaganda pieces designed to make foreign nations, especially those with Communist or Socialist leanings, into an amorphous, villainous "Other," a faceless, all-purpose enemy easily identified and demonized by the U.S. audience, in fictional contests which often ended in nuclear-fueled world annihilation.[2] With allusions both to the Nazis and Communist Russia and to the horrible killing potential of atomic warfare, the recurring message in these films, as in much postwar U.S. media, posited that it is fortunate that "we" got the A-bomb before "they" did, or the world would have been destroyed long ago. (Some later, more ironic thrillers of the genre claimed that whomever owned the A-bomb, good or evil, would eventually use it, against all better judgment.) *Bride* shares, in part, this paranoia for a supposed battle between the U.S. and Russia for atomic supremacy, a battle which was subsequently revealed to be largely inflated, if not wholly fabricated.

Although not political in content nor overtly revolutionary in essence, *Bride* does contain key elements which recall aspects of the philosophy of "epic" theatre formulated by German playwright Bertolt Brecht (1898–1956). While it would be disingenuous to suggest that Wood consciously applied these somewhat radical techniques to his screenplay for *Bride*, it is exciting that, perhaps intuitively, he did manage to convey a certain sense of radical theatre in *Bride* and subsequent films. As will be seen, *Bride* uses certain "shock" or "alienation" techniques which destabilize the film's attempt to remain a straightforward melodrama, and certainly carry the spirit, if not the letter, of the basic philosophy of Brecht.

The credits for *Bride* roll over a scene of an "old, dark house" at night, during a raging thunderstorm. The scene clearly evokes the mystery and horror thrillers of yore, most specifically B-level horror movies of the 1940s, a genre which the star of *Bride*, Bela Lugosi, frequently occupied. The trees in the foreground sway realistically in the wind, yet some lightning flashes reveal a static scene with house and other foliage standing stock still, and the viewer notes with curiosity that the scene is difficult to read as either real or fake. Various observers have claimed that the setting appears to be a matte painting, a rear-screen projection, a miniature set, or even a half-scale stage set, yet in the Rudolph Grey book, Scott Zimmerman claims that Wood himself told him that the house was a real house in L.A.: "A canvas tarp was rigged up behind it to serve as a gray sky, because I didn't want the other houses in the background to show."[3] While this claim is certainly feasible, it is hard to believe that Wood and company had the resources and inclination to mount what must have been 30-foot high canvas tarpaulins around a two-story house in a crowded neighborhood. Oddly, whether the house is a painting, a model or a cropped slice of real life, the effect is the same, as its sterile and static quality creates a notably "fake" ambience, a Brechtean touch which foreshadows the overt theatricality of *Bride*.

The credits sequence ends with a stock thunder-and-lighting shot, an ubiquitous Wood touch which occurs with similar metaphoric intent in virtually all of Wood's directorial efforts, and will feature prominently in *Plan 9 from Outer Space*, in each case symbolizing the machinations of, or commentary by an angry supernatural universe. In a bleak, dark woods teeming with rain, two men wearing raincoats and carrying rifles are getting drenched. One yells, "This is the worst storm yet!" The other responds, "Yeah, it's been doin' it every night for the last three months," a disturbing statement which suggests that something is very wrong with the local climate, with allusions to the Great Flood of the Old Testament, in which neverending rain sent by an angry God washed away all sinners. This notion of something foreboding about the rain is underscored by a final comment: "It sure ain't *natural!*" In fact, it may well be *super*natural. The two men are presumably hunters, as witness their firearms, so one might readily assume that they are being punished for their grievous sin of killing innocent animals, and may well represent sinful Man, whom "God" is trying to cleanse of evil.

A lightning bolt strikes an immense tree nearby, knocking it over. The hunters look at each other in dread; these woods have become a primordial forest of evil. Approaching a clearing, Hunter #1 suggests they might make it over to "the old Willows place," an idea that Hunter #2 finds preposterous: "Are you out of your mind?" The hunters exchange further expository dialogue, revealing that there is supposed to be a "monster" at the old Willows place, that local newspapers have often told this story, and that the place has likely been unoccupied for years. The hunters cautiously trek onward and, punctuated by another stock footage lightning bolt, they finally arrive at the house.

Standing before a front door, Hunter #1 states with surprise, "I thought you said this place was deserted." Hunter #2, equally as shocked, replies, "It was supposed to be; I don't get it!" It is unclear what the men are alarmed about, although a brief, earlier process shot did suggest that there might be lights on in the house. Hunter #1 knocks on the door, and soon the door opens. A glowering old man (Bela Lugosi) answers, growling, "What do you want?" Hunter #2, frightened by the creepy elder, wants to leave, but Hunter #1 holds his ground, asking if they may come in out of the rain. The old man bellows, "No, no, you can't stay!" The hunters plead with the old man, but he insists: "You are not welcome in my house! Go away! Now! Go! Go!" The old man quickly grabs Hunter #1's rifle, suggesting that the desperate man might have been preparing to force entry into the house at gunpoint, again underscoring their sinful nature. From out of the foreground, an immense, lumbering giant (Tor Johnson) waddles towards the two men, menacing arms outstretched. The old man yells, "Lobo! No! Just see that they go!" The giant stops his advance. Hunter #1 yells, "The monster!" and Hunter #2 replies, "So now you *believe* those newspaper stories?" as they run off in terror. The old man smiles with satisfaction at having the intruders scared off his property, and observes with amusement, "You hear that, Lobo? *You're* the monster!" Shouting out to the hunters, he adds, "Perhaps one day you will *meet* the monster!" In this bizarre hellworld, the hulking mute giant is *not* a monster; something much more horrible is granted that label. This scene at the door is one of Wood's first "big" shots, recorded in one long, theatrical take, with four characters exchanging a good deal of dialogue, accented by some rather complicated effects. It is one of the first of many great, that is, *large* scenes in the micro-budget cinema of Wood.

The old man returns inside and passes a foyer which appears in disarray, complete with a broken chair, a busted steamer trunk, a picture hanging askew on the wall, and a stairway that appears to lead nowhere. He advances into a dark, dingy living room and triggers a switch within the false mantle of a fireplace, which activates an automatically opening door, presumably to a secret lair (a loving reference to a familiar narrative cliché of the 1930s–1940s horror film, the trap door which hides entry to a secret lair). As it symbolized in both *Glen or Glenda?* and *Jail Bait*, the domestic hearth setting in *Bride* represents a setting of duplicity, conflict and secrets; in *Bride* it further serves as a portal to a world of evil, suggesting a hidden malevolence lurking beneath the complacent facade of domestic suburbia. Lobo enters the living room, and the old man stops him in his tracks with a wave of his hand; the lumbering giant obediently turns and retreats. The old man is apparently in complete control of his natural environment, possessing extraordinary powers including hypnosis, a skill which will become pivotal shortly. This scene effectively negates our introduction to the two characters on the front porch, wherein the old man was seen as the passive individual, and Lobo the aggressor; the binary has now shifted equivocally.

The old man enters his laboratory, and here is where *Bride* first rises above its nostalgic horror-film underpinnings and becomes something poetic and allegorical. The first thing one notices is the patently artificial walls of the lab, studio flats which are primitively painted to look like stonework, but are so literally illustrative they convey no realism at all, but make the entire set look not just fake, but *deliberately* and *consciously* fake, another nod by Wood to Brechtean theatre, in which audience engagement in the piece is largely predicated upon the notion that the scenario is *theatre*, and not a narrative analog to real life, or in other words, non-representational vs. representational theatre.[4] Other touches in the laboratory set which, due to meager resources primarily consist of familiar found objects, also accent the theatrical fakeness which makes the set memorable and unique, in essence *iconic*. These include the lab table on stage right, which consists of two well-worn wooden workbenches, casually placed one atop the other, and upon which rest a haphazard aggregation of perfunctory chemical lab equipment. The main piece of instrumentation, placed stage center, is a somewhat impressive console of unidentified machinery and equipment, with a neon light and a television screen and various knobs and controls, a passable facsimile of modern laboratory equipment, yet looking more like broadcast paraphernalia than scientific apparatus. At the front of the set is an operating table, draped in a white sheet, immediately recognizable as the ubiquitous scene of barbaric crimes of Outlaw Science in countless cinema thrillers. Two elements of this set-up draw attention to themselves: a piece of equipment which looks like it is used on patients on the operating table consists of what is clearly a boom microphone stand with rolling "dolly" legs, upon which some sort of photographic enlargement unit has been hung. Also, sitting on the table is a helmet, again presumably to be worn by the unwilling patient on the table, and this helmet is a photo-flood light shield, a common fixture in both professional and amateur photography, and easily recognizable as fake by many members of an audience. On stage left stands an entire kitchen ensemble, consisting of a sink, cabinets, and a large refrigerator. While a refrigerator may well have been an actual item in many a scientific laboratory, in which controlled temperatures were essential to certain compounds used in experimentation, its casual placement in this patchwork laboratory seems anachronistic and confusing. It makes the lab seem somehow entirely domestic, referential to a suburban home environment, and makes the events occurring there seem both more familiar, and yet ultimately more sinister. Another juxtaposition of the mundane and the sinister is contained with two props that hang, side by side, next to the refrigerator: an institutional wall clock and a pair of shackles. All in all, the laboratory set draws attention to itself, and would confuse any but the most casual observer, who wonders whether it is meant to be taken as literal or fanciful, dramatic or satirical, real or unreal.

As the old man slowly, deliberately walks across the phony set, again giving the audience a chance to ponder its singular artifice, he removes his dark dressing coat and puts on a white lab coat, changing before the audience's eyes from a grumpy, even misanthropic, yet ostensibly benign old man to an evil scientist of formidable, diabolical power, changing in fact from a realistic to a fantastic character. The scientist looks through a small rectangular

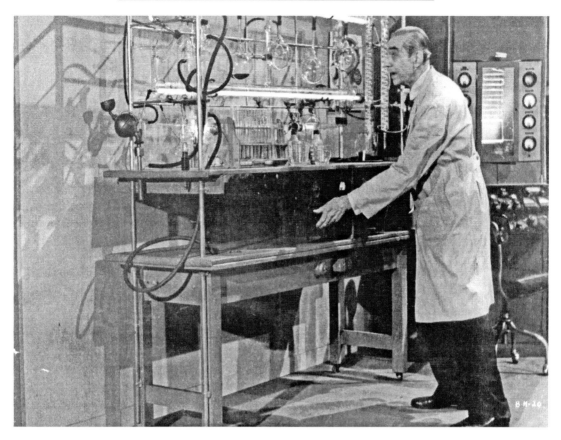

Thanks to a lurid screenplay and the talents of horror great Bela Lugosi, Wood managed to evoke the stark mythos of a 1940s Poverty Row horror film in his decidedly threadbare *Bride of the Monster*.

portal with satisfaction at the supposed inhabitant within, a patently fake rubber octopus prop which sits impossibly propped up against a black backdrop, defying the audience to take it seriously.[5]

Grinning maliciously, the scientist approaches his neon-lighted generating equipment and flicks a switch, presumably to activate the iconic sea creature. Returning to gaze into the light-infused window, the scientist looks on lovingly, almost hypnotized by his creation, and for a brief second his reflection appears, staring back at him in the window; it is the image of a sad, lonely old man, a chilling foreshadowing of what will be revealed anon about this tragic character. The scene inside the window now shows stock footage of a very large, and quite ugly, *real* octopus swimming around a marine aquarium tank. The Scientist reacts with shock at his creation's sudden animation, and more stock footage shows the octopus swimming off to parts unknown.[6]

Another stock footage lightning and thunder crash returns the scene to the rainy woods, where the two hunters are trying to beat a hasty retreat. One terrified hunter shouts, "What I wouldn't give to see a couple of cops right now!," setting up an introduction to the police officers who will make a significant impact on *Bride* shortly, as well as reinforcing the omniscience of law enforcement as a force of good, of *the law*, in Wood's films. As they pass by a flooded aqueduct, one of the hunters slips and falls in. More stock footage of the octopus finally suggests that these two discordant scenes are in fact supposed to be happening simultaneously, and as the fallen hunter screams, the audience realizes with a shudder that this benign stock footage octopus is "the monster" everyone is whispering about. Shots of the hunter flailing about in the aqueduct alternate with completely mismatched stock shots of the octopus, and the illusion of reality is brazenly shattered by Wood. A dramatic music cue and an abundance of screams from the hunter almost manage to merge the disparate units together, and then Wood surprises the viewer with a shot which, for all its phoniness, does dutifully merge the two sequences into one glorious, fantastically awful whole: The hunter writhes in the murky water, surrounded by the tentacles of the fake octopus prop introduced briefly earlier, and rolls back and forth, screaming, and trying vainly to make the inanimate tentacles look like they are gripping him. Granted, two of the tentacles appear to be moving under their own power, presumably via unseen wires, yet the illusion of strength, of menace, is utterly absent. In fact, the shot is so stunningly false that it conveys a creepy uber-realism of its own, and is one of *Bride*'s greatest illusions; in true Brechtean form, it completely undermines suspension of disbelief, and thrusts the audience into a much more confrontational world of fake melodrama and unbelievable theatrical illusion. Here, as elsewhere, Wood boldly *dares* his audience to believe. Hunter #2 recklessly shoots at the monster, presumably hitting his fellow in the process. Suddenly, Lobo appears out of nowhere and seizes the hunter. Lobo opens his mouth to scream, and a wheezy, dubbed-in lion's roar can be heard, lending the mute giant a comically savage patina.

After yet another thunder-and-lightning punctuation, the scene returns to the Willows place. Hunter #2 wakes up to find himself in the laboratory, shirtless and strapped to the operating table, with the ridiculous photo-flood shield attached to his head. The prop looks even more phony in close-up, as *Bride* becomes less literal, more unreal by the minute. (As well, the bare-chested man serves Wood's apparent need for homo-eroticism.) Lobo silently wheels the boom microphone stand over to the prisoner, who demands to be released. The scientist enters and informs his prisoner, "Lobo hears, but he cannot speak. He is mute!" Combining pathos and menace, Lobo is a much more effective character as a mute than he would be were he to speak. (As well, Tor Johnson's thick foreign accent would have instantly shattered any pretensions to brute savagery.) Being mute, Lobo comes across as a completely passive and powerless individual, a "slave" of sorts, easily manipulated by his demonic, outspoken "master." However, in line with the master/slave dialectic of Hegel, it will subsequently be revealed that Lobo is not purely passive, and his charismatic master is not infallibly aggressive, that in fact each character has a good deal of the other's power within them.[7]

Examining a wound on the hunter's body, the scientist slaps Lobo on the face and shouts, "Lobo! You are too rough with my patients!" brutally illustrating the savage power dynamics of the pair, set succinctly in traditional master/slave mode for the moment. Finally, the hunter asks who his captor is, and the scientist replies grandiosely, "Vornoff! Eric Vornoff! The name will mean little to you...." Vornoff returns to his equipment and turns on an atomic ray which shines onto the hunter's face. The laboratory really comes to life in this scene, with many flashing and pulsating lights and some impressive sound effects. When the hunter begs to know what diabolical process he is undergoing, Vornoff exclaims, "You will soon be as big as a *giant*! With the strength of twenty men! Or, like all the others: *dead*!" Lugosi hams it up mercilessly here, imparting all the lurid theatricality these precious pulp fiction lines deserve. Soon, the hunter dies on the operating table, and Vornoff checks his heart, brain *and* pulse with a stethoscope. A saddened Vornoff pats Lobo on the shoulder and walks forlornly over to the aquarium portal. Pointing again at the stock footage octopus, Vornoff ponders, "Isn't it strange, Lobo, how our friend always returns home after his long, tiresome swim," followed by a sad, poignant fade-out.

The next day, the *Daily Chronicle*'s headline blares, MONSTER STRIKES AGAIN!, while *The Daily Globe* shouts, MONSTER TAKES TWO! The scene moves to downtown police headquarters where, in a nicely staged dolly shot, the camera approaches a police officer who is questioning an arrogant, drunken tramp (Ben Frommer as another of those recurring peripheral characters, the angry, outspoken drunk, which may well mirror filmmaker Wood himself). The drunk refuses to cooperate, so he is dragged off to jail. The impressive set used in this scene cleverly incorporates two planes of action, the first being the office with desk and chairs and, thanks to a conveniently placed window with open Venetian blinds, the hallway directly behind it. Some fascinating action takes place in this second plane of action, beginning with the two cops hauling off the angry drunk and bumping into another character who is just entering the building.

A newsboy (William Benedict) enters with the morning paper and tries to enter another office, but the officer at the desk insists that all newspapers to the captain must go through him first. As this is occurring, another character enters the hallway behind the window. The newsboy, who identifies the police officer as Kelton (Paul Marco), finally acquiesces to the cop and throws the newspaper at him. Kelton gathers up his courage, rolls up the newspaper, and enters his boss' office, identified by a sign which reads, "HOMICIDE: Det. Tom Robbins." Inside, Robbins (Harvey B. Dunn) is playing with his pet parakeet, while Kelton pleads with him to let him work on the "Lake Marsh Monster" case. Robbins dismisses him with a curt, "Get back to your desk." A dejected Kelton turns to leave, and Robbins calls him back; Kelton enthusiastically returns, only to be told by Robbins that the newspaper boy should bring the papers in himself. A twice-rejected Kelton grumpily leaves. This, the first scene wherein one of Wood's recurring characters, "Kelton the Cop," is played for comedy, shows that Wood had a penchant for light comedy which was sadly interspersed with his (at least intentionally) serious screenplays. Due perhaps to the inept readings of the actors, or the rushed nature of low-budget film production, these comedy scenes rarely play out well, and often emerge as embarrassing misfires.

As Robbins awaits his subordinate, Detective Craig, the viewer gets a chance to peruse the lawman's office, which contains many significant icons, not the least of which is his pet parakeet, which the gruff lawman cherishes as a love object throughout most of his scenes. This notable prop, along with the lawman's unusual surname, recalls foremost the cultural notion of the pirate or buccaneer, who often carried a cherished parrot that acted both as companion and mouthpiece. This likely apocryphal partnership, which many attribute not to factual history but popular fiction, specifically Robert Louis Stevenson's novel, *Treasure Island*, has nonetheless become an icon which endures in popular culture to this day. To overlay this cultural myth over Robbins and his little pet may suggest that the bird represents not only a love object to a lonely man, but also a tempering and humanizing influence to one whose daily labors include the violent harnessing of evil incarnate. Robbins and his "robin," like Lobo and his master, are another couple who symbolize the notable binary which populates *Bride*, that of a "master" and "slave" who, sharing a close and undeniably interdependent relationship with an overt passive and aggressive power dynamic, nonetheless challenge this dynamic in true Hegelian form. While the parakeet is obviously dependent on Robbins for his immediate survival, the beloved pet clearly provides the aggrieved lawman with much-needed companionship and affection, and in this vital way, "masters" his master and equalizes the relationship.

On two shelves behind Robbins' desk are several trophies, a portable radio set, and several odd sculptures. One appears to be either an Indian shooting an arrow, or perhaps Diana of mythological fame, shooting her "golden arrow." Either way, in many shots the sculpture eerily replicates a Christian cross, as no Wood film seems to be complete without some overt or covert instance of this most familiar Judeo-Christian symbol of death and resurrection. Over Robbins' other shoulder is a figurine of a resting woman, a sculpture which immediately brings to mind Psyche, the goddess of purity in Greek mythology, who was saved from a terrible fate by a magical elixir.[8]

While waiting for Craig, Robbins reads the newspaper headlines again, and then offers his little pet a glass of fresh water, upon which it happily perches. Wood even takes the time to insert a brief close-up of the bird drinking, showing how important this character is to Robbins (perhaps even to reinforce the significance of water to the scenario, which does, after all, focus on an ill-used body of water, and evil men's exploitation of it). The importance of the bird to Robbins is underlined when Lieutenant Craig (Tony McCoy) arrives and Robbins states, "That's the one thing about birds: They never cause anybody any trouble." This endearing pet does represent something innocent, pure and free of sin to the world-weary policeman, qualities which would be rare indeed in the fallen world he inhabits.

Robbins reveals that Craig's girlfriend is a reporter, as he compliments her on the recent news stories. Craig fills in even more for the audience: "Twelve disappearances and nothing to go on," an interesting number as it suggests both the twelve apostles of Christ, and that the next victim of the unknown killer will be #13, a number of drastic metaphysical import. The implication in both cases is that the victims were, in some sense, sacrifices to evil. Robbins identifies the murdered hunter as Jake Long, and his companion, whose coat alone remains, as Blake McCreigh. Craig asks Robbins point blank if he believes in "these monster stories," and Robbins emphatically states, "The police don't believe in monsters. *Facts* are our business! Facts and only *facts*, and don't you forget it!" This recalls Dr. Gregor's similar emphatic statement in *Jail Bait*: "The proof is in the *fact*!" suggesting that truth is of great significance, even in the avowedly fantastic Wood film universe, as well as mimicking a common catchphrase of the day, due to the preponderance of crime shows on television, that good policemen were interested in "just the *facts*, ma'am."

After easily deflecting an ever-whining Kelton, Craig's fiancée Janet Lawton (Loretta King in a stunning performance) enters, yelling accusations, and the mood of *Bride* changes entirely. The heretofore dreary theatrics of the scenario shift radically at the entry of this first female, who breathes much-needed life into the stuffy patriarchal universe of good and evil males. Janet is immediately poised as one of Wood's archetypal, opinionated heroines, begun with Wood's alter ego, Glenda, and continued with the long-suffering, duty-bound Marilyn Gregor in *Jail Bait*. The brassy girl reporter, another ubiquitous pulp-fiction stereotype, stands in stark contrast to her mate, the lackluster Craig, whose deadpan emoting borders on the comatose. To Wood, the female is clearly the life of the party, as well as the real hope of potential societal change.

As a couple, Janet and Craig are yet another example of *Bride*'s recurring binary of passive and aggressive personalities. In their case, they represent a clever reworking of the traditional domestic couple of the day, which stated that the male was supposedly the "master" or aggressor of the heterosexual unit (i.e., breadwinner), while the female was the passive "slave" in said unit (i.e., "housewife"). This social tyranny is, in *Bride*, turned simplistically yet dramatically on its head. Janet could not be more clearly drawn as an autonomous, even aggressive character, while Craig's anemic passivity throughout is notable. The power dynamic of the 1950s heterosexual unit is thus subverted as astutely in *Bride* as in Wood's more radical treatise on the role of gender, *Glen or Glenda?*, and *Bride* proudly carries on Wood's agenda of challenging and revising outmoded, restrictive gender roles in modern society.

An agitated and frustrated Janet demands to know "the scoop" on the Lake Marsh Monster, and Robbins readily spars with his perceived mental equal, bellowing, "There's no such thing as monsters; this is the 20th century!" to which Janet replies, "Don't count on it!" After a pregnant pause, she adds, "The monsters, I mean," clarifying that there *is* such a temporal notion as "the 20th century." The hilarious misunderstanding in the comment suggests that the scenario in *Bride* is not to be seen as contemporary and literal, but timeless and allegorical, a demure wink from the author to the astute viewer.

The now-angered Janet threatens to break off her engagement with Craig, and Robbins calls her bluff by suggesting she make it "official" by returning her engagement ring. Janet backs down and returns to the subject at hand, revealing herself to be not quite yet completely emancipated from her repressive phallocentric environment. Were Janet able to easily break this entanglement to overbearing patriarchal culture, it is unlikely she could subsequently be manipulated into being the "Bride of the Atom." Janet and Robbins spar back and forth, while Craig sits, limp and impotent and worthless, watching his mental superiors battling. Janet crows, "That makes 12 in three months! Everything points to an inhuman violence! Or are you still sticking to the 'alligator devouring' routine?" Robbins sputters back: "Monsters! It's *fantastic*, you know that!" Janet picks up one hunter's coat and mocks, "What's this, a dancing costume?" She next picks up the other hunter's rifle, and smirks, "And this? A pogo stick?" By denigrating these cherished emblems of male-hood, Janet has not only shamed her immediate peers, but struck a blow against rationalist, short-sighted phallocentric society in general.

Janet calls the recalcitrant policemen's bluff once again, by stating that she is going out to Marsh Lake by herself to see what she can find. The men, expectedly, think it's a terrible idea, and thusly reveal not only their cowardice, but their secret belief in "monsters" and "inhuman violence." Craig ineffectually wheezes, "Over my dead body," and Janet, tellingly aroused by the thought of her boyfriend's demise, pulls suggestively on Craig's lapel and murmurs, "*That* can be arranged!" Janet leaves, and Robbins quips snidely, "You know what? I think she's just crazy enough to do what she says!" Craig agrees; only an *insane* woman would have the courage of her convictions, and defy male authority, in this patriarchal stronghold of female repression.

Janet drives off to her newspaper office, visiting the archives where old news clippings are stored, a library commonly called a "morgue" (another subtle nod to the post-mortem world, always on the mind of the death-obsessed Wood). Janet converses with the morgue's librarian, Tillie (Ann Wilner), and requests certain old news clippings related to the Willows place. Tillie points out the location of the requested articles and, pointing in the direction of the files, quips, "Take your time! I'm not going anywhere, and *neither are they*!" The comment seems somehow morbid, as if she is the caretaker at an actual morgue, and the "they" she is talking about are dead bodies. Upon leaving the morgue, Janet bumps into Marge, a co-worker (Wood protégé Dolores Fuller, reduced here to a thankless bit role), who says that these "monster stories" are causing quite a panic around town.[9]

The scene returns again to Robbins' office, where he interviews a strange-looking person called Professor Vladimir Strowski (George Becwar), a comic caricature of an Old European doctor, *a la* Sigmund Freud. Strowski wears a fancy vest, suit coat and bow tie, and sports a full beard. Most telling, his suit jacket holds a tiny rose perched in his jacket lapel, commonly known as a boutonnière, which he dramatically sniffs as he boasts proudly, "I am considered an authority on the subject of prehistoric monsters...." This is an marvelously absurd portrayal by Wood of arrogant Science, or pretentious, pseudo-intellectual European dandies entranced by their perceived self-importance. One even wonders if the man's name is an allusion to that of famed acting coach Lee Strasberg (1901–1982), whose philosophies on stage acting Wood thoroughly despised.[10]

Strowski informs Robbins that in his opinion, the Marsh Lake Monster and the Loch Ness Monster cases bear certain striking similarities, and that he might be of assistance to the police. It is agreed that Strowski and Craig will investigate the marsh together, but Strowski, for reasons unknown, seems unwilling to visit the place at night. Is he a coward, or does he hide a secret agenda? After the professor leaves, Craig shares with Robbins, "Strange sort of *bird*...," an interesting reference considering with whom he speaks.

Janet leaves her house and dons an angora beret, making her officially an iconic Wood heroine. Amidst creepy thunder rumblings, Janet drives off to Marsh Lake. The sinister weather both foreshadows her dire fate and recalls the earlier observations of the hunters that the weather has been unnaturally violent in the area for an extremely long time, again alluding to a brewing, biblical-sized apocalypse. As Janet drives down a dark, winding country road, the storm worsens, and her visibility drops so badly that she swerves off the road and crashes in a gully. As she exits her vehicle, the scene changes to that of a dark, primordial forest setting, with a twisted tree in the foreground. Janet has forgone the relative safety of the city only to become trapped in the savage environs of a veritable jungle hell. The disoriented, and possibly injured woman removes her beret and falls to the ground to rest. Unbeknownst to her, in the gnarly tree before her lies an immense snake ready to strike, and the scene becomes a post-modern incarnation of the biblical Garden of Eden, with Janet a beleaguered Eve about to be accosted by the Devil in serpent form, an inhabitant of the deadly Tree of Knowledge. The intensity of the thunderous storm worsens, further enhancing the biblical motif of the scene, and Janet finally looks up to see the hideous serpent staring at her from only inches away.

Janet screams and faints, and seems all but ready to be devoured by evil, when Lobo rushes in from off-screen, bashing the serpent (actually now a rubber prop) against the tree with extreme violence, then approaching the female. Lobo grabs the angora beret, fondles and smells it and, with a look of pure joy on his face, stuffs it in his pocket, probably for future erotic uses. Wood's overt fashion fetishism is lucidly outlined in this marvelous touch. Lobo then proceeds to carry off the woman.

Later, back at the Willows place, Janet groggily wakes up to hear a disembodied voice saying, "You are all right, now my dear!" It is Vornoff. Janet comes to as the camera dollies back, revealing her to be sitting on the leather couch in Vornoff's laboratory, with the doctor crouching next to her. Vornoff insists that what she needs is rest, and against Janet's protestations, he waves his hand slowly over the woman's face and commands, "Sleep! Sleep!" Vornoff hypnotizes the woman in an act common to the thrillers of the silent and early sound film era, but notably out of date in the mid–1950s, an era of emerging gender equalization. The act does, however, paint Vornoff as an evil, diabolical being, and the audience knows now that Janet may be in imminent peril from this sinister emblem of Old Europe. As Vornoff hypnotizes Janet, there are several close-ups of Vornoff's mesmerizing eyes, deliberate attempts by Wood to recapture the magic of similar close-ups of Lugosi's eyes in the magnificent voodoo thriller *White Zombie* (1932, d: Victor Halperin). Unfortunately, the staging and the lighting of these new scenes, along with the fact that the actor had aged over twenty years, make these close-ups, while evocative, far less effective than those in the Halperin masterpiece. The scene fades out as Janet loses consciousness, and Vornoff grins wanly, with the sinister implications of unwitting sexual violation clear.

The next day, Craig and his new partner, Marty (Don Nagel, essentially reprising a similar role in *Jail Bait*) drive out to Lake Marsh, unaware of Janet's fate. Stopping at the fork in the road, the cops share a cigarette and meditate on the creepy swamp. Accompanied by a beautiful, slow tracking shot of an actual swampland, Monty ruminates: "The wind, the rain, gives this place a gleam that just isn't *natural*. And the ground, alive with crawling things—crawling *death!*" Craig concurs: "This swamp is a *monument* to death! Snakes, alligators, quicksand, all bent on one thing—*destruction!*" This poetic scene gives Wood yet another opportunity to pontificate on his favorite subject, death, or rather, "Death." When contemplating why Wood was so obsessed with the shadow of the death instinct over modern society, recall what Freud, Marcuse and others had observed: "In a repressive culture, death itself becomes an instrument of repression." In Wood's art, "Death" is undeniably the *deus ex machina* of much, if not all, of doomed human activity.[11] Noting the unearthly thunder and fast-moving black clouds, Monty continues, "Something strange about all this rain." Craig adds, "Lightning's been going crazy too." Monty muses, "Maybe its like the papers say—all these atom bomb explosions, distorted the atmosphere," a most interesting statement which likely reflects some real fears of the mid–1950s, amidst the rampant, reckless above-ground nuclear testing being carried out by the U.S. military. The cops finish their discussion by revealing that Professor Strowski, suddenly and without warning, took off for Lake Marsh early this morning, by himself, a fact which makes the queer "professional" even more suspect. After discharging three important expository duties in this marvelously efficient scene, the two cops hop back in the car and drive on.

Further down the road, the two cops see Janet's car in the ditch. Finding the car empty and fearing for Janet's safety, they speed on to a "coffee joint about ten miles back." Else-

Over tea and toast, *Bride of the Monster*'s Bela Lugosi reveals his hypnotic power over Loretta King in this amusingly domestic scene, an ostensibly familiar setting which, as in much of the Wood film canon, turns the notion of polite, well-ordered suburbia on its head.

where in the swamp, Professor Strowski arrives in his rented Studebaker and begins prowling the swamps by his lonesome. Soon arriving at a rest stop-gas station called "Cafe & Cabins," Craig puts a call in to Robbins, who admonishes the detective for letting Strowski out of his sight. As Robbins reluctantly informs Craig that Janet is officially missing, the parakeet perches on Robbins shoulder, and the figurine of Psyche hovers closely above them, emphasizing the preeminence of the female principle in this key exchange. Psyche is perhaps positioned here as a guardian angel, summoned to protect these mortals from the impurities of the evil swamp. Craig and Marty finish a slug of coffee and move on, while Robbins calls Janet's newspaper to find out who saw the girl last.

The scene returns to the Willows place, where Janet awakes with a start, horrified at her surroundings. Vornoff enters the lab, followed by Lobo, who carries a tray with a teapot and cups. Janet is repulsed by the obese giant before her, so Vornoff cheerily states, "Don't be afraid of Lobo; he's as gentle as a kitten!"[12] (Actually, a cornered kitten can be surprisingly vicious.) Ordering Lobo to leave, Vornoff is incensed when the giant stares lustily at poor Janet. Fingering again the woman's angora beret, and breathing heavily, obviously in a state of erotic arousal, Lobo slowly edges towards the terrified girl. Vornoff picks up a nearby whip and begins whipping Lobo into submission. Janet stares on in sheer horror, witness to a barbaric scene most bestial, which paints her "host" as a vicious tyrant hiding just underneath a (barely) charming exterior. This scene, while underscoring the ostensive master/slave power dynamic between Vornoff and Lobo, also hints at the first signs of the slave's brewing rebellion. Returning to his assigned role of passive helpmate, Lobo timidly retreats, while Vornoff amusingly placates a horrified Janet with a dismissive, "That is all!"

Vornoff sits next to Janet and implores her to eat something, but the woman is still in shock. The cozy little tea set which sits before the couple, a comforting emblem of civilized Anglo-centric relations, stands in mocking contrast to the savagery just witnessed, again reinforcing a sense of domestic suburban life vainly attempting to repress its cruel underpinnings. When Janet demands to know what happened to her, Vornoff describes her automobile accident, and reintroduces himself. Slowly, Janet comes to realize that she is the prisoner of a madman, who has set up his lair at the old Willows place. From searching the real estate records, Janet knew that a Dr. Eric Vornoff had purchased the Willows place back in 1948, and Vornoff nods understandingly at this disclosure. Janet unwisely decides to lay her cards on the table, and confesses that she is a newspaper reporter covering the Lake Marsh Monster. At the mention of the word "monster," Vornoff laughs and places his hand gently on Janet's shoulder, calling her "Miss Lawton." She recoils, demanding to know how he knew her name. Vornoff admits, "I didn't, but since you were unconscious, I took the liberty of looking in your purse," another none-too-subtle reference to possible sexual invasion.

Janet demands to know more about her captor, and in answering, Vornoff reveals some fascinating background about Lobo: "Oh, he is entirely human! I discovered him in the wilderness of Tibet. He is quite useful to me, at times." Vornoff insists that Janet must still be exhausted, and once again against her wishes, and with the aid of more close-ups of the eyes, Vornoff asserts his will over the female and puts her into a hypnotic trance, transforming again from doddering old man to fearsome monster. Janet falls back on the couch, unable to defend herself against such diabolical, aggressive evil. Vornoff goes to the door and yells, "Lobo! Take the girl to my quarters!" Vornoff's sinister smile at this command reflects much more than satisfaction over his complete conquest of his adversary, but in the knowledge that he is also giving his Tibetan monstrosity the opportunity to finally have his way with the poor girl, a violation that will undoubtedly be depraved in nature.

Meanwhile, Strowski stealthily approaches the Willow house, in a shot which gives the viewer another good look at the house exterior. Oddly, even with the actor approaching the house, the scene looks counterfeit — the roadway and path to the house in the lower foreground look especially illustrative. And as in earlier scenes, the conspicuous flatness of the scene is notable. If a real house was used, as Wood claimed, why does it look so unreal? As one observer noted, "Why does it look as if it were some kind of artificial phantasm rather than an authentic structure?"[13] As the absolute genesis of the set remains elusive, it would appear that Wood has here performed a truly Brechtian magic trick for his bewildered audience.

Finding the front door unlocked, Strowski sneaks inside. In a fascinating set of dolly-driven shots, Strowski explores first the foyer, and then the living room, and the audience gets to see much more of these settings than previously. What is notable about both rooms is that they appear in complete disarray, as if they have not been lived in for decades. Most prominent are several busts of perhaps-famous figures, paintings both lopsided and askew, and broken furniture. This setting of stark abandon goes against the assertion made by Janet, and not denied by Vornoff, that he and Lobo have resided here for almost a decade. Nevertheless, these rooms give the impression of decadence, decay and death, and are a significant part of the dread atmosphere of *Bride*. They also suggest a very dark fate for postwar suburbia which, according to these symbols, is decimated by the barbarism of war, and doomed to decay and demise.

Lobo enters the foyer from the creaky stairwell that appeared to lead nowhere; the viewer now assumes it leads to the giant's living quarters. In the living room, Strowski snoops about, and appears to be all but ready to discover the trick mantel-piece, when Vornoff appears, shocking him by stating, "Professor Strowski! It has been a long time!" The two apparent colleagues timidly shake hands, and Strowski confesses he has been tracking Vornoff for years: "In Paris, I missed you by a month! In London, a week! At Loch Ness, by only one day!" Strowski admits he was sent by "his country" to seek Vornoff in order to learn more about his groundbreaking experiments in atomic energy.

The two gentlemen sit down and continue their discussion. Vornoff haughtily states, "So, my dear country now *believes* in my work!" Vornoff is either an ex–Nazi or a Russian Communist, or for the allegorical purposes of *Bride*, a fanciful melding of both. Strowski states that his government wants Vornoff to return, to complete his experiments for their glory. Vornoff confesses his true feelings towards his former country in a lovely Wood soliloquy: "Twenty years ago, I was banned from my own country, parted from my wife and son, never to see them again. Why? Because I suggested using the atom elements for producing superbeings! Beings of unthinkable strength and size! I was branded as a madman! A charlatan! Outlawed in the world of science, which had previously branded me as a genius! Now, in this forsaken jungle hell, I have proven that I am *all right!*" Strowski pleads with Vornoff to forget his country's "tragic error" in exiling the great scientist, and begs him to return "home" with him. Vornoff replies, with great poignancy, "Home? I have no home! Hunted! Despised! Living like an animal! The jungle is my home! But I will show the world that I can be its master! I will perfect my own race of people! A race of atomic supermen, which will conquer the world!"[14] (Lugosi here occupies much the same position as he did in *Glen or Glenda?*, a pseudo-god figure who wishes to lord over a race of puppet-people.) Strowski responds enthusiastically, "Yes! A truly great *master race*," revealing his National Socialist loyalties. He again begs Vornoff to come with him, but Vornoff insists he works only for himself now. Strowski asks the megalomaniac scientist if he has lost his mind, and Vornoff replies with more perfect Wood dialogue, which might as well apply to many avant-garde artists, the author included: "One is always considered *mad*, when one discovers something that others cannot *grasp!*"

Realizing he will not be able to convince Vornoff to return voluntarily, Strowski pulls out a revolver and reveals he was ordered to bring Vornoff back to their country, one way or another. Vornoff is more amused than concerned, however, as he knows his secret weapon, Lobo, waits in the wings. Lobo grabs Strowski as Vornoff takes his gun. The foreign agent is dragged through the laboratory and thrown into the pit with the monster octopus. As Vornoff and Lobo look on with unabashed delight, Strowski wrestles valiantly with the unmoving rubber prop, but he has to actually throw himself against it several times and scream unceasingly to even approximate the illusion of menace or attack. This is another of Wood's wonderfully fake, Brechtean scenes, highly unconvincing and thus purely iconic, its patent artificiality enhanced even by the black barrenness of the set, which looks somehow very stage-like, thus reinforcing the sense of watching *theatre*, not narrative.

As he watches his enemy perish, Vornoff states, "Your country offers fame and fortune for my return, but my price is much more great!" Returning to his atomic-generating equipment, Vornoff triggers the power switch, and back at the aquarium window, notes with satisfaction that the monster has come alive; Strowski still struggles with the rubber octopus, but now some of the tentacles are moving of their own accord, thanks to invisible wires being manipulated off-screen. Wood has brilliantly made this "fake" scene "come alive."

Soon, Craig and Marty arrive in the area and discover Strowski's rental automobile. Craig tells Marty to investigate the nearby area, while Craig proceeds alone to the Willows place. Craig puts on his trenchcoat and heads out on foot, promptly falling into some quicksand; he is soon accosted by (stock footage) alligators. Craig finds a felled tree branch and extricates himself.

Meanwhile, at the Willows place, Vornoff summons Janet into the laboratory with a mere wave of his hand. The door opens, and Janet enters, now inexplicably dressed as a beautiful bride in a flowing white gown. As the swelling main theme music plays, Lobo and Vornoff look in pure ecstasy at this vision of loveliness. Vornoff gushes, "Dear! You look *lovely!*" and escorts Janet, via mental telepathy, to the operating table; presumably she is about to become yet another sacrifice in Vornoff's mad scheme to create a race of "atomic super-beings." This is a wonderful, highly symbolic scene, preposterous on its surface, but rich in allegorical import. In addition to indulging Wood's fashion fetishism, this entrance of Janet as a slave-bride suggests the inevitably disastrous wedding of the principles of Eros, god of Love and Thanatos, god of Death. As well, it underscores the recurring notion in *Bride* that the apparently passive slave, vividly represented by the zombie-bride of the Evil Scientist, is not a mere captive of aggressive, demonic masters, but a dynamic and crucial part of a somewhat equalized power dynamic. This dynamic, shown most clearly in *Bride* by the sado-masochistic and entirely symbiotic partnership of Vornoff and Lobo, again bears allusion to Hegel's master/slave dialectic, in which true consciousness is attained when master and slave both realize they need the other, and so are power equals.[15] As well, Vornoff is doomed from the start with this ill-advised attempt at harnessing Janet as a "Bride" to Evil; he naively assumes her to be a "passive" figure in the heterosexual world, thus easily manipulated, while she is an aggressive figure, and will in fact clash with aggressor Vornoff and trigger his downfall.

Vornoff orders a reluctant Lobo to strap the young beauty to the operating table. Lobo, knowing her dire fate if Vornoff actually experiments on her, refuses, and Vornoff again savagely whips him into obedience, in plain view of the comatose "bride," with the savage genius, the dumb animal, and the sacrificial virgin tossed together in one amazing tableau. Craig soon arrives and enters without knocking as did Strowski. Craig finds Strowski's portfolio, inside of which are some 8x10 publicity stills of Lugosi, amusingly "non-representational" stock photos of the actor which serve as "representational" identifications of the character called

The poster artist for Wood's *Bride of the Monster* took great pains to suggest that Bela Lugosi would be reprising his famous vampire role, when in fact he played nothing of the sort. The copywriter's tagline "The Screen's Master of the Weird … in His Newest and Most Daring Shocker!" could certainly apply to either Wood or Lugosi.

Vornoff. Craig next stumbles onto the secret passageway to the laboratory and enters, gun in hand. Janet revives and finds herself surreally strapped to an operating table in a wedding gown, surrounded by human monsters. Vornoff assures her, "It hurts, just for a moment, but then you will emerge a woman of super-strength and beauty: the Bride of the Atom!" (The comment alludes not only to scientific torture but to a virgin's momentarily painful first encounter with vaginal intercourse.)

Vornoff's delusional plans for Janet, the desire to make her into a super-being both strong and beautiful, belies his own stated intentions of world conquest, for he obviously wants to create a woman who is *stronger* than he is, who will finally be able to *overpower* him emotionally and help him *end* his madness; at root, this wildly ill-advised experiment is a pathetic but understandable attempt to bring back the wife Vornoff had to abandon so long ago, when he was exiled from his homeland. What Vornoff fails to see is that by "energizing" his foe, he seals his doom, for as Marcuse notes, "The uncontrolled Eros is just as fatal as his deadly counterpart, the death instinct."[16]

Night has fallen. Robbins and Kelton arrive at the swamp in their squad car. They get an update from Marty and head out to the Willows Place. Robbins makes a point of telling Kelton, "This is your first time out — don't mess it up!" Kelton responds in the affirmative, exasperating Robbins. This tired comic set-up, awkwardly delivered, seems out of place in the preposterous, yet ostensibly grim scenario which is building up, again illustrating that Wood's attempts at overt comedy are not nearly as successful as his unintentional ones. Back in the lab, Craig is chained against the wall by shackles, and watches in horror as Vornoff strokes Janet, cooing, "I hope the straps are not too tight. Such lovely skin should not be marred." (This scene, in which a young woman in bridal gown is lashed to a table by leather straps, well serves a creepy sado-masochistic impulse.) Vornoff triggers his atomic reactor, and the process of radiating the subject begins as Craig struggles helplessly.

Lobo takes out Janet's beret again and fondles it like a treasured love object, and referencing Lenny and his rabbit in John Steinbeck's *Of Mice and Men*. Lobo is painfully torn between blind obedience to his savage master, and love (or at least lust) for this winsome innocent he has helped endanger. Janet's angora beret has triggered radical intellectual growth in Lobo, and he suddenly realizes that he can, and must, forgo his passive leanings and finally take action. As Marcuse might amusingly note, Janet's beret has slowly made Lobo aware of his thankless life of alienated labor, his erotic and creative energies subverted to the service of society's performance principle.[17] Lobo now sees that, as the unwitting and hopeless slave in a dysfunctional relationship, he is an integral part of that partnership, with powers unexpressed or ill-targeted, and must now manifest this repressed power to balance the lopsided scales of justice.

In a long, theatrical take with the raw beauty of poetry to it, Lobo turns against his master, roaring at him like a lion. Vornoff sees that his servant has turned traitor, and shoots at him repeatedly. During this struggle, Craig and Janet both struggle against their respective restraints. Vornoff keeps shooting, and Lobo keeps approaching, in a shot where *Bride* turns winningly into fantastic theatre. Through an awakening of consciousness triggered by the contrapuntal stirrings of savage lust and tender love, Lobo realizes that he has not merely been Vornoff's dumb mule, but a very real source of his power, a power which, now accessed, can be turned towards good, again a salient illustration of Hegel's master/slave dialectic in action.[18] Vitalized by this emancipating self-knowledge, Lobo easily fells his cruel former master, and gently unstraps Janet from her bondage, as the swelling theme music plays yet again. Craig fears the worst, but the gentle Lobo merely strokes Janet's hair and leaves her in peace. As Lobo approaches the comatose Vornoff, Janet retrieves Craig's gun and unshackles him; she has become an "atomic superwoman," as she and only she is able to restore her man's stolen masculinity. Lobo, accessing his instinct of jungle justice, drags Vornoff's body to the operating table, straps him in, and prepares to give him a taste of his own medicine. (It is encouraging that this lumbering mental defective knows how to operate such complicated machinery, showing that the "dumb" servants of evil masters may be learning more than they let on.) Suddenly stricken by conscience, Craig tries to get Lobo to stop this murder, and stupidly decides to toss away his gun and fight *mano a mano*, but the emaciated policeman is no match for the well-fed behemoth, who fells the wimpy cop easily, managing also to rip off his shirt, in another instance of Woodian homo-eroticism.

As Janet hovers over her fallen man, Lobo completes the ghastly procedure, and Vornoff awakens to find himself being doused with deadly atomic rays. Vornoff pleads for mercy, but receives none from his assembled victims. Lobo approaches his master, with an odd grimace which may express either satisfaction or remorse, and adjusts the dials on the equipment. The atom-energized Vornoff, played now not by Lugosi but a stand-in whose face is obscured, easily breaks his own restraints, and, smoking like an A-bomb, approaches Lobo. The two super-beasts battle it out, throwing lab equipment, fixtures and furniture at each other in a stagy grand action finale worthy of silent cinema. (The Vornoff stand-in, as well as Tor Johnson, gamely endure these physically challenging stunts, which include shattered glass and breaking furniture.) Finally, Vornoff knocks Lobo over the head with a beaker; the giant falls back onto the atomic generator, and soon the entire lab bursts into flames. Vornoff grabs Janet and drags her off, leaving Craig to die in the flames. The flames soon awaken Craig, however, and he rushes out of the building.

Simultaneously, Robbins and the other policemen arrive. Robbins orders Kelton to stand guard at the front door, while he and Marty go inside. In the living room, smoke billows out of the fireplace; as the fireplace in the Wood universe is never used for its literal purpose, Robbins knows that something is wrong, and he and Marty beat a hasty retreat. Outside the house, Kelton points out to Robbins and Marty a strange vision: a mad scientist carrying off a woman in a wedding dress. Following them is Craig, now completely topless, in another bit of gratuitous beefcake that is quickly becoming a Wood trademark. As Vornoff carries Janet further into the swamp, Craig runs up to his partners and whines pathetically that it is his beloved who is being carried off. Kelton nervously aims his pistol to shoot at Vornoff, but Craig tells him to stop, as he might hit Janet. Again, the comedy elements of Kelton's scenes are simultaneously rushed and belabored, and do not work, yet lend the scene a pathetic sort of immortality. As the cops run off, Craig borrows Marty's gun; he doesn't even bother to remove his tattered shirt which, wrapped around his arms as it is, would clearly make accuracy difficult. Here is Wood's homo-eroticism at its most blatant, as it completely undermines logical plot structure; it does, however, restate Craig's passivity, as he runs through the woods, his masculinity hilariously mocked by the shredded fabric, which flaps impotently in the breeze.

The angry heavens open up, as thunder and lightning punctuates the night sky. By now the viewer may assume that this unearthly cataclysm in the sky is a function of Vornoff's diabolical experiments with the Atom, closely connected to the runaway chain reaction now occurring in the laboratory. A momentous lightning bolt, another metaphorical comment from an angry god, hits the Willows house, which explodes. As Vornoff looks on in horror, the house, and all his hopes for world conquest, burst into irradiated flames. Vornoff runs off, leaving Janet behind. The cops soon converge on Janet. Robbins again asks Kelton to do something, and Kelton tiresomely mutters a pseudo-comical reply, but mutters it so badly it is inaudible, again ruining any potential for farcical comedy, and again turning the scene from mere failed comedy into wildly memorable "badfilm."

As Vornoff shares one last angry close-up of misanthropic malevolence with the world, the cops open fire, assailing him with a barrage of gunfire. Vornoff stands tall against this assault, however, and via Lugosi's stand-in, is able to make his way to an immense prop boulder. More belabored, foundering comedy ensues when Kelton follows Vornoff, and stumbles and falls next to the big rock, resulting in a reaction shot of Robbins, shaking his head in complete disgust. Back at the gully, Craig revives Janet. Finally removing his shirt in toto, he runs off to help his partners fell the monstrous East European beast. Craig comes to the aid of the stricken Kelton, who labors on the ground with a sprained ankle. Juxtaposed with these chase-and-battle scenes are somewhat incongruous close-ups of Lugosi as Vornoff, grimacing wildly, supposedly as he is being pelted with multiple bullets. The incongruency and sheer theatrically of Lugosi's queer expressions make the scene ever-more bizarre and ridiculous. It is as if Lugosi is reacting in convulsive dismay to the sheer absurdity of the scenario which is climaxing haphazardly all around him.

In an extraordinary climax, badly staged and awkwardly filmed, Vornoff approaches the prop rock. Craig launches said rock, which dutifully tumbles onto Vornoff, who falls into the viaduct where his pet octopus monster lies, and proceeds to struggle with it, as did Strowski.

Contrary again to Wood legend, it is Lugosi's stand-in, and not Lugosi, who struggles with the rubber octopus prop, actually grabbing the tentacles and wrapping them around himself to lend some iota of menace to the perfectly absurd scene.[19] As Janet and Craig cuddle, and Robbins watches in disbelief, the chain reaction at the laboratory reaches critical mass, and the entire compound explodes. As Craig lifts Janet up to her new future as an obedient wife to tyrannical maledom, they witness the most horrible specter of the post-war world, a nuclear explosion, via government stock footage of a hydrogen bomb blast at night.[20] As the continuity of the shots attempts to convey that it is the house that is exploding in this miles-wide atomic fireball, the audience likely knows by now that the conflagration is allegorical, that the "Bride of the Atom" is Man, and that Man is now doomed to a marriage with unstoppable technological Evil, a union made in Hell and which can only end in utter catastrophe. As predicted, when the life force Eros and the death instinct Thanatos are forcibly "wed," the resultant "honeymoon" is calamitous, a truth of which modern history can attest. Robbins joins the older, perhaps wiser lovers, and accents this notion with a profound Wood bon mot: "He tampered in God's domain," a parting word which clearly punctuates *Bride* as an anti-war, anti-nuclear protest from the great poet-philosopher Wood.

Bride stands as a most extraordinary achievement in the annals of low-budget independent filmmaking, not only in that a film so small and threadbare actually got made, but that the finished product works so well, and reflects so many profound and fascinating themes and ideas. As in *Glen or Glenda?* and *Jail Bait*, *Bride* clearly shows not only Wood's talent as scenarist, but as complete orchestrator of fantastic narrative melodramas with a unique signature and an indelible *mise-en-scène*. Most exciting is *Bride*'s thoughtful and vivid, if inconclusive discussion of passive and aggressive personalities in the postwar world, which at least hints at some of phenomenological work of Hegel, specifically his master/slave dialectic. In *Bride*, the traditional aggressive and passive parties, having seen their essential unity for better or worse, radically shift their roles and literally transform the world with this bountiful unleashed energy, symbolized most masterfully by the ravishing stock footage holocaust at film's end. Vornoff and Lobo, Janet and Craig (even Robbins and his parakeet to some degree) come to revelatory terms with their obsolete master/slave power dynamics and their emancipatory, if catastrophic antitheses, and through painful but mandatory adjustment of these dynamics, forge a wholly new, if frightening world of profane forces unleashed. Perhaps one of the reasons Kelton the Cop sticks out like a sore thumb in *Bride* is that he has no counterpart, no co-conspirator to give him balance and meaning. He is a true outsider in *Bride*'s scenario of coupled binaries; he may in fact combine *both* master and slave, combining aggression and passivity, Eros and Thanatos in one neurotic, ineffectual lump of annoying flesh. This may be why he fails as a force for good in *Bride*, and also fails as a comic object; he is a damned, lost soul who battles endlessly with himself, and can thus have little impact on his world.

The truly amazing tale of *Bride*'s filming, including numerous budget crises and mutinies by several of the cast members, including Bela Lugosi and George Becwar, is a fantastic pulp-fiction narrative in itself, well chronicled in Rudolph Grey's *Nightmare of Ecstasy*. It was none other than Samuel Z. Arkoff, soon to become vice-president of prolific B-movie factory American International Pictures, who helped to get *Bride* finished and released. According to various sources, Arkoff made enough money off *Bride*'s (none of which reached Wood, incidentally), to start his momentous movie factory AIP.[21] Wood's fate throughout his career was to make bad deals with shady people, another inevitable fact in the ruthless world of independent filmmaking. That films as gloriously plaintive as *Bride* even got made, and released, and preserved for future generations to marvel at, is in itself almost miraculous, and shows the strength of Wood as an artist whose extraordinary work, against all odds, managed to endure.

Bride of the Monster is the biggest canvas upon which Wood had worked thus far, coming dangerously close in aesthetic temper, if not in revolutionary intent, to the "epic" theatre envisioned by Bertolt Brecht, by the use of various shock and alienation techniques designed to jar the audience into overt awareness of *Bride* as an "epic" theatre of cinema. The reformist spirit of Ed Wood hovers unceasingly over *Bride*, in the angry drunk who flaunts the law, in the angora beret which inspires the passive beast towards rebellion, in the loyal parakeet which humanizes lonesome tyranny, in the cardboard dungeon which mocks the secrets of evil even as it harbors them, in the fiendishly radiant stock footage holocaust which ignites the very heavens, all of which denote a fantastic, non-representational world in which Wood apes narrative tradition only to shatter it beyond recognition. With *Bride*, Wood stretches genre melodrama to its breaking point, and in so doing sets the stage for his definitive break with traditional narrative, a leap which inaugurates his magnificent excursion into Absurdist cinema, *Plan 9 from Outer Space.*

5

Sex and the Subversive Screenplay

Although he was fortunate enough to be offered the rare opportunity to direct a handful of feature films in his lifetime, a bounty which future generations of film lovers still enjoy, Ed Wood was first and foremost a writer. On record as being an extraordinarily fast typist,[1] and perpetually fueled by alcohol (and possibly stimulant drugs), the prodigious Wood managed to create a dizzying literary output of over 40 screenplays,[2] 80 novels, and hundreds of short stories during his fevered lifetime.[3] A look at two of Wood's produced screenplays during his "golden age" will reveal how this prolific artist managed to insert certain unusual, even subversive elements into his yarns, which make the resultant films stand apart from their contemporaries. Although filmed by others, they bear the indelible stamp of Ed Wood. In each, Wood's pet themes of Sex (gender perplexity) and Death (sacrifice and resurrection) are brightly drawn, and in each, certain other Woodian quirks manage to remain intact even through the creative filtering of other hands.

The Violent Years (1956)

According to Rudolph Grey, *The Violent Years* was based on an original story by producer Roy Reid, under the pseudonym "B.L. Hart." Reid may have in fact produced little more than an outline or treatment for the production before handing over screenwriting chores to Wood, as no record of the published story has surfaced.[4] Wood is not credited on screen, so his exact contribution to the piece can only be intuited, although it is likely that the overt emphasis on errant parents as the architects of corrupted, wayward youth comes directly from the mind of Wood, who surely had an emphatic opinion on the subject. Much of the trite yet lyrical dialogue in the film sounds clearly like the voice of Wood, as do the many preachy and punitive speeches on the part of the judge and the lawman. Certain plot points might be assigned to the original short story, and director William Morgan, a veteran of television production, had much to say about the visual look of the piece. Yet considering the virtually obsessive fixation on the culpability of errant parents in the troubles of modern society, and the marvelously contradictory nature of the assuredly "masculine" female protagonist, it can be confidently stated that *The Violent Years* is, in spirit, an Ed Wood creation.

As will be seen, the protagonist of the film, Paula Parkins, is most assuredly a Woodian archetype, a gender-bending female whose entirely masculine persona, and undeniably schizophrenic personality mark her as a veritable poster girl for Wood's ongoing discussion of gender reassignment, so clearly outlined in *Glen or Glenda?* and carried on through *Jail Bait* and *Bride of the Monster*. Also, this anti-heroine's inevitable yet still tragic death, and symbolic resurrection via her newborn baby girl, illustrates Wood's chronic obsession with death and resurrection as formenters not only of tawdry narrative thrills, but revolutionary societal apotheosis. Finally, the almost comical fixation in *The Violent Years* on bad parenting as the sole cause of society's ills hilariously mirrors the simplistic thoughts of a bitter, self-pitying screenwriter apparently still stinging from the smart of his own morbid upbringing.

The credits for *The Violent Years* roll over an impressive painted cityscape, a generic metropolis which well represents "Anytown, USA" (although it probably depicts good old Hollywood, California). As the film opens, four teenage girls walk in sequence by a school chalkboard, upon which is written, in pretty cursive script, "Good Citizenship = Self-Restraint, Politeness, Loyalty," the very mantra of repressive 1950s society, especially to the obedient female of patriarchal culture. As jazzy theme music plays, the girls walk up to the blackboard, read its contents and laugh or gesture mockingly; the viewer is simultaneously introduced to them via on-screen graphics: Paula (Jean Moorhead), Phyllis (Gloria Farr), Geraldine (Joanne Cangi) and Georgia (Theresa Hancock), the four horse-girls of Wood's strange apocalypse. During this scene, a narrator (Timothy Farrell) solemnly, even mournfully intones, "This is a story of violence, a violence born of the uncontrolled passions of adolescent youth, and nurtured by this generation of parents, those who in their own smug little worlds of selfish interests and confused ideas of parental supervision refuse to believe today's glaring headlines. But it has happened. Only the people and places have been given other names." Already, Wood has cited the parents of the younger generation as the culprits in the upcoming scenario, and the viewer may rightly intuit a personal agenda on the screenwriter's part.

The scene changes to show a large portrait of the father of our country, George Washington, whose famous anecdotal motto, "I cannot tell a lie," underscores the quest for objective (perhaps unknowable) truth which haunts Wood's cinema. The camera dollies back to a door, upon which a sign reads, "Judge Raymond Clara." (Assuming that Wood created the character names for *The Violent Years*, the judge's feminine surname may be yet another clue of Wood's ongoing gender-bending agenda.) The sour-faced judge (Stanford Jolley, yet another veteran of the B-Western genre whom Wood coaxed out of semi-retirement to perform what would be one of his last roles) exits his chambers and enters the courtroom. Clara asks a man and a woman to approach the bench, and they stand before the judge so that the viewer can only see the backs of their heads; they are immediately archetypal, standing in as parents for all wayward youth. Clara sadly states, "Law is law, and it must be ministered to one, just as another." He then chastises the pair for being bad parents, as the two bow their heads in shame. He continues, "In all fairness to the society which you have so miserably failed," denying an unstated request to the two. This deliciously heavy-handed condemnation of the pair, whose crimes are still unknown to the viewer, offers an aggressive distaste on the part of Wood towards that citizen of society known as the parent, and the film soon reveals a reason for that hatred.

The camera dollies into the back of the woman's head, covered in a hat and veil almost like funeral garb, and in voiceover she says, "Where can I have failed? I remember I gave her everything she ever wanted...." Clearly, the postwar parent is guilty first and foremost of spoiling their children. The shot of the mother's head dissolves into the back of another head, a person with short blond hair, and sporting frilly loungewear. As the viewer cannot see the person's face, or most importantly *gender*, the first thing which might occur to the viewer is that he is seeing the back of Wood himself, dressed up as Shirley, his transvestite alter ego.

The superficial similarity of this unidentified figure to the "female" which Wood played in *Glen or Glenda?* is uncanny. This is a most interesting clue or bluff on the part of the filmmakers, as *The Violent Years* will subsequently be revealed not only to be Wood's astute if simplistic harangue on the corrupting and decadent state of postwar capitalism in America, as evidence in citizens' lousy upbringing of their kids, but most excitingly a personal diatribe by Wood against his own birth parents, whom he declared had abused him emotionally as a child. This fantastic, melodramatic treatise against bad parenting is in many ways an abstracted confession of Wood's own sorrowful childhood. With this insert, which cannot be attributed to Wood personally as he did not direct the film, Wood magically manages to insert himself into the scenario, and the astute viewer now knows that Wood inhabits *The Violent Years* in spirit.

The blond head finally turns and the viewer now sees that it is an attractive, if somewhat masculine, young woman, Paula Parkins (played well by Jean Moorhead), dressed in a sexy negligee, and sitting in a nicely furnished living room. The viewer may assume that Paula is Wood's surrogate in the film, and her subsequent behavior will reinforce this. Paula asks her mother (Barbara Weeks) if she has time to talk this evening. Mother mockingly dismisses her, stating that she has much charity work to do, and has no time for her own daughter. Mother condescendingly adds, "Besides, what can be so important in *your* young life to warrant my attention so drastically?," a line which hilariously sums up, in awkward Wood prose, that generation's complete lack of understanding of the significant emotional needs of youth. Paula begs Mother to reconsider, saying, "It's been a long time since we've had a heart-to-heart," but Mother insists it can wait, adding, "What is more important than our charities?"

As Paula helps Mother put on her fur coat, an adroit symbol of the barbaric heart of decadent capitalistic affluence, Mother confesses, "I'll tell you a secret — I think I like it down at the club so much because I get such nice flattery." Mother is here revealed to be, at heart, not a compassionate philanthropist, but merely a self-centered, superficial attention-seeker, arrested in emotional infancy. Mother tries to instill guilt on Paula by bringing up Father and his grueling hours at work: "That newspaper will be the death of him!" Mother seems to intuit that the mercenary and exploitative nature of the Fourth Estate will be instrumental in the tragic downfall of the Parkins family. As Mother fiddles with her purse, she off-handedly states, "Thank goodness you aren't one of those character types your father's paper is always talking about!" With this bizarre revelation, the viewer knows full well that Paula will assuredly be one of those "characters types."

Mother asks Paula coyly if she needs some "mad money," and against Paula's protestations, offers her a check, buying her love and nicely symbolizing one of the corruptions of capitalism, the blind worship of money as the magical talisman to solve all emotional and societal wounds. It may even be significant that Mother writes Paula a *blank* check, suggesting that no amount of money can fill a ruptured emotional void. Paula reveals that, as usual, she and Mother are going to swap cars, an interesting observation which suggests that their emotional roles have been switched: Mother is the irresponsible child, while Paula is, in many ways, the emotionally burdened adult.

As soon as Mother closes the door behind her, the mood of not only Paula but the film itself changes drastically. Ominous music fills the soundtrack as Paula's expression changes from polite resignation to creepy, sullen anger. Paula picks up the phone and calls one of her contacts, barking at her in language more fitting of a deranged hoodlum than a sweet teenage girl. This radical change in Paula's personality, which appears able to switch from innocence to degeneration in a breath, is not dissimilar to certain characters used in classical Greek drama and elsewhere, and even has a touch of the characterization found in the theater of Bertolt

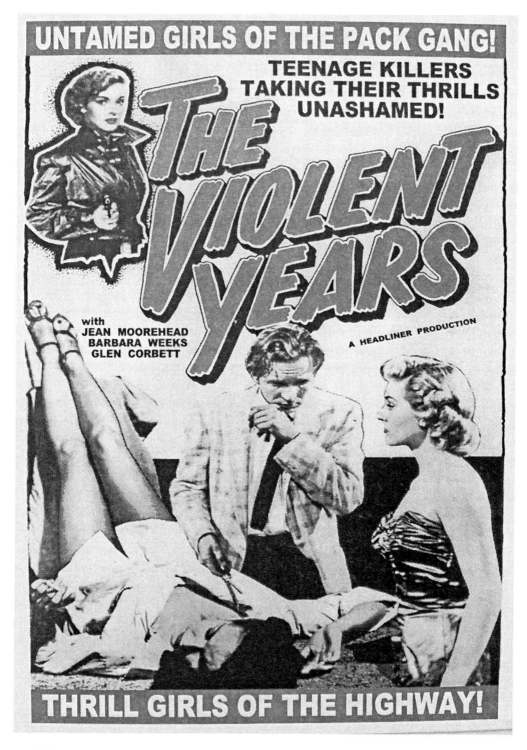

Lurid theatrical poster for *The Violent Years,* an early example of exploitation film's successful transformation to mainstream cinema. Wood's violent, subversive screenplay glorified an unusual new anti-hero: the female teenage sociopath. Like James Dean in *Rebel Without a Cause* (1955, d: Nicholas Ray), she was an antagonist both sexy and deadly.

Brecht, whose schizophrenic characters (Mother Courage, from *Mother Courage and Her Children*, for example) reveal not only deep-seated emotional imbalance in the individuals, but also represent contrapuntal political forces in the society in which they live. For Brecht, the split personality proclaims a battle between common sense and instinct, a battle which, in Paula's case, leads to an ever-ascending instability between the self-preserving principles scrawled on the schoolroom chalkboard, and the nihilistic qualities associated with the most self-destructive members of "throwaway" mass culture.[5]

Soon, a dark Cadillac drives through the dusky California night, arriving at a filling station. The male attendant is shocked to be met at gunpoint by the driver, who wears a kerchief and cap to disguise herself. The viewer can easily see that it is Paula, by her heavily made-up eyes. Three other girls, all dressed also with cap and kerchief, rob the station as Paula holds the attendant at bay. Finally, one girl knocks out the attendant with her pistol, and they drive off with their booty. The sheer absurdity of these spoiled teenage girls, hilariously dressed like urchins from a Dickens novel, robbing a big-city gas station, in plain view of the neighborhood, is a lovely absurdist touch which shows Wood's bizarre melodramatic bent.

As in much drama, notably in Brecht's theatre, this use of somewhat bizarre, comical or expressionist costumes or "masks" to drape the protagonists symbolizes the destruction of the legitimate self and the ascent of a specious imposter, of a character completely the opposite of the actual personality. As will transpire, this "fake" personality seeks to negate, thwart, and ideally destroy the person's primary personality, to completely envelop it in order to harbor and accomplish its own nefarious, and purely self-destructive goals. That the costuming used here suggests not only personality but gender transformation is another delicious touch of socio-cultural sabotage on Wood's part.[6]

Later, at a hospital, a doctor tells policemen Lt. Holmes (Timothy Farrell) and Detective Artman (F. Chan McClure) that the filling station attendant will likely not survive. The cop says, "These fool kids—when will they learn?" His companion amusingly blurts a none-too-subtle condemnation of the generation: "These aren't kids—they're *morons!*" The scene changes to the big-city newspaper office where Paula's editor-father works. Carl Parkins' (Arthur Millan) large office, boasting a large library of books, is reminiscent of Dr. Alton's office in *Glen or Glenda?* and Dr. Gregor's office in *Jail Bait*, ostensibly settings for truth and learning, and perhaps even justice. Carl and a reporter called Barney (Glen Corbett) share a cigarette while discussing their mutual fatigue and how difficult it is to run a newspaper. The topic soon comes around to the recent holdups, and Barney reveals to Carl that it's the same gang: four people wearing masks. Carl seems both fascinated and reluctant to discuss the affair, but resignedly moans, "It's news." He is beholden to obediently report every seedy and demoralizing event occurring in his fallen community, and the effect of chronicling and, in many ways, glorifying Evil in his society is obviously wearing on the morally upright man.

The film switches moods abruptly again, returning to the upbeat jazz theme which introduced the girls at film's start, and which recurrently stands for the untamed libidos of this thrill-crazy girl gang. The giant Cadillac goes roaring down country roads, finally pulling up next to a couple of teenagers smooching in a car, in a field next to a high tension tower. One girl forces the frightened teenage girl out of the car, as another compliments her on her nice furry sweater. The gang then demands that she take the sweater off, in a manifest acknowledgment of Wood's notorious fur fetishism. This Wood signature is further reinforced when the girl's name is revealed: Shirley. Shirley was Wood's transvestite alter ego, as well as one of his most frequently recurring character names, and most assuredly his primal muse. Wood has managed yet again to insert himself irrevocably into the scenario, and makes the film unequivocally his own.

Shirley's terrified boyfriend Johnny, noting the crazed look in the criminals' eyes, as well as their threatening guns, insists that Shirley do as they say. Meanwhile, Paula makes Johnny exit the car and frisks him. After finding only $11 on the poor youth (which well symbolizes how "worthless" capitalism is to its jaded members), one gang member suggests another way they might "utilize" Johnny. While one gang member agrees that the boy might be sexually serviceable "under conventional circumstances," the other quips, "Why wait for conventional circumstances?" The gang ties up Shirley with ripped shreds from her own skirt, in scenes which approach the borderline of good taste in terms of sado-masochistic bondage imagery, which was probably still somewhat taboo in mid–1950s cinema. Some shots, especially a provocative close-up of Shirley's legs being tied together with the rags, have an unusually fetishistic, almost pornographic spirit, and here is where *The Violent Years* descends into pure exploitation film.

The girl-gang drags poor Johnny behind the bushes to perform some nefarious deed on him, as Shirley struggles to free herself. Paula acts as lookout while the other girls forcibly strip the horrified youth. Paula, apparently the "queen bee" of the gang, gets first dibs on ravaging the captive male, and she approaches the camera while disrobing, with a look of pure lust in her eyes. Shirley finally breaks free and runs down the road in her bra and slip. As she runs, pitiful, girl-like screams fill the soundtrack. The viewer at first assumes that these screams come from Shirley, screaming for help as she runs down the road, but as Shirley turns and looks back at the direction of the screams, she and the audience simultaneously realize that it is poor Johnny who is screaming!

Apparently, Johnny is being gang-raped by the vicious girl-gang, and suddenly *The Violent Years* has taken a truly bizarre and somewhat sinister turn. Here, Wood's ongoing ruminations on shifting gender qualities, dealt with so sublimely in *Glen or Glenda?*, and touched on elsewhere, are mutated into something simultaneously hilarious and depraved. The female, the "weaker sex" in modern society, has here been turned into something powerful, dominant, and undeniably savage, while the supposedly "stronger" male is completely emasculated, exploited, in fact "violated," most importantly in the area of sexual conquest, exactly the area in which he had heretofore claimed complete dominance. Wood has cleverly, and catastrophically, shifted gender assignment, and its accordant power dynamics, by merely switching the traditional gender of rapist and victim, a simple yet devastatingly subversive act. Johnny's pathetic

A gang of "bad girls" (unidentified) overpower a teenage male in a pivotal moment from *The Violent Years*. Wood's subversive screenplay featured an elemental yet radical switching of traditional gender roles.

screams thus symbolize not only his personal terror at being attacked and compromised sexually, but his humiliation at the awareness that he, as a gender, has been completely emasculated and compromised by the aggregate female gender, and the revolutionary politics they represent. Johnny's screams symbolize the fall from power of patriarchy, at least in this fanciful scenario, a fall epitomized by complete sexual humiliation.

The next day, *The Daily Chronicle* headline reads YOUNG MAN CRIMINALLY ATTACKED. A sub-headline is even more revealing: "Man Attack in Lover's Lane." This amusing headline suggests not only that a man was attacked, but that the gender known collectively as "Man" was attacked, by an aggressive, ascendant female body politic. The postwar world is one of provocative and (to the male at least) frightening new power shifts, and Wood here suggests that patriarchy may well be doomed to extinction by the likely revolutionary shifts in gender assignment and their subsequent power transfer. At the Parkins home, as Paula's parents share breakfast, Mother reminds Father about their daughter's birthday party this coming evening. Father, unfortunately, cannot attend, as he has a newspaper to run. As he states ironically, "With these young hoodlums on rampage through the town, I'm kept pretty much on the go!" In a marvelous depiction on Wood's part of parental neglect and its societal repercussions, again as always stated in elemental, almost child-like form, this ignorant parent's incessant need to spend all his time "at the office," neurotically keeping track of all the evil in his community, is precisely the cause of evil in his community. In Wood's simplistic scenario, the elders' inability to harness and nurture the adolescent forces run amok in their own homes is a major cause of their community's predicaments, as the author takes another playful swipe at his own parents.

Mother, chagrined at Father's almost obsessive dedication to his work, sadly states, "Sometimes you sound more like a policeman than a newspaper man!" Father replies, ominously, "Sometimes there isn't much difference!" This noted synchronicity between law enforcement and the Fourth Estate, a recurring alliance seen in much contemporary film and literature, underlines the necessary focus on a community's outlaws and their actions by both occupations, as well as the sometimes morbid obsession with same which comes with the job. As in *Jail Bait*, here Wood briefly notes the visible brotherhood between the law and the lawbreaker, who in a certain way need each other for survival. In the case of Paula, the fact that her counterpart in this weird bond is her own biological father brings up certain Oedipal considerations which are largely bypassed in Wood's screenplay, but do supply some tension to the piece.

Mother adds that she can't attend Paula's party either; both are thus portrayed, rather comically, as absolutely terrible parents, guilty of abject neglect and willful abandonment, and responsible not only for their daughter's bitterness, split personality and criminal behavior, but the crumbling of their beloved "society." Mother reveals that Paula is having a pajama party this evening with some of her girl friends, and insists to Father: "No boys invited!" Ironic gender-centric *bon mot* notwithstanding, the audience immediately anticipates, and correctly so, that the ensuing un-chaperoned soiree will be a coed booze-and-sex orgy. Before Father leaves for work, Mother muses wistfully, "Paula is such an understanding child." She really means that Paula is understanding about their terminal neglect, whereas the objective truth of the statement is that Paula "understands," all too well, some very dark lessons about the adult world, and has furthermore learned how to act on this sobering wisdom. Father grabs his briefcase and exits from one door, as Paula emerges from another, nicely emphasizing the contrary worlds they occupy. Insists on making Paula breakfast, Mother absurdly coos, as if Paula were an infant, "You're a growing girl — you need your vitamins!" As Mother exits the dining room, a glowering Paula beats a hasty retreat, abandoning Mother just as Mother has abandoned her child.

Paula next calls on Father at his office. Father is delighted, but surprised to see her, and the viewer senses both discomfort and guilt on his part. After exchanging some banal niceties, Paula coyly starts grilling Father for information about the gang which is terrorizing the community. Father dismisses her curiosity with a condescending, "Don't you worry your pretty little head about it!" proving him to be completely oblivious to her daughter's real personality. Paula then reveals something amazing to both Father and audience: She is running for student body president at her school! The delicious irony of this sociopathic, likely schizophrenic thug leading a double life as a community do-gooder is perfectly drawn Woodian wit, absurd yet profound.

Paula cons Father into revealing sensitive information about the current crime wave by claiming that with this information, she can better run her political campaign, in spurious logic which could only emanate from the mind of Wood. The adoring patriarch falls for Paula's bluff, easily swayed by devotion and guilt, a naïve idiot to the end, and guilty of egregious parental sin in the eyes of Wood. Father then reveals that the police think the crimes are being committed by four young *males*, a revelation which Paula finds especially intriguing. Paula's flawlessly innocent behavior in this scene is quite disarming, obviously to Father, but to the audience as well; she is already a cunning sociopath of some import. Father, alternately, represents entrenched patriarchal culture, which automatically assumes that criminal gangs, as well as all significant power groupings, must by nature be male, because "girls don't do such things."

Later, Paula informs the gang that the heist at Clinton's gas station for that evening is cancelled because "the coppers" are onto them. They decide instead to visit their "fence," Sheila, to cash in last week's booty. Residing in a swanky hotel apartment, Sheila, dressed in a sexy silk dress, is a "tough broad" several years the teens' senior. Sheila immediately chastises the girls for their reckless behavior, and sullenly examines the stolen merchandise. As the gang share alcoholic beverages, they bicker with Sheila over various aspects of their relationship. The group finally strikes a bargain, and as Sheila leaves the living room to fetch the money, Paula boasts to the other girls that the money isn't important to her: "It's the principal of the thing." Here, Paula reveals herself to be, even at this tender age, a career sociopath; her goal is not amassing a fortune but consciously hurting the society which she feels has abandoned her. Paula adds proudly, "It's the thrill that gets me — the thrill of the chase." Paula, like all of society's washouts, indulge in evil for evil's sake.

When Sheila returns with the cash, she insults Paula, calling her a punk, which incenses the gang leader. Paula excuses the other members and has a "private" discussion with Sheila. Now alone, Sheila confesses to Paula that there are people who dislike school even more than the students, a bizarre thought which intrigues Paula. Sheila intones mysteriously, "It's worth a lot of money to a certain organization, if certain damages are reported. If you can wreck a few schoolrooms you could make yourself a pack of dough." Paula, skeptical, wonders out loud why anyone would pay to have a school wrecked. Still an innocent at heart, Paula hasn't yet entered the world of *big* evil. Sheila then offers the punchline: "And don't worry if a few *flags* get destroyed in the process...." The viewer, and presumably Paula, now know that Red Communists are the "certain organization" who pay disenfranchised American thugs to deface their country. The Communists want to destroy American infrastructure and shatter confidence in the democratic lifestyle — at least according to Cold War propaganda. Sheila reinforces this notion with her final word on the matter: "Let's just say it is part of a well-organized *foreign* plan." References to conspiratorial Communists and red-baiting was all the rage during this time period, especially rampant on television, so this reference, although somewhat obscure today, was common at the time, and Wood now has revealed *two* sources of evil influence on the "modern" teenager — bad parents and Red Communists!

That night, Paula and the gang have boys over to the house for their pajama party — which, as anticipated, is a drinking and smooching and wild music party, a Dionysian orgy celebrating, again in simplistic exploitative terms, the alleged decadence of the young generation. Paula apparently has been assigned a greasy gigolo named Manny (Bruno Metsa) by her good friend, Sheila. Manny molests Paula as Paula declares, somewhat unconvincingly, her independence. Soon, Father's star reporter, Barney, shows up at the house. Paula becomes visibly disturbed here, as she doesn't know which personality to play. Father's world has infected her world, which shows how foolish she is at heart to think she could keep the two worlds separate. Paula really is still a child at heart, as witness her flawed logic in making such an egregious mistake as having a sex party at her parents' house. A psychologist might even suggest that Paula *wants* to get caught in the act of being bad.

Paula reluctantly introduces Barney to her guests, all of whom look at the old guy with pure disgust. Barney reveals the reason for his surprise visit, and gives Paula a birthday gift from Father. Paula indifferently thanks Barney, who asks why she isn't even interested in opening it. Paula wearily replies that she already knows what it is—a fancy watch, the same gift Father gives her every year. Paula then whines about her sad fate as the spoiled daughter of doting but emotionally absent parents—every year a watch from Father, and a new sports car from Mother! As presumptuous as it may be for her parents to assume these fancy baubles compensate for their physical and emotional absence at her birthday parties, which merely symbolize active participation in the youth's emotional life overall, it would be hard to paint a convincing argument that Paula here is anything but a spoiled brat—surely, a new watch and a new car every year compensate for many missed birthday parties. The children of capitalism as painted here and represented by Paula, are nothing more than greedy, insatiable consumers, addicted to the products of society by their parents, trying to fill holes with stuff that no emotional void could possibly fill. At this point, perhaps unwittingly on Wood's part, sympathy for Paula is rapidly declining.

A teenage sociopath (Jean Moorhead) observes two males (unidentified) enacting the regressive confrontational posture as Wood's screenplay comes to life in *The Violent Years*.

A disgusted teen turns the music back on, and the smooching continues as Barney looks on, horrified — this new world of kissing, spoiled teens is evidently loathsome to him. Paula orders Manny to tell Barney to split. Manny threatens Barney, so Barney punches him, knocking him on the floor. Barney tells Paula she's in bad company, and Paula tells the old fool to mind his own business and get out. Manny comes to and prepares to go after Barney, but as the camera dollies in, Paula gets him to stay by cooing, "But the night's just beginning," with a lecherous look in her eyes.

Soon, the big black Cadillac is barreling through the night to the public school. The girl-gang easily breaks into the building and, entering a darkened schoolroom, start wrecking the joint. As one girl messes up the teacher's desk, swirling papers and writing instruments around and ripping up the desk blotter, she yells, "I hate you! If was this was your scrawny neck...!" Obviously, this girl is releasing some long pent-up rage with her hilariously impotent acts of vandalism. She then walks up to the blackboard, which bears a message similar to, but not the same as, one that started the film: "Good Citizenship: Restraint, Politeness, Self-Discipline." "Self-Restraint" has now become simply "Restraint," and most tellingly, "Self-Discipline," has somehow morphed into "Loyalty." The difference between the life-changing utility of self-discipline over the soul-crushing complacency of blind loyalty is so vast, the viewer may wonder if this drastic change has anything to do with the girls' absentee bosses, the Commies, who would likely place loyalty well above self-discipline as an asset to the State. As the girls continue to noisily wreak havoc, the ruckus alerts the night watchman (longtime Wood compatriot Bud Osborne in an uncredited cameo, reprising the "Mac" role he played in *Jail Bait*, and reinforcing Wood's influence on the film's production), who investigates.

In a marvelous scene, Paula runs up to a bookcase and throws all the books on the floor, obviously a nod to anti-intellectualism and the ascendancy of ignorance in postwar culture. Paula next picks up a world globe, the perfect representation of "tamed" and codified civilization, and instead of tossing on the floor, does a double take and throws it out of the window, loudly shattering glass as she does. This wonderfully nihilistic act starkly symbolizes the young sociopath's true agenda: complete world annihilation. Another girl slowly approaches the sacred American flag, with the obvious intense of desecrating it, but she backs off when police sirens are heard. In this surprisingly tense moment, the film tantalizingly approaches a true taboo, knowing exactly when to back off, aware that the movie audience of 1956 was not yet ready for the wholly revolutionary act of flag-molesting.

Several police cruisers converge on the scene. Like seasoned outlaws, Paula and her gang crouch by the windows and start shooting wildly at the policeman. This amazing scene, lifted verbatim from countless Western movie scenarios, is as exciting as it is ludicrous, and one can only imagine Wood, a lifelong lover of the Western genre, having a twinkle in his eye as he inserted this homage to a Wild West shoot-out into his ostensibly "modern" screenplay. Much to the girls' chagrin, the cops shoot back, and the gang become unnerved, apparently for the first time. Perhaps the adolescents thought the shoot-out was fantasy, like an old cowboy picture they saw on television, and not reality. Hard-as-nails Paula instructs the gang to barrage the coppers with bullets, so they can make a run for their car. As they pelt the lawmen with bullets, Geraldine laughs, "Look at them, running like rabbits!" A cop shoots back and hits Geraldine, who falls melodramatically to the floor while moaning, "It ain't ... supposed ... to be ... this way!" in a clichéd, over-dramatic death worthy of any B-western of the 1930s. As Geraldine expires, an enraged Paula shoots the cop who felled her sister, and Paula now crosses that line from spoiled brat to incurable sociopath.

As Paula and the gang head for the car, Phyllis is also shot dead, and Paula tellingly clutches at her abdomen in pain. The viewer first intuits that Paula was also shot, but the pain will be soon be revealed as being far more metaphorical in nature. Amazingly, Paula and Georgia are able to hop into the Cadillac and drive through the police barricades without a scratch. A lethargic nighttime chase ensues, a slow-motion scene reminiscent of similar scenes in *Jail Bait*, as Paula easily loses the sluggish law-enforcement personnel. Paula and Georgia hightail it to Sheila's apartment, telling her they are on the lam and demanding immediate payment for their act of political sabotage. When Paula sniffs, indifferently, "I killed a cop tonight!," Sheila picks up the phone to call for help; Paula shoots her in cold blood. Soon, Paula and Georgia are dressed in some of Sheila's finest trashy garb, becoming fully "grown-up" in the worst sense of the term, and prepare to make off with a large cache of cash to leave the country. Paula again grabs her abdomen theatrically, but insists it is just a cramp; the viewer, however, has by now intuited that Paula has been not only overtaken, but literally impregnated by Evil, via the slimy Manny, and her fate is now sealed. (Other observers have theorized that Paula was impregnated not by Manny, but by Johnny, the rape victim, an eventuality which would radically alter the consequence of the pregnancy and the subsequent child's character development.)

Paula and Georgia leave on foot and soon arrive at a used car lot to pick up a getaway car. They drive off in a spiffy white Thunderbird convertible via a nice montage in which their getaway is interspersed with scenes of the cops gathering clues. At a stoplight, Paula doubles over once again in pain, and Georgia suggests, "Maybe it's something you ate at the party." Paula tellingly replies, "Or something I *drank*," as in man's evil "seed." A cop car pulls up beside the girls and, recognizing them, tells them to pull over. Paula panics and speeds the car into the plate glass window of a nearby department store. Through crude animation, it is implied that both of the girls are seriously injured, if not killed, by a torrent of flying glass. Paula next wakes up in bed, fully bandaged, in what appears to be a prison hospital. It is revealed that Georgia was killed instantly, while Paula is in rough shape. Father Parkins shows up in time to hear the whole sordid story.

The story finally returns to the courtroom, as the viewer remembers that this entire melodrama has been a flashback. Judge Clara asks the jury for their verdict, and a sole man stands up to represent the collective jury (as well as the community at large), declaring its verdict: "Guilty!" The judge orders Paula to rise, and restates that she's been found guilty of murder in the first degree, as her parents look on pure horror, perhaps realizing for the first time the reality of the situation. Several days pass, and the scene returns again to the courtroom, where Judge Clara is about to pronounce sentence. First, however, the judge must harangue Paula at length, in an amazing bit of priceless Wood polemic:

> Paula Parkins, you have had all that money can give you, but it wasn't enough! You became a thrill-seeker, with an over-inflated ego! This thrill-seeking became the one great thing in your life, piling one thrill on another until, with ever-increasing intensity, you became much like the drug addict, with his continual increases of dosage, until the climax — a murder! To kill for the love of killing. To kill for a thrill! The thrill-seeker comes from all walks of life, the rich as well as the poor. They come from the home, the home where the parents are too busy in her own affairs to take time to teach their children the importance of self-restraint, self-discipline, politeness, courtesy, love for the mother and the father, the church and their country. It all adds up to that one great essential of living: self-respect, and regard for the property and feelings of others. Yet it's through this utter disregard for life itself that the thrill-seeker finds his eventual end. A prisoner of the state, standing in a courtroom, convicted of murder in the first degree. Because of your youth, Paula Parkins, its impossible for me to give you the sentence you so rightly deserve. You are hereby mandated to the proper institution until you become twenty-one years of age, at which time you will be transferred to the state penitentiary for women, where you will spend the rest of your natural life.

Sensationalistic aspects aside, this hilariously punitive speech definitely shifts blame from the spoiling parents squarely onto the jaded adolescent's shoulders, virtually canceling out Wood's principal thesis, that the cause of juvenile delinquency rests squarely upon the shoulders of recalcitrant breeders. The emphasis on the somewhat amusing term "thrill-seeker" underscores the corruption inherent in an affluence-oriented, consumer-based culture, i.e., capitalism. Citizens of such a society can all too easily become jaded because, as Clara pontificates, whatever society offers its lucky recipients, "it wasn't enough!" Even worse, capitalism creates self-centered monsters with "over-inflated egos," a quirk of materialism which any casual observer can even today attest to. The heart of Clara's speech, which proffers a solution even while diluting it with further rumination, is a quintessential Woodian line: "It all adds up to that one great essential of living: self-respect, and regard for the property and feelings of others." The "one great essential of living" is apparently at least *two* essentials of living, each at odds with the other. This pivotal line shows not only Wood's predilection for submitting sloppy, uncorrected first drafts, but reflects Wood's ambivalence over the reasons for society's ills; perhaps it is, after all, a fragile balance between enlightened self-interest *and* other-directed sacrifice which best sustains a community, which after all can only be as healthy as its individual citizens.

The scene returns to the Parkins home. Mother brings a tray of coffee to the living room, but Father, slumped in a chair, declares, "I couldn't take another drop." Mother insists, "It passes the time," adding, "It's all my fault. If only I had thought less of my outside interests than in my own daughter." Father verifies, "It's a hard lesson we've been taught. We're certainly a fine pair of parents!" Mother then coos, "We still have each other — that's some consolation." Even in their grief, the Parkins' sheer self-centeredness comes to the fore. They appear more worried about how they're going to get along now, rather than their daughter's horrific fate, self-absorbed and myopic to the bitter end. Mother even states, "It almost seems like such a bad dream!" Is she referring to her daughter's sad tale, or the fact that this couple even had a child? The Parkinses seem dangerously close here to mutually agreeing that they never had a daughter, to writing her off as "a bad dream," a shared existential delusion which would qualify as the apex of bad parenting. Mother states, in a whine of pure self-pity, "We've given her everything but real love — a dress, instead of a caress— a new car instead of a heart-to-heart talk." Father says, with all the emotion of a clam, "It does no good to look back — it can only bring more hurt. We must now look forward, using the past only as a pattern of judgment for the future." Mother adds, as if in a drugged stupor, "Paula's lesson to us was strong, but her child will profit from our mistakes." The cramps which debilitated Paula earlier have been revealed to be due to impregnation by either the corrupt Manny or the innocent Johnny; will this newborn thus carry on the seed of reckless sociopathy, or will it become a better citizen because of its tragic heritage?

The Parkinses soon visit Paula at the prison hospital. Paula's first words to them are, "I don't want my baby in a place like this!" Does she mean merely the shame of birthing her child in the ignominy of this institutional setting, or the larger esoteric crime of bringing a life into such an evil, sinister world, one Paula knows only too well? Soon, a nurse tells the parents to split. Mother impotently wheezes that "everything will be all right now," but even her half-hearted delivery of the edict suggest it will not. After the parents leave, the camera dollies up to Paula's face, as she utters a bitter "So what?" Paula is now resigned to the payoff for her nihilistic, wasted life.

Later, the Parkinses wait outside the surgery suite to await their dear daughter's fate. A doctor enters and informs them that the baby, a girl, was born healthy, but Paula has died. Paula now becomes one of Wood's great sympathetic characters, whose tragic death and subsequent resurrection (through the birth of her baby girl) leads to significant repercussions throughout her troubled community. As a sobbing Mother Parkins is hugged by a shocked Father Parkins, the scene dissolves back again to the first scene in the film, the back of Mother Parkins head as she stands in the courtroom, and the viewer realizes that the preceding section was a flashback *within* a flashback, one of Wood's most interesting and quirky narrative devices, in which exposition is offered in ever-accruing layers, an aesthetic conceit which leads to significant temporal and expositional disorientation. Considering the *two* "returns to the present" which close *The Violent Years*, Wood has led the viewer one layer *above* the reality which started the film. Begun with the miraculously circuitous *Glen or Glenda?* and achieving perhaps its finest showcase in the mesmerizing *Plan 9 from Outer Space*, Wood's chronic shifts in levels of narrative reality highlight the highly allegorical nature of Wood's cinema, and underscore the tendency towards non-representational theatre inherent in Wood's films, another interesting synchronicity between Wood's cinema of absurdity and Bertolt Brecht's "epic" theatre. The somewhat "shocking," or certainly disorienting, aspect of Wood's puzzling detours of expositional structure may enhance and baffle the viewer's understanding, but not enjoyment, of the piece.

Judge Clara now admonishes the Parkinses, whose pain the viewer is now fully aware of, with another hearty chunk of signature Wood polemic:

> Some people think newspapers exaggerate juvenile crime, or that is it is confined mostly to large cities. This is far from being the case. From coast to coast, in small communities as well as the largest cities, juvenile delinquency is on the rise. No child is inherently bad. He's made what he is by his upbringing, and his surroundings. It is thus apparent that something has gone wrong in the environment of a great many of these children or we wouldn't have this present delinquency problem. Adults create the world children live in, and in this process, parents play the key role. When children grow up among adults who refuse to recognize anything that is fine and good, or worthy of respect, it's no wonder that many of these children fail to develop high moral standards, or to distinguish right from wrong. Their attitude is summed up in two callous words: "So what?" Juvenile delinquency is always rooted in adult delinquency, and only through general acceptance of higher moral values can we hope to solve the problem. The easiest way to bring this about is through a return to religion. If all people would join this "Back to God" movement, and train their children to respect the Ten Commandments, or other moral laws laid down by all the great religions, we would soon bring delinquency under control. But the time has come that we must impose sterner penalties and restrictions against the young lawbreaker, to protect the law-abiding. His mere youth is no excuse for letting him remain at large. Some young criminals are just as vicious and dangerous as older criminals and lawbreakers. No young offender should be released in the custody of his parents unless an investigation shows the parents are capable of controlling his behavior. If they are not, his supervision should be entrusted to a more responsible agency. And in making parents financially liable for property damage caused by their children, could be especially helpful against the wave of vandalism which has been sweeping across our country. For this responsibility, we're sure that parents would keep a closer eye on the kind of fun their children are having. And if the old-fashioned wood-shed would receive more use, then vandalism would decline. Some parents refuse to recognize the moral obligation to the child they bring into the world. When that is the case, we must take stronger measures to make them realize their responsibilities.

This final speech of Clara's restates three prevalent themes of *The Violent Years*. Firstly, it emphatically restates, yet again, the crime of errant parents against their children, reinforcing the notion that Wood's screenplay was, in some respect, a nasty letter home to his own parents, admonishing them for their own ill treatment of him in youth. Lines like, "No child is inherently bad. He's made what he is by his upbringing...." and, "Adults create the world children live in, and in this process, parents play the key role," could not be more clear in their indictment of parents' actions in children's fates. Somewhat more unusual is the suggestion for society to "return to religion," although this is, in some way, in keeping with the overt Christian emphasis on death, resurrection and redemption in Wood's films. Wood's mention of a "Back to God" movement may have been apocryphal during the 1950s, a period which saw a mass exodus of church congregations, but his belief that Judeo-Christian mythology offers much moral guidance to one and all could not be more clearly stated. Finally, Wood amusingly suggests a reinstatement of parentally administered corporal punishment as a means to correct wayward youth, a strangely punitive act towards the youngsters he seemed to be primarily championing and defending throughout the film. One wonders if the "old-fashioned wood-shed" Wood speaks of was a memory of his own troubled youth (Wood's shed?).

Clara concludes this long-winded, hilariously judgmental speech by denying the Parkins their request for adoption of Paula's baby; they have lost their opportunity for a second chance at child-rearing and, according to Wood, rightly so. The parting shot shows the shadow of the window in Paula's prison cell shining against an opposite wall. The grilles of the window cast a shadow oddly like a grouping of crosses, in what appears to be the obligatory symbol of Christian sacrifice and redemption in a Wood-influenced film. Over this somber scene, the viewer hears the soulful cries of Paula's new baby as THE END appears on screen, and one cannot help but wonder what type of world the new child will be entering.

The Violent Years is an excellent example of how Wood could, even when not occupying the director's chair, manage to imbue a grade-B melodrama with his own unique voice, through a fantastic scenario which coupled lurid melodramatics with uncannily poetic dialogue and indelible, larger-than-life characters, resulting in a narrative which indelibly bore the author's signature. Here Wood achieves in his taut and elegant screenplay nothing less than a provocative, even subversive treatise on some pet themes of the day, gender questioning and the relative significance of nature vs. nurture in character formation amongst them. Wood's infantile, yet perhaps understandable obsession with bad parenting in *The Violent Years* is, in some aspect, a furthering of the discussion in *Glen or Glenda?*, in which the age-old "nature vs. nurture" question is brought up as the reasons for one's eventual adult personality. Wood seems determined to blame parents for childhood trauma; in both films, he blames the parental and cultural environment with the adult's tragic anti-societal neuroses. In *Glen or Glenda?*, the neuroses dictate relatively harmless sexual orientation and behavior, whereas in *The Violent Years*, the crimes against the child are immediately turned back against the parents, in crimes against society. And, as happens so often in the Wood universe, Death is the great equalizer, functioning as the *deus ex machina* of the protagonist's fate, a fate which, tragic though it may be, leads to the creation of new life, of new hope, and thus, of new myth for a culture which so badly needs this.

Paula is one of Wood's classic anti-heroes, the proverbial good person with a bad habit, a spoiled and corrupted innocent, like Don Gregor in *Jail Bait*. Both Paula and Don suffer most of all from the corrupting influence of a decadent society created before they were born. Paula may be seen as an incarnation of Wood's sexually charged alter egos, Shirley aka Glenda, a stand-in for the author and an expression of the darkest side of gender reassignment. Paula is, like Shirley, a magnificent Woodian manifestation of radical gender-shifting, who yields equally provocative results, and Jean Moorhead does an admirable job of portraying these two selves. Most excitingly, as a wholly masculine female who has pushed obsolete gender demarcation to the breaking point, Paula (note the masculine name) represents not only a surrogate for Wood-as-Shirley, but an agent of the female gender accruing power heretofore denied them, albeit in ill-advised, morally bankrupt ways.

To be sure, plucky females were *de rigueur* in 1950s cinema and television, yet Wood refused to blindly follow mere trends; his heroines are, to a "man," males in drag, even when played by a woman, with Paul/Paula being a fine example. Paula represents something much more than the spunky female stereotype of 1950s pop culture; she embodies an ersatz revolution, an unwitting trailblazer of the nascent woman's liberation movement, which had not yet located its best means of entry into phallocentric culture, and so in this instance was content with *destroying* phallocentric culture. Even this, one might say, was a step in the right direction, although Paula ends up being a sacrifice to this cause of female emancipation, then becoming the iconic Wood heroine, perhaps the Joan of Arc of the Ed Wood canon. Paula follows the template in so much Wood cinema, where the hero suffers a tragic if inevitable death, and is "risen up" by literal or symbolic resurrection, this time through offspring, to get a second chance to do right by their community, in Wood's fascinating interpretation of the Christian concept of redemption and atonement.

As for Paula's two-faced character, which may or may not represent an actual split personality, but does well symbolize its more socially significant aspects of the phenomenon, it follows closely certain elements which align it somewhat with the revolutionary theatre of Brecht. As a tragic character, Paula certainly stands for the opposing elements of aspiration and certitude, the insoluble chasm of fantasy envisaged vs. reality suffered, and the opposing split in the psyche and destabilization of the person's environment well illustrates the net effect of this deadly fissure in the person's mental make-up.[7] Also following the philosophy of Brecht, whose thesis declared that human beings were essentially good until corrupted by their surroundings, Paula is a sharp example of Wood's recurring "good person with a bad habit," and reinforces Brecht's notion that it is the cultural environment which perverts the inherited righteousness of humanity into its antonym.[8] As hinted at in the opening scenes, this character template could easily apply to Wood himself, in his characters of Glen and Glenda, who may be the perfect Brechtian archetypes, another incident which may strengthen the as-yet unexplored parallels between Wood and the giants of the Theatre of the Absurd.

The Bride and the Beast (1958)

The Bride and the Beast, based on an original screenplay by Ed Wood delightfully entitled "Queen of the Gorillas," is a wild and (literally) woolly romp through several bizarre B-movie landscapes, an unwieldy combination of steamy melodrama, simplistic jungle adventure, and preposterous horror film, triggered by a pseudo-scientific motif suggested by topical events of the day. As to the basic scenario, the film rewrites the "Beauty and the Beast" fable as a strangely erotic and modern "anti-romance." Wherein most modern horror films used the "Beauty and the Beast" motif to pit innocence against degradation, in *Bride and the Beast* Wood almost diabolically reverses the scenario and shows innocence voluntarily embraced and claimed by what man considers "bestial." In this film, which was perhaps influenced in a sense by Jean Cocteau's immortal 1946 adaptation of the tale, *La Belle et la bête*, innocence rightly ends up with her desired beastly mate, and the male kingdom can collectively "go to hell," having been replaced by their "savage" betters and rendered thus obsolete.

In *Bride and the Beast*, Wood reflects, rather effectively, on the ironic and disingenuous nature of the modern male, in many ways more "savage" than those he systematically fells in his delusional pretense to "protect" his kingdom. The ostensible hero of the piece, newlywed Dan Fuller, is revealed throughout the film to be nothing more than a dumb killing machine, obsessed with the capture, subjugation and expiration of anything/anyone whom he considers "the other," the animal kingdom first and foremost, but apparently womankind as well. Tongue not entirely in cheek, Wood positions the male hero as the "Beast" of the piece, far more murderous and savage than either ape nor bride could ever be, and in this way sagely prophecies much feminist writing on the subject of male dominance and violence towards women and animals, his pathological assault on the natural world.

As he denigrates the male, Wood simultaneously elevates the female to absolutely mythical proportions, giving the heroine all of the charm and strength and wit and insight that he denies the hero. Wood consistently attacks traditional, sexually oriented gender roles in his film work, and *Bride and the Beast* is no exception. As in *Glen or Glenda?*, wherein the male and female archetypes of modern culture are overlapped and mutated until one is unrecognizable as the opposite of the other, in *Bride and the Beast*, Wood switches the power dynamics of male and female so successfully that at the film's end, the viewer realizes that the female was the real power figure all along, while the male was a mere frightened child, albeit dangerous with his killing weapons. As in so much of Wood's work, gender roles in *Bride and the Beast* are critically explored, only to be radically revised.

On the more lurid side, Wood also mischievously plays with certain somewhat tawdry erotic elements. Firstly, the scenario addresses, somewhat provocatively for the time period, the concept of bestiality, the phenomenon of humans in sexual congress with non-human animals. By film's end, the subject is more than implied, and the sheer absurdity of the potential act, which would place a sexy young woman in furry sweater in carnal rapport with an unseen actor in a threadbare gorilla suit, only adds to the delicious absurdity and sheer theatricality of the piece. Perhaps the incongruity of the sexy female and the shabby costumed "other," in addition to never showing the act, but only implying it, makes the avowed taboo discussed somehow tame, and safe for late 1950s drive-in audiences. As seen previously in Wood's scenarios, this erotic absurdity again suggests elements of Bertolt Brecht's alienated, non-representational theatre, wherein wholly unbelievable scenarios evoke a distancing on the part of audiences, who then become aware that what they are watching is artifice, allegory, with the potential at least for political commentary.

Allied with this is the insistence of the female's wearing of animal-like clothing throughout the film. While the stated reason for this is that the heroine, having an intense symbiotic relationship with animals since childhood, would likely adopt certain elements of the animal kingdom into her immediate environment, the primary reason for the woman's parading around in some garish angora sweaters is mere projection on the part of author Wood, who fixated on angora and other materials for his own cross-dressing wardrobe, and inserted this fetish into virtually everything he ever wrote. Yet Laura's wearing of angora throughout *Bride and the Beast* is much more than a little inside-joke or signature on the part of Wood; although it serves this playful, essentially selfish purpose well, the symbolism of the sweater also tags Laura as a stand-in for the author himself. Wood, having accessed his "feminine" side so radically in his art early on, writes best for his female characters, who essentially mouth his own somewhat revolutionary feelings about the gender-centric universe. Thus, Laura is Wood's mouthpiece in *Bride and the Beast*, and as such, it makes sense that she even looks like the author, in a crude sense. When Laura describes her obsession with fur and fur-like material in one of her induced trances, again, Wood is speaking of himself, and not coincidentally, of the sensitive being's inherent connection to the animal kingdom, whence said material is cruelly seized. Wood, and perhaps others with the sensitivity to appreciate the uncanny sensation of animal fur against human skin, were aware on a deep intuitive level of their own animalistic nature, perhaps even their "bestial" prehistory in former incarnations. Having made this discovery, the sensitive person, such as Wood-as-Laura, would logically try to *connect* with the animal kingdom, likely becoming an animal lover and animal advocate in the process, as opposed to the typical phallocentric male, with *Bride and the Beast*'s Dan Fuller a fine example, who obsessively tries to *abolish* the animal kingdom. Seeing non-human animals as "the other," as a threat to their unearned and unwarranted dominance of their environment (political, cultural and sexual), these predatory men become, primarily, animal haters and animal killers. This is one reason why sensitive, intuitive persons such as Laura, although originally attracted to such men due to dumb biology or pre-scripted cultural roles, eventually find them vile and offensive, i.e., "the enemy," and do whatever it takes to leave them to their pathetic killing clubs.

The main credits to *Bride and the Beast* roll over footage of a violent thunderstorm; whether this was indicated in Wood's scenario or not, it invokes the spirit of Wood, as so many of his horror scenarios feature angry heavens tossing lightning and deluge down upon a sinful, fallen mankind. After the credits, the camera pans briskly from a wooded setting to a two-pronged road sign which strangely states "Route 42" in one direction, and "Dan Fuller" in another. Assuming that "Dan Fuller" indicates the film's main character, does this unusually "possessive" sign suggest that this person deserves his very own road sign? Further, does Dan Fuller warrant his very own road? This striking conceit on the part of the filmmakers, who may well have created this peculiar signage in blind obedience to Wood's screenplay, suggests something further — that "Dan Fuller" is more than a man, but represents patriarchy in toto, a thought which foreshadows much in the ensuing film. Soon, a snazzy convertible sports car drives up to the sign and stops. A man, who in fact is the legendary "Dan Fuller" (played with lackluster zest by Lance Fuller), and a woman, Laura (scintillatingly played by Charlotte Austin[9]), comment on the brewing storm. Laura states, "Thunder and lightning scare me," implying that she is still in touch with the elements of nature. Dan, oblivious to both Laura and her canny connection with nature, orders her to get out of the car and help him put up the convertible top. Laura innocently asks, "What's it really like in Africa?," their destination for an upcoming trip, but Dan ignores her curiosity as well, issuing instead further orders.

Laura exits the car, and the viewer notes that she wears a garish, striped fuzzy sweater, topped with what appears to be a dark fur collar. One might readily assume that the material in question is angora, Wood's favorite, and that if Wood did not select the garment personally, he had some voice in its selection. It is a truly ugly and ostentatious garment, and paints its demure wearer as somehow animalistic, as will be revealed anon. As the storm intensifies, Laura confesses, "You know, this is hardly the honeymoon I dreamed of!" Dan replies, apparently only half-jokingly, "Leave them out in the middle of nowhere, take their shoes away, and you'll have a wife who will do very nicely," a boldly sexist comment which makes Laura look down at the ground in shame, only to mutter, "So, you think you'll keep me?" It is revealed that this bold woman and sad man were recently married, and both of their comments illustrate poignantly their respective viewpoints, and to a large degree their ultimate incompatibility. Thus, Laura's deferential comment, "So, you think you'll keep me?," means less her insecurity that Dan will remain devoted to her, and more that, as callous patriarchal overlord, as witness his previous vile comment on brides, he might literally "keep" Laura, as a prisoner, as a caged animal of his idiot macho craving. This ominous note is quickly reinforced by Dan's cavalier reply: "That marriage license cost me six bucks! You know I can get six wives for that in Africa!" To this obstinate heel, life is cheap, and a woman's life is worth about one dollar.

The two "lovebirds" embrace passionately, and the woman vulnerably coos, "I love you," to which the cold-hearted Dan only mutters, "I think we better get home." Commenting on the beauty of the surroundings, Dan states that there are dangerous wild animals, like panthers, around, and the viewer wonders whether the setting is Southern California or South Africa — the scenario thus far appears to deliberately confuse the two. To this revelation, the confident Laura replies, "Oh, animals don't frighten me. I had a pet monkey when I was a little girl — he loved me but hated everybody else." This is the third clue revealed as to Laura's empathic connection with the natural world, which will ultimately embrace and rescue her from her captivity in vile male-dom. Dan then mentions Spanky, a gorilla he captured as a baby and has kept caged in his house until adulthood; apparently, Dan is either some sort of zoologist, hunter, or maybe just an animal-hating madman. Still, this comment prompts an unusual interest on the part of Laura, who seems suddenly contemplative. When Dan mentions that Spanky is going to the zoo next week, Laura bites her lip, pondering something, and is awoken out of her fantasizing only by a violent lightning crash, perhaps from an angry god who wants to interrupt her perverse thoughts.

Driving up to the gloomy household, Laura ponders, "Imagine, a mansion in the middle of nowhere," which reinforces the peculiar sense of not knowing whether we are in California, or even the U.S.A., or on the outskirts of some unnamed jungle; the earlier mention of the panther has confused the viewer, lending an archetypal nature to the setting, which may have been either intuitive, or merely sloppy on the filmmakers' part. As the newlyweds enter the house, the camera pans to a basement window, and as the storm bursts into torrential rain, the viewer sees Spanky, a caged gorilla (played by a man in a gorilla costume, an ubiquitous horror character in countless horror films and comedies of cinema since the early 1930s, and occupying much the similar role here, in one of its later incarnations).

Spanky seems terribly aroused by the entrance upstairs of this thrilling female with whom he apparently shares some primordial connection; even the torrential rain seems a symbol of something ominous occurring, as these two star-crossed souls first share the same living space. As Laura walks into Dan's study, which is peppered with revolting stuffed animals from his many hunting excursions, including a stuffed lion in the center of the room, she folds her arms and rubs the soft fur of her sweater, to gain warmth and/or solace. She states, "It's chilly in here," referring to the emotionless nature of her new husband, his cold-blooded nature as witness the carcasses of dead animals strewn about the place, more than the temperature. Dan quickly fixes some drinks in order to dull Laura's perceptions, and the two share an awkward embrace, which further enrages Spanky, who has seemingly claimed Laura as his own.

Laura is surprised, but not uninterested, to learn that Spanky is downstairs; this leads her to further contemplation on subjects soon revealed. She requests to see the gorilla, and as Dan can't think of a good reason not to, not yet seeing the beast as his rival, the two depart to visit the animal. Oddly, the door to the basement is a secret trap door, implying that Dan's activities are secretive and malicious, fully in keeping with his pastime as unrepentant animal-killer. The fully stocked gun rack next to the entrance reinforces the deadly agenda of this all-too-human beast.

When entered, the basement looks like a torture dungeon out of a period horror film, replete with gruesome stone walls and anachronistic torch, adding to the tacky nature of the scenario, but also to Dan's highly questionable personality; it may remind the viewer of a stripped-down version of Dr. Vornoff's sinister lab in *Bride of the Monster*. Dan is here further painted as a denizen of the old patriarchal order by the decidedly malevolent motif of his suburban "basement." In contrast, when Spanky and Laura first meet, it is "love at first sight." Both are rendered mute, as the music swells up tellingly. Laura grabs herself and rubs her sweater seductively, gushing, "He's beautiful!" Spanky and Laura stare meaningfully into each other's eyes — the woman and the animal have recognized each other as peers. As Laura slowly walks towards the suddenly tame beast, the torrents of water cascading by the basement window somehow reflect an aroused female sexuality.

Laura and Spanky continue to flirt with their eyes, and Laura finally moans, "Fascinating!" She starts to move closer, desperate to touch this magnificent male so unlike the heartless dud she married, but the heartless dud, perhaps beginning to see the threat which Spanky represents to his own happiness, which after all is predicated entirely on the subjugation of the natural world, grabs Laura and pulls her away. Spanky becomes enraged by this intervention, and starts to hoot and jump all over his cage, as Laura continues to stare, obsessed by this creature of prehistory. Soon, Laura ventures too close to Spanky, who grabs her wrist. As Dan watches in horror, Laura manages to talk Spanky out of hurting her, saying, "You don't *want* to hurt me." With that statement, Spanky begins to stroke Laura's hair with his other paw, a blatantly erotic gesture which disgusts Dan.

Laura, although concerned, does not panic, and in fact seems to enjoy it as Spanky moves his furry arm down from her hair to fondle her sweater, and the breasts underneath. After getting "a good feel," Spanky lets go of Laura upon her verbal command, demonstrating that she does have empathy with this beast, and thus rapport with the bestial. Only when the situation seems sufficiently diffused of immediate danger does cowardly Dan finally rush to Laura's rescue, chastising her after the fact for her recklessness. Dan has to then virtually force Laura upstairs, as she cannot take her eyes off the now-violent gorilla; even this dullard seems to understand that something is seriously amiss in his marriage, as his new bride seems to have a thing for his pet monkey. After the pair exit, Spanky goes berserk, trashing the fixtures inside his cage, as he now knows that happiness lies only on the outside, with a strange and beautiful fur-covered beast called "Laura."

Later, the storm still raging, Dan sits in front of a roaring fire, smoking, and trying to figure out what strange behavior has overtaken both his wife and his beastly prisoner; his heretofore successful conquest of all objects in the natural world seems to be hitting a snag. As he is dressed in a robe and pajamas, and smoking a cigarette, it may also be assumed that Dan is nervous about his upcoming honeymoon night, and how he will perform, in comparison to his new, "savage" competition. Soon, the beautiful Laura enters the room, dressed in a frilly nightgown, and approaches Dan, who beams with delight at his now-obedient bride. As Laura lets Dan pick her up, the viewer cannot help but notice that her smile is half-hearted, as if her thoughts are elsewhere. On cue and with a particularly loud thunder clap, Spanky again roars with rage from the basement, so loud that the couple upstairs hears it, prompting Laura to suggest, "Do you think Spanky is afraid of the storm?" Dan replies, tellingly, "He never was before!" No, it isn't the storm which enrages Spanky — it is the storm brewing in his heart over Laura. Dan carries Laura over the threshold, completing a ritual by which the patriarchal buffoon claims a woman as property, and the scene fades out as the couple seal their nuptials, with Spanky howling in impotent rage.

Later that night, Dan and Laura sleep in separate beds, perhaps a nod to movie censorship taboos of the day, but also a sign of the emotional distance of the couple, perhaps even suggestive of a sexual mishap on this, the most hallowed of nights for newlyweds. The endless storm rages on, as the aroused heavens continue to protest against a quickly approaching misadventure. As the camera slowly tracks into the fitfully sleeping Laura, a swirling graphic is superimposed over her face, and tense, string-based music triggers what at first appears to be a dream sequence. Yet as Laura tosses and turns, Spanky breaks out of his cage downstairs, bending the steel bars with an impressive acquisition of supernatural strength. Spanky exits the basement, easily finding the trigger for the trap door. Simultaneously, Laura awakens, and goes to the still-roaring fire to warm up. Elsewhere, Spanky walks through the house, and eventually arrives upstairs.

By now, the viewer realizes that this is not a dream sequence at all, but a strange twist of reality. Did Laura actually manifest this turn of events, by sending some sort of sexually charged mental energy downstairs to the gorilla, giving him the strength and focus needed to manage a strange midnight encounter? Such seems to be the case as Laura sits by the fire, smoking a cigarette, looking over her shoulder at the bedroom door repeatedly, as if she expects someone to enter. As Laura finally senses Spanky's presence outside the door, she deliberately faces away, so that he may approach her from the rear, a deferential position which suggests many things, sexual submissiveness amongst them. Spanky enters the room and soon reaches Laura, gently pawing her slinky negligee. Laura gasps, but it is a gasp of erotic thrill, not fear; she stands in complete submission as she lets Spanky fondle her aggressively. Unfortunately, as the odd couple appear to finally clinch their affections in a truly bestial embrace, sad-sack hubby Dan wakes up and, seeing a true nightmare of phallocentric betrayal before his eyes, leaps out of bed and grabs his trusty pistol. After shooting a warning shot into the air, Dan shoots his rival in cold blood. The wounded gorilla retreats and falls off a stair railing to his death.

This horrid behavior on Dan's part, which makes little sense from a rational perspective, paints him in part as the stereotypical batterer of women. As many social workers and feminist authors especially have observed and chronicled, the male who physically abuses women also often performs hurtful or deadly acts on non-human animals.[10] In this case,

Another steamy scene from *The Bride and the Beast* boasts a palpable sexual tension, as the predatory beast silently approaches his sexual prey from behind. The female (Charlotte Austin) is unaware of the imminent threat, although the coyly lifted heel suggests that she does, perhaps, anticipate that something dangerous and thrilling is about to occur.

A shockingly sensual production still from the Wood-scripted *The Bride and the Beast* features a clearly flirtatious female (Charlotte Austin) in the embrace of the bestial, who appears all but ready to ravage her. The gorilla hand pawing the woman's bare back exudes a scintillating, even perverse sexual tension, and the woman's taunting, bold stare could only add to the beast's, and the audience's, ascendant lust.

Spanky the gorilla, although acting strangely, was not a dire threat to either Dan or Laura, and certainly Dan could have corralled or tranquilized the animal as easily as slaughter him. The killing performed several important functions for Dan, however: As an act of terror against Laura, the shooting right before her demonstrated clearly his uncontested control over his environment, including women and animals, and has the likely effect of keeping her in submission to him.[11] The act also vividly illustrates Dan's maintenance of *sexual* domination over his "other" objects of desire, Laura foremost.[12] Further, there is some allusion in the previous scenario that Spanky might have actually been Laura's childhood pet, grown-up. Even the nostalgic name suggests a childhood friend, and Laura's uncanny symbiosis with the gorilla hints at a relationship previously forged. Whether Spanky was Laura's pet monkey as a little girl, he certainly came to represent that figure for the adult Laura. Thus, the shooting of the gorilla by Dan, in addition to being an act of violence towards the animal most assuredly, was also an act of psychological cruelty towards Laura's memory of a cherished childhood pet, in effect destroying that perceived relationship.[13] In addition to potentially instilling grief in Laura by crushing her naïve mate before her eyes, Dan has effectively reiterated how authoritative he is in the power dynamic of the relationship, and how dangerous he can be when threatened or crossed.

The scene dissolves to a later time, and Laura is sipping some tea, and wearing a fuzzy white bed-jacket, apparently unmoved by the tragedy which just occurred; perhaps she is in shock, or perhaps she is, after all, as cold-hearted as her deadly mate. Yet Laura ponders, "I still shudder at the strange sensation I had when the gorilla was trying to be tender." Dan agrees it was "strange, very strange," yet he does not know yet how strange. Dan notes that the storm has finally ended, an event which coincides with Spanky's death, and the removal of the fated lust connection between he and Laura, a bestial lust which angered the very heavens. Laura continues to ruminate on the ordeal, much to Dan's chagrin; Laura insists that Spanky wasn't trying to hurt her. Dan suggests that tomorrow they consult their good friend, a psychiatrist called Carl Reiner(!).

Laura then ruminates, "Have you ever had the feeling that you've been somewhere before, or that you've done something that you know you hadn't?" This introduces the second motif of *Bride and the Beast*, that of past live regressions, and Wood's most unusual take on the "Bridey Murphy" craze of the mid–1950s, which was inspired by a woman who was purportedly regressed via hypnosis to a past life incarnation, a life which she was able to articulate to various audiences.[14] Laura continues: "That's the way I felt with the gorilla — almost as if it had happened before, a long time ago." Here, Wood eschews the popular-but-boring notion of recent, *civilized* past lives, which was the general emphasis of the "Bridey Murphy" phenomenon and its many cultural references and imitators, and delves into the much more interesting notion of ancient, *prehistoric* past lives, before man walked the earth, and men's innocent souls were embodied in the beasts of the field. The two retire, as Laura quips, "Fine wedding night I've given you," to which Dan somberly intones, "We're going to be married *a long time*," an ominous statement which causes Laura some concern, for she knits her brow upon hearing it.

Laura falls asleep, wearing a fuzzy bed-jacket, and soon has another "episode" which may be a dream, a hallucination, or a tapping into deep psychic wells within the sensitive woman. In the fascinating vision, Laura sees images of the animal kingdom in all its horror and glory, conveyed effectively via a montage of stock footage shots of various animals, including rhinoceros, zebra, elephants, lions and snakes, all seen cavorting in their natural habitats. Several studio-set tracking shots in staged jungle environs add to the otherworldly ambience, and there are several shock moments, including a scene of a native spearing a zebra, and a brief shot of the gutted zebra carcass, skeleton exposed. Throughout, Laura's troubled, sleeping face is superimposed over the animal montage, clearly connecting the two in spirit. The montage sequence ends with a shot of a white gorilla looking into a pool, as Laura believes that she is looking at herself, from a past incarnation. This montage is annotated with a lovely Wood-penned speech, narrated by Laura largely in the form of a question, which again references the past lives fad of the time period:

> How many of us, searching our minds, our conscience, our hearts, would admit that in another life, perhaps even another *kind* of life, we have lived before? *I've* lived before — I *know* I have. I've know I've been here before, and I've seen them before. A long, long time ago — I can remember them! Why do I see strange things? Why do I see animals, animals, animals? There must be a reason, reason, reason! Why? Why do I remember these things? Now I know. Now I know. I am a part of all this. A part of this whole scheme of things....

This amazing bit of prose, in addition to alluding to the topical "Bridey Murphy" phenomenon as mentioned, also suggests that Laura, clearly a sensitive and psychically attuned soul, is clearly connected with the natural world via the animal kingdom, as would any human being who realizes and understands their mutual genesis and heritage. Laura understands this intuitively, as she states, "I am a *part* of all this." Because she is someone who feels allied with the animal kingdom, it would certainly follow that Laura finds these visions of a possible past life as an animal disturbing yet compelling. As intriguing as these accruing revelations may be, a most disturbing fact, which causes her such fright at the vision's end, is the notion that she, as an animal in the past, as well as an "animal" to her current patriarchal lord, may be captured, tortured, subjugated, and even killed under this heinous phallocentric empire she has fallen into. In short, if Laura is an animal, and her husband hunts and kills animals, she is doomed to be mere sport for this monster, and her marriage mere imprisonment. This, as much as the unnerving revelations that she may have been a prehistoric gorilla, are what likely cause Laura to awaken from the dream screaming. Laura has seen a clear, if coded, vision of her history and thus perhaps her destiny. And as many writers have noted, the world of the predominantly male hunter, and his "targets," women and animals, are not only at odds with each other, but diametrically opposed — in fact, mortal enemies.[15]

Dan rushes to Laura's side, insisting that her psychic experience was merely a "bad dream" (as it surely would be to him), and that her intuition should be disregarded. Laura shares with Dan a summary of her animal-centric "dream," and Dan affirms that everyone dreams of animals, and tellingly admits that he himself often has dreams of being chased by a lion, clearly a guilt-induced nightmare to someone who hunts and kills animals for sport. Although Laura declares she doesn't want to, Dan insists that she take a sedative. Dan realizes that Laura is exhibiting more intellectual curiosity and emotional freedom than he would like, and that it is important to drug her, the better to enslave her as the animal he insists that she is. Dan states that in the morning, he will fetch his psychiatrist friend, declaring, "*He'll* know what to do about this *dream* of yours." Clearly, Dan needs more male allies to squash Laura's emerging "dream," which may well be a dream of awakening, awareness, emancipation.

As the drugs begin to take effect, Laura coos, "I'm sorry to be so much trouble," for the moment the obedient pet of patriarchy. Dan callously responds, "After that Spanky affair, you are entitled to *one* bad dream." It is notable that Dan refers to the experience with Laura and the gorilla as an *affair*, underscoring his suspicion that the tryst was, in some ways, sexually infused. Laura queries Dan as to her previous experience: "Do you think we can come back, after death? Do you think that, perhaps, we've lived before? Maybe somewhere else as somebody else? Maybe even something else? That life really never stops for anyone, it just sort of goes on, and on, and on, one existence after another?" Wood here ponders some of the great questions of life, and some of the tenets of all world religions, in innocent, even adolescent, yet not unmoving terms.

Dan fully reveals his sheer idiocy by stating bluntly, "I never *thought* about it before!" It seems likely that all sentient beings, at some point in their life, have pondered what happens after death, and whether the life he currently lives is the only possible one. Clearly, a person so dull as to have never considered these universal existential issues is a myopic, psychologically crippled buffoon, and arguably the only type of blind soul who could hunt and kill other beings for sport. Laura seems thoroughly disgusted by Dan's response and curtly bids him a good night. The two again retire to their separate beds, now an overt sign of a doomed marriage's impending dissolution.

The next morning, a dark-skinned man wearing native costuming, complete with head turban and waist sash, wheels a breakfast cart into the Fullers' living room. This is Taro (Johnny Roth), the servant mentioned earlier but unseen until now. It is notable that Taro, representing a somewhat racist stereotype seen in jungle-centric melodramas since the earliest days of cinema, and fairly anachronistic in the late 1950s, appears only after Laura's intense vision of the night before, which did include scenes of jungle natives chasing animals. Taro's appearance does reinforce the escalating notion that Dan is nothing more than the stereotypical "Great White Hunter," replete with obedient native lackey, and that Laura will end up being prey in this increasingly ominous scenario.

Laura exits the bedroom as Taro looks up the stairs at her; their first moment of eye contact is punctuated with a bold orchestral cue, suggesting a significant, as yet unnamed, connection. Laura stands on the landing in front of the section of the stair railing which had broken last night, leading to Spanky's fall and demise; this removal of a safety barrier also hints at possible future sexual opportunity. Taro pours some coffee for Laura, and informs the woman that her husband has gone to town to fetch the "headshrinker," another assuredly jungle-centric aside. Furthering the sad racist stereotype of the role, Taro even refers to Dan as "Bwana." Taro offers at least two compliments to his boss' wife which could be construed as flirting, again underscoring a potentially sexual aspect of the relationship.

Soon, Dan arrives with Reiner in tow. In the first outside shot of Dan's "mansion," which looks almost like a castle, there hangs over the gate a sign which inexplicably reads, "Dan Fuller's Jungle." The viewer may be confused as to whether this is an in-joke on Fuller's part, or meant to be taken seriously. However, the sign does eerily reinforce what has been developing thus far in the power dynamics of the scenario; Dan Fuller has undeniably been acting like a lord and master over his domain, in which innocent animals (and women?) are seduced, captured, imprisoned and unceremoniously murdered. The place, a bonafide hellhole for animals, certainly qualifies as a "jungle." The sign also recalls the strange road sign seen at the film's beginning, which pointed to "Dan Fuller," apparently a road, and a world, unto itself. These consequential signs suggest the tendency of patriarchy for "branding," that is, identifying everything with one's own identifiable trademark. Thus, there is Dan Fuller's road, Dan Fuller's car, Dan Fuller's house, Dan Fuller's jungle, Dan Fuller's wife, Dan Fuller's gorilla, Dan Fuller's slave, etc. One would not be surprised to find an actual brand emblazoned on the butt of either wife or slave, so possessive and paranoid is patriarchy as to what "belongs" to it. (It may be an even further nod to this notion of branding that the main character, Dan Fuller, utilizes the actual surname of the lead actor playing him, Lance Fuller!)

The conceit also vividly illustrates the patriarchal agenda to own and possess all elements in his environment, whether earned or not; especially important in this imperialistic domination is the appropriation of non-male members of the world, i.e., women and animals, who, if not adopted voluntarily, may be taken by force. As Marti Kheel notes in her admirable essay "License to Kill: An Ecofeminist Critique of Hunters' Discourse," "historically, men have transcended the world of contingency through exploits and projects, that is, through attempts to *transform* the natural world."[16] This "transformation," too often describes forced assimilation, if not outright annihilation.

Dan and Dr. Reiner enter the foyer, while Laura sits alone in the living room, uncomfortably listening as the men discuss her without her participation. As the camera dollies intimately into Laura, she seems aware that a conspiracy against her may be brewing, but seems unable to do anything about it. She appears trapped, like any other of "Dan Fuller's Animals." Soon, Reiner exchanges pleasantries with Laura, and then abruptly orders Laura to sit down, an order which Laura obeys. All of the men in *Bride and the Beast* share the same aggressive habit of ordering animals and women around. As Reiner prepares Laura for hypnosis, he slowly shuts the curtains, ostensibly to darken the room but also to hide from prying eyes whatever transgressions may occur, and to remove a means for Laura to communicate with the outside world, should the need arise. Dan sits on a nearby couch, watching with voyeuristic interest as Reiner "takes over" his wife. Laura declares passionately, "I'll do anything if there's a chance to get rid of that dream." Rather than embracing her memory of a powerful prehistoric autonomy, it seems that Laura wants to squash it, to remove it from her troubled consciousness so that she can go about being the obedient lackey of a humorless prick. The viewer hopes that Laura may be only "playing dead" with these ruthless men in order to appease them for the time being.

As Reiner whispers for Laura to close her eyes, Laura smiles seductively and says, "Well, where do we go from here?" It comes across as flirtatious, almost seductive, as if she is fantasizing that she may be sexually overpowered by the two males. As if to challenge the meaning of her comment, Reiner declares, "That's what *you* are going to tell *me!*" Reiner places his thumb on Laura's forehead, and asks if she feels it. She replies yes, and when Reiner soon removes it and asks again, Laura again replies in the affirmative. It seems that Laura is, after all, still suggestible to phallocentric imprinting. Under Reiner's direction, Laura soon falls into a deep sleep. Reiner performs some parlor tricks for Dan's benefit, like asking Laura to reach for her coffee cup while her arm is stiffened. Dan cannot help but be aroused while his lovely wife is under his good friend's complete and utter control, apparently more than willing to "perform" for their entertainment. Drifting further into deep sleep, Laura is asked her name, and she tellingly says, "Laura Carson," her *maiden* name. Only when Reiner prompts her again does Laura reveal her current, *married* name, "Laura Carson. ... Fuller," stumbling over her husband's surname as if in distaste. Laura's inner self obviously has not resigned itself to this repressive bond so recently forged. The scene ends with a cutaway to a disturbed-looking Dan, who seems to see that Laura's unsullied subconscious is rebelling against this marriage.

The scene dissolves into a later moment in Laura's hypnotic adventure. Dan and Reiner are both standing near Laura now, a switching of position which recalls the previously noted notion of the men taking sexual advantage of the comatose woman. Laura describes, with great passion, her subconscious fetish with fur-like objects: "Angora! The sweater was such a beautiful thing! Soft, like kitten's fur! Felt so good on me, *as if it belonged there.*" Wood here cleverly introduces his pet fetish into the proceedings, but more importantly, clarifies a possible reason for this fetish—fur against a woman's (or man's) flesh reminds him, pleasantly, of his jungle prehistory, when as an animal he ran through hill and plain covered in the protective covering of fur. Wood may thus be suggesting that his all-consuming, publicly declared predilection for furry garments, so vividly illustrated in his passion for angora, is merely an attempt to mimic an ancient, buried memory of himself, and by extension, all modern men, as his ancestor, an ape or ape-like creature.

Laura concludes her bizarre revelation, which doesn't seem exactly connected to any particular past life, but more a rumination of the subconscious mind, by stating, "Felt so bad when it was gone..." which may mean that her collective memory of lives lived felt bad when this portion of her evolution had passed, when the animal eschewed fur for flesh, and began to stand upright, naked and ashamed in the light. The two men exchange a meaningful glance, and Reiner instructs Laura to go into a deeper sleep. Considering Laura's virtually erotic expression of fur-fetishism, the viewer may rightfully wonder whether this further violation of Laura's psyche is, in sum, for her edification, or the men's prurient amusement? As Laura idles in deep-sleep mode, Reiner takes Dan aside to clarify what he desires to do to her next. As the two share a cigarette near the now-open window, Reiner casually asks Dan where he got the magnificent stuffed tiger which sits in the living room, and Dan, just as casually, explains that he originally wanted to take it home alive, but a native taboo demanded that it be destroyed. Reiner replies enthusiastically, "Fascinating business!"

The unnerving quality of this callous affirmation of obliviousness to the sanctity of life, while the comatose, almost corpse-like woman sits nearby, illustrates the largely malevolent role of the hunter in modern culture. For many participants, hunting is seen not merely as a sport or recreation, but more importantly a mission, in effect a "business." Aside from the immediate financial gain hunters accrue by trapping and killing certain animals and selling their carcass, in whole or in part, to interested parties, many hunters feel that they are performing a vital service for the natural world, for the "biotic whole" as some writers have coined it, by killing certain predators so that other animal populations may flourish. The hunting lobby has been noted as playing a vital, if ironic, role in the early conservation movement in the United States. The conservation-oriented hunter's ethic maintains that the main purpose of modern hunting is to "manage animal populations for the benefit of the natural world." Truthfully, this statement and philosophy is entirely disingenuous, as the "management" cited is designed primarily to maintain sufficient number of certain species for hunters to hunt and kill.[17]

Reiner says, "Dan, I'd like to try *regression* on Laura!" as a close-up of Laura shows her to be visibly disturbed, as if she can plainly hear what the men are plotting against her, yet cannot act, a perfect metaphor of the entrapped female prisoner of patriarchal culture. Dan readily agrees to Reiner's bold experiment, suggesting a most casual approach to his new wife (i.e., "do whatever you want with her"). Soon, Reiner is directing Laura to return to any previous life she is able to access, and via an evocative close-up of Laura, her eyes brilliantly highlighted by spot lighting, she intones, with some distress, "It's dark, very dark, and so cold — I'm so cold!" Laura appears not to be describing merely a past environment, but the existential black void of the very cosmos, an eternal land of the spirit which existed before time (and an obligatory Woodian nod to his grand muse, Death). Reiner seems to sense that Laura is stuck in some sort of primordial limbo, for he hurriedly encourages her, "Go on through your journey — to the next light of day that you remember."

Reiner coaxes Laura ever onward, commanding, "You will tell me what you are now seeing — back, back to the endless reaches of time." As the close-up of Laura fades into complete blackness, the scene shows largely the same montage as seen in Laura's earlier fever dream, but now offset by using the film negative, setting the images in an eerie "reverse" mode, a nice cheap optical trick to convey a vision other than a normal waking state (and also cleverly hiding the rougher edges of the stock footage compilation). Over this engaging montage, Laura and Reiner exchange some meaningful dialogue:

> REINER: Where are you now?
>
> LAURA: I'm in a jungle. I see brush, trees, lions. I see animals!
>
> REINER: What kind of animals?
>
> LAURA: All kinds! There are many zebras by the water! Elephants moving! There is a snake crawling in the underbrush! Leopards moving in the jungle! Lions — so very many lions! The giraffes seem frightened! They're running away! Running from something!
>
> REINER: Why are they frightened?
>
> LAURA: All the animals are frightened now.
>
> REINER: Why are the animals frightened?
>
> LAURA: They're frightened of ... of ... of *me*!
>
> REINER: Why are they frightened of you?
>
> LAURA: I don't know, but all the animals run when I'm near!
>
> REINER: Are you hurting the animals?
>
> LAURA: I *have* hurt them, but I'm not hurting them now.
>
> REINER: What are you doing now?
>
> LAURA: I'm walking through a jungle. Trees and vines don't seem to bother me — I push right through them.

REINER: You are very strong?
LAURA: *Very* strong...

As a prehistoric beast, autonomous and feral in the jungle, this eternal female acknowledges thus her tremendous power, a power now thwarted in her contemporary servitude to domineering male-dom. She even acknowledges her power to harm, quickly adding that she has tried to use discretion with this power. This paints the prehistoric Laura as a fascinating metaphor of the unbridled, untrammeled female spirit, before it was harnessed and subjugated by male-dominated socio-political power structures.

Further annotations of the jungle montage follow; one interesting observation by Laura concerns again the importance of tactile experience to reinforce one's identity, as she makes another reference to fur: "Cool wind brushes my fur!" As she states this, the viewer sees a gorilla, obviously Laura's early incarnation but currently unbeknownst to her, rubbing itself with pleasure, an image which can only remind the viewer of author Wood and his beloved angora. The conversation does seem to be heading in exactly that direction, as Reiner coaxes her with a question: "What kind of fur is the wind brushing?" Oddly, the film cuts abruptly here (at least in the recently restored Retromedia DVD), and there is no answer to the question, but the viewer can easily fantasize Laura moaning, "Angora! Angora!," a line that may well have died on the cutting room floor. The montage ends in a most shocking (to her, anyway) revelation: "I see my reflection. I'm ... I'm a *gorilla!*" While the audience has certainly pondered this eventuality by now, it most assuredly causes the woman some concern. Laura finally comes to consciousness, screaming of pain at being shot by grinning savages, and yet exhibiting what looks like the signs of a sexual orgasm, complete with low, long moans, and frantically clutching at herself. This journey to a "better" self seems to have triggered many conflicting feelings within the woman, not the least of which is untamed lust.

Dan, upset or aroused also, orders Reiner to extract Laura from this disturbing limbo-state, but Reiner insists on bringing her out of it slowly. The viewer wonders if Reiner is being wise with his reluctance, or merely enjoying the spectacle of Laura's largely erotic fantasizing, as assuredly is the audience. Reiner does subsequently put Laura into a deep sleep, which settles her down quickly, like a sweet, post-coitus nap. Reiner soon instructs Laura to come back to consciousness with recall of what she discussed in her altered state. Reiner significantly instructs Laura to awaken as "Laura Carson Fuller," the obedient married slave, not the autonomous maiden, and coyly adds, "And you will want a cigarette!"

Reiner tells Dan that he is certain they have just witnessed Laura recounting a past life, and most amazingly a past *death*, while Dan still dismisses the whole thing, understandable as Laura's other selves directly contradict the subservient role he has in mind for her. Based on the traumatic experiences Laura has just undergone, Reiner recommends that Dan keep Laura out of the jungle for awhile, but obstinate Dan insists that they had made plans to honeymoon in the jungle, an entirely fateful choice of venue considering what has transpired, and he intends to keep his plans intact, regardless of how it might disturb his lovely young bride. Little does Dan guess that his selfish decision will ultimately backfire on him, and lead his wife into the freedom and emancipation she is seeking here. Perhaps that is what Reiner feared — that putting Laura back into her earlier setting of autonomy and power might give her ideas. Reiner brings Laura to consciousness, and the first thing she asks for is a cigarette. Dan and Reiner share a grin, acknowledging the cheap phallic trick they have perpetrated on the unwitting female, and illustrating how easy it may be to brainwash certain females into compliance with phallocentric dogma, symbolized by that not-so-harmless cigarette.

The tenor of the film changes radically at midsection, as the scenario deals very little with the major themes of the first and last sections, acting as pleasant but uninspired melo-drama. Much of this middle section is comprised of stock footage of various activities, most notably a tiger attack extracted from an earlier production, *Man-Eater of Kumaon* (1948).

Soon, Laura, Dan and Taro are making their way across the globe towards Africa, their honeymoon destination. Laura wears her garish angora sweater with the fur collar, an odd choice unless Laura has intuited that this trip will bring her back to her fur-clad "roots," and wants to be easily recognized by her "peers." Arriving in Africa, Dan and Laura visit Captain Cameron, a friend of Dan's who is head of the region's gaming commission. After exchanging some banal pleasantries, including sexist drivel regarding Laura's beauty, Cameron calls Dan "the greatest white hunter of the area," a comment which should send Laura packing. Cameron enthusiastically asks Dan, "What's it to be this time—capturing, or killing?" Dan coyly replies, "Oh, a little livestock. We'll go in for a little shooting, though." The whole time, Laura sits there, quiet as a mouse, in her little angora suit, looking like a giant decoy bunny rabbit, ready to be targeted for extinction by the great white hunter and his gang.

Soon, Laura and Dan are setting up camp in the jungle, aided by a small community of blacks, led by an older woman named Marka. Dan seems to have managed to successfully manifest a slave plantation business model in the modern world, no mean feat, even for a boor. That evening, as they sit around the campfire, a tarantula approaches Laura, and Dan bravely steps on it with his shoe, crushing the life out of it like one would squash a cigarette. Rather than painting Dan as the "great white hunter," it serves to show how petty and over-reactive Dan is, as flicking the spider safely back into the brush would have served the same purpose. Yet Laura pokes the squashed carcass of the dead spider with the tip of her own shoe, perhaps trying to connect with it, or even offer some sort of apology, and she states, "I'm afraid some of the jungle's romance is leaving me." She refers here not only to her recent near-death experience, but the sadness of this dangerous-but-diminutive threat having been unceremoniously crushed by the belligerent foot of male-dom, seeing it as metaphor for terrified phallocentric culture literally crushing anything it deems as "other." Marka offers the distraught Laura a hand-made shawl, and Laura comments on the material. It isn't angora, but it does evoke the sense of animalistic fervor which the jungle is unleashing in her.

At dawn the next morning, a cheetah approaches the camp, and this intrigues Laura. (This scene is composed of severely mismatched day-for-night scenes with daylight stock footage, and is quite disorienting.) Strangely, Laura suggests, "Why don't you shoot him?" and uber-capitalist Dan replies, "He's worth more to us alive." Laura, visibly aroused, says, "This is exciting!" Laura's personality is changing radically in this new setting—her empathy for animals is shifting into a more predatory stance, not unlike that of her husband. Triggered by the spider attack, it would appear that Laura is slowly evolving into the reluctant predator she was in prehistory.

Laura seems utterly fascinated as Dan chases down and lassoes a zebra, via rented truck; the more "predatory" instincts which Laura tapped into through hypnosis have thoroughly overtaken her, as her virtually bloodthirsty attitude towards animals at this point seem diametrically opposed to her empathic attitude towards animals in the first reels. Possibly these scenes, which as mentioned seem largely added as "padding" to extend the scenario's skimpy running time, were not written by Wood at all, or scribbled quickly by Wood without noting his screenplay's overriding motif of animal empathy. Still, Laura's notable shift in attitude during her "jungle phase" is significant in terms of her eventual revolutionary lifestyle choices at film's end, when she is literally embraced by the jungle and its citizens. Laura soon states, "The jungle really gets in your blood, doesn't it? Just one week here, and I feel ... I feel as though I've always *belonged* here." Dan acknowledges, "You seem to have a way with the birds, too," and Laura dutifully responds, "Well, *we speak the same language.*"

Soon, Dan and Laura, with the assist of stock-footage natives, are headed straight for "gorilla country," which Dan coyly and accurately describes as "beautiful, but dangerous." Unbeknownst to our travelers, several fearsome escaped Indian tigers prowl nearby. That evening, as they pitch camp, the group members hear the fearsome growls of the tigers, and know that they are lurking nearby. Dan and Taro grab their rifles and enter the night jungle. Marka tries to ease Laura's obvious discomfort by stating, "Bwana is the best hunter of all," but the remark does not appear to console Laura. Dan and Taro fail to kill the beautiful tiger, and return to camp pouting like children.

Amongst other jungle-centric events which comprise the movie's padded mid-section, poor Marka is attacked and killed by one of the tigers. Some time later, Dan sits alone in a tree at night, pondering this diabolical kingdom which completely ignores his edicts to conquer it, and waits for the escaped tigers to emerge from the brush. Soon, dawn arrives, and a groggy Dan awakens. Elsewhere, safe in her tent, Laura awakens also, to the sound of chattering chimpanzees swinging in the trees, a sound which perhaps awakens something deep in Laura's psyche. Laura walks out into the jungle, alone, barefoot and with shawl. Is it to find her husband, or her real family, the chattering monkeys? The viewer by now assumes that Laura is walking to meet her destiny. (Laura's ill-advised excursion into the jungle in shawl and bare feet is soon explained by the appearance of a similarly dressed woman in dark, grainy stock footage again from *Man-Eater of Kumaon*, attempting to match Laura's visage).

Meanwhile, Dan rests groggily under a large rock. Again through the astute use of stock footage, a tiger sneaks up behind him, preparing to jump; however, Dan manages to see him in time and rolls to safety, firing off several shots at the beast. The shots alert Taro, who comes running, rifle in hand, as Laura continues preposterously to tramp through the deadly shrubbery in some sort of stupor; she and the tiger meet in a clearing, and Laura screams. Soon, the tiger chases a woman dressed similarly to Laura in yet another stock footage montage. Finally, the tiger manages to push a screaming "Laura" (via stock footage again) off the edge of a cliff. Laura has finally been "touched" by the jungle, which will very soon make her its own. Dan and the tiger meet and fight it out via another stock footage montage; inexplicably, the wimpy Dan bests the strong tiger. Taro brings the comatose Laura back to camp, and Dan and Taro fret over her. Both men are now significantly topless; Dan has joined Taro in going "native," and vainly attempting to show his animalistic side by baring his flabby chest. As Dan worries over Laura's immanent demise, Taro narrowly escapes encounters with crocodiles and leopards as he treks through the jungle to fetch a doctor, conveyed again via plentiful amounts of stock footage.

Laura's wound-induced comatose state recalls her earlier somnambulistic states in which she dreamt and/or relived through hypnosis, visions of animal adventures which may have been fantasy, hallucination, or actual memories of past incarnations. The sleeping Laura now suffers another "episode," signaled by the swirling circle of deep unconsciousness. In the vision, a massive, angry gorilla tromps through the jungle, seeking an object. The viewer originally intuits that this vision is from Laura's mind, a dream or a fantasy, yet Dan clearly hears the gorilla's roar, and the viewer soon accepts that, as before with the episode with Spanky, Laura is not dreaming at all, but is actually summoning the gorilla to her, by sending out powerful, primordial waves of psychic (and presumably sexual) energy in order to lure the desired beast. As Laura convulses in a fit of what may be mental or sexual arousal, the gorilla comes ever closer to camp, as Dan looks around, aware that his kingdom is under attack from all quarters. Laura slowly awakens and rises out of bed, a determined look on her face; she walks out of the tent and sees Dan. She quickly looks away from the scrawny, topless buffoon and turns towards her real desire — the gorilla, which even now approaches. Laura and the gorilla are soon close enough to exchange meaningful eye contact, and the two connect as kindred spirits, sent through time and space to this fateful destiny.

Laura takes one last, withering look at poor Dan, who washes his face with a dishrag, looking the miserable sad sack that he is. Dan finally turns around and sees the Bride and the Beast together, and screams for "his woman." Alas, Laura never *was* "his woman," as the gorilla beats his chest to claim his possession. Dan grabs his puny pistol and tries to shoot the ape, but the pistol is empty, white male impotence perfectly personified. Dan tries to strike the beast with his useless phallus-surrogate, but the beast easily knocks over his obsolete rival. Laura looks down at her fallen "husband" with a mixture of pity and scorn, and then readily lets the gorilla pick her up and carry her off into the jungle, where she will gladly be his sexual mate, for life.

What is suggested throughout *Beast*, and cleverly accented in this, the film's "climax," is not merely Laura's symbiotic connection with the animal kingdom, but her sexual attraction to same. This nod to the sexual proclivity known as bestiality, in which humans participate sexually with non-human animals, has a seemingly inexhaustible cultural record, albeit largely suppressed and hidden. In antiquity, the taboo practice was often legally cited as "the offense the very naming of which is a crime."[18]

The threat of the bestial supplanting the human (i.e., the male) in terms of male sexual fantasy towards woman has led to much insecure fantasizing on the part of the chronically insecure male, that his woman would be better satisfied with an animal than with he. From proverbial lore such as "A woman who has tasted a dog will have no more use for a man," to documented chronicles of animal-human copulation, the specter of bestiality as a threat to male sexuality especially, has a long history which Wood cleverly taps into here, giving *Bride and the Beast*'s scenario much of its undeniable sexual tension.

Historically, occurrences of bestiality have overwhelmingly involved males involuntarily taking animals as their sex partners, so the preeminent male sexual fantasy of women with beasts seems to be equal parts wishful thinking and guilty conscience. As for men copulating with animals, the documented history on this phenomenon is legion, from time-honored tales of lonely shepherds mingling fraternally with their flock, to observations by anthropologists such as Sir Richard Burton who noted that the urban Chinese of the latter 19th century were notorious for their indiscriminate sexual dalliances with "ducks, goats, and other animals."[19] Further, sociologist Paolo Montegazza observed, "The Chinese are famous for their love affairs with geese, the necks of which they are in the habit of cruelling (sic) wringing off at the moment of ejaculation, in order that they may get the pleasurable benefit of the anal sphincter's last spasms in the victim."[20]

To focus on the woman's sexual attraction to a non-human "beast," this emphasis in Wood's delightfully naughty screenplay for *Bride and the Beast* serves as a useful metaphor for dull Dan's obvious phallic insecurity, illustrated most obviously by his bloodlust for animals (his competition, after all) and his obsession with deadly-potent, uber-phallic firearms (which reliably perform where he, assumedly, cannot). Add to this the highly significant fact that the scenario brings together a man and a woman on their honeymoon, the archetypal heterosexual scene of sexual discovery and first performance, and it is easy to see why Dan is so threatened by Laura's relative coolness towards him, and her peculiar hankering for furry apes. Not merely other men, but the entire animal kingdom, are Dan's rivals, and thus enemies, in his desired conquest of the strong female known as Laura; Dan's homicidal paranoia at this realization greatly fuels his accelerated bloodlust in the ensuing melodrama.

Eventually, Dan "wakes up" (perhaps in more ways than one) and, eschewing his puny pistol for his far more impressive rifle, runs out into the jungle to regain his rightful property. As the gorilla carries off Laura, the woman looks at her new mate with a mixture of drowsy curiosity and awakening lust, a most steamy moment in a film veritably dripping with an almost perverse sexual tension. The gorilla eventually reaches his lair, a cave, and brings Laura inside. Two more gorillas soon enter the cave, suggesting that Laura is meant to be partner not to one, but a whole gaggle of apes, a lurid notion only briefly sketched. Laura looks at the two gorillas who flank her, groaning enthusiastically. Dan arrives at the cave just in time to see two gorillas leave; he carefully enters the foreboding chasm, symbol of all that Laura has denied him sexually, her voracious and bestial sexual appetite, and is astonished to see Laura, surrounded by two more gorillas, seemingly fully at ease with the situation.

Laura glances over at Dan, and now gives him a look of undisguised hatred; Dan has now truly become the enemy, the intruder, the unwanted "other." Laura has obviously made her choice, and Dan's presence only threatens her newfound freedom. Dan manages to shoot one gorilla and knock over another, but when he tries to grab Laura to take her with him, she fights him ferociously, emphasizing her changed viewpoint. He is the ugly beast now. Realizing that the only way to take back what he feels belongs to him is by force, Dan does what any insecure phallocentric buffoon in similar circumstances would do—he punches Laura in the face, knocking her out.

In this one vile act, Dan is summarily recognized as patriarchy's golden child, he whom attempts to take that which he desires by force, even deadly force if necessary. The history of male violence towards women and its connection to male violence towards animals has been well-documented, especially in recent years, so it is reprehensible, but not at all surprising, to see Dan act thus. With that one punch, Dan succinctly illustrates everything that is wrong with the established heterosexual social construct, one which emphasizes a dominant-male ideology which sees all "others," i.e., non-males, as "feminized" and thus inferior, subordinate, and acceptable prey for conquest. As Carol J. Adams states in her astute essay, "Women-Battering and Harm to Animals,"

> [G]ender is an unequal distribution of power; interconnected forms of violence result from and continue this inequality. In a patriarchy, animal victims, too, become feminized. a hierarchy in which men have power over women and humans have power over animals, is actually more properly understood as a hierarchy in which men have power over women, (feminized) men and (feminized) animals.[21]

Luckily, the gorillas come to just in time to save Laura from what would now be certainly a fate worse than death; Dan's pitiful girl-punches are no match for the gorilla's brute strength, and Dan is soon rendered unconscious and finally, harmless. In a truncated coda, which takes place back in the living room of "Dan Fuller's Jungle," the viewer learns that the entire film, in hallowed Wood tradition, was a lengthy flashback, which in addition lacked a forward framing device to set it in time, showing Wood's temporal mischief in fine form. Dan and his compatriot-in-oppression, Dr. Reiner, share some booze and discuss the previous traumatic experience with all of the emotion of two cads sharing sexual war stories. Swigging a drink, Dan indifferently states, "And that's where I left her." Reiner casually restates his original thesis, that Laura had been a gorilla in a past life, concluding, "I believe she's gone, Dan. Back where she came from...." As Dan looks on in a state which can only be described as complete indifference, superimposed over him is one final vision of his lovely, lost wife, being held tenderly in the arms of the beast who took her from him, back to the jungle she prefers. Woman and Animal have aligned themselves together in perfect harmony, eschewing the murderous, possessive world of patriarchy for a blissful, truer, natural state of existence, while it would appear that Man couldn't care less, for there are always more animals to hunt and kill, and more women to seduce and enslave.

It seems almost incredible that Ed Wood could write such a prophetic, largely feminist screenplay during the gender-phobic 1950s, but *The Bride and the Beast* stands as a glorious, black-and-white testament to its unlikely existence. Eerily prophesying the controversial discourse on the role of hunting as metaphor to violence against women, and more universally as symbolic of phallocentric culture's hostile agenda towards women and animals, i.e., "the natural world," a dialogue which would not become predominant until some forty years later, *Bride and the Beast* stands as a proud example of the truly unique, iconoclastic Wood's character as a writer without peer. Once again, Wood stands traditional gender-centric roles (and their socio-political assumptions) on their respective heads, and offers a radical gender-switching scenario, not unlike *Glen or Glenda?* in many ways, in which the female and male "genders" are modified and realigned, especially in terms of their inherent and adopted power dynamics, and rendered virtually unrecognizable by film's end.

Specifically, the scenario for *Beast* takes direct, devastating aim at the sacred notion of the hunter as a natural predator somehow contributing to the overall well-being of the natural environment, and reveals how self-absorbed, delusional, and ultimately sexual is the hunter's intrinsic primary motivation. Marti Kheel uncovers the hidden erotic agenda of hunters' stated philosophy in terms which uncannily describe the prevailing sexual tension in *Bride and the Beast*: "[T]he primeval, animal-like aspect of hunting is experienced as an instinctive urge which, like the sexual drive, cannot and should not be repressed."[22] Dan Fuller's obsessive, highly neurotic attempts to harness both the animal kingdom, and his untamable wife, both ultimately with violence, underscore the highly sexual component of both endeavors.

As well, the violence eventually inflicted upon Laura by Dan, an inevitable crossover of Dan's chronic and institutionally sanctioned violence towards animals, perfectly mirrors the observed occurrences of violence to women being all too often connected with violence towards animals. These events also cleverly illustrate the ever-fragile, mercurial nature of anyone seen as "the other" by violent patriarchal culture, beings who may go from cherished objects of protection to targeted objects of extermination in a moment's notice, or as Carol J. Adams articulates, "battering exposes how contingent is the status of women and animals in patriarchal culture: one moment 'pet' or 'beloved,' the next injured or dead."[23]

Finally, Wood's scenario vividly exposes the prevailing flaws in patriarchal culture towards both women and animals, and how these two groups can and must align themselves in solidarity if any progress towards eventual safety and equality for all parties is to be attempted. From this perspective, it is not only morally but politically correct that Laura ends up as the love mate of the gorilla gang, for with this newly forged alliance, a group energy may emerge which might someday successfully challenge the ongoing threat to the natural world from the male hunter, who seems determined to annihilate it with extreme prejudice. Wood again seems to have uncannily recognized the universality of male violence towards all non-male "others," as his scenario ultimately conveys much the same message as author Adams, who concludes in her essay, "[R]ecognizing harm to animals as interconnected to controlling behavior by violent men is one aspect of recognizing the interrelatedness of all violence in a gender hierarchical world."[24]

Laura intuitively recognized this fatal connection early on, perhaps from the moment she entered Dan's lair, replete with stuffed carcasses of Dan's felled foes. From the moment when Laura covered her breasts and commented on the coldness of Dan's world, to the defining

Another provocative production still from the Wood-scripted *The Bride and the Beast* features leading man Lance Fuller and his pet gorilla in a curious embrace, which accents both the fierce competition between two "animals" over a prized female, as well as suggesting a sort of "dance" between adversaries who may have more in common than they would care to admit.

moment when Dan shot Spanky the gorilla in cold blood right in front of her, Laura realized that it would only be a matter of time before she, too, would be the target of this violent oppressor's gun or fists. Laura thus ends *Bride and the Beast* as an unusual pre-feminist archetype, a woman who was emancipated, via survived violence, towards self-autonomy and affinity with the animal kingdom.

Although highly entertaining and a virtual gold-mine of Woodian insight and philosophy, *Beast* is overall a strangely haphazard film, with much padding, as discussed. Certainly the film fulfilled the requirements for a low-budget potboiler for distributor Allied Artists, which was having its "Golden Age" from 1957–1959 with a string of highly successful genre-centric double bills. Taking a page from their nearest competitor, American-International Pictures, Allied Artists contracted and purchased many single features, and some ready-made double bills, from producers such as Roger Corman and William Castle, and other independents, and marketed them to the teenage and youth crowd in rural drive-ins and urban grind-houses, sometimes with astonishing returns on their investments. *Bride and the Beast* was undoubtedly one of the cheaper, and presumably less successful, of these products, but considering the budget on which it was made, it undoubtedly made back more than its investment for its producers, and likely also fared well during the 1960s bonanza of syndicated feature films for television. Producer-director Adrian Weiss was the son of prolific B-movie producer Louis Weiss, who apparently oversaw much of *Bride and the Beast*'s production. It appears to have been Adrian Weiss' only directorial credit, although he had a hand in earlier Weiss productions, including the impossibly incoherent *Devil Monster* (1946) a decade earlier, acting as producer and editor on that unbelievable sea-faring yarn. The younger Weiss had little experience as a director, however, and this may explain the slipshod nature of the production. However, in addition to the highly engaging scenario by Wood, there are the competent performances of Charlotte Austin and Lance Fuller, both of whom give their roles an energy and respect far above the production's spirit. As well, a soulful and stirring music score by talented, prolific composer Les Baxter adds greatly to the surprisingly lush ambience of *Bride and the Beast,* making it appear more polished than its low-budget could reasonably dictate.

Yet *Bride and the Beast* is essentially a one-joke premise, expanded to feature length via its untidy stock footage mid-section; it perhaps would have worked better as a half-hour television episode, along the lines of Wood's *The Final Curtain* and *The Night the Banshee Cried* (ca. 1957). Still, with its resplendent undermining of noxious phallocentric culture, and provocative positioning of Woman and Animals as the rightful inheritors of the earth, *The Bride and the Beast* can proudly take its place amongst Ed Wood's timeless cinematic achievements.

6

Plan 9 from Outer Space (1959)

Infamy is a mixed blessing. If an artist and his or her works are objectively critiqued, the reputation gained may be considered equitable. But when an artist and his or her works are judged subjectively, prejudicially, even maliciously, by those with self-serving agendas, the resultant notoriety, although specious, may be all but impossible to revise. Such may be the case with Ed Wood's magnum opus, *Plan 9 from Outer Space* (henceforth referred to as *Plan 9*), long considered by many "the worst film of all time." What exactly would it take to view the film more objectively? Alas, perhaps a reputation thus gained is irrevocable, and one can only attempt to discuss the film anew by starting from scratch. Thus, there will little incorporation here of the vast storehouse of popular opinion and oral history regarding the film, and its makers, the better to freshly revisit the subject.

In the Medved brothers' ostensibly punitive treatise on failed films and overreaching filmmakers, *The Golden Turkey Awards: The Worst Achievements in Hollywood History* (1981), they infer, with tongue fully in cheek, the unsung, if eccentric, artistry of Wood. Addressing via crude satire the trend at the time in some quarters to worship and over-interpret what were generally considered "trash" films unworthy of serious consideration, the Medveds surely meant to mock and taunt their object of veneration, not elevate him; the audience of the book, and subsequently of Wood's films, gleefully pounced on the abundant flaws, eccentricities and inaccuracies in the Wood film canon. Yet, when the dust settled, Wood and his canon remained, seemingly untouched, and many of the Medveds' parodic "observations" about Wood seemed not so bizarre after all. In the segment devoted to Wood in a chapter entitled "The Worst Director of All Time," condescending section headings such as "A Poet's Ear for Language and Dialogue," "A Hard-Edged, Documentary Narrative Style" (sic), "A Deliberate Attempt to Blur the Line Between Art and Artifice," and "A Tragic, Unsentimental View of Man's Doomed Struggle Against Elemental Forces," seemed not so far off the mark as they might have originally been intended.[1] From our exploration of Wood's astounding cinematic output, one might confidently state that all the above observations, originally intended perhaps as little more than patronizing asides, are in essence true, and therein lies the uncanny endurance of Wood's legacy, which seems impervious to sustained attacks or attempts to discredit.

To give credit where due, the Medveds did introduce the man and his works to a larger audience than Wood could have conceivably dreamed of. What many film buffs took from the Medved books, again underscoring their overall contribution to popular culture, was a curiosity towards the filmmakers and films discussed. To many film lovers, the dire verdicts assigned the films and filmmakers in the books laid down a gauntlet, so to speak, to seek out

138

these works and to view them objectively, in many instances for the first time. What many people took with them from further exploration of the undeniably fascinating Ed Wood and his films was that here was not necessarily the *worst* director of all time, but certainly one of the *oddest*, and most idiosyncratic; likewise, his films, amongst the lowest of mainstream cinema product, were not necessarily the worst films of their time period or genres, but most assuredly the *weirdest*. To some, this was not a cause for scorn, but celebration.

Perhaps the Medveds even called their audience's bluff; perhaps they, too, felt that Wood was a fascinating auteur awaiting rediscovery, yet also knew that the only way to sneak this obscure filmmaker into the popular consciousness was not to prop him up as an unsung genius, but as a delusional clown with artistic pretensions. Even at the time of the books' release, many read between the lines and suspected that the Medveds' virtual obsession with Wood suggested that he may well have been an as-yet unheralded artistic genius. But their overtly critical and denigrating stance led many away from seriously considering Wood's films as art for years. The integrity of the films has nevertheless endured.

The Medveds brought public awareness to *Plan 9* in a way few others could. Although the film had gained an unconnected cult following thanks to frequent television broadcasts in the 1960s, it was still obscure enough to be resident on many film lovers' "to see" lists. The Medveds' claim that their choice of *Plan 9* as "The Worst Film of All Time" was based in part on votes submitted by readers of their earlier work, *The Fifty Worst Films of All Time* (1978), suggests that there was already a healthy grass-roots fan club for the film. Thus, the Medveds' almost blow-by-blow account of *Plan 9* brought the film to life for many who had been unable to find the film on television or elsewhere. If their object was to scare people away from the film by claiming it "the worst film of all time" (which seems doubtful), the Medveds failed in this task, for the obvious effect of glorifying the film thus was to make it a highly sought-after, increasingly popular cult film attraction, on television, in theatrical revivals, in college and institutional screenings, and soon on home video. In short, after reading about *Plan 9* in *The Golden Turkey Awards* (and in Danny Perry's excellent *Cult Movies* [1981]), everybody wanted to see it, and for a while, *Plan 9* was one of the easiest of obscure older films to access.[2]

Ostensibly, *Plan 9* is a fascinating yet unwieldy combination of two popular cinema genres of the day, the science-fiction or "space" picture, and the gothic horror film. Both genres had existed virtually since the birth of cinema, yet each had gone through significant changes in the previous decades. Triggered by the discovery and unleashing of the atomic bomb, 1950s cinema was utterly obsessed with the topic of science-fiction, often reflecting on the evil or dangerous results of untamed scientific misadventure. Allied to this was the ever-growing fascination with space travel and the possibility of alien civilizations, prompted in part by accelerating research in both areas by science and industry, and fueled by the continuing popularity of science-fiction in popular literature.

Gothic horror, on the other hand, was suffering a demise in the 1950s, having had impressive peaks of popularity in both the 1930s and 1940s. Possibly due to the emphasis on the more modern aspects of science and outer space, it had become a minor genre during the mid–1950s. Thus, *Plan 9*'s gothic horror aspects give it much of its anachronistic charm, making the film seem quaint, naïve, and mysterious; it appears to take place in a time period too ancient to be the 1950s, yet too modern to be the 1940s. This awkward synthesis of science-fiction and gothic horror does much to give *Plan 9* its wholly unique ambience, and makes the film seem, significantly, "timeless." As will be seen, this nod to antiquity in *Plan 9* evokes a most interesting connection.

The final genre which influences *Plan 9* is not at first apparent, yet becomes pivotal as the film progresses, and surfaces in notable subtextual ways. The film's opening and closing

The evocative poster art for Wood's magnum opus, *Plan 9 from Outer Space,* hints but little at the film's wildly Absurdist canvas, although it does suggest its glorious theme, the ritual resurrection of the deceased beloved.

framing devices are the most obvious clues, for they effectively parody and mimic the verisimilitude and ambience of programming (taking primary aim at local religious programs and children's science-fiction serials) in that most insatiable, soon-to-be omnipresent cultural monster known as television.

With this "holy trinity" of genres (science-fiction, gothic horror and television), Wood cooks an utterly bizarre narrative stew which, although purporting to be a "science-horror adventure," is nothing of the sort. Surely, anyone who happened upon *Plan 9* in theatres upon its limited release in 1959, tucked almost apologetically in a double-bill beneath a lackluster adventure yarn called *Time Lock*, could not have fathomed what they were watching and, unfamiliar with the filmmaker and his creative idiosyncrasies, likely thought that they had, in fact, stumbled upon a film so horrible as to be virtually un-releasable.[3]

Wood's screenplay is in essence a script for a big-budget, epic adventure of mammoth proportions, a playful conceit of the fertile writer's mind; to mount the screenplay successfully would have taken a sizable budget underwritten by a major Hollywood studio. That Wood then filmed this epic story himself, with virtually no finances or studio resources, shows the author's folly and his genius, for *Plan 9* filmed in any other way would not have created the artfilm masterpiece which it is. The very absurdity of the epic elements in *Plan 9* being depicted in such a threadbare way make the resultant film utterly unique and unabashedly charming, and no increase of budget or talent or resource could have done anything but diminish this singular charm. This balmy overreaching on Wood's part, seen before in *Bride of the Monster*, becomes an art form in and of itself in *Plan 9* which, in purporting to paint the grandest of spectacles on the tiniest of filmic canvases, creates an end product which is philosophically and aesthetically revolutionary.

The notion of grand melodrama on a minuscule budget is in itself very much in the tradition of Bertolt Brecht and his notion of "epic theatre." There is also more than a hint of the spirit of the Theatre of the Absurd in many of *Plan 9*'s more "shocking" elements: abstract, "symbolic" special effects; shameless, incongruous clowning on the part of several characters; a treasure trove of nonsense verbiage; a scenario largely infused with dream and fantasy imagery, hinting at cogent allegorical content; unceasing and ultimately baffling narrative discontinuity.[4] This is not to suggest that Wood was consciously trying to create a dramatic shock-piece along the lines of a Samuel Beckett or Eugene Ionesco, only that it is peculiar and intriguing that some of the most striking and unique elements of post-modern Absurdist drama managed to find their way into *Plan 9*, either by accident or intuitive foresight on the part of its author. Martin Esslin thus describes Absurdist Theatre: "[T]he audience is confronted with actions that lack apparent motivation, characters that are in constant flux, and often happenings that are clearly outside the realm of rational experience," a definition which could be applied almost verbatim to Wood's magnum opus.[5] As well, underneath the cynical, comedic nonsense which informs Absurdist theatre lies the dark truth of man's journey from life into death — "The Theatre of the Absurd expresses the anxiety and despair that spring from the recognition that man is surrounded by areas of impenetrable darkness, that he can never know his true nature and purpose, and that no one will provide him with ready-made rules of conduct"[6]— this too describes well the essence of *Plan 9*.

The obsession which Wood had with all things religious and metaphysical is expressed purely and integrally in *Plan 9*, so much so that it often looks like a religious drama, and evokes memories of the theology-oriented Mystery Plays of antiquity, liturgical dramas enacted throughout Europe and England before countless communities, theatrical presentations dealing with Good and Evil, God and the Devil, Sins, Sinners, Noah and Jesus and other Christian Bible "superstars." These stark allegorical melodramas boast some uncanny parallels with *Plan 9*, and considering the film was funded by a Christian church group, one cannot help but ponder the significance Judeo-Christian tradition in the postwar environment may have had on the filmmaker when he was inspired to create this wildly existential treatise on life, death and resurrection.

This largely haphazard combination of wildly disparate elements, along with Wood's notoriously fragmented narrative structure, makes the resultant dizzying film much more than another straightforward, threadbare melodrama of the day. In many ways, *Plan 9* is more satire than melodrama, taking clever aim at its intended genres of cheap science-horror pictures, religious drama, and television programming. In fact, it may by viewing it as satire that *Plan 9* immediately becomes brilliant, if flawed.

Much has been chronicled about *Plan 9*'s remarkable genesis, so it will not be discussed at length here; two recommended sources of information are Mark Patrick Carducci's excellent documentary *Flying Saucers Over Hollywood — The Plan 9 Companion* (1991) and Rudolph Grey's *Nightmare of Ecstasy*, a treasure trove of historical tidbits on this and other Wood-related subjects. Suffice it to say that *Plan 9* was primarily produced by transplanted Southern Baptists, who also played several key parts in the film, and in addition insisted that the performers be baptized before production commenced. The overt religious patina which accompanied *Plan 9*'s birth thus eerily foreshadows the film's striking resemblance to both the ancient liturgical drama and the more recent English mystery plays, motifs which seem not merely fortuitous or coincidental, but absolutely integral to the film's phantasmagoric thesis.

Plan 9 opens with one of its most shocking conceits, and to the observant viewer, one of the more obvious clues as to its real intent. Certainly, any standard melodrama of the day would open either with the main credits, or a narrative-driven prologue introducing the main action of the piece. *Plan 9*, however, opens with a title graphic, "Criswell Predicts," superimposed over a barren set with a fan-like pattern of lights set against a black backdrop. A lone figure, silhouetted against the lights, can be vaguely seen. Swelling orchestral music rises as a light illuminates the silhouetted figure, whom the viewer may or may not recognize as the popular Los Angeles–area television personality, Criswell, prognosticator of future events. Criswell wears a silly bow tie and a funereal suit, and with his spit curls, he looks very much like a slightly demented undertaker. Addressing the confounded viewer directly, Criswell pontificates, in his most grandiose manner:

> Greetings, my friends!
> We are all interested in the future,
> For that is where you and I are going to spend the *rest* of our lives!
> And remember, my friends—
> Future events such as these will affect *you* in the future!
> You are interested in the unknown, the mysterious, the unexplainable!
> That is why you are here!
> And now, for the first time,
> We are bringing to you the full story of what happened on that fateful day!
> We are giving you all the evidence, based only on the secret testimony
> Of the misable souls who survived this terrifying ordeal!
> The incidents! The places!
> My friend! We cannot keep this a secret any longer!
> Let us punish the guilty!
> Let us reward the innocent!
> My friend!
> Can your heart stand the shocking facts
> About *graverobbers from outer space*?!

Popular prognosticator Criswell graces the cover of this 1954 science-fiction magazine, with a rendering of his predicted miles-wide space station that will someday carry all of humanity off an atomically decimated Earth. In Ed Wood's *Plan 9 from Outer Space*, Criswell played himself, filling the film with similar apocalyptic pronouncements.

This bombastic, utterly surreal bit of polemic clues in the observant viewer that what is about to transpire will not be a standard B-level space picture or zombie yarn. Wood seems to take great pains to thus signal his audience. Criswell does not, by any stretch of the imagination, appear like the narrator or story teller of a melodrama, however fantastic it may subsequently be. He does, however, sound uncannily like one of the fire-and-brimstone preachers who were just then beginning to populate the television airwaves through local late-night and Sunday programming, and here is where Wood first takes clever aim at the cultural monster of television. *Plan 9* was conceived and filmed circa 1956, the exact moment when "televised evangelists" (later to be cynically dubbed "televangelists"), featuring early pioneers such as Rex Humbard, A.A. Allen and Bishop Fulton J. Sheen, were starting to command the video airwaves.[7]

As for Criswell (1907–1982, aka Jeron Criswell King), he had managed to forge an auspicious career for himself from an implausible genesis: In order to fill extra time on a local television program he had purchased to hawk a line of vitamin pills, Criswell began his "Criswell Predicts" segment as a lark, and likely with tongue in cheek. Understandably, this more exotic portion of the program became the most popular, and soon "Criswell Predicts" was a popular Los Angeles–based production, broadcast from KLAC, Channel 13, and for a time syndicated nationally as well. Criswell's predictions were also nationally syndicated for newspapers, and several popular books followed.[8] While the opening segment of *Plan 9* may actually mirror Criswell's television program of the time period, a comparison which cannot be verified as no films have surfaced for comparison, certainly Criswell himself was borrowing the bombastic polemic and melodramatic sentiment of those religious preachers for his own, somewhat mystical predictions in this bizarre opening segment. What Criswell, and Wood, astutely gleaned from the "televised evangelist" phenomenon was not the subject matter, but the more important "cult of personality," which dictated that a charismatic spokesman could sell pretty much anything via the intimate medium of television, from vitamins to God to "The Future."

Ironically, Criswell does also act as storyteller in *Plan 9*, as the entire film is posited as his tale told, or possibly even a delusional fantasy, as the man surely seems possessed of something. As such, this clever framing device on Wood's part, while setting up the fantastic scenario in part, also adds to its unreality, as the viewer is aware, from the prologue and epilogue as well as Criswell's intermittent narration throughout the film, that the story may be nothing more than this madman's delusional fever dream. This makes the subsequent scenario both more believable as fantasy, and yet less acceptable as standard melodrama; Criswell's participation does add to *Plan 9*'s sense of being more allegory than narrative.

As mentioned, from this very first scene, *Plan 9* seems to be forging a connection with a specific, quite ancient form of drama — the religion-based plays of the fourteenth and fifteenth centuries, collectively known as the "Mystery," "Morality" or "Miracle" plays.[9] This series of plays, themselves derived from earlier church services which entertained and educated congregations with reenactments of tales from the Christian Bible, evolved as a separate theatrical phenomenon, adding "dramatic interpretation and scenic setting" to the church-bound liturgical services.[10] These plays had a specific overriding purpose: to dramatize and celebrate significant events in Christian lore, the foremost being the resurrection of Christ. Plays such as *The Creation of Man, The Garden of Eden, The Fall of Man, Noah's Flood* and *The Sacrifice of Isaac* are self-explanatory in their subject matter, while other dramatic productions such as *Everyman* and *The Woman Taken in Adultery* incorporated much from their source material while adding new dramatic effects and philosophical insights, all geared to educate a wayward audience about the wages of sin and the eternal rewards of repentance and atonement. These exceedingly popular plays were eventually grouped together and performed in series or "cycles," dubbed posthumously with their location of origin in England (i.e., Chester, York, Coventry, Wakefield).

They are often lumped together as aspects of the same liturgically based dramatic tradition, but this series of plays actually fall into three somewhat distinct categories, although there is considerable overlap within: The "Mystery Play" connoted a religious drama fueled by biblical tales and more or less "literal" narrative; the "Miracle Play" focused principally on the legendary lives of the saints; the "Morality Play," the most allegorical of the trinity, was based on the discord of abstract metaphysical notions, enacted via corporeal manifestations of Good and Evil.[11]

As will be seen, *Plan 9* incorporates elements from all three of these dramatic forms, but borrows most heavily from the Mystery Play and Morality Play ethos. Compare the opening speech by Criswell with the prologue to *Everyman*, a fifteenth century Dutch Morality Play (considered a masterpiece of the allegorical Morality Play genre, and a personal favorite of George Bernard Shaw),[12] spoken directly to the audience by a peripheral character known only as "The Messenger":

> I pray you all give your audience,
> And hear this matter with reverence,
> By figure a moral play,
> *The Summoning of Everyman* called it is,
> That our loves and ending shews
> How transitory we be all day.
> This matter is wondrous precious;
> But the intent of it is more gracious
> And sweet to bear away.
> The story saith: — Man, in the beginning
> Look well, and take good heed to the ending,
> Be you never so gay!
> Ye think sin in the beginning full sweet,
> Which in the end causeth thy soul to weep
> When the body lyeth in clay.
> Here shall you see how *Fellowship* and *Jollity*,
> Both *Strength*, *Pleasure* and *Beauty*,
> Will fade from thee as flower in May;
> Calleth everyman to a general reckoning.
> Give audience, and here what he doth say![13]

While the narrative specifics admittedly bear little comparison, the overtly preachy, shamelessly didactic quality of the two pieces share an uncanny similarity, and the structure of the prose shares rhythmic congruence as well. In each, an emotionally invested narrator is virtually pleading with his audience to hear well what he is saying, to watch carefully the unfolding scenario, for the benefit of their very souls. The scenario to come will eerily mirror certain aspects of *Everyman* in particular, and the Mystery Play and Morality Play genres in general; considering the eventual financial rescue of the picture by fervent Baptists, the overt religiosity in *Plan 9* will seem by film's end neither mere coincidence nor reluctant consequence, but the very core of its existence, and the key to its enduring, unearthly charms.

Everyman follows a single, archetypal man as he is met by Death and forced to face the reality of his own mortality and, most importantly, to see the error of his ways, in order to avoid eternal punishment when he crosses that threshold between life and death. The synopsis is articulated succinctly in the play's introduction: "Here beginneth a treatise how ye high Father of Heaven sendeth Death to summon every creature to come and give account of their lives in this world, and is in manner of a Moral play." As will be seen, *Plan 9* is utterly fixated upon Death as the *deus ex machina* of all earthly affairs. *Everyman* takes place largely at the entrance to a grave site, as Death beseeches Everyman to utilize the spiritual tools of penance and confession to prepare for his maker; inarguably, *Plan 9*'s most significant setting is the cemetery, with its open crypts and compromised graves astutely symbolizing the proximity to death which haunts all mortals.

As for Criswell's introduction, there are several points worth noting. The frequent evocation of "my friend," used to ingratiate the viewer and establish an intimate bond between speaker and audience, was likely a phrase used by Criswell in his televised predictions; it also, however, sounds exactly like the phraseology used by the aforementioned television evangelists, who attempted, after all, to befriend their electronic congregations, the better to embrace their message (and contribute to the preacher's ministry collection). Used in *Plan 9*, the effect may be ironically to confuse and distance an audience which did not expect to be approached so directly in a vehicle advertised as cheap, fantasy-oriented entertainment.

The iconic line, "We are all interested in the future, for that is where you and I are going to spend the *rest* of our lives," at first seems absurdly self-evident, but it signals one of *Plan 9*'s most exciting conceits—that art in general, and especially avant-garde art which may only be appreciated outside of its own time, may blossom and flourish at some future point. The line thus underscores Wood's faith that his art, and *Plan 9* particularly, would find its grateful and abundant audience in that vast temporal mystery known as "the future," where he and his audience (the aforementioned "you and I") would share, in spirit, the bounty of this remarkable cinematic achievement. This faith in salvation for art via the passage of time is reinforced by the subsequent line, "Future events such as these will affect *you* in the future!" Long attributed to Wood, these introductory lines actually belong to Criswell, as they were part and parcel of his standard opening in both his television show and newspaper and magazine columns.[14]

The following lines, "You are interested in the unknown, the mysterious, the unexplainable! That is why you are here!" again suggest lines taken directly from Criswell's prognostication act, and its intended audience, those who from time immemorial have been fascinated with the notion of life after death, ghosts, reincarnation, and all the metaphysical mumbo-jumbo which shares such an affinity with the tenets of the world's organized religions. Yet these subjects were also obsessed upon by Wood himself, whose lifelong, adolescent fixation on all things "spooky" fueled much of his most fantastic writing. As Criswell rants on, "And now, for the first time, we are bringing to you the full story of what happened on that fateful day!" his voice now sounds like a parody of a tabloid newspaper headline which "screamed" its shocking news-flashes to its readership, or one of the many *True Confessions*–type magazines which promised to reveal lurid secrets to a terminally morbid public. The further admonition, "We are giving you all the evidence, based only on the secret testimony, of the miserable souls who survived this terrifying ordeal!" combines this tabloid sensibility with a slight nod to popular television crime programs such as *Dragnet*, which based many of their stories on true incidents, evidence gathered, and testimony recorded. Criswell seems about to lose control as he virtually screams, "We cannot keep this a secret any longer!" and thus uses his best pitch-man skills to keep the viewer in a state of high anticipation. As Criswell then chants, "Let us punish the guilty! Let us reward the innocent!" he sounds again very much like a fire-and-brimstone preacher of perhaps Calvinist bent, chastising his congregation for their inevitable moral transgressions in order to whip up guilt and moving his listeners toward confession and repentance.

Finally, Criswell fairly shouts the prologue's summation: "Can your heart stand, the shocking facts, about *Graverobbers from Outer Space*?!" Again alluding both to tabloid journalism and fundamentalist Christian preaching, with its emphasis on horrible fates in hellish ethereal worlds awaiting vile sinners, this proclamation immediately cuts, for fullest dramatic impact, to an almost subliminal stock footage sequence which fully acknowledges Ed Wood as the author of the piece: a thunder-and-lightning shot, which startles the viewer even as it introduces the main credits. It is almost as if the mere uttering of the biblically-blasphemous word "graverobbers" has angered the very heavens.[15] The original title of *Plan 9* was *Graverobbers from Outer Space*, a delightful pulp fiction title, and it is nothing short of travesty that the paranoid Baptists who funded much of *Plan 9*'s post-production costs insisted on changing the name from what they considered, inevitably, something blasphemous and offensive. The film's release title, although it has become iconic, was likely seen at the time as lackluster and without character, and may have had a good deal to do with the film's difficulty in finding even the most cursory theatrical distribution. Ironically, by changing the film's title thus, the Baptists not only sabotaged their own plans for making money on the project, but insured that the film would only be able to find an appreciative audience in the future.

The main credits roll with the main cast and crew's names engraved on cartoon tombstones. The final screen credit is conspicuously separated from the others by a blast of thunder, accompanied by a blinding flash which blanks out the screen for several frames. Another lightning bolt crashes down upon a woodsy natural landscape, conveyed either via an impressive miniature set or matte painting, from which a mountain stands majestically, only to be attacked by a violent bolt of lightning. This virtually subliminal sequence, lasting only 23 frames, nonetheless conveys much dramatic and narrative power, and subconsciously suggests an angry god-head summoning judgment upon mere mortals, and perhaps even traditional Hollywood. The subsequent credit, superimposed over a winsome matte painting of a galaxy full of stars, reads, "Written-Produced-Directed: EDWARD D. WOOD, JR." Without question, this is the bold signature of a filmmaker who is deliriously proud of his work, and who obviously fancied it high art.

As Criswell moans in narration, "All of us on this earth, know that there is a time to live, and a time to die," again reflecting the liturgical prejudices of *Plan 9*, the narrative proper begins at a funeral service at a cemetery.[16] Wood begins *Plan 9* with Death, and fully indulges his career-long fixation on Death as the *deus ex machina* of all melodramatic narrative, the vital energy animating life itself. A small group, including Bela Lugosi, stands around an open grave replete with marble tombstone; the setting is accented with several other makeshift wooden crosses, suggesting this cemetery to be of the working class, if not a veritable potters' field. Shots of the mourners, and Lugosi with the minister (Reverend Lyn Lemon, one of several Baptist church leaders who participated in the film[17]), alternate with cutaway shots of two gravediggers sitting and watching, shovels in hand, ready to do their part in this barbaric ritual preserved for modernity. The scene is given expositional clarity with further flowery narration: "Just at sundown, a small group gathered in silent prayer around the newly opened grave of the beloved wife of an elderly man. Sundown of the day, yet sundown of the old man's heart. For the shadows of grief clouded his very reason." Lugosi is apparently the bereaved party. The mourners leave the grave as Criswell offers a segue: "It was when the gravediggers started their task that strange things started to take place...."

The scene changes to a stock shot of an in-flight DC-7 commercial airliner which is identified as "American Airlines Flight #812, non-stop to Burbank, California." In the interior of the airliner cockpit, pilot Jeff Trent (Gregory Walcott) and co-pilot Danny (David

DeMering) attend to business. DeMering was chosen for the role because he was, at the time, "personal secretary" to John "Bunny" Breckenridge, who plays "The Ruler" in *Plan 9*. As Breckenridge invested in *Plan 9*,[18] it may be assumed that the use of DeMering was either a favor, or a way to fill a role with free labor; several sources claim that DeMering was also Breckenridge's lover at the time.[19]

As the viewer gets his first glance at the notorious airline cockpit, composed almost entirely of found objects and unrelated ephemera, one may be taken aback by its sheer crudeness; yet one must also agree that it does effectively convey the essence of the scene intended, albeit allegorically as opposed to realistically. This is yet another example of Wood's brilliant use of non-representational imagery to convey representational objects and settings, clearly in the spirit of Brecht's "epic theatre." As will be seen, Wood's predilection for sketchy imposters to create *mise-en-scène* is, in addition to being merely the hasty, lazy efforts of an impatient, cash-poor producer, also one of his most enduring and indelible artistic touches. As author Brad Linaweaver astutely observes, "Ed Wood invented symbolic effects to take the place of special effects. [They are] a symbol of the effect he would have if he had the money."[20] While these "symbolic" effects were certainly economically prudent, they are one of the many quirks which raise the films of Ed Wood to the level of art.

The back wall of the airplane cockpit, supposedly a sheet of "Masonite" spray-painted white, does look sufficiently metallic to pass for a real wall, Spartan though it be. The rest of the props are what give the scene away as cheesy and timeless. The doorway to the passenger compartment is conveyed by a hole in the wall covered with a loosely draped shower curtain. On the cockpit wall, the complicated instrumentation of a modern airliner is conveyed via two pathetic props. On one side is tacked a simple flight computer or "whiz wheel," a calculation wheel used by pilots in training for calculating various figures including wind, speed and altitude. On the other side is tacked a garden-variety clipboard with papers. Yet perhaps the most non-representational elements in this astounding set are the pilots' steering columns, which seem to be comprised of nothing more than wooden stands with curved pieces of darkly painted wood meant to symbolize steering apparatus. That these Absurdist props wobble about from the least touch of the actors make them seem all the more unreal. These spare props, desperately mimicking the authentic items one might find somewhere in the baggage of a commercial airline pilot, by no means effectively convey the actual interior of a real-life airplane cockpit, and look nothing but apologetic in the scene, unless the viewer begins to sense that what Wood is trying to convey here is not reality at all. This hunch is immediately confirmed as the scene catapults completely into Absurdist territory, when the pilots are shaken up by a loud noise and a blinding light from outside. As they look out their non-existent window, the scene cuts to the first shot of the legendary, iconic *Plan 9* flying saucer, a glistening silver disc floating serenely over a matte painting of billowy white clouds.

The *Plan 9* flying saucer, which has been called everything from a paper plate to an automobile hubcap to a balsa wood prop to a trash can lid, even by some of the film's creators (Wood included), is in fact an easily identifiable cultural product. It was first identified to a mainstream audience in Mark Carducci's documentary *Flying Saucers Over Hollywood — The Plan 9 Companion* (1991); any self-respecting Baby Boomer was likely already aware of the prop's genesis. During the height of the UFO craze of the early to mid–1950s, popular culture addressed this fascination with all manner of homage, movies and books being foremost. One of the most interesting responses to the trend was marketed by Chicago-based toy manufacturer Paul Lindberg, who in 1956 created a mass-market plastic hobby kit, called simply "The Flying Saucer." The simple construction kit portrayed the common popular conception of a "flying saucer," that being a silver disc-shaped craft with a clear dome on top, inside of

The famous *Plan 9 from Outer Space* flying saucer — which reviewers called everything from a paper plate to an automobile hubcap — was in fact a plastic children's toy. It is immortalized above in the original digital artwork *Flying Saucer Resurrection* by graphic designer Curt Pardee (courtesy of the artist).

which sat a "little green man." The kit, originally selling for 50 cents, was extremely popular in its original release, and in several re-issues in the 1960s and 1970s. More recently, the molds for the kit were purchased by Glencoe Models, and a further re-issue of the iconic kit was still in production well into the 1990s, and can be easily located today.

Edie the stewardess (Norma McCarty) pushes through the shower curtain just in time to see what the pilots are seeing, and asks, "What in the world?" to which Danny replies, "That's nothing from *this* world!" Danny sends out a Mayday to Burbank headquarters. As the saucer flies over some more matte paintings, the careful viewer may note that it is not now portrayed by the Lindberg plastic model first seen, but a similar prop. This revised spacecraft was likely a modification of the original saucer model, as it retains the basic disc-and-dome design, but now with different proportions and somewhat less detail than the original craft. This newer saucer is that which appears to land in the cemetery.

The two gravediggers seen earlier are played by J. Edwards Reynolds and Hugh Thomas.[21] Reynolds was the film's producer, and one of the leaders of the Southern Baptist Church of Beverly Hills, which basically sponsored *Plan 9*[22]; in a most salient case of poetic justice, not only would Reynolds' machinations to wrest control of the finished film from Wood backfire on him, leaving him hopelessly in debt, he would, a few years hence, drink himself to death.[23] Hugh Thomas was another member of the church, so the Baptists' presence clearly under-

scores the theological underpinning which energizes *Plan 9*. As they hear strange noises emanating from the nearby flying saucer, they discuss the situation in hilarious Wood dialogue,
including the following exchange:

> GRAVEDIGGER #1: Don't like hearin' noises—'specially where they ain't supposed to be any!
> GRAVEDIGGER #2: Yeah! Sorta spooky-like!

What makes the conversation most comical is that the scene, shot silent, seems to have
been under-cranked while filming, so it plays back at a faster-than-normal speed, similar to
how many silent films were sped up to show on television. The dialogue, which was then overdubbed at a later time, comes across as rushed and comical, enhancing somehow the absurdity of the exchange, and the silliness of the characters.

The gravediggers walk into another portion of the cemetery, in which a tiny mausoleum
lies. This new set is stage-bound, simplistic yet quite expressive, with a black backdrop serving as the background, a lone tree accenting the prop mausoleum, and everpresent fog-
machine smoke softening the *mise-en-scène*, making the setting look literally "otherworldly."
It is at first jarring for the viewer to realize that this engaging yet patently false setting is supposed to depict the same space as the previous exterior scenes of the cemetery, filmed in broad

Perhaps unwittingly, Wood fashioned an indelible icon in the somber Maila Nurmi, who portrays
a resurrected corpse in ***Plan 9 from Outer Space***. The silent character conveys the existential
tragedy of spiritual desolation, as well as invoking the exalted spirit of silent cinema, a genre
which well illustrated the mystical wisdom inherent in non-verbal expression.

daylight. At first blush, it appears that Wood was either too lazy or too poor to darken the exterior scenes with post-production laboratory work, so they at least somewhat approximated the gloomy studio scenes. Yet the resultant disparity creates both a narrative tension and an aesthetic dichotomy which resonates throughout *Plan 9*, and gives the film much of its "otherworldly" verisimilitude. Further, this shocking and reckless juxtaposition of virtually neo-realistic location settings with haphazard stage-bound fantasy-scapes is one of *Plan 9*'s most exciting and vivid binaries, literally pitting the real against the false or, as one might term it, contrasting the "live" and the "dead." The incompatibility of representational and non-representational theatrical aesthetics is nicely illustrated here as well, and this incompatibility as mentioned supplies *Plan 9* with much of its compelling creative friction. The mausoleum is a tiny, makeshift thing, hardly big enough to conceivably house even one lone coffin, and in the medium shots, its hasty wood-and-paint construction can be easily identified, making it yet another in a rapidly increasing list of allegorical or "symbolic" icons which provide *Plan 9*'s unearthly charm. The top of the crypt sports the obligatory cross of Jesus, as Wood takes every opportunity possible to recall this magnificent Christian fable of death and resurrection, a theme so dear to his heart.

As the gravediggers, again in the daylight exterior setting, walk towards camera, in theory towards the stage-bound mausoleum setting, a ghoulish woman, dressed all in black, walks from behind the studio-set crypt. With her stringy black hair, tattered funeral dress, morbidly small waistline, cadaverous face and creepy long fingernails, this vile creature immediately makes the viewer sense that, although in motion, she is not of the living. This "ghoul woman," labeled "Vampire Girl" in the cast listings, is Maila Nurmi, dressed as her famous horror character, Vampira. That Vampira is a beloved and enduring cultural icon is without question; how this fame came about is a story unto itself, addressed thoroughly in several places. Mark Carducci's *Flying Saucers Over Hollywood — The Plan 9 Companion* (1991) and Kevin Sean Michael's essential *Vampira: The Movie* (2007) are the best sources for the truth about this miraculous anomaly of 1950s culture.

Nurmi's Vampira character was a heady, eclectic mixture of many pop culture female archetypes; at various times, Nurmi had listed all of the following as direct influences on her creation: "Dragon Lady" from the "Terry and the Pirates" comic strip; the evil queen in Walt Disney's *Snow White and the Seven Dwarves* (1937); the morbidly sexy woman in Charles Addams' *New Yorker* cartoons; the dominatrix mythos of the dominant, aggressive, even fatal female; the bondage-and-dominance pin-up women depicted in John Willie's *Bizarre* magazine; Theda Bara; Norma Desmond from *Sunset Blvd.*; Tallulah Bankhead; Marilyn Monroe; Katharine Hepburn; Bette Davis; Billie Burke; and Marlene Dietrich.[24]

Born in Finnish Lapland and brought to the U.S. by her parents at age two, the spiritually minded Nurmi originally wanted to become a traveling evangelist called "Sister Mary Francis," and her fitful acting and modeling career was an attempt to raise funds for this grand dream, which never materialized as such. Trying to create a character which might catch the eye of local television and movie producers, Nurmi stumbled on the Vampira character after some trial and error, and eventually landed a fateful job at Los Angeles TV station KABC in 1954, where Vampira acted as host for old horror films. With her arresting presence and sense of autonomous menace, this strange stab at fame became an overnight sensation, and Nurmi-as-Vampira was soon even seen nationwide thanks to a *Life* magazine article. Unfortunately, male conspiracy was afoot, and Nurmi was fired after less than a year as the world's first TV horror host, as ABC wanted to create a television series about Charles Addam's "family," and decided to steal her character in order to achieve this. In addition, Nurmi was blacklisted in Hollywood, and found making the jump from television to motion pictures difficult.[25] According to Nurmi, Wood's protégé Paul Marco approached her in late 1956 with $200 in cash (mostly singles), and asked her on behalf of her boss to play a vampire in his new movie, *Graverobbers from Outer Space*.[26] The down-and-out actress readily agreed, and showed up for her one day of shooting wearing her now-threadbare royal costume of former, fleeting glory. Again according to Nurmi, she insisted on playing Vampira as a mute, as she didn't at all like Wood's dialogue. However, as neither of the other "dead" people speak in *Plan 9*, it is also possible that no dialogue was ever written for them.

The iconic creation Vampira, as resurrected by Nurmi for *Plan 9*, evokes much about the female principle in postwar culture. As an autonomous, and undeniably dangerous, female archetype, Vampira incorporates Man's two premier obsessions, Sex and Death, in a most combustible fusion. Film historian David Skal has noted that Vampira invoked, "Eros and Thanatos at the same time,"[27] a combination which, as philosophers have long observed, leads to notably erotic aspects of destruction. As the complete antithesis of the "normal" or "safe" female of the 1950s, Vampira and her cultural ilk represented something alluring yet frightening to the male collective, and presumably a certain female audience as well, a novelty at least and perhaps a counterpoint to the stifling roles assigned for women during this most punitive and sexist decade. The rather extraordinary power of non-verbal communication is conveyed in breathtaking manner via Vampire Girl's mute role in *Plan 9*; her regal presence and highly theatrical mannerisms in the cemetery scenes recalls a similar authority conveyed by iconic female performers in silent cinema, with Nurmi's acknowledged influence Theda Bara being a prime example.[28]

The Vampire Girl walks slowly around the mausoleum, then turns and walks towards camera. A quick cutaway to the gravediggers expressing surprise verifies that they are supposed to be witnessing this studio-set scene, as is the viewer. As the scene returns, one last time, to the studio set, and the Vampire Girl gets ever closer to the camera, her spidery arms outstretched, the scene fades out with the sound of a man's blood-curdling scream. The implication is that the gravediggers have either fainted from sheer fright at the sight of this hideous ghoul from the grave, or have in fact been attacked and assaulted by same. The viewer is likely by now completely bewildered at the unfolding scenario, which seems to be taking place on different planes of existence, and utilizing footage with such antithetical ambience. The dire warning of Criswell seems to be coming true, and it might be paraphrased thusly: "Can your heart stand the shocking facts of Ed Wood's complete undermining of cinematic reality?" This egregious ripping asunder of narrative convention, which had been building up steam quickly since Wood's tumultuous subliminal montage placed directly before his authoritative credit, has finally all but fatally undermined traditional narrative structure. One might even fantasize that the off-screen screams which punctuated this scene were more intended as a symbol of *Plan 9*'s definitive break with cohesive exposition and integral aesthetic than as a mere plot point annotated via cheap audio effect.

The next scene shows Bela Lugosi skulking about outside a modest house. This footage was shot by Wood outside the home of Tor Johnson's son Karl for one of his many unfinished film projects, possibly *The Vampire's Tomb*.[29] According to Wood, Lugosi badly needed money, and Wood paid the ailing actor $1,000 to appear in these scenes and several graveyard scenes which will be peppered throughout *Plan 9*. This poignant footage is all the more extraordinary as it is the last filmed record of the iconic actor, and is cannily used by Wood as the great man's memorial.[30] As Lugosi, in cape and hat, wanders around the front lawn aimlessly, eventually picking up a flower and smelling it, Criswell attempts to superimpose some vestige of expositional import on the scene with poetic Wood narration:

The grief of his wife's death
Became greater and greater agony!
The home they had so long shared together
Became a tomb!
A sweet memory
Of her joyous living!
The sky, to which she had once looked,
Was now only a covering for her dead body!
The ever-beautiful flowers she had planted,
With her own hands,
Became nothing more than the lost roses of her cheeks!
Confused by his great loss,
The old man left that home,
Never to return again!

Lugosi walks off-camera; when he has left the frame, the scene freeze-frames, as an off-screen car crash is heard. This cuts to an ambulance driving towards a hospital, sirens wailing, and the scene fades out. Clearly, the old man has been hit by a motor vehicle, but it is left unclear as to whether he absent-mindedly stumbled out onto the busy highway near his home, or decided to end his lonely existence, which had become too great to bear, in order to join his beloved once again, in death. The notion of suicide is reinforced by Criswell's observation "the old man left *that* home," implying that he desired to journey to a *new* home, that being the graveyard, where he could once again be united with his darling spouse.

Back at the studio cemetery set, several mourners emerge from the tiny mausoleum, almost an unbelievable act considering the prop's diminutive size, and more evidence of Wood's almost magical ability to make even the most absurd action seem somehow legitimate in his scenarios of ever-accruing impossibilities. A female mourner asks, "Why was his wife buried in the ground, and he in a crypt?" and her companion replies, "Something to do with family tradition, a superstition of some sort." This mention of a family tradition or superstition may refer to the ancient practice for burying kings, priests and other social "royalty," wherein the (male) personage was elected to be forever enshrined in an elaborate above-ground chamber built especially for him, while the notable's deceased "others" (spouse, children, servants and other "inferiors") could rot in the cold ground along with the common folk. That the Old Man, and his wife, were interred this way suggests the possibility of an Old World sexism at work, but also enforces the notion that Wood saw Bela Lugosi, the actor who initiates this character, as possessing an undeniable "royal" bearing.[31]

As the two mourners stroll through the stage-bound cemetery, the viewer gets a good chance to see the artistry of Wood in his capacity to create fantastic artificial worlds out of meager resources. By judicious placement of grass mats, a black backdrop, a fog machine, carefully posed tree limbs, the pasteboard prop crypt and some wooden and/or cardboard tombstones, Wood manages to create not only a reasonable facsimile of an actual graveyard, albeit one more symbolic than literal, but invokes an ethereal, evocative "cosmic void" with this strange "dead space." God's laboratory in *Glen or Glenda?*, the atomic laboratory of Vornoff in *Bride of the Monster*, and the entire scenario of *Jail Bait* also illustrate this peculiar Woodian milieu. This recurring space is Wood's manifestation of "the other world," the world of the spiritual, of all which is beyond the reach of death. This emblematic "dead space" in the Wood film canon can also be seen as a fanciful metaphor for the religious concept of purgatory, wherein the recently deceased wait for final judgment; in Wood's version, souls both living and dead occupy the craven space, and their behavior within dictates their final temporal destination. The studio cemetery set in *Plan 9* is perhaps Wood's ultimate manifestation of this "other world"; it is undoubtedly one of Wood's finest artistic compositions.

The female mourner spots the bodies of the gravediggers, now transposed to the studio cemetery set and thus connected to the narrative "proper." The woman screams—another patently fake scream which mirrors the earlier scream of the gravedigger(s)—and again suggests a reaction to the inchoate temporal elements which Wood recklessly yet magically tosses together to form his exhaustively circuitous patchwork narratives.

Plan 9 catapults abruptly to epic melodrama with the next scene, in which the police are brought in to investigate the cemetery murders. With the addition of the obligatory law enforcement characters, *Plan 9* becomes an archetypal Wood film, with the filmmaker's queer obsession with "the law" and some form of earthly justice taking center stage. Several police officers exit a police station, hop in a car and drive off in glaringly inconsistent day-for-night footage. In these two shots, day and night are switched indiscriminately, and the police car itself switches between two radically different makes and models. The police car which enters the studio cemetery scenes seems to be yet a third vehicle, as witness the different paint scheme from the vehicles used in the exteriors. This sequence fully reinforces the earlier juxtaposition of the location graveyard scenes with the stage-bound cemetery set, and the reckless switching of vehicles alludes to Wood's playful switching of reality with artifice, most recently illustrated by the octopus in *Bride of the Monster*. In Wood's capacity as film "magician," he constantly dares the viewer to distinguish the "real" object from the symbol, the stand-in, the surrogate.

Back at the cemetery set, which exists in an ethereal, eternal nighttime, regardless of the time experienced by the outside world, Police Lt. Daniel Clay and several of his subordinates investigate the strange happenings. Clay, played by inimitable former-wrestler Tor Johnson, is a "bigger than life" character in more ways than one. The hulking giant of a man, well-utilized by Wood in *Bride of the Monster* as a lumbering mute, here is given a "human" role with character attributes and significant dialogue, and it was in this role that the "Super Swedish Angel" became a true cultural giant. Giving a foreign-born actor with an extraordinarily thick accent meaningful dialogue, with a touch of American slang to boot, would seem foolhardy to the point of sabotage in the hands of another, but Wood's dialogue for Johnson seems also designed to be made deathless by the actor's distinct enunciation. Tricky and abrupt to begin with, and virtually indecipherable through Johnson's hasty delivery, this remarkable dialogue has become, itself, iconic instances of Absurdist performance without peer. Wood must have had some form of light comedy in mind when he penned Clay's response to his co-worker asking what he was going to do, to which Johnson dutifully responds in deadpan, "Knock around a little...." And Wood undoubtedly had tongue fully in cheek when he had Lt. Harper (played by another Wood perennial, Duke Moore) warn his boss to be careful, to which the immense Clay playfully mutters, "I'm a *big boy* now, Johnny!" Not only Wood's mischievous writing talents, but his dear love for his big pal, come into play in this precious scene, one of few in Johnson's film career where he actually speaks. This is a key scene in *Plan 9* which hints at Wood's Absurdist leanings as this bizarre dialogue, filtered through a performer uniquely ill-equipped to deliver it, becomes virtually nonsensical, and suggests the appalling balderdash of a Eugene Ionesco, who said of language, "[T]he words themselves must be stretched to their utmost limits, the language must be made almost to explode, or to destroy itself in its inability to contain its meaning."[32]

The scene shifts to the backyard patio of airline pilot Jeff Trent, who is relaxing with his wife Paula (Mona McKinnon). Both are enjoying a cup of tea when an ambulance siren is heard. Paula notes, "That's the fifth siren in the past hour!" Jeff notes, "Something's happening down at the cemetery." It may take the casual viewer by surprise, but not the carefully attuned Wood fan, to note that *Plan 9*'s leading man and his wife live in precarious domestic bliss, *next door to a graveyard*. Realistically, none but the terribly poor or chronically morbid would buy property directly adjacent to a "boneyard," and this amazing fact, although narratively expedient on Wood's part, gives rise to contemplation. The brutal reality of dead flesh rotting in the dirt right next door to the cozy shelter of the Trents' backyard nicely conveys the precarious nature of the myopic postwar suburban experiment, which tried, with some success, to create innumerable pockets of fanciful autonomy and unruffled tranquility within the dangerous, unstable outside world, which carried on its agenda of endless strife and sudden death just beyond the feigned boundary of suburbia's proverbial white picket fence. At least in Wood's morbid philosophy, blissfully ignorant middle-class America lies in close proximity to "the other world" of danger, death and terror, just as Life ever resides next door to Death.

Paula notes Jeff's emotional distance, stating, "You seem to still be *up there* somewhere. I don't think I've ever seen you in this mood before." Jeff retorts, in shockingly existential Wood dialogue, "Maybe it's because I've never *been* in this mood before!" Paula's reference to "up there" may be a clue to the observant viewer that Wood's agenda is primarily spiritual, as religious symbology and references to mythological lands like "Heaven" seem to be building up speedily. As Paula pushes her husband for further details, Jeff finally confesses, "I saw a flying saucer!" Paula incredulously injects yet another "Heaven" reference by asking, "You mean the kind from *up there*?" Jeff then oddly states, "It was shaped like a *huge cigar*," when it was obviously a flying disc that both he and the viewer have witnessed. This suggests that Wood didn't bother to alter his screenplay after the design of the on-screen saucers was finalized; the extant gaffe does, however, reinforce the tendency of males in a patriarchal society to view everything in terms of phallocentric ideology. Perhaps Jeff did "see" the alien craft as saucer-like, yet chose to recall it later only in relation to his own phallus, that beloved object which he, and his brethren, attempt to imprint on all culture.[33]

Newlyweds Jeff and Paula Trent (Gregory Walcott and Mona McKinnon) ponder some ominous signs, in the form of flying saucers from outer space and graverobbers from the cemetery next door, as the sanctity of their cozy suburban fortress is shattered in Wood's apocalyptic *Plan 9 from Outer Space*.

Jeff continues to unburden himself to his partner: "Oh, it burns me up. These things have been seen for years. They're *here*! It's a *fact*! And the public oughta know about it!" As the camera meaningfully dollies into Jeff, he laments, "I can't say a word — I'm muzzled by Army brass!" This consequential line in the

Wood canon is nearly ruined by Walcott's mumbling through his annoying Southern accent, but luckily the line survives the actor's uninspired reading. This allusion to government conspiracy in general, and the military's cover-up of documented UFO sightings, taps into a popular notion of the day, and Wood's inclusion of it in *Plan 9*, expanded in profound manner shortly, was a daring, even radical act on the filmmaker's part; it would be almost a decade before government conspiracy became an accepted (and safe) topic for mainstream culture. Just as Jeff moans, "I can't even admit I saw the thing!" a blinding flash of light swoops over the patio, accompanied by a whooshing noise and a gust of wind which knocks over much of the wicker patio furniture. This perfectly timed phenomenon is meant perhaps as an omen to Jeff to reveal all he knows, regardless of consequence, or perhaps it is merely a mocking by the "gods" of flying saucers, hinting that no matter how many times he has seen them, he cannot share his knowledge with the world, for fear of mockery, persecution, or worse. It is at this point that the flying saucers seem positioned by Wood as some form of angelic surrogate, spiritual messengers from Wood's "other world," sent to earth to reveal a profound spiritual message, and/or save mankind from his fatal and endless sins. The fact that they arrived on cue to enlighten Jeff, after his vocalized lament, reinforces their allegorical, "angelic" nature, and shares much with similar dramatic tropes in the historical "Mystery Play" canon.

Back at the cemetery, the saucer passes overhead just as the gravediggers' corpses are brought via stretcher to the morgue wagon. Conveyed via a swooping spotlight, a blast of wind, and a loud roar, the commotion causes one of the corpses to drop from the stretcher and fall back to the earth where it rightfully belongs. It is also at this moment, when the saucer "reveals" itself to mankind, that one of the tombstone props in the graveyard set wobbles conspicuously. This glaring visual gaffe was not corrected by Wood in the editorial process, yet the reason, universally attributed to sloppiness or laziness, may be something more. It is at this moment when humanity in toto must take as fact this intervention by aliens, by impossible emissaries of "the other world." Considering the saucers, and their inhabitants, to be angel-surrogates, this is the moment when *Plan 9*'s scenario most vividly embraces Christian symbology. It is at this singular moment when a nearly subliminal reference would have the most impact, and a wildly gesticulating cross, that symbol of the "superhero" of Christian mythology, would effectively serve that purpose. This scene, reshot or re-edited to omit the faux pas, would mean nothing; letting it stand as it is alternately means everything in acknowledging and abetting Wood's metaphysically possessed narrative universe.

The various lawmen, also thrown to the ground by the blast, rise slowly, like corpses rising from graves, and gather their senses. Elsewhere, Inspector Clay watches in horror as the saucer lands almost directly in front of him. Bravely trekking forward, Clay soon encounters the tiny mausoleum. As he passes it, the door opens and the Old Man (henceforth referred to as listed in the cast credits: "Ghoul Man") emerges, now apparently another reanimated corpse, the face covered by his cape. As Bela Lugosi had by now passed to the great beyond, this character is played by another man, Wood's chiropodist, Tom Mason, who is conspicuously taller and younger, than the Hungarian. Although seen as a cheap stunt and a sham by many historians, this clever conceit on Wood's part was his way of not only keeping the character, but the memory of Lugosi himself alive after death, an homage done perhaps in desperation, but also out of love for the fallen thespian. As well, this "resurrection" of Lugosi, through "the magic of motion pictures," gives *Plan 9* much of its creepy metaphysical import, an observation which will lead to a miraculous revelation by film's end.

Clay continues to tromp through the barren cemetery, which in some shots is conveyed by nothing more than a black backdrop accented by some casually placed shrubbery and studio fog, looking not much like an earthbound location, but very much like Wood's beloved "other world." Finally, Clay enters an awful space where he is completely surrounded by things un-living: the Ghoul Man on one side and Vampire Girl, the Ghoul Man's wife, on the other. Both ghouls approach the man slowly, inexorably. Through an astute use of disparate editorial elements, Wood conveys the notion that Clay is simultaneously being attacked by both walking specters, and as he shoots impotently at them, they both approach menacingly from different angles. One shot in particular of Vampire Girl approaching the camera is breathtaking — arms extended, fangs exposed, she looks convincingly like a beautiful, bloodthirsty fiend.

The other cops hear gunfire and rush to their comrade's aid, but alas, it is too late — Clay is dead, and must now return to the "clay" from which he was fashioned. As the cops gravely absorb the shock of their leader's death, and the viewer accepts the murder of this sympathetic character, Harper carelessly scratches his chin with the point of his pistol and delivers another existential Woodian bon mot: "One thing's certain — Inspector Clay's dead, *murdered*, and somebody's responsible!" Harper barks orders to Officer Kelton (Paul Marco), who inevitably bungles his comic reply, being the obligatory Wood buffoon.

Clay's funeral appears to take place in the same primordial, stage-bound void as the previous action, and furthermore perhaps even in the same night, a grotesque and ghoulish thought, and another of Wood's ubiquitous temporal gaffes which adds to the utter ethereality of his film universe. This notion of "another world" is reinforced by inserted shots of the Vampire Girl observing the funeral from the wings, and appearing to be actually moved by this man's death at her own hands. Perhaps her mortal soul and its allied emotions have not been completely erased by her unholy reanimation.

As the funeral concludes, a flying saucer flies overhead, followed by another, and then another, for the first time introducing the "holy trinity" of saucers which lends to *Plan 9* much of its religious underpinning. In a marvelous Wood montage, the trio of saucers are seen flying over various stock footage landmarks of the Los Angeles area. A hilarious shot of people in a car, pointing ludicrously at the sky, is annotated with narration by Criswell: "People turning south on the freeway were startled to see three flying saucers, high over Hollywood Boulevard." This reference to Hollywood, the Culture Industry's mythical land of mass-produced "other worlds," cannot be coincidental.[34] Three subsequent stock shots reveal Wood's editorial mischief in full swing: a saucer wobbles over the CBS-TV headquarters building, in broad daylight; a saucer flies by the NBC-TV headquarters building, again in daylight; now at night, a saucer flies by the ABC-TV headquarters building. What possible reason could Wood have had for utilizing scenes identifying all three major television networks, and uncannily in their order of relative importance at the time? The last shot, of the ABC building, is delayed for a moment, so the viewer might initially surmise that the first two shots were mere coincidence, that Wood forgot about ABC, which was at that time the struggling "dark horse" of the three networks. But suddenly, there it is, completing a most unusual "trinity" of commercial broadcasting. This triad of iconic American businesses nicely reinforces the trio of saucers so recently unveiled in *Plan 9*, and considering the film's overt Christian symbology thus far, one cannot help but recall Christendom's "holy trinity," the Father, the Son and the Holy Ghost. Wood seems absolutely obsessed with inserting religious symbolism, heavy-handed though it may be, in every nook and cranny of *Plan 9*, a conceit which makes parallels to the Mystery Plays of antiquity seem ever stronger. As well, in this remarkable sequence Wood shrewdly associates the then-emerging "one-eyed monster" of television, at that very moment challenging theatrical Hollywood's hegemony in the entertainment industry, with an invading force, an almost-spiritual revolution which threatened, with its "holy trinity" of networks, to reshape modern entertainment culture in its own image and to its own advantage.

Outside a cocktail bar, another drunk looks up in the sky and sets down his bottle of whiskey, as Criswell intones amusingly, "There comes a time in each man's life when he can't even believe his own eyes!" This tongue-in-cheek comment could as well reference *Plan 9*'s by-now befuddled viewer, unsure how to respond to Wood's kaleidoscopic montage sequences. In another mischievous, and completely self-serving, use of montage in *Plan 9*, a saucer just happens to fly by the Crossroads Theatre, where the marquee claims that the head-liners are Frances Faye and June Christy; following this is another night-time scene of the Mocambo Theatre, next to Larry Finley's famous restaurant, where Eartha Kitt is the star attraction. By hitching the fantastic happenings in *Plan 9* to these familiar Hollywood haunts, likely also Wood's own stomping grounds, the filmmaker manages to connect the topograph-ical Hollywood with the myth known by the same name, and makes his intrusion of aliens into this land of self-made "stars" all the more notable and romantic. The three saucers finally swoop down convulsively against a starry outer space backdrop, as Criswell reinforces this connection, screaming ecstatically, "Saucers seen over Hollywood!" Perhaps it is Hollywood, after all, not the metaphysical land beyond death, which is truly Wood's "other world."

Plan 9 changes gears radically at this juncture and becomes, for a moment, what appears to be something akin to a traditional science-fiction melodrama; yet even here, in this most perfunctory segment of the film, Wood takes great pains to insert his own agenda. Wood's singular aesthetic quirks can likewise be seen throughout the sequence which, although look-ing superficially like any number of other "aliens vs. the military" sequences in genre films of the day, upon closer inspection stands proudly apart from its contemporaries in sheer odd-ness and insertion of fringe philosophy. As Criswell shouts, "Flying saucers seen over Wash-ington, DC!," Colonel Tom Edwards (Tom Keene, a veteran Western actor first used by Wood in his TV pilot *Crossroad Avenger*) is introduced as being "in charge of field activities." Edwards' scenes are set against a bleak, uniformly gray backdrop, another "dead space" of Wood's meant to vaguely convey the desert setting of much of the military-oriented stock footage, yet moreso conveying another visage of "the other world" which seems to reside in no identifiable time or space. Wood's use of stereotypical, peripheral characters like Edwards, more symbolic of type than of individual, is one of *Plan 9*'s most interesting dramatic quirks. What ensues after Edwards gives the signal is a violent, somewhat orgasmic montage, with stock footage of artillery shooting at nothing in particular juxtaposed with effective scenes of the model saucer(s) in the sky being accosted by flashes of light. The overtly phallic mis-siles of death are fired at the decidedly feminine spaceships, creating a most interesting abstrac-tion of the male/female binary, as acted out in an advanced technocracy. The alien ships are seemingly untouched by the Earthlings' weapons of destruction, hovering unscathed amidst the explosions, in mockery of man's futile attempts to reach them.

Criswell then chimes in, "Then, as swiftly as they had come, they were gone," another somewhat wistful observation which reinforces the notion that these craft are somehow con-nected to all things spiritual and other-worldly. As the saucers fly off-screen, a soldier walks into Edward's "dead space," at first a somewhat startling entrance, as Edwards seemed self-contained in this monochromatic womb. Edwards comments that these "visitors" have come before, to which the suddenly pacifistic soldier treasonously quips, "Are big guns our usual way of welcoming visitors?" Edwards retorts with a bizarre, cryptic comment which suggests suppressed history at its most nefarious: "We haven't always fired at them. For a time we tried to contact them by radio, but no response. Then they attacked a town; a small town, I'll admit, but nevertheless a town of people, people who died." Edwards then drops a bomb which reinforces a popular paranoia of the day: "It was covered up by the higher echelon." Government conspiracy, as mentioned, is always on the mind of Wood, and here it is presented as a key narrative point which will be expanded upon shortly.

Edwards concludes with another disturbing edict: "Take any fire, any earthquake, any major disaster, then wonder...." In response to the soldier's distress, Edwards concludes with, "Flying saucers are still a rumor, captain — *officially*." This revelation of government duplicity cuts to a stock shot of three U.S. Air Force F-86 Sabre Jets flying off in formation, and most significantly flying *away* from the viewer, perfectly illustrating how a surreptitious government's technocratic dominance is sustained via secrecy and subterfuge. Returning to Edwards' "dead space," he mutters with uncharacteristic vulnerability, "What do they want? Where are they from? Where are they going?" The soldier, having quickly picked up his superior's message, and more than willing to perpetuate the systemic program of silence and conspiracy, responds coyly, "*They*, sir? Why, this is a training maneuver, sir! We only did a little practice firing at the clouds!" Without acknowledging the soldier's complicity, Edwards signals a scene change via an antique plot device: "I wonder what their next move will be?"

The "holy trinity" of saucers now return to their "other world," i.e., outer space, and specifically to a large mother ship, an impressive if simple globe-like model set against a starry cosmic backdrop. This and other miniature scenes in *Plan 9*, thoroughly mocked by detractors over the years, are in fact no worse than many miniatures-based special effects scenes for similar science-fiction pictures produced during the decade obsessed with space travel, and are arguably better than some.[35] The interior of the "mother ship," either ironically or intuitively, is decidedly "female" in character. The background of the ship's control room are glistening stage curtains; the alien furniture is easily identified as a random cobbling of garden-variety Early American; the main figure, who sits at a large desk adorned with war-surplus electronics paraphernalia, will turn out to be flamboyantly homosexual.

A man dressed in what looks like modified silk pajamas makes a grand entrance through the curtains, gestures by crossing his arms, and announces, "Your space commander has returned from Earth." Two more "aliens" (Dudley Manlove and Joanna Lee) enter, also dressed in the silk jackets. The Ruler (John "Bunny" Breckenridge), feigning indifference, wheezily asks, "What progress has been made?" The male alien, known as Eros, reports haughtily, "We contacted government officials — they refuse our existence!," which recalls General Edwards' observation that the U.S. military had tried to communicate with the aliens, but were met with silence. Obviously, either one party is lying, or there is an utter lack of communication between species, an interesting comment on the inability of different races and species to transmit common goals and thus peacefully co-exist, a universal defect symbolized here by the barrier of language.

Breckenridge, another of Wood's "larger than life" characters, brings to his role as The Ruler all the foppish pomp attendant to a Hollywood-based libertine, and perhaps unwittingly infuses the characters of the aliens with an arrogance which may not have been delineated in Wood's original script. Many lurid details of Breckenridge's fascinating life can be uncovered in Rudolph Grey's *Nightmare of Ecstasy*.[36] The Ruler, placing his tongue firmly in cheek, almost as a cue to the viewer, queries, "What plan will you follow now?" Eros confidently barks the iconic answer, "Plan 9!"[37] The Ruler picks up a sheaf of papers which may well be his shooting script and reads, stumblingly, "Plan 9? Ah yes. Plan 9 deals with the resurrection of the dead. Long-distance electrodes shot into the pineal pituitary glands of recent dead." As well as sloppily giving away *Plan 9*'s basic plot point, the line cleverly reveals the film's major theme, for "Plan 9 deals with the resurrection of the dead" and more importantly, attendant spiritual and moral concerns. Eros reports that he has "risen two so far," and the viewer now makes the connection between the walking Vampire Girl and Ghoul Man and alien intervention. Far from diminishing the supernatural import of the undead couple which prowls the Hollywood cemetery, this revelation makes their reanimation even more heinous and unearthly, and makes these seemingly genteel aliens seem all but necromantic; they are, literally, graverobbers from outer space. As well, the aliens' ability to resurrect the earthbound dead makes them certainly more than mortal, super-human by definition, and reinforces the notion that they are some form of spiritual messengers from "the other world."

Leaving the Ruler's "office," Eros and his female colleague, Tanna, converse in an outside corridor which is dressed similarly to the airplane cockpit seen earlier. Discussing what obstacles they may encounter, Eros hilariously pontificates, folding his arms for heightened dramatic effect: "You know, it's an interesting thing when you consider the Earth people, who can *think*, are so frightened by those who *cannot*—the dead." This is a sublimely absurd yet profound thought, in sum a brilliant existentialist meditation which underscores one of *Plan 9*'s core themes, that Man is demonstrably terrified of Death, and cannot progress spiritually until he makes peace with this black terror which, in this scenario, *literally* hounds his every waking step. It may likewise have been insight or serendipity that encouraged Wood to dub his angelic aliens Eros and Tanna, names which cannot help but evoke the names of Eros and Thanatos, the gods of Sex and Death.

Via more impressive miniature work, the saucers leave the mother ship and return to Earth. The scene returns to the Trents' patio with the view of the cemetery. Jeff emerges from the house in full uniform, about to depart on another flight. He advises Paula to go home to Mother (perhaps referencing the just-seen "mother ship") for protection after all the gruesomeness at the next-door boneyard, but the feisty woman holds her ground. As Jeff grabs Paula in his arms, the camera dollies in, and Paula cracks, "If you see any more flying saucers, will you tell 'em to pick another house to buzz?" The humorless Jeff retorts, "There's *something* in that cemetery, and that's too close for comfort." The ever-present specter of mortal death, which haunts the human soul from birth to grave, is that "something" in the cemetery, and their creepy proximity to the place assures that this young couple will have morbidity on their minds throughout their matrimonial career. The comment also reinforces the earlier notion of staid suburbia forever attempting to strike a precarious balance between serenity and danger, symbolized by the close proximity of middle-class America to war, destruction, and death, occurring just beyond the relative, and patently false, security of the fenced-in backyard.

Playing the obedient 1950s-era wife, Paula attempts to soothe Jeff's nerves, and ego, by stating another clever Wood line: "The saucers are *up there*, and the cemetery's *out there*, but I'll be locked up *in there*!" Here, Paula has just bolstered the shaky argument of suburbia being a tranquil, safe harbor against the dangers of the "outside world"; as long as she stays "in there," and not "out there," Paula assumes she will be fine. This myopic faith in the impenetrability of her pasteboard domicile will be severely shattered in short order. Paula then coyly adds, "Besides, I'll have your *pillow* beside me...." Jeff is confused, so Paula clarifies: "Well, I have to have *something* to keep me company while you're away!" Here, the pillow is clearly posed as a sexual surrogate for the missing male, and hints at sexual frustration by the female, or sexual inadequacy by the male. Paula extrapolates: "Sometimes at night, when it does get a little lonely, I reach over and *touch it*. Then it doesn't seem so lonely any more." This ambiguous statement likely refers to the aforementioned pillow-surrogate, yet it could as easily refer to Paula's untouched genitals, implying the need for female masturbation in the absence of a live, willing sex partner. This allusion to sexual barrenness in suburbia will have a most devastating illustration shortly, as the female in question will be threatened by sexual violence emanating from the dangerous world "out there."

Meanwhile a saucer, now with its landing cylinder extended, descends towards the cemetery, followed by a most rare occurrence in a Wood film — a passionate kiss between a man and a woman. Jeff kisses Paula, and as he leaves he orders his wife, whom he obviously considers property, to lock herself inside the house. As Jeff walks to his car, which sits in another of *Plan 9*'s abundant ethereal voids, Paula playfully shatters Jeff's presumptuous peace of mind by popping out of the locked door and jesting, "If you're especially nice, I *may* even lock the side door," a comment which coyly suggests the possibility of sexual infidelity. Paranoid Jeff responds with, "And be sure you keep the yard lights on," but Walcott's enunciation is so sloppy, it sounds like he is saying, "And be sure you keep the *urine* lights on," another odd subliminal reference to a (largely repressed) obsession with his wife's genital region.

The American Airlines DC-7 is soon airborne, with Jeff and Danny back again in their "pretend" cockpit. Danny notes Jeff's quietness, and Jeff admits that he is preoccupied with Paula's safety, and fidelity, at home; her sexually loaded remarks were not lost on the dullard after all. Edie the stewardess bursts through the shower curtains at this sexually tense moment, almost a manifestation of Jeff's disembodied guilt, and suggests that Jeff attempt to communicate with his wife via radio. Danny then boldly propositions Edie: "Hey, Edie, how about you an' me ballin' it up in Albuquerque?" Edie graciously declines, and the discussion turns to the innate morbidity of taking residence next to a graveyard. Edie scolds Jeff with a remark which reveals her intrinsic wisdom: "I tried to get you kids not to buy too near one of those things—*we get there soon enough as it is.*" Edie then scurries off to make coffee for the men, and eventually accepts Danny's proposition for a later date. After this stereotypical female has obediently fulfilled all possible duties to the assembled males, serving them in every way imaginable, the scene's closure with another stock shot of the shiny phallic airliner soaring proudly through the heavens seems almost diabolically sexist on Wood's part.

Next comes another stock shot of thunder and lightning, which alerts the viewer to the scene which follows, amazing footage of the real Bela Lugosi as the Ghoul Man, suddenly "resurrected" from the dead as prophesied by the introduction of Lugosi's double earlier, and seen moving in broad daylight through a real graveyard. Accented by two giant wooden crosses, Lugosi walks majestically to mid-frame and raises his caped arms dramatically, for a brief moment recreating his iconic pose as Dracula, the Prince of Darkness, and invoking, for one last time mere months before his death, his dramatic masterpiece. It is nothing short of stunning that Wood managed to bring Lugosi to this grand moment near the end of his life, and to record it for posterity. Lugosi smiles grandly, unable to contain his joy at being briefly able to capture this most beloved character on film one last time. Lugosi then covers his face with the cape, turns and exits the graveyard, in effect bidding farewell to his audience. Criswell annotates this momentous scene thusly: "Residents near the cemetery paid little attention to the blast of thunder and the flash of lightning, but from the blast arose the moving figure of the dead Old Man..." and the viewer realizes retroactively that in this case, the stock footage of a thunderstorm was not intended merely as an aesthetic point or author signature on Wood's part, but as *narrative*, again showing Wood's astute editorial mischief in full play. Not only does the viewer never know whether a scene depicted is intended as real or metaphorical, but footage may be intended as exposition, documentary or ambience, as Wood switches between modes effortlessly and with flair.

Lugosi is next briefly seen as the Ghoul Man, walking to the back door of a real house, which the viewer assumes is the Trents'. The next scene takes place inside their bedroom, where Paula sleeps soundly, an open book lying near her, apparently having satisfied her sexual loneliness in some manner. Paula wears a sexy, frilly nightgown, as only Wood would have his heroine, and which reinforces the notion of possible sexual play. The phone rings, waking Paula up from her dream reverie. Paula answers the call from "Mac" (a recurring Wood character name), the airport control tower operator. Assuring him that she's all right, Paula briskly hangs up, more disturbed than relieved at her husband's concern, which has all the flavor of an insecure mate's checking up on a wayward spouse. Suddenly the Ghoul Man, now represented by Lugosi's stand-in, enters the sacred space of the bedroom, his face covered by his cape in a vain attempt to obscure the obvious switching of actors. Paula looks on in sheer horror and runs screaming out of the bedroom, with the undead "thing" following slowly behind. This scene is a primitive yet viable depiction of dark sexual fantasies on the part of the American middle class, combining various elements, including the fear of sexual attack from a stranger, an older man and, most provocatively, a foreigner. Also, the awareness on the viewer's part that this dark predator is, in fact, *dead*, underlines the previous allusion (by the Trents' proximity to the cemetery) that postwar life was not merely precariously close to death, but was in fact actively stalked by death. Even worse, this undead thing has forced Paula out of the fake security of her suburban fortress into the black terror of "the other world."

As Paula runs through the studio cemetery set, her frilly nightwear flowing in the ethereal fog, *Plan 9*'s main theme music plays, suggesting that perhaps "plan 9" is much more than the mere resurrection of the dead, but involves the sexual conquest of Earth as well. After another brief shot of Lugosi as the Ghoul Man, running out of the house, the scene returns to the studio cemetery, and Paula continues to run past the same grave markers over and over again, a temporal disorientation which evokes the common dream motif of running while standing still. An insert shot of Vampire Girl, watching as always from the wings, shows her eyes widening in apparent concern or anger; she appears disturbed to see her "dead" husband chasing a living blonde! This unlikely reaction from the she-zombie suggests that earthly emotions linger in the newly dead, and that there may be such a thing as adultery after death. In a time-honored if sexist narrative cliché, Paula then trips and falls on a patch of cemetery weeds; in patriarchal lore as well as male-dominated popular culture, the female must always be drawn as defective, fragile, prone to accident, in order to be the "inferior" love object — in need of constant rescue — which dominates collective male fantasy.

Returning briefly again to a daylight exterior scene, Lugosi as the Ghoul Man tromps around the location cemetery, in a shot which further derails the narrative thread of the already inchoate scene. This aesthetic jolt serves to prepare the viewer for the following, wildly artificial shot of a miniature grave, complete with tiny grave marker, and the earth surrounding it convulsing like it were alive, or breathing. This is arguably the *worst* shot in *Plan 9*, that is, the least convincing from a traditional perspective. The already precarious suspension of disbelief, brutally assaulted thus far in the film, is shattered beyond repair here, and this shot signals the film's irrevocable collapse into allegorical, non-representational territory. Some have thus argued that this shot is the *best* in the film, as it is the most obtuse and false.

Back at the studio cemetery, awash in eternal darkness, Vampire Girl walks away from the camera, and then turns and looks directly back at it, in an overtly flirtatious gesture. Now portrayed via stand-in, the Ghoul Man prowls the same dead space, as Paula continues to run through the same section of graveyard, caught in some horrible time warp of the master Wood's creation. Returning to the impossible model gravesite, the grave now vomits forth mounds of heaving earth, and soon, the grave caves in, leaving a gaping black hole where a coffin should be. Vampire Girl, unawares, walks across the cemetery. Paula runs in the opposite direction, through the same patch of cemetery, her cruel Sisyphisian travails annotated with a crudely overdubbed scream.

One of *Plan 9*'s most beloved scenes follows, the veritable jewel in this extraordinary montage, as the corpse of Inspector Clay, now animated by the aliens, rises out of his grave. It is only now that the viewer realizes that the preposterous model shots of the tiny grave caving in were meant to symbolize the grave of Clay, opening up to release his "resurrected" corpse. This shocking cheat is perhaps the best example thus far of Wood's "symbolic" special effects, meant as a mere sketch of what he might have committed to film given more time, money and talent. The scene reverts to the studio cemetery set as Clay slowly, and quite awkwardly, attempts to pull himself up out of his grave. The first thing the viewer notes is that his grave appears to be *illuminated from within*, a poetic touch on Wood's part which suggests the abundant spiritual energy still attached to recently deceased, their spirits literally co-habitating with the lost flesh in this final resting place. The 400-pound Johnson understandably has difficulty climbing out of the makeshift pit created for him, and the shot cuts just as it appears he is about to either keel over, or knock over the tombstone directly behind him. The continuity shot which follows shows Clay, his face now set in a ghoulish grimace, already outside the grave pit, standing upright. Clay's eyes are now rendered eerily vacant, thanks to contact lenses furnished by makeup man Harry Thomas.[38] Johnson's blank stare, with a gaping black mouth, is one of those uncanny shots in *Plan 9* which are actually effective in conveying a sketchy horror-film verisimilitude. (It was undoubtedly veteran director of photography William C. Thompson who gave *Plan 9* its uncanny visual flair; Wood had the foresight to know that good cinematography covers many ills.)

The following scene shows Paula running yet again along the same patch of studio-bound gravesites. This time, the viewer can clearly see one of the primitive wooden crosses used as a grave marker lying flat on the ground, the wooden dowel used to anchor it to the studio floor sticking up impotently. Once again, the viewer is faced with the stark, ironic "reality" of Wood's shameless non-representational universe. The startling montage continues: Clay looks around, in a zombie-like trance; the Ghoul Man, conveyed via stand-in, skulks about; Clay finally gets his bearings and trudges off, stage left. In another brilliant touch of raw filmic poetry, after Clay leaves his open grave, the scene returns ever-so-briefly to the horrible model gravesite again, just long enough to see the now-compromised tombstone falling into the pit. Almost as a reaction to the patent artifice of the scene, there follows a brief shot of Vampire Girl looking displeased, even disgusted, at Wood's daring subterfuge of all reasonable editorial and narrative sensibility. Paula runs, finally, through a demonstrably different patch of cemetery, her frilly nightgown still flowing seductively in the fog-machine ether. Clay walks menacingly towards camera, arms outstretched and face in full grimace. The Ghoul Man tromps through the same cemetery patch, carefully walking around the various tombstones and markers as a lumbering, brain-dead zombie would never do.

Finally, this ghastly, claustrophobic sequence opens up via a shocking exterior scene of Paula running through a field and falling, and being spotted by a motorist in a fancy convertible. Yet the scene mercilessly cuts *back* to the gloomy studio set, where the Ghoul Man continues his advance. Back again to the exterior setting, where the motorist rushes to assist the fallen woman. Recognizing her, the motorist shakes her, shouting, "Mrs. Trent! Mrs. Trent! What's wrong?" The motorist looks in both directions and, judging by insert shots of Vampire Girl and Inspector Clay, the viewer must assume that the driver has spotted these ghouls from hell himself, each enveloped in their own secular zones. The driver picks up Paula, puts her in his car, and prepares to beat a hasty retreat.

Following this is another exterior shot featuring Bela Lugosi, one last time, as the Ghoul Man, looking off-camera with anger. Back in the "real" world, the driver has difficulty starting his car, and one final studio-bound shot of the Ghoul Man, portrayed via stand-in in the

An iconic image from Wood's hyper-religious *Plan 9 from Outer Space*. The man and the woman (Tor Johnson and Maila Nurmi), voiceless archetypes of society degraded, wander aimlessly through an existential netherworld, unaware that their resurrected spirits will become the mechanism by which civilization narrowly escapes from utter oblivion.

graveyard set, breaks this singular scene beyond all repair. This accruing and glaring discontinuity shares much with Wood's fantastic editorial trickery in *Bride of the Monster*, wherein he recklessly juxtaposed imagery of his rubber octopus prop against stock shots of a real octopus, to strain the limits of credibility and playfully taunt his audience by asking, "Which one is real, which one is not, and *does it matter?*" The motorist finally starts the car and drives off, just as the Ghoul Man, once again played by the stand-in, approaches, yet this time in an *exterior* shot, which even further subverts the aesthetic and temporal coherence of the piece. Heretofore, a shaky subjective constancy was achieved by the viewer's understanding that it was Lugosi who played the Ghoul Man in the exterior scenes, while stand-in Mason played them in the studio-bound interiors. With this one brief shot, which shows this character crossing the supposedly sacred line between exterior and interior, inner and outer, representational and non-representational, Wood removes even this meager point of narrative security, and with an almost diabolical gusto warns the viewer that no set boundaries are ever to be taken for granted in his subversive "cinema of cruelty."

Their prey safely rescued from their clutches, and their tasks in the subversion of narrative cinema completed for now, the Ghoul Man, Vampire Girl and Inspector Clay all turn and stumble back to the cemetery, all entrenched in their own distinct, antithetical spatial worlds. This harrowing, irrational montage engages multiple characters in a remarkable editorial choreography, and is as deft a use of disparate film elements as Wood's magnificent montages in *Glen or Glenda?*. Here, the random juxtaposition of interior/exterior, day/night, dead/alive and other assorted dichotomies underline Wood's absolute fixation on real vs. unreal, on earthly existence versus the quixotic allure of "the other world." The constant aesthetic and narrative tension in Wood's films address in simplistic yet undeniably memorable form the eternal tension between material and spiritual planes of existence. This lifelong obsession, noted often in Wood's writings, may be the primary muse in his film work as well; the recurring motif of death and resurrection, often of sympathetic main characters, attests to this fixation.

Some time later, the police again return to the studio cemetery "stage," as before driving an automobile which changes make and model right before the viewer's eyes, with Wood again indiscriminately switching "symbols" meant to evoke, in some expositional netherworld, "the real thing." The car which arrives at the studio set, in fact, has no official markings of any kind, and affords its occupants a certain generic, "everyman" quality. As several cops prowl about, an exterior cemetery shot of Lugosi as the Ghoul Man continues to upset the viewer's sense of temporal and narrative continuity. Here, Lugosi shakes his fist in anger, wraps his cape around him, and makes a grand exit. Back at the studio cemetery, Inspector Clay and Vampire Girl, now for the first time seen as a couple, plod through the graveyard, arms outstretched. As visually different as night and day, the hulking, dumpy Johnson and the emaciated, sexy Nurmi come as close to a living embodiment of Charles Addams' creepy bourgeois cartoon couple as anything since committed to screen, yet aesthetically they go together well, and invoke yet another unique binary in the multifarious universe which is *Plan 9*. This unlikely yet inimitable duo creates a playful parody of the postwar suburban couple who appear to be "sleepwalking" through life (or in this case, death); they cast a humorous, yet devastating light on the traditional heterosexual unit, portraying the 1950s-era heterosexual couple as soulless, mindless, obedient ghouls who are easily made the zombie-servants of phallocentric technocracy.

The next scene introduces what will soon be verified as the interior of the alien's flying saucer, although no continuity shots are offered to confirm this. As Eros and Tanna look out the rectangular portholes of their craft, the viewer gets a baffling glance at the spacecraft furnishings. Several disparate pieces of electronics equipment, including an electric-arc generator commonly known as a Jacob's Ladder, sit on two shabby wooden workbenches, with no attempt whatsoever made to make them appear extraterrestrial. Wood's bold daring in submitting these obviously terrestrial emblems as signs of supra-intelligent life from other worlds again shows the author's predilection for complete indifference to traditional verisimilitude in his melodramatic *mise-en-scène*, wherein the barely passable must pass as "symbols" of what a spaceship set might look like given the resources to do it "correctly." By bravely crafting these patently artificial worlds, Wood enlightens his audience to the beauties of "artistic license," as he constantly referred to it,[39] which in his case really described a unique filmic poetry. These fake worlds as well remind the viewers, *a la* Bertolt Brecht's non-representational "epic" theatre, that they are watching a play, not witnessing reality, yet ironically suggesting at the same time that this "fantasy" may contain more poetic truth in it than the barren, mundane reality of the "real world."

As Tanna strolls across the spaceship cabin, the viewer spies more evidence of *Plan 9*'s reckless abandon at conveying atmosphere. The wall which contains the outer door of the spaceship is easily seen as the same wall, and porthole, first seen as the American Airliner cockpit. Even worse, the same flight computer or "whiz wheel" which hung on the wall of the airliner cockpit also hangs on the alien's wall. Other props, such as a common office chair, a wooden ladder, and what appears to be a railroad timetable taped to the wall, further add to the delirious non-reality of the set. As Inspector Clay and Vampire Girl enter the spaceship, the angle of the scene changes, and even more exciting patchwork *mise-en-scène* can be espied, the most exciting revelation being that the same large wooden desk used by the Ruler has been transplanted verbatim into this spaceship interior. The desk boasts two commonplace electronic instruments which appear to be a ham radio set and an oscilloscope, and on the middle of the desk sits a pile of papers and a fountain-pen holder. This striking attempt by Wood to convey the notion that the aliens are thoroughly humanoid, and very much like us, will have an interesting conclusion by film's end.[40] Eros reinforces this notion with his observation, "They can't tell *us* from anyone else!"

Eros watches as Tanna quickly switches off the electrode impulses to the two ghouls, who enter the ship and then de-animate, standing comatose. A memorable close-up of Inspector Clay and Vampire Girl reveals impressively vacant expressions, a vibrant Woodian sketch which again portrays the postwar heterosexual couple as dumb automaton sheep. Outside the ship, the Ghoul Man, portrayed via stand-in, approaches the entry hatch. The spaceship exterior is even more threadbare than the interior, portrayed by two flats positioned at a right angle, with the hatch and the same wooden ladder the only visible details. Meanwhile, police officers Jamie (Conrad Brooks) and Kelton (Paul Marco) skulk about the cemetery; Jamie soon utters another delightfully philosophical Wood remark: "It's tough to find something, when you don't know what you're looking for!" Soon, the saucer model ascends in front of a photograph of an actual cemetery, assisted in the subterfuge by some wispy smoke and a "whooshy" sound effect.

Kelton and Jamie join Inspector Harper and Patrolman Larry (Carl Anthony) and discuss the recent bizarre phenomena. Kelton casually mentions finding a recently opened grave, and the group rushes off to investigate. Here, Marco again tries to imbue the scene with some comic import, and again fails miserably. Kelton's inclusion in *Plan 9* seems a vain attempt to make the scenario serio-comic, when in fact Wood has already achieved "high comedy" with the bizarre editorial conceits and daring *mise-en-scène*; using Kelton as a conscious effort at comic relief here, as well as in *Bride of the Monster* and *Night of the Ghouls*, seems either a misguided dramatic endeavor, or a careless afterthought. Yet for better or worse, Marco is Wood's "imp," a Skid Row analog to "Puck" of Shakespeare's *A Midsummer Night's Dream*, a quasi-demonic creature whose caustic comments on the proceedings attempt to enlighten and inform both fellow characters and the audience.

Elected to go into the grave to read the tombstone, sad-sack Kelton pseudo-comically replies, "Why do I always get hooked up with these spook details? Monsters! Graves! Bodies!" Kelton climbs down into the open pit, which is conveyed metaphorically again, via two planks of wood at right angles, with some shrubbery attached to the top. Kelton timidly discloses, "Casket's here, but nobody's in it!" Harper throws Kelton a pack of matches; lighting one, Kelton discovers that it is the grave of their beloved boss, confirming, "It's Inspector Clay's grave, but he ain't in it!" With this revelation, the flickering match thus acts as a memorial to their fallen hero.

The scene changes to the Pentagon building in Washington, D.C. An Army general (Lyle Talbot, a prolific character actor who had also appeared in Wood's *Crossroad Avenger*) inhabits a tiny office which is decorated primarily with photographs of outer space scenes and inexplicably, a Santa Fe Railroad map of the United States. This same map can also be seen as a backdrop in Phil Tucker's striptease comedy *Baghdad After Midnight* (1954), also filmed at Quality Studios, so the map was likely an in-house prop available to anyone shooting there. "The general," who is given no surname and who subsequently comes across as an archetypal representative of the Military-Industrial Complex, is first seen concluding a clandestine phone conversation with another party identified only as "G2," a delightfully paranoid reference to occlusive government conspiracy.

Colonel Edwards enters, and in a fuller shot of the office, further simplistic props are observed, including several missile models, a framed painting of the solar system, and what appears to be a plaque for undisclosed meritorious service. The general baits Edwards by asking him, point blank, "Do you believe there are such things as flying saucers, colonel?" Edwards hesitantly replies in the affirmative, aware that the answer may be construed as treason, punishable by court-martial. The general, lighting a cigarette, finally admits to his nervous colleague, "There *are* flying saucers. No doubt they are in our skies. They've been there for some time." Edwards' apparent incredulity at this admission by his commanding officer is out of place, as the viewer recalls that he recently told a soldier about flying saucers attacking a town and killing its inhabitants. Either Edwards is forgetful, or playing it safe in this potentially treacherous meeting with "the higher echelon."

The general reveals, "We've had contact with them, by radio," and acknowledges that the U.S. military has received messages which at first appeared to be "just a lot of jumbled noise." Now, the government has developed a "language computer" which "can break down any language into our own." The general turns on a reel-to-reel tape recorder, and the message unspools, spoken via the didactic voice of Eros. The message reveals that the aliens desire peaceful coexistence with the earthlings, but fear Man's penchant for creating ever-increasing weapons of mass destruction. The aliens have intervened at this juncture in order to halt this accelerating tendency towards self-destruction and to forge a mutual alliance. Failing that, the aliens threaten to destroy mankind, so that Man cannot contaminate the universe with his neurotic "death wish." This cautionary "message from the stars" was ubiquitous in 1950s science-fiction cinema, and popular literature before that, with its first manifestation in the movies possibly being *The Day The Earth Stood Still* (1951, d: Robert Wise). As well as venting a knee-jerk misanthropy on the part of its authors, it cleverly delineates in abstracted form the essential message of many of the world's religions—that man is too much of the flesh, too impulsive, destructive and headstrong, i.e., sinful, and must change his ways, i.e., repent, if he is ever to find peace amongst his fellows and salvation for eternity. As did many science-fiction films before it, *Plan 9* also adheres to the notion of using space aliens as surrogate religious representatives; this film, however, takes this conceit in some unusual directions, as seen. As the message plays, Edwards and the general smirk and grimace and shake their heads at Eros' arrogance and misanthropy, but in fact he is correct: Humanity is everything he accuses them of, and more. Man is in fatal denial about his innumerable flaws, as illustrated so well by the military men's mockery of both message and messenger. The general summons Edwards over to the Santa Fe Railroad map, as the camera dollies in, and asks, "Ever been to Hollywood?" Responding in the negative, Edwards is assigned to go there to solve these recent mysteries of opened graves, resurrected dead and flying saucers over Hollywood. Handing Edwards a top secret portfolio, the general bids the man adieu.

Now returning to the mother ship, the aliens report again to the Ruler. This fuller shot of the mother ship interior boasts a newly seen, fascinating feature—a valance at the top of the back curtain, which gives the set an overt sense of being a "stage," and gives the resultant drama the unshakable sense of being "theatre." An amusing gaffe reinforces the notion that Wood always filmed in a hurry, and rarely re-shot a scene unless absolutely necessary: As the Ruler enters, he waves his hand for his "secretary" to depart, yet the man stands by the curtain, unmoving. It is only when the Ruler finally sits down and clicks an equipment switch does the inferior briskly leave the set, obviously having been cued by Wood to do so at this time. As the man leaves, the Ruler gives him a brief, withering glance which can only be described as a dirty look, an interesting sketch of failed power dynamics and orders unheeded, at both the character and actor level.

Eros defensively informs the Ruler of their travails on Earth, explaining that their tardiness in implementing Plan 9 on the Earthlings' discovery of their saucers. As the Ruler sits back in his chair to absorb this information, the camera dollies in, and the viewer can clearly see the ax-and-handle insignia on his vest, verifying that Wood grabbed this Arthurian garb off the rack at the local costume shop, and reinforcing the assumption that Wood saw his aliens as spiritually attuned humanoid analogues. The Ruler desires to see a resurrected corpse, so Eros orders Tanna to bring in a "victim" using her small electrode gun. As Tanna leaves to fetch the subject, the Ruler informs Eros that he has taken two saucers from his command, leaving him only the one. Eros complains, but the Ruler duly lectures Eros about his need to prove himself before earning a larger army. Breckenridge, as the Ruler, once again looks to the script, hidden behind an electronic apparatus, as he gives this speech; his reliance on the physical script, alongside his melodramatic portrayal, outlandish costume and woebegone interior furnishings, elevates all of the "mother ship" scenes to the level of pure Brechtian theatre.

Suddenly there is a close-up of the curtains, and a heavily made-up Tor Johnson walks in, as the risen corpse of Inspector Clay. The zombie has milky white contact lenses for eyes, and several amateurish scars on his face, but his dull, open-mouthed grimace conveys much terror. High drama ensues as Clay lumbers menacingly towards Eros, who whimpers to Tanna to "turn off your electrode gun!" A clumsy insert shot of Tanna shows her futilely fumbling with the (probably toy) firearm. Clay is about to strangle Eros, when the Ruler finally intervenes, telling Tanna to drop the gun to the floor so that the electrical contacts will be short-circuited. Tanna does this just in time and Clay loosens his grip on Eros, who wobbles to stage center and wheezes, "That was ... *too close!*" The Ruler rolls his eyes, apparently bemused by his subordinate's ineptness and woeful line delivery.

The Ruler slowly walks to his desk and sits down, once more rolling his eyes in hilarious affectation, and stumbles over his next line, "Bring the giant here, that I may ... get a better look at him." Following an impressive, brief close-up of Clay, eyes wide yet blank, mouth in a hideous expression of ghoulish terror, Eros carefully walks the giant over to the Ruler's desk. The Ruler contemplates Clay's hulk for a moment, and then says excitedly, "This gives me a plan!" Tanna removes Clay from the operations chamber with her suddenly repaired electrode gun, and the Ruler fills in Eros: "The old one must be sacrificed." This odd aside has portent, as Wood uses the death and rebirth of Bela Lugosi in *Plan 9* almost in a ritual sense. The Ruler's ridiculous plan involves sending the Ghoul Man into an Earth dwelling, turning off the animating charge, and using a "decomposing ray" to turn him into a pile of bones and ashes, which he feels will scare the humans into believing that the aliens mean business. As the Ruler gushes, "The result will astound those watching!" the reference could refer as well to *Plan 9*'s audience, who will shortly be astounded at another of Wood's fantastically symbolic, magical transformations. The Ruler rises and walks to the curtain's edge, followed by the camera. He gives Eros the following scenario: "As soon as you have enough of the dead recruits, march them on the capitals of the world. Let nothing stand in your way!" The Ruler slowly turns and walks through the curtains, and the viewer marvels at how Wood has managed to imply an epic-level apocalypse merely with a line of lyrical, poorly emoted dialogue.

Back on Earth, the cops return to the cemetery, now taking Colonel Edwards along with them. Once again they proceed in differing automobiles, and once again they arrive in pitch darkness. While Kelton and Jamie wait at the car, Edwards and Harper visit the Trents on their cozy patio, Wood's emblematic setting of postwar domestic bliss. Edwards questions

Jeff about his sighting of the flying saucer. On cue, a model saucer descends on the nearby cemetery. Paula also tells her saucer story to a befuddled Edwards. Edwards then asks the couple whether the gust of wind which accompanied the saucer was hot or cold, seemingly a trivial point, yet Jeff tellingly maintains that the wind was *neither* hot nor cold. This observation may strengthen the viewer's hunch that the saucers in *Plan 9* are symbolic spirits, angels or messengers of a sort, and that they came not from outer space, but from some parallel universe, i.e., "the other world." Back at the cemetery, the saucer's landing cylinder door opens and the Ghoul Man, now reanimated (and portrayed by Lugosi stand-in Tom Mason), leaves the saucer to play the Ruler's trick on the humans. However, the subsequent shot returns to the actual Sacramento cemetery, where Lugosi reprises his role as the Ghoul Man, stomping menacingly through the grass.

On the Trents' patio, Edwards concludes, "That's the most fantastic story I've ever heard." Jeff replies, "And every word of it's *true!*" Edwards confirms, "That's the fantastic part!" In Wood's "other world," the "truth" is stranger than any possible fiction. The group at the cemetery continue to investigate, and Harper confesses, "I can't help thinking that *the answer* is out here somewhere." Wood suggests here that the answers to the mysteries of life are to be found in his cosmic void, which represents the thin line between life and death, astutely illustrated in *Plan 9* with this highly "symbolic" graveyard.

The group on the patio soon feel the presence of something evil approaching, and the music ominously builds until Kelton points his gun at a horrifying cloaked figure (Tom Mason as the Ghoul Man) which approaches the police car. Soon, Kelton is seen backing up onto the patio, with the Ghoul Man following close behind, as the others look on in terror. Finally, the Ghoul Man judo-chops Kelton, momentarily losing his cape but quickly catching it. Harper fires at the Ghoul Man, but bullets cannot fell the dead. A glow is seen coming from behind a grove of trees at the outskirts of the cemetery, and a beam of light shoots out from behind the trees. The "decomposer ray" reaches the Ghoul Man, who falls to the ground like a stone. Edwards flips aside the cape from the still figure, and all are shocked to see that what once walked the earth is now nothing more than a perfectly clean human skeleton. Harper revives the fallen Kelton, who delivers more tired comic dialogue as the scene ends. This wonderfully metaphoric scene shows Death *literally* assaulting Life, represented by an amazing societal microcosm which *Plan 9* assembles at this iconic suburban locale: male, female, peace officer, war monger, boss and laborer. The community as a group gathers together, and cowers before, this specter of their own mortality, conveyed so purely, so simply, by Wood's "walking skeleton." And certainly the real *magic* trick on Wood's part is the bold, shockingly theatrical substitution of Bela Lugosi, first with the stand-in, and finally with the medical-lab skeleton. This miraculous scene perfectly embodies the spirit of the Theatre of the Absurd, whose creators attempted to enlighten and inform, "based on suddenly confronting their audiences with a grotesquely heightened and distorted picture of a world that has gone mad."[41]

A short while later, the group returns to the cemetery, in their incessant, seemingly ill-fated quest to find some tangible answers to life's insoluble riddles. As the men prepare to explore the graveyard, Harper orders Paula to stay by the police car, but the plucky 1950s heroine replies, "Stay here alone? Not on your *life!*" Harper snottily replies, "Modern women!" Edwards counters, "Yeah, they been *that way* all down through the ages—especially in a spot like this!" By "that way," the misogynist military man means stubborn and stupid, but Paula's decidedly nonconformist actions more accurately illustrate actions which might be described as brave and autonomous. Patriarchal culture being what it is, Harper orders his inferior, Kelton, to "guard" (i.e., detain) the woman, and Jeff quickly reinforces this edict, in order to "protect her" from the evil world out there. Paula is clearly upset by this decision made without her input. Seeing the clownish half-man who is guarding her, Paula implores her husband, "I'd feel safer with you!" Immediately following this declaration, there is a marvelous insert shot of Vampire Girl walking slowly through the thick fog, passing by the mausoleum where her husband formerly rested. She even touches the crypt briefly, to make sure it is there, making this a depiction of the more autonomous potential for woman, which Wood contrasts to the obedient, and presently imprisoned Mrs. Trent.

Paula acknowledges the male conspiracy, stating, "Well, I don't like it, but I guess there isn't much I can do about it." Surrounded by a perhaps well-meaning, yet still-threatening male collective, a single female cannot effectively fight this entrenched cabal of solidarity known as patriarchal culture. After locking the prized woman-object in the police car, with half-man Kelton standing "guard," Harper asks Jeff if he knows how to use a gun. In an absurdly machismo voice, he boasts, "After four years in the Marine Corps?" (In this line, one can hear Wood proudly referencing his own military career.) The three males don their pistols and slowly walk off-camera, their destructive pseudo-genitals dangling before them. After the "men" leave, Kelton tries to calm himself with his own, significantly self-destructive phallus surrogate—a filter-tip cigarette. Significantly, though, Kelton does not attempt to converse with Paula; this could reflect misogyny on his part, or perhaps merely a fear of women.

Back at the saucer, Eros enters his ship and strolls briskly across the set. In addition to the silk-like blouse and leotards, he can now be seen wearing black leather boots, making these "aliens" possibly the most fetishistic portrayal of extraterrestrials ever captured on film. The aliens anticipate the Earthmen's immanent arrival, and Eros orders Tanna, "Send the big one to get the girl and the policeman. I'll turn on the Dicto-Robo-Tary [a hilarious Woodian coinage for Robot-Dictionary], so we can converse with them." Meanwhile, back at the police car, Kelton nervously smokes, while Paula appears to be napping in the back seat. Out of the mist, the zombie Clay lumbers towards camera in another of several effective scenes in a film which pits an abundance of genuine atmosphere against a backdrop of avowed silliness. Poor Kelton suffers another attack from the undead, as Clay approaches and knocks him to the ground. Paula screams for her life, unheard by her supposed protectors, and Clay easily opens the car door and extracts the woman.

Elsewhere, the three male "stooges" see the glowing light of the saucer in the distance and dutifully head out to investigate. Soon, the men reach the outer hull of the saucer; inside, Eros watches their approach, stating breathlessly, "A moment or two more, and you will be the first *live* Earth people ever to enter a celestial ship!" Tanna enters, and Eros instructs her to open the outer hatch. The men bang on the side of the saucer and hear a weird twang. When the hatch suddenly opens, the three men draw their guns and decide whether to venture inside. Jeff quips, gun cocked, "I tell ya one thing: If a little green man pops out at me, I'm shooting first and asking questions later," a most succinct declaration of the cowardly, destructive philosophy of homo sapiens.

The men now enter the spaceship. Eros introduces himself, and explains that his race does not want war with Earth, but understanding. He explains that they have been trying to communicate with men for some time, but have been met with complete silence. Edwards cautiously asks why the aliens so badly want to talk with them, and Eros' answer reveals all: "Because of Death!" Here, Wood underscores brilliantly the base thesis of his, and perhaps all narrative: the issues of life, against the fear of death. Eros goes on to clarify his somewhat prejudicial, yet not indefensible, position: "Because all you of Earth are idiots!" Jeff, the macho Marine, bleats, "Now you just hold on, *buster!*"

Eros interrupts him, somewhat cattily, "No, *you* hold on!" Eros then segues directly into a long speech about man's history of developing and then utilizing destructive weaponry against himself and his planet home, again an argument which has much truth to it. Still, the choice of symbolic developments in weapons of mass destruction is odd, to say the least, beginning with, "First, was your firecracker." Perhaps Wood meant dynamite. Then hand grenades are mentioned, then a bomb, then "a larger bomb — many people are killed at one time." Eros then turns towards Tanna who, in an insert, turns away from Eros almost as if embarrassed, as he states: "Then your scientists stumbled upon the *atom* bomb." Here, Wood seems to be somehow equating atomic weaponry with the female principle. Eros continues on, passionately: "Then the hydrogen bomb, where you actually explode the *air* itself," not an entirely accurate statement, but one with great lyrical effect. Eros then drops his own bomb: "The only explosion left is the *Solaronite!*" This ridiculous name, awkward and uninspired, was supposedly coined by Wood and his wife Kathy with great effort, and by referencing the Christian Bible.[42]

Colonel Edwards counters gravely, "There's no such thing." Eros replies, in a strangely wistful manner, "Perhaps to you ... but we've known it for centuries. Your scientists will stumble upon it as they have all the others. But the juvenile minds which you possess, will not comprehend its strength, until it's too late." The reference to "stumbling" is a nice touch, implying that man's scientific progress is more attributable to luck than to talent. Edwards deferentially confesses, "You're way above our heads," a comment which suggests not only intellectual but *spiritual* superiority, reinforcing the hunch that the aliens in *Plan 9* are primarily intended to be seen as spiritual beings, i.e., "angels." Jeff, the dull xenophobe, grunts, "So what if we developed this bomb? We'd be an even stronger nation than now!" In a rage, Eros sputters, "You see? Your stupid minds! *Stupid! Stupid!*" This immortal line is a quite-accurate assessment of the then-burgeoning Military-Industrial Complex, which has turned out exactly as Wood and others in 1950s fantastic cinema had long postulated: mercenary, explosion-happy uber-patriots without a whit of sense or ethics.

To completely prove Eros' point, and also Wood's thoughts on the subject, Jeff shouts, "That's all I'm takin' from you!" and slaps Eros across the face. Eros falls across one of the wooden workbenches; as he rises, he growls, "It's because of men like you that all must be destroyed! Headstrong! Violent! No use of the mind God gave you!" It is most interesting that this first *overt* mention of the concept of God in *Plan 9* comes from an alien, again reinforcing the notion of the aliens as heaven-sent messengers, angels with a mission. Colonel Edwards, visibly uncomfortable at the direction the conversation is taking, asks, "You speak of Solaronite, but just what is it?" Eros, again perhaps unwisely, decides to explain the entire principle of this super-weapon to his ignorant, war-like enemy, in wonderfully absurd elucidation:

> Take a can of your gasoline. Say, this can of gasoline is the sun. Now, you spread a thin line of it, to a ball, representing the earth. Now, the gasoline, represents the sunlight, the sun particles. Here, we saturate the ball with the gasoline the sunlight. Then we put a flame to the ball. The flame will speedily travel around the Earth, back along the line of gasoline to the can, or the sun itself. It will explode this source, and spread to every place that gasoline, our sunlight, touches. Explode the sunlight here, gentlemen, and you explode the *universe!* Explode the sunlight here, and a chain reaction will occur direct to the sun itself — and to all the planets that sunlight touches! *To every planet in the universe!*

Actor Dudley Manlove was proud to do this long speech in one long take, in order to save his boss and friend the costs of re-shooting, and Wood saw fit not to cut the scene, so it stands as a testament to a talented actor giving even the most abstract and un-engaging lines the seriousness he felt they deserved.[43] Several sources maintain that Wood was very proud of this speech, saying "I never worked so hard on anything," and even with its logistic loopholes and redundancies, it is fairly memorable, and has become a veritable mantra for fans of bad scientific exegesis, many of whom can easily recite it by heart.[44] Metaphorically, the speech cleverly suggests the dangerous assumption that whenever Man tries to expand his presence in his immediate or abstracted environment, that is, express his collective ego beyond himself, he will inevitably poison these new environs, because his myopic, greedy self-interests are not allied with the peaceable maintenance of the natural world, or indeed the universe.

Eros concludes, "This is why you must be stopped. This is why any means must be used to stop you — in a friendly manner, or, as it seems, you want it!" The reactionary Harper responds to this erudite speech with a perfunctory "He's mad!" This angers Tanna, who finally breaks silence and counters, "*Mad*? Is it *mad* that you destroy other people to save yourselves? You have done this! Is it *mad* that one country must destroy another to save themselves? You have also done this! How then is it *mad* than one planet must destroy another who threatens the very existence...." Tanna's passionate oration is interrupted by an agitated Eros, who forcefully pushes her aside. It appears odd that Eros doesn't support Tanna's utterance, as she is merely voicing what he was saying earlier. Perhaps Eros likes to be the only speaker in a conversation, and may be as sexist as his earthbound rivals. Eros clarifies this notion thusly: "In my land, women are for advancing the race, not for fighting man's battle!"

Having regained the floor, Eros continues, "Life is not so expansive on my planet. We don't cling to it like you do!" This summation goes to the heart of *Plan 9*, its main thesis being a mediation on life and death. Most importantly, *Plan 9*'s animated ghouls are attempting to educate Man not to fear death, but to accept and even embrace it. As many philosophers such as Ernest Becker have noted, Man's chronic individual and collective fear of Death leads him down many unwise avenues in attempts to fashion an impossible material "immortality" for himself. In addition to relatively harmless "monument-building" such as the legacies created through family and good works, Man has a tendency to destructively manipulate his environment in order to make an enduring impression on it and to assure him a place in some perceived eternity. This tendency towards battle and environmental devastation is one of the most ill-advised, assuredly neurotic attempts by Man to ignore, conquer or nullify death. As Eros has stated succinctly, the advanced race does not "cling" to life so pathetically as do homo sapiens, and are thus far less destructive of self and others.[45]

Meanwhile, back at the cemetery, patrolman Larry arrives to assist the still-agitated Kelton. The two cops run off to find the others. In another unexpectedly beautiful shot, Clay carries a comatose Paula slowly towards camera, a classic image of the living and the dead, of Life and Death, Eros and Thanatos, in one poetic composition. Back at the spaceship, Eros stares forlornly out the porthole. As the camera slowly dollies back to reveal Tanna and Harper listening, Eros states, "Then one day, it could all be gone, in one big puff of smoke and ball of fire. All that out there. The stars, the planets. All just an empty void." Here, Wood clearly, poetically references the cosmic void, the "other world" he so obsessed on. Harper, gun in hand, orders the aliens to accompany him to the police station, the only location of justice the dullard knows. Eros laughs at the Earthman's "juvenile" mind. Eros commands Harper to look out the porthole, and the lawman sees a horrible vision — his boss, Inspector Clay, is now an undead walking ghoul, carrying an unconscious woman in his arms!

Elsewhere in the cemetery, Kelton and Larry sight the glowing spaceship in the distance, and soon see Clay and Paula. A horrified Kelton mutters in exasperation: "Clay is dead, and we buried him. How we gonna kill somebody that's already dead? Dead! And yet there he stands!" Wood's buffoon, Kelton, understands little about Life and Death, the almost-invisible thread which separates yet binds the two, yet he obsesses on same. His befuddled declarations succinctly underscore Man's eternal quandary over these literally "life and death" issues and here again, Kelton is posited as one of the key archetypes in the Wood film canon, the clown-philosopher who voices in literal, ostensibly ignorant terms the sheer terror of life facing death.

Kelton and Larry sneak up behind Clay and slug him over the head with a big stick; they soon locate the spaceship, and prepare to enter just as Harper attempts to escort the aliens out. The cops knock on the spaceship door, which distracts Harper and causes a fight to ensue between aliens and Earthlings. Eros and Jeff stoop to the lowest of form of conflict resolution, hand-to-hand combat, in the process knocking over one of the workbenches with its lone piece of electronic paraphernalia. Eros and Jeff slug it out like two drunken gunslingers in an old cowboy picture, while the upturned table stands improbably erect in the foreground, passive counterpoint to the animated battle.

As the Earthmen seek the exit switch, Tanna fumbles with some machinery in an attempt to launch the spaceship with their "guests" aboard. Meanwhile, Eros tosses various pieces of electronics equipment at Jeff, oddly exhibiting the destructive behavior the alien had so recently denounced as barbaric. Edwards finally finds the knob to the outside door, understandably adjacent to it, and urges his colleagues to escape quickly, as the ship is now on fire. Eros falls to the floor, unconscious, as the Earthmen flee from the ship. Tanna tries to awaken Eros, as more machinery bursts into flames. As the assembled Earthmen watch from the cemetery, the saucer ascends to the skies, and speeds off, in flames. One preposterous scene shows the smaller of the saucer models rising above a photograph of the cemetery location; absurdly large flames engulf the tiny miniature, ruining any attempt at realistic proportion in the scene. A more effective effects shot follows, showing the larger Lindberg flying saucer, soaring against a backdrop of Hollywood at night, and boasting slightly more proportionate flames.

Kelton points out to the others that his beloved superior, Inspector Clay, has become a skeleton, and now, returning to the earth once again, he can finally "rest in peace." On a similar note, Colonel Edwards offers, "We gotta hand it to them, though, they—they're *far* ahead of us." By now the viewer knows that he means *spiritually*, not technologically. One final return to the spaceship interior, now completely engulfed in smoke, is accented by the sound of Tanna screaming, suggesting the unpleasant assumption that the alien messengers are being burnt alive, victims of their own peculiar "Hell." Finally, the model saucer explodes, and Criswell's voice can be heard over the now-empty Hollywood night sky, reiterating, "My friend...."

The scene now reverts to *Plan 9*'s opening set, the ethereal "primal void" wherein Criswell originally and accurately "predicted" all that has transpired; he now concludes:

> You have seen this incident,
> Based on sworn testimony!
> Can you prove that it didn't happen?
> Perhaps on your way home,
> Someone will pass you in the dark,
> And you will never know it,
> For they will be from outer space!
> Many scientists believe that another world is watching us this moment.
> We once laughed at the horseless carriage,
> The airplane, the telephone, the electric light,
> Vitamins, radio and even television!
> And now, some of us laugh at outer space!

Meaningfully, the camera dollies back, as Criswell rises from his seat and ends this prophetic melodrama with his trademark sign-off: "God help us, in the future." The lights which introduced this exalted spiritual figure come on again behind him, as Criswell's figure again becomes a black silhouette, against which is superimposed the end title, with its infamous proclamation: "Filmed in HOLLYWOOD, U.S.A."

Criswell, our ersatz "televangelist," thus ends this monumental spiritual fable with an admonition for his audience to approach life with the utmost solemnity. His queer observation that "some of us laugh at outer space" refers to the superficial mortal who refuses to take the spiritual side of life seriously, with its attendant perils of sin, ruination, punishment and eternal damnation. This nicely segues with the essential message inherent in the historical Mystery and Morality Plays, with *Everyman* a salient example. As noted, *Everyman* depicts a generic soul as he encounters Death personified, and is summoned to face the certainty of his own mortality. The remarkable similarity in setting between *Everyman* and *Plan 9*, both of which transpire primarily over the graves of fallen men, reinforces the analogous theme of each, that "every man" faces Death in his life, and existentially at least, by his lonesome. This awareness, which can lead either to terror or celebration depending on the soul's spiritual outlook, is elaborated on in great detail in both pieces, but the concluding moral in each is to correct one's behavior while one still has the opportunity, for calamity will follow otherwise. Judging both works after the fact, it now seems likely that poor, comedically challenged Officer Kelton is Ed Wood's "Everyman," for he alone seems the most moved by Death, even "scared to death," and most aware of the sheer terror of the graveyard and all it suggests; he even encounters these undead terrors, by and large, alone, recalling the fate of "Everyman." Finally, the echo of *Everyman* is heard in Criswell's epilogue, whose beseeching of favor from the gods bears similarity to the final lines of the Mystery Play: "Thereto help, the trinity! Amen, say ye, for Saint Charity."[46]

That *Plan 9* is simply awash in religious symbology and reference, and follows the structure and synopsis of the ancient mystery plays can be no mere accident or folly; these elements are intrinsic to the heavily metaphysical, avowedly occult spirit of *Plan 9*, and impart to the literally "magical" film much of its energy. One might even say that the impact of Baptist theology on the film's genesis gives *Plan 9* much of its supernatural esprit, and fuels its vividly morbid interpretation of Christian mythology. In a decade in which genre films were assuredly obsessed with death as the wages of sin, *Plan 9* takes this notion a good deal further, and ruminates on the horrors, and joys, of that land occupied after death, and Wood is clearly in his glory as he illuminates for us "the other world," in what may be dubbed his own "Mystery Film."

The accruing career-long evidence of Wood's fascination with the theme of death and resurrection, whether enacted metaphorically through gender reassignment or the legacy of good works or offspring, or literally through atomic or alien reanimation, seems to be heading somewhere, and in *Plan 9*, Wood's clandestine agenda is finally activated. Many ancient cultures, haunted by superstition, were convinced that the only way to preserve the spiritual dignity of a reigning monarch or priest was to remove it from the authority figure's ever-aging material body. As Sir James Frazier has noted:

> The divine life, incarnate in a material and mortal body, is liable to be tainted and corrupted by the weakness of the frail medium in which it is for a time enshrined; and if it is to be saved from the increasing enfeeblement which it must necessarily share with its human incarnation as he advances in years, it must be detached from him before, or at least as soon as, he exhibits signs of decay, in order to be transferred to a vigorous successor. This is done by killing the old representative of the god and conveying the divine spirit from him to a new incarnation. The

killing of the god, that is, of his human incarnation, is therefore merely a necessary step to his revival or resurrection in a better form. Far from being an extinction of the divine spirit, it is only the beginning of a purer and stronger manifestation of it.[47]

For the artist, a similar procedure is used, in which the thoughts, insights and inspirations of the mortal creator are transferred onto physical works or "texts" which may live on long after their creator has passed on. This process is always a gamble, and the artist can never know whether their works will survive or flourish in the great beyond known as "the future"; therefore certain artists have traditionally taken steps which they feel might bend fate in their favor. Wood, for one, seems to have considered the notion that by enacting the death-and-rebirth ritual *within* one of his artistic creations, as performance, the resultant work, and its creator, stood a better chance of surviving and prospering in cultural history.

In addition to the various resurrected characters in *Plan 9*'s scenario, there is the purely ritualistic "resurrection" of Bela Lugosi in the film. Shown first in his last filmed performances, and then re-created via an implausible stand-in who wears the mortal cloak which immediately evokes the actor's eternal spirit, Lugosi is literally "killed" and "resurrected" by Wood in *Plan 9*, and it is this arguably "magical" act which sparks *Plan 9*'s uncanny omnipotence. Far from exploiting Lugosi in *Plan 9*, Wood made his dear pal immortal, a promise which he has kept; as Lugosi was a "king" amongst actors, seen by many as virtual royalty,

Plan 9 from Outer Space has understandably inspired many an artistic homage; pictured here is Elisa Vegliante's tribute, entitled *Vampire Girl & Ghoul Man: One Last Show* (courtesy of the artist).

Wood's editorial magic in keeping him alive in *Plan 9* can be seen as directly referencing the "killing of the divine king" ritual of antiquity. Bob Burns has mentioned that Wood dedicated *Plan 9* to Lugosi at the film's premiere, so the deceased thespian was verifiably foremost on the filmmaker's mind.[48]

This bold move on Wood's part may have been merely a pre-conscious fancy or a carefully thought-out subterfuge, yet still the intent can easily be seen when viewing *Plan 9* from this angle: *Plan 9* is a consciously designed ritual performance of the ancient death-and-rebirth rites, designed to help the film itself endure and survive the cruel weeding process of culture, and to preserve the artist's legacy in perpetuity. That *Plan 9*, fifty years after its "birth," enjoys a notoriety and devotion from many quarters far in excess of its original cultural reception, and beyond even the wildest dreams of its creator, is a certainty; that Wood's metaphysical manipulations on the film's behalf had anything to do with it cannot be verified, and should not be taken as a given. Yet, in the eerily prophetic words of Criswell, "Can you prove it *didn't* happen?"

This glorious revelation now leads us directly to the secret of *Plan 9 from Outer Space*. There is a dizzying, ultimately overwhelming array of binary oppositions which inhabit the film, each complementing and overlapping the other in an intricate web of accelerating philosophical import. *Plan 9* offers innumerable lucent examples of various structural dyads, both in harmony and in conflict: males work with and also battle females; Earthlings encounter and try to first understand, and then vanquish, visitors from another world; neo-realistic exterior scenes clash harshly with tattered, surreal studio sets; the constant shuffling of daytime and nighttime footage creates a baffling *mise-en-scène* which is unidentifiable as either day or night, or even earthbound; the neo-realist, documentary-style ambience of certain montage sequences both augment and negate the Absurdist stagebound narrative passages. Finally, the various traumatic, highly symbolic interchanges between the living and the dead underscore the fundamental dialectic addressed brilliantly in *Plan 9*, arguably the consummate binary opposition — life and death.

This rudimentary deduction points out something obvious yet elusive in man's quest for individual and collective harmony: It is the eternal creative frission between dichotomous elements which animates life's terrifying yet fascinating journey into inevitable darkness. This dialectical tension is inarguably the author of the vital energy which inhabits *Plan 9*. Wood's astounding treatise on the subject reveals a fundamental, yet obscure truth: Life and death are not, as often postulated by fearful human beings, irreconcilable antagonists to the other, but essential creative partners in the other's very existence. For life certainly can have no possible meaning or conceivable purpose without the absolute eventuality of death, just as death is, by strict definition, merely a life ended.

Plan 9's wild meditation on the subject explores man's perpetual conundrum regarding his seemingly dire fate, and finally celebrates, through the allegorical resurrection of the dead, the revealed knowledge that life and death are not two, but one, and that none living should fear death, which is merely life's reward. Just as Wood's dear friend Bela Lugosi changes from living man to dead man to impossible stand-in to costume shop skeleton before our eyes, so does man's physical being evaporate effortlessly into "the other world," and is none the worse for that, as his spirit and memory may live on. *Plan 9* is, indeed, a "magic act," but assuredly Wood had something miraculous up his sleeve: the divine secret of man's temporary residence on this planet called "Earth."[49]

Reinforcing this irrevocable connection between the living and the dead is the spirit of "the Vampire" which hovers over *Plan 9*. Bela Lugosi will be forever associated with this magnificent horror creature of mythology, and his Ghoul Man character, perhaps fortuitously, is dressed as such to remind the viewer that, as Lugosi himself once stated, "Dracula never ends!" The Ghoul Man's wife, specifically called "Vampire Girl" in the credits, prowls Wood's patchwork purgatory dressed, and acting, exactly as would a vampiress. As storytellers from Bram Stoker onward have clearly elucidated, the cultural legend of the vampire is "the ghostly link between the living and the dead."[50] The line between the horror story and the fairy tale is a thin one, and for all its apparent ghoulishness, *Plan 9* is in essence a fairy tale, a post-modern mythology, and one with a happy, albeit twisted, ending—the "bad guys" (the "angelic" aliens) die, while the "good guys" (the "war-like" Earthlings) get another chance to correct themselves, in a canny inversion of traditional narrative scenario. Yet the delusional, ignorant Earthlings of *Plan 9* are not really the good guys, an insight well articulated by Eros; they only fantasize that they are. Thus, *Plan 9*'s overriding lesson is as dark as pitch, and quite unsettling: We humans think we are good, but we are actually evil. Illuminated brilliantly within *Plan 9*, and echoed throughout most of the world's religions, this lamentable mass hallucination is Mankind's curse, his fatal flaw, his absolute guarantee of mortality.

In its attempt to utilize both genres in the service of metaphysical enlightenment, *Plan 9* ironically becomes one of the most successful examples of the decade to engagingly combine horror and science-fiction themes. Using the most cynical and opportunistic pulp-fiction scenario possible (flying saucers invade a graveyard and bring back the dead), Wood fashions a magnificent, melancholic satirical sketch of America, postwar and post-mortem. Further, the revelation of *Plan 9*'s pretense to be a spiritually infused cautionary fable in no way contradicts its more Absurdist pretensions, for that genre was ultimately obsessed with the very same thing, as Martin Esslin noted: "In trying to deal with the ultimate of the human condition not in terms of intellectual understanding but in terms of communicating a metaphysical truth through a living experience, the Theatre of the Absurd touches the religious sphere."[51] It is even profound and ominous that *Plan 9* seems obsessed with television, and its birthing of the phenomenon of the "cult of personality," well illustrated through the use in the film of not one, but two television icons, Criswell and Vampira, both of whom come across as Absurdist mass-culture evangelists of a sort, through their immortal and inimitable portrayals in this unique film. With *Plan 9*, Wood merged narrative film, documentary, liturgical drama, Absurdist theatre and television "infotainment" to create a wholly unique viewing experience, perhaps even a wholly unique cultural creation. This lurid-yet-revelatory cautionary fable, this glorious "Mystery Film," magnificently pulls back the curtain of earthly existence to give the viewer a startling glimpse of "the other world." It is thus no wonder that to the day he died, Ed Wood called *Plan 9 from Outer Space* his "pride and joy."[52]

7

Night of the Ghouls (ca. 1959)

With *Plan 9 from Outer Space*, Ed Wood pulled aside the veil of postwar reality to give his audience an Absurdist-tinged glimpse of the metaphysical plane; with his next film, he completely immersed both character and audience into this hellish parallel universe, from which escape is only possible through a most peculiar death. This film, originally produced as *Revenge of the Dead*, is in many ways a follow-up to Wood's biblically fueled outer space parable, although it is not a sequel from a narrative point of view. Several characters from *Plan 9 from Outer Space* (henceforth called *Plan 9*) make an appearance in *Revenge of the Dead*: Tor Johnson returns to his more familiar role of Lobo, the lumbering, mute flunky of evil seen in *Bride of the Monster*; Paul Marco reprises his unique clowning one last time as Kelton, Wood's miserable imp; most tellingly, Criswell returns, once again as himself and once again introducing and framing the narrative with allusions to the priesthood and/or televangelism (with significant modification). In many ways, *Revenge of the Dead* is the quintessential Ed Wood film, as it takes the morbidity, religious fixation and Absurdist pretensions of *Plan 9* and other previous efforts to dizzying new heights. The entire film is set in the now-familiar cosmic void seen in *Jail Bait*, *Bride of the Monster* and *Plan 9*; the scenario is completely immersed in this bleak netherworld, the characters swallowed whole by it.

Also noteworthy is the film's rescue from certain oblivion. After finishing principal photography and rough editing of the film in late 1957, the always-destitute Wood could not raise the money to do post-production work, so the original 35mm negative of the film remained at a film laboratory, a hostage to unpaid bills, for over twenty years, unscreened, unreleased and unknown. It was considered by film historians either a lost film, or a figment of Ed Wood's fertile imagination, until film archivist Wade Williams tracked it down, paid the film's extant bills, and released it in the early 1980s to home video under Williams' own title, *Night of the Ghouls* (henceforth referred to as *Ghouls*). That Williams was able and willing to undertake this audacious rescue is cause for celebration, as the Ed Wood film canon would be irredeemably poorer without this extraordinary post-modern "ghost story," told as only the spook-obsessed Wood could.

The basic plot-line of *Ghouls* follows a police investigation of a spooky suburban house which is purported to harbor ghosts and monsters. It is discovered to be a front for a "phony" fortune-telling racket, one which successfully bilks naïve people out of their life savings in exchange for the chance to speak with loved ones from beyond the grave. Wood's obsession with the binary opposition of life and death, so ingeniously depicted in *Plan 9*, is *Ghoul*'s very essence. Although the charismatic "swami," another peculiar sketch by Wood of an ambivalent religious figure who relies on a manipulative "cult of personality" for their questionable gains, does turn out to be a fake, Wood always has tricks up his sleeve with his cinematic "magic acts," and offers the viewer a glorious reward at film's end which positions *Ghouls* as a fantasy of the most morbid kind. In *Ghouls*, Wood once again tricks both characters and audience into misreading what is "real" and what is "not real," astutely merging the representational and the non-representational into a nonsensical, profound "epic."

Wood may have gotten the germ of the idea for *Ghouls* from the obscure *Sucker Money* (1933), a low-budget melodrama produced by exploitation legend Willis Kent and released under his True-Life Photoplays banner. *Sucker Money* stars Mischa Aueur as Swami Yomurda, a petty con-man who mounts an elaborate fortune-telling swindle with the help of his minions. The gang manages to extort a considerable amount of money out of gullible bereaved persons until exposed by an intrepid reporter. Yomurda and company use clever, cutting-edge technology, including a hilarious use of surreptitiously obtained surveillance film, to trick their "patsies" into thinking they are actually receiving audio-visual communication from "the other world." *Ghouls* shares much with *Sucker Money* in its basic scenario, including the aforementioned use of bizarre audio-visual gimmickry to fool victims. If Wood never saw *Sucker Money* in the theatre or on local television, the similarities between the two films are even more remarkable. Regardless, Wood used *Sucker Money*'s straightforward melodrama template to manifest something completely unique, so *Ghouls* cannot be called a remake of the 1933 film.

As with *Bride of the Monster* and *Plan 9*, with *Ghouls* Wood exercises his uncanny knack for incorporating, perhaps intuitively, notable elements from the tradition of Absurdist theatre, with some interesting parallels to the work of Samuel Beckett; most notable is the film's enervating, non-linear structure, in which characters seem stuck in limbo rather than participating in a narrative progression, and Wood's iconoclastic use of language not to clarify or communicate meaning, but to obfuscate and obliterate same.[1] Some of the pessimism, and even nihilism of Beckett also seeps into *Ghouls*, albeit in the roundabout way one might expect from a creatively muddled artist such as Wood. Still, the spirit of the Absurdist reigns in *Ghouls*, and one would not be surprised to find the film considered as Wood's own *Waiting for Godot* at some future time. Also interesting is the fact that *Ghouls*' production, and *Waiting for Godot*'s premiere, occurred within months and possibly weeks of each other, between late 1957 and early 1958, suggesting that the Absurdist spirit was alive and well in both film and theatre at this time.

Ghouls begins exactly as did its "big brother," *Plan 9*, with an introductory segment featuring Wood's metaphysical spokesman, Criswell, which will act as a framing device for the subsequent story. In *Ghouls*, however, Criswell leaves the stage-like set which posited him as an ersatz televangelist in *Plan 9*, for a most significant substitute: The camera dollies towards a coffin, which sits in one of Wood's trademark cosmic voids, a "dead space" which illustrates Wood's recurring purgatory. As the camera approaches, Criswell sits up, rather awkwardly, in the coffin, his hair mussed, his eyes half-closed — the viewer may get the suspicion that Criswell was dead and just came back to life, a notion which certainly foreshadows the film's finale, or that he was perhaps asleep in the coffin and had just woken up. This latter notion is not discouraged by apocryphal stories that the popular entertainer, a self-proclaimed "freak," enjoyed napping and/or sleeping in actual coffins.[2] In either case, the unearthly action comes across as a metaphoric birth of sorts. As in *Plan 9*, Criswell then speaks directly to the audience, conveying via hyperbolic narration the tale about to ensue:

> I am Criswell! For many years, I have told you the almost unbelievable, related the unreal, and shown it to be more than fact! Now I tell you a tale of the "threshold people," so astounding that some of you may faint! This is a story of those in the twilight time — once human, now

monsters—in a world between the living and the dead. Monsters to be pitied! Monster to be despised!

A signature Woodian thunder-and-lightning stock shot, as usual suggesting god-heads incensed with man's chronic wickedness, is the segue to the main credits. Over an exterior shot of the outside of the "County of Los Angeles Sheriff's Department, East Los Angeles," illuminated by a visible movie light sitting in the lower right frame, Criswell continues: "For our talk, I must take you to your town, *any* town. A police station. Activity of the day and night. Activity—some of which, the police are quite willing to admit." Here, Criswell consciously states that his "talk," suggesting again the sermonizing of the televised evangelist as in *Plan 9*, tells a tale which, although purportedly taking place in East Los Angeles or thereabouts, could in fact be occurring anywhere, in *any town*, again directly referencing the viewer with language which mirrors that used by Criswell in his print predictions.[3] Thus the tale which unspools is meant to be taken as allegorical, a key point which will gain importance anon.

The studio interior of the police station is concocted, in true Wood fashion, via two walls, and a padded, rounded counter which looks lifted from a cocktail lounge, perhaps a most obscure reference by the filmmaker to the omnipresence of booze in his aesthetic universe. Most conspicuous in the lobby is an 8x10 publicity photograph of Wood tacked to the wall, an overt parody of typical F.B.I. WANTED posters. This tongue-in-cheek self-reference by Wood is another bold signature by the filmmaker, who obviously took playful, loving pride in his work. Via the portrait, Wood is literally "overseeing" the progression of his scenario, humorously poised as the "guiding spirit" of the piece. To accent this revelation, another Wood signature immediately follows: A cop drags an ornery drunkard into the police station. This recurring, abstracted Wood "cameo" is repeated almost verbatim from similar scenes in *Bride of the Monster* and *Jail Bait*.

As the drunkard continues to cause trouble, Sergeant Crandel (Don Nagel) escorts a distraught elderly couple out of his office; they are Henry Edwards (Wood ensemble regular Harvey B. Dunn) and his wife Martha (Margaret Mason, wife of Wood's chiropodist–Bela Lugosi's *Plan 9* stand-in Tom Mason). Crandel orders Patrolman Kelton (Paul Marco) to escort the couple home. As they prepare to leave, Henry shouts, "Oh, it was a nightmare of horror!" Martha concurs: "Oh, it was horrible! Oh, that horrible face! And those long fingers! Oh, I'll never forget it the longest day that I live!" This hilarious dialogue, ineptly emoted by rank amateurs, is lovingly watched over by Wood, whose face hovers directly above via his photograph on the wall, creating an Absurdist signature most touching.

The scene, and the pace, of *Ghouls* now changes radically, with an impressive montage, augmented by wild, drum-based jazz music, and Criswell's pedantic annotation. As a police car roars down a country highway, its sirens blaring, Criswell attempts to stabilize the dizzying segue thusly: "This is how it began. An incident that the police were fearful to admit. Your daily newspapers, radio and television dares to relate the latest in juvenile delinquency...." The scene changes to show teenagers dancing at an outdoor café, in footage filmed by Wood for an unfinished project called *Rock and Roll Hell*, footage from which can also be seen in *The Sinister Urge* (1961).[4] The police car continues down the street as Criswell continues: "At times it seems that juvenile delinquency is a major problem for law enforcement officers!" Now is shown more unrelated footage, this time of a fistfight in a trench between two males (Ed Wood himself, battling with long-time colleague Conrad Brooks), a scene witnessed by a cheering gang of teenagers. As the police car returns as the montage's connecting narrative thread, Criswell ponders, "But, is this the major horror of our times?" More fighting footage follows, as two men battle in a deserted alley, while a young girl watches. Criswell further baits his audience: "Is this violence and terror the small few perpetrate, the most horrible, terrifying of all crimes, our civil servants must investigate?" The montage concludes with a most amazing sequence—an automobile swerves along a mountain road, soon careening down a hillside and crashing, followed by a grimly staged shot of the bloody, apparently dead driver staring blankly at the viewer. Criswell comments thusly on this horror: "The National Safety Council keeps accurate records of all highway fatalities—they can even predict how many deaths will come on a drunken holiday weekend!" This astounding, macabre montage is, in sum, Wood's microcosmic collage of postwar culture, a skewed and prejudiced snapshot of American society circa 1957, whose problems are crudely, darkly listed as: rampant crime, unleashed anger, violent youth, drunken adults, and sudden, bloody death.

The grim portrait of the tragic randomness and meaninglessness of human mortality, portrayed by the motorist who dies right before the viewer's eyes, goes straight to the heart of Wood's cinema, which is unflinchingly fixated, not merely on contemplation of life and death, as is much of narrative cinema, but of that cryptic correlation *between* life and death, portrayed in Wood's films as a biblical-style purgatory given visual expression via one of his many cosmic voids. Yet perhaps Wood's central passion on the subject, conveyed via the hideous blank stare of the dying motorist, is the heart-stopping shock of the *moment* of death, that specific temporal point of pure horror where life and death are inextricably entwined.

Criswell now attempts to escalate his laundry list of society's ills with the following: "But what statistics are kept, what information is there, how many of you know the horror, the terror, I will now reveal to you!" The scene changes to show two teenagers necking in a convertible parked at night at a local lover's lane. At first it appears that this sequence is a part of the montage of civilization which just transpired, but as the sped-up film shows the male getting more and more aggressive, followed by the female slapping him and getting out of the car, it appears that *Ghouls* has now, rather sneakily, returned to narrative territory. The girl runs, almost comically fast due to the under-cranked camera, into the woods, and spots a dingy old house. Out of nowhere, a strange female creature, dressed all in black veils and featuring an odd crown on her head, stares from behind some bushes. (This creature, played by Jeannie Stevens, will henceforth be referred to as The Black Ghost, as stated in the cast listings.)

The boy gets out of his car to find the girl and searches the woods, again in fast motion, while the Black Ghost prowls a different aspect of the woods in slow motion footage which creates a nice contrast to the comic running of the youths. In an amazing shot, the girl runs past some hedges, and right behind her follows what now appears to be a crude stand-in for the Black Ghost. This absurd (or Absurdist?) clone, although wearing similar veils and crown, has "her" face completely covered by the veils, making it likely that this is a substitute for actress Stevens, another daring substitution of the genuine by the fake, along the lines of *Plan 9*'s preposterous "cloning" of Bela Lugosi. Paul Marco stated in an interview that this "mock" Black Ghost was none other than Wood, a revelation which makes the character's crude metamorphosis all the more significant.[5]

In several subsequent scenes, the Black Ghost walks through an impressively atmospheric set amidst shrubbery and studio fog, another evocation of the abundant, if morbid, atmosphere of *Plan 9*. The girl trips and hurts her ankle, and soon the Black Ghost is upon her. The boy soon stumbles upon his mate, and is also attacked by the Black Ghost. As he succumbs to the undead thing, the boy lets out one of Wood's patently artificial dubbed-in screams which may, as before, be self-effacing commentary by the filmmaker regarding his scandalous use of bold artifice to both convey and subvert traditional aesthetic verisimilitude.

Back at police station, a medium shot of Crandel reveals a piece of tape over the photograph of Wood, with the word WANTED hastily scrawled on it. Another ornery drunk stumbles into the police station, wobbling precariously close to the Wood WANTED poster, only to stumble right out again; this is surely Wood reminding his audience not to forget who made this Absurdist spectacular. In another example of Wood's desire to portray *Ghouls* as archetypal melodrama which could occur anywhere, Criswell reveals, "The work of a maniac was credited for the murder of this boy and girl. You remember the stories your newspapers carried of the incident ... but let us see what really happened."

Inspector Robbins (John Carpenter) barks at Patrolman Kelton to send in Detective Bradford as soon as he arrives. Kelton, of course, is a recurring character in the Wood film canon playing the same role in *Bride of the Monster* and *Plan 9 from Outer Space*; Inspector Robbins was also a character in *Bride of the Monster*, but in that film he was played by Harvey B. Dunn, who here plays the distraught farmer just seen leaving the police station. Why Wood didn't think to ask Dunn to reprise his role as Inspector Robbins in *Ghouls* is open to conjecture, but it does add to the several fascinating instances where Wood used two, and sometimes more, actors and/or props to play the same character, with *Plan 9*'s "Ghoul Man" the preeminent example. These switching of persons who play similar characters may in fact be the human equivalent of Wood's "symbolic" effects, where one or more cheap props are offered to portray what was actually intended. In Absurdist theatre, this practice was deliberate and celebrated, well expressed by actors instructed to play their character as a clichéd archetype, not as an actual person; the practice was also expressed via the conscious switching of the actor playing the part, usually within the same play. In the "epic" theatre of Bertolt Brecht, this exercise was meant to impair the omniscience of the actor, and the venerated significance of characterization in conventional theatre. As Brecht himself articulated in his *Little Organon for the theatre*, "the actor should not be a single unalterable figure but rather a constantly changing figure that becomes clearer through the way in which he changes."[6] Wood assuredly had a similar notion with his wildly vacillating characters, which magically "changed their spots" before the viewer's eyes.

A woman seen at the film's opening, arriving to report a stolen automobile, now exits, thanking an officer for his help. This latter appearance of a peripheral character may momentarily disorient the viewer — has she been in the police station overnight, or did the gruesome murder occur in the same time period as Edwards' traumatic experience just before? The viewer then realizes that the just-seen montage of civilization in upheaval gave the impression of much time passing, when in fact everything seems to be occurring thus far in almost real time, an observation which will be carried through to film's end. This newest example of radical temporal dissociation well displays Wood's genius at altering cinematic time and space. Next, a handsome man walks into the police station, dressed in top hat and tails, instantly perceived by all as incongruous, if not downright anachronistic. This is Inspector Bradford (faithful Wood player Carl James "Duke" Moore).

The addition of this odd, out-of-time character, who appears to be a refugee out of a period gothic drama (or perhaps an undertaker, in keeping with *Ghouls'* overriding spirit), may trigger an uneasy recognition on the part of the careful viewer — this assemblage of disparate characters, mulling about in a bleak, flavorless, generic setting (which Criswell has reminded the viewer to consider archetypal, and taking place in "your town"), is quickly becoming one of Wood's trademark cosmic voids, a Skid Row purgatory where all of humanity must pass at various points of life, towards death. This pasteboard limbo, furthermore, is presided over by the vividly drawn spirit of its "creator," Ed Wood, who literally hovers over his chosen "damned" via his "graven image," tacked to the wall and with the enigmatic word WANTED adding to the cryptic clues in this accelerating occult mystery.

Bradford enters Robbins' office and another barren space, including a door which doesn't have a doorknob, just a hole where one should be. Bradford reveals that he was on his way to the opera, and this is why he was dressed in the fancy duds; the "real" reason for Wood dressing his character thus will be seen anon. Over Bradford's protests, Robbins assigns Bradford what is being called "The Black Ghost Murder" case. As Robbins fills Bradford in, he coyly whispers, "It might be *ghosts!*" It is revealed that the house in question is, in fact, "the old house on Willows Lake," and the observant Wood viewer will recall that this is the same location as Dr. Vornoff's laboratory in *Bride of the Monster*, another interesting reference to an earlier Wood screenplay. Bradford reinforces this connection: "Oh, you mean that old road that goes by that old house I investigated a few years ago — the one that was destroyed by lightning?" Wood thus connects *Ghouls* to *Bride of the Monster* in a very specific narrative way. Explaining the apparent discrepancy of strange happenings occurring at a supposedly destroyed house, Robbins casually states, "You knew someone rebuilt it, right?" Elaborating, Robbins states, "A little while ago, a farmer and his wife charged in here..." which leads to a flashback in which we see the elderly Edwards couple driving along a lonely country road at night; in traditional Wood form, the scene alternates between exterior establishing shots at dusk, and studio-bound interiors shot against a pitch-black backdrop.

Robbins continues, "The old couple were driving along and the storm was coming up..." as the scene shows the bickering couple. Martha wails, "It's dark as pitch out there — I can't see a thing." Henry reminds Martha that they must "cross the mountain before the storm comes"—clearly alluding to biblical symbology. Henry soon points out the legendary house of Vornoff, and Martha asks, "You mean that place where the mad doctor made *monsters?*" Announced by a signature thunder-and-lightning segue, there follows a shot of a dilapidated old shanty, a complete wreck which quickly contradicts the possibility that this tumbledown shack was recently "rebuilt"— it looks like a hold-over from the Great Depression.

Out of the house through a screen door walks Wood's newest "pride and joy," his very own "ingénue," 15-year-old Valda Hansen as "The White Ghost." According to an interview conducted shortly before her death, Hansen first met Wood during a local theatre production in 1957. Immediately impressed with the vivacious and alluring actress, Wood asked her to consider being the female lead in his next production, *Revenge of the Dead*. The aspiring teenage starlet readily accepted, and Wood convinced her to bleach her hair for the production so that she would appear "legal."[7] The comely teenager walks, zombie-like, wearing a tacky white gown which looks somewhat like a prom dress. This vision of entranced innocence may remind the viewer of "bride of the monster" Janet's entrance into Vornoff's lab in *Bride of the Monster*; both grand entrances established the summoning of obedient, ritually dressed virgins into the clutches of evil.

The couple's car comes to a sudden halt for an undisclosed reason, followed by a gorgeous shot of the White Ghost slowly approaching the camera, enveloped by fog. Henry can't restart the car, and Martha looks out the window only to see the White Ghost approaching. Martha screams, and she and Henry stare in horror as we see a close-up of Valda's pretty hands with long fingernails, not an image of horror at all, but perhaps frightening to the couple as an ominous summoning of the unleashed feminine principle. Regarding this extraordinary shot, Valda Hansen recalled, "Funny, Ed Wood told me to do that — and he loved it! He triggered emotions into future expression that aren't fully understood at the time it's shot."[8]

Post-flashback, Robbins offers Bradford bumbling Patrolman Kelton as his assistant. Bradford moans: "Kelton! If I was expecting any trouble, he'd be the *last* man I'd want!" This pregnant dialogue is a conscious segue into Kelton's "grand entrance" as a main character in

The sublime Valda Hansen, who stars as "The White Ghost" in Wood's surreal send-up of religious dogma, *Night of the Ghouls*, had a sporadic and underappreciated acting career. Valda is pictured here (center, with unidentified cast members) as a frontier prostitute in *Cain's Way* (1970), a low-budget Western which also featured the ubiquitous John Carradine.

Ghouls, not merely reprising but significantly expanding his character from *Bride of the Monster* and *Plan 9*. In *Ghouls*, Kelton's "shining moment," Wood paints his cosmic buffoon with broad strokes; the cowardly cop's constant, terrified commentary on the proceedings succinctly reflects the unexpressed sentiments of his community, especially regarding the ever-present fear of death.

Kelton scurries into Robbins' office and makes a wisecrack about going to the opera with Bradford, perhaps an oblique reference to homosexuality and high culture. After discovering that he is to accompany Bradford to the old Willows Place, where he had previously been sent to help destroy Vornoff's monsters, Kelton exits the office in deadpan; but when the door is closed, he yells at the top of his lungs, "*Willows Lake!*" Although the timing is poor, this is one the few instances where Wood succeeds in pulling off a consciously "comic" scene. It appears that Wood may have been veering towards comedy as a genre with *Ghouls*, as seen by most of Kelton's scenes, which are played overtly as comedy, and also suggested by other strange throwaway "bits" like the drunk who stumbles into and out of the police station. One of Wood's next projects was going to be a parody of giant monster movies called *Invasion of the Giant Salami*, a title which Wood purportedly found deliriously funny.[9]

Kelton runs back into the office and moans, "The old house on Willows Lake? You mean where all those *monsters* come from?" Kelton expands his connection not only to *Bride of the*

Monster, but also to *Plan 9,* with this reference: "Monsters! Space people! Mad doctors! They didn't teach me about such things in the police academy! And yet that's all I've been assigned to yet I became on active duty!" This exciting revelation, almost destroyed by Marco's consistently terrible line delivery, connects *Bride of the Monster, Plan 9 from Outer Space,* and *Night of the Ghouls* as a trilogy of sorts, with this pathetic example of humanity its main connecting thread. In the first two films, Kelton's cowardice and wisecracking were his primary behavioral traits, but in *Ghouls* Wood expands this key character to include what might be called maturity; there are at least flashes of self-confidence not seen in the earlier two portrayals. After lamenting, "Why do I get picked for these screwy details all the time?" Kelton threatens to resign, and Bradford threatens him physically. Kelton dashes out of the room, ranting, "You're against me! The whole police force is against me! The whole city's against me!" This notable reference to expansive paranoia suggests that perhaps the male collective are trying to kill this "runt," this embarrassing clown of the police force, this idiot cosmic "seer" who voices all that his community represses and considers taboo. Kelton has wisely intuited that his real enemy is not the spooks and monsters on a lonely lake road, but his peers, who seem to wish only pain and terror for him. Wood's "everyman" is beginning to see that his real enemy is not the alluring peace of Death, but the very real, human-made terrors of Life.

Bradford soon arrives at Willows Lake in his Pontiac Bonneville, still dressed for the opera, while the Black Ghost watches from nearby. A near-dusk pan shot of the "rebuilt" Willows Lake place shows it to be a wreck, and the front "lawn" appears to be a veritable junkyard. Inside, Bradford is met by a strange man wearing a business suit and a turban. Bradford asks if there are others in the house, and the turbaned man cryptically states, "Many — the living, and those gone beyond, the dead...." Sensing a scam, Bradford replies wistfully, "The living and the dead. Well, yes, yes. Then, I've found the right place at last!" Now feeling less threatened, the house owner introduces himself as "Dr. Acula." Acula leads his new "sucker" to the "resurrection chamber" in a sub-basement of the house, close to the earth which holds man's deceased loved ones. Acula is played by Kenne Duncan, prolific B-Western villain in one of his finest, albeit most bizarre, roles. Wood considered Duncan his "friend and partner in many enterprises."[10]

Back at the police station, Inspector Robbins is startled when someone slams his door shut — it is Kelton, who walks in angrily and announces that he is (still) quitting the force. Obviously, he wants somebody to comfort him, tell him how valuable he is to society, but Robbins ignores Kelton's pleas. Kelton informs his boss that nobody will give him a patrol car, an example of unprofessional peer behavior which suggests that Kelton's sense that everyone on the police force is against him is accurate after all. Robbins moans about wanting to get home to his wife and her roast, announcing that it is "nearly midnight," a telling point considering what is about to transpire. Robbins makes a phone call and gets a patrol car for Kelton. As Kelton leaves, he tries to save face by stating, "Well, you're an *inspector!*"; apparently, rank matters. As Robbins tells the front office that he's going home, the viewer can see that his shirt is completely unbuttoned in front, revealing his chest, which imparts to the previous antagonistic encounter with the recalcitrant subordinate an almost violent sexuality.

As Robbins exits the scene stage right, the scene dissolves quickly to a bare black backdrop. Dr. Acula enters stage right, nicely counter-pointing the relative ethics of these two diametrically opposed characters. As Bradford follows, Acula states, "Watch your step — the passage ahead will be very dark." This admonition could as well be for the viewer, as he enters this latest in Wood's ethereal cosmic voids. The two walk further into this apparently endless black void, traversing what appears to be the same space over and over. As elsewhere, this

scene illustrates the persistent phenomenon that Wood's characters are not so much participants in a story, as beings trapped in recurring circumstances. This emotionally draining fate
may remind the viewer of the Absurdist tradition, especially the works of Samuel Beckett,
whose characters suffer "types of situations that will forever repeat themselves."[11]

The scene dissolves to show an exterior setting, a patchwork graveyard, which combines
real tombstones with some makeshift wooden crosses, as Wood never misses a chance to reference that most utilitarian emblem of Christian iconography. To punctuate the symbolic
import of this "holy trinity" of crosses, Wood next inserts his signature thunder-and-lightning stock shot. Shots of the Black Ghost and the White Ghost alternate, as Criswell intones,
"Near the old bell tower of the ancient cemetery, another strange incident was about to happen." The Black Ghost now encounters her supposed spiritual alter ego, the White Ghost,
conveying the concept of binary opposition in perfect allegorical form. The White Ghost
"sees" the Black Ghost, screams and runs off. Has "Good" thus encountered "Evil," or have
these winsome sketches of the conscious and the subconscious psyche seen their cerebral
opponent? This initial meeting of binary opposites will soon conclude in a most amazing way.
Back inside that primordial void known as "the Willows Place," Bradford and Acula both hear
the White Ghost's scream, and Acula annotates thusly: "To the untrained mind, it is the
scream of the White Ghost. She died two centuries ago—the first I raised from the other side
of the grave. She has never left in all these years." As Acula appears to be a con man yet to
be revealed, this "knowledge" of ghosts in his backyard leads the viewer to suspect the authenticity of these pretty specters.

Now passing another, especially dingy portion of the house, Bradford and Acula meet
an old man named Darmoor (another Wood ensemble regular, Bud Osborne), who enters
the scene through a door and expresses concern that the raising of his dead wife, Lucille,
seems to be taking so long. Acula consoles the grieving man with more soothing double-talk:
"Those that are gone longer, are much more difficult to raise. However, I am in touch with
the spirit world, and you may see your wife on the second Friday of the fifth month." Darmoor clarifies this cryptic reference by observing, "Well, that's in two days," a revelation
which places this Night of the Ghouls somewhere in the middle of the month of May. The
viewer may recall that in the original Roman calendar, the month of May was named after
Maia, the fertility goddess of Roman mythology. The earth goddess was associated with the
ascending fecundity of the spring; the middle of "her" month, when Ghouls' séance takes place,
was considered sacred.

Acula surprises the forlorn widower by stating, "Even now, she rests in this room." Following is a startling insert close-up of a door, and doorknob, both of which are slightly trem-
bling, another shoddy optical trick which nonetheless disturbs both the men in the hallway,
and the viewer, who is again taken by surprise by Wood's clever manipulation of obvious
props to convey the essence of the supernatural. Acula confirms this new revelation with a
notably didactic statement: "Patience is the only rewarding virtue." However, Darmoor pleads
to have a "peek" at his wife, and Acula offers him a brief look, from the doorway. Darmoor
opens the door, and the scene cuts to the inside of a room in which what appears to be a body
is lying on a table, covered with a canvas tarpaulin, and surrounded by four burning candles,
set against a drab, generic wall. The contours of the sheet-draped object suggest a head,
breasts, and the pointy toes of high heel shoes. This suggestion of death in repose, although
crudely drawn, is somewhat startling, and as the scene cuts back to Darmoor, whose eyes
widen, he swallows hard and closes the door briskly. Acula adds this poetic touch to the scene:
"Even now, life is being restored to her, through the scented candles, the spices, the oils, and
a shroud from the ancient tombs of Egypt."

As Acula shoos the befuddled men down the corridor, the scene cuts abruptly to another startling vision — a pair of giant feet, with ankles covered in torn fabric. As Criswell moans, "The house was not all that remained of the old scientist's horrors," the camera tilts up to a hulking, shabbily dressed figure who is none other than the mute giant Lobo, from *Bride of the Monster*, as essayed brilliantly by Tor Johnson. Wood has now thoroughly connected *Bride of the Monster* to *Ghouls*, not only by the crudely planted mention of former plot points, but by "resurrecting" not one but two characters from the former screenplay. In *Ghouls*, Lobo's face is far more deformed and scarred than when the viewer last saw him — Lobo even turns and shows the viewer what appears to be almost half of his face disfigured by the horrible burns suffered in the atomic fire which destroyed Vornoff's evil kingdom.

Patrolman Kelton soon arrives, notices Bradford's car, and walks towards the gloomy house, as the Black Ghost watches. Criswell helpfully enlightens the viewer as to the background and character of Wood's cosmic buffoon: "Patrolman Paul Kelton, 29 years of age, four years with the department, eager for the glory of the uniform, but wide-eyed with fear, at the thought of actually being on special duty. Unfortunately, though eager, not what the department usually looks for in officers." As Criswell thus denigrates Wood's "everyman," the indisputable hero of *Ghouls* stands next to an immense, brightly lit and oddly horizontal tree branch, hilariously emblematic of phallocentric culture, which hangs in grotesque "erection" next to this emasculated "non-man," nicely illustrating how the puny Kelton is an infinitesimal, thoroughly feminized "outsider" to the entrenched patriarchy, which seems here extended even to the natural world.

When Kelton looks off-screen, there is a cutaway to the three wooden crosses lined up in perfect symmetry in the old cemetery referenced earlier, another consciously crafted insert shot designed to recall the crucifixion of Jesus in Christian mythology, with the two thieves on either side of him. Upon seeing this, Kelton hears a mournful wail from beyond, perhaps the moaning of his crucified "savior." Kelton then espies both the White Ghost and the Black Ghost in different parts of this "dead space." Interestingly, Kelton fires his pistol not towards the various inserted demons, but directly at the camera, in effect trying to kill the viewer, so as to remove from his vision the nightmare which Kelton alone must see and suffer. Kelton calls headquarters and reports that he just saw some ghosts ("There's a *nest* of haunts — a whole *mess* of 'em!"), to which the sarcastic communications officer barks, "Who's been spiking your beet juice?," a wisecrack which reinforces the notion that Kelton is seen by his peers as a weak, feminized "health nut," not a "real" man worthy of entry into patriarchal culture.

Accompanied by the sound of a gong, the scene dissolves to show a human skull encased in a clear globe, sitting on a table, and flanked on each side by burning candles. The camera dollies back to reveal a most extraordinary scene: Sitting at the head of the table is Dr. Acula, resting in a chair which boasts two more human skulls on either side of its back. On his right sits a woman, who will be revealed to be Mrs. Wingate Foster (Marcelle Hemphill), apparently trying to seek her lost husband via the machinations of Acula. Next to Mrs. Foster is an as-yet unidentified young man (Clay Stone), and the elderly Darmoor seen earlier. Across from these "humans," in complete and utter mockery of them, are three human skeletons, all sitting in chairs, and with their arms resting on the table, as if they are "actively" participating in this weird séance. A truly remarkable Woodian touch is that one of the skeletons, presumably a female, wears a dark-haired wig. The viewer may thus assume that these absurd props are supposed to represent characters.

This scene catapults into pure Absurdist territory with the following shot: A trumpet floats in front of some curtains, playing loud fanfare blasts all by itself, presumably being played by a spiritual messenger, a notion which recalls the mythical horn of archangel Gabriel, whose heavenly sounds heralded the coming of the Messiah. The apparently megalomaniac Acula pontificates at length about his great ability in summoning the supernatural, in some delightful Wood prose which evokes the morbid poetry of Edgar Allan Poe: "Through my powers of the supernatural, I and I alone can bring him to this room tonight, from that place in the deep blackness of death from which no visitor is to return. Where the sun is seen to rise, and the sun is seen to set. Where the gracious moon comes from the east, on its long journey to the night sky, in the west." As Acula speaks, Mrs. Foster and the obviously bored young man look off in opposite directions, with the two candles flickering between them, nicely emphasizing the concept of spirituality as a potentially divisive element between persons.

Another trumpet fanfare, followed by avant-garde guitar-plucking, introduces the next "vision" from the other world: Accompanied by a comedic slide-whistle, a person dressed in a white sheet dances gayly across the set. This is a time-honored, comical "imitation" of a ghost, a trick used by small children and bad theatre productions since time immemorial. That Wood (and, for that matter, Acula) dared to use it to convey a diplomat from the spirit world reveals both Acula's ultimately self-destructive cynicism about his illegal and immoral venture, but more excitingly Wood's playfulness with his audience. Wood assuredly wants the viewer to see this image as fake and silly; if the sheet-covered demon itself doesn't alert the viewer to Acula's sham enterprise, the incongruous dancing of the apparition and the goofy whistle which accents its prancing clues the viewer that this image is designed to be fraudulent. Wood will call the viewer's bluff shortly, by introducing "spooks" which, in comparison, appear all-too-authentic. The use of "fake" spooks versus "real" spooks in *Ghouls* is another of its fascinating binary oppositions, recalling similar contrasts between representational/non-representational and male/female in *Bride of the Monster, Plan 9* and elsewhere.

Next up in this pseudo-spiritual "performance" for the benefit of Acula's guests is a model of a human eyeball, of the type used for medical training, which bounces awkwardly along the curtained ether, a clumsy attempt to convey the enhanced "vision" offered to the gathered mortals, in order to see into the desired "other world." After another trumpet blast, Acula says, "Many questions need to be asked by those left behind, can only be answered by those gone on." Mrs. Foster takes the hand of the younger man, whom we assume is the matriarch's newer, younger lover. Acula continues: "The light of mortal existence will die, only the spiritual light may prevail within this room. We are waiting, oh spirits of the dark world beyond. We are waiting your judgment, your all-glorious knowledge of truth and righteousness."

After another floating-trumpet fanfare, the dancing ghost in the billowy sheet now returns back whence it came, again reminding the viewer that Wood can juggle patently fake and effectively real imagery in subtle and disarming ways. Apparently, Acula has in fact summoned something from "the other world," for the next sequence defies belief or easy description: In yet another black void, without any anchoring reference, the disembodied head of a man gyrates, rolls his eyes, grinds his teeth and pokes out his tongue in a crude yet effective depiction of dementia, convulsion or demonic possession. The head is topped with a jungle explorer's pith helmet, which is illustrated with an amateur drawing of a skull and crossbones, the universal symbol for poison. The accompanying audio features a slowed-down voice moaning, "Mondo! Mondo! I am your spirit guide!" It seems that this "spirit guide" is calling from "the other world" to communicate with the world of the living; accenting the uncanny vocals is a free-form bongo-drum solo. The talking head continues: "From the everlasting pit of darkness, Dr. Acula calls— and I appear! Mondo! Mondo! Mondo! I will lead you into the dark world beyond! Mondo! Mondo! Mondo! Mondo! Mondo!" The reaction shots of the gathered show them to be rather complacent, even bored with the astounding performance enacted before them, which further accents the extraordinary absurdity of the sequence. The ghost-head's incessant chanting of "Mondo" (Italian for "world") can also be seen as Wood's ethe-real mantra regarding all things "super-natural"—the endless existential exploration in his films, and to some degree his writing, for the precarious balance between the "real" or mate-rial world, and its parallel spiritual counterpart, alternately posited as near-death, purgatory, the cosmic void, real vs. non-real icons and emblems, etc.

After summoning the spirit world through the use of this weird spokesman, one of Acula's assistants opens the lid of a before-unseen coffin, set against a backdrop of curtains, that most pragmatic of Wood's recurring backdrops. To the amazement of the gathered, a male corpse inside sits up. A subtle tracking shot circles the coffin, as the "corpse" (Tom Mason, of *Plan 9* stand-in fame) speaks to his beloved, in a voice filtered through an echo filter. He tells his wife, Maude, to by all means hook up with the young man who sits beside her, and to furthermore "permit him a free hand in leading you always." The vulnerable, dis-traught Widow Foster takes her gigolo's hand, and tells the "ghost" how glad she is to have his blessing on this upcoming, inevitably doomed partnership. The "ghost" concludes his com-munication thus: "Well, I grow weary—weak—the strain of spanning the everlasting is so tiring." Bidding his wife adieu, the "ghost" lies back down in the coffin, and the assistant care-fully refolds the shroud and closes the lid.

In this pivotal scene, Wood has performed another in his endless bag of magic tricks: He has brought the dead back to life. The viewer is fairly certain that the performance was a trick, and not genuine, but there was the hint of creepy authenticity to it, in the strangely altered voice, the ghoulish makeup on the "ghost," and the lyrical, cryptic statements of same. If the characters in the "resurrection chamber" are not at all sure of what they are seeing, nei-ther is the devoted viewer, who is so used to being tricked by Wood, he never knows whether to take anything posited by the filmmaker as verifiable narrative "reality." Yet Wood seems determined to undermine our confidence in discernable reality at all costs. One could only assume that bereaved loved ones who believed in an afterlife for their dear departed would be of a Christian bent; unless the gathered were devout devil worshippers, what possible rea-son would there be to insert a comment such as this, uttered by Acula: "I have consulted with the prince of darkness, who rules my destiny." This allusion to loved ones consorting with devils would surely offend the pious truth-seeker, strong in the love of Christ, yet Wood makes his "ghost's" affiliation clear through the constant revelation of a grim alliance, identified at one point as "a truth which all those of the dark world believe." Here, Wood's loyalty to Christian mythology seems in conflict with other, darker hobbies.

This scene impresses itself upon the viewer, who yet assumes the "ghost" is in fact a stooge, a fake set up by Acula to trick the bereaved woman out of her money. Yet the uncanny look of the ghost, which after all must look at least somewhat like the "real" Mr. Foster in order to fool the widow, is not easily dismissed. Add to this the eerie voice of the specter, which invokes the arcane ethos of "the afterworld," and the subtle tracking of the camera towards the character, as if alternately afraid and fascinated by it, and the scene becomes unidentifiable as either successful cinematic fantasy or well-mounted melodramatic trickery. Compared to the deliberately comical dancing ghost seen earlier, Foster's ghost certainly does "appear" authentic, and Dr. Acula's performance takes on all the dire import of religious rit-ual.

As Bradford parts yet another curtain in this endless void of fabric which veils portals to the unknown, Criswell elucidates: "The momentary distraction of Dr. Acula gives him time to locate one of the many secret doors in the draped room. Lt. Bradford had seen the

Kenne Duncan, who plays bizarre con man "Dr. Acula" in Ed Wood's *Night of the Ghouls* was a familiar face in hundreds of B-Westerns, in a career which spanned over four decades. Here, Duncan is pictured (on left; others unidentified) in *The Texas Rangers* (1951), one of many uncredited "bad guy" roles.

workings of Dr. Acula in the meeting — now he must find proof of this vicious, crooked racket, which preys on the innocent!" Now that the viewer "officially" knows that these séance sequences were faked, the more bizarre of them take on an even more uncanny quality.

This assault on the line between "real" and "fake" is further shattered in the next scene, in which not one but two characters "break character" and become something other than that which they have thus far portrayed. In a wallpapered room, which looks downright domestic next to the unearthly generic settings which predominate in this "spook house," the woman whom the viewer knows as the White Ghost confronts the man whom the viewer knows as Dr. Acula and pleads, in an all-too human voice, "Oh, I'm frightened, Karl! There's a policeman hanging around outside! But there's something more, there's something else out there, something I don't understand. I think ... ghosts!" Dr. Acula, aka "Karl," is a hardened cynic, as well he should be considering his occupation, and he barks back, "Sheila, you're a fool! I'm the one who creates ghosts around here. Me, me, nobody else!" The rather obvious con scheme is now revealed to the viewer, and both Karl and Sheila are unveiled as petty criminals and nothing more. Yet mysteries remain, as Sheila reiterates her observation of "black shapes that mill through the fog...." Apparently, the Black Ghost which scared her previously was not part of Acula's "gang," so *Ghouls'* primary genre of crime melodrama, horror or fantasy remains undeclared. Karl reminds Sheila, and reveals to the viewer, his plan to get Mrs. Foster to hand over her substantial wealth to the charismatic young gigolo, who will then share a portion with Acula and associates; he also reveals plans to fleece Darmoor in similar fashion, and orders Sheila to prepare for the night's "performance." This scene between Karl and Sheila nicely illustrates a recurring theme in the films of Wood, that of decadence and corruption in a suburban setting. This couple, which appears at this juncture to be a domestic married couple in the middle of a garden-variety argument, have shown to the viewer that they are not at all the kindly, sincere characters they portray to the community, but depraved sociopaths, vicious and conniving and rotten to the core. The fact that they perpetrate their misanthropic crimes against society using an iconic, if dilapidated homestead as headquarters fully emphasizes Wood's cynicism and disdain for the suburban experiment. Even the haphazard pile of junk which passes as a front lawn suggests a desolate, degraded suburban environment.

Back in the curtained catacombs, Bradford slips though an atypical white curtain to investigate this chamber of fake horrors and phony players. As Criswell narrates, "He entered into a hall he did not remember from his previous visit there," Bradford continues to investigate, and ends up in what looks like the back rooms of a theatre. Here is where *Ghouls* incorporates the only known extant footage from Wood's lost short subject *The Final Curtain*. This half-hour film, which featured Duke Moore (billed as "C.J. Moore") was purportedly shot in 1957 along with the also-lost *The Night the Banshee Cried*; both were intended as pilot films for a proposed television anthology series called *Portraits in Terror*. The footage used in *Ghouls* can be verified as material shot for *The Final Curtain* by comparing it with Wood's short story of the same name, which follows the footage in *Ghouls* almost exactly. The short story details the wanderings of an actor in a darkened theatre following the last performance of a play, after the cast and crew have departed. The unnamed actor wanders around the spooky place, looking for something he is only vaguely aware of. The strange sights and sounds that the actor experiences, he attributes to "a new world ... that of the spirit and the unseen,"[12] one of the more literal invocations of the cosmic void seen in nearly all of Wood's films, as well as writings. *The Final Curtain* was probably shot silent and then over-narrated, as the footage used in *Ghouls* is silent with narration by Criswell. As "the Actor" in the *The Final Curtain* segments is dressed similarly to Bradford in the *Ghouls* footage, the reason for Bradford's conspicuous "over-dressing" in *Ghouls* now becomes apparent.

Criswell annotates the scene thusly, in an attempt to connect it to the scenario of *Ghouls* which, as previously seen, also boasts references to the screenplay for *Bride of the Monster*: "Lt. Bradford found the staircase — a staircase he remembered so well from the days long ago when he had been investigating the mad scientist and his monsters...." Bradford is first spooked by a light bulb that goes out without seeming cause, and a cat that screams (both incidents are referenced in the short story[13]). Soon, Bradford finds a metal spiral staircase. He places his hand on the railing and jerks it back, as if it gave him an electric shock. Bradford thinks out loud, "It's only a metal railing. Ha! This Dr. Acula character probably has this railing rigged up too!" Criswell annotates the scene thusly: "He remembered the cold, clammy sensation of the railing — cold, clammy, like the dead." Yet in the short story, the actor's description of the incident differs: "The moisture from my hand causes the railing to feel clammy, unearthly. It is moving in my hand like a cold, slimy snake!"[14] As he walks up the stairs, Bradford notes to himself, "Now that's strange — the ringing of the staircase is so much louder at night than during the day." This simplifies the avowedly metaphysical reference in the short story: "I find myself wondering why it sounds so much louder in the night than during the day. This is another strange thing that only the night can answer and I must learn." After reaching the second floor, which contains, according to the story, the "dance and rehearsal studios,"[15] Bradford finds more theatrical equipment: lights, props, a dumpy couch and an organ. He thinks out loud, "I wonder what a theatre group could do with these," in another oblique reference to the short story.

With the introduction of this fascinating yet askew subplot, *Ghouls* becomes narratively derailed, and it never regains its earlier expositional focus. At the police station, Robbins and Crandel mull over Kelton's ridiculous reports. At the Willows Lake region, Kelton finally musters enough courage to peek out of the police car, only to crawl back inside after seeing the Black Ghost again.

Finally returning to the house, *Ghouls* utilizes another scene from *The Final Curtain*. Bradford walks slowly down a long corridor and finally reaches a door which he identifies through another over-dubbed voiced thought as "the scientist's control room." Bradford opens the door and stares intently at what occupies the space: a beautiful female mannequin, dressed all in white and wearing a white wig. Bradford, drawn to the lovely vision, approaches it slowly, strokes its chin and ogles the fabric, in apparent erotic arousal. Bradford marvels out loud at the odd, life-like quality of this waxen statue — he even wonders if it could be a "fancy type of embalming job." Bradford leaves the room, stopping at the door to take one last look at the haunting beauty. He is shocked when the apparently living corpse smiles at him coyly, and gestures with an outstretched hand. Horrified, Bradford closes the door, stating to himself, "That Acula guy's a genius!" Criswell cryptically retorts: "A genius? More than you'll ever know!"

This startling, hallucinatory scene, which has nothing whatsoever to do with the plot of *Ghouls* but fits in brilliantly with its diabolical juggling of representational and non-representational elements, is also a key scene in the short story, which unfolds in largely the same way, with some notable differences. In the story, the actor is at first startled by the weird white beauty which stands in the middle of the room, until he recognizes it as "the dummy of a vampire — her long flowing shroud we'd been using these many weeks in act three of our horror play!"[16] The actor then proceeds to approach and fondle the "dummy," but in the story, he becomes so aroused that he considers having sex with the mannequin — he even fingers the mannequin's vagina, which he is thrilled to learn is "warm and wet!" Debating whether he should "stick it into this blonde creature, who smiled and stared straight into space...," the actor finally decides that it would be too weird; it is then that he leaves the room, turns, and sees the "dummy" smiling back at him, presumably either in gratitude for not violating "her," or perhaps in mockery of his last-minute timidity regarding same.[17] Yet even without the dramatic import of the sexual tension inherent in the short story, the scene as it stands in *Ghouls* is still powerful, if disincarnate.

In the hallway, Bradford is soon met by Lobo and Acula, as the film returns to original footage shot for *Ghouls*. Lobo grabs the cop as Acula frisks him; when it is discovered that he's a cop, Acula orders Lobo to take him to "the mortuary room," where he is imprisoned. Outside, Kelton eventually summons the courage to force himself inside the spook house. He walks down a corridor and opens a door; a human skeleton hangs on a hook, while a dubbed-in scream forces Kelton to run from this cheesy spook-show illusion, which again mirrors his perpetual fear of mortality. Kelton soon enters the room where Bradford is detained, and another scream accompanies his discovery of a human skull sitting on an incongruous fence-post. Unbeknownst to the cop, Lobo follows him, softly moaning. Back at the "resurrection chamber," another séance commences, this time apparently for the benefit of Darmoor. As Mrs. Foster watches the proceedings with the utmost sincerity, the gigolo smirks at the silly sham until the widow turns and looks at him, at which time his expression effortlessly changes to one of the utmost solemnity, in a marvelous if simplistic depiction of the two faces of human duplicity. Soon, Sheila enters the room disguised as the White Ghost, walking in a zombie-like trance, yelling for one of Darmoor's dead relatives. Kelton (another "white ghost"?) follows Sheila into the room, amazed by the incredible scene before him. Kelton attempts to arrest the gathered group, but Lobo pops through the misty white veil and attacks the cop. Kelton shoots thrice, but bullets cannot fell the lumbering beast, who drags Kelton off with orgiastic grunts. Acula attempts to continue with the séance, again resorting to priceless Wood dialogue: "Again, a salute to the prince of darkness! Always, there is an unbeliever to defile the supernatural! The unbeliever is a scourge to the world! Down with them whoever they may be!"

Elsewhere, Bradford escapes his flimsy prison and walks down a hallway, ducking into a side door when he spots Lobo. Bradford trails the human monster, soon stumbling into the last of the footage from Wood's aborted *The Final Curtain*: In a nondescript room, Bradford approaches a coffin and slowly lifts the lid, shocked to find the body of a man lying within. In the short story of the same name, the actor walks into a dark room, sees a coffin and lifts the lid. The actor then realizes that this room, and this coffin, was his destination all along, "the reason for my sudden adventure this night. The real reason."[18] The story ends as the actor accepts his fate: "It is in that moment I know I am going to climb into this cushioned box and permit the lid to close over me — THE FINAL CURTAIN.... FOREVER. ... forever. ... forever...."[19] The charming if simplistic use of allegory, sketching the actor's play as a metaphor for his life, and noting that when the play ends, the actor's life is also ended, is portrayed fairly well in Wood's story; it is unfortunate that he could not impart more of this aspect into *Ghouls*.

The scene dissolves back to the "resurrection chamber," where Acula tries to complete the séance before more mischief can occur. Elsewhere, Kelton has caught up with his boss Bradford and describes his encounter with Lobo. Sharing a cigarette, Bradford is now sympathetic towards his inferior, having now "seen the light" of the supernatural world, and man's cruel exploitation thereof. Kelton muses, "Why do I get beat up by these goons? You know, sometimes I feel I'm the whipping boy of the whole police force!" This confession again notes the paranoia Kelton feels, as the persecuted outsider of the group; there is also a hint of masochism in the statement, suggesting that the outsider may invite at least part of his perceived oppression. Bradford leaves Kelton to relax on a couch and enjoy a well-earned cigarette, a rare moment of repose and reward for Wood's tortured "everyman."

The scene dissolves into a location not yet seen, apparently the "dressing room" for the diabolical con artists. In addition to the obligatory makeup table with mirror, there is a silhouetted human skull hung on the wall, a bizarre decoration for a room certainly not meant to be seen by the public. This seemingly gratuitous decoration suggests that perhaps these crooks are taking their chosen scam a bit too seriously, an almost subliminal foreshadowing of what will occur shortly. As Acula enters and removes his makeup, becoming Karl, the White Ghost walks up behind him and hugs him, becoming Sheila, the two necromancers now poised as a garden-variety, if corrupt, domestic couple.

Elsewhere, Bradford returns to fetch the still-woozy Kelton. They reach the resurrection chamber, now called "that draped room." Kelton notes, "You know, this crazy room has more doors than a funhouse!" Lobo is about to attack the two when Lt. Robbins bursts into the room and, firing four more shots into the giant, fells him. Back in the dressing room, the two con artists hear the shots, and again refer to the resurrection chamber as "the draped room." Karl and Sheila plan to escape through "the mortuary room" — are they subconsciously aware that their only escape from a sinful life is through a repentant, purifying death? Soon, Sheila bursts through some unidentified curtains and throws on her wig in advance of escape. Looking up, Sheila is startled to see a gaggle of dead men, with Criswell in the middle, standing directly in front of a coffin! Karl also bursts through his own "final curtain," also staring in disbelief at the horrific vision before him.

Affixing Criswell to the narrative of *Ghouls*, a genius stroke on Wood's part, not only erases the boundaries of the framing device in which he resides as storyteller, but also strengthens the notion that the tale is the coffin-sleeping prophet's own delusional tale, as it features himself, most conveniently, as its hero. Criswell now speaks, in an echo-enhanced voice similar to that used by the scam artists: "Greetings, Dr. Acula, we have been expecting you! You ask who we are, yet it was you who called for our return! Your powers were even stronger than you yourself realized! You have brought us back from the grave! Once every thirteen years, when called by a strong medium such as you, we are given a brief twelve hours of freedom from our deep pit of darkness. Those few hours are almost gone. We must return to the grave. You will accompany us there!"

Apparently, Acula's fake séances were so well-mounted, so "convincing," they summoned that which they were pretending to convene. This exquisite touch of poetic justice from beyond the grave implies many things. In an ironic, almost comical sense, the uncanny turn of events illustrates that any endeavor pursued with sufficient vigor will achieve results, those results potentially surpassing the endeavor's original intention. Metaphorically speaking, the plot twist underscores the underlying truth that Man can never successfully exploit (and thus deny) Death, whereas Death can always exploit Man, over whom it triumphs in each and every instance. Criswell's intriguing comment that this window of occult opportunity lasts only for twelve hours, and occurs only once every thirteen years, may remind the viewer of Acula's cryptic comment which anchors the scenario of *Ghouls* to "the second Friday of the fifth month," that is, the middle of May. As mentioned earlier, the month of May was named after Maia, the fertility goddess of Roman mythology, and the middle of the month was considered a time of great metaphysical import, perhaps a good time to raise ghosts.

The horrified Karl/Acula, for the first time dimly aware of his own diabolical and horribly misdirected "powers," tries to rush the ghouls, but they surround him and throw him to the floor. As Criswell supervises, the ghouls pick up Acula's body and place him in the coffin he so richly deserves, the destination he has been exploiting, and thus avoiding for so long, as a triumphant musical fanfare plays. Acula's turban, his emblem of phony supernatural authority, falls off his head as he is lowered to his destiny. Criswell slowly, and with great flourish, closes the lower coffin lid, arranges the funeral shroud, and lowers the upper coffin lid just as the dethroned Karl comes to consciousness; the charlatan screams piteously as Criswell closes the coffin. As Criswell orders his fellow ghouls to take the coffin to the crypt, one of the ghouls carefully retrieves the turban, emblem of its wearer's abject failure as a moral being, and places it on top of the coffin, after which the group carries the death box to an unknown destination.

Outside, another poetic instance of cosmic justice is about to occur. The Black Ghost wanders the fog-shrouded woods, while the White Ghost, aka Sheila, attempts to escape the area. The real ghost soon stands face to face with the fake ghost, who screams at the sight of her sister-in-spirit. Sheila now sees her own mortality in the face of her dark sister, as well as finally understanding the depths of her own egregious sin in defaming the dead. Following a signature thunder-and-lighting stock shot, the Black Ghost appears to hypnotize Sheila, who stands motionless before her; alternately, Sheila may be remaining voluntarily, perhaps accepting her fate at the hands of this genuine apparition whose spirit and suffering she so thoroughly mocked and exploited. The Black Ghost intones, "It is time for you to join the others— in the grave!," leading the entranced Sheila towards her final destiny, to confront the fate she had so ruthlessly abused in life.

A rare photograph of a young Jeron Criswell King (a.k.a. Criswell) and his wife, Halo Meadows, as they appeared in the local stage production *The Sins of Dorian Gray*, circa 1943 (courtesy of Rylan Bachman).

Back in the mortuary room, the cops look down at a haphazard heap of human skeletal remains, apparently all that is left of the "ghouls" who delivered Acula to his maker, and just reward. Bradford poses many unsolved questions to his peers: how did Acula die, where did the bones come from, etc.? The enlightened Kelton knows: "Maybe the bodies have gone back where they came from!" Likewise, the cops surmise that the White Ghost may still be around, until Kelton insightfully adds, "Unless she's become a *real* ghost!"

Criswell concludes: "File closed. The police had only their opinion as to the true ending — it was only patrolman Kelton's guess that could be considered the closest." Truly, only the outsider, the cosmic fool sees the truth behind man's precarious existence, his ominous proximity to that terrifying nothingness known as mortality. In an amazing parting shot, Sheila walks through Wood's eternal night of purgatory, now truly become a White Ghost; as she walks solemnly into the distance, her image finally disappears from view altogether. The White Ghost, the mortal soul of Sheila, has finally reached "the other world." For the epilogue, *Ghouls* returns to Criswell, who still rests in his coffin, the viewer only now recalling that *Ghouls* may have been this daft madman's tale. As before, Criswell directs his attention towards the viewer, pointing his finger as he declares, "And now we return to our graves, the old, and the new, and *you*, may join us soon...." Criswell again reclines down in the coffin, his arms folded like a contented corpse in quiet repose, reconciling his metaphoric birth at *Ghouls'* opening with its inevitable complement, in this instance a literal death. The lights fade as the end title appears; as did *Plan 9*, *Ghouls* proudly announces, "Filmed in Hollywood, U.S.A."

Ghouls is Ed Wood's ultimately profound, if somewhat daffy and admittedly circuitous, meditation on death, balancing scenes of Absurdist metaphysical lunacy with moments of sublime import to create a text of memorable prudence on this eventuality all mortals share. Criswell threateningly, yet correctly, reminds the viewer that the living will soon join the dead, restating the obvious yet chronically repressed existential truth that all men die. Likewise, Acula and his gang have exploited death to their own gain, yet were summarily swallowed up by death's inscrutable might at film's end, again conveying the verity of death's certain triumph over life. If *Plan 9* is Wood's ritual resurrection of the beloved king, then *Ghouls* is Wood's requiem, a sublime narrative "hymn" honoring the dead, or more specifically, death as Man's curse, and the poet's muse. The bizarre resurrection ritual in *Ghouls* reminds the viewer of Paul's words to the Corinthians, from the Christian bible: "Lo! I tell you a mystery. We shall not all sleep, but we shall be changed, in a moment, in the twinkling of an eye, at the last trumpet. For the trumpet will sound, and the dead will be raised imperishable, and we shall be changed."[20] It seems incontestable that Wood, as well as being fixated on that thin veil separating life and death, was certain of their eternal, highly poetical connection. Valda Hansen verified Wood's apparent obsession with all things supernatural: "He was very metaphysical and believed strongly in life after death. I believe he's still with us, I've sense his presence any times."[21]

What Wood was specifically mourning in *Ghouls,* that which his requiem honored, will now become clear to the astute viewer. Returning to a theme addressed in *Bride of the Monster, The Violent Years* and *Plan 9 from Outer Space,* and touched upon in *Jail Bait* and *Bride and the Beast,* an isolated house on the outskirts of suburbia, supposedly a sanctuary of solidarity, harmony and tranquility, is revealed to be a corrupt and morally bankrupt place of horror and upheaval, in many cases a refuge for evil. In film after film, Wood upturns the quaint notion of the suburban household as being both incubator and repository for society's heroes and champions, and instead posits that this iconic location is a veritable incubator for misanthropes, criminals, and psychopathic monsters. Vornoff's house of horrors in

Bride of the Monster, although burned to the ground, was "rebuilt," obviously by the spirit of evil, only to rise again, phoenix-like, to continue its baneful work in *Ghouls*.

The rebuilt Willows Lake "house," replete with an ersatz "atomic family" (Acula = father, White Ghost = mother, assistants and/or "spirits" = children) mimics and mocks the traditional suburban household of the day with vicious clarity, excepting that these souls are malevolent, and practice evil as their livelihood. In *Ghouls*, Wood virtually celebrates what he perceives as the perpetual rottenness of the suburban experiment, which he apparently disdains as a presumptuous exercise in unrepentant self-obsession and pitiful solipsism. Also noteworthy is the assumption in *Ghouls* that those living within suburbia are by definition myopic and spiritually stupid, thus vulnerable to the ills visited upon the unreflective.

Allied with this theme is a sustained attack in *Ghouls* on organized religion, particularly a cynicism towards any dogma which preys on people's beliefs for personal gain. The ghoulish "family" in *Ghouls* exploits both the mystery and fear of death to their own immediate financial advantage, not realizing that in the end, they will inevitably be enveloped by that which they manipulate and mock. Acula's gang, the real "ghouls" in the film's title, understand too late that there is after all a spirit world to be acknowledged, respected and feared. That Wood, by all accounts a spiritual man, was able to successfully argue such a devastating attack on religious institutions of the day is impressive, to say the least, and echoes the oft-observed phenomenon that the truly spiritual person eschews all religious institutions, for the two are diametrically opposed.

Again referencing the Absurdist tradition, *Ghouls'* somewhat bleak assessment of the religious experience may remind the viewer of the plays of Samuel Beckett, most notably *Waiting for Godot*, in which the characters wait in vain for deliverance from their apparent purgatory, imprisoned in a hellish limbo which is, figuratively, "life." As Martin Esslin noted Beckett's bleak appraisal of spiritual yearning, "[T]he hope of salvation may be merely an evasion of the suffering and the anguish that spring from facing the reality of the human condition," a stark reality which the con man Acula has now seen, being literally dragged into his own mortality by those deceased souls gone before.[22] As well, the poor souls who trusted Acula to redeem their own existential pain through supernatural means learned a similar lesson, through much pain and loss.

As seen, *Ghouls* showcases Paul Marco as Patrolman Kelton in his shining moment as Wood's cosmic buffoon, facing alone the black terrors of that netherworld between life and death. Kelton suffers many scenes alone in Wood's generic purgatory, shaking like a leaf and muttering gibberish, while moths buzz around him like vultures waiting for their prey to expire, in little set pieces which are nothing short of stunning. The reason Kelton, who as seen in *Plan 9 from Outer Space* is Wood's "everyman," is so terrified of the spooks and noises outside the Willows place is that they represent to him, in stark allegorical terms, the encroaching upon life of death, reminding him that his fate is the tomb, and its unrevealed black terrors. The constant assault on Kelton in *Ghouls* by the forces of evil is, in essence, Kelton experiencing, over and over again, that ever-threatening *moment* of death which resides, always, in Wood's perennial "cosmic void," his cartoon purgatory from which his sorry, fallen souls can never hope to escape. It is at first glance frustrating that many of Wood's choice lines are all but obliterated by Marco's consistently sloppy, rushed line delivery, yet this too may have been a clever conceit on Wood's part, similar to what he did with his lines for Tor Johnson as Inspector Clay in *Plan 9*. By reducing language to indecipherable gibberish, Wood may be suggesting that human communication is severely defective, and possibly meaningless, an avowed position of Brecht's "epic" theatre. These failed attempts at communication also convey the Absurdist truth that, when man is faced by the bleak horrors of death, language as a means of enlightenment or rescue becomes completely worthless. Wood's iconic dialogue, in most cases delivered poorly by under-rehearsed non-professionals, is an Absurdist touch worthy of note, and certainly recalls the Absurdist obsession with the demystification of language as a means of effective communication. As Martin Esslin wrote of Samuel Beckett's ambivalence to language, "[S]ometimes it appears to him as a divine instrument, sometimes as mere senseless buzzing."[23] Patrolman Kelton's irritating, incessant bemoaning of torment by demons both inner (paranoia, self-doubt and fear) and outer (peers, crooks and ghosts) illustrates this use by Wood of language both as "divine instrument" and "senseless buzzing."

Still reeling from *Ghouls'* kaleidoscopic collage of disparate narrative elements, which seemed to cover a great distance of time and various temporal planes, the viewer may be stunned to realize that the film has in fact unspooled virtually in *real time*, covering just a period of a few hours before and after midnight, somewhere in the middle of May. Wood really did create, with this epic poem of morbidity and madness, a *night* of ghouls. This, too, is *Ghouls'* uncanny genius, making it, like *Plan 9*, another postmodern incarnation of the antique Morality Play of liturgical bent. The weaving of three separate "mysteries" (the police station, outside the house, inside the house) all unraveling simultaneously and merging finally in an orgiastic raising of the dead, shares much with the traditional religious drama, albeit radicalizing it in notable ways.

Notable also is the life-and-death binary opposition, eventually synthesized and reconciled in *Plan 9*, which are again brought into play in *Ghouls*. This dialectic is most vividly drawn by the remarkable dance between the Black Ghost and the White Ghost, who appear at film's start to be similar creatures, occupying the same narrative and metaphysical space, yet turn out by film's end to be diametrically opposed, as their opposite coloration suggested. As the White Ghost turns out to be no ghost at all, but pretty con artist Sheila, she is finally humbled, lured and enveloped by the authentic Black Ghost, who easily hypnotizes her into accepting her moral transgressions and subsequent fate as a "real" ghost, who will resignedly walk through Wood's iconic fog-machine purgatory until the end of time; this is a most poetic synthesis of opposites, possibly Wood's most brilliant.

As noted, *Ghouls* falls directly in line with the Absurdist theatre tradition, in many aspects mirroring the work of Samuel Beckett and others. Most notable is the lack of coherent expositional structure in *Ghouls*. Although a plot of sorts does eventually unwind, it is halting, self-negating, haphazard, and ultimately indecipherable as a story told in linear fashion. *Ghouls* instead deposits tragically inclined characters into a self-contained space, Wood's cosmic void, an avowedly Absurdist dramatic purgatory in which characters gnash their teeth and wail for deliverance, seeking an escape route forever elusive. As Martin Esslin noted of the plays of Samuel Beckett, "Instead of a linear development, they present their author's intuition of the human condition by a method that is essentially polyphonic; they confront their audience with an organized structure of statements and images that interpenetrate each other and that must be apprehended in their totality...."[24] This could well describe much of the cinema of Wood, and suggests *Ghouls* and *Plan 9* most specifically.

Wood's wondrous use of language in *Ghouls,* and elsewhere, also taps into the Absurdist tradition of both overvaluing and negating language as a tool for communication. Kelton's gruesome rants and Acula's prosaic chants both prominently display the overvaluation of ritual language and the concomitant, insane muttering of the demented inner mind, in dialogue as exquisite as it is ultimately fraudulent and meaningless. Esslin's observation regarding Beckett, and his use of language, could certainly be applied to Wood: "He may have devalued language as an instrument for the communication of ultimate truths, but he has shown himself a great master of language as an artistic medium."[25] It is, in fact, the combination of Wood's precious dialogue, portrayed by cartoon-like characters who are mercilessly placed in a desolate, enervating purgatory of the soul, which makes *Ghouls*, and Wood's cinema in general, so akin to the Absurdist theatre tradition.

According to Paul Marco, *Ghouls* did have a theatrical premiere in 1959, after which Wood decided to make editorial changes; in a letter to associate producer Anthony Cardoza, Wood stated: "I want to add some Lugosi footage at the beginning-ending-and middle instead of the Criswell stuff we now have — and also take out the junk in the first reel — and possible (sic) change the title — this should do it — because the rest of the picture is not bad."[26] It would appear, however, that Wood never made the stated changes, and that *Ghouls* never progressed past this hopeful first showing, falling prey to bill collectors, and resting in limbo until rescued by Wade Williams some years later. This rescue should be celebrated by fans of Wood and devotees of original independent cinema, for *Ghouls* is a priceless film treasure. The dizzying combination of raw poetry, religious allegory, temporal alchemy and stark, mystifying imagery makes *Ghouls* much more than an aesthetic and thematic restatement of *Plan 9*; in *Ghouls*, Wood clarifies many of his daring cinematic procedures from *Plan 9*, honing them to virtual perfection. Just as *Plan 9* may always stand as Wood's most popular film, and his personal pride and joy, time may yet expose *Night of the Ghouls* as Wood's unrivaled masterwork, a zenith of low-brow film art which displays the cinematic singularity of Wood in absolute form. Even the film's improbable existence today, rescued from the fires of oblivion by a lone film collector, adds weight to observations by colleagues who felt that Wood had a special quality not easily defined; Maila Nurmi, for one, stated on several occasions that she believed Wood had "a gilded karma."[27] Valda Hansen noted of she and Wood: "We were on this earth, but not of it...."[28] The fact that Ed Wood's daft, clumsy, unbearably odd "spook show" never found the financing for distribution is not surprising, but the fact that a penniless alcoholic bum managed to commit to celluloid such an ominous, unparalleled meditation on human mortality is nothing short of miraculous.

8

The Sinister Urge (1960)

Apparently undeterred by the financial and critical failures of the barely released *Plan 9 from Outer Space* and the unreleased *Night of the Ghouls*, the indefatigable Ed Wood continued to crank out screenplays, ever hopeful of mounting his next production. According to Wood biographer Rudolph Grey, in 1959 Wood completed a script called *Racket Queen*, which he revised for producer Roy Reid of Headliner Productions in early 1960. The revised screenplay was shot primarily in mid–July, 1960.[1] This timing is significant, because the resulting film, *The Sinister Urge* (henceforth referred to as *Sinister*) owes some debt to Alfred Hitchcock's blockbuster psychological thriller *Psycho*, which was released in midsummer of 1960. It seems likely that both Reid and Wood were aware of the Hitchcock film even pre-release and, with *Psycho*'s extraordinary success at the box office, rushed to get *Sinister* to theatres posthaste.

Hitchcock's *Psycho* is a deft and dazzling thriller without peer, and Wood's take on the phenomenon of sexually motivated psychopaths is comparatively infantile, yet it is always fascinating to see what one artist does when inspired by another; each brings their own particular sensibility to the project, the results being inevitably divergent. As suggested by the additional filming of some sexually infused scenes for *Sinister* later in the year before its December, 1960 release, it seems probable that Reid and Wood were consciously capitalizing on the success of *Psycho* with their minor entry into a genre which would grow exponentially in the wake of the Hitchcock blockbuster.[2]

Sinister is in many ways Wood's most accomplished film. It unreels primarily as a straightforward, surprisingly coherent crime melodrama; it is only the somewhat schizophrenic insertion of disarmingly perverse sex scenes which makes it an unusual film for the time period. With the added elements of crude, vividly expressed attacks on women, *Sinister* may be one of the first, if not the first, example of an exploitation genre known colloquially as "roughies," sexually oriented films which gained much of their dubious entertainment value from the dramatization of sexual violence towards women. This genre, which blossomed in the mid–1960s before more explicit, less loathsome "normal" sexual activity predominated in the exploitation narrative, was primarily inspired by Hitchcock's *Psycho*, although the genre, with few exceptions, offered none of the aesthetic charm or psychological insight which graced that dark masterpiece.

Sinister's essentially conservative, not inaccurate position regarding the sociological connection between pornography and violence towards women in some ways echoes *Psycho*'s fixation on same; although the Hitchcock thriller focuses on the psychological motivations behind sexual violence, with voyeurism taking a primary role in its incubation and manifes-

At the end of a nihilistic decade, five years after *The Violent Years* (1956), Wood applied the same psychosexual leitmotif and came up with *The Sinister Urge*, a damning sketch of the emerging pornography industry.

tation, *Sinister* forges a naive cause-and-effect argument which, although oversimplified, has an element of truth to it. Social observers such as radical feminist Andrea Dworkin have long noted the connection between pornography and sexual violence towards women; Dworkin chronicled an intrinsic causal relationship between the two purportedly disparate phenomena. In her seminal treatise on the subject, *Pornography: Men Possessing Women*, she maintained that pornography was not merely an incidental analog to patriarchal culture, but a systemic manifestation of phallocentric culture's largely successful attempt to exploit, subjugate and dominate women in general. Dworkin stated this function of pornography thusly: "The major theme of pornography as a genre is male power, its nature, its magnitude, its use, its meaning."[3] This certainly seems to be one theme of *Sinister*, where women are invariably exploited and abused, often unto death. Granted, the exploitation of women in sexploitation films is a given, as it is one of the genre's primary narrative threads, yet it will be seen that what Wood does with the theme in *Sinister* mirrors the observations of some of the genre's fiercest critics.

Sinister is easily identifiable as a Wood film. Several of Wood's ensemble cast members make appearances, in some cases as characters reminiscent of those portrayed in earlier works. Although there is a conspicuous lack of convoluted framing devices in the remarkably linear narrative, there are more subtle expositional departures which reveal the hand of this unique artist. The use of footage from earlier, unfinished Wood projects is a primary example; *Sinister* also boasts at least one notable temporal disorientation which marks the scene as indelibly "Woodian." Finally, *Sinister* contains some of the most memorable and iconic Wood dialogue ever captured on film, and is certainly one of his more overtly "poetic" works, where the verbal takes precedent over the visual.

Sinister starts off with a bang, via an extraordinary reverse tracking shot wherein the camera precedes a young blonde woman (Betty Boatner) who runs, terrified, along a mountain road, dressed only in her undergarments. This exquisite scene sets the pace for the subsequent film, as the woman, in obvious fear for her life, stumbles *away* from her unseen tormentors, yet *towards* the viewer, in a perfect expression of that inviolable dialectic which infuses sexually oriented narrative, the convergence of objective narrative threat with subjective prurient voyeurism. That the viewer can ogle this winsome creature, who approaches him tantalizingly even as she faces imminent danger while running half-naked in public, illustrates the dark vicarious thrill which is the voyeuristic experience. Narrative film in general contains this voyeuristic element, and films of the period, such as the aforementioned *Psycho* and Michael Powell's remarkable *Peeping Tom* (1960), explored the darker aspects of the primarily male preoccupation of observing females in private situations both provocative and threatening. *Sinister*'s opening shot expresses in lucid form this preoccupation, and when the film's main title is superimposed over this female victim of unnamed crimes, the viewer is told in no uncertain terms that his prurient and morbid fascination with this woman's travails, his potentially erotic arousal over her sheer vulnerability, is indeed a "sinister urge." *Sinister*'s major theme, that the viewing of "smut pictures," aka pornography, especially by unstable and/or psychologically vulnerable members of a community, is a dangerous voyeuristic act which may precede antisocial thought, and trigger violent assault, is heralded loud and clear in this exemplary opening shot.

The terrified young woman dashes hopefully to the sanctuary of a city park, but she is accosted by a male who kills her and dumps her body at the edge of a lake, where she is soon spotted by passerby. This gripping scene, which has all the dark thrill of similar scenes in *Psycho* (admittedly sharing none of the aesthetic subtlety of same), signals that something is very wrong in this community, that relations between male and female, always precarious, have deteriorated into brute antagonism; what remains to be seen is the catalyst for this rift between the sexes.

The scene changes to an iconic Wood locale: police headquarters. The preeminence of peace-keepers in the films of Wood, as representatives and upholders of "the law," reveals the author's naïve belief that peace officers are, by and large, incorruptible moral arbiters of society, and a priceless resource to same. Police Lieutenant Matt Carson (long-time Wood colleague Kenne Duncan, in a role diametrically opposed to his demonic presence in *Night of the Ghouls*) hears about the latest "lake murder" and asks a subordinate, Kline (Fred Mason), to gather information on the case. (The obedient flunky Kline appears to be a humorless stand-in for the clownish Officer Kelton of previous Wood infamy. One wonders if it was producer Reid, or Wood himself, who thought that the injection of a comic observer to violent sexual death might be too much, even for the sexploitation crowd, as the absence of this element of absurd wisdom in *Sinister* is conspicuous.) Carson summons his associate, Lt. Randy Stone (C.J. "Duke" Moore, essentially reprising his role from *Night of the Ghouls*), and they venture to the lake. Examining the corpse, Stone notes how young and innocent the victim looked, while Carson counters, "Maybe she grew up during that moment of truth," that "truth" being the violent nature of the predatory male in a degraded community. Stone offers, "I'll give ya 50 to 1 that girl's connected to that smut picture racket!" and *Sinister's* main theme is introduced: Sexual violence towards women is largely due to, and inflamed by, the proliferation of mass-produced pornographic materials. As observers such as Dworkin have noted, pornography in itself is a form of sexual violence towards women, a "system of dominance and submission,"[4] which perfectly encapsulates man's seemingly intrinsic need to terrorize women even as he objectifies and worships them, that terror being "the outstanding theme and consequence of male history."[5]

Almost as a conscious counterpoint to this dark allusion, the mood of *Sinister* changes drastically in the next scene. Three pretty young women pose together in what appears to be a film studio, while an old man standing behind a camera gives orders. A comical music cue accents the intended light-hearted nature of the scene, which appears playful and harmless, the complete antithesis of the brutal reality just witnessed. Jaffe, the apparent "director" (Harry Keatan), fusses about and orders stagehands around in a scene which mocks the artistic pretensions of the filmmaker. This is the first of several instances in *Sinister* in which Wood makes light of himself as a director, as well as his peers in the exploitation film industry, who churn out "trash" while pretending to make "art," an interesting comment on the propensity for male delusion and rationalization, especially in areas which tend to objectify and exploit women.

Johnny Ryde (Carl Anthony) enters and tells Jaffe that their boss, a woman named Gloria Henderson, wants her inventory moved elsewhere for safekeeping; the viewer can well imagine this "inventory" to be films and/or pictures of a prurient variety. As the men talk, the models take a break elsewhere in the studio. Suddenly, a shirtless man (Henry Kekoanui) enters this area. He is short and muscular, and sports dark hair and a bushy mustache. He ogles a model standing next to him with undisguised lust, and quickly injects this virtually comic scene with an element both fearsome and potentially sinister. He appears to be Wood's manifestation of something akin to pure male libido, the unbridled sexual lust of man incarnated in vivid, if simplistic form.

Jaffe prepares to finish his photo shoot, ordering a lackey to bring him his chair, in another nod to artistic pretension. Suddenly, the door bursts open and police raid the place. As the model standing next to the shirtless brute runs in terror, she loses her frilly robe, which the brute grabs and fondles lustily, reinforcing his role as the personification of male lechery. Carson, Stone and Kline gather up all the participants in a shot which illustrates well how Wood could choreograph a scene when he cared to take the time. Jaffe reluctantly gives the cops the keys to the storeroom; when Carson and Randy peer inside, there is a cutaway to an actual motion picture editing room, complete with 35mm splicer and rewinds, and numerous metal film cans. It would not be surprising to learn that this was a rare glimpse into the room where Wood edited his films.

Back at police headquarters, the inspector (Reed Howes) chews out Carson and Stone for not exposing the "smut picture racket." Yet before he finishes, the man takes the time to carefully pore over a stack of dirty pictures just confiscated. This is the first instance wherein *Sinister* acknowledges the purely voyeuristic elements of pornography, how it may be vicariously "enjoyed" by disparate members of the community, even those who are purportedly against it; it could even be suggested that the viewing of the pictures by the inspector triggered some innate lust within, and that this was the cause of his subsequent angry outburst. Kline enters the office to inform Carson that "a taxpayer named Romaine" would like to see them. An elderly gentleman enters (Wood regular Harvey B. Dunn, in a marvelous bit part) and rants about the high taxes he pays as a local businessman. Romaine then gets to the main point of his visit: He thinks it is foolish to spend taxpayer money on cleaning up "this silly dirty picture business!" The agitated citizen insists that the cops should spend less time on what he considers a harmless deviance, to spend more time on "important crimes" like "robberies, murders, and gangs of young hoodlums that roam the street."

Romaine can't fathom why the police are so concerned about squashing those who produce "a few girly pictures that never hurt anyone!" Romaine clearly represents the social liberalist viewpoint regarding pornography, which is viewed as a beneficial expression of free speech, merely innocent fun for all parties concerned. As Wood's mouthpiece, Carson proceeds to disavow Romaine of that delusional notion posthaste: "For your information, Mr. Taxpayer, the dirty picture racket can be directly connected to a goodly percentage of the major crimes in this city!" Romaine, sincerely moved, asks how this could be possible, and Carson states, "We'd need a psychiatrist to explain it to you," an interesting point as the sociological and psychological connections between pornography and violent crime are circuitous. To press home his point, Carson shows Romaine some photographs of the victims of pornography, young women, who were "tortured — mutilated — murdered!" As dramatic music rises, Romaine stares in utter disbelief at several somewhat erotic scenes of posed bondage, into which is mixed one actual "death photo," of the blonde assaulted at the film's start. Certainly, the sheer absurdity of cops allowing an anonymous citizen to view such gruesome photographs, which after all are evidence in a murder investigation, is a breech of protocol unlikely in real life; Wood is using the device to underscore his main thesis, which is articulated vividly by Carson as Romaine ogles the "snuff" imagery:

> Not a pretty sight, is it? Let these pictures get in the hands of certain characters, and they just have to go out and try it themselves! You know what pictures like this can cause? Sex maniac headlines! Murder! Some characters will steal or kill, just to get this stuff! It's worse than dope for them! Mr. Taxpayer, the smut picture racket is worse than kidnapping or dope, and can lead to the same place for somebody — the morgue! Show me a crime, and I'll show you a picture that could have caused it!

The scene also restates one of *Sinister*'s main themes, that a community infested with such vile imagery also engages in and is responsible for it, vicariously participating through individual and collective acts of voyeurism. The viewer can never know what the cops, or the taxpayer, is thinking or feeling as they pore over these depictions of the debased and abused female body, yet the cops allowing Romaine to view the pictures has all the qualities of the pornographer showing same pictures to his paying customers, and also of filmmaker Wood offering them to his audience. Wood is thus vividly stating that all men are voyeurs of the debased arts, all men are guilty of participating, all men are responsible for its proliferation. In order to bring the point home even more brutally, Carson asks Romaine if he has any daughters. The still-shocked man appears to have been rendered speechless by this shocking revelation of pure evil residing in his community. As he opens the door to leave, he utters, "Yes—I have *two* daughters."

This fascinating scene offers much in terms of illustrating the interrelation between ostensibly opposed factions of a community. The cops and the average citizen are as obsessed with pornography as are the manufacturers and consumers of same, thus revealing their underlying solidarity. As many have noted, and as Wood himself sketched previously, especially in *Jail Bait* (1954), both law-keeper and law-breaker have much in common in their overriding zeitgeist, being in essence two sides of the same coin, and both are perceived as romantic heroes of a sort by their community, and assuredly in popular culture. Dworkin states this phenomenon succinctly: "In male culture, police are heroic and so are outlaws; males who enforce standards are heroic and so are those who violate them."[6]

Romaine's revelation "I have two daughters" identifies him as merely another patriarch in patriarchal society, a microcosmic cog in the macrocosmic cultural wheel which dominates women even as it purports to cherish and protect same, from daughters and wives to models and whores. Further, these disparate male members of the community have more in common with society's outlaws than they may care to note, as dominion over women, either for personal gain or personal glory, seems to be their overarching agenda; Dworkin notes, "It is a mistake to view the warring factions of male culture as genuinely distinct from one another: in fact, these warring factions operate in near-perfect harmony to keep women at their mercy, one way or another."[7]

The scene changes, tellingly, to a modern household in suburbia, that supposedly tranquil and moral postwar citadel which in the films of Wood instead fuels dysfunction, harbors corruption, and breeds evil. From *Glen or Glenda?* onward, the suburban domicile in the Wood film canon is a not a location of peaceful society and moral upbringing, but discord, deception, and even diabolism. Thus, when the scene enters the living room of the house, and attractive blonde Gloria Henderson (Jean Fontaine) is seen at a desk, the viewer may assume that this is not a typical domestic housewife, but a much darker character. Outside, a shiny new automobile pulls into the driveway; thus far, the scene depicts a stereotypical domestic setting in postwar suburbia, with the passive housewife waiting at home until the breadwinner husband returns from work. The man, who can be recognized as Johnny Ryde, the thug seen earlier, enters the house as the woman wisecracks, "Honey, you're letting the flies out, " significant in that it paints the woman not as a typical, nurturing *hausfrau*, but something contradictory, even antithetical. The notion of letting bacteria-carrying pests *out of*, not into the house also suggests that, in contrast to the typical domestic household, portrayed in popular culture as a bastion of moral purity and obsessive cleanliness, a sanctuary whose members doggedly attempted to keep the messiness of the "dirty" natural world outside its doors, here the flies, representing both the unruliness and the dirtiness of the natural world, are *inside*, liable to contaminate the outside world should they escape. Surely what exists inside this household is "dirty," in both the literal and figurative sense, so with this clever exchange, *Sinister* paints the ostensibly tranquil suburban domicile as filthy and malevolent, adding another ingenious portrayal of suburbia as a corrupt dystopian world to the Wood film canon.

Johnny informs Gloria of the police raid on her film studio, and the woman reacts with an anger which borders on viciousness, turning from benign housewife to hateful criminal before the viewer's eyes. Gloria then asks Johnny, "Now, what about Shirley?" Johnny replies that someone named "Dirk" has "taken care" of this person, and the viewer may assume that Shirley was the poor blonde murdered at the film's opening, and that Dirk was the killer. Apparently, Shirley had learned too much about Gloria's business, and had to be liquidated. (It is always amusing to find reference to "Shirley," Wood's transvestite alter ego in his works, a reference which occurred with increasing frequency with Wood's prolific writings in the 1960s.) Johnny wonders aloud if their relationship with the killer Dirk might be a source of trouble down the line, noting, "That knife of his— he enjoys using it too much." Dirk's knife is used here as a simple yet effective metaphor for violent phallocentric society, which literally disembowels the objectified women it desires and abuses with its phallus-shaped weaponry. Perhaps "metaphor" is inaccurate as a descriptor here, as the phallocentric weapons of patriarchy (gun, knife, spear, etc.) are used literally, not metaphorically, against women by the unstable, misogynist male, attempting to sever the male-female binary via violent force. Here, *Sinister* elucidates one of the main observations of critics of phallocentric culture; for example, Andrea Dworkin states, "The symbols of terror are commonplace and familiar: the gun, the knife, the bomb, the fist, and so on. Even more significant is the hidden symbol of terror, the penis."[8]

Discussing business, Johnny requests "a hundred 4 × 5s, for the local high school outlet." As quaint as this enterprise of passing out recycled bondage photographs to teenagers might seem to the viewer today, the institutional corruption of minors through the desensitizing influence of mass-produced and distributed pornographic imagery is real and documented, and in the decade(s) following *Sinister*'s release came to pass in unforeseen ways. The scene changes to Jake's Pizza Joint, one of the outlets for pornographic material as described earlier. According to several sources, much of this footage was filmed several years earlier for an unfinished project called *Rock and Roll Hell*; Wood managed to incorporate this footage in both *Night of the Ghouls* and *Sinister*.[9] The impressive establishing shots show a large group of teenagers happily dancing and eating at an outside cafe, in what is possibly the "biggest" single scene ever mounted by Wood. Inside, two young men approach each other, switchblades open, preparing to fight. This amazing historical footage features Conrad Brooks, Wood's long-time associate, and Wood himself, again in footage filmed five years previously for the unfinished *Rock and Roll Hell*. As Wood and Brooks prepare to fight, owner Jake breaks the top off a wine bottle as a threat, causing the two warriors to back off. Outside, another party enters the scene: Dirk, *Sinister*'s "psycho killer" (well-played by 18-year-old newcomer Dino Fantini). Dirk stares through a window at the action supposedly occurring inside. Inside, the entire gang of youth leaves with Brooks, as Wood sits alone, looking forlorn. Wood watches as Jake makes a transaction with a woman at the counter. Dirk listens in, as an overdubbed conversation verifies that Jake has paid the woman, Janet, for more smut pictures, but complains that he needs new material. As for his current pornographic inventory, he declares, "Everyone from 7 to 70 has 'em!" Wood and Janet leave together, so it may be assumed that Wood's peripheral character in *Sinister* is involved in the smut picture racket, either as a bodyguard to peddler Janet, or perhaps just a boyfriend. Once outside, Brooks again threatens Wood, whom he calls "Danny," and the two engage in a rough-and-tumble fistfight which ends up in a ditch. In cutaway shots, Dirk watches the violence, completely unmoved, nicely illustrating his sociopathic nature and reinforcing the voyeuristic theme of *Sinister*, that the viewing of sex and violence can be as arousing to some as participating in same. Perhaps ironically, it is Dirk who calls the police to intervene.

To the police's delight, Jake and gang are caught red-handed with the dirty pictures. It

turns out that Danny (Wood) and the other man (Brooks) are low-level smut peddlers battling for territory; Wood thus places himself directly into *Sinister* as a pornographer, one of
several instances in the film of critical self-reference on the part of the author. Back at Gloria's corrupted suburban homestead, the female thug relaxes on the back porch. Johnny calls
to inform her that an ice cream seller named Clauson, another distributor of dirty pictures,
is "holding out on them," and she orders Janet and her gang to "rough him up." The following scene depicts Janet and three other females visiting Clauson's business, which is a hot dog
stand on the outskirts of town. This footage, shot silent and overdubbed, is purportedly from
another unfinished project of Wood and Conrad Brooks, entitled *Hellborn*.[10] Its use here,
although expedient, is somewhat jarring as it differs wildly from the virtually professional
look of the main narrative sequences in *Sinister*. Still, the sight of four well-dressed teenage
girls, replete with purses, beating the crap out of Clauson is classic Wood imagery and in its
crude and simplistic way does add to the accruing imagery of the redefinition of gender roles
in postwar America which Wood was so adept at sketching. The young women surprise Clauson as he eats one of his own ice cream cones. Two of the women attack the man, apparently
choking him with his own confection, while another raids the cash register, retrieving the
withheld funds.

Back at Carson's office, the lawman views more pornographic pictures. One assumes he
is viewing them for official purposes only, but here again *Sinister* suggests the universal pastime of male voyeurism, to which no member of a community is immune. Carson receives
a call stating that Clauson is in the hospital, in "serious" condition. Apparently, Janet's gang
of female teenagers were highly effective in committing violence against a male they deemed
an exploiter of females, both through his distribution of imagery depicting the degradation
of the female body, but also through his embezzlement of funds from an organization apparently run by a woman. As with the male rape scene in the Wood-scripted *The Violent Years*
(1956), here is a disarmingly simple yet effective reversal of traditional gender roles, as young
females take on the characteristics, albeit momentarily, of the brute power of entrenched
patriarchy.

The scene returns to Gloria's living room, where she and Johnny are watching some
16mm movies projected onto a screen, another completely innocent and ubiquitous suburban activity, here given a most "sinister" twist, as the movies are pornographic. Perhaps Wood
is also suggesting that the movies which the average domestic couple watched in the privacy
of their own home weren't always of the squeaky-clean "home movie" variety usually assumed.
Oddly, this new film features Janet, Gloria's tough female fence, and Dirk, the killer psychopath; the inference of placing these two unstable individuals in a choreographed sexual
situation is unsettling, to say the least. Gloria reminds Johnny how "unstable," i.e., deadly,
Dirk is when sexually aroused by pornography (seemingly either as participant or voyeur),
but Johnny maintains that he can keep Dirk in check. In this scene, Gloria wears a clingy
bathing suit topped by a frilly robe, a trademark Wood fetish.[11]

As illustration of the conversation just ended, the scene changes to a local park, where
Dirk encounters a trampish young woman, who openly flirts for his attention. Dirk offers her
a cigarette but then refuses to light it for her, showing in simple relief his complete disdain
for females. The insulted, yet intrigued woman follows Dirk to a picnic bench, where she
strokes her leg seductively. Dirk embraces the woman, who responds passionately. When Dirk
becomes enraged with wanton lust, the woman escapes from his menacing clutches, tearing
her blouse as she does. Dirk follows the woman and rips off her bra, rendering her topless in
a brief scene which catapults *Sinister* into pure sexploitation territory, amusingly mirroring
the "smut pictures" the film purportedly rails against. In an emblematic act of gender-based

hatred, the misogynist Dirk slugs the fully exposed female, who falls to the ground. Dirk retrieves his beloved knife, his deadly phallus surrogate, and attacks the woman, in that most vile analog of rape, the sexually fueled stabbing death.

Back at the Henderson ranch, Gloria and Johnny enjoy another pornographic film. This time, the viewer is allowed to see the film being projected, set in a self-reflexive frame by a home movie projection screen. The scene shows the brutish, shirtless man seen earlier, beating two scantily clad females. The man coils up a whip, which he has presumably recently used on the women, as the females approach their abuser and embrace him passionately. This stunning segment clearly illustrates a dominant male fantasy, that woman not merely endure but *enjoy* violent abuse by males, even inviting it, and that it arouses them sexually. As fantasy, the film sequence would assuredly be arousing to a sizable portion of the male population; as social narrative and a reflection of reality, it is inane and erroneous. The sado-masochistic tradition notwithstanding, the violent abuse of females by males for sexual arousal, although ubiquitous in popular culture, is not acknowledged or celebrated by the female collective. According to commentators such as Dworkin, the male perception of the female is wildly askew, in terms of her motivations, desires, and even physical presence, and the male depiction of women in popular culture is "bizarre, distorted, fragmented at best, demented in the main,"[12] descriptions which accurately characterize the previous scene. As for the use of the whip on the women, this tiresome emblem of male erotic fantasy most assuredly stands in as an analog to the penis; even such traditional male commentators as Havelock Ellis celebrated the whip as "a logical and inevitable expression of the penis,"[13] a comment which plainly exposes man's desire not to please, but to punish women with his phallus and its surrogates. That the women in the porno film scene react so positively to having been whipped by this faux-penis perfectly underscores how "bizarre, distorted, fragmented" is the pornographer's depiction of female pleasure, and as the pornographer is creating mass-produced fantasy for the male consumer, one must assume that a large portion of the male audience feels the same way.

As the lurid film unspools, Johnny watches in complete deadpan, apparently unmoved by the prurient scenes unfolding before him. If anything, the "director" appears ashamed or depressed. Johnny subsequently reveals his emotional state: "I look at this slush, and I try to remember, at one time, I made *good* movies." This certainly sounds like the voice of Wood in a serious moment of self-reflection wherein the promising filmmaker, once seeing in himself the potential to mount glorious science fiction epics and horror film masterpieces, is now reduced to peddling little more than his own brand of smut pictures, *Sinister* being a salient example. As Wood would soon be forced by alcohol-fueled economic hardship into writing hard-core pornography, both in the form of novels for the popular press, and in R-rated and X-rated movie screenplays, the statement is eerily prescient.

That evening, Carson returns to his office to relieve Stone. The two begin a discussion which digresses from specifics about the current case to generalities about all the young women who come to the big city searching for stardom, but who end up being prey for various scam artists, including said pornographers. Carson states dramatically, "They come from 'Everywhere, USA' to star in the movies. Somewhere right now, a 'Mary Smith' is graduating, head of her class! She was great in the school play. And now her starry eyes are looking to the far horizon—Hollywood!" The general theme of the following sequence is similar to Wood's *Hollywood Rat Race*, a 1964 book which purports to be a cautionary tale for young starlets who are considering leaving their small town to head for the bright lights of Hollywood. Although the book is filled with numerous tips and insights for the young performer contemplating such a move, it is far more rewarding as a virtual treasure trove of anecdotes about Wood's life and career, with innumerable references to colleagues, projects both finished and unfinished, and favorite hang-outs for the author and his gang. *Hollywood Rat Race* is the closest thing to a memoir Wood ever penned, an essential document for the true Wood devotee.

The scene changes to show a Southern Pacific passenger train racing towards Hollywood, and fame and fortune for one such "Mary Smith." Superimposed over the scene are numerous "No Casting" signs. The simple montage dissolves into an office where a young woman (Jeanne Willardson) is patiently sitting as a man looks over some of her photographs. This archetypal female, who is in fact named in the cast listings as Mary Smith, is Carson's casual stereotype literally brought to life. She pleads with the man to take her on as a client, as she has had no luck in getting any of the movie studios to look at her portfolio. The agent regretfully states that the woman's limited experience in local theatre doesn't qualify her for work in the entertainment industry, and he ends the interview. Later, Mary strolls aimlessly through a city park and happens upon what appears to be a film production in progress. Inevitably, it is Johnny Ryde and Jaffe filming some filler material for their smut pictures. Johnny approaches Mary and introduces himself as "John Ryde, motion picture director," a misleading although technically accurate description. Jaffe notes Johnny's smoothness with women to a subordinate, who observes, "You lost your accent." Jaffe replies, tellingly, "But I'm not *directing* now!" This is another wonderful snipe at artistic pretension, a nice bit of self-deprecation on Wood's part.

Later, at Johnny's office, Mary arrives for an appointment with the exalted "motion picture director." Johnny offers her a part in his next production without so much as an audition, and Mary is beside herself with terminally naïve joy — she even states, "I'll work *ever* so hard!," a comment which evokes the memory of Shirley Temple, and equates the naive innocence of these fresh actresses to the cloying myopia of a simpering child star like Temple. Johnny mentions all the expenses which are needed in order to promote and train a new performer, but expectedly, Mary Smith is broke and unemployed. Johnny chastises Mary: "That's the trouble with you young girls — you come out here with little or no money, and expect to be discovered in the drop of a hat!" Johnny lists all the things Mary will need to make it in this business (new clothes, hairstyles, acting lessons, nice apartment, reliable automobile, etc.), and offers to front her the money for these expenses. Simultaneously, this will indebt Mary to the male and his organization, the better to manipulate her into the unpleasant activities they have in mind for her. As Mary prepares to leave the office, she notices several movie posters on the wall, which all happen to be half-sheets of previous Wood productions: *Bride of the Monster*, *The Violent Years*, *Jail Bait* and *Plan 9 from Outer Space*. Mary comments, "Are gangster and horror pictures all you produce?" and Johnny responds, "Those are made by friends of mine. I think you'll find *my* type of picture entirely different." This allusion to his previous cinematic triumphs is a marvelous expression of well-deserved pride on Wood's part, and Johnny's response is yet another attempt by Wood to distance himself from *Sinister*, which he himself perhaps perceived as a lowly "smut picture." As well, this important scene accurately conveys some of the unbalanced political dynamics of the pornography industry, and the entertainment business in general, in which a woman seeking gainful employment is pitted in unbalanced alliance with the predominately male business owners, who can easily exploit them. The ability of patriarchal culture to exploit and abuse females is largely predicated on their deliberately suppressed earning potential, making them vulnerable for manipulation through economic means. Mary Smith, like so many other "young girls" who are dazzled by the bright promise of Hollywood, arrive penniless and jobless, in effect in poverty, and it has been well-documented that the use of women in the pornography industry is heavily based on the sustained poverty of the women who are utilized in same. Some commentators on pornography maintain that economic domination of the female in male culture is cannily echoed in the economic exploitation of the model in the pornography industry. Andrea Dworkin maintains that this inevitable economic peril is an intrinsic part of the model's allure, as it adds to the aura of humiliation so essential to the genre: "The female model's job is the job of one who is economically imperiled, a sign of economic degradation."[14]

All too soon, Mary Smith meets "the big boss," Gloria Henderson, and reality comes crashing down on her. The brassy dame introduces herself, but significantly does not ask for Mary's name, stating that names are "unimportant," grimly reinforcing the generic nature of these sad "Mary Smiths," used as faceless, nameless objects by their exploiters. Not only do not these victims of the industry not have a name — they in fact often do not even possess an identifiable self. Gloria immediately barks at Mary to expose her legs. Mary blushingly lifts her skirt up a tiny bit, unaware of what is really being asked of her — to expose her body and her very soul to these pornographers. Gloria shouts indignantly, "Oh, brother — what's with her?!" Johnny tries to calmly explain the situation to Mary, but the impatient Gloria will have none of it, and yells at Johnny for his inability to pick the "right" kind of girls.

An increasingly distraught Mary sees her dreams shattering before her eyes, unaware that the entire scene is likely being choreographed expressly to manipulate her into acquiescence. Poor Mary falls right into their trap, pleading, "Give me a chance — at least let me try!" The naif has taken the bait, and now literally begs to be abused by these monsters. Gloria decides to give her another chance, barking, "Now, when I say let's see those legs, honey, I mean just that! Let's see those legs from your toes, right up to your hat!," a strange little couplet that rhymes in spite of itself. However, Mary still doesn't "get it," so Gloria shows her the cancelled checks and says, "You're in the hook to me for plenty!," reinforcing the pornographer's economic hold over its female victims. Now realizing her dire situation, Mary does lift her skirt, and shows the mean people her legs, all the way to her "hat." Economically dependent and socially isolated, Mary Smith has now become the archetypal object of men's pleasure, rendered impotent by male economic dominion, and forced to perform to ensure future survival. An Dworkin notes, the male system has made Mary "economically, socially, and sexually degraded as a given condition of birth...."[15]

Soon, a conspicuously resigned-looking Mary is posing for pictures in a frilly nightgown, with Jafee "directing" her. The viewer may wonder whether Mary has finally resigned herself to her fate, or whether unseen coercion, such as drugs or physical abuse has helped her apparent "transformation." A grip turns on a fan, which adds to the scene the sheerest pretense of art. As Johnny watches, Mary stands proudly, yet mournfully, in her nightgown, which flutters in the fake breeze. Following is a most unusual and haunting shot, in which the silhouette of Mary, her bare skin visible beneath her flowing, diaphanous veils, is cast against an equally "bare" wall. Suddenly, the brutish, shirtless man walks directly in front of the woman's shadow, setting up a vivid dialectic of the faint, ethereal, perhaps even spiritual "shadow" of the female set against the hard, brute, very "material" threat of the sexually aroused male. The man walks off-screen and grabs the nightgown from Mary in an action which the viewer sees taking place in silhouette. The man then returns on-screen, again standing next to Mary's shadow, which now reveals her exposed, naked glory. The systemic assault by the predator male via pornography on the exploited female body, in an act which renders her naked, isolated and powerless, is portrayed beautifully in this ironically "arty" scene. As Dworkin would observe, Mary now represents a symbol of all the women whose pornographic images "graphically embody devotion to the male sexual system that uses them."[16]

A voyeur to the last, psychopath Dirk waits until he sees Gloria leave and then easily breaks into the house through the patio door. Snooping around the joint, Dirk finally finds what he seeks— more dirty pictures. Apparently, in addition to being a psychopathic killer, Dirk is also a sex addict, and here *Sinister* makes a clear connection between the two. Emblematic of the psychologically arrested, sexually obsessed terminal adolescent, Dirk is literally a walking "dick"— or as Dworkin would note, "the penis is the man."[17] Dirk produces his cherished dick-knife and rubs it suggestively over several photographs of naked women, clearly reinforcing the connection between sexual arousal and brute violence, and eliminating any perceived distinction between man's "real" phallus and his weapon-analogs. To even further illustrate the inextricable connection between pornography and violence, Dirk kisses his knife, almost a masturbatory gesture, as he symbolically achieves orgasm through viewing the smut pictures, and obviously fantasizing the deadly violence he wishes on the subjects therein, as symbolized so well by the wandering knife, which caresses the images on the paper as would his phallus prowl the restrained female body in actual physical contact. This stunning scene reiterates an enduring notion of phallocentric culture, that the penis is perceived primarily not as an agent of pleasure, but of pain; as Dworkin observes, "Throughout male culture, the penis is seen as a weapon, especially a sword."[18] Dirk's rather comical, yet enlightening, inability to distinguish between his knife and his penis illustrates this with shocking clarity, and his ritualistic defaming of the erotic photo with his "junior penis" unveils the underlying meaning of all male erotica, as Dworkin notes: "Sex as power is the most explicit meaning of the photograph."[19]

Through an unusual dissolve which spins the scene in a circle, suggesting the descending spiral of madness and debauchery which the addiction to pornography may cause in the mentally unbalanced, the scene returns to the city park, where a sexually aroused Dirk awaits his next victim of untamed lust. Soon, a young woman approaches to feed the ducks. Dirk crouches behind a tree, hiding behind the sheltering sanctuary of patriarchy as it were, and periodically refuels his lustful desires by continuing to view some pornographic pictures which he holds in his hand. Here, *Sinister*'s theme of the connection between pornography and violence is blatantly, even comically drawn, so that even the dullest in the audience could not mistake the film's thesis. Dirk ambushes the woman from behind, stabs her, and the two fall into the duck pond, where Dirk drowns the woman.

Back at police headquarters, Carson eagerly shows Stone new pictures of the latest victim. It seems inescapable at this point that amongst the lawmen's more noble duties are the questionable fringe benefits of being able, voyeuristically, to relive all these horrible murders, through careful viewing of the photographed corpses. As many have noted, images of death are indeed a form of pornography, and are sexually stimulating to many. These viewings of pornography throughout *Sinister* by those who are purportedly fighting it reinforces the dark truth that all men achieve vicarious thrill from woman's debasement. The implicit sanction of pornography, even by those publicly opposed to it, is endemic to phallocentric culture, which relegates females to the constricted role of "Man's lust-maker," and there are no innocent male parties in this gender-wide conspiracy. To paraphrase Dworkin, all ostensibly disparate factions of male culture function in concord to maintain dominance over women.

Fortunately for the cops, Dirk Williams left behind the photographs which fueled his latest murderous rage, and his fingerprints have been identified; it might even appear that Dirk left the pictures on purpose, as a calling card to the cops, his unnamed partners in this darkest conspiracy against the female. The cops decide to set a trap for Dirk by placing an undercover policeman in the park, dressed as a woman.

Gloria returns home only to find two members of her sponsor, "the syndicate," waiting for her. It is significant that Gloria is not the mastermind behind the pornography business, but merely a functionary of organized crime, a collective of amoral capitalist males functioning in essence as an underground "corporation." Pornography is, with notably few exceptions, a male-sponsored phenomenon, and ill-advised women like Gloria are little more than "madams" of the "girls" who fuel the industry, "middle managers" at best. Although not guiltless in their contributions to the industry's maintenance and prosperity, they are victims as well, utilized by their male supervisors and discarded or removed when no longer useful. Although the bossy, very "male" Gloria appears to be in charge of this vile operation, she is in fact no more than a puppet of largely unseen male masters, another nice touch on *Sinister's* part which again echoes the thoughts of some of male culture's more severe critics, such as Dworkin, who maintains, "The power of the male is affirmed and omnipresent and controlling even when the male is absent and invisible."[20]

The thugs show Gloria the late edition of the *Hollywood Chronicle*, whose headlines economically reveal the whole story: "ANOTHER SEX MANIAC MURDER! SMUT PICTURE RACKET BLAMED! POLICE SEEKING DIRK WILLIAMS." They insist that their "middle manager" take care of the unruly employee, who is drawing negative attention to their enterprise; they absurdly believe that evil enterprises such as theirs can be perpetuated and contained without poisoning the community at large, and incurring tragic consequences. Gloria offers to send Dirk out of town, but the thugs clarify their desire to "get rid of," that is, kill him. Later, Gloria rests on the porch, still agonizing over the bad news. When Johnny arrives, Gloria chews him out for his inability to manage his "staff." Amusingly, in this scene, the two felons argue over their wayward employee as would any postwar domestic couple over their recalcitrant child. Johnny comes up with a plan to send Dirk out of town in an old car with faulty brakes, which should insure a fatal accident. After Johnny assures Gloria that "nothing can go wrong," the two share a passionate embrace, a rare thing in the films of Ed Wood, and here emphasized as a moment of passion triggered by evil motives. Clearly, the two business partners seem to be sexually aroused by the impending death of their surrogate "son," an event which paints this couple, and by extension the suburban couple archetype which inhabits Wood's film universe, as nihilistic sociopaths guilty of wishing death in their own "children."

Soon, an odd-looking woman strolls through the park, as Dirk again hides behind a tree for safety. The "woman" is an undercover policeman. Even odder, the character is played by Clayton Peca, not Wood himself. However, Wood inserts himself, in spirit, into *Sinister* with this incarnation of his alter ego, Shirley, that benevolent transvestite who symbolizes the filmmaker's career-long agenda of radically obfuscating traditional gender roles. As this socially approved transvestite passes by Dirk, the psychopath pounces and attacks as usual, but the quick-thinking lawman instead knocks Dirk to the ground. However, an unseen male subsequently hits the policeman on the head, knocking "her" out. Dirk comes to and thanks his assistant, who unsurprisingly is Johnny. Johnny gives Dirk some cash and tells him about the plan to get out of town for awhile. Dirk readily agrees, and is soon driving an old sedan down a winding mountain road. Some of the footage in this scene was also used in Wood's *Night of the Ghouls*, and fans of that film may expect the car to crash, as it did in that film's opening montage. Yet as the brakes fail, Dirk leaps out of the car before it rolls off a cliff to its destruction. An injured Dirk, now aware of the plot against him, stumbles away from the wrecked vehicle.

Later, as Johnny returns to Gloria's house, Dirk springs out from behind a chair and pulls a knife on him. In an impressive tracking shot, the action moves from the patio to the living room, with the camera following, as Dirk pins Johnny down on the couch. Dirk reveals his awareness of his boss' plans to kill him and yells, "I don't dig the angel bit!" Johnny tries to bide his time by betraying his partner, insisting that Gloria was the architect of the plan, and that he and Dirk should now work together to topple Gloria's evil empire. Johnny insists that if Dirk gets rid of Gloria, the two of them could become the heads of this lucrative operation. For the moment, Dirk falls for this all-too-obvious Oedipal plot against this "mother" of pornography.

When Gloria arrives, Johnny tells her the bad news about Dirk. Gloria slaps Johnny in the face, another markedly "domestic" expression of anger at a mate for their "child's" misbehavior. Johnny then tells Gloria that he has "heard" that Dirk has survived and is looking for both of them; in this dysfunctional family, it appears that the reigning principle is "every man for himself." Johnny fixes himself a drink and tells Gloria that they should bring in the syndicate to take care of Dirk; the distraught artisan reveals that he has never even met his dark sponsors. As Dirk watches from outside, like a child hearing his parents quarrel, Gloria agrees to Johnny's plan, but her inability to convincingly disguise her emotions leads the viewer to anticipate further duplicity on her part. Gloria retires to the bedroom to change her clothes, and Johnny meets Dirk on the porch, preparing for the ambush. Johnny tells Dirk to hide until Gloria reveals the names of her backers, at which time the planned killing may commence. Dirk is unconvinced of Johnny's intentions, however, and shuts out the patio light, plunging the two into near-total darkness. Johnny asks why he did this, and Dirk ominously replies, "Maybe I *like* the dark..." Dirk's psychological world is undeniably a very dark one, and as the camera again tracks from the exterior patio to the living room, which is also plunged in darkness, the viewer realizes that here, in *Sinister*'s final moment, Wood has again manifested his trademark cosmic void, his purgatory for lost souls where fallen mankind hovers between sin and redemption, between life and death, between salvation and damnation. With this archetypal suburban domicile now plunged into literal as well as moral darkness, the destruction of the souls within cannot be far off.

Gloria, wearing new clothes and carrying a pistol, now enters this dank netherworld, the failed suburban matriarch summoning her two-timing mate towards their mutual fate. A figure approaches, and although the face is not visible in the pitch blackness, Gloria knows it is Johnny and shoots him, point blank. Gloria shouts at the dying man, "Whatever gave you the idea I'd cut you in, Johnny? You knew I could never stand a blackmailer. You *knew* that!" This is a significant statement, as it underscores the assault and murder which started *Sinister*, that of the blonde Shirley, seen running down the road at the film's start; Shirley was subsequently revealed to be blackmailing Gloria, and this revelation led to her demise. With this revelation and the murders attached to it, *Sinister* comes full circle. Gloria calls Lt. Carson and informs him that Dirk has just shot Johnny. Gloria hides the murder weapon under a couch pillow, and the police soon arrive. Investigating the corpse, they discover it is Dirk, dressed in Johnny's suit. Too late, Dirk tried to "grow up," tried to be like his daddy, even wearing his garb, but alas, he was felled by a monstrous mother figure who couldn't tell her mate from her spawn, and in the end, couldn't care less.

The cops now ask Gloria to repeat her story, and afterwards they show her the body of Dirk. Seeing the "son," not the "husband," lying on the ground causes Gloria to suffer a mental breakdown. Meanwhile, a police officer searching some shrubbery on the patio discover Johnny's corpse hidden by foliage. Seeing that the jig is up, Gloria rushes for her pistol, but the cops are too fast for her, and take her into custody. Wrapping things up, Carson contemplates, "Two young hoodlums. Two wasted lives. You know what? If Johnny stayed honest, he might have been a big man in the motion picture business!" This is another self-deprecating reference by Wood, perhaps alluding to failed ambitions to be "bigger" than he felt he was. As for Dirk, Carson notes, "Gloria's gun gave him a providential release from his compulsive madness." That is, it was his surrogate mother's unwitting but necessary intervention which led to Dirk, the fallen "son," finally finding peace. Carson sums up *Sinister*'s theme nicely with his final utterance: "Pornography — a nasty word for a dirty business!" The cops lead Gloria outside, turning off the living room lights as they do, leaving a lone police officer to stand guard over two corpses in Wood's purgatory of fallen souls.

It is admirable that Wood managed to impart so much thoughtful, highly self-critical thematic content into this threadbare treatise on the "smut picture racket." Although the exploitation film genre was largely a politically conservative enterprise, a quaint anomaly in that its product was ostensibly prurient, still *Sinister* stands apart from the others due to its engaging, penetrating ruminations on the function of pornography in society. While admittedly taking a page from Hitchcock's *Psycho* in its elemental premise, *Sinister* approaches sexual violence from a socio-political perspective, with surprising conclusions which include some harsh self-judgment on the part of filmmaker Wood towards himself and his professional peers. It is almost as if Wood's more feminine (or feminist?) side, his alter ego "Shirley," were invoked through the screenplay, which seems to be uncharacteristically sympathetic towards the female. While many critics have noted that in *Psycho* and subsequent films, Hitchcock seemed to take great pride in subjecting his narrative heroines, and their actor counterparts, to cruel tortures and horrifying fates, in *Sinister* Wood seems to have downplayed the most egregious expressions of the male lust for violence towards the female, making no bones about his actual opinion on the subject at hand: "A nasty word for a dirty business!"

As the ubiquitous popularity of pornography proves, men are endlessly fascinated by sexually vulnerable depictions of women, a fascination which, according to some, is considerably enhanced by the awareness of the economic transaction which precipitated it; i.e., the model got paid to perform these sexual acts in public.[21] As many critics of pornography have noted, the purpose of "erotica" is not stimulation through harmless sexual play, but by the assumed, or enacted, domination of the models within; as noted above, the economic coercion of the models is an indelible part of that domination. Thus, according to Wood and others, including Andrea Dworkin, pornography in and of itself is a violent act against women, which would certainly tend to reinforce and inflame violent behavior elsewhere in the community, with Dirk's "killing penis" a lucid emblem of same. States Dworkin: "The force depicted in pornography is objective and real because force is so used against women."[22] As Wood so cleverly illustrates in several scenes, especially in the scene where the cops "share" their pornography, including gruesome death photographs, with taxpayer Romaine, the ultimate object of pornography is not the depiction of woman's pleasure, but woman's punishment; as Dworkin observed, "Terror is finally the content of the photograph...."[23] Wood apparently believed, along with many others, that pornography (original meaning, from the Greek: "the graphic depiction of vile whores"[24]) was never intended as a celebration or elevation of its female subjects, but as the humiliation and degradation of same.

Sinister also offers another wonderfully spiteful portrayal of the postwar suburban household in complete dysfunction, undeniably a major obsession of Wood. Pornographic wrangler Gloria is portrayed as a tyrannical, if manipulated matriarch, with Johnny playing the obedient but degraded husband, and Dirk standing in as their hilariously wayward son. These recurring stabs at corrupted, delusional domestic bliss by Wood likely reflect some misgivings on the author's part about not only his economically precarious urban existence throughout his own life, but may reflect some unkind light regarding Wood's own upbringing in Poughkeepsie, New York; the monstrous, overbearing matriarch and the lackluster, largely passive patriarch in *Sinister* may represent Wood's own parents in spirit, if not in fact.

As seen, *Sinister* is an engaging and coherent melodrama, with more than a hint of social

This collage of images from Wood's *The Sinister Urge* offers a panoply of sexual situations, from the tame (a girl lifting her skirt) to the savage (female bondage and torture), well in keeping with the film itself, which teeters wildly between the quaint conservatism of the burlesque film, and an angry ethos of sexual degradation more akin to the violence-infested "roughies," a genre triggered, perhaps ironically, by Alfred Hitchcock's *Psycho* (1960).

philosophy to it. Wood managed to shoot this charismatic, heartfelt treatise against female exploitation in less than a week, and for approximately $20,000, which shows that the filmmaker was at his creative peak during this time.[25] *Sinister* has an aesthetic richness which belies its meager production schedule and Skid Row budget, thanks again to cinematographer William C. Thompson, whose artistic eye enhanced so many of Wood's directorial efforts. (Unfortunately, Thompson was losing his eyesight at this time, and *Sinister* would be his last production.[26]) Sadder still, *The Sinister Urge* is the last mainstream film which Wood would write and direct; his "direction" of the hard-core pornographic film *Necromania* (1971) some ten years later is a pathetic, cruelly ironic epitaph to an artist who held such promise, and overcame so many obstacles both personal and professional. Following *Sinister*, Wood would primarily earn his living by penning exploitation screenplays for other producers, and by writing pornographic novels, in essence becoming the villain of his own *Sinister* screenplay. Perhaps Wood's own destiny loomed before him, a grim specter of doom, as he wrote this screenplay which so eerily predicted his own failed future, as well as the culture's extraordinary deterioration through the contaminating onslaught of mass-produced pornography.

9

Orgy of the Dead (1965)

From any traditional entertainment perspective, *Orgy of the Dead* is inexplicable. Even within the eclectic "adults only" genre, *Orgy of the Dead* (henceforth referred to as *Orgy*) is an anomaly; it falters miserably as narrative melodrama, and also fails as prurient erotica, its original intent. The remarkably odd *Orgy* is neither fish nor fowl, a baffling and excruciating experience for many viewers. Judging from published and anecdotal reviews and comments, after viewing *Orgy* audiences seem to either worship the film with fierce reverence, or loathe it with near-visceral disdain. Such a marked disparity of response suggests that *Orgy* taps into some deep cultural well, and elicits responses according to the viewer's particular mindset. The genesis of *Orgy* may shed some light on the zeitgeist behind this remarkable production. In a very broad sense, *Orgy* is an example of an "adults only" film genre known colloquially as the "nudie cutie," a narrative-based film featuring attractive young women in various stages of undress (predominately, topless) inserted peripherally into the story. Notably, the "girls" in the "nudie cutie" were, with few exceptions, set up as objects of worship and observation by the male characters in the narrative, and by extension, the male audience members; they were rarely integral to the plot. By contrast, the liberal, less polarized sexploitation films of the late 1960s and the 1970s featured a democratic merging of males and females into the narrative, engaged in nudity and simulated sexual activity. The "nudie cutie" was an inevitable extension of earlier "adults only" genres such as the striptease/burlesque film, in which the film itself was little more than a recording of stage performances of female dancers and strippers, often stitched together with a shaky framing device to give the film the appearance of narrative. *Orgy* borrows much from the striptease/burlesque template and, but for the color cinematography and bizarre plot-line, could have been made a decade previously, when the striptease/burlesque genre was preeminent. The "nudie cutie" in general, with *Orgy* a fine example, took the objectification of woman to new heights; however, *Orgy* was produced in 1965, smack dab in the middle of the 1960s, the decade of the so-called "sexual revolution," an era in which sexploitation film moved from the exploitation film ghetto into mainstream culture. As awkward and quaint as *Orgy* appears today, it was an accurate reflection of the somewhat schizophrenic culture of its time, mixing liberal philosophy with regressive socio-political sensibilities in ways which mirrored the current convulsive trends.

Ed Wood was commissioned to provide the screenplay for *Orgy*—a screenplay which producer-director Stephen Apostolof doggedly followed, within the inevitable financial and aesthetic restraints of the production—and the resultant film is inarguably an Ed Wood film in spirit. Wood aficionados may thus celebrate *Orgy* for many reasons, not the least of which is that here is *an entire film* set overtly in Wood's cosmic void, his very Christian purgatory

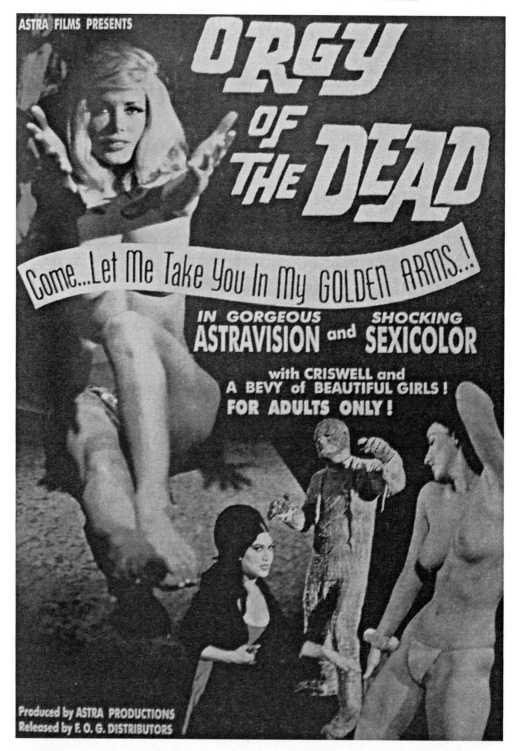

As illustrated in this theatrical poster art, Wood gleefully returned to his apocalyptic roots in his screenplay for the striptease-horror anomaly *Orgy of the Dead*. As witness the recycling of much of the dialogue, *Orgy of the Dead* is essentially a color, sex-infused remake of Wood's unreleased labor of love, *Night of the Ghouls*.

of fallen souls, who are there expressly to seek judgment for their eternal spiritual destination. The dancers are, in fact, being punished for their sins in life. This is the "real" biblical purgatory, where a patriarchal government judges and punishes sinful women, primarily for their sexual power over men. The delicious irony of *Orgy* is that the audience, many of whom may find the film to be excruciating, are also being "punished" for their prurient interests. In *Orgy*, Wood has magically expanded his slapdash spiritual netherworld not only to imprison his characters, but also his audience, in a most amazing creative act.

Orgy's main protagonists, Bob and Shirley, serve several important functions in the scenario, the first being that the couple represents the hallowed heterosexual unit which Wood both worshiped and denigrated in his films, presented here as before as a dysfunctional suburban couple in the throes of painful dissolution. Yet in *Orgy* this sacrificial couple is wrested out of the relative safety and comfort of their domestic domicile, coerced into a fight for survival in a most punitive patriarchic microcosm. The couple is subsequently punished for their sins, which may be ultimately political, made a captive audience to the proceedings in *Orgy* and "forced" to watch female beauty degraded *en masse*. Bob and Shirley are thus clever narrative stand-ins for *Orgy*'s unfortunate audience, who certainly "suffer" the film as well. Finally, Bob and Shirley are brightly drawn contrapuntal aspects of Wood himself, as vivid in many ways as his Glen and Glenda, and each person's reaction to their dire predicament reveals much about the conflicted yet fascinating mindset of their creator, a lucid comic war between Wood's male/female sides in eternal struggle.

Orgy's preeminent quirk, and perhaps one of Wood's most clever subterfuges, is its extraordinary thematic thrust. In spite of its original intent as mere prurient titillation for male thrill-seekers, in effect just "business as usual" for the female-exploiting adult entertainment industry, the poignant conceit of *Orgy* is that it doggedly, even fiercely invokes not the male but the *female principle*, ultimately celebrating it in most glorious terms. *Orgy*'s stark and memorable invocation of the mythological "World Mother" of prehistory, in her trinity of manifestations, may be part of the reason why *Orgy* has become such an enigma in cult cinema circles, both loathed and adored, and why the film curiously fails only in its original mission to sexually arouse males. As will be seen, the Virgin aspect of the ancient mythological Goddess trinity is incarnated as both Shirley and the dancers, all of whom serve largely the same function in the proceedings—to serve male ego and lust. The Mother aspect is conveyed by the Holy Mother of God, Mary, who watches over the entire proceedings from her perch in the Devil's sepulcher. The law-giving, destroying Crone aspect is well portrayed by the Princess of Darkness, whose apocalyptic agenda will summon the end of the world as she knows it. Whether Wood, as scenarist, had any notion that this is what he was invoking, or whether it was a purely intuitive act on the part of this creative artist's highly developed anima can only be assumed, yet the result in *Orgy* is an amazing symbolic enactment of endangered matriarchy battling entrenched patriarchy in a most marvelous metaphorical setting.

Conversely, while the female principle in *Orgy* is elevated, worshiped and enabled, the male principle is remarkably denigrated: All the "men" in *Orgy* are notably defective, failed creatures, in sum quite pathetic. The elder patriarch, Criswell/The Emperor, is a tottering, bloated, pompous old buffoon, a harsh if amusing critique of failed patriarchal society in rapid decline. The "hero" of the piece, Bob, is a marginally talented hack and an unrepentant cad, guilty of bad acting and worse intent, a moral coward who can barely summon up the courage to rescue his mate from the savagery of the assembled multitude. The Wolf Man and the Mummy are absurd depictions of failed men, comical in the extreme; both reveal their cowardice numerous times. The other male symbols in *Orgy* are all deceased, impotent nonselves, ineffectual in the extreme: skulls, skeletons, and tombstones of non-entities like "Harry

Ruben." This is a most damning portrait of male-dom, suggesting its imminent demise, and it is easy to extrapolate this disdain for the human male in *Orgy* towards its intended subject, the male viewing audience. *Orgy* is, in large part, a slap in the face to its intended beneficiaries, a fine example of Wood's career-long ambivalence towards the modern male in postwar culture.

As *Orgy* opens, two muscle-bound young men approach a tomb with steel doors; both wear nothing but short wrap-around skirts over their groin area. The garments seem to be a conscious attempt to mimic the linen loincloths worn by workers in ancient Egypt. As worn by these "workers" in *Orgy*'s supernatural netherworld, the anachronistic garb thus immediately, if sketchily, suggests ancient Egypt, and certainly that civilization's notorious and elaborate burial and funeral rituals; as well, the skirts which conceal the workers' "manhood" illustrates perfectly the inherent sexist hypocrisy of the exploitation film of the day, which modestly hid men's private areas while brazenly exposing those of the females.

The workers open the doors and enter the crypt. Near a glowing red circle of light in the center of the tomb is a marble bust of Mary, the virgin mother of Christian fame, and the first symbol of the female principle which will haunt *Orgy* from start to finish. Ancient matriarchal culture's mythological goddess construct, coined by some the "World Mother," who in her trinity of aspects presided over birth, life and death, had as her anchor the Mother figure, sustainer of all earthly mammalian life. Later patriarchal belief systems such as Christianity embezzled this useful icon, repackaging her as Mary, a virtually diabolical combination of the Virgin and Mother aspects of the "World Mother."[1] As well, Mary and her son, Jesus Christ, are both myth-figures extracted from similar icons of ancient Egypt, Isis and Horus, so *Orgy* already seems to be forging a subtextual connection with that august civilization which, history notes, literally worshipped the female principle as the source of all life and fortune.

This Mother of God serenely watches over a coffin which sits in the center of the tomb. The two goons remove the coffin lid and walk out of the tomb, glancing briefly at the camera. A black-clad corpse lies in the coffin. Through a dissolve, the corpse now sits up; it is Wood's colleague and spokesman, Criswell, resurrected once again by Wood's magical pen. Mary looks lovingly over Criswell's shoulder, as he gives his opening narration:

> I am Criswell! For years I have told the almost unbelievable, related the unreal, and shown it to be more *than a fact*! Now I tell a tale of the Threshold People, so astounding that some of you may faint! This is a story of those in the twilight time — once human, now monsters — in a void between the living and the dead. Monsters to be pitied! Monsters to be despised! A night with the ghouls, the ghouls reborn, from the innermost depths of the world!

The astute Wood fan will recognize this prologue as being remarkably similar to that which began *Night of the Ghouls*. There are but two notable changes in the speech as given here; firstly, the phrase "in a void between the living and the dead" tellingly replaces "void" for "world" in the original speech, signaling that *Orgy* does take place, literally and consciously, in Wood's cosmic void. Also notable is the addition of the last line — "A night with the ghouls, the ghouls reborn, from the innermost depths of the world!" — a very poetic line which one would think might have worked admirably in *Night of the Ghouls*. As Criswell speaks, the scene cuts away from him several times, to show a headstone with a skull next to it, a close-up of a stuffed raven surrounded by billowing smoke, and oddly, the tombstone of one "Harry Ruben" together with another human skull.

The main credits roll over a statue of an immobile young woman clad in gold — an iconic image likely influenced by the recent blockbuster *Goldfinger* (1964, d: Guy Hamilton), in which a madman turned everything he coveted, including females, into gold. Certainly, the

In addition to sporadic appearances in Wood films such as *Orgy of the Dead*, Criswell maintained his popularity in print as an entertaining, if not entirely accurate, seer of future events, mostly of a lurid, apocalyptic nature. Here, he is pictured on the cover of his 1969 book of predictions.

image reflects the cherished notion of man's prized possessions, gold and women, being merged into one magnificent lifeless totem.

A burgundy Corvair drives through a sunny California desert. A close-up of the occupants of the motor vehicle shows them inexplicably set in pitch blackness. The man is Bob (William Bates), the woman is Shirley (Pat Barringer).[2] The two bicker like a prototypical Woodian domestic couple:

> SHIRLEY: We sure picked the wrong night to find a cemetery!
>
> BOB: No! It's on a night like this when the best ideas come to mind.... Seeing a cemetery on a night like this can stir in the mind the best ideas for a good horror story!
>
> SHIRLEY: But there are so many wonderful things to write about, Bob.
>
> BOB: Sure there are — and I've tried them all! Plays, love stories, westerns, dog stories ...

This awkward yet telling dialogue reveals much more than mere exposition of what will prove to be a most threadbare plot. Bob and Shirley, in addition to being Wood's latest and perhaps greatest manifestation of a dysfunctional domestic couple, one of the artist's favorite tropes, are seen here as clever and lucid stand-ins for Wood himself. Bob is obviously Ed, arguing with "Shirley," his transvestite alter-ego. In short, Wood is here talking to himself, his anima battling its antithesis if you will, trying to convince himself that his fitful, ostensibly failed life as a creative artist is nonetheless valid, and that what he is creating has intrinsic worth, even though society thinks his "horror stories" i.e., bad movies, are worthless. Attempting to justify his strange sexual proclivities, and perhaps even his alcoholism, which undeniably fueled his creative energies for better or worse, Bob/Ed further states, rather defensively, "My monsters have done well for me..."— that is, his *inner demons* have served him. This is a most exciting act of confession, and the insertion of self into art.

As mentioned, Bob and Shirley are Wood's archetypal domestic couple, his problematic take on the heterosexual social construct, seen in many of his previous films yet here significantly brought out of their safe and cozy (if dysfunctional) suburban environment into the "cold, cruel world." The fact that their personal, subjective world is completely dark, as witness the peculiar blackness which surrounds them in the car, as opposed to the bright sunshine which surrounds the car when seen objectively in the establishing shots, clearly states that this couple is engulfed by the darkness of their personal dysfunction. Perhaps it is Bob's avowed allegiance to the "dark things" of the world which has doomed the couple to destruction, although Shirley's lack of compassion and understanding also plays a part. This sketching of the twin poles of an artist's psyche is a marvelous bit of critical self-reflection on Wood's part.

The sexist Bob chastises Shirley: "Your Puritan upbringing holds you back from my monsters, but it certainly doesn't hurt your art of kissing." This illustration of Shirley's contradictory nature, simultaneously conservative and liberal, pure and debased, suggests the universal symbolism of the female as both virgin and whore, expressed most directly in Christian mythology as the "virgin mother" called Mary; that this Mother of God is invoked twice in *Orgy* in the first five minutes is nothing short of remarkable.

Shirley whines, "I can't see a thing," which suggests the couple's spiritually blindness. Bob finally acquiesces to the female's legitimate fear of the unknown and agrees to turn back, not realizing that his "monsters," the subconscious demons which rule his life, will not let him. Bob, seeming almost possessed, inexplicably speeds up instead of slowing down, a contrary act which suggests that he is being piloted by his "monsters," that is, his subconscious, which has no intention of breaking his rendezvous with fate. A final point-of-view shot of the vehicle diving off a mountain cliff in bright sunlight perfectly counterpoints the occult bleakness within the car, and confirms that this couple's personal spiritual sphere is drenched in absolute gloom. The scene changes to a rapidly spinning dissolve, suggesting the car toppling over the cliff, but also serving as a clichéd cinematic signature, often used to introduce a dream sequence into a narrative. Bob and Shirley lie on the ground, surrounded by fake leaves on a fake field. Slowly, Shirley comes to, and tries to revive Bob. Bob and Shirley are now unwitting citizens of Wood's materially fake, yet spiritually alive cosmic void.

The scene dissolves to a dark, fog-shrouded cemetery, the iconic location of Wood's cosmic void in *Plan 9 from Outer Space*, invoked yet again by this master of cinema metaphysics. Criswell narrates: "It is said on clear nights, beneath the cold light of the moon, howl the dog and the wolf, and creeping things crawl out of the slime. It is then that ghouls feast, in all their radiance. It is on nights like this, most people prefer to steer clear of, uh, burial grounds! It is on nights like this, that the creatures are said to appear — and to walk!" As Criswell speaks, a man emerges from the shadows and walks slowly across the cemetery set, his cloak draped over his face in an act similar to the Ghoul Man in *Plan 9 from Outer Space*. When the man sits down on a marble altar, we see that it is Criswell, now revealed to be both storyteller and character in *Orgy*, in a dual role which seems ever-similar to that portrayed in *Night of the Ghouls*. Criswell, who is unnamed in *Orgy*, but billed as "The Emperor," and will be seen to portray an all-powerful devil figure, continues: "The day is gone — the night is upon us — and the moon, which controls all of the underworld, once again shines, in radiant contentment! Come forth, come forth, oh Princess of Darkness!" From out of the mist walks another ghoulish creature, a female with pasty white skin, draped all in black, with red sleeves and a black beehive hairdo. She walks slowly, regally towards her companion. The female bows before the male, the two joining hands in a significant close-up which suggests the attempted synchronicity of this pair, who will be revealed anon to be almost prototypical binary opposites. The Emperor declares, "If I am not pleased by tonight's entertainment, I shall banish their souls to everlasting damnation!," and his diabolical, omniscient nature is thus revealed. The female (Fawn Silver)[3] nods in silent agreement.

The Princess of Darkness is a pivotal figure in *Orgy*, perhaps *the* pivotal figure. First seen as a mere sidekick to the elder patriarch in this ghoulish societal microcosm, this "princess" of the dark world summarily sheds her subordinate role and becomes, by film's end, powerful, even omniscient, and the eventual sating of her bold desires will have a profound impact on the patriarchy which she purportedly serves. The Princess of Darkness, as portrayed in *Orgy*, seems a conscious invocation of one aspect of that ancient and revered "World Mother," that hardy mythological construct which was formulated and nurtured by ancient civilizations to represent both the entire natural world, and as an homage to the mammalian mother, who gave birth, literally and figuratively, to the whole extant animal kingdom. This hallowed Goddess figure, an indelible fixture of many disparate female-oriented "pagan" cultures, was most often manifested as a trio or "trinity" of aspects: the Virgin, the Mother and the Crone. These three symbolic females, representing the creation, preservation and destruction of life in a cycle never-ending, brought meaning and sense to much of ancient matriarchal culture, until the advent of patriarchal-based communities appropriated this "holy" trinity, eventually confiscating it for such phallocentric belief systems as Christianity, with its Trinitarian "Father, Son & Holy Ghost."[4]

The Virgin aspect of the Goddess was most often represented by a sexually powerful being (for instance, in Tantric Buddhism represented in mortal form by the *yogini*, a female who combined the arts of teaching, dancing, and prostitution in the service of the great Goddess).[5] Western patriarchal culture has deprecated the Virgin aspect of the Goddess mythos into the maligned, objectified "sex goddess" archetype, merely a servile functionary of men; the upcoming dancers in *Orgy* definitely serve that function.[6] The Mother aspect of the Goddess mythos, that elemental preserver of all sentient life, was again appropriated by patriarchal culture and eventually emerged, in truncated and mutated form as the Holy Mother of Christendom, Mary.[7] It is thus very exciting that the Virgin Mary makes such an overt and pivotal appearance in *Orgy*, for her guardian presence in the crypt of Patriarchy truly signals the preeminence of the World Mother in Wood's hellish netherworld, and states in no uncertain terms the significance of the female principle in same. Finally, the Crone aspect of the Goddess trinity is most vividly evoked by the Princess of Darkness, who after all is the female in charge of the death-dealing aspects of this purgatory of lost souls, quite specifically carrying on the destruction aspects of her mythological mentor.

Even the name, "Crone," was originally inspired by the word crown, as "she represented the power of the ancient tribal matriarch who made the moral and legal decisions for her subjects and descendants," a description which succinctly describes the Princess of Darkness' dark duties.[8] The Princess' behavior suggests strength, power and confidence, behaviors sorely lacking in the other females in *Orgy*, and this moral vigor aligns with the notion of the Crone, who was invariably perceived as the most powerful of the Goddess trinity, with her unquestionable power over life and death itself.[9] A final clue as to the Princess' alignment with the Crone aspect of the World Mother is the notable fact that her coloration — pasty white skin, funereal black dress, and blood red fingernails, lipstick and clothing accent — perfectly mirror the "famous" three colors of the female trinity throughout Europe and Asia (white, black, red) which, according to historian Barbara G.

Orgy of the Dead's alluring "Princess of Darkness," Fawn Silver (a.k.a. Fawn Silverton), as she appeared in a 1966 issue of *Millionaire,* a men's magazine (courtesy of Rylan Bachman).

Walker, represented "[white] radiant, pure tranquility; [red] blazing energy and passion; and [black] weight and darkness, the silent night of the tomb."[10] White also symbolized the purity of the Virgin, red the holy, birth-giving blood of the Mother, and black the eternal night of the death-dealing Crone.[11]

As *Orgy* unfolds, the Princess of Darkness will reveal herself to be fully aligned with the ancient mythic archetype of the Crone, or "the World Mother in her Destroyer aspect."[12] Immediately following the Princess' entrance is a close-up of the full moon, accompanied by a loud cymbal crash, a significant variation of Wood's trademark thunder-and-lightning signature, meant here to signal the start of the evening's entertainment. More importantly, this introduction of "Luna" into *Orgy*'s scenario clearly positions the Princess as a manifestation of the World Mother in her Crone aspect (later codified in Christian governmental systems as a "Witch"), whose "magical" powers of healing, birth-giving, and even death-summoning were believed to be extracted from the moon. These women's "magical" menstrual blood, believed by the ancients to be the sole source of life, was more commonly termed "lunar blood."[13]

In the middle of the cemetery, bright flames encircle a young woman in Native American garb (Bunny Glaser[14]). The Princess elucidates: "One who loved flames! Her lovers were killed in flames! She died in flames!" The scene returns to this "Indian Girl," who now dances topless, wearing only a red bikini brief and white moccasins, the flames surrounding her. Odd chant music accompanies the dance; at one point, a male voice chanting, "Yahoo! Wahoo!" comes across more as mockery than an authentic depiction of tribal Native American culture. However, this "Fire Dancer" does crudely mimic the actions of the vestal virgins, those holy dancers of the Roman Empire who danced before a "perpetual fire" to maintain the spiritual health of the community. Soon, the camera pulls slowly away, revealing that the threadbare *Orgy* employed tracking crane shots, an unusual aesthetic conceit to find in such a low-budget (and low-brow) production. (This use of crane shots in *Orgy* will be spare, but meaningful, leading to a most spectacular finale.) The "Indian Girl" soon finishes and walks off into the fog-machine ether of Wood's purgatory.

The scene briefly cuts back to Bob and Shirley, who are both now conscious. The Princess of Darkness announces the next "entertainment" in voiceover: "One who prowls the lonely streets at night in life, is bound to prowl them in eternity." A red-haired woman (Coleen O'Brien[15]), dressed in a red dress accented by blue scarves, begins her performance, making ridiculous "come-hither" gestures in an attempt to convey the actions of a common street prostitute. Bob decides to investigate the music coming from the old cemetery, against Shirley's wishes— Bob's "monsters" seem to have completely captured Bob's common sense. The scene cuts back to the streetwalker, now naked but for a string bikini brief. Bob and Shirley creep closer to the cemetery, peeking from behind some fake shrubbery, another interesting glance at another iconic, artificial suburban setting, the pretentiously lush "backyard." Shirley offers: "Could it be some kind of college initiation?" Bob retorts: "It's an initiation, all right. But not of a college as you or I know it. Nothing alive looks like that!" Watching these ghoulish rites of the undead, Bob is unsure whether he and Shirley are still mortal, or have passed into Wood's cosmic void. The streetwalker, now with a bold red light cast on her, cavorts seductively with a human skeleton which hangs on a nearby tree, suggesting the live consorting with the dead, and certainly a nod to necromancy, the sexual attraction to the dead. Seeing the "live" female in harness to a very "dead" male is another interesting illustration by Wood on the upheaval of traditional gender roles, almost a post-apocalyptic redux of *Glen and Glenda*; here, the female principle boasts sentience and animation, while the male principle is shown as nothing but bones and ash.

The Streetwalker exits, and the Emperor declares, "I would see for approval, the one who in life worshipped gold above all else!" The Princess points her bony white finger, and the two faux–Egyptian goons return to the crypt. The goons have now exchanged their earlier shorts for ones with an odd red-and-white striped pattern; this new pattern evokes the decorative design found on the Egyptian *klaft*, rectangular headpieces worn by Egyptian royalty of the old kingdom. In the coffin where Criswell introduced *Orgy* lies a woman with platinum blonde hair, dressed in a golden gown. She is played by Pat Barringer, the actress who also plays Shirley, in an interesting modification of Wood's propensity to use stand-ins and two performers playing one role. Here, one woman plays two roles which seem, at first blush, diametrically opposed, yet Barringer's portrayal of both characters symbolically bonds the erotic dancers with the suburban female into one unified motif of the Virgin aspect of the mythological "World Mother" trinity. The Golden Girl rises and dances naked, while the goons watch, in a classic "nudie-cutie" composition. (As the camera follows the Golden Girl towards stage left, the hand of the camera operator can be briefly seen at the edge of the frame, another intriguing, albeit unintentional, sketch of the literal and figurative "hand" of the pornographer in the scenario.) Unfortunately, Barringer's "Golden Girl" dance is even more lethargic and disengaging than previous performances, and not even rescued by another impressive but superfluous craning shot.

As the Golden Girl sits down, the Emperor orders "More gold!" and the faux–Egyptian goons obediently retrieve a gaudily painted bushel basket, from which they toss handfuls of "gold coins," which are plainly yellow poker chips. The Golden Girl lustily gathers up the "gold" as the Emperor repeatedly chants, "More gold!" The ascending absurdity of the sequence, with its artless depiction of the compulsive accumulation of wealth for its own sake which is the defining principle of Capitalism, culminates in the Emperor smugly declaring, "For all eternity, she shall *have* gold!," to which the Princess of Darkness applauds in approval. As the Emperor laughs maniacally, the goons forcibly remove the Golden Girl to a large cauldron, inside of which boils a mass of liquefied gold. The goons lower the woman into the boiling vat, as the Emperor nods, this head of patriarchy heartily approving of the diabolical torture of woman. The scene certainly evokes the memory of the Christian-based witch-burning of old, the cauldron being codified as both tool and symbol of the so-called "witch." As well, the scene suggests the savage torture-murder of women by cruel means such as boiling them alive, a most ill-advised expression of "love" enacted by the bloodthirsty followers of Jesus Christ. Yet previous to being misrepresented by Christianity as a tool of evil, the cauldron was revered, as historian Barbara G. Walker notes: "[T]he vessel was an important and central symbol in pagan religion."[16] Contrary to its purported function as defined by Christianity, the Crone's "endlessly-churning" cauldron was seen as "the source of life, wisdom, inspiration, understanding and magic."[17] Although the Princess of Darkness has no direct dealings with the cauldron, nonetheless its presence in her midst, as well as her approval of its usage, reinforces that character's accruing affinity with the Crone figure of antiquity.

When the goons lift the Golden Girl out of the cauldron, she is now literally a "Golden Girl," that is, a stiff statue of a woman, presumably either covered in, or turned to gold. This new Golden Girl is a marvelous depiction of sexist Man's coveted prize, his "trophy wife," literally an embalmed statue of his beloved sex object, who is immobile and likely dead. The goons parade the Golden Girl around the graveyard as if she were a parade float, and then place her lifeless form back on the slab in the crypt, as the bust of the Virgin Mary appears now to mourn over her fallen sister. The "Golden Girl" sequence in *Orgy* is one of its most interesting, both in its relatively elaborate *mise-en-scène* and its socio-political import. Ostensibly, the scene is a nod to the box office hit *Goldfinger*, in which the titular madman turned female beauty, via Shirley Eaton, into a gold-covered corpse. Another scene with some interesting parallels to this sequence can be found in *Serpent of the Nile* (1953, d: William Castle), wherein a young Julie Newmar (billed as "Julie Newmeyer") performs an elaborate dance covered entirely in gold paint.

As Bob and Shirley continue to crouch impotently in the foliage, the Emperor intones, "And both couldn't help but remember a line from one of Bob's stories—'The sadden wind howls—the night things are all about me—every shadow, a beckoning invitation to disaster! I know I should think of other things, of pleasant things, but I can't! How can I think of other things, of pleasant things, when I am in a place surrounded by shadows and objects, which can take any shape, here in the darkness—any shape my mind can conceive....'" Accenting this most poetic bit of self-reflexivity on Wood's part, two monsters from a child's nightmare suddenly burst through the plastic shrubbery: a "Wolf Man" (John Andrews) and a "Mummy" (Louis Ojena), twin icons of the classic horror film, and universally recognized cultural ephemera. The monsters seize Bob and Shirley and drag them away. It may be that the Emperor's narration was a virtual invocation of the monsters, who can be seen as Bob's comic-story "monsters" literally coming to life, his inner "demons" finally coming to get him.

The Emperor orders the captives brought to him, and appears shocked by their presence: "These are live ones? Live ones, where only the dead should be?" Apparently, Wood's cosmic void has suffered an egregious split, and the living and the dead now occupy the same metaphysical space. The Mummy now speaks, in an overdubbed voice which sounds artificial, as if it were recorded through a tin can, and which emphasizes the fact that these are not "real" but metaphorical monsters, Bob's comic-book monsters, his personal creative demons come to life. The Emperor orders the Princess of Darkness to "put these intruders to the test." The Princess complains, "But they are not yet one of us!," emphasizing that these living beings are an anomaly, a mistake in this purgatory for the damned. Bob and Shirley are summarily roped to two extremely phallic headstones, in effect anchored symbolically to their own imminent mortality in this violent patriarchal microcosm. An insert shot of the Princess shows her in apparent erotic arousal, fondling a large, phallus-shaped knife as she watches the torturous bonding of these poor souls, and reinforcing the omniscience of savage phallocentrism in this hellish netherworld. Even Shirley knows as much, as she mumbles unconvincingly, "Fiends ... fiends...."

As the Princess now intones, "To love the cat, is to *be* the cat!," the most absurd, and sexist dance in *Orgy* follows, in which a woman (Texas Starr[18]) dressed in a cheesy leopard costume, replete with cat-like headpiece, prances about the cemetery to dull music which mimics the dance-hall perennial "Alley Cat." The blatant, almost comical sexism of the segment is illustrated by two notable things. Firstly, the dancer's costume is awkwardly cut at the chest, so that only her breasts are exposed; the effect is the complete antithesis of the erotic one intended. Secondly, as this "Cat Woman" dances about listlessly, one of the goons, who has now changed his Egyptian skirt back to the leopard-skin one seen in *Orgy*'s prologue, in order to better to align with his foe, follows the woman around, thrashing her periodically with a bullwhip. The implication is that the male and the female are engaged in a voluntary, mutually enjoyable sexual ritual, and that the woman's dancing is even inspired by the periodic stings of violent prodding from the male, a most elemental metaphor for violent sexual intercourse, and troubled, confrontational male-female sexual relations in general. As the Cat Woman approaches a giant tombstone and scratches it as a domestic cat might scratch the arm of a sofa, with the goon whipping the poor creature ever more ferociously, the camera dollies in, the better to capture the bizarre dialectic of the performance. The

Emperor underscores the assumed sado-masochistic, as well as fatalistic nature of this crude ritual thus: "A pussycat is born to be whupped!" (sic).

In this and subsequent dances in *Orgy*, an added element makes them more significant in terms of their overall symbolic meaning: Not only is the audience "forced" to watch these lethargic and seemingly interminable performance pieces drawn from the Skid Row of the adult-oriented "entertainment" industry, but now Bob and Shirley, tied to grave markers, are forced also to watch the proceedings, which to them are purely horrible. Bob and Shirley are thus posed nicely as stand-ins for *Orgy*'s also-captive theatrical audience.

An amazing shot follows, as the camera peeks over the Emperor's shoulder, showing the Cat Woman dancing, with the goon following, as the Emperor, the Princess, the Wolf Man and Shirley watch, a most rare occurrence in *Orgy* of subject and object, dancer and audience, seen in the same space, which further reinforces the embracing of the audience into Wood's cosmic purgatory, depicting the sexual revolution gone to seed. A subsequent cutaway to the Emperor and the Princess depicts them as looking bored. Perhaps watching an endless procession of the damned, dancing to save their souls, becomes tiresome after an eternity, a notion which reinforces the sense of ennui and fatigue which haunts *Orgy*. At some point, perhaps even devils seek release from their evil reign, and both audience and character may be finally sated, cured of their addiction to meaningless sexual activity having suffered the aesthetic "hell" which is *Orgy*.

Finally, the Cat Woman removes her ridiculous costume, dancing in the nude but for a G-string brief and her absurd cat hood, a thoroughly humiliating and infantile portrayal of woman. A cutaway to a horrified-looking Bob begs the question: Does this male find these dances erotically arousing, or repulsive? Again, the dancing sequences in *Orgy*, ostensibly designed to be titillating to at least its original theatrical audience, seem to have exactly the opposite effect, in essence assuming a crude form of aversion therapy, wherein that which the addict craves is offered in portions both sufficient — and most importantly modified — enough to cure the subject of his lusting for same. The original promotional posters for *Orgy* challenged the potential movie patron with the amusing question: "Are You Heterosexual?" Although presumably intended as a rhetorical, tongue-in-cheek query at the time, *Orgy* might be extremely useful in defining one's sexual leanings. Is the viewer to be considered "manly" if he finds this deadening procession of lifeless dances erotically charged? Or is he more of a "man" if he sees through this charade, and feels nothing but pity or amusement? Certainly, any reasonably intelligent viewer would question the erotic quotient of such a painful cultural artifact as *Orgy*, and ponder the significance that at one time, pathetic performances such as this were wildly popular and eagerly sought. *Orgy*'s audience stand-in, Bob, seems to find this string of "erotic" dances anything but, and his expressions of pained horror beg the question of his own declared heterosexuality, which seems to be thrust back at him, almost as a weapon, in Wood's diabolically clever inversion of traditional male heterosexual beliefs.

After an abrupt end to the Cat Woman dance, the Emperor crudely segues, "It will please me very much to see the slave girl with her tortures!" This is followed by a somewhat shocking medium close-up which may make the viewer suddenly realize that one of the reasons the previous scenes have been so uninviting is that they were filmed from a distance, almost never in close-up, thus appearing stagy, theatrical, emotionally uninviting. Now, in a much tighter composition, one of the goons mercilessly whips the back of the Slave Girl (Nadejda Dobrev[19]), dressed in a peach tunic and with her hands chained to a stone wall. This is a sheer, unadulterated moment of dark male fantasy of violence to the female, usually couched in less brutal and literal terms, here given free expression. The Emperor underscores man's innate need to see females violently treated with the iconic utterance, "Torture! Torture! It *pleasures* me!" Wood's significantly arcane line underscores the sad fact that torturing females gives some men great pleasure. Here, Wood was likely alluding to the malefic philosophies of the notorious Marquis deSade (1740–1814), the libertine author revered in male liberalist circles as a prototypical champion of socially acceptable torture and exploitation of the female, wherein the violent actions of the male sexual predator are couched within the apologetic term "sado-masochism."[20] As feminists such as Andrea Dworkin have noted, however, and as Wood, the author of the virtually pornographic *Orgy* may have unwittingly confessed, man's obsession with domineering sexual activity with obliging, passive females reveals his actual desire: to brutalize, assault, even kill his desired "objects." Thus, even innocent "fun" such as *Orgy* may tip its hand, so to speak, in scenes such as the Slave Girl's whipping, which could only be seen as erotic by a twisted misogynist mind such as deSade's. Yet everyone involved in creating *Orgy*, including Wood, presumably thought the scene was acceptable male fantasy of the day, and this acceptance reveals the male group's inherent denial of their darker aims. As Dworkin states, "In Sade, the authentic equation is revealed: the power of the pornographer is the power of the rapist/batterer is the power of the man."[21]

The Slave Girl, improbably animated by a sultry "Arabian Nights" music cue, breaks free of her literal and symbolic chains and begins a dance, supposedly to appease her male tormentors. The girl dances through a door, and the viewer sees that her whipping took place inside the crypt, as the Virgin Mary watched over her. (The Slave Girl's dance most readily evokes the phenomenon of Hindu temple dancers, an ancient ritual performance still carried on, in truncated form, to this day.) As usual, the first portion of the dance is clothed, and the second portion is nude but for underpants. The camera finally tracks in to the Slave Girl as she writhes on the ground, the closest thing to an "erotic" scene that the lifeless *Orgy* has to offer. The Slave Girl slinks back into her crypt, presumably for eternity.

A telling exchange between Bob and Shirley follows. Shirley confesses that she is "so frightened!" and Bob responds, "You've a *right* to be — we're trapped by a bunch of fiends!" After a few more exchanges, Bob declares, out of the blue: "Easy, Shirley, easy! Panic won't do us any good!" Shirley is notably mute as Bob says this, clearly not panicking, so it appears that Bob is projecting his own fright onto his female partner. (Even Bob's garish yellow shirt seems to symbolize the man's cowardice in this admittedly unsettling situation.) When the viewer sees Bob and Shirley as Wood's male and female sides, the author's inner self in battle, the exchange has much meaning, for Shirley is evidently the source of strength and courage for the beleaguered couple. This exhibition of female vigor attracts the Princess, who now approaches Shirley, grinning seductively, and starts to unbutton the woman's blouse. The Princess may certainly be seen as overtly lesbian, yet more significantly, this female power figure, this Crone aspect of the "World Mother," is more interested in the female principal as represented by the stoic Shirley, than the male principal, as represented by the befuddled Bob. Even in erotic partnership, the Princess knows that her sister-in-spirit is manifestly more energizing than the dull male-female binary so listlessly portrayed in *Orgy*. The Princess of Darkness scratches a bloody "X," in effect the bloody cross of Jesus Christ, on Shirley's stomach, removes her phallic knife, and seems all but prepared to stab the poor woman to death, in a sadistic act of pseudo-phallic intercourse, but the Emperor intervenes: "Let her continue to learn. The time is not yet right, that they should join with us!" The Crone thus reluctantly defers one more time to patriarchy. The Princess returns her phallus-symbol to her "sheath" and, after ogling Shirley for a moment, returns to her current "master."

The Emperor retrieves a nearby human skull and shows it to the Princess, asking a rhetorical question: "What is this?" The Princess dutifully replies, "A symbol, master." The Emperor presses her: "What kind of symbol?" The Princess then segues into the next dance, only circuitously answering the question: "She loved the bull ring and the matador. She danced to their destruction — now she dances to her *own* destruction!" The Princess tosses the skull into the middle of the graveyard-stage-performance space and soon, Latin-tinged music is heard, and a woman (Stephanie Jones[22]) presumably of Spanish heritage enters, dressed in a red dress with black veils. The woman dances around the skull, using it as her muse, her prop and her anchor. Eventually, the dancer picks up the skull, kissing it seductively, fully embracing Death. In a marvelous master shot, the dancer twirls as Bob, Shirley, the Wolf Man and the Mummy all watch, the entire cast of the living and the dead, literal and symbolic characters tossed together in an most-literal "orgy of the dead." The Emperor elaborates on the dancer's fate: "She came to us on the 'Day of the Dead.'" The Princess confirms this: "*El Dia de los Muertos*— a celebration in her country!" The dance now has enlarged meaning, for in Mexico the "Day of the Dead" is a time-honored festival, carried over from ancient Aztec civilization, in which the living honor their deceased relatives in a colorful festival which celebrates the recurrent cycle of birth, life and death, in contrast to Western culture's morbid fear of and denial of the omnipresence of death (*El Dia de los Muertos* is a notable "pagan" analog to the morbid Catholic holy day "All Souls Day").

The dancer now cavorts in the nude, but for a G-string undergarment and black-lace headgear, a minimalist costume both fetishistic and absurd. The dancer picks up the skull and carries it with her, fondling the cranium and kissing its mouth — as she might caress a living lover — in a simplistic yet vivid portrayal of Eros in league with Thanatos, a sublime living cartoon of Sex and Death joined together in pure ecstasy and, incidentally, a vital answer to the Emperor's original question as to what the skull symbolized. Not incidentally, the skull is a venerated icon in "Day of the Dead" celebrations, often depicted in artworks adorned with candy or flowers, as it symbolically represents not merely the bones, but the living presence of those passed on. This homage to Death via interpretive dance clearly aligns itself with Wood's career-long obsession with human mortality as an inevitable, glorious, emancipating adjunct to life for the enduring soul of Man.

The Princess snaps her fingers, and the next dancer struts out between *Orgy*'s two primordial couples, Bob and Shirley, and Wolf Man and Mummy. This dancer (Mickey Jines[23]) is attired in vaguely Polynesian costume, as the Princess explains that this damned soul was "a worshipper of snakes, and smoke, and flames!," a revelation accented via a cutaway to a (badly overexposed) stock library shot of an agitated rattlesnake. The dancer soon loses her costuming and gyrates convulsively in the near-nude. A subsequent cutaway to the angry rattler, its tail fully extended and twitching, suggests male penile erection, as this dancer's gyrations, shot in medium close-up, has an erotic quotient conspicuously lacking in the majority of *Orgy*. This scene effectively if crudely reinforces the notion of the serpent, in myth and psychology, as representing a most primal symbol of phallocentrism at its most deadly, seductive, even surreptitious. This ritual between fallen female and seditious serpent most immediately recalls the biblical tales of Adam and Eve, that apocryphal genetic duo of Judeo-Christian lore; as Eve and the serpent did their little "dance," civilization supposedly fell, and man became damned for all time by woman's weakness and duplicity. Yet before "modern" patriarchal religion demonized the serpent-as-tempter even as it fetishized same, certain matriarchy-based cultures worshipped the snake as "embodiments of divine female wisdom."[24] Some Christian Gnostics even maintained that the "unholy" liaison between Eve and the Snake sparked the liberation of humanity from darkness and ignorance.[25] Again in the realm of myth, the ancient Egyptians made much of a demon called *Apep* (*Apepi* in Babylon), a multifaceted serpent who controlled the night, and endeavored to keep daylight away from earth. An arch-enemy of Ra, the Sun God, Apep was conquered only by the most intricate recurring ritual performances enacted on the part of the Egyptian coterie.[26]

The importance of the snake in *Orgy*'s scenario is quantified by an extended comic exchange between the Wolf Man and the Mummy which reveals much about the monsters' essentially craven nature. In his tinny, virtually indecipherable voice, the Mummy states, "I don't like snakes! I remember the one Cleopatra used. She loved the little rascal, until it flicked out that red tongue, with those two sharp fangs! You'd never think such a little thing could pack such a wallop!" The Wolf Man, playing straight man to the Mummy's shtick, mumbles something in response, to which the Mummy delivers a most bizarre punch-line: "Hurt her? Hell, it *killed* her!" This absurdly failed attempt at comic relief, delivered terribly by its most pathetic characters, evokes the memory of Officer Kelton, that font of idiot wisdom from three of Wood's earlier efforts. That these bad comic mouthpieces utter some of *Orgy*'s most significant dialogue underscores their essential efficacy in the cinema of Wood, where the lousy delivery of lousy dialogue is part of an Absurdist-tinged subversion of conventional theatrics.

The joke itself, wherein the infamous Egyptian royalty is killed by a vicious, poisonous snake, is merely a bad retelling of a hoary old sex joke, with the snake representing nothing more than a large penis on the person of one of Cleopatra's many lovers, possibly even Marc Anthony. That this mammoth phallus not only hurt, but killed the woman, undermines revered phallocentric propaganda that the penis, as seen by its owner, is meant as an instrument of pleasure and service for the woman. The joke, perhaps unwittingly, profoundly reinforces the feminist position that males primarily see their phallus not as an instrument of pleasure, but as a weapon of domination and punishment towards its female target.[27]

The Mummy continues: "We had lots of snakes in my ancient Egypt. Slimy, slinky things! When I was alive, they were the things nightmares were made of!" The Wolf Man howls, either in disgust or approval. That these "monsters" are afraid of snakes reveals that they are afraid of the whole natural world (and by extension, the female principle)—they are monsters literally scared of their own maternal shadows. The fact that the Mummy obsesses negatively on snakes, with apparent aversion to their phallo-centric symbolism, suggests that this "Mummy" is in fact female in character, in essence a "Mommy" to "his" sidekick, the Wolf "Man." With this revelation, the Wolf Man and Mummy can easily be seen as a third couple in *Orgy* which portray, in twisted form, the heterosexual couple which Wood loved to bring to life, only to dissect and even dismantle same. As do Bob and Shirley and the Emperor and the Princess, the Wolf Man and the Mummy represent another of Wood's archetypal suburban couples, tossed into an antagonistic environment and reduced largely to fighting amongst themselves as a reaction to the pressures of the outside world.

As this latest dancer finally exits, the Emperor passes judgment: "She pleases me. Permit her to live in the world of the snakes"—in other words, permit this woman to live in the service of males' erotic needs, eternally, a most dire sentence for any woman. The Emperor next summons the Wolf Man and Mummy, who are immediately nervous and racked with guilt. Being the insecure buffoons that they are, they are certain that they did something wrong to warrant attention from the elder patriarch, who apparently would not normally bother with such low-born flunkies. The two failed horror-creatures present themselves to the Emperor, who asks why they are shaking in fear. The Mummy defers, "It's not often an Emperor like *you* calls on creatures like *us*," suggesting the vast class system of hierarchy which exists, even in this world of the dead. The Emperor puts the monsters' minds at ease, and informs them that he tires of the normal entertainment and seeks their advice on something unusual. Yet the Princess of Darkness notes anxiously, "The moon is soon gone. There is little time left for the remainder of the evening's pleasures!" The line is accented by a stock-footage shot of a full moon, an interesting replacement of the more phallic (and violent) thunder-and-lightning shots which punctuate most of Wood's directorial efforts. This shot of the round, wholly female moon is in keeping with the female principle which is quickly becoming the guiding spirit in *Orgy*. The Princess then reveals what will be a significant plot point: "At the first sight of the morning sun's rays, we must be gone!" Here, Wood lumps together much ancient mythological tradition, including that of the vampire, in a reckless touch of editorial conceit which will nonetheless serve *Orgy* well. The Princess' acknowledgment of the moon, and its immutable power over the natural world, underscores her function as an incarnation of the mythological Crone figure of prehistoric matriarchy, whose affiliation with the moon was legendary.[28]

While the Emperor and the Princess of Darkness bicker like any self-respecting domestic couple, Bob and Shirley bicker as well. Even though Bob has loosened his restraints, and now has the potential for escape, Shirley still fears the worst. Bob tries to be optimistic, but Shirley has much darker, and likely more realistic thoughts: "These heathens probably have a open grave for us!" Bob has an odd response to this: "They wouldn't dare put *both* of us in the same grave — or would they?" Seemingly, Bob has no desire to spend eternity with his life partner, which reveals again his cowardice and his essential misogyny. In essence, Bob has no desire to be united with his "other half." Quite possibly triggered by this statement of potential abandonment on Bob's part, Shirley finally reveals her true feelings about being trapped by Bob's monstrous, infantile, phallocentric hell-world: "I hate you." Shirley rightly blames Bob and his "monsters," that is, his adolescent worldview, for their current precarious situation. Shirley is apparently highly intuitive, for even as she fears for her life, the Emperor and the Princess of Darkness are arguing over her impending fate. The Emperor scolds the Princess: "I will tell you when and if you may have her," which emphasizes the man's exalted position in this microcosmic patriarchy society, as well as again referencing the Princess' ostensibly lesbian leanings.

The Princess, ultimately a slave to men, defers to the head patriarch and returns to her duties as "hostess," announcing the next dancer as "the woman who murdered her husband on their wedding night! Now she dances with his skeleton!" A dancer (Barbara Nordin[29]) dressed in a makeshift bridal gown fondles a human skeleton which hangs unceremoniously on a hook near the crypt doors. According to the Princess, the skeleton is the dancer's deceased husband, so the subsequent dance can be seen as a rather extraordinary, and avowedly sexist, symbolic depiction of marriage as viewed by male-dominated society, which sees the union to woman as some form of diabolical punishment, from which the only escape is death and complete bodily disintegration. The Bride does a silly frug-like dance, as the Princess of Darkness looks on fondly, in obvious admiration of this female's homage to the female principle, so joyous and full of life. For the majority of the dance, the Bride wears nothing but her bridal veil, dancing almost convulsively in front of her skeleton patriarch, and making a mockery of the ill-fated "union" of the modern married couple with her performance before her "mate." The Bride continues her increasingly bizarre dance, making weird, bird-like motions with her arms, and jiggling her breasts in medium close-up. The Bride accelerates her dance steps, looking at times virtually in the throes of demonic possession, and at one point almost violently shaking her breasts towards the camera. All the while, bland instrumental music accompanies her, in itself very much an emblem of the WASP experience of the time. In medium close-up, the Bride dances next to her "husband's" skeleton, thrusting her breasts before "him" in a mocking gesture, as "he" can never again access his wife's erotic charms. In sum, the Bride's dance is her personal triumph over this domestic tyrant, who seems pained even in death. Bob and Shirley look especially displeased at this particular dance, which mirrors, and mocks, their own failed domestic partnership. Yet this "Skeleton Dance" also illustrates in vivid relief *Orgy*'s ever-ascending theme, that of the triumph of the vibrant, life-embracing female principle over the weak, static, decayed male principle (aka phallocentric death culture), most comically depicted here by a stack of bones.

Perhaps vaguely sensing the threat to his patriarchal reign which the accumulated dances portend, the Emperor addresses Shirley directly for the first time: "Have you not enjoyed the evening's festivities?" Seeing her horror, he continues: "Ah, that will soon change, when you've become one of us!," that is, when Shirley is embraced not as a member of the female collective which dances before her, but as obedient slave to Bob, the Wolf Man, the Emperor, i.e., the assembled male collective. The Wolf Man howls in ecstasy at the moon, his muse and his ruler, at the very thought of the luscious redhead ending up as part of this hellish entourage of imprisoned humanity. The Emperor underscores the thought, "It would seem that the Wolf Man would have you for his own," the cue for Shirley to scream bloody murder. Bob calls the Emperor a fiend, realizing perhaps for the first time that patriarchy bears no loyalty to its own, stealing that which it covets without logic or remorse. Reinforcing the betrayal endemic to male-dominated culture, the head patriarch replies, "Fiend, is it! You will not be so fortunate! Your existence will cease within moments!" The Emperor then utters a remarkable aside, which vividly underscores the prominence of the female principle in *Orgy*: "No one wishes to see a *man* dance!" This declaration reinforces the notion that both men *and* women covet the sexual spirit of the female, seen clearly by both genders as the vibrant creative force which powers the mammalian world, if not the entire universe; likewise, no one could conceivably gain inspiration from the objectification of the male. The Empress reinforces this zeal for the female, flesh and spirit: "*She* is to be *mine*! It is thus spoken!"

The Emperor finally defers to the Princess of Darkness and offers Shirley to her. The Princess, increasingly nervous about the approaching daylight, is reprimanded yet again by the Emperor, who haughtily declares, "I know the laws of the night." As the finale of *Orgy* will reveal, this arbiter of patriarchal wisdom apparently does *not* know the laws of the night, or has interpreted them incorrectly, whereas the Princess, representing the "World Mother," all-knowing creator to the natural world, most assuredly does know the "laws of the night," and has intuited that disaster waits just ahead. Emboldened by this awareness of her superior knowledge, the Princess even dares to challenge her "superior": "I would have time for my *own* pleasures!" Yet the Emperor, bloated emblem of patriarchal greed and arrogance, demands the entire night for himself: "Your own pleasure comes only after mine!" The line perfectly expresses the self-centered, infantile emotional hierarchy of patriarchal culture: The male always gets his jollies first, with the female's needs coming afterwards, if at all. The Emperor reinforces his tyrannical reign: "I am the sole ruler of the dark world! There is none to challenge my authority here! My word is the law! All-powerful!" The Emperor again reveals his own blindness with this declaration, which suggests both that he rules over the world, when he is merely half of the equation, and that also, he knows all that there is to know, a most dangerous, and eventually fatal, delusion.

Having put the matriarch once again in her place, the elder patriarch commands that the seemingly endless string of *Orgy*'s performance pieces proceed. *Orgy* could have easily ended here, at the 70-minute mark, without theatre patrons complaining that they hadn't received their money's worth; that this "divine torture" continues for another two reels painfully reminds the viewer that he is irrevocably trapped in Wood's stultifying cosmic void. This may represent an example of one of Wood's most profound messages, that if one plays too passive a role in one's community, one may eventually become trapped in its entrenched dogma, victim of its enervating vortex of socio-political inertia. This notion is illustrated well in *Orgy*, in which both viewer and protagonist become virtually interchangeable, indistinguishable prisoners in a horrifying limbo. The viewer of *Orgy* becomes an unwilling recipient of the same punishment meted out to the film's "heroes," Bob and Shirley, in effect becoming a narrative character himself, a fate which in *Orgy*'s case is not a blessing but a curse.

The next dancer is introduced thusly: "She lived as a zombie in life — so she will remain as a zombie in death!" This admonition suggests that this female was non-actualized as a human being, repressed and suppressed by her community, living her life in an emotionally dead stupor, a most common fate for the postwar woman. A brunette woman (Dene Starnes[30]) enters, dancing around the graveyard with arms outstretched, looking barely prescient, in effect sleepwalking. This interpretive dance crudely yet effectively evokes the docile, obedient female of patriarchal acclaim, a non-autonomous "object" rendered virtually comatose by a punitive, sexist culture, ultimately more dead than alive. As the Zombie dances, the Emperor and the Princess continue their night-long squabble over the approaching dawn.

Introducing the final (we hope?) dancer, the Princess of Darkness declares, "All others were but infinitesimal bits of *fluff*, compared to her ... this one would have died for feathers, fur and fluff — and do she did." A dancer (Rene De Beau[31]) bursts through the crypt doors, wearing a gaggle of colorful scarves, trimmed with red fur or feathers. Rather than have her remove each scarf separately, seductively, meaningfully, as even any self-respecting striptease artist would have done, the doggedly dull-witted *Orgy* suffices with the usual abrupt cutaway and return to the dancer, suddenly minus her symbolic garmentalia. This rare opportunity to indulge in Wood's fetish for all things "fluffy" by draping the exotic dancer in all manner of alluring garb is completely missed, and one wonders if producer-director Apostolof had the slightest inkling whatsoever about using even the most rudimentary aesthetic garnish to enliven and distinguish his stultifying parade of interchangeable female body-objects.

When the Fluff Dancer finally backs awkwardly into the crypt whence she sprung, the Emperor crows, "The time is short — for *your* pleasures, of course! You may take her now!" When the Princess of Darkness breathlessly ponders whether there is enough time left for fulfilling her own emotional and sexual needs, the Emperor ominously states, "You better *hope* there is!," reinforcing the preeminent notion of patriarchy, that the female's needs come well after all male-oriented needs and desires are satisfied, in effect nothing more than an afterthought. As the Emperor subsequently crows, "I will watch! Your desires may be my pleasure also!," the viewer is reminded that not only does the female agenda come dead last in patriarchal culture, but it might not be addressed at all but for how the male-dominated society may still benefit directly from it. It appears that the Emperor "allows" the Princess of Darkness to realize her own pleasures at least in part because he can enjoy them also, as a voyeur. Thus, even the autonomy of the female in entrenched patriarchy may ultimately be allowed to blossom and flourish only when it also serve males.

The Princess now dances in front of Bob and Shirley, using her phallic knife as symbol and surrogate partner in her own interpretive dance of the maligned, mutated heterosexual dyad which haunts the dark world of *Orgy*. Even though the Princess remains fully clothed, her dance is easily the most erotically charged dance in *Orgy*; she stares directly, even defiantly at the viewer, whereas the other dancers casually glanced at the camera when they remembered to. The erotic energy which inhabits the Princess' dance again reinforces the notion that she represents, via an incarnation of the Crone aspect of the "World Mother," the life-affirming female principle brought to life, giving her actions all of the energy and thematic impact the other dancers could not summon. The Princess here readily invokes the mythos of Kali the Destroyer, the venerable Hindu black goddess of death; the Princess is an actual

Criswell hams it up in a rare publicity photograph from *Orgy of the Dead* (courtesy of Rylan Bach-man).

character in *Orgy*, whereas the other dancers were mere objects, and therefore the Princess' actions carry greater narrative and symbolic weight than those who went before. In the same stunning shot, the Princess approaches Bob and Shirley, and starts to remove the mortal woman's blouse, as the Wolf Man and the Mummy enter the scene also, watching in a voyeuristic fever. The Princess again taunts Shirley with her knife, and prepares to stab her as before. Bob finally makes his move, only to be felled by the Wolf Man. This extraordinary scene, lasting a full 2½ minutes without a cut, brilliantly merges the performance aspects of *Orgy* with the narrative elements, and all but compensates for the haphazard structure of the previous scenario.

It is dawn, and the sun has begun to rise. The Princess of Darkness falls to the ground, as would a vampire under similar circumstances, and (via a quick cutaway) turns into a fully clothed skeleton, one of Wood's favorite stand-in archetypes, and a vivid illustration of two of his favorite binaries—real/fake, life/death. Another cutaway to the merciless sun reveals the Emperor, the Wolf Man and the Mummy also reduced to bones. A close-up of the skeletal Emperor fades out, signaling an end to the microcosmic patriarchy which ruled *Orgy*.

An exceptional final scene, which sums up the entire narrative of *Orgy* in another long take lasting well over two minutes, fades in on Bob and Shirley, lying on the ground as they were at the film's start, when they were flung from their car. Two paramedics hover over their bodies, recalling similar death scene tableaus in *Glen or Glenda?* and *Jail Bait*. A photographer and a police detective enter the scene. Shirley comes to and cries out for Bob. She starts talking about monsters and ghouls, but the assembled lawmen chalk it up to shock. This neophyte patriarchal assemblage still does not believe in the wisdom of the female principle, as Wood suggests that patriarchy wins, after all. As the paramedics dress the wounds, Shirley confesses to Bob that she *does* love him after all, especially as they weren't damned forever to Bob's adolescent monster-hell. Bob acknowledges Shirley's vow and negates all that went before, saying, "It was all a dream!" In a magnificent final use of a crane shot, the camera pulls up and back to reveal an ambulance on the set, as Wood's tortured domestic couple are led away to heal their psychic wounds, and ruminate on the nihilistic hallucination they have just endured.

The Emperor returns, now again as "himself," as Criswell, sitting once more in his womb-like coffin and offering an epilogue which completely fuses the narrative and "documentary" aspects of *Orgy*:

> Yes, they were lucky, those two young people. May you be so lucky! But do not trust luck, at the full of the moon, when the night is dark. Make a wide path around the unholy grounds of the night people. Who can say we do not exist—can you? But now, we return to our graves, and you, may join us soon!

Criswell lies back peacefully in his coffin, to sleep, to die, and the camera pans up to the blessed virgin Mary, mother of all mothers, as THE END is superimposed over this ultimately celebratory meditation on human mortality. One cannot help but feel that the message is partially that all life ends, and that this is good, for just as *Orgy* has finally ended, a torture for all but the most twisted, who would want life to perpetuate endlessly? That life is mortal is a blessing, not a curse, just as the end of *Orgy* has released the viewer from this peculiar anti-aesthetic hell-world. Further, the main theme of *Orgy* becomes crystal clear with this epilogue: Patriarchy, represented here by Criswell/The Emperor, is only given life and sanctuary by virtue of the female principle, as essayed by many in *Orgy*, and capped at beginning and end by Mary, Christendom's notorious Super-Virgin. Matriarchy, the essential mothering of mankind, is the inarguable progenitor of society in toto, including any patriarchal system, without which it would not, and literally *could not* exist.

For many viewers, *Orgy* is dull, tiresome, and ultimately meaningless. It may be that *Orgy* is best viewed not as story, but as ritual, and not as a narrative experience, but as a meditation, similar to the "no-thought" enlightenment of Zen Buddhism. Certainly, time stops, or appears to stand still, in *Orgy*, which not only expresses the temporal stasis of Wood's eternal hell of the damned, but also Zen's recommendation to be always "in the present," to experience the "here and now," detached from chronic temporal acceleration. Lacking any semblance of narrative rhythm, *Orgy* lurches along in its own purgatory of locked time. At the film's end, the viewer realizes that the "narrative" of the film has unfolded *in real time*: The audience has spent 90-odd minutes with the living and the dead at the end of the world, a captive audience to an excruciating occult ritual, Wood's "divine torture" for damned souls.

As seen, Bob and Shirley are Wood's archetypal dystopian suburban couple, invoked in some fashion in every Wood film, and brought to vivid life here, in "living" color. In *Orgy*, Bob and Shirley are violently thrust into Wood's cosmic void, his purgatory of judgment for fallen souls. As punishment for their sins, the couple is made a captive audience and forced to watch the sexual revolution unfold before their horrified eyes, in effect to see the results of their crimes which, in Wood's tale of unearthly woe, is the disintegration of rationalist modern culture, and a return to superstition-fueled barbarism. As mentioned, Bob and Shirley also stand in for *Orgy*'s audience, who assuredly "suffer" the film as do the film's heroes. In *Orgy*, Wood has ingeniously merged protagonist and audience as one, and sentences them both to what could only be described as a "divine torture."

The unique *Orgy of the Dead* boasts legions of fiercely devoted fans; here, artist Kalynn Campbell captures its indefinable supernatural aura in his illustrative tribute *Dead & Reburied* (courtesy of Kalynn Campbell).

As seen, *Orgy* also features two other "domestic couples"—the Emperor and the Princess of Darkness, and the Wolf Man and the Mummy—each of whom fret and moan and wail in their failed microcosmic "suburbias." The Wolf Man and the Mummy serve several purposes in *Orgy*: They are not only Bob's "monsters" come to life as cheap characters from cheap pulp fiction, but they are also Wood's inner demons (alcoholism and sexual perversion) brought to comical life by their tormented creator, who was also their prisoner.

Overall, the main thematic thrust of *Orgy* seems to be patriarchy's chronic, self-destructive inability to embrace the female principle, to bridge the enigmatic gap between life and death, expressed symbolically as the difference "between night and day," a denial and oversight which, at least here, leads to complete annihilation. One might effectively argue that the dialectical tension which inhabits all of Wood's films is, for all intents and purposes, resolved definitively in *Orgy*. That dialectic, between the male and female, or more correctly between the male and female *principles*, was conspicuously, even brilliantly evoked by Wood in his inaugural feature, *Glen or Glenda?*, essayed by the author himself in a canny autobiographical characterization of the traditional heterosexual unit, in which Wood significantly played *both parts*. This ostensibly antagonistic set of binary opposites, brought to life in subsequent Wood films in such guises as the squabbling suburban couple, the crafty swapping of fake and real symbols, Wood's chronic temporal dislocation, where day and night merged indiscriminately, and even the perpetual existential battle between Life and Death, is summarily, if not amicably, resolved in *Orgy*'s finale, in which the Crone's hard-won attainment of her own pleasure unleashes the violent forces of the natural world, ending not only in the destruction of the entire patriarchal universe, but all female members within, the matriarchal myth-figure included. It would not be out of line to suggest that the Princess of Darkness, seeing the irredeemable rottenness of the governmental system which she inhabited and promoted, decided that it was obsolete and beyond repair, and must be destroyed in order for a more healthy system of government to take its place. In this way, the Princess' apparently greedy act was actually an august self-sacrifice, a suicidal gesture done for the good of the community, a necessary suicide both noble and emancipatory, for now a new cosmic purgatory may be built, perhaps along more egalitarian, female-centric lines. The Princess-as-Crone would surely be aware that dissolution was not a finite end to existence, but an inevitable precursor to new life, so only by her sacrifice would the female principle be able to rebuild and flourish in an environment now cleansed of all patriarchal error. This may also explain why the parade of interpretive dancers in *Orgy* fail so miserably in their "stated" goal of exciting male lust, instead inviting contemplation of a most philosophical kind: By film's end it is clear that they were in the service of the female principle all along. It may even be that the reason that there were "too many" dancers, and each took "too long" to perform, was a deliberate plot mounted to subvert the Emperor's primarily exploitative agenda, and to sabotage the chance for all to escape in the dead of night, before they had a chance to be judged and sentenced by the harsh truth of the natural world, as represented by the morning sun. *Orgy* thus gloriously ends Wood's career-long rumination on the male-female binary opposition, with the female principle, always championed, now emerging victorious and ascendant, ready to wrest the world back from the caustic phallocentrism which has brought it to the brink of extermination.

For better or worse, the dances are the focal point of *Orgy*, making up the majority of the film's leisurely running time. Depending on the viewer, they are either the main point of interest, or of extremely limited interest. Aside from the physical attractiveness of the female performers, the dances are listless and presented without any aesthetic embellishments, just as a burlesque review or live striptease stage show would be mounted. As such, they are historically important as time capsules of live stage performance of the day, and as mediations on beauty and interpretative dance, as codified for the adult entertainment crowd. The potentially exciting striptease element of these erotic dances is eliminated in the *Orgy* dance sequences, which signals the progression of the times to more "bold" adult entertainment and removing, for many, the most alluring feature of the erotic dance genre — the tease. Even the droning, canned generic music which accompanies the dancing sequences reduces the erotic quotient of same, while elevating the symbolic bourgeois quality of the pieces, suggesting that the supposedly "erotic" dancing in *Orgy* is the visual equivalent of "Muzak" — boring, interchangeable performances with the cultural impact of stultifying "elevator music," also ubiquitous in that era.[32]

Just as Christianity merged Creator and Preserver aspects of the female principle into a hybrid dubbed "Mary, Mother of God," the dancers in *Orgy* are positioned as a symbolic amalgam of these Virgin and Mother aspects of the "World Mother" mythology of ancient matriarchy. They serve primarily as sexual objects for the male, a function which aligns them with the Virgin aspect; there is also the emphasis in *Orgy* (indeed, in all "nudie cuties" of the era, as well as most "adults only" entertainment of the day) in showcasing the women's breasts, which are featured prominently in the dance sequences. The ubiquitous adult male fetish with the female breast is a descendent, if altered expression of the infantile boy's wish to perpetually suckle the mother's nurturing teats. This fixation with breasts pinpoints the *Orgy* dancers as occupying the same metaphorical space as the bust of the Virgin Mary, as they simultaneously arouse and "mother" *Orgy*'s audience by offering their collective bosom as both fetish object and symbol of comfort.

Ultimately, the *Orgy* dances are less a meditation on female beauty than an illustration of how men viewed women at the time — as "damned whores." The *Orgy* dancers, in sum, evoke the mythos of the fabled "temple dancers" of ancient India, young women who were proscribed to perform at Hindu religious ceremonies. The practice of these dancers, also known as *Devadasis*, dates back to at least the 6th century CE, and was originally a purification ritual designed to amuse the temple congregation, but more importantly to impart spiritual purity to the dancer herself. The original *Devadasi* dances were designed to save the dancer's soul by "wedding" her to God; as such, the *Devadasi* were believed to be mortal incarnations of *Apsaras*, female spiritual beings who danced in the heavens to entertain the gods and their permanent guests. This noble, if superstitious practice, which peeked circa the 11th century CE, eventually degenerated into something akin to human trafficking, wherein *Devadasis* were enlisted by reigning monarchs to provide entertainment in their courts. These dancers, now called *Rajadasis*, provided prurient entertainment, and often sexual services on the side; the occupation purportedly still exists today. Although they do commit to dancing in order to save their souls, a la *Devadasis*, the later *Rajadasis* most clearly evoke the spirit of the *Orgy* dancers, as they primarily appear to function as erotic entertainment for their reigning monarch, the Emperor. The dancers' checkered sexual pasts even hint at the prostitution aspect of these "holy" dancers; as noted in the endnotes, many if not all of the *Orgy* dancers also boasted extensive work as nude models and nude dancers, activities very much in line with their historical mentors. Ultimately, Hindu religious doctrine seems to have considered their *Devadasis* as little better than *Orgy*'s "damned whores." As well, the *Orgy* dance sequences evoke the character of primitive ritual dancing, such as that found at the ancient festival called *Saturnalia*, where orgiastic dancing was specifically designed to enhance the fertility of the crops and the well-being of the community.[33]

As seen, the basic template for *Orgy* is the striptease and burlesque films of the previous decade, wherein a string of performances were framed by vaguely narrative or comic relief "filler" segments, a format which itself owed much to the staged vaudeville or burlesque review of antiquity. Yet *Orgy*'s particular narrative structure bears some improbable similarity with a most incredible peer: Tchiakovsky's beloved ballet, *The Nutcracker*. As implausible as it may seem, *The Nutcracker* and *Orgy* share some amusing, if broad parallels: In each, an elder patriarch with supernatural powers (Herr Drosselmeyer, the Emperor) animates non-living entities (toys, the recently deceased) to perform ethnically oriented interpretive dances for the benefit of a young couple (Clara and the Prince, Bob and Shirley), late at night, on a holiday, during the full moon. Giant Mice attack Clara in *The Nutcracker*, also acting as Greek Chorus; the Wolf Man and the Mummy render a similar function in *Orgy*, with their assaults on Bob and Shirley. Furthermore, both productions end with the young couple emancipated from their waking dream/nightmare to re-enter the "real" world. While no direct comparisons can be made between the thematic content of the two admittedly disparate works, this superficial resemblance makes one wonder whether Wood had viewed a performance of the ballet, either on television or at a local theatre, shortly before penning his own version of a magical purgatory where the "dead" are made to dance, and which both imprisons and emancipates its youthful heroes.

As bizarre as *Orgy* is, it is even more fantastic to realize that, for likely economic reasons, Wood expanded his threadbare screenplay into a full-length manuscript and released *Orgy of the Dead* as a novel which was published in 1966 by Greenleaf, a notorious distributor of literary sexploitation. Boasting an amazing piece of cover art by the unsung pulp-art genius Robert Bonfils, the *Orgy* novel went on to modest sales, soon becoming as obscure as its film father. In the novel, Wood cleverly substituted the numerous dance sequences with short horror stories, many written earlier, creating in essence a horror anthology similar in spirit to many television programs of the day including *The Twilight Zone* and *The Outer Limits*. Some of Wood's best short stories, abrupt and awkward though they are, appear in the novel, including "The Night the Banshee Cried" and "The Final Curtain," and it is in sum a pleasant if unexceptional reading experience, combining cheap horror and crude erotica in a utilitarian, yet ultimately effective way. One extraordinary story, which also made its way into men's magazines as "Into My Grave," chronicles in excruciating first-person detail the protagonist's horror at being buried alive, likely reflecting similar fears on Wood's (and the reader's) part. Although one can understand the reasons *Orgy* was made as it was, it would have been nonetheless amazing had Wood and Apostolof been able and willing to film *Orgy* as Wood wrote the novel, as a fantastic horror anthology, a sub-genre which was in the mid–1960s just beginning to find favor with theatre audiences via the British films *Dr. Terror's House of Horrors* (1964, d: Freddie Francis) and *Torture Garden* (1967; d: Freddie Francis). A less sexy, more "horrific" *Orgy* would have likely found an enthusiastic audience, and with Wood's screenplay in harness to Apostolof's shoddy production values, the resultant film might have resembled a delirious, color-soaked redux of *Plan 9 from Outer Space*.

With the publication of the *Orgy* novel, Wood became virtually indistinguishable from his paperback horror-writer hero, Bob, and the many parallels to Wood in the character, both in film and novel, become all but autobiographical. In the novel, Wood allowed himself to expand upon the spare, utilitarian dialogue of the film. When Shirley first asks Bob whence he gets his morbid and bizarre ideas for his paperback horror fiction, the author reveals a creative process which is certainly his own: "Sometimes I dream them. Most of the time, in fact, a figure forms itself in my brain. Then if it doesn't define itself I search out old wives' tales, occult books. Sooner or later the creature ... the picture is clear."[34] The Emperor character, called "The Black Creature" in the novel and described fantastically as a floating black cloak topped by a grinning skull, pontificates at length on various and sundry subjects: "Profits, massive profits, overindulgence, under any and all circumstances, are the downfall of most!"[35] Even the Mummy, who is given an entire short tale in the novel, has a pacifist bent unseen in the film: "What is this madness of destruction?!"[36] But Wood tellingly gives his female half, his alter ego, "Shirley," the best lines: She philosophizes at length about existential matters of life and death: "Those creatures out there are what nightmares are made of. How can they be real? But they are. How can we be here? But we are."[37] Wood even indulges in his favorite fetish in the novel: "I can feel the soft fur of my angora against my cheek. How can that be if I am dead?"[38] Yet it is humbling to realize that Wood saw fit to end his novel as he did his screenplay, with the Criswell character pointing at his audience to declare that great existential truth, "And you may join us soon...."[39]

According to Rudolph Grey, "Orgy of the Dead began life as an eighteen-page script called Nudie Ghoulies," which suggests that Wood and producer-director Apostolof were consciously attempting to forge in Orgy an example of the popular "nudie cutie" genre of the time period.[40] According to Apostolof, Wood also performed duties as production manager and casting director on Orgy.[41] Apostolof also claimed that he kicked Wood off the Orgy set after a particularly egregious drinking binge, but whether Wood was "present" or not during the week-long filming of Orgy makes no difference, as the spirit of Wood resides inexorably in the magnificently weird and revelatory screenplay to this most fantastic amalgam of male sexual fantasy with female liberation, wherein Eros and Thanatos are irrevocably wed in an ecstatic convulsion of mutual preternatural exaltation.[42]

A notable "cousin" to Orgy is The Bachelor's Dreams, a 1967 "nudie cutie" also produced and directed by Apostolof. What is intriguing about this film is that it uncannily mirrors the basic plot structure of Orgy, without Wood's fantastic supernatural elements. Also significant is the fact that The Bachelor's Dreams features four of the erotic dancers who appeared in Orgy, each performing nearly the exact same routine, suggesting that the dancers had just performed their established night club "act," intact and unmodified, for both films. Also of interest is an enigmatic cast listing for one "Shirley Wood." This may be a nod of appreciation from Apostolof to Wood, but it is a fitting label to describe Wood's extraordinary incorporation of both male and female principles in one utterly unique individual.

10

Necromania — A Tale of Weird Love (1971)

Ed Wood's career-long (and likely lifelong) obsession with Death as the ominous, paradoxical analog to Life is brought to a glorious conclusion in *Necromania — A Tale of Weird Love*, a hardcore sex film (also released in a softer, R-rated version) which still manages to embody much of Wood's most notable thematic content, even within a minuscule (even by Wood's own standards) *mise-en-scène*, and the potentially deadening influence of extended sex scenes. Produced, written and directed by Wood under the pseudonym "Don Miller," *Necromania — A Tale of Weird Love* (henceforth referred to as *Necromania*) signals its fixation on mortal dissolution in its very title. Although the traditional meaning of the related word, necrophilia, denotes a sexual compulsion for the deceased, Wood's fitting modification of the word for his film suggests that this "tale of weird love" will be a philosophic rumination on the symbology of Death, rather than a mere depiction of an obscure sexual fetish. The devoted Wood fan will certainly expect as much from their hero, and Wood does not disappoint in *Necromania*, which virtually obsesses on the subject of Death as a means of not only spiritual, but sexual emancipation, emerging as an excellent example of finding "high art" in "low places."

Necromania is an early example of the hardcore sex feature, a subgenre of sexploitation which started a year earlier with films such as *Mona: The Virgin Nymph* (1970, d: Howard Ziehm) and *Sex: U.S.A.* (1970, d: Gerard Damiano). The perhaps-inevitable evolution of the soft core sex film, which now included graphic depictions of intercourse and other intimate sexual acts, burst on the scene with the start of a new decade, and became both mainstream and iconic with the release of the infamous blockbuster hit *Deep Throat* (1972, d: Gerard Damiano), starring the ill-fated Linda Boreman (aka Linda Lovelace). With few exceptions, the early hardcore sex features attempted, at least peripherally, to integrate the sex scenes into a fully developed narrative story, and Wood's *Necromania* follows this template. The early promise of graphically depicted sex used as an integral, meaningful part of an adult narrative, a short-lived experiment which reached its zenith in films such as *Last Tango in Paris* (1972, d: Bernardo Bertolucci), *The Opening of Misty Beethoven* (1975, d: Radley Metzger as "Henry Paris"), and *Sodom & Gomorrah* (1974, d: Artie Mitchell) was soon exhausted. Presumably coaxed by uncaring audiences and mercenary producers, filmmakers decided to emphasize and extend the sex scenes, and all but dismiss the narrative element, so the genre quickly devolved into pornography, which functioned as little more than a mass masturbatory aid. Thus, 16mm micro-budget gems like *Necromania* are all the more precious as they represent an extremely brief cultural phenomenon — the narrative-driven sex film where the narrative, not the sex, predominates.

Necromania is "based on" a novel by Wood, *The Only House*, purportedly published by Gallery Press in 1970.[1] To confuse matters further, Wood produced and directed a feature film about this time with the name *The Only House*, and although this obscure film has not surfaced as of this writing, it is thought to be a completely different film than *Necromania*, and not based on the novel of the same name. As will be seen, however, certain elements of the novel *The Only House* were slavishly reproduced for the *Necromania* film, while other elements were altered radically, or removed altogether.

The very first shot in *Necromania*, pre-credits, shows a gaggle of naked bodies writhing in sexual congress in a garish red netherworld; the scene is replicated several times in the frame by the use of an optical prism, so that the "orgy" being depicted seems to be repeating itself endlessly. This, of course, is yet another manifestation of Wood's cherished cosmic void, his purgatory for sinners, brought to life quite vividly here. After the credits, a Cadillac moves aimlessly through a California suburb, looking for something. Insert shots of a large old mansion, and a hand knocking with a lion door knocker, and soon a young man (Rick Lutze) and a young woman (Rene Bond) are inside the house, cautiously walking down a narrow hallway. Immediately, they start bickering about whether they should be entering this mysterious place, which boasts a devil's pitchfork on the door. They are Wood's suburban couple in discord, that tumultuous, tragic yet ultimately radicalized male-female binary always in search of socio-political correction. The young man quips, "Any minute, I expect Bela Lugosi as Dracula!" — and Wood thus "resurrects" his dear, departed friend one more time. The couple eventually finds the main room of the house, a rather bizarre interior landscape adorned in red, and boasting an odd, entirely Woodian assemblage of disparate objects: two Chinese signs, a skull on a pedestal, a rubber snake, a prop pick-axe and, most notably, a mahogany coffin, which sits square in the middle. The items in this seemingly random collection of occult-oriented artifacts all carry much symbolic weight, as will be revealed anon. After more bickering, a buxom young woman enters, dressed in a frilly red negligee, and asks if the young couple is Danny and Shirley Carpenter. (Observant fans will immediately note that Shirley, Wood's transvestite alter ego, is again used as a stand-in for Wood.) After they acknowledge that they are the entirely generic "The Carpenters" (a perfect name for these bland, bourgeois ciphers), the sexy woman introduces herself as Tanya. Tanya informs the Carpenters that the "master" of the house, Madame Heles (pronounced "heals") does not receive "guests" until midnight — the time chosen suggesting that the Carpenters have agreed to participate in some sort of occult ritual.

Tanya leads the Carpenters to their room, which looks like a garish hotel room of the period, replete with a king-sized bed adorned with screaming yellow bed-sheets, and two strange gargoyle figures on the bedstead. Most notable, however, is a large plastic dildo which, Tanya informs her guests, is to be used as a ringer in order to summon service. Tanya squeezes the faux-member, explaining, "All you just do is squeeze this little doll for attention." This is a significant, amusing little aside, as this literal phallus analog is not employed for its traditional purpose, as a penis surrogate for sexual pleasure, but specifically to summon the female master or "spirit" of the house. As the dildo ringer is not seen again for the balance of *Necromania*, its sole appearance here reinforces that its placement is purely symbolic, representing a disembodied phallocentrism rendered impotent and comical, harnessed and/or emasculated solely in the service of the female principle. (The dildo does, however, feature prominently in the novel, becoming a pivotal prop in a love scene between two men. This understandably did not get filmed for *Necromania*'s "straight" market.[2]) Danny doesn't care for the current situation, understandable as he has just seen phallocentrism radically appropriated; even Shirley confesses, "I admit its a strange place, but strange happenings come from strange happenings," a seemingly redundant, even superfluous line which in the world of Wood may subsequently mean much, firstly that radical change may only be triggered via considerable risk-taking.

The perspective changes, and the viewer sees the room from a new angle. On the wall, there is a pop-art painting of two owls, a crude yet effective reinforcement of *Necromania*'s numerous binary couplings. The plot finally kicks in, as Shirley threatens to leave Danny if tonight's events aren't successful. The viewer may intuit that Madame Heles has been solicited to help with the Carpenters' sexual dysfunction, which surely echoes more dire, devastating emotional discord. The defensive Danny mutters, "I never had any complaints before you came along, you mother!" as he flips his beloved the bird. As Shirley shakes her head in dismay at her partner's entrenched infantilism, the camera zooms in on the eyes of the owl painting, suggesting that the couple is being spied upon. Shirley continues to deride Danny's manhood in a somewhat cruel and shrewish manner, and the viewer may begin to see at least part of the reason Danny can't perform satisfactorily. Danny soon reveals the real reason for their visit: "A witch! Bullshit!" Shirley elaborates: "Madame Heles is not a witch — she's a *necromancer*" as the owl eyes become human eyes, which are indeed watching our couple, in a playful updating of a venerable "old dark house" trope, the spying eyes behind the patriarchal portrait. (This plot point is translated verbatim from the novel.[3]) Judging from the thick, full lashes on the eyes, one surmises that they belong to Tanya, the hostess; furthermore, the entirely feminine quality of the eyes suggests that this couple, and perhaps the heterosexual unit as encompassed in *Necromania*, are being watched over by a benevolent female spirit, the mythological World Mother of matriarchal prehistory. Shirley ends her tirade with an ultimatum: either Danny become sexually vital after the weekend's therapy, or she is leaving him. This is a simplistic, somewhat misogynist depiction of the cock-hungry heterosexual female, the sexually obsessed harridan, and not one of Wood's kinder character sketches. Shirley then threatens Danny: "You're going to do what I say, or I'm leaving right now!" This declaration not only posits the female as the absolute power figure in this particular duo, but also reinforces the omnipotence of the female principle in *Necromania*, which rules with a benevolent, but assuredly firm hand.

Tanya returns to the main parlor, gets down on her knees and prays to a bronze skull sculpture (a fascinating Wood icon also seen in *Take It Out in Trade*). It is clear by now that there are definitely occult rituals being performed within this phantasmagoric house. Tanya picks up the skull and kisses it, then rubs it over her body, using its cold, hard, metallic essence to achieve erotic stimulation. (The novel expands on this moment meaningfully: "She lowered the skull to her navel. 'Take it and I imagine the tongue which was once there attacking my navel, the most ignored spot in the human body ... the spot where so many nerve endings have had their electrical points awaiting so very long for those electricians who know how to connect their own electrons....'"[4]) This crudely played but intriguing depiction of a simple sex magic ritual is intensely erotic, a most rare thing in the cinema of Ed Wood (and in the world of pornography in general, for that matter). Tanya states, while looking at the audience, "They are as you suspected — not married. They are now ripe for our purpose." (The fixation on marital status in *Necromania* is curious, especially as the Carpenters in Wood's novelization are happily married. Perhaps a bit of Wood's reactionary conservation is at play with his apparent condemnation of the Carpenters' "blasphemous" status.)

Tanya leaves the parlor, and the viewer sees something not seen before — an immense stuffed black wolf, fangs bared in a ferocious grimace, a startling evocation of bestial (i.e., male) lust, ossified, which eerily foreshadows *Necromania*'s apocalyptic finale. As Tanya strolls down another corridor, a young man wearing nothing but briefs stops her and asks, "Is it time yet?" Tanya tells the man, Carl, that he will have to wait for another sexual bout with her, as new arrivals have precedence. Carl whines, like a small child, "But I wanna be first! I *must* be first! I paid plenty to be first!," an extraordinary illustration of the childish self-centeredness of the heterosexual male. The ever-merciful Tanya agrees to service Carl, and the two run to a nearby bedroom to begin sexual relations. Their sexual escapades are accompanied by a goofy music score which suggests that traditional, male-centered lovemaking is a pathetic, comical thing. Carl performs cunnilingus on Tanya, and Tanya soon reciprocates, in the first truly graphic sex scenes in the cinema of Ed Wood. Tanya then mounts Carl and they proceed to engage in garden-variety intercourse, all the while accompanied by the comedy music and absurdly exaggerated dubbed-in moans and groans, a truly farcical depiction of sex.

That scene dissolves into another binary coupling, Danny and Shirley, who are getting frisky in the rarified atmosphere of a strange bed. Danny is determined to prove his virility to his partner. As before, cunnilingus precedes fellatio which precedes intercourse, an entirely predictable sequence which reinforces the earlier notion that traditional heterosexual intercourse is in many ways a tiresome social ritual, and nothing more. While Danny and Shirley attempt sexual self-healing, Tanya again watches them from behind the "wise" owl. (The iconic image of Tanya's eyes peering through the "mask" of an owl effectively serves as metaphor for the all-seeing spirit of female wisdom which presides throughout *Necromania*.). This act of observation by the female principle does seem to seal Danny's doom, as he summarily goes limp, disappointing Shirley yet again. Leaving a deflated Danny in bed, the dejected Shirley roams the halls, dressed in a frilly negligee, in search of something that might fulfill her sexually. Caught unawares, Shirley is startled by the stuffed wolf, which now resides far from its original location, suggesting that this conspicuously mobile inanimate object serves primarily not as prop or character, but as metaphor for the spirit of the bestial which haunts human sexuality. Shirley mutters unconvincingly, "You nearly made me wet my nightgown, old boy — it's new, too!" a terribly corny and endearing line which might sound cute coming from Wood himself, but seems entirely artificial emanating from Shirley. But since Shirley *is* Wood's alter ego, perhaps she is the only person who could effectively utter such a line.

A young woman enters the hallway, also sporting a frilly nightgown; she strokes the head of the stuffed wolf and mutters, "He died of *rabies*, you know," a revelation which underscores the malignancy of bestial (read: male) lust, which may condemn its hapless victims to a horrible death. A brief close-up of the wolf's face, frozen forever in a moment of pure terror, of sudden, horrific death, accentuates this notion (and also may uncannily mirror Wood's own tragic, untimely moment of death, which occurred so shortly afterwards). The attractive brunette introduces herself as Barb, one of the "inmates" of Madame Heles' bizarre hotel for sexual therapy. The bold woman stares at Shirley, stating, "I must say, you are a good-looking one." Barb begins to pet Shirley, who doesn't mind at all; this is evidently what Shirley was missing sexually all these years. Barb is soon kissing Shirley all over, and Shirley, who becomes sexually stimulated like she never did with Danny, returns the passionate maneuvers. This amazing moment of female homosexual alliance fully embodies a prevalent theme throughout Wood's films, all of which, to some degree or another, emphasizes the omniscience of the female principle as a vital source of socio-political power. The two women soon make sweet love, accompanied by a sexy bossa nova (i.e., "new beat") instrumental, cleverly reinforcing the progressive nature of this ascension of collective female power. This pivotal coupling, which occurs at *Necromania*'s midpoint, signals a reversal of thematic polarity which plays out in some remarkable ways. (Granted, lesbian scenes such as this were ubiquitous in sex films of the day, and also, perhaps even primarily, served the male audience and thus the male principle, reinforcing phallocentrism through voyeuristic sexual performance; this is one of the contradictory dualities which haunt sex-centered films in general, and most assuredly Wood's cinema.)

The scene cuts to a close-up of Tanya's eyes spying through the owl peephole, and the film returns to the guest bedroom, where Danny arises from a fitful sleep. Finding himself alone, and most importantly with a flaccid, useless penis, Danny mutters, "Oh, shit!" and decides to track down his lover, his last hope of staying a rapidly decelerating manhood. Danny's abject failure as a man is comically reinforced by the next sequence, in which he has extreme difficulty putting on his trousers. This problem appears to have been an actual gaffe captured on film, but as retained it emphasizes the narrative thrust of the scene, for just as the previous lesbian scene emphasized the empowerment of the female principle in *Necromania*, Danny's limp noodle, laughably accentuated by his inability even to put on his pants like any self-respecting toddler, clearly illustrates that the male principle, especially phallocentric ideology, has been rendered completely and utterly impotent, in every sense of the word, by Madame Heles' all-powerful sex magic. When Danny finally moans, "I better go find her...," the "her" he speaks of is that matriarchal power source which might potentially save Danny from his impending fate as a failed and abandoned penis-holder. (This notable reversal of psycho-sexual polarity in *Necromania*, initiated by the empowering lesbian coupling and underscored by Danny's bedroom humiliation, is further reinforced by another, possibly inadvertent event: As Danny struggles to put on his pants, the viewer cannot help but notice that the owl picture, and the dressing table, which in the first scene were on stage left, have now magically shifted to stage right. Since redecoration of the set in such a quickly shot production is unlikely, it appears that the film itself was reversed in laboratory processing. Whether an innocent gaffe, or a crafty bit of "magic" on the part of the filmmaker, this notable aesthetic jolt goes far to accentuate the switching of sexual and political loyalties from male to female which fuels the narrative in *Necromania*.)

When Barb takes Shirley back to the house bed and continues to seduce her, she states, "Trust in me — put your whole body and soul into my hands," a somewhat pretentious statement to make were this just another pick-up, but completely appropriate for one coaxing a reluctant but inquiring soul into a ritual initiation into the female principle, undoubtedly a moment of great import to the student. (Barb is a most important character in *Necromania*, and even moreso in the novel; there she has one of the best bits of dialogue, which unfortunately was not filmed: "Take all the joys you can from this life.... There are so few joys on the outside world. We are here for only the one purpose. To give joys in the only way we know how ... and in the only way where thorough enjoyment may come to the human being ... may come to all the inhabitants of the earth."[5]) The two women kiss, and as Shirley passionately, even aggressively draws Barb closer, it is apparent that Shirley has now embraced this new belief-system, which may yet save her from the dull thrust of phallocentrism. Meanwhile, poor Danny walks down the hallway where Shirley and Barb met, and the polarity has again changed, as the emblematic stuffed wolf is now on stage right. Danny backs into this metaphor for ossified bestial lust, in effect getting "goosed" by the ever-stiff corpse of the philosophy to which he has foolishly pledged allegiance. Tanya finally encounters Danny and drags him to yet another bed. She declares cryptically, "Your wife was much more demonstrative when she saw the wolf-mummy," assigning a wonderfully cryptic name for the stuffed wolf, which reinforces the notion that the beast does represent a spiritual and psychological "test" for all whom "it" encounters. As seen, immediately after Shirley encountered the wolf-mummy, she was seduced by Barb and initiated into her new matriarchal world of sexual and political freedom. Danny's response to the beast's goosing was typical male timidity, and running away; when Tanya brings this fact to his attention, the best this male dud can do is grunt. Clearly, he is unenlightened, and likely beyond redemption. Tanya now makes a pass at Danny, merely performing her duties as a good sexual hostess, but Danny protests about his "wife," and Tanya scolds him for the lie, which is public knowledge by now. *Necromania* seems to take clear aim at what Wood considers the "lie" of promiscuous premarital sex, a somewhat parochial viewpoint which clashes harshly with the primarily progressive spirit of *Necromania*. (As noted, this harsh judgment is all the more odd as Wood's novel depicts Danny and Shirley as happily married.)[6]

The scene returns to Shirley and Barb, who states, "You come quickly." Shirley responds, "I have a good teacher," as the experience has been primarily educational for the bright young woman. Barb notes casually, "Danny's in training." Shirley asks to confirm this, and Barb quips, "Bet yer sweet bippy!" in a brazen theft of a corny catchphrase from the popular television series *Rowan and Martin's Laugh-In*. During cunnilingus, Barb states dramatically, "Union of two bodies—*that* is what we strive for," and here Wood's agenda is succinctly declared, for this is exactly the message of Wood's cinema since *Glen or Glenda?*: the attempted ritual reconciliation of male/female, Eros/Thanatos, Life/Death, into one stable, balanced socio-political entity, a daring progressive philosophy applicable both to individuals and societies. Barb now virtually shouts, "Love me Shirley —*love me!*"— that is, embrace the matriarchal imperative, adore the female principle, accept all that "she" represents— and Shirley takes the cue, for the first time in her life climbing on top of another body and taking full charge of her own sexual and political destiny.

Meanwhile, back in the doomed heterosexual bed, Tanya fellates Danny, who moans, "Duh, that feels good," a predictably imbecilic comment. This sex scene is again accompanied by goofy instrumental-with-chorus elevator music, illustrating the tiresome bourgeois quality of the act. Tanya soon commands Danny: "I need you to come!" Judging by a close-up of Danny's barely erect cock, the phallocentric world has lost the ability to please anyone. A loud, off-screen gong sounds, while a disembodied voice emanating from the coffin echoes, "It is time." Tanya leads Danny over to a curtained window and tells him to look within. Inside, a number of indistinguishable bodies are having group sex. The scene is shot through a primitive optical prism, which replicates the original image numerous times, in a crude attempt to symbolize that this "gang bang" entails hundreds, if not thousands, of souls, in what is apparently an endless repetitive act of involuntary copulation, an eventuality which would be torture to some. (Group sex, at least as posited during the faux-spiritual Sexual Revolution, was considered a highly metaphoric phenomenon, the goal of which was to dampen the individual psyche in an attempt to merge all members of a community into one harmonious, ego-less "godhead." The reality was that this promising phenomenon was quickly and decisively appropriated by phallocentric interests and used primarily as a lure for readily available sex for compulsives, and as a virtually endless source of visual material for the pornography industry.) Tanya annotates the scene: "Not all react to the treatment successfully; there are those who will never find satisfaction in their, their universal language — sex! Some want too much, others too little." Danny, in a rare moment of self-awareness, responds, "I didn't react too well, did I?" Tanya gives him a knowing grin, and some words of comfort: "There is always the future." Danny, unsure of whether this "future" of which she speaks is a godsend or a horror, asks, "Like them, and their future?" Tanya puts his mind at ease: "Not like them — they're lost forever. They can never return to a world which will reject them.

They are happy here." Tanya thus pinpoints this sex-saturated universe beyond the "final" curtain as Wood's cosmic void for lost souls come to life yet again, in what is perhaps his final, most poignant sketch of this recurring psycho-spiritual landscape, Wood's ethereal "bus station" on the road to eternity. (The novel offers an awkwardly lyrical description of this sexual purgatory: "Danny felt he was looking down into a snake pit of humans who had lost all contact with life except pleasing themselves through a horror of mentally disturbed lust.")[7]

Tanya next leads Danny by the hand, like a mother and her little boy, to the "Red Room," where Madame Heles holds court. The stuffed "wolf-mummy" has returned to its rightful place, by his master's side, having completed its various metaphorical tasks. Shirley and Barb soon join the others. The first thing Danny asks his life-partner is, "Where have you been?" and Shirley responds, "I could ask you the same question!" In their first meeting in several hours, the first emotions expressed by this ill-fated couple are hostility, accusation and jealousy; surely this relationship is doomed, a verdict reinforced by the fact that they stand on opposite sides of the room, next to their mentors. Danny, a chronic slave to the infantile ego of the idiot male, boasts, "Well, I had a delightful time." Shirley goads him with a response which underlines his problem of compulsive self-centeredness: "Yes—but did *she*?" The implication, of course, is that "she" did not, and Danny couldn't care less, as long as his own terminally adolescent, short-term needs (i.e., quick orgasm) have been met.

Tanya and Barb kneel before their sacred altar of matriarchal coition and pray to their masters, Madame Heles and the spirit of the World Mother. Tanya and Barb slowly undress each other, for nakedness is pure and beautiful in a world uncontaminated by Judeo-Christian concepts of shame and loathing. At the sight of the two naked beauties, Shirley nearly swoons in erotic stimulation; the sight of this dyad of female sexual empowerment is too much for her. Amusingly, the same sight terrifies Danny, who runs to his lover's side, almost hiding behind her, so frightened is he of this powerful expression of female sexual emancipation. Barb now services Tanya, accompanied by crudely dubbed-in moaning, which suggests the disembodied spirit of female lust unleashed. In the foreground, atop the bronze skull, a skinny red candle now seems an apt, all-too-peripheral stand-in for the absent, unmissed phallus. Tanya then performs cunnilingus on Barb, and as the two writhe in pleasure, the stuffed wolf-mummy stands nearby in paralysis, forced to watch this act of sweet love occurring without, in fact benefiting from its absence. Understandably, any sexual activity which ignores him infuriates Danny, who groans, "I don't dig any of this crap"; Danny is likely beyond hope if he doesn't find exhilarating this sight of two attractive females innocently petting. The problem, again, is that the act does not include him, painting Danny as a childish egotist to the last. Danny defensively declares, "I might have problems, but it looks like these people have a hell of a lot more problems than me!"; Shirley counters, "Nobody's got more problems than you—and that's the *truth*!" As a representative of sexually compulsive, terminally myopic patriarchy, Shirley's verdict may be correct (even though her response may have been, to Wood, merely another failed attempt at copping a line from *Laugh-In*).

Finally concluding their ritual lovemaking, which invoked the spirit of the all-powerful female principle, Tanya summons Madame Heles and escorts Shirley to switch places with her, so that male/female and female/female are once again aligned. This last-minute reversal of polarity back to its original position signifies that the sexual magic performed for this couple has been completed, has come full circle as it were, and all that remains is the judgment from the master as to the ritual acts' efficacy. Unearthly groans emanate from the coffin, as the lid opens and Madame Heles (Maria Aronoff) sits up. The viewer might be surprised to note that Madame Heles is not played by an older woman, which would makes sense as she is obviously meant to portray the elder, Crone figure of the World Mother trinity

(destroyer and sexual healer), but by an attractive young woman. Still, an angled shot showing Heles rising from her crypt, while the wolf-mummy scowls close by, is revealing. and as
it is accompanied by Wood's signature audio effect — thunder — the viewer knows this is the
pivotal moment in *Necromania*, in which god and mortal, Life and Death, are merged in an
apocalyptic, potentially liberating apotheosis. This sequence is reminiscent of similar opening sequences in *Night of the Ghouls* and *Orgy of the Dead*, in which Criswell rose out of his
coffin to spin his grandiose tales of Life and Death. For *Necromania*, Criswell purportedly
donated a coffin which he owned, so even here the spirit of Criswell is undeniably evoked.
Ted Gorley, who photographed *Necromania*'s hardcore scenes, stated in *Nightmare of Ecstasy*
that they in fact borrowed the wrong coffin, an older relic "from Lincoln's time," which may
explain why the prop has such an "antique" look to it.[8] This revelation also suggests that
Criswell did not own just one coffin, but a collection of them, making the dark entertainer
even more mysterious. Additionally, Maila Nurmi (aka Vampira) was approached to play the
part of Madame Heles, but declined after hearing that it was a sex film.[9]

Madame Heles asks news of the progress of her newest "students," and Barb states of
Shirley, "She has made tremendous progress— she has *learned her sex* well." Shirley has not
merely learned *about* sex, but has learned the tremendous untapped power of *her gender*, has
in fact "learned her sex" well. Pleased, Madame Heles proclaims, "Then she shall be removed.
Henceforth, she will live for sex, and sex alone," as she fondles her own ample breast, symbolically the nurturing breast of the World Mother. Barb tells Shirley, "You've graduated,"
also baring and fondling her breast, an act which Wood seems to be presenting almost as a
"secret sign" of identification between emancipated females. Barb walks off and Shirley obediently follows, uttering not one final word to her now-useless male partner. Danny, understandably, is horrified by this abject betrayal, and says the only thing his tiny mind can think
of: "What about *me*?" Tanya declares, "We still have some work to do on you," knowing that
to wrest the world from the insidious clutches of patriarchal domination, much work remains.
Madame Heles declares, "Then he needs the personal sex teachings of Madame Heles," as she
again fondles her breast.

Madame Heles reclines in her coffin, crossing her arms in a posture of death, while
Danny, suddenly nauseous, holds his stomach. Tanya snaps her fingers, and Barb and Carl
(the impatient male seen earlier) enter the Red Room, grab Danny, strip him nude, and force
him into the coffin with Madame Heles. Forced to face his own very special "death," the death
of failed phallocentrism, Danny is now forced to enter the ego-dampening world of the
community-oriented female principle. Struggling unsuccessfully, Danny is soon dragged into
the dark crypt with Madame Heles. As the lid closes over them, Danny screams bloody murder, for only now he sees the gaping void which is all that he has heretofore avoided or
repressed in his sexual affairs, and in his very psychology. The coffin lid lifts briefly to show
Danny and Heles kissing, and as the lid closes yet again, Danny screams, "I'm a man! I'm a
man! Oh, great!" Madame Heles' matriarchal magic has healed Danny, in an unexpected
happy ending for him.

The soft core R-rated version ends here, but the hardcore X-rated version features an
extended scene, wherein Heles fellates Danny while both are in the coffin, an indelibly ritual act which merges Eros and Thanatos in a most pure, virtually alchemical form. Heles soon
brings the possessed Danny to orgasm, an act again accompanied by Wood's trademark thunderclap, marking the moment as of great metaphysical import. As Sigmund Freud, and followers such as Herbert Marcuse maintained, the alchemical marriage of the life instinct with
the death instinct would be catastrophic, at least on the psychological level, and Wood's thunderclap may thus portend socio-political apocalypse.[10] Alternately, this highly significant "cli-

max" of *Necromania* may suggest the ultimate triumph of phallocentrism, which by film's end is still being serviced by the obliging female; yet perhaps the finale after all remains true to the prevailing theme of *Necromania*, in that many cultures believe that the coaxing of vital seminal fluid from the male is primarily an act of emasculation on the part of female succubae, who drain the life-fluid from males in order to render them weak and impotent. As such, the ascendancy of fellatio as the preeminent act in pornography, with *Necromania* a significant early example, may attest more to its socio-political functioning as a symbol of mass male enervation, than to its relative aesthetic popularity in sex media. As well, Freudians may see the omniscience of oral sex in pornography as illustrating a cultural infantilism, a systemic codification of the male collective mentally arrested in the earliest, "oral stage" of psychological development.

Necromania's end title offers one last, truly iconic Wood image: a human skull wearing a female wig, with the words THE END pasted on the skull's forehead with plastic letters. This marvelous appropriation of a typical "Day of the Dead"–style adornment of dead bones, with the hilariously poignant "message" branded on the skull of the deceased, is almost too good to be true, as it is so perfectly captures Wood's alternately gruesome and whimsical fixations on Death, the dead, and that enigmatic "moment of death" which haunts virtually every frame of his films. As John d'Addario observes in the liner notes to the Fleshbot Films DVD release of *Necromania*, "Eros and Thanatos are inextricably linked in *Necromania*..."[11] and as this endeavored alliance between Sex and Death appears to have been Wood's creative mission all along, the shabby, lackluster *Necromania* may ironically stand as one of his finest achievements. As mentioned, from the Freudian perspective of basic psychoanalytic theory, the desire to merge the life instinct (Eros) and the death instinct (Thanatos), or the pleasure principle with the reality principle, must perforce augment destruction, so one might perceive this passion of Wood as a somewhat self-destructive aim. Yet as Herbert Marcuse interprets Freud's theory, "The death instinct is not destructive for its own sake, but for the relief of tension. The descent toward death is an unconscious flight from pain and want."[12] From this angle, Eros and Thanatos seem in to be in the service, at root, of the same thing—an achievement of pleasant mortal stasis, a "Nirvana" which erases all torment and strife. As Wood (and many others) picture Sex as a potentially healing and emancipating socio-political force, Death, far from being a fearsome enemy to be avoided, may be a sought-for achievement or "reward" for a life well-lived; both are thus seen in the service of easing the existential "tension" of life. This is the essence of much matriarchal philosophy, which preaches the eternal, entirely mutual cycle of Life and Death, and this main thematic point in Wood's films is strikingly acted out in *Necromania*.

According to several sources, *Necromania* was made on a budget of approximately $7,000, and utilized a script barely 20 pages long. As might be anticipated, Wood purportedly went on a drinking binge the week before production, but according to Charles Anderson, who worked with Wood on some of the 8mm sex films he produced at this time, Wood dutifully showed up the day before shooting, wearing his "embroidered western outfit," with script in hand.[13] An enduring enigma concerning *Necromania* is the assertion by several that Wood played a Wizard in the film. Charles Anderson stated of his colleague, "He acted in *Necromania* as a sort of Orson Welles type, a wizard. He had some sort of weirdness going on with his scene, an evil doctor kind of thing."[14] As Wood does not appear in any of the several versions of *Necromania* released on home video, one wonders what happened to this footage of the artist in performance. If anything could make *Necromania* an even more iconic Woodian treasure, it would certainly be the appearance of Wood as a malevolent magi. Even *sans* personal appearance, the ever-optimistic Wood was proud of the finished product, even boasting that *Necromania* "will set a new trend in sexploitation type of films (sic)."[15]

As mentioned, *Necromania* shares much with Wood's novel *The Only House*, following the plot-line almost exactly. As might be expected, the novel goes into greater detail about the protagonists' mindset, and offers some marvelous Wood philosophizing. Especially intriguing is a vaguely Puritanical perspective throughout the novel, which seems to simultaneously take aim at promiscuous, hedonistic breeders, and yet disparages historical attempts to take all the erotic enjoyment away from the sex act. Consider this passage: "In some religions the wife was dressed entirely, her entire body in coarse sackcloth. There was only a small hole over her pubic region to where the male would insert his penis. This was to aid in keeping the possibility of enjoying the affair at a minimum."[16] Later in the novel, when Tanya recalls her sad childhood, her alcoholic father and her abused mother, the tone has completely changed: "And she was knocked up ... pregnant ... with child ... going to lay another 'house ape, screaming brat, fuck-head, stinking ass kid on the doorstep of the world.'"[17] There is also plenty of cock-eyed Woodian observation on the inherent contradictions of life: "I wonder why if something feels good it's all wrong ... but when a piece of shit is too hard and it hurts your ass when it comes out, that's alright?"[18] There is also some surprisingly violent imagery in the novel, which may have reflected Wood's actual experience in the sexual underground of Hollywood; particularly unsettling is this account of homosexual rape: "Once she had seen a beautiful drag queen raped by six men in an alley. It was a sight of pure terror because they ripped the young boy's ass right out. The blood and the gore was a horrible sight to witness. But after the initial pain shot through her voyeuristic eyes she felt pleasure in all they did to him."[19] Finally, Wood takes time in the novel to comment on the Demon Rum, obviously a subject of great personal interest to him: "We are not so stupid as to destroy our liver with such disturbing influences. We have much more use for our bodies than to make them the swill receptacle of worthless crap."[20] In sum, *The Only House* is one of Wood's strongest, most coherent novels, eminently readable and full of profound insights and reflections on modern culture. (The basic scenario of *The Only House* was also shortened by Wood into a short story, with the typical "pun" title "Come Inn," which was published in a 1971 men's magazine.)

As astounding as it may seem, Wood's thematic agenda remains intact and vital, even in such a pathetic showcase as *Necromania*, proving that this remarkable craftsman could successfully insert his philosophical agenda into even the most unlikely vehicle. *Necromania* consistently, if not clearly, champions that integration of the male and female sides, of both individuals and societies, which Wood had been preaching since *Glen or Glenda?*, a passionate rumination on the "yin" and "yang" of both material and spiritual existence which fascinated Wood, as it has fascinated artists, lovers and thinkers throughout history. *Necromania* makes clear, as does *Glen or Glenda?*, *The Bride and the Beast*, and *Orgy of the Dead*, that it is the omniscience of the male principle, as systematized by entrenched patriarchy, which has caused much if not all of modern man's existential and political dilemma, and it is only the embracing of the female principle, through an acceptance of matriarchal participation, which may save mankind after all. *Necromania* positions the emancipating joys of sexual intercourse as the key to balancing male/female equality, yet the novel greatly expands on this theme with some exemplary passages, such as: "Think of the wars and we then think of unhappiness. Would it not be better if all these men were in bed with some woman ... or with themselves for that matter? There would be no time for wars in such a case."[21] And there is no mistaking Wood's viewpoint on the matter when Tanya tells Danny, "You have been the problem all along."[22] Thus, *Necromania* continues Wood's proselytizing towards a sexually egalitarian world, represented first and foremost by the artist himself, as his alter ego Shirley, and brought to life so vigorously, and tirelessly in this artist's extraordinary works.

11

Sexploitation Superstar

Faced with ever-diminishing chances for mounting his own film productions, due to dwindling financial opportunities, radical changes in the entertainment industry and undoubtedly also the author's increasing alcoholism, Ed Wood continued to write with seemingly superhuman vigor, churning out many written works, including novels, short stories and film screenplays for other producers. Herewith are brief observations on several Wood screenplays which made it to finished film, as well as a few instances where Wood graced the screen himself as performer.

Revenge of the Virgins (1959)

Ed Wood's participation in this low-budget film is disputed; it is included on the assumption that Wood wrote, or contributed to the screenplay, which is credited to a "Pete LaRoche." The only other screenplays credited to LaRoche are *Wetbacks* (1956) and *Outlaw Queen* (1957), but there are at least two magazine articles during the time period with a similar by-line, dealing with Western movie stars William S. "Bill" Hart and Tim McCoy. Pete LaRoche may in fact be a separate individual, or one of Wood's many pen names, as Wood was an avid fan of the Western film genre, and could have easily been the author of all extant "LaRoche" pieces.[1] *Revenge of the Virgins* (henceforth referred to as *Virgins*) is a threadbare western melodrama, with the added conceit of the "Indians," i.e., the Native Americans, depicted as attractive young women who happen to be topless. This makes *Virgins* one of the first in the sexploitation genre known as "nudie cuties" which, in contrast to earlier genres such as striptease, burlesque and nudist camp films, featured nudity that was at least marginally justified by a narrative storyline. Russ Meyer's *The Immoral Mr. Teas* (1959) is often considered the first "nudie cutie," but *Virgins* may predate it. There is also reason to believe that fellow producer-director and Wood colleague Ronald V. Ashcroft was involved in *Virgins*, as uncredited producer. *Virgins* boasts several parallels to Ashcroft's 1958 science fiction film *The Astounding She-Monster*, including the same stock music score, compiled by Guenther Kauer, at least one of the same players (Kenne Duncan), and a scenario largely filmed in deep, shadowy woods. Also, the production company, R.V.A. Productions, improbably identified by some sources as "Radio Voice of America," more likely got its name from Ashcroft's initials. Also noteworthy is the fact that Peter LaRoche's other screenplay credits, *Wetbacks* (1956) and *Outlaw Queen* (1957), were both Ashcroft productions. *Virgins* unfolds primarily as a straightforward melodrama, crudely but evocatively filmed, with the noted addition of the topless maidens. Uncredited narrator Kenne Duncan informs the viewer that this band of females is all that is left from a once-noble tribe of Native Americans, whose men were slaughtered by white men who brought with them the bloodthirsty myths of Christianity. This is an interesting point, which hints at Wood's involvement, as Wood had profound opinions on the subject of organized religion, as seen elsewhere. Significantly, the leader of the female warriors is a white blonde, who apparently was left by others and brought up by the Native Americans as their own. (Truth be told, all of the maidens look fairly "white.") The story involves a dandy from the East and his shrewish wife, who hook up with an alcoholic gold prospector and two escaped convicts to search for a large gold deposit in the desolate hills; eventually two deserters from the U.S. Cavalry join them. Ruby, the wife, is clearly a potential Wood archetype, an emasculating harridan who is completely, unashamedly mercenary; she crows to her husband, "I wanna be queen of the beehive!," a line which sounds like pure Wood. During the group's excursion, they are constantly shadowed by the Native Americans, who crouch behind trees and bushes, rising just enough so that the viewer can see their bare breasts. The simplistic plot has the white men killing each other off, while the remaining members are killed by arrows from the topless warriors. Another touch which suggests the hand of Wood are the makeshift graves two of the men make for their fallen comrades. One of the men wonders if it wouldn't be proper to add a cross or marking to the mounds of dirt, just to be proper; as the astute viewer knows by now, Wood is all about graves, marked or unmarked. As the female warriors drag the last white man off to his death, Kenne Duncan sums up: "This is the revenge of the virgins! Beware the savage guardians of the golden horde!" Most notable about *Virgins* is that it essentially pits two microcosmic matriarchies against each other. Ruby is decidedly the leader of the "white" group; with her constant badgering and threatening of the assembled males, she clearly rules the men, and it is primarily her lust for wealth and power which leads these men to their demise. Contrasting this is the entirely female society of the Native Americans, also headed by a white woman, who guides her sisters to seek a very poetic justice for the murder of their mates. The matriarchy of the Native Americans wins out, entirely erasing their rivals, and in effect reclaiming the land which was so violently wrested from them. To call *Virgins* a pre-feminist tract would be stretching things, but the spirit of Wood is evident in this somber scenario which revolves around the deadly machinations of women on missions both noble and vile.

Married Too Young (1962)

Ed Wood's participation in this well-mounted but predictable exploitation entry is disputed. According to Greg Luce at Sinister Cinema, a producer for Headliner Productions claimed that Wood was brought in to finish up the troubled production, and can be credited with the last 15 minutes or so of the completed film. Elsewhere, the daughter of credited screenwriter Nathaniel Tanchuck has insisted that Tanchuck was the sole scenarist.[2] Unless an annotated screenplay turns up, Wood's participation can only be intuited, but there are reasons to believe that he did have a hand in the finished product. Most importantly, Wood had just the previous year finished *The Sinister Urge* (1960) for Headliner Productions, acting as both scenarist and director, so he was undoubtedly familiar with Headliner at the time. Also, some scenes in *Married Too Young* are similar to scenes in *The Violent Years* (1956), a film which Wood scripted for Headliner Productions some years earlier. *Married Too Young* is somewhat of an anachronism, a fairly tame melodrama about impulsive youth gone astray. This was a recurring motif in the exploitation genre of the 1930s through the 1950s, but it had become virtually obsolete by the 1960s, all but replaced by stronger subjects such as the "nudie cutie" and the "roughie," genres more accurately termed sexploitation, which featured abundant nudity, sexual deviance and violence as their main narrative conceits. (*The Sinister Urge* was arguably one of the first "rough" sexploitation films to be released; in comparison, *Married Too Young* seems positively archaic.) The scenario follows high school student Tommy Blaine (played by the son of famed comedian Harold Lloyd) and his devoted girlfriend, Helen Newton (Jana Lund). Blaine is a popular race car driver and mechanic, but his real aspiration is to become a doctor and a member of good standing in his community. Contrasting the sickeningly sweet morality of Tommy and Helen are a lawless, charismatic couple who act as tempters to the heroes—Grimes, a seedy gangster, and his teenage tramp of a girlfriend, Marla. It turns out that Tommy and Helen are "secretly engaged," and one night while necking in the back seat of the car, they decide they cannot control their passions any longer. Rather than commit the unforgivable sin of premarital sex, the pair hurry to a justice of the peace on the outskirts of town to get married. The notion of evil awaiting to ensnare reckless youth just outside the borders of their safe suburban community is an old one in the exploitation genre; in these films, many a wayward youth was led to his or her destruction with the assistance of out-of-town (i.e., "foreign") abortionists, bar-keeps, drug pushers, slave traders, etc. Tommy's parents are hapless underachievers, while Helen's are ruthless social climbers. When they find out about this teenage marriage, they confront the justice of the peace who, instead of admitting guilt, gives the parents a stern lecture on their abdicated responsibilities as parents. This scene echoes similar segments in the Wood-scripted *The Violent Years,* although the stern moral lecture was a fixture of exploitation film in general, and is by no means a Wood trademark in and of itself. Tommy soon buys a house for his teenage bride. Of course, domestic life turns out to be anything but bliss. The evil Grimes makes a deal with Tommy, and soon, the financially strapped youngster is fencing stolen cars to make ends meet, awash in the darker side of adult independence. A later night-time scene features Helen meeting with Tommy in the living room, to discuss their future. In this scene, Helen wears a flowing, frilly nightgown; the viewer may wishfully imagine Wood's influence here, as it is perhaps the sexiest moment in a truly sexless film. The last reel of the film is fairly exciting; it seems likely that this is Wood's work, either primarily as scenarist-director, or via significant post-production work. A distraught Helen suffers a weird nightmare in which she sees, through superimposition, all of the images which led to her present sorry fate. Helen runs to the garage at midnight, confronting Tommy. The two drive off in a stolen automobile, and are soon tailed by police. After a high-speed chase, the car hurtles off a cliff, and the viewer assumes that the heroes have died. Miraculously, they survive, and in fact appear none the worse for wear. At the probation trial, the judge scolds the parents for their failure in raising responsible citizens, in a scene which could have come, almost verbatim, from the Wood-scripted *The Violent Years.* But Wood's voice can perhaps be most clearly heard in the judge's plaintive summation: "Very few of us ever get a second chance!" The bizarre dream-montage, the midnight rendezvous, the apocalyptic car crash, the miraculous "resurrection" from certain death of the heroes, the stern moral lecture—surely, the spirit of Ed Wood hovers over this final reel of *Married Too Young.*

Shotgun Wedding (1963)

Ed Wood's participation in this engaging medium-budget sex farce is based on the filmmaker's inclusion of the title on a list of his feature writing credits, which he compiled for Fred Olen Ray in 1978, shortly before his death.[3] The influence of the early 1960s media obsession with all things rural, largely fueled by the smash CBS television series *The Beverly Hillbillies*, is evident in *Shotgun Wedding*, which combines a bucolic hillbilly sensibility with the ruthless, contradictory backwoods politics of Al Capp's *Li'l Abner* comic strip, in which men are ineffectual, drunken buffoons, while women are sexy, gold-digging "man-traps." Amongst many other films which exploited this obsession with rural sexuality were *Poor White Trash* (1957, d: Harold Daniels), *Lorna* (1964, d: Russ Meyer), and *Jennie, Wife/Child* (1966, d: James Landis, Robert Carl Cohen). *Shotgun Wedding* is a well-produced, attractive film which features a good deal of effective comic banter between characters. Familiar character actor J. Pat O'Malley stars as Buford Anchors, head of a hillbilly clan which lives, significantly, on a houseboat which has been swamped on dry land for years. This notable portrait of a downwardly mobile family "anchored" to a stagnant land-based existence does mirror Wood's recurring theme of failed suburban families and their dysfunctional ways. Expectedly, Buford is an idiot tyrant, a common sketch of clownish patriarchy who bellows his orders to his totally dysfunctional suburban household, which is truly "sub-urban." His live-in partner, a shrewish sex kitten named Melanie, is actually "Tiger Rose," a carnival performer who may have murdered a man. It is revealed that Melanie is "with baby," but she was impregnated by Buford's son, not by Buford, a plot point which reinforces the tiresome stereo-

Itinerant Preacher William Schallert (front left) officiates for Buford Anchors and his bride-to-be Melanie (Pat O'Malley and Valerie Allen, center), as reluctant Maid of Honor Honey Bee (Jenny Maxwell, right) and a host of unidentified cast members look on, in Boris Petroff's *Shotgun Wedding* (1963), co-authored by Ed Wood.

type of rural families being awash in incestuous partnerships. The titular "shotgun wedding" ensues, presided over by a mercenary evangelist, played by William Schallert.[4] At the wedding's consummation, much to the guests' horror, it is the son who passionately kisses the bride, his new mother. The balance of the film centers around the son and the mother in conspiracy against the father, in classic Oedipal fashion, until the townsfolk rise up en masse to rid their community of this enclave of incest and amorality. The film ends as Melanie and the preacher, the two "urbanites," escape death by lynch mob, and ride off together to continue their grifting ways in that carnival of corruption known as "the big city." Notable are references by Melanie and the preacher to life at a big city carnival. Wood liked to toss in references to carny life wherever possible; they are especially abundant in his writings. Assuming this is partially a Wood screenplay, one can see that he did, in fact, have a flair for light comedy, and this may be his most successful comedy venture. *Shotgun Wedding* is an entertaining if cynical portrait of the modern family in upheaval; it features snappy dialogue and clever wordplay, performed by actors who know their lines and have a good sense of comic timing, a fairly rare occurrence in the Wood canon. Additionally, there are lines of dialogue in *Shotgun Wedding* which evoke the spirit of Wood. One such line is uttered by Buford as his trampish live-in partner packs to leave the Anchor household; she tosses a furry sweater into her suitcase, and Buford, seeing feathers everywhere, exclaims, "What, did you just pluck a chicken in here?!" Reinforcing Wood's disdainful position on modern marriage are comments such as, "There's more to marriage than four legs and a bed!" One might attribute Buford's exclamation, "Doggone, ya just can't be good to a woman!" to knee-jerk misogyny on Wood's part, but in the context of the scenario, Buford is an abusive and over-possessive mate, and he makes the comment after realizing he has "lost control" of his wildcat concubine. A line created for pure comedy, which also addresses rural ignorance, comes after a young man learns that his partner is pregnant; the stunned male asks her to repeat the troubling disclosure, and she screams, "Baby! B-a-b-b-y!" Yet Wood's voice, succinctly expressing his frustrated-underachiever philosophy, may be most clearly heard in the disgruntled character who observes, near the film's cataclysmic end, "What a *fink* world!"

The Love Feast (1969)

Joseph F. Robertson's *The Love Feast* might have fallen through the cracks of history as just another no-budget sex film, were it not for one remarkable conceit — it features Ed Wood as the leading man. Wood declares that his character's name is "Murphy," but it is obvious that Wood is just playing himself — an effeminate, sexually obsessed boozehound. Posing as a photographer, the sex-addicted Murphy lures models to his house to strip for him. As model after model joins him in bed, the scene turns into a sexual free-for-all, a "love feast." The film's basic narrative template is taken from the early "nudie cutie" genre, with a lone male "capturing" females on camera as a pretense for conveying nakedness on screen. *The Love Feast* mutates the obsolete genre by grafting onto it nearly pornographic depictions of sexual intercourse and total nudity. Placing Wood as the male lead in this sorry debacle removes all pretense at erotica, for he is depicted as a bloated old man, with slurred speech, greasy long hair, and a propensity to stumble around — in short, a drunken bum. The end result of tossing this flabby old stumblebum into a sea of taut young bodies is that *The Love Feast* comes across as a crude and cynical sex farce, a total mockery of its intended genre and a slap in the face to the then-ascendant Sexual Revolution. Here, Wood-as-performer immerses himself headfirst into the female principle, summoning it into his personal bed; at one point, he even chants, "Now I love girls! Girls! Girls! Girls!" Several extended lesbian sequences reinforce the ascendancy of the feminine in *The Love Feast*. As the orgy grows ever larger, at one point it is impossible to tell the bodies apart or to clarify gender, as *The Love Feast* manages to evince the mystic's "sacred marriage" of spirit and matter, yin and yang, anima and animus into one homogeneous and androgynous societal unit. Yet Wood's compulsive escapades ironically conveys the utter fatigue inherent in sexual obsession; early on, Wood pays a cab driver to join the orgy and give him respite. Between sexual escapades, Wood retreats to his backyard, where he smokes and drinks liberally, essentially reprising in toto his archetypal dysfunctional suburban couple, here escaping from the invasive Sexual Revolution by retreating to the sanctuary of his debilitating, but comforting personal wilderness. It is significant also that *The Love Feast* is a shameless celebration of alcoholism — Wood's frequent trips to the back patio to refresh himself with liquor suggest that booze is essential in maintaining an artificial interest in chronic recreational sex. In a prevalent conceit of male pornographic fantasy, the females are portrayed as succubi, mythical she-demons who drain a man's soul through endless sexual intercourse. Mid-film, the increasingly exhausted Wood even utters a telling revelation: "My God! The energy of youth!" The withering elder has seen the "energy of youth" not as something winsome or envious, but as predatory and debilitating, in effect a cruel "god" to the sexual compulsive. Again as a form of narrative "rescue" for the fatigued Wood, two male plumbers intervene at one point, in a parody of a typical pornographic trope, the solicitation of a "service man" to "service" the on-screen woman, and by proxy the male audience. Meanwhile, back on the bed, the sorry, ever-expanding gaggle of social defectives listlessly grope and fondle each other. Photographic depictions of group sex are invariably dull, and *The Love Feast* is no exception. Ultimately, the film seems a most unusual invocation of Wood's perennial cosmic void except that here, Wood has trapped not only his characters and his audience, but *himself* in this sinners' hell of his own creation, suffering "the wages of sin" in a most personal way. In the last reel, three dominatrixes arrive via Cadillac expressly to intervene on Wood's behalf; they have been sent specifically to punish Wood for his sexual sins. They force the poor man to wear a dog collar, a frilly pink nightie and high heels, emasculating him in front of his guests with this "holy trinity" of sado-masochistic garmentalia. Now thoroughly humiliated by those whom he has exploited, Wood becomes mythic via his fetish-fueled punishment and atonement. Wood has become his anima, "Shirley," the female principle incarnate, through a painful ritual invocation of the Sexual Revolution, which as depicted here is a cruel and predatory force. (Throughout the movie, Wood also "humiliates" himself with shameless mugging and corny voiceover lines such as, "From the top of your head to the bottom of your toe, you make me want to go, go, Go!") Wood is subsequently asked if he has ever licked boots, and he playfully responds, "I was in the service!" More than mere reference to his fetish-fueled Marine days, the comment underscores the essentially masochistic nature of military service, which remains one of the last overt forms of the barbaric "slave/master" dialectic in modern society. Wood then dutifully gets down on his hands and knees, like a dog, and licks the dominatrix's shiny black leather boots, a sacred act of humbling repentance. These painfully humiliating scenes of Wood's debasement and correction by the female collective could not conceivably serve any erotic purpose to the audience; they function primarily as ritual acts meant to elevate Wood as a cultural figure of note. The lead dominatrix finally removes Wood's underpants, rendering him completely naked against his gods. She then picks up Wood's "holy" briefs and fondles them, achieving erotic stimulation from the act. This fetish worship of the sacred fabric which contained Wood's "manhood" is an early petition for the positioning of Wood as a sort of "love god." Wood is finally embraced by the female collective, who surround him in purple silk and perform a dance which reinforces the ritual nature of *The Love Feast*, for here Wood is not just figuratively, but literally absorbed by the female principle, in effect, becoming one with it. Back outside, Wood utters his most revealing bon mot: "The girls back there don't know it, but I'm loving them *to death!*" By connecting Sex and Death yet again, and aligning the destructive aspects of the female principle with the creative/sexual, Wood has by film's end declared his emergence as a Love God, master of the Sexual Revolution, and one of the few to successfully escape his own purgatory, his own sinners' paradise. Apparently, Wood was allowed to largely dictate the course of *The Love Feast*, for the film ultimately emerges as his "portrait of the artist as an old man," a wildly successful attempt to document a prosaic memoir or archive of his later life, and capture the essence of his creative spirit during this time. The film also vividly reinforces the preeminence of artistic creation while in drunken stupor, an enduring socio-cultural stereotype portrayed brilliantly here. Like *Glen or Glenda?*, *The Love Feast* showcases Wood in all his fearless exhibitionist glory, depicting an artist entirely confident of his impact on culture, playfully portraying the drunken, divine idiot of religious renown. Wood's ability to completely expose himself onscreen enables him, in *The Love Feast*, to absorb this narrative "divine idiot" within himself, essaying a remarkable instance of atonement-as-performance. Subsequently, *The Love Feast* is an exceptional, essential part of the Wood canon, wherein the artist is summarily elevated to that exalted cultural icon — the Love God.

One Million AC/DC (1969)

A fascinating screenplay by Ed Wood (as "Adkon Telmig," a virtual inversion of "Vodka Gimlet," presumably Wood's drink of the moment) fuels this low-budget, softcore sex film which playfully satirizes popular prehistoric-era films of the day, such as *One Million Years B.C.* (1966, d: Don Chaffey) with Raquel Welch. The entire scenario takes place almost entirely in a mountain cave, certainly suggestive of the female principle, the harboring womb of the "World Mother." This emphasis on matriarchal concerns is conveyed throughout the film by numerous depictions of female sexual pleasure, albeit as filtered through the prejudiced lens of male sexual fantasy. Thus, during a virgin sacrifice, the subject is tormented by female guards who eventually sexually service the young maiden; she subsequently becomes erotically energized by her torture. Only in male pornography could such a ritual rape turn into mutual lust. The male component is evident also in several lesbian lovemaking scenes, all of which include a phallus surrogate as a stand-in for the absent, voyeuristic male audience "member." A good deal of screen time is spent watching females achieving orgasm, so one might intuit that the energizing of the female principle is at hand, but recalling that the scenario is unspooling purely for the benefit of the male, this seems unlikely. The majority of the film depicts males and females coupling frequently, and seemingly at random. The sex scenes suffer from the usual clinical obsession with body parts, and are not helped by a grating synthesizer-and-drum musical score. A fat chief watches the ongoing sexual orgy with bemusement; it is amusing to see Wood portray entrenched patriarchy as an obese glutton, in a role which is not far removed from those of Criswell in Wood's previous efforts. Soon, the patriarch mumbles an enigmatic declaration: "Gradually, it is happening. Gradually, it is done..." — what "it" is will be revealed anon. Throughout the film, a bemused scribe captures the carnal activity via crude hieroglyphics, and by the film's end, it is revealed that this "artist" has been preserving these "dirty pictures" for the benefit of the male collective, in essence becoming the world's first pornographer, in an interesting touch of self-reflexivity on Wood's part. Meanwhile, out in the cruel natural world, a gorilla (or more accurately, a man in a gorilla suit) kidnaps a young cavewoman, drags her back to his lair, and has his way with her. Later, the woman escapes, but the gorilla summons her back to his haunt by crooking his finger. The woman shrugs her shoulders while glancing at the (male) audience, accepting her fate and returning to bestial sexual servitude. Elsewhere, a fake toy dinosaur attacks another cavewoman, rips the top of her blouse off in service to the male audience, then proceeds to eat her as a toy fashion doll, in a vivid depiction of the objectification and trivialization of the female in phallocentric culture. Later, a topless cavewoman is chased around the jungle by a handsome blonde stranger. The two eventually mate in a beautiful green garden. They are Adam and Eve, symbolizing the figurative, even literal (assuming impregnation) birth of Judeo-Christian mythology, an essential propaganda tool of patriarchal culture. Amazingly, Wood has depicted here a microcosmic subjugation and conquest of prehistoric matriarchal culture by emergent patriarchy. This truly "sexual" revolution is clarified as the film ends with the making of the first spear, the first phallus-analog weapon derived from man's penis, with which man may now conquer nature. As a ritual affirmation of this, Caveman and Cavegirl sing, to the audience, "The spear goes into the monster, the spear goes into the monster, the spear goes into the monster, and the monster loses his mind." The monster, representing the natural world, does lose its mind to this deadly rising of the male principle. The elder confirms this with a proclamation so blatantly sexist it could be dubbed a veritable Patriarchal Manifesto: "Nothing has changed much, down through the ages. Man has to kill. Man has to eat. Man has to have his woman." These "truths" are true only in male-dominated tyranny. The cave clan finally emerges into the daylight, for they have conquered the natural world with the aboriginal ascendancy of their phallocentric societal system, a system which plagues us to this day. In spite of itself surely, *One Million AC/DC* shows in indelible cartoon form the conquest of the ancient matriarchal society by domineering phallocentric culture, an amazing feat by scenarist Wood and a remarkable achievement for any sex film. As suggested by the title, the male and female principles are set against each other in both a literal and metaphoric fight to the death, and as this is male fantasy, the male principle must by definition win. Still, there is much to ponder and contemplate, not the least of which is the entirely Woodian omnipresence of Death, as depicted via the skulls and skeletons which abound in the cave as a constant reminder that death inhabits the brutal pre-modern world. During the orgy sequence, food and sex are vividly shown as virtually indistinguishable and thoroughly interchangeable appetites, and when accented by the gluttonish elder, whose appetites have obviously caused his physical demise, there is more than a hint of cynicism towards the hedonist and the sex addict on Wood's part. And although the men "win" at film's end, the absolute preoccupation with female sexual pleasure seems an attempt by Wood to honor the female in all her radiant, life-affirming glory — even if she is depicted here as an exploited, and thus endangered species.

Take It Out in Trade (1970)

In *Nightmare of Ecstasy*, Rudolph Grey tells about the "exciting" discovery of a print of *Take It Out in Trade* (henceforth referred to as *Trade*), a 1970 sex film directed by Ed Wood, so it may be assumed that Grey owns or has access to such a print, although it has yet to appear on home video; as of this writing, all that is available for public viewing are 69 minutes of outtakes, released by Something Weird Video.[5] From this randomly stitched sampling of scenes (which ironically may run longer than the finished film), it is possible to put together a reasonable approximation of *Trade*. Grey summed up the plot nicely: "A private eye's search for the missing daughter of wealthy socialites bears fruit when she turns up working in 'Madame Penny's Thrill Establishment.'" The wealthy socialites are played by Donna Stanley and Carl James "Duke" Moore. Moore, of course, was Wood's colleague and drinking buddy, appearing in all of Wood's later film efforts. From the extant footage, it would appear that Detective MacGregor (Michael Donovan O'Donnell), who may be seen as the audience's alter ego or stand-in (in effect a surrogate "Dick"), beds an abundance of women in his search for this runaway escapee from an apparently oppressive domestic environment. In a narrative trope similar to Wood's *The Sinister Urge*, a problematic suburban couple try to retrieve and tame an errant offspring who seems to be either slave or willing victim of the Sexual Revolution. It seems that MacGregor's world travels are conveyed by nothing more than shots of planes landing along with static shots of various world travel posters. In the outtakes there are several minutes of exterior scenes, including airplanes landing at a local airport, and scenes outside the famous Brown Derby Restaurant in Los Angeles, a favorite hang-out for Wood and his entourage.[6] Yet *Trade* is undeniably a product of its time, as it intersperses its perfunctory plot with some virtually hardcore sexual scenes. Also somewhat shocking are comical scenes of a crusty old dame (Nona Carver) shooting up heroin on a dilapidated bed. Many scenes feature a group of young prostitutes ascending and descending a red-carpeted staircase, and also sitting around a shoddy living room, practicing isometric exercises and dancing to Santana records. Although perfunctory male/female sexual relations comprise the bulk of *Trade*, most notable from a socio-cultural standpoint is the inclusion of a young homosexual couple, who appear to figure significantly in the plot. The showcasing of these male lovers suggests foremost that Wood was as sensitive as any other artist to the emergence of gay culture during the time period, with gay rights finally beginning to achieve long-sought, hard-won recognition. The appearance of the couple may also suggest a closer fraternity with the local gay community by Wood than had been previously noted; considering Wood's lifelong preoccupation with transvestitism, it would be more surprising to find out that Wood did *not* have any dealings with the gay community, so the couple pictured in *Trade* were likely friends of the director. Yet MacGregor, *Trade*'s resident "dick," has several extended scenes with the gay men, and he appears to treat the men with utter disdain. This likely reflects MacGregor's role as stand-in for the predominantly heterosexual male audience, but it also suggests some ambivalence on Wood's part, an attempt to distance himself from the homosexual community similar to certain aspects of *Glen or Glenda?*. In a dinner scene, one of the gay men dresses as a woman, and one cannot help but note a passing similarity to a younger Wood, regally attired as Glenda. And speaking of Wood-as-Glenda, perhaps *Trade*'s primary historical consequence occurs with the appearance of Wood also as a character, Alecia, a drag queen. This extraordinary reincarnation of Wood's Glenda, almost twenty years later, shows a bloated and older Wood ridiculously clad in the colorful, trendy clothing of the dominant "hippie" youth culture of the time. Wood's Alecia is seen primarily sitting on a couch, dressed in bright green blouse and skirt, dark stockings, and garish white "go-go" boots, a uniform one might expect to find on a winsome teenage girl, not a middle-aged man. The effect is startling, to say the least. In one outtake, MacGregor rips off Alecia's blonde wig, in a scene which evokes memories of Glenda's self-loathing unmasking of herself in *Glen or Glenda?* This ritual act of exposing the man behind the woman, expressed in similar fashion in Wood's two "drag movies," underscores the artist's ambivalence about the pastime, and a back-handed defense of his status as heterosexual male. In typical Woodian irony, at some point, the young prostitutes who have embraced the runaway capture, bind and gag MacGregor, and the runaway has to rescue the "Dick" from certain death. This inversion of the traditional male rescue of an endangered female cleverly, if simply, underscores the ascendant power of the female in culture, certainly a dear theme to Wood. Scene 62, which comprises the finale of *Trade*, recurs an astonishing eight times in the outtakes, which shows that Wood considered the film's climax of utmost importance; it is unlikely that Wood shot any other particular scene during his career multiple times, if at all possible. The scene, which even silent is quite revealing, depicts MacGregor returning the runaway to her relieved parents. After some small talk, the runaway opens her top coat and reveals herself to be naked (but for panties) underneath. The runaway has essentially "flashed" her parents and, in so doing, celebrated the female principle, and also announced her escape from the punitive restraints of the old world and her emancipation into the ascendant Sexual Revolution. In a witty depiction of Wood's archetypal parental duo, Mom reacts with overstated horror, while Dad stares in dumb amazement. After more banter, the disgusted MacGregor tosses a wad of cash, his payment for services rendered, back at the elders. He then picks up the runaway and carries her off. In this brave new, sexually infused world, the female is far more important than money. (That "The Girl" is the prize in *Trade* also nicely reinforces the preeminence of the female principle in the films of Wood.) The cinematographer for *Trade* was Hal Guthu, who also shot Joseph F. Robertson's *The Love Feast* a few months earlier; that film shares many visual similarities with *Trade*, not the least of which is the primitive "home movie" look of both. Two notable props in *Trade* also occur elsewhere: A metal devil-skull sculpture is also seen in *Necromania*, and a metal cobra statue is seen in the opening sequence of *The Love Feast*. The frequent shots of film slates in *Trade* (meant to help the editor sync sound to picture) gives an accurate chronicle of when it was shot: January 14, 15 and 16 of 1970 — a Wednesday, Thursday and Friday in the dead of winter, two weeks into a new year, a revelation which gives *Trade* a salient historical resonance. The slate even states the film's production number as "010" (likely an arbitrary number), a novel combination which almost suggests that *Trade* will be two parts female and one part female, a suggestion which pans out by film's end. According to Nona Carver, Wood obtained the $2,000 budget for *Trade* from a private investor who just wanted some pornographic films for his personal collection.[7] According to Grey, *Trade* was never officially released by its distributor, MarJon Distributors, but did play the Los Angeles–based "Pussycat Theatre" circuit.[8] Despite the sloppy "home movie" look of *Trade*, which mimics the careless *mise-en-scène* of most sex film of the era, it looks like a promising addition to the Wood canon which, despite its low-reaching narrative, manages to suggest in rudimentary form several familiar Wood themes, and shows in bright relief how the filmmaker, almost two decades after starting his career, was still able to fashion remarkable micro-budget narratives under the most unlikely conditions.

Venus Flytrap (ca. 1970)

Verifying Ed Wood as scenarist for this bizarre U.S.–Japan co-production is simple, as Wood listed it as one of his credits on a filmography he complied for Fred Olen Ray in 1978;[9] even without this verification, the spirit of Wood is evident in the film's astonishing dialogue, hackneyed plot twists and tasteless detours into tacky grue.[10] As of this writing, the only extant print of *Venus Flytrap* is a 1980s home video release with false credit listings, retitled *Revenge of Dr. X*. James Craig, an actor with a remarkable resemblance to a middle-aged Clark Gable, plays Dr. Bragan, the head of NASA, whose ongoing stress leads him perilously close to a nervous breakdown. As a hurricane threatens his latest rocket launch, Bragan shouts out the window, "How on earth can anybody be so *utterly stupid*, to build a rocket base on the coast of Florida!," a line dripping with pure Woodian insolence. Bragan doubles over in pain, and his Japanese colleague suggests he take a long vacation in Japan. Taking his colleague's advice, Bragan is soon taking an inexplicable detour through Wilmington, North Carolina, on his way to the airport. Suffering car trouble, Bragan stops at a roadside garage. Looking for the owner, Bragan approaches a barn which bears a sign reading "Snake Kiosk"; he opens the door and a crusty old coot waddles out, carrying a snake in each arm, in a marvelously Absurdist depiction of phallocentrism-as-lunacy. (The snake handler looks a lot like Wood's frequent colleague and actor, Harvey B. Dunn, and it is certainly his type of role.) Bragan professes no interest in snakes, but the old coot counters, "Ah, snakes is of interest to *everybody*, even if they is scared of 'em," a line which reinforces the omnipresence of phallocentric ideology, introduced by the snake handler's notable entrance. Reluctantly venturing inside the barn, Bragan finds, amidst the serpents, one thing of extreme interest: an assuredly "feminine" Venus's-flytrap plant. Mesmerized by the alluring growth, the old coot directs Bragan to the swamp out back, to fetch his very own Venus's flytrap, for in his rapidly increasing dementia, Bragan somehow senses that this flora, which embodies the female principle in virtual perfection, will "complete" him. In a scene played for comic relief, Bragan dodges a veritable sea of snakes in order to reach his desire. Soon en route to Japan via airliner, Bragan takes a peek at his prized plant. It bites him, which prompts a stewardess to quip, "It's a good thing that's so small — a *big* one could take an arm off!," an amusing allusion to the plant as metaphor for the female vagina. Bragan soon arrives in Tokyo, where he is greeted by Noriko, a pretty female assistant. (The unidentified actress who plays Noriko speaks her lines with a heavy accent, and often appears to be reciting the lines phonetically, which adds an uncomfortable, unintentional comic factor to dialogue like, "*Frattery* will get you everywhere, Dr. Bragan.") Noriko and Bragan soon arrive at an attractive, albeit isolated, villa in the mountains, significantly residing next to an active volcano.[11] The caretaker is a ridiculous hunchback who relaxes by playing grim tunes on an immense pipe organ, an absurd combination of the Hunchback of Notre Dame and the Phantom of the Opera. Bragan sets up a laboratory in the villa's immense greenhouse; his charming manner when introduced to Noriko quickly descends into arrogance and exploitation, as he orders the poor woman around. (Bragan's wild, chronic mood swings suggests undiagnosed bipolar disorder.) While Bragan browbeats Noriko, the hunchback tends to peek, voyeur-like, from behind shrubbery. Odd for a Japanese co-production, the depiction of Asians in *Venus Flytrap* is somewhat racist and disdainful; the hunchback is portrayed somewhat as a "sneaky Jap," an unfortunate racial profile which may have stemmed, subconsciously at least, from screenwriter Wood's experiences (and prejudices) during his World War II stint in the Pacific Rim. (The creeping racism in *Venus Flytrap* may also partially explain its obscurity.) Eventually, Bragan shares his plans with Noriko: Via his Venus Flytrap, that enigmatic creation which Charles Darwin called "the most wonderful plant in the world," he wants to prove an intrinsic link between plant and animal life. (Here is another interesting Wood binary — plant/animal — which, although unexplored seriously in *Venus Flytrap*'s scenario, does illustrate in crude form the synthesis of two antithetical groups into a synergistic merging of dualistic opposites.)

That night, as Bragan reads, the caretaker plays the familiar Bach Toccata in D minor on the organ (the infamous "Phantom of the Opera" cue). Perhaps the creepy organ music inspires the mad doctor, for he suffers a hallucination, conveyed via a peculiar montage. Bragan shouts at his plant, "Your mother was the soil ... perhaps the lightning will become your father," alluding to a diabolical merging of the matriarchal World Mother with the phallocentric god of the patriarchal heavens, undoubtedly an ill-advised "sacred marriage" doomed to failure. Bragan takes a short detour to Tokyo's National Science Museum to observe a

"Venus Vesiculosa," apparently the underwater analog of the Venus's-flytrap.[12] This "female" partner to his mutation is what Bragan feels is needed to create the most powerful creature in the world: half man, half plant! Soon, Noriko locates some topless "Diving Girls of Japan," and they agree to conduct an underwater search for the elusive plant. Bragan places the retrieved specimen into a large, coffin-like glass case, and the diving girls, now wearing fuzzy sweaters (surely a nod to the screenwriter), carry the glass case off the beach as Bragan follows, an iconic image which suggests the fairy tale wake of "Sleeping Beauty," as well as the impending *death* of the female principle at the hands of this patriarchal loon.

Back at the lab, Bragan injects his mutations with super-vitamins, preparatory to his plan to fuse the two plants together. Finally, Bragan stitches together parts from the two plants, a la *Frankenstein*, during an obligatory thunderstorm. Bragan hoists the monster skyward (in a scene lifted directly from the 1931 Universal production of *Frankenstein*), while shouting another variant of what is quickly becoming his mantra: "The earth was your mother, your blood will be the rain, your father's the lightning!" That night, as dogs howl at the moon, the improbable creature begins to stir, and Bragan removes its protective covering, revealing a magnificent and bizarre man-in-suit creation: a humanoid man-plant with fly-trap hands and feet, a superlative example of 1960s Japanese creature design. Bragan revises his mantra once more: "Your mother was the earth, the rain your blood, the lightning your power!" Bragan cackles in demented glee before collapsing from exhaustion. Inexplicably, the caretaker places one of his cherished puppies in front of the monster, and the carnivorous plant soon attacks and devours it, in a scene both ludicrous and shameful. The next morning, the monster has grown considerably, and is full of vim and vigor (and puppy). (At this point, *Venus Flytrap* is starting to bear a similarity to Roger Corman's legendary 1961 black comedy about a man-eating plant, *The Little Shop of Horrors*.) Bragan soon figures out the creature's new energy source and grabs another nearby puppy to feed to his monster, but Noriko rescues the poor baby. (It seems strange that Wood, a long-time dog owner and devoted animal lover, would resort to such a seedy use of infant canines for his narrative.) A subsequent montage shows the monster's paws grabbing mice and rabbits, while slurping noises anoint the soundtrack, in another ridiculous and tasteless scene. Bragan now wants to make his bloodthirsty flora ambulatory, a decidedly bad idea which reveals his increasing dementia, as revealed by this declaration: "All I need is the blood of a human being to prove the fact that human beings are descended from plant life!" That night, Bragan sneaks over to the nearby Asama Sanitarium, where he cruelly jabs a needle into a sleeping young woman's bared breast in order to extract blood. As hoped, injecting the stolen blood into the monster immediately invigorates it.

Noriko is horrified by Bragan's descent into insanity, and shouts at him, "You are no longer Dr. Bragan, scientist — you are becoming Dr. Bragan, *madman*!" That night, during a violent thunderstorm, Bragan transplants the monster outside, where it becomes fully ambulatory and starts stalking the grounds, soon attacking the caretaker's dog. In order to prove that the monster is in fact ambulatory, Bragan decides to sit up all night to watch its actions (another direct theft from *Little Shop of Horrors*). Alas, the clever monster produces a mist which incapacitates its intended prey, and soon both Bragan and Noriko are in a dead sleep (a plot point not dissimilar to "Audrey Junior's" ability to hypnotize Seymour Krelboin into abject obedience). The monster sneaks off and invades a nearby village, where it attacks and kills a small girl who just happens to be skipping down the main road after dark (yet another example of the tacky exploitation of the innocent for crude dramatic purpose in *Venus Flytrap*). The villagers gather and walk through the countryside carrying torches (in another nod to the Universal *Frankenstein*), with the father of the dead girl leading the way, carrying the

child's body in his arms. This vision of horror shocks Bragan into finally realizing his mis-
deeds, and he runs off to confront his creation, grabbing a small goat as bait. As dawn
approaches, Bragan reaches the top of the volcano, carrying the goat. He calls out to the creature, and promises to run off with him elsewhere to continue their diabolical partnership.
(Bragan calls the creature by name several times, and although nearly indistinguishable on
the muddy video soundtrack, it sounds alternately like "Insect-a-vorous" and "Drac-a-
vorous," the latter an especially fanciful moniker which merges "Dracula" and "Carnivorous"
into a most "Woodian" appellation.) When the creature reveals itself, Bragan lures it to the
volcano's edge, where both fall to their death. Miraculously, the goat survives (again referencing Abraham's biblical "scapegoat," also used to good effect in Wood's *Jail Bait*) and Noriko
clutches the innocent to her breast, sheltering it from the further cruelties of evil men.

From at least two viewpoints (the overt racism, and animals and children used as cheap
dramatic props), *Venus Flytrap* is not one of Wood's shining moments, but it is a formidable
addition to the Wood canon nonetheless. Wood manages to insert at least two oblique, ham-
fisted references to Judeo-Christian ideology into his scenario (the creepy garden of snakes,
and the sacrificial goat). The impossibly naïve and comical plot (nicely augmented by the
bizarre, organ-based music score, which underscores *Venus Flytrap*'s lurid melodrama) is
pure Wood dementia. *Venus* is also a treasure trove of prime Wood dialogue, including the
aforementioned mantra of Bragan, but also via other revealing tidbits such as, "It's always
best to bury one's mistakes," "Could-be's I cannot use! I want the *facts*, the *facts*, do you
hear?," "I *refuse* the word impossible!," "You will become the most powerful thing *on* this universe" (sic) and, perhaps most iconic of all, "Well, *think* of it, girl, *think* of it!" Incidentally,
Venus Flytrap shares many interesting parallels with *The Manster*, a 1958 U.S.–Japan co-production, not the least of which is the fact that both films share the same director, Kenneth G.
Crane. Also, both films feature roughly the same plot synopsis: an American is seduced by,
and subsequently exploits, Japanese culture. Both films take place primarily in a secluded
mountainous region and both end with the monster falling into a volcano. Both films showcase Japanese females in provocative, even exploitative ways. Also, both films were purportedly co-produced by United Artists of Japan.

Drop-Out Wife (1972)

Ed Wood's recurring "suburban couple-in-discord" comes to vivid life in a remarkable
screenplay, virtually buried beneath one of Stephen Apostolof's dull sex films; yet Wood's
light shines bright even in such a dim-witted atmosphere, and *Drop-Out Wife* courageously
champions several preeminent Wood themes, the most striking being the continued denigra-
tion of phallocentric culture, and the empowerment of the female as a possible cure for runaway patriarchy, seen here as the author of a decidedly malevolent sexual freedom. In fact,
Drop-Out Wife's protagonist couple seems doomed to failure, first and foremost, by their
seduction into the then-rampant Sexual Revolution, which promised diversity and sexual
freedom, but delivered cynical exploitation and emotional isolation. Truth be told, *Drop-
Out Wife*'s crude stabs at feminism and the counterculture are problematic, but not without
interest. *Drop-Out Wife* is told largely in flashback, as an unhappily married woman, Peggy
(Angela Carnon), leaves her dolt of a husband Jim (an uncredited Christopher Geoffries) and
two unseen kids, turning to her best friend Janet (Terry Johnson) for shelter and guidance.
Early on, Peggy frets to Janet about her children, addressing understandable guilt over abdi-
cating her "duties" as a mother. Janet cracks, "At least you weren't out to propagate the race!,"

Theatrical poster for *Drop-Out Wife,* one of several screenplays Wood cranked out for sexploitation producer Stephen Apostolof, credited as A.C. Stephen.

a sly anti-family comment by Wood, who often took similar aim at "dumb breeders" in his writings.[13] The contradictory nature of the doomed relationship is revealed in the first flashback, wherein newlyweds Peggy and Jim make out in a hotel room to the strains of Mendelssohn's Wedding March, amusingly but succinctly counter-pointing the spiritual and carnal aspects of marriage. A later flashback shows Peggy and Jim forcing sexual relations during a thunderstorm, which nicely mirrors their accruing marital discord. As Jim frets about the rain, Peggy reassures him, "It's only a summer storm," but Jim ominously replies, "Summer storms have been known to last for days," intuiting that this trouble in the bedroom is not a passing thing, but a symptom of something grimmer and more obstinate. Yet Jim convinces a reluctant Peggy to have sex in the rain, and they are soon screwing on the grass like a postmodern Adam and Eve. An angry thunderclap punctuates Jim's forceful insemination of Peggy, who moans in true despair, "Number three!" This cryptic comment not only refers to the creation of a third child to suffer this loveless marriage, but also suggests that this pregnancy will be the third strike, "the last straw" for the doomed couple. Commenting later on this doomed act, Janet hurls an iconic Wood rant: "Men! They can be the most disgusting creatures the Creator ever put on this crazy, mixed-up planet!" By now it is clear that Janet will be Wood's mouthpiece throughout *Drop-Out Wife*.

Returning to flashback, things deteriorate further and during an argument, Jim punches his wife, a seemingly inevitable event in the course of patriarchal domination. The violent act triggers a painful miscarriage in Peggy, proving that this was the "last straw" which Peggy prophesied during that impregnation. During a subsequent failed sexual encounter, Peggy blurts out a pre-feminist mantra: "There's got to be more to life than kids! Dirty diapers! Washing dishes! Making beds! Kitchens!" Yet poor Jim can think of nothing better to save their marriage than joining a wife-swapping club, naively believing that more bad sex might somehow cure emotional incompatibility. But Peggy is deep into her own repressive despair, moaning, "I feel like I'm dead without being buried...." Ironically, however, Peggy's eventual experimenting with group sex does open the door to an attempted liberation; the most significant discovery she makes is that she enjoys sex with another woman. As with Wood's *Necromania*, Peggy's first lesbian encounter invokes the female principle, as well as acting as metaphor for the invigorating solidarity of the then-powerful "Women's Liberation" movement. This spirit of liberation is also echoed in Peggy's quip to one of her anonymous partners: "When I started on this, I thought it was to save a marriage. Now? *What's a marriage?*"

Peggy soon has second thoughts about her woman-woman encounter, but Janet is nothing but supportive: "You've gotta do your own thing." Segueing cannily into feminist dogma, Janet continues: "We've gotta tame 'em — and you know who I'm talking about — the male of the species," perfectly articulating the overarching agenda of a resurgent matriarchy, further reinforced by Janet's follow-up: "Put *women* onto things, and there wouldn't be any more wars." Clearly, Janet is pushing a feminist agenda to her curious, if timid "student." Peggy even apologizes for her confusion and missteps, which causes Janet to reveal her alliance overtly: "Sorry! Why? Our *movement* says you should never be sorry about anything you really feel, or anything you really wanna say!" Janet is clearly a Woman's Libber, and as Wood's chosen stand-in reveals Wood's sympathies with the cause, which after all is largely in line with the pro-female stance of his works since the beginning. This revelation of a new philosophy to Peggy seems to empower her, for the next scene depicts the actual breakup of the couple. The now-emboldened Peggy finally stands up to Jim, who conspicuously wears a red, white and blue robe, now representing not just the archetypal male, but the archetypal *American* male, in all his tyrannical, self-serving splendor. Jim accuses Peggy of becoming promiscuous, a laughable assertion as it was he who virtually forced his wife into the arms of anonymous sex partners. Jim goes even further, clearly perceiving Peggy's momentous life change: "You can't make it with men anymore. It's the *broads* you wanna shack up with." As the two continue to bicker, Jim resorts to accusing his wife of being a spendthrift, of not "valuing" money, the one true god to the capitalist male. The argument deteriorates until Peggy utters the iconic line, from which the title was inspired: "I dropped into your life — now I'm *dropping out!*" As always, Janet later comments astutely on the previous scene: "You get all hung up on one guy, and your life is over before you know what's happened to you!" Janet then ponders, "I can understand everything, except why it took you so long to leave," a pivotal question for the nascent feminist.

Arguably, the sheer inertia of the comfortably dull heterosexual unit, along with the woman's inevitable economic marginalization, can make the choice to free one's self extremely difficult. Peggy puts it well, "Guess it's the old thing called the rut — and probably, the kids," and history does reveal that the bearing and raising of men's children has been a salient force of women's enslavement for centuries. When Peggy confesses to Janet, "The future — that's what I'm afraid of," Janet pontificates grandly: "The future, the past, haven't you ever heard? There's no such thing as the future! The only thing you have to remember is, there's only the present!" This is a truly existential pronouncement, reflecting the mystical outlook of many Eastern-based belief systems; perhaps not coincidentally, this is also a centerpiece of prehistoric matriarchal philosophy, which preached the concept of life and death as being an eternally repeating process or circle, not the dire linear progression outlined in patriarchal belief systems. However, the still-confused Peggy continues to tramp around with charismatic bums in her as-yet unfocused quest to find herself (and perhaps partly as a guilt reaction to her newfound passion for women). In *Drop-Out Wife*'s last half, the viewer is subjected to a seemingly endless procession of male-female groupings, which was certainly the film's original intent yet today looks like a dreary parade of dumb mammals in rut. Soon, Peggy is disillusioned, for while she is looking for sexual, emotional and spiritual fulfillment from these random encounters, she discovers that the men are just looking for a hole. Peggy is, in fact, seeking female companionship, but doesn't know it yet. Having mistaken promiscuity for emancipation, Peggy realizes that all this partying and whoring is taking its toll on her, leaving her physically and emotionally depleted. Peggy still misses her children, so she foolishly calls Jim, who harangues her, calling her "a bitch, and an unfit mother!" Jim also announces that he is suing for divorce, revealing the shunned male to often be a vindictive adversary. Peggy now realizes that she has made an irreversible decision. Janet shows up just in time to remind her to have the courage of her convictions, and to move forward with her new life.

Janet escorts Peggy to the Cameo Club, where they are picked up by two musicians, and are soon engaging in more meaningless sex. This dull orgy concludes with the long-anticipated sexual encounter between Peggy and Janet. As in the aforementioned *Necromania*, this essential Woodian merging symbolizes the ascension of the female principle, both as a new personal paradigm for Peggy, and as a specter of progressive social change for the community. Peggy eventually rejects Janet, and storms off. Throughout *Drop-Out Wife*, Peggy has attempted to break through to feminist freedom, but she is still anchored to the heterosexual prerogative, a slave to its phallocentric ideology. A perhaps-inevitable, yet punitive epilogue shows *Drop-Out Wife* to be (Wood's progressive sexual politics notwithstanding) a predictable cultural product of its time. Now completely alone, Peggy ruminates over her catastrophic life changes as she watches happy children romp at a playground. She thinks out loud: "I left them — and for what? To be free? To live? *They* are what's real! Maybe I can go back. They've *got* to take me back! We'll make it work this time — I just know we will!" In *Drop-Out Wife*'s depressing closing shot, Peggy scurries back to her patriarchal prison, still run by the abusive dullard she so rightly left, and to a life which contains all the problems she abandoned. This deflating reversal in *Drop-Out Wife*'s precarious, but hopeful, feminist stance may represent nothing more than a male-oriented "happy ending" tacked onto Wood's screenplay by Apostolof, or it may be an example of Wood's problematic sexual politics which, as seen, veer wildly between thoughtful progressivism and parochial conservatism. Certainly, *Drop-Out Wife* was produced primarily as a sex film for males, so the ultimate adherence to patriarchal philosophy should not come as a surprise. Yet it is unfortunate that the poignancy of Wood's screenplay is so severely diluted by Apostolof's dreadfully dull sex scenes; one might call the insightful, at times even lyrical screenplay an added bonus. This aesthetic and philosophical dichotomy underscores the inherent contradiction of splicing feminist philosophy in a male-oriented sex film, and *Drop-Out Wife*'s narrative awkwardness is largely due to this philosophic incompatibility. Yet there is much to enjoy, not the least of which is Wood's doggedly determined attempt to praise the charms of the female in any subject he tackles. Perhaps unwittingly, films such as *Drop-Out Wife*, which obsess on depictions of male-female sexual couplings, may ultimately serve to denigrate the hallowed heterosexual social construct, revealing it to be an ridiculous and exhausted socio-political paradigm. Thus, *Drop-Out Wife* and films of its ilk are illuminating examples of the problematic nature of the sex-based narrative, whose ostensible emphasis is on the enthusiastic coupling of men and women, while the narrative tends to focus on the emotional and philosophical problems inherent within said couplings. Yet, while thoughtful screenplays by Wood and others may have effectively belittled the heterosexual couple as an obsolete social model, this would not in any way reduce its popularity, which in the very same narrative texts is seen as hardy, omnipresent, and virtually indestructible. The eternal fixation on the "magic" of insemination and the short-lived joys of dumb lust will fuel the dyad's socio-political omniscience into the foreseeable future, a future which Wood cleverly exposes as a chimera of an eternal, immutable "now."

The Class Reunion (1972)

The Class Reunion boasts a rough, yet often remarkable Ed Wood screenplay, again buried within one of Stephen Apostolof's stillborn sex films, which touches on some trenchant social issues of the day, including feminism, the counterculture and the dubious allure of the sexual revolution, and ends on a stunningly metaphysical note, bringing much of Wood's pet themes to thrilling conclusion. The threadbare "plot," merely an excuse for the usual sex scenes, involves the "Class of '69" reuniting at a hotel. Just as producer-director Apostolof uses the sketchy, halting narrative to insert his redundant, tiresome sexual couplings, so does Wood use *The Class Reunion*'s paltry narrative framework to pontificate on several of his pet themes. The "Class of '69" alludes to a common slang phrase denoting mutual oral servicing, yet the significant number also evokes the prevalent Eastern mystical notion of Yin and Yang, that perfect balancing of male and female cosmic energies, which is one of Wood's main thematic thrusts throughout his work — the attempted balancing of the male principle and female principle in individuals and society — so even this throwaway touch acts as code to *The Class Reunion*'s preeminent issue.

  The Class Reunion's first shot depicts a beautiful blonde woman taking a shower, the camera taking great care to note the woman soaping and caressing various body parts, the breasts most significantly; this is also code by Wood revealing that *The Class Reunion*, like so many of his films, will be about the female — not merely the protagonist(s) of the story, but all women, and symbolically about the female principle. Several close-ups of the woman's ecstatic face suggests that this ritual act of bathing also serves as an invigorating, perhaps even empowering act of erotic self-arousal; in essence, the woman is not merely serving herself, but honoring her gender with the nurturing act. The woman is soon standing in front of a mirror, brushing her long golden locks, and she talks to herself, reinforcing the notion that she represents not a woman, but all women. Naming herself "Rosie," she ponders out loud, "I wonder what this day has in store for me." The next 72 hours, when Rosie is significantly separated from her husband, portends something momentous, so when the doorbell soon rings, it is clearly intended as Fate calling, with life-changing news. Granted, the lengthy prologue, which dutifully records the woman tediously drying herself, also serves another, less noble purpose, the sexual arousal of the predominantly male audience. This chronic dichotomy illustrates the ongoing, contradictory nature of the sex film of the day, especially those penned by progressive thinkers such as Wood, who managed to inject much sexually egalitarian philosophy into what was ostensibly, and admittedly, base prurient entertainment for the male collective.

This inherent contradiction in the genre is nicely addressed subtextually with the next scene, as a mailman brings a special delivery letter which announces the titular class reunion. While the "male" man is delivering his fateful message of special import, one which promises significant ramifications for Rosie, he takes care to ogle Rosie in overt, lecherous terms. The mailman thus symbolizes two aspects of the male presence in sexploitation film, that of potential deliverer/enabler of change to women, yet invariably also their exploiters and abusers. Post-credits, the film proper begins with a close-up of a tumbler of bourbon on a waiter's tray, thus signaling the preeminence of alcohol in *The Class Reunion*, not merely as an in-joke homage by the booze-hound scenarist, but also addressing its omniscience as a social lubricant and, apparently, as key ingredient for casual sexual interludes. With several members of the "Class of '69" imbibing and reminiscing in a banquet room of the Century Plaza Hotel, someone asks Rosie why her husband didn't attend, and she ominously remarks, "I'd be crazy to bring Angel-Baby to a boozefest like this!" The other responds, "A teetotaler?" but Rosie clarifies, "A lush!" as Wood effortlessly inserts alcohol-as-muse into the scenario twice in the first reel.

One conspicuous member of the alumni party is Thelma (Rene Bond) who, wearing a red dress to signal her sexual shame, will turn out to be a notorious lesbian; Thelma pairs up with the flamboyantly gay Bruce, as they are largely excluded from the celebration of the "straights." In an astonishing scene, which has no ostensible narrative reason other than giving Wood an excuse to rant, the partygoers look out of a window and watch a huge anti-war demonstration, represented by authentic newsreel footage of a Vietnam-era protest march, and featuring a multitude of young protesters marching, chanting and carrying signs such as AFTER VIETNAM, WHO'S NEXT? This is an amazing time capsule of authentic American dissent, an endangered species and perhaps doomed even then. A partygoer with the hilariously symbolic name of Wimpy Murgatroyd (Christopher Geoffries) groans, "I tell ya, nothing like those street-apes ever happened when we were their age. And to think — I helped pay their school tax!" This disparaging comment about the politically active youth of the day sounds like it is coming from someone much older, and more conservative, than the character who speaks it and indeed, it is coming directly from Wood, in one of many instances of shameless lecturing within narrative. However, fellow alumni Charlie Knight (Forman Shane) comes to the protestors' defense, asserting that his peers didn't act so much different when they were "young," a strange assertion as the group is clearly in their early twenties, being fresh out of school.[14] At best, this exchange shows that Wood was perhaps ambivalent about the counterculture, yet his reactionary equation of political conscience with sexual licentiousness is an amusingly prejudicial view of youth by an elder, and well illustrates the battling of progressive and conservative sentiments within the artist. Charlie announces that he brought "a little movie" with him which will prove the alumni were once as wild and reckless as these hilariously named "street-apes."

The gang is next seen up in Charlie's room, imbibing more alcohol and watching themselves having what appears to be a wild Dionysian orgy at a fraternity house, in reused footage from Apostolof's *College Girls Confidential* (1968). Projected on a 16mm projector Charlie conveniently brought with him, the footage imparts an interesting bit of self-reflexivity, both to the assembled characters, who are seeing themselves "as they were," but also to the film's audience, who watch a "film within a film" and note with irony the difference, and similarity, of sex "then and now." However, the conceit that it is amateur "home movies" that the characters, and audience, are watching is immediately shattered by the professional quality of the footage, which features zoom shots, angle changes and frequent cuts. Also depicted are a man jumping off a balcony while pretending to fly (presumably high on LSD), and a forced sex scene which depicts a rape — all of which are annotated aurally by giggles amongst the gathered, lending a banal quality to these somewhat traumatic acts. After the film ends, Charlie suggests that they can do *now* what they did *then*, and the group immediately disrobes and copulates, rendering their earlier claims to maturity absurdly false. Filmed as artlessly as possible, the orgy comes across as utilitarian and dull, and several inserted close-ups of an uninterested Bruce may accurately reflect the boredom of at least a portion of *The Class Reunion*'s audience, who would be hard-pressed to find anything of erotic value in these underlit, badly composed sex scenes. The orgy does inspire Thelma to disrobe and fondle herself, reinforcing the potential for female self-actualization in the decidedly reflective setting.

Subsequent footage of the sexual acts are virtually indistinguishable from the college-era footage shown earlier, disclosing that for all their posturing, they are still ruled by dumb lust. In fact, the care taken to distinguish this mass grope of "straights" from the two isolated, decidedly sympathetic homosexual characters suggests that this mass orgy of unenlightened individuals may be a latter incarnation of Wood's purgatory for lost souls. Wood's problematic incarnations of the heterosexual unit, if not outright malevolent in *The Class Reunion*, are painted here at least as redundant and regressive, and possibly obsolete. Still, the scene does give the audience what they came for, depicting a "class reunion," that "class" being the American middle class, the heterosexual bourgeoisie.

Later that night, the first of several highly metaphorical couplings follows: Wimpy and a woman named Fluff copulate, with omnipresent alcohol acting again as social lubricant. Fluff and Wimpy connect sexually several times, in scenes intercut between other couplings, and as Wimpy becomes evermore fatigued, unable to keep up with Fluff's apparently boundless sexual appetite, the scenes rapidly digress from ostensibly erotic to consciously comic, nicely mirroring in microcosm the declining sexual compatibility of the average heterosexual partnership throughout a long relationship. While depicting the heterosexual unit as simultaneously inexhaustible and exhausted, these scenes also cleverly denigrate the heterosexual unit via these characters' absurd nicknames: The man turns out to be literally "wimpy," as he cannot chronically service his insatiable partner, who is depicted as so much "fluff." Elsewhere, Thelma visits a girlfriend at her room, using a classic Wood pickup line ("Got a drink?") to which the woman replies, "Doesn't every room?" Like all good Wood heroines, the women down stiff shots of bourbon. Thelma easily seduces the bored housewife, preaching Wood's special brand of matrist philosophy while fondling her subject: "Men are all beasts! They don't care what a woman likes or dislikes — they just wanna get their own climax and go home." This is an observation not far from the mark, perhaps not coincidentally being the film's original theatrical audience, which consisted largely of socially retarded men who were comfortable masturbating in a public venue, and were attending specifically to "get their own climax and go home."

Thelma next ventures even further into feminist territory: "Have you ever thought about what a woman really needs, and wants?" The loaded rhetorical question suggests that what a woman "needs and wants" is not just sexual, but social, political, spiritual, etc. Thelma then coos, "Tell *Momma* what it is you need," revealing herself to be representative of matriarchal culture, of the nurturing mythological World Mother archetype who wants to help a way-ward sister find her feminist way. The subsequent tryst between the two beautiful women carries an erotic energy conspicuously lacking in the numerous "straight" sex scenes which surround it, reinforcing the transcendent power of the female principle in anything Wood seemed to touch. Thelma is effortlessly able to bring her willing new pupil to sustained cli-max, as she has the power of the matriarchal imperative behind her, with its empowering and nurturing energy.

At the bar, Liza meets Charlie and they share an obligatory bourbon while reminiscing. Liza wants to turn in, but Charlie declares, either targeting the alcoholic class or his gener-ation en masse, "We don't turn in — *we turn on!*" This careless equating of the consciousness-expanding experiments of Timothy Leary and others with common drunkenness could come only from the cynical pen of a career alcoholic like Wood, yet Wood's art does illustrate that alcohol can be harnessed as artist's muse, leading him to fitful flights of awkward creative brilliance, albeit at terrible personal cost. Liza and Charlie stumble upstairs and perform sloppy, drunken sex — presumably the kind Wood and his audience were intimately familiar with — yet the scene implies that the heterosexual unit might not function at all if not dead-ened by booze, and hints that male-female couplings are accidental, perhaps even unnatural social constructs. As if positioned explicitly to augment this observation, the following sex-ual encounter, considering the time and audience it was created for, is nothing short of remarkable.

Bruce enters a hotel room with another gay man. The two share a ritualistic glass of bour-bon and proceed to fondle each other. This depiction of gay sex in a "straight" sex film of the day was extremely unusual, as the heterosexual male audience was traditionally timid, if not outright hostile, towards homosexual behavior. This prejudice, significantly, does not carry over to female-female sex, which is acceptable to men as it is erotically charged, aesthetically pleasing, and does not threaten phallocentric hegemony. The two gay men are comically over-played, in what is essentially an unkind parody of what "straight" men think "faggots" act like, although the comic relief aspect is seriously diminished as the men disrobe and fondle each other, and the viewer may feel that the scene, or the "joke," has gone on too long. The filmmakers', and by proxy the audience's, loathing of homosexuality is strikingly revealed as the two men are about to caress: The camera zooms out suddenly and swiftly, as if it were actually afraid of what it was about to witness. The two men do eventually start groping each other lasciviously, again a most unusual moment in the traditional sex film of the day, which aggressively polarized genres into "straight" and "gay." The straight male audience, in fact, might have gotten somewhat worried at this point, fearful they might be exposed to the hor-rifying vision of men having sex. Luckily for them, the filmmakers mask this "taboo" act by having it take place under (significantly, *pink*) satin sheets, where the act remains hidden, comical and safe. An act of oral sex is depicted by a head ridiculously bobbing up and down underneath the pink sheets, a vision neither erotic nor aesthetic, and by now not even comic, but merely grotesque. Assuming Wood to be the author of this scene, his problematic stance on homosexuality is disappointing, as elsewhere in his art he champions sexual difference with a vengeance. But as shameful as the scene thus far is, Wood has an even darker trick up his sleeve, well in keeping with the genre's essential philosophy that wanton woman, and certainly "faggots" must be punished for their indiscretions. As the men cuddle, post-fellatio, and just as it seems the audience might be able to stand no more, there is an ominous knock on the door. The pick-up wonders out loud if it's the house detective, but Bruce reassures him, "Not in this age of the sexual revolution!" The pick-up then utters, sheepishly, "It could be my wife!" This first plot twist in the scene confuses both Bruce and the audience, suggesting that the pick-up is a promiscuous bisexual. When Bruce gingerly opens the door, an angry redheaded woman enters and immediately starts browbeating the both of them. This introduction of the woman into the scene is significantly seen in reverse, through a reflection in the hotel room mirror, nicely accentuating both the startling shift in power dynamics of the participants, as well as the duplicitous nature of certain persons in the room, to be soon revealed. (Also, the woman enters just in time to "rescue" the homophobic audience from this traumatizing scene.) The woman starts to thrash both men with her purse, in a hilariously dated take on the "henpecked husband and shrewish wife" stereotype of the 1950s. The woman yells, "I'll pluck you leaf from leaf, you *pansy*!," clearly acting as stand-in for the male audience member in her role of punisher of (homosexual) sin. The woman threatens to call the police to report this "lewd" interval, another anachronistic touch by Wood, as gay sex was not an illegal act by this time. The husband cowers under the sheets and whimpers, "I thought you were going to your *Woman's Liberation convention*!," Wood taking an uncharacteristically disparaging swipe here at the feminist movement. The woman continues to bash Bruce with her handbag, comically illustrating the sad reality of physical violence fated for many exposed homosexuals during the gay community's tumultuous "coming out" period. When the woman subsequently threatens legal action against Bruce for ruining her "poor husband's" reputation, he offers her his wallet as a pay-off for her silence, which prompts the enraged woman to shout: "I'm a member of the Woman's Liberation group, and we don't stand for that sort of thing!" (What they don't "stand for" is unclear. Bribes? Money? Capitalism?) Bruce continues his peace-making efforts, suggesting that the money be used as a donation for her "group." The woman greedily grabs all the money Bruce has, as he beats a hasty retreat.

Shortly after Bruce leaves the man and the woman break into sinister, conspiratorial laughter. Apparently the entire event was staged, a scam to fleece money from homosexuals! This cruel depiction of the heterosexual unit as purely mercenary, duplicitous, and decidedly predatory towards any progressive sexual movement, is a damning portrait of the postwar couple, and the most evil portrayal yet of Wood's recurring "suburban couple in discord." (The only comparable example in the Wood canon is the mobster couple in *The Sinister Urge*, whose sociopathic solidarity is based solely on exploiting their community through criminal activities.) Even stranger, the patent absurdity of the scam is downright breathtaking. After all, what normal man would have sex with another man in order to gain petty cash? The husband here represents at least a career sociopath with serious mental problems, or more likely a closet homosexual with schizophrenic tendencies. Either way, this may be the most dysfunctional couple Wood ever manifested. When this despicable pair subsequently makes love to celebrate their victory over sexual and political diversity, it comes across as a ritual between jungle beasts who have savaged some prey, and now gorge on their conquest, which in this case may be all progressive socio-political thought.

As if to rescue heterosexual reputation from this vicious portrayal, *The Class Reunion*'s final scene starkly reverses that malignant polarity. In the sole sequence which takes place outside of the hotel, at a lovely nearby park featuring lush foliage, babbling brooks and abundant animal life, a man and a woman meet at a bench and decide to take a stroll, away from the others. As they walk deeper into the beautiful woods, the male states, "It's so nice to be back in the woods, and feel nature so close to you"—in other words, it is healing to get back to one's roots, to reconnect with one's primal nature. Both express their mutual distaste for the "rat race," and when the man declares, "This is just like out of a storybook," it is clear that this scene is meant to allude to that great fairy tale treasury—the Holy Bible—and its primordial fantasy-scape, the Garden of Eden. The pair finally reach a luxuriant field of wild-grass, and the woman states, "This is a perfectly *divine* spot," designating it as sacred, blessed by the gods. The man next brings up memories of college biology class, an odd reference unless it is meant to preface that which is forthcoming. The conversation next turns to an extraordinary, if awkward discussion of life's great existential mysteries, as the woman asks, seemingly out of the blue, "What makes people like us tick? Why are we here, and why are we so miserable at home?" The man responds emphatically, "I don't question it; I just accept it. If there's got to be a reason, we'll find out sooner or later." The couple now guiltlessly fornicate on a natural bed of soft green grass, and the viewer realizes that this modern couple have symbolically walked back in time, to the very beginning; they have in fact reverted to the prototypical Adam and Eve, alone and ecstatic in their own personal Garden of Eden. Having shed the stress, debauchery, cynicism, despair and corruption which enthralls their peers and defines their world, the two have become momentarily pure and innocent, have become whole once more. Post-coitus, the man offers a final philosophical observation: "Yeah, life is so wonderful, and you are so beautiful—maybe that's the reason, the only reason...." In so doing, he has perhaps unwittingly stated the core mantra of the seemingly imperishable male-female social construct, whose essential philosophic core is nothing more, yet nothing less, than the biological mystery of mutual attraction.

Although other films remain to be released and reviewed, *The Class Reunion* may stand as Wood's last great screenplay. Within all the deadening sex and pointless plot twists lies the true soul of the poet-philosopher, featuring contradictory yet fascinating observations on sexual mores, socio-political phenomena, and the deathless existential riddles shared by the entire human race.

Fugitive Girls (1974)

It is difficult to ascertain just how much input Ed Wood had in creating this exploitation film, as he is listed as co-scenarist with producer-director Stephen Apostolof; yet it is likely that Wood invested much into the screenplay, which features a number of Wood-themed dramatic moments and motifs. Rudolph Grey maintained that the screenplay for *Fugitive Girls* was solely Wood's creation, and the film evokes the spirit of the artist in its circuitous, confrontational scenario.[15] Wood was also enlisted as assistant director in *Fugitive Girls*, and his duties likely included creating the particular *mise-en-scène* of the film. Wood's presence in *Fugitive Girls* is even more literally etched by performance, however, as he plays *three* small roles, and displays impressive acting skills that he rarely got a chance to exercise during this time period. It is thus both homage and favor on Apostolof's part that he lists Wood's role as "Pop" as a "Guest Appearance" in the credits.[16]

The basic scenario follows a familiar exploitation template of the era, the "Women in Prison" subgenre which featured female inmates of corrupt penal institutions pitted against evil, often sexually debased authority figures, each other and, after an inevitable escape, the even harsher cruelties of the outside world. Many film historians say that the first movie in this exhilarating genre was Jack Hill's *The Big Doll House* (1971), followed shortly by the equally impressive *The Big Bird Cage* (1972), and capped off with Hill's remarkable *Switch-blade Sisters* (1975), which is considered a bonafide exploitation masterpiece. As always in the exploitation world, scores of imitations followed, none of which carried the aesthetic charm, cinematic integrity or narrative insight of the Hill trinity. Also noteworthy is Tom DeSimone's idiosyncratic but entertaining trilogy *Prison Girls* (1972), *The Concrete Jungle* (1982) and *Reform School Girls* (1986). Kiddie matinee king K. Gordon Murray released his last film, *Thunder County* (d: Chris Robinson), a wretched and baffling potboiler which boasts some interesting parallels to *Fugitive Girls,* also in 1974.

Fugitive Girls follows certain elements of the "Women in Prison" template slavishly (lesbian love, corrupt law enforcement officials, etc.), yet likely due to Wood's influence, other elements veer wildly from formula. The most notable set-piece in the film is a scene wherein the escaped inmates encounter what appears to be a friendly gang of hippies in the wilderness. The gypsy-like troupe invites the women into their camp, offering them food, drink, entertainment and shelter for the night. Yet the next morning, the two groups clash with their inevitable cultural differences. The hippies offer the inmates some herbal tea, which the convicts find absolutely disgusting. Tempers flare, and the kindly hippies suddenly produce large chains and swing them menacingly; a fight ensues, and the inmates beat up the hippies. This is a most bizarre take on the youth movement by Wood and/or Apostolof, two middle-aged men who rather prejudicially (and indiscriminately) merged the pacifist hippie movement with the outlaw biker gang phenomenon. Another scene which captures the spirit of Wood occurs late in the film, when the inmates stumble upon an isolated house in the desert. Seeking refuge from the law, they break into the house, only to find the owners, a young man and a woman, fast asleep in their respective chairs. So still are the two that when the inmates, and the audience, first see them, there is the assumption that they may in fact be dead. The woman soon wakes up, followed shortly by the man, and both are horrified at this home invasion. The man, in fact, is a cripple, confined to a wheelchair due to injuries inflicted while serving the military in Vietnam. This is a latter incarnation of Wood's "suburban cou-ple in discord," here unable to manifest progressive change within themselves or their community as they are literally and figuratively comatose and paralyzed.

As for Wood, his portrayal of "Pop," a doddering old mechanic who runs an isolated airstrip, is imbued with both pathos and humor, and his timing and delivery are impressive. "Pop" is constantly harassed and assaulted by the younger generation, represented both by the female inmates and also a roving male biker gang,

In this evocative production still, escaped female convicts (unidentified) commit an ill-fated home invasion in Wood's intriguing *Fugitive Girls.*

and one may assume this reflected the aging Wood's feelings about the youth of the day. Wood's portrayal of the sheriff, although perfunctory and brief, is also professional, and after seeing Wood performing thus, one might wish he had more opportunities to act during his few remaining years. Also impressive in the cast is Rene Bond, who would eventually make a name for herself as an adult film star. Previously seen in Wood's *Necromania*, Bond gives what can only be called a bravura performance, defying the critics who maintained that performers in pornographic films lacked any real acting talent. Considering *Fugitive Girls* is a Stephen Apostolof production, it is pleasantly surprising to find that it is fast-moving, relatively expansive, and even boasts an attempt at a car chase, an obligatory moment in any self-respecting 1970s action film.

Fugitive Girls may be Wood's proudest achievement towards the end of his career, and is a significant time capsule showing the artist still in fine form both as writer and performer, and happy to work within the confines of the exploitation motifs of the day.

12

Ed Wood Rises from the Dead!

Although Ed Wood had already developed a tiny cult following amongst fans of the bizarre via telecasts of some of his films throughout the 1960s, the "Wood Revival" proper started in the late 1970s, perhaps not coincidentally coinciding with Wood's demise in 1978, with theatrical screenings of films such as *Glen or Glenda?* and *Bride of the Monster* in New York City and Los Angeles. Soon, the brothers Medved released *The Golden Turkey Awards* which proclaimed Wood's *Plan 9 from Outer Space* to be "the worst film of all time," and the Cult of Wood was born. As much as the Medveds put down Wood's films, they inadvertently created an impressive groundswell of interest in them; many Wood movies, including *Plan 9 from Outer Space*, were subsequently recognized for the primitive film treasures they are. Wood's films quickly outgrew their reputation as "bad films" to become something else; not good films, but eccentric, charming and engaging outsider art from a filmmaker who became more fascinating, it seemed, by the hour. Aided by the simultaneous advent of home video, Wood's films soon reached a grateful, enthusiastic mass audience who relished the discovery of each new obscurity. As most, if not all of the Wood films were in the public domain, many were released on various home video labels, some as early as 1982, and the true renaissance of Wood arguably began at this exciting moment, when classics such as *Plan 9 from Outer Space, Bride of the Monster, The Violent Years* and *Glen or Glenda?* could be found at video stores, department stores and even supermarkets, as well as on cable television.

In 1993, inspired by the burgeoning popularity in Wood, Adam Parfrey's iconoclastic small press Feral House published Rudolph Grey's patchwork biography *Nightmare of Ecstasy: The Life and Art of Edward D. Wood Jr.*, a bestseller which underlined Wood's arrival as a bonafide cultural icon. Flawed and disjointed, Grey's book consisted of snippets of interviews with various surviving members of Wood's family and social circle, arranged haphazardly in a vaguely chronological format. Surely, a filmmaker and writer as fascinating as Wood deserved a traditional, narrative-fueled biography, not this rough draft passing as historical tome. Indeed, the definitive Wood biography remains to be written. Yet Grey's book did feed the insatiable appetite of an audience desperate to find out anything they could about their new cultural hero, grateful for this information even when presented in such cynical fashion. Grey's book has gone through several printings and, over a decade later, remains popular.

What the Grey book does offer the patient reader is essential raw data about Wood, man and artist, information neither embellished or annotated, but salient facts and loving remembrances which bring the subject to vivid life. Among topics luridly obsessed upon in Grey's book are Wood's cross-dressing and alcoholism, neither placed into any kind of sympathetic light or historical perspective, but played for sheer sensationalism. Still, when one reads between the lines in many of the interview clips, one can see the soul of Wood rising out of the ashes of these potentially damning proclamations, and one aches to see a fuller portrait of this most astounding visual and literary artist. Grey's book did enlighten Wood's fans as to his most prolific, yet previously obscure side, that of the indefatigable author of nearly countless sex and exploitation novels; this revelation of Wood's creative alter ego was a most exciting discovery.

Nightmare of Ecstasy's reception soon led to a major motion picture, *Ed Wood* (1994), produced and directed by eccentric Hollywood filmmaker Tim Burton, and (very loosely) based on the Grey book. The Touchstone Pictures release did much to catapult Ed Wood into the cultural mainstream, and the film's many flaws can be largely forgiven, for here was a bonafide cultural hero brought to vivid, implausible life through the magic of motion pictures. *Ed Wood*, devotedly filmed in monochrome, purports to be a semi-biographical account of the filmmaker's life during the mid–1950s, the peak period of his career. Specifically, it focuses on Wood and his gang as they prepare for his greatest production yet: *Graverobbers from Outer Space.*

The emergence from obscurity of several actors from the Ed Wood universe, including Conrad Brooks, Paul Marco, Maila Nurmi and Dolores Fuller, helped to solidify the notion of Wood as a venerable, even increasingly mythological, cultural hero, and numerous Wood-related memoirs followed in short order. Interest in at least two deceased performers in Wood films, Bela Lugosi and Tor Johnson, rose exponentially. Wood has also inspired a number of film documentaries, which range from slapdash hack jobs to loving video biographies; the best thus far are Mark Patrick Carducci's *Flying Saucers Over Hollywood: The* Plan 9 *Companion* (1991) and Bret Thompson's *The Haunted World of Ed Wood* (2005). With the emergence of the World Wide Web, fansites run by advocates of Wood have sprouted like weeds; the two best are Steve Galindo's lovingly devotional "The Church of Ed Wood" (www.ed wood.org) and Philip R. Frey's exhaustively researched "The Hunt for Edward D. Wood, Jr." (www.edwoodonline.com). Although quality and themes range widely in this panoply of Wood shrines, there is no doubt that these "virtual" tributes will have a lasting influence on the legacy of Edward D. Wood, Jr.

In *Hollywood Rat Race*, Wood's haphazard memoirs disguised as a guide to young actors, he writes a surprisingly vicious anecdote about attending the premieres of several low-budget films by Hollywood compatriots. Specifically, Wood tells of attending the opening night of a 3D picture circa 1953, which was "so horrible it closed the next night," going straight into oblivion until sold to television. This reference probably refers to Phil Tucker's legendary *Robot Monster* (1953).[1] This acknowledgment of Wood attending the premiere of a colleague's production, fully living the 1950s Poverty Row Hollywood experience, is significant. Wood was undoubtedly motivated by the raw, unfocused energy that was floating around Hollywood during this period. Arguably, this exciting creative atmosphere would inspire even the mediocre artist or craftsman to do their very best, to set high standards for themselves; one might even confidently theorize that *Robot Monster* was a significant influence on Wood as he created, three years later, his own Skid Row sci-fi apocalypse, *Plan 9 from Outer Space.*

In many ways, Wood's films are the missing link between personal, or amateur movies, and slick corporate (i.e. "Hollywood") fare. Against all odds, several of Wood's hopelessly fragile, literally "impossible" films were made, released, and eventually received by a large audience. Wood's ability to create feature films out of literally "nothing," to have them embraced by audiences well into the future, make him to many fans a hero of popular culture. Yet if Wood's films are so popular now, why were they discarded "at birth"? Unconventional film tends to distance an audience expecting generic, predictable entertainment, even as it attracts those who seek something challenging and different. This may explain why Wood's films fell flat with their original first-run theatrical audiences, who were likely disappointed that they hadn't happened on yet another instantly familiar Hollywood clone. The aesthetic, dramatic and narrative roughness of a Wood melodrama must have come as something of a shock to the typical drive-in or grindhouse audience of the 1950s, and one doubts whether this audience was sophisticated enough to appreciate and enjoy a "bad" or "weird" movie on its own singular merits, like a piece of baffling, yet compelling modern art.

Like many, if not most creative persons, Wood may have intuited that he was not ultimately creating a product for the contemporary entertainment marketplace, but cultural artifacts for the future, and it is here, "in the future," where Wood's art shines. Through Criswell, Wood even clued in his audience: "We are all interested in the future, for that is where *you and I* are going to spend the rest of our lives." In this line from his magnum opus *Plan 9*, Wood seems to be signaling his audience that he knows he will be with them, *in the future.* Wood may have truly believed that his works would live on, may have even fancied himself a spiritual master, like his good friends Criswell, Jesus Christ and God. Wood seemed to also intuit that the successful artist is one who is able to create new myths, to bypass business and history and enter the culture subconsciously, through primal collective fantasies which act as the official "stories" of the age. Popular Fiction, and Popular Cinema, the twin godheads of Popular Culture, have always been the main repository for these, and Wood, intimately familiar with the culture of his time, was able to extract and rework many cultural myths to his own design, as few others with his finite resources were able to do.

In Wood's films, many contrasting, even antithetical themes are poured, often at random, into a maddening, confrontational, Brechtian verisimilitude which baffles its audience even as it engages it. Simplistic, awkward, even adolescent to a fault, Wood's film universe is a clumsy theatre of the Absurd, endearing but under-rehearsed high school plays captured on 35mm film for mass distribution, freak accidents of quirky personal art that happened to sneak into mainstream culture. That the films of Ed Wood capture the spirit, if not the letter, of the Theatre of the Absurd has, I hope, been demonstrated. Wood's magnificently unreal yet evocative dreamscapes, his ominous limbo netherworlds, are inhabited by peculiar and gruesome figures both realistic and fantastic, who change their costumes, as their very essence, without rhyme or reason, capturing the Absurdist spirit in full measure.

Discussing the inviolability of human mortality, Wood manages to disarm mere melancholy by pinning his most dismal revelations to his most absurd, clownish characters, Kelton the Cop foremost, safely distancing his audience from these dark truths. In the Absurdist tradition, comic characters are essential, yet they are always maligned and alienated by the audience, who experiences, through them, "embarrassment and shame"; these same characters are then, inevitably, the repository of all qualities which the audience denies or represses.[2] Wood was also a master at simultaneously honoring and ridiculing language as a means of effective communication. This is a key element in Absurdist theatre, which meditated endlessly on the phenomenon that reality was far too enigmatic to be genuinely conveyed merely via idea and rhetoric. Wood's cataclysmic juxtaposition of well-articulated, lyric prose against insane, mumbled gibberish clearly mirrors this obsession, this disenchantment with language as a means of codifying reality.[3]

Throughout his films, Wood suggests that to be happy, productive and fulfilled, individual men must accept their anima, their "female" side, in order to ensure proper psychological balance. This theme is expressed most succinctly in *Glen or Glenda?*, but appears elsewhere as well. As his vision matured, Wood furthered this notion to embrace society as a whole, suggesting that male-dominated society must collectively embrace and celebrate the female principle, and its emphasis on life cycles over a morbid and myopic obsession with death, in order to counteract patriarchy's obsession with self-destruction, in an attempt to reorder its dangerous psychological imbalance. *Orgy of the Dead* states this theme vividly, for in that film, patriarchy's inability to bridge the enigmatic gap between life and death, expressed symbolically as the difference "between night and day," leads to its complete annihilation.

The cinema of Wood is deeply immersed in dualistic philosophy, brought to life via myriad symbolic dialectical couplings such as man/woman, fake/real, day/night, life/death, and other assorted ideological and aesthetic binaries. Wood's unceasing fixation with man's obsession with dualistic thought process, with its restrictive "either/or," "self/other," "right/wrong" perspective, may be most clearly understood as the mystical concept of the illusory separation between spirit and matter, in which mortal beings are stuck in believing themselves to be an isolated "thing" without connection to others, the natural world, or the universe. This dangerous yet obstinate chimera has led to most if not all of mankind's problems, and a convergence of the spiritual and material sides of man has been advocated by thinkers throughout the ages. Wood expresses this wish for a merging of these two selves most overtly through his depiction of the male and female principles at first in conflict, but ultimately forging an uneasy but hopeful alliance. In *Glen or Glenda?*, Wood himself plays both parts of this extraordinary cosmic equation; in other films, the male/female binary is often essayed by a squabbling suburban couple.

At first blush it may appear that with this recurring theme, Wood is championing the ascendancy of the female, and thus the female principle, *over* the male principle, which has caused so much havoc in the modern world. Yet upon further inspection, Wood's seems to be hinting at an amicable *synthesis* of these apparently disparate elements, a conjoining of male and female, spirit and matter which might be coined a "mystical androgyny" or, as the mystics themselves labeled it, "the sacred marriage." Like the mystics, Wood saw the spirit behind the flesh in all things, yet few modern artists were able to depict that vision so distinctly, so elementally, as does Wood in his films and writings.

The heterosexual social construct as essayed in the majority of narrative cinema is an exalted, even sacrosanct unit, fundamentally well-intentioned, empowered and indestructible. Wood revised this cherished formula radically, crafting male/female couplings with antithetical, even diabolical agendas, and with tumultuous, even apocalyptic destinies.

Ed Wood and his muse, Dolores Fuller, share a posed moment of tranquility in this production still from *Glen or Glenda?* Wood's radical reflections on the traditional heterosexual dialectic resonates throughout popular culture to this day.

Ultimately, Wood's films illustrate that gender in itself is meaningless as a marker of identity, reflection of personality, or agent of social evolution. Ethical character is not forged due to, but in spite of, an individual's gender assignment or biological markings; any championing of gender-centric doctrine thus falls into the same myopic, exclusionary trap as discarded religious or political ideology, eventually regressing into useless, isolationist dogma.

Yet Wood's fixation on the heterosexual unit, most often represented by a squabbling, notably sexless suburban couple, might simultaneously be little more than an unconscious invocation of the man's parents, a problematic portrait of "Mom and Dad." From this perspective, Wood's continual narrative punishment of this archetypal couple likely acted as a psychological catharsis for the author (and likely too for certain members of the audience), whose obvious antipathy for the pair wrestles with an overriding love for same, resulting in the couple's frequent rescue at film's end from a perilous fate. Although Wood may have primarily denigrated patriarchal institutions while elevating the female to virtual godhead, still he may have ultimately forgiven "the father" for his sins, finally realizing that his existence was after all due to the hardiness of the problematic yet enduring male-female binary, represented to every living being by its immutable archetype: parents. Wood's "Mom and Dad," although flawed, at times even despicable creatures, are each ultimately redeemable, and as every audience member shares this couple, Wood's ambivalent ruminations may be edifying to all.

Wood appears to have also largely forgiven patriarchy, the collective father, for its sins, taking the prime edict of its premiere religion and sincerely, if recklessly embracing Christianity's prime metaphysical concept, yet ultimately its fatal flaw as a progressive belief system — and therein lies one of Wood's prime thematic contradictions. This vacillation between conservative obedience to the male-dominated socio-cultural imperative along with a progressive, even subversive alignment with all things female fuels the dizzying creative energy which elevates Wood's weird works to the level of art, and which threatens to render meaningless all gender-centric social theory. Yet even if the incarnations of Wood-as-Shirley and Glen-as-Glenda are in the final analysis trivial, are finally nothing more profound than a neurotic adult male "playing mommy," still the foreboding specters of their psychological underpinnings and sociological functions haunt culture to this day, goading it to response and reflection.

Regarding Wood's purgatory for lost souls, his recurring cosmic void, it is in some ways a return to the metaphysical womb of birth, a recycling of life, through death, into its next incarnation. This too is in keeping with the female principle which Wood almost compulsively invokes in his films. The continual cycles of death and rebirth which the female principle so clearly stands for are enacted chronically in Wood's omnipresent death-and-resurrection scenes. Wood's ultimate message may be that humans are, at root, divine beings, and if they ever learned to equalize their out-of-balance male/female, spirit/matter aspects, they would be privy to the great secret that life, which is unceasing, is by definition eternal.

The fact that Wood's art has been largely reviled and ridiculed suggests that his primary message — an attempt towards both psychological and societal gender balance, with an emphasis on reintroducing matriarchal philosophy, to invoke a progressive socio-political egalitarianism — strikes an errant, runaway patriarchy to its very heart. Historically, any attempt to even gently criticize entrenched phallocentric ideology is met with hostility and marginalization, if not outright exile, and Wood may represent a trenchant example of this prejudice, for the same commercial and cultural enclaves which rejected Wood are specifically those cultural institutions (Hollywood, the publishing industry) which serve their masters by promoting their malevolent, self-serving agenda.

As seen, Wood's films' preoccupation with Death and Resurrection as the trigger for so many narrative events hints at many things. Aside from the adolescent fixation on death and the morbid things of the natural world as seen in Wood's movies (and writing), there is also present the almost constant fear of demise which hovers over the chronic alcoholic, who sees the shadow of the Reaper behind every drunken hallucination, wheezing cough and stoned fever dream. Yet Wood was channeling truths even more profound. As he suggested time and again in his highly ritualistic works, death is not the antithesis to life, merely its evolution, again a nod to the female principle of ancient matriarchal myth. Death, at root, is a celebration of life, for only through death is the "spirit" of being released into immortality. Wood may have intuited that a life's work may only be catapulted into cultural history with the creator's passing. Life only becomes history when punctuated by death, so death *must* be the essential partner to life. A person's life, relived endlessly by his survivors through his creative works and living memory, thoroughly "resurrects" the person in spirit, and this "living death," his resurrection, may last well into eternity, as so many myths in the world's great religions suggest.

Wood's legacy assuredly proves this; perhaps he knew this formula all too well. Yet certainly this serene philosophical acceptance of death wrestled alongside the tenacious dread of expiration all mortals share, and it is likely this gruesome anxiety which fueled Wood's more adolescent (read: male) ruminations on the subject (ghouls, graveyards, the walking dead, etc.) When Wood himself passed away in December, 1978, after having been evicted forcibly from his last home, could he have possibly known that he would, in short order, become a bonafide cultural icon, a virtual godhead of the popular arts? No, it is more likely that as his bewildering, scattershot life passed before him, all he saw was a homeless, penniless, drunken bum, wretched and terrified, an abject failure and a subject worthy of the deepest ridicule and scorn.

This liable moment of horrifying self-discovery is given some credence by Kathy Wood's observation that when Wood died, there was a look of pure horror on his face, as if he had finally seen the dark, ugly truth, not only of the road to death, but of his own failed and laughably unresolved life, and that this, not the immortal he might become, was his last vision of self in consciousness.[4] What Wood knew then, in all its stark glory and terror, was that one must die before one can be resurrected, and it is at that singular moment of death that a person is absolutely and utterly alone, with no one to save him, as he faces the bleak void of the eternal cosmos, exposed and afraid. At the bitter end, Wood had come face to face with his own cosmic void, a cruel if inevitable poetic justice.

The astute viewer of the Wood canon may ponder whether the frequently murdered characters in Wood's films are more correctly labeled slaughters or sacrifices. Do their deaths benefit the greater good? It seems likely that they do. In his life as his films, the holy trinity of death, resurrection and transformation forms the essential ontological and aesthetic triptych of the Ed Wood universe. The Japanese soldier slaughtered by a horrified Wood, temporarily in harness to primal blood-lust, comes back to haunt his killer countless times in Wood's nightmare art. In his films, Wood constantly assaults the viewer with the stark truth of his own mortality, in images equal parts horrific and comic. Yet again, his ultimate message is hopeful, even celebratory: "Do not fear death, for life and death are agreeably reconciled in that vast eternity known as 'the future.'"

It is well known that Wood idolized filmmaker Orson Welles, and fancied himself an unofficial protégé of the culture giant. This pretension on Wood's part was a source of amusement amongst both friends and detractors, who thought the sheer audacity of a "hack" like Wood comparing himself to one of film's great geniuses was delusional beyond measure. Yet

Ed Wood *was* Orson Welles in a way; he was the "home movie" Orson Welles. Indeed, perhaps Wood did more than admire Welles; perhaps he thought he *was* Welles. Wood was, according to many sources, drunk during much of his creative activity in both writing and filmmaking. Could he have also been delusional, and actually thought he was something greater than he was? Did this, in fact, give him the courage to create his astounding personal art? Did Wood in fact create his body of unique work almost entirely in an alcoholic stupor? His peers were aware that Wood was a sad, unrepentant alcoholic, but it was much later when many realized that he might also be a bonafide Dharma Bum, an artistic savant of import, a spiritual teacher merely masquerading as a flop filmmaker. Some adherents have convincingly suggested that Wood hovers intriguingly above the mere mortal plane; Maila Nurmi, for one, did not hesitate in her assessment of his implausible infamy: "It was karma. He was a chosen one...."[5] The almost "worshipful" behavior of his legion of followers also suggests something mystical about the man. A representative comment by outsider artist Kalynn Campbell shrewdly captures both the "everyman" and deity-like aspects of Wood: "Ed was a maverick, an outcast, a Saint. Ed is us."[6]

It is his timeless thematic content in harness to quirky aesthetic motifs which mutate Wood's films from the low-brow commercial product they were born as, into the high art which his devotees always knew them to be. Arguably, the overriding goal for any artist is to expand his audience for compensation; all else, at root, is mere practice of craft. Wood managed to amass his impressive, ever-growing audience after his death, the legacy of any successful artist. Like his main characters, who have the greatest impact on their community after their death, Wood himself became a bigger-than-life character in popular culture, with an ever-expanding legacy, starting significantly at the very moment of his death in 1978, when the first theatrical revivals of his films occurred. Since that remarkable moment of synchronicity, the legacy of Wood has grown exponentially, his profound effect on popular culture by now undeniable. Through death, Wood became imperishable, a giant of popular culture whose voice reverberates across the world, and towards the very heavens.

And what of the future? What can one say about a man whose career, uncelebrated in his lifetime, grows in stature exponentially with the wide distribution of his raw, troubled, at times dazzling motion pictures? One can call Wood a vagabond genius or a drunken fool. One must, however, concede he is an enduring artist. If Edward D. Wood, Jr., is not an artist, who is? His troubled yet indefatigable creative ingeniousness shines through even the most tawdry and flawed vessel. By heroically merging limited financial, technical and intellectual resources, Wood reached more people than any other filmmaker with similar options and, in so doing, blazed a trail in crafting that most rare commodity, "mass art." One could even make the argument that Ed Wood is the outsider artist version of Orson Welles, creating a singular, iconoclastic and baffling independent cinema against Jobian trials both external and internal. This is why so many devoted fans declare, "Wood is God!" This is why Wood ought be recognized as a notable poet-philosopher, a drunken, lunatic mythmaker who himself became mythical. Similar to many creative souls throughout history, Wood gave his heart, his soul, his very life for his art. Although his prolific literary output has yet to be fully appreciated by a mass audience, Wood's films, with their creative virtuosity, courageous philosophical content and boundless entertainment value, have truly become legend. Merging personal art with consumer product in a way no other filmmaker has yet to approach, Wood may yet be claimed a godhead of entertainment, as large in import as Orson Welles or any comparable peer. In that vast chasm called "the future," Edward D. Wood, Jr., may yet metamorphose from mere freak or fringe hero into a cherished cultural entity — the patron saint of Hollywood, U.S.A.

Filmography

Full production credits are listed for films in which Wood performed two or more functions, screenplay and director, or was a participating and verified screenwriter; other films which included Wood are listed under "Additional Credits." Where there are discrepancies between a person's professional name, this filmography favors the on-screen credits.

The Streets of Laredo (1948)

Directed by Edward D. Wood, Jr.; Screenplay: Edward D. Wood, Jr.; Produced by Tony Lawrence, John Crawford Thomas; Cinematography: Ray Flin, Edward D. Wood, Jr.; Music (1995 restoration): Ben Weisman; Music Director (1995 restoration): Dolores Fuller; Associate Producer (1995 restoration): Dolores Fuller; Wood-Thomas Pictures; aka *Crossroads of Laredo*, 23 minutes. (Unreleased; first issued in 1995 as *Crossroads of Laredo*).

Cast: Duke Moore (Lem), Ruth McCabe (Barbara), Don Nagel (Tex), Chuck LeBerge (Sheriff), John Crawford Thomas (Sheriff's Deputy), Edward D. Wood, Jr. (Young Cowboy), Christopher Longshadow (Parson), Paula Evans (First Dance Hall Girl), Leme Hunter (Second Dance Hall Girl), Carol Crisner (Third Dance Hall Girl), Mrs. Magee (Basketwoman), Bill Ames (Bartender), Ramina Rae (First Flower Girl), Patsy Martin (Second Flower Girl), Bob Paul (Cowboy), Nish Tara (Cowboy), Bob Burke (Cowboy), Charles Davidson (Cowboy), Kate Flannery (Barbara's Voice, 1995 restoration), Cliff Stone (Narrator, 1995 restoration)

The Sun Was Setting (1951)

Directed by Edward D. Wood, Jr.; Screenplay: Edward D. Wood, Jr.; Produced by Milton Bowron, Joe Carter, Don Davis, Edward D. Wood, Jr.; Cinematography: Ray Flin; Editing: Daniel A. Nathan; Makeup: Curly Batson; Hair Stylist: Josephine Sweeney; Production Manager: Don Davis; Sound: Glen Glenn; Produced by Empire Productions, WDBC Productions; aka *The Sun Also Sets*, 20 minutes.

Cast: Angela Stevens (June), Phyllis Coates (Rene), Tom Keene (Paul) (as Richard Powers)

Boots (1953)

Directed by Edward D. Wood, Jr.; Screenplay: Edward D. Wood, Jr.; Produced by Tucson Kid Productions, 25 minutes, b/w.

Crossroad Avenger (1953)

Directed by Edward D. Wood, Jr.; Screenplay: Edward D. Wood, Jr.; Produced by John E. Clarke, Lew Dubin, Edward D. Wood, Jr.; Cinematography: Ray Flin; Editing: Lou Guinn; Art Director: "Cowboy Slim"; Sound: John E. Tribby; Produced and Distributed by Tucson Kid Productions; aka *The Adventures of the Tucson Kid*, 50/24 minutes, color

Cast: Tom Keene (The Tucson Kid), Tom Tyler (The Deputy), Lyle Talbot (Bart), Don Nagel

(Dance), Harvey Dunn (Zeke), Forbes Murray (Roger), Kenne Duncan (Lefty), Bud Osborne (Max), Edward D. Wood, Jr. (Pony Express Rider)

Glen or Glenda? (1953)

Directed by Edward D. Wood, Jr.; Screenplay: Edward D. Wood, Jr.; Produced by George Weiss; Music: William Lava (from *The Courageous Dr. Christian*, uncredited); Cinematography: William C. Thompson; Editing: "Bud" Schelling; Music Consultant: Sandford Dickinson; Makeup: Harry Thomas; Settings: Jack Miles; Sound: Ben Winkler; Produced and Distributed by Screen Classics Inc.; aka *Glen or Glenda?, He or She, I Changed My Sex, I Led 2 Lives, The Transvestite*, 74/68/65/61 minutes, b/w

Cast: Bela Lugosi (Scientist), Lyle Talbot (Insp. Warren), Timothy Farrell (Psychiatrist), Dolores Fuller (Barbara), Edward D. Wood, Jr. (Glen-Glenda) (as "Daniel Davis"), "Tommy" Haynes (Allan-Ann), Charles Crafts (Johnny), Conrad Brooks (Banker/Reporter/Pickup Artist/Bearded Drag) (as Connie Brooks), Henry Bederski (Man with Hat and Receding Hairline, uncredited), Captain DeZita (The Devil/Glen's Father, uncredited), Helen Miles (uncredited), Shirley Speril (Miss Stevens, uncredited), Harry Thomas (Man in Nightmare, uncredited), William C. Thompson (Judge, uncredited), Mr. Walter (Patrick-Patricia, uncredited), George Weiss (Man at Transvestite's Suicide, uncredited), Evelyn Wood (Sheila, Glen's Sister, uncredited)

Trick Shooting with Kenne Duncan (1953)

Directed by Edward D. Wood, Jr.; Produced by Edward D. Wood, Jr.; Presented by the MacLachlan Brothers; Produced by Ronald V. Ashcroft; Music by Gene Kauer; 10 minutes, color.

Cast: Kenne Duncan (Himself), Ruth Duncan (Herself)

The Lawless Rider (1954)

Directed by Yakima Canutt; Screenplay: Edward D. Wood, Jr. (as Johnny Carpenter); Cinematography: William C. Thompson; Distributed by United Artists, 62 minutes.

Cast: Johnny Carpenter (Rod Tatum), Frankie Darro (Jim Bascom), Douglass Dumbrille (Marshall Brady), Frank Carpenter (Big Red), Noel Neill (Nancy James), Kenne Duncan (Freno Frost), Bud Osborne (Tulso), Bill Coontz (Red Rooks)

Jail Bait (1954)

Directed by Edward D. Wood, Jr.; Story and Screenplay: Alex Gordon, Edward D. Wood, Jr.; Produced by Edward D. Wood, Jr.; Executive Producers: J. Francis White, Joy N. Houck; Music: Hoyt S. Curtin (as Hoyt Kurtain); Cinematography: William C. Thompson; Editing: Charles Clement, Igo Kantor; Makeup: John Sylvester, Harry Thomas; Sound: Dale Knight, Charles Clemmons; Special Effects: Ray Mercer; Production Assistant: Esko; Dialogue Coach: Vicki Cottle; Lighting: Harl Foltz; Knitwear: Westwood Knitting Mills, Los Angeles; Ladies' Suits: Jerry Mann, Los Angeles; Dresses: Gene D. Evans, Los Angeles; Lingerie: Chic & Pandora, Los Angeles; Locations: Larry Moses, Monterey Theatre, Monterey Park, Calif., Hunters Inn, Temple City, Calif.; Distributed by Howco Productions Inc., aka *Hidden Face*, 72 minutes, b/w.

Cast: Lyle Talbot (Inspector Johns), Dolores Fuller (Marilyn Gregor), Herbert Rawlinson (Dr. Boris Gregor), Steve Reeves (Lieutenant Bob Lawrence), Clancy Malone (Don Gregor), Timothy Farrell (Vic Brady), Theodora Thurman (Loretta), Bud Osborne (Paul "Mac" McKenna), Mona McKinnon (Miss Willis), Don Nagel (Detective Davis), John Robert Martin (Detective McCall), La Vada Simmons (Miss Lytell, Gregor's Nurse), Regina Claire (Newspaper Reporter), John Avery (Police Doctor), Henry Bederski (Suspect in Police Station, uncredited), Conrad Brooks (Medical Attendant/Photographer, uncredited), Ted Brooks (Policeman, uncredited), Chick Watts (Nightclub Performer, uncredited), Cotton Watts (Nightclub Performer, uncredited), Edward D. Wood, Jr. (Radio News Announcer, uncredited)

Bride of the Monster (1956)

Directed by Edward D. Wood, Jr.; Story & Screenplay: Edward D. Wood, Jr., and Alex Gordon; Executive Producer: Donald E. McCoy; Associate Producer: Tony McCoy; Music: Frank Worth; Cinematography: William C. Thompson, Ted Allan; Editing: Mike Adams; Camera Operator: Bert

Shipham; Technical Supervisor: Igo Kantor; Makeup: Louis J. Haszillo, Maurice Seiderman; Assistant Directors: Bob Farfan, William Nolte; Property Master: George Bahr; Sound Recordists: Dale Knight, Lyle Willey; Sound Effects: Mike Pollock; Special Effects: Pat Dinga; Stunts: Red Reagan; Key Grip: Thomas J. Connolly; Electrician: Louis Kriger; Produced by Rolling M. Productions; Distributed by Banner Productions Inc., presented by Filmakers Releasing Organization (sic); aka *Bride of the Atom, Monster of the Marshes, The Atomic Monster*, 68 minutes, b/w.

Cast: Bela Lugosi (Dr. Eric Vornoff), Tor Johnson (Lobo), Tony McCoy (Lt. Dick Craig), Loretta King (Janet Lawton), Harvey B. Dunn (Capt. Tom Robbins), George Becwar (Prof. Vladimir Strowski), Paul Marco (Officer Kelton), Don Nagel (Det. Marty Martin), Bud Osborne (Mac), John Warren (Jake), Ann Wilner (Tillie), Dolores Fuller (Margie), William Benedict (Newsboy) (as William Benedict), Ben Frommer (Drunk), Conrad Brooks (uncredited)

The Violent Years (1956)

Directed by William M. Morgan; Story: B.L. Hart ("Teenage Killers," uncredited); Screenplay: Edward D. Wood, Jr.; Produced by Roy Reid; Associate Producer: William M. Morgan; Cinematography: William C. Thompson; Editing: Gerard Wilson; Wardrobe: Victor Most of California; Makeup Artist: Steven Clensos; Set Director: Jack Miles; Music Supervisor: Manuel Francisco; Sound: Glen Glenn; Electrician: Frank Leonetti; Produced by Dél Productions; Distributed by Headliner Productions of Hollywood; aka *Female, Girl Gang Terrorists, Teenage Girl Gang*, 65/58 minutes, b/w.

Cast: Jean Moorhead (Paula Parkins), Barbara Weeks (Jane Parkins), Arthur Millan (Carl Parkins), Theresa Hancock (Georgia), Joanne Cangi (Geraldine), Gloria Farr (Phyllis), Glenn Corbett (Barney Stetson), Lee Constant (Sheila), I. Stanford Jolley (Judge Clara), Timothy Farrell (Lt. Holmes), F. Chan McClure (Det. Artman), Bruno Metsa (Manny), Harry Keaton (Doctor), Bud Osborne ("Mac," the Night Watchman, uncredited)

The Final Curtain (1957)

Directed by Edward D. Wood, Jr.; Screenplay: Edward D. Wood, Jr.; Produced by Walter Brannon, Anthony Cardoza, Tom Mason, Ernest S. Moore, Edward D. Wood, Jr.; Cinematography: William C. Thompson; Sound: Dale Knight; Editorial Supervisor: Edward D. Wood, Jr.; Music Supervisor: Gordon Zahler; Distributed by Atomic Productions Inc., 20 minutes, b/w.

Cast: Duke Moore (The Actor) (as C.J. Moore), Dudley Manlove (Narrator), Jeannie Stevens (The Vampire)

The Night the Banshee Cried (1957)

Directed by Edward D. Wood, Jr.; Screenplay: Edward D. Wood, Jr.; Produced by Edward D. Wood, Jr.; Produced by Atomic Productions Inc., 22 minutes, b/w.

The Bride and the Beast (1958)

Directed by Adrian Weiss; Story: Adrian Weiss; Screenplay: Edward D. Wood, Jr.; Script Consultant: Dr. Tom Mason; Produced by Adrian Weiss, Louis Weiss; Music: Les Baxter; Cinematography: Roland Price; Assistant Directors: Harry Fraser, Harry Webb; Editing: George M. Merrick, Samuel Weiss; Production Design: Edward Shiells; Set Decoration: Harry Reif; Makeup Artist: Harry Thomas; Special Effects: Gerald Endler; Camera: Keith Smith; Assistant Cameras: Don Lopez; Gaffer: Bobby Jones; Script Supervisor: Diana Loomis; Key Grip: Doty Steels; Wardrobe: Adolph Weiss; Sound Mixer: Harold Hanks; Prop Man: Monroe Liebgold; Rifles and Trophies by Weatherby's; Miss Austin's Wardrobe by Emerson's, Studio City; Produced and Distributed by Allied Artists Pictures Corporation; Distributed by Weiss Global Enterprises, aka *Queen of the Gorillas*, 78 minutes, b/w

Cast: Charlotte Austin (Laura Carson Fuller), Lance Fuller (Dan Fuller), Johnny Roth (Taro), William Justine (Dr. Carl Reiner), Gil Frye (Captain Cameron), Jeanne Gerson (Marka), Steve Calvert ("The Beast," uncredited), Slick Slavin (Soldier), Eve Brent (Stewardess), Bhogwan Singh (Native)

Revenge of the Virgins (1959)

Directed by Peter Perry, Jr.; Screenplay: Edward D. Wood, Jr. (as Peter La Roche); Produced by

Bethel Buckalew; Music: Guenther Kauer; Cinematography: Gene Cropper, Vilis Lapenieks; an R.V.A. Production, 53 minutes, b/w.

Cast: Charles Veltman (Mike Burton), Jodean Russo (Ruby Burton), Stan Pritchard (Van Taggart), Hank Delgado (Barman), Lou Massad (Stan), Ralph Cookson (Wade), Del Monroe (Deserter), Hugo Stanger (Deserter), Joanne Bowers (Yellow Gold), Pat O'Connell, Jewell Morgan, Betty Shay, Jan Lee, Nona Carver, Romona Rogers (Golden Hord Guards), Kenne Duncan (Narrator, uncredited)

Plan 9 from Outer Space (1959)

Directed by Edward D. Wood, Jr.; Screenplay: Edward D. Wood, Jr.; Produced by Edward D. Wood, Jr.; Associate Producers: Hugh Thomas, Jr., Charles Burg; Executive Producer: J. Edward Reynolds; Music Supervisor: Gordon Zahler; Cinematography: William C. Thompson; Editing: Edward D. Wood, Jr.; Costume Design: Dick Chaney; Makeup: Tom Bartholemew, Harry Thomas; Production Manager: Kirk Kirkham; Assistant Director: Willard Kirkham; Set Constructor: Tom Kemp; Property Master: Tony Portoghese; Set Dresser: Harry Reif; Sound: Dale Knight, Sam Kopetzky; Special Effects: Charles Duncan; Production Assistant: Donald A. Davis; Script Supervisor: Diana N. Loomis; Grip: Art Manikin; Wardrobe: Richard Chaney; Electrical Effects: Jim Woods; Picture Vehicles: Karl Johnson; Produced by Reynolds Pictures Inc.; Distributed by Distributors Corporation of America Inc.; International Film Distributors; Grand National Pictures Ltd., aka *Grave Robbers from Outer Space*, 79 minutes, b/w

Cast: Gregory Walcott (Jeff Trent), Mona McKinnon (Paula Trent), Duke Moore (Lt. John Harper), Tom Keene (Col. Tom Edwards), Carl Anthony (Patrolman Larry), Paul Marco (Patrolman Kelton), Tor Johnson (Insp. Daniel Clay), Dudley Manlove (Eros), Joanna Lee (Tanna), John Breckinridge (The Ruler), Lyle Talbot (General Roberts), David De Mering (Danny), Norma McCarty (Edith), Bill Ash (Captain), the Reverend Lyn Lemon (Minister at Insp. Clay's Funeral), Ben Frommer (Mourner), Gloria Dea (Mourner), Conrad Brooks (Patrolman Jamie), Vampira (Vampire Girl), Bela Lugosi (Ghoul Man), Criswell (Himself), Donald A. Davis (Drunk, uncredited), Johnny Duncan (uncredited), Karl Johnson (Farmer Calder, uncredited), Tom Mason (Lugosi's Double, uncredited), J. Edward Reynolds (Gravedigger, uncredited), Hugh Thomas Jr. (Gravedigger, uncredited), Edward D. Wood, Jr. (Man Holding Newspaper, uncredited)

Night of the Ghouls (1959/1983)

Directed by Edward D. Wood, Jr.; Screenplay: Edward D. Wood, Jr., from his novel; Produced by Edward D. Wood, Jr.; Production Executive: "J.M.A."; Executive Producer: Major J.C. Foxworthy, (U.S.M.C.R. Ret.); Associate Producers: Marg. Usher, Tony Cardoza, Tom Mason, Paul Marco, Walt Brannon, Gordon Chesson; Cinematography: William C. Thompson; Editing: Edward D. Wood, Jr.; Consolidated Editorial Service, Editorial Supervisor: Donald A. Davis; Art Director: Kathy Wood (as Kathleen O'Hara Everett); Costumes: Robert Darieux, Mickey Meyers; Makeup: Harry Thomas; Assistant Directors: Ronnie Ashcroft, Scott Lynch; Sound: Harry Smith; Music Supervisor: Gordon Zahler; Costumes: Mickey Meyer; Camera Operator: Glen R. Smith; Stills: Larry Smith; Lighting: John Murray; Accountant: John Jarvis; Film Developed as Directed by Film Service Laboratories, Inc., Hollywood; Produced by Atomic Productions; Distributed by Wade Williams Productions, aka *Dr. Acula*, *Revenge of the Dead*, 70 minutes, b/w

Cast: Criswell (Himself), Kenne Duncan (Karl/Dr. Acula), "Duke" Moore (Lieutenant Daniel Bradford), Tor Johnson (Lobo), Valda Hansen (The White Ghost), Johnny Carpenter (Police Captain Robbins) (as John Carpenter), Paul Marco (Patrolman Kelton), Don Nagel (Sargent Crandel), Bud Osborne (Darmoor), Jeannie Stevens (The Black Ghost/Mannequin), Harvey B. Dunn (Henry), Margaret Mason (Martha), Clay Stone (Young Man), Marcelle Hemphill (Maude Wingate Yates Foster), Thomas R. Mason (Wingate Foster's Ghost), James La Maida (Hall), Tony Cardoza (Tony), John Gautieri (Boy), Karen Hairston (Girl), Karl Johnson, Leonard Barnes, Frank Barbarick, Francis Misitano, David DeMering (as David De Maring) (The Dead Men), Henry Bederski (Drunk, uncredited), Mona McKinnon (Juvenile Delinquent Girl, uncredited), Conrad Brooks, Edward D. Wood, Jr. (Men in Fight, uncredited)

The Sinister Urge (1960)

Directed by Edward D. Wood, Jr. (as E.D. Wood); Story & Screenplay: Edward D. Wood, Jr. (as

E. D. Wood); Produced by Roy Reid; Associate Producer: Edward D. Wood, Jr. (as E.D. Wood); Cinematography: William C. Thompson; Assistant Director: Jim Blake; Editing: John Soh; Sound Mixer: Sam Kopetzky; Set Designer: Jerome Lapari; Set Dressing: J.B. Finch; Sound: Jim Fullerton; Special Effects: Ray Mercer; Musical Arrangement: Manuel Francisco; Miss Fontaine's Wardrobe: Eileen Younger; Distributed by Headliner Productions, aka *Hellborn, Rock & Roll Hell, The Young and the Immoral*, 76 minutes

Cast: Kenne Duncan (Lt. Matt Carson), Carl James "Duke" Moore (Sgt. Randy Stone), Jean Fontaine (Gloria Henderson), Carl Anthony (Johnny Ryde), Dino Fantini (Dirk Williams), Jeanne Willardson (Mary Smith), Harvey B. Dunn (Romaine), Reed Howes (Police Inspector), Fred Mason (Officer Kline), Conrad Brooks (Connie), Vickie Baker, Jean Baree (Policeman), Henry Bederski, Honey Bee, Judy Berares (Frances), Betty Boatner (Shirley), Toni Costello (Model), Carole Gallos, Claudette Gifford, Harry Keatan (Jaffe), Henry Kekoanui (Dark stud), Dick Lamson, Carmen Lee, April Lynn (Model), Paul Main (Paul), Sylvia Marenco (Model), Candy Paige, Clayton Peca (Policeman Undercover in Drag), Kathy Kendall (Model), Nick Raymond, Vic McGee (Syndicate Men), Oma Soffian (Nurse), Raphael Sporer, Vonnie Starr (Secretary), Rhea Walker, Lisa Page Ward), Kenneth Willardson (Theatrical Agent), Edward D. Wood, Jr. (Danny)

Married Too Young (1962)

Directed by George Moskov, Edward D. Wood, Jr. (uncredited); Story by Nathaniel Tanchuck; Screenplay: Nathaniel Tanchuck, Edward D. Wood, Jr. (uncredited); Cinematography: Ernest Haller; Editing: Maurice Wright; Assistant Directors: Lindsley Parsons, Jr., George Batcheller; Music: Manuel Francisco; Wardrobe: Forrest T. Butler; Makeup: Fred Phillips; Property Master: Karl Brainard; Chief Electrician: Norman McClay; Recording Engineer: Woodruff H. Clarke; Set Continuity: Hope McLachlin; Set Decorator: Ted Driscoll; Distributed by Headliner Productions, aka *I Married Too Young*, 76 minutes, b/w

Cast: Harold Lloyd Jr. (Tommy Blaine), Jana Lund (Helen Newton), Anthony Dexter (Grimes), Trudy Marshall (Marla), Brian O'Hara, Nita Loveless, Lincoln Demyan, Marianna Hill, Cedric Jordan, Jamie Forster, George Cisar, Joel Mondeaux, David Bond, Richard Davies, Irene Ross, Frank Harding, Tom Frandsen

Shotgun Wedding (1963)

Directed by Boris L. Petroff; Story by Edward D. Wood, Jr.; Screenplay: Edward D. Wood, Jr. (as Larry Lee); Produced by Boris L. Petroff; Associate Producer: Lloyd R. Bell; Assistant to the Producer: Herb J. Miller; Music: Alexander Starr; Dance Music: Jerry Capehart; Cinematography: Paul Ivano; First Assistant Director & Production Manager: Harold Lewis; Editor: Fred Feitshans; Camera Operator: Ned Davenport; Assistant Cameraman: John Jones; Sound Recorder: Ray Bisordi; Sound Mixer: Charles Wallace; Boom Man: Dean Hodges; Script Supervisor: Kenneth Gilbert; Gaffer: Les Miller; Grip: Tex Hayes; Construction and Art Supervisor: John LeSabora; Makeup Director: Bob Mark; Wardrobe: Marguerite Curry; Choreography: Clair & Glenda Folk; Produced by Boris Petroff Productions; Pat Patterson Productions; Distributed by Arkota, 62 minutes, color

Cast: Pat O'Malley (Buford), Jenny Maxwell (Honey Bee), Valerie Allen (Melanie), Buzz Martin (Rafe), William Schallert (Preacher), Nan Peterson (Lucianne), Peter Colt (Shub), Jack Searl (Silas), Jan Darrow (Mountain Gal), Art Phillips (Curley), Edward Fitz (Steelo), Jack Riggs (Silas' henchman), Lyn Moore (Girl at Meeting)

Orgy of the Dead (1965)

Directed by Stephen Apostolof (as A.C. Stephen); Screenplay: Edward D. Wood, Jr., from his novel; Produced by Stephen Apostolof (as A.C. Stephen); Associate Producers: William Bates, L.S. Jensen, Neil B. Stein; Music: Jaime Mendoza-Nava (uncredited); Cinematography: Robert Caramico; Editing: Donald A. Davis (uncredited); Art Direction: Robert Lathrop; Set Decoration: Ernest Bouvenkamp; Costume Design: Robert Darieux; Makeup Artist: Margaret Davies; Hair Stylist: Nancy Sandoval; Post-production Supervisor: Donald A. Davis; Production Supervisor: Tad Stafford; Assistant Directors: Ted V. Mikels (uncredited), Edward D. Wood, Jr. (uncredited); Sound: Dale Knight; Choreographer: Marc Desmond; Assistant Camera: Robert Maxwell; Still Photographer: Robert Wilson; Produced by Astra Productions; Atomic Productions Inc.; Distributed by F.O.G. Distributors;

SCA Distributors; Crown International Pictures; Wade Williams Productions Inc. (1988 re-release), aka *A.C. Stephen's Orgy of the Dead, Orgy of the Vampires*, 92/82 minutes, color

   Cast: Criswell (The Emperor), Fawn Silver (The Black Ghoul), Pat Barrington (Shirley/Gold Girl) (as Pat Barringer), William Bates (Bob), Mickey Jines (Hawaiian Dance), Barbara Nordin (Skeleton Dance), Bunny Glaser (Indian Dance), Nadejda Klein (Slave Dance) (as Nadejda Dobrev), Colleen O'Brien (Street Walker Dance), Texas Starr (Cat Dance), Rene De Beau (Fluff Dance), Stephanie Jones (Mexican Dance), Dene Starnes (Zombie Dance), Louis Ojena (The Mummy), John Andrews (The Wolfman/Giant), Edward Tontini (Doctor), William Bonner (2nd Doctor), Rod Lindeman (Giant), John Bealey (Detective), Arlene Spooner (Nurse)

Gun Runners (1969)

   Directed by Donald A. Davis; Screenplay: Edward D. Wood, Jr.; Produced by Donald A. Davis; Produced by Don Davis Productions, color

The Love Feast (1969)

   Directed by Joseph F. Robertson; Screenplay: Harry Kaye, Joseph F. Robertson, Edward D. Wood, Jr. (uncredited); Produced by Joseph F. Robertson; Cinematography: Hal Guthu; Titles: Granville Murphy; Produced by Robertson-Kay Productions, aka *Pretty Models All in a Row, The Photographer,* 59/63 minutes, color

   Cast: Mia Coco (Black Model), Linda Colpin (Linda), Casey Lorrain (See-Through Clothing Model), Edward D. Wood, Jr. (Mr. Murphy)

One Million AC/DC (1969)

   Directed by Ed De Priest; Screenplay: Edward D. Wood, Jr. (as Akdon Telmig); Produced by Ed De Priest; Cinematography: Ed De Priest, Eric Torgesson (as Les Stevens); Sound: Mike Stange; Produced and Distributed by Canyon Films, 65 minutes, color

   Cast: Susan Berkely, Gary Kent, Billy Wolf, Sharon Wells, Jack King, Natasha, Nancy McGavin, Tod Badker, Tony Brooks, Pam English, John Lee, Harry Stone, Gail Lavon, Larry Vincente, Shari Stevens, Bonnie Walker, Mary Doyle, Greg Mathis, April O'Connor, Jacqueline Fox (uncredited), Maria Lease (uncredited)

Operation Redlight (1969)

   Directed by Don Doyle; Screenplay: Edward D. Wood, Jr., from his novel, *Mama's Diary*; Produced by Jacques Descent Productions, 90 minutes, color
   Cast: Edward D. Wood, Jr.

Excited (1970)

   Directed by Edward D. Wood, Jr. (as Akdov Telmig); Screenplay: Edward D. Wood, Jr. (as Akdov Telmig); Produced by G & J Productions; Distributed by Canyon Distributing Company, 53 minutes.

Take It Out in Trade (1970)

   Directed by Edward D. Wood, Jr.; Screenplay: Edward D. Wood, Jr.; Produced by Edward Ashdown, Richard Gonzalez, Roy Corrigan; Assistant Director: Don Nagel; Cinematography: Hal Guthu; Editing: Edward D. Wood, Jr., Michael J., Sheriden; Produced by Ashdown-Gonzalez Productions, 80 minutes, color

   Cast: Nona Carver (Sleazy Maisie Rumpledinck), Linda Colpin, Monica Gayle, Duke Moore (Frank Riley), Michael Donovan O'Donnell (Mac McGregor), Donna Stanley (Shirley Riley), Edward D. Wood, Jr. (Alecia, as Ed Wood), Casey Lorrain, Emilie Gray, Donna Young, Lynn Harris, Andrea Rabins, James Kitchens, Hugh Talbert, Judith Koch, Phyllis Stengel, Elaine Jarrett, Linda Spheres, Lou Ojena, Jack Harding, Herb Webber

The Double Garden (1970)

   Directed by Kenneth G. Crane; Screenplay: Edward D. Wood, Jr.; Produced by Toei Co. Ltd., aka *The Devil Garden, The Revenge of Doctor X, Venus Flytrap*, U.S.-Japan, 94 minutes, color
   Cast: James Craig (Dr. Bragan), James Yagi (Dr. Paul Nakamura)

The Only House (1971)

Directed by Edward D. Wood, Jr.; Screenplay: Edward D. Wood, Jr.; Camera: Ted Gorley; Produced by Cinema Classics; Distributed by Stacey Films, 60 minutes, color

Necromania: A Tale of Weird Love (1971)

Directed by Edward D. Wood, Jr. (as Don Miller); Screenplay: Edward D. Wood, Jr. (uncredited), from his novel, *The Only House*; Produced by Edward D. Wood, Jr. (as Don Miller); Cinematography: Ted Gorley, Hal Guthu; Editing: Edward D. Wood, Jr. (uncredited); Sound: George Malley (uncredited); Grip: John Andrews (uncredited); Produced by Cinema Classics; Distributed by Stacey Distributors, aka *Necromania*, 54/51 minutes, color

Cast: Maria Aronoff (as Marie Arnold) (Madame Heles), Rene Bond (Shirley), Ric Lutze (Danny)

The Class Reunion (1972)

Directed by Stephen Apostolof (as A.C. Stephen); Adaptation: Pierre Legay; Screenplay: Stephen Apostolof (as A.C. Stephen), Edward D. Wood, Jr.; Produced by Stephen Apostolof (as A.C. Stephen); Cinematography: Allen Stone; Production Coordinator: S.B. Cooper; Script Supervisor: Nelson Lowe; Still Photographer: Errof Lyn; Art Director: Mike McCloskey; Sound Recorder: Nick Raymond; Chief Gaffer: Brink Brayman; Assistant Camera: John Pratt; Makeup: Harry Page; Produced by Valentine Enterprises; Distributed by SCA Distributors, 90/83 minutes, color

Cast: Marsha Jordan (Jane), Rene Bond (Thelma), Sandy Carey (Fluff), Starline Comb (Rosie), Terry Johnson (Liza), Forman Shane (Charlie), Flora Weisel (Henrietta), Fred Geoffries (Wimpy), Rick Lutze (Harry), Con Covert (Bruce), Ron Darby (Tom), Mark Nelson (Bellboy)

Drop-Out Wife (1972)

Directed by Stephen Apostolof (as A.C. Stephen); Screenplay: Stephen Apostolof (as A.C. Stephen), Edward D. Wood, Jr.; Produced by Stephen Apostolof (as A.C. Stephen); Cinematography: R.C. Ruben; Camera: R.C. Ruben, Jr.; Sound: Dick Damon; Gaffer: Brink Braydon; Makeup: Jerry Sussi; Music: J. Mendozoff; Associate Producer: S.B. Cooper; Assistant Director: Harvey Shain; Script Supervisor: Jo Henry; Stills: R.C. Ruben, Jr.; Post-Production Supervisor: Luigi Rogatoni; Produced by A-A Productions; Distributed by SCA Distributors, aka *Pleasure Unlimited*, 94/82 minutes, color

Cast: Angela Carnon (Peggy), Fred Geoffries (uncredited, as Jim), Terry Johnson (Janet), Forman Shane, Lynn Harris, Douglas Fray, Jean Louise, Corey Brandon, Sandy Dempsey, Duane Paulson

The Undergraduate (1972)

Directed by Jacques Descent; Screenplay: Edward D. Wood, Jr., 68 minutes
Cast: Cindy Hopkins, Eve Orlon (as Sunny Boyd)

The Snow Bunnies (1972)

Directed by Stephen Apostolof (as A.C. Stephen); Screenplay: Stephen Apostolof (as A.C. Stephen), Edward D. Wood, Jr.; Produced by Stephen Apostolof (as A.C. Stephen); Cinematography: Allen Stone; Distributed by SCA Distributors; Marden Films, color

Cast: Marsha Jordan (Joan), Rene Bond (Madie), Terri Johnson (Brenda), Sandy Carey (Tammy), Starline Comb (Carral), Forman Shane (James), Christopher Geoffries (Chris), Marc Desmond (Bartender), Ric Lutze (Paul), Ron Darby (Fred) (as Mark Desmond)

Fugitive Girls (1974)

Directed by Stephen Apostolof (as A.C. Stephen); Screenplay: Stephen Apostolof (as A.C. Stephen), Edward D. Wood, Jr.; Produced by Stephen Apostolof (as A.C. Stephen); Associate Producer: S.B. Cooper; Editing: Louigi Rogatoni; Makeup: Gerald Sucie; Assistant Director: Edward D. Wood, Jr. (as Dick Trent); Props: Budd Costello; Sound: Dick Damon; Camera Operator: Robert Birchall; Script Supervisor: Marlene Buckalew; Animal Trainer: Karl Miller; Karate Supervisor: Jerry Morrey, Gaffer: Guy Nicholas, Produced by A.F.P.I. Productions, Apostolof Film Productions; Distributed by SCA Distributors, aka *Five Loose Women, Hot on the Trail, Women's Penitentiary VIII*, 92/84 minutes, color

    Cast: Jabie Abercrombe (Paula), Rene Bond (Toni), Talie Cochrane (Kat), Dona Desmond (Sheila), Margie Lanier (Dee), Forman Shain (Kyle), Nicole Riddell (Jan), Douglas Fray (Presser), Sunny Boyd (Tears), Gary Schneider (Bat), Flash Storm (Crack), Maria Arnold, Armando Federico, Janet Newell, Con Covert (Sunshine), Edward D. Wood, Jr. (Sheriff/"Pop")

The Cocktail Hostesses (1976)

    Directed by Stephen Apostolof (as A. C. Stephen); Screenplay: Stephen Apostolof (as A.C. Stephen), Edward D. Wood, Jr.; Produced by Stephen Apostolof (as A.C. Stephen); Camera Operator: R.C. Reuben; Music: J. Mendozoff; Distributed by SCA Distributors; Marden Films; Eurogroup, 80 minutes, color

    Cast: Rene Bond (Toni), Rick Cassidy), Starline Comb, Sandy Dempsey, Douglas Frey (Tom), Susan Gale, Lynn Harris, Kathy Hilton (Lorraine), Terri Johnson (Jackie), Jimmy Longdale, Ric Lutze, Duane Paulsen (Howard), Candy Samples, Forman Shane (Larry)

The Beach Bunnies (1976)

    Directed by Stephen Apostolof; Screenplay: Stephen Apostolof (as A.C. Stephen); Edward D. Wood, Jr.; Produced by Stephen Apostolof (as A.C. Stephen), S.B. Cooper; Art Direction: Bud Costello; Assistant Director: Harvey Shain; Sound Recordist: Dick Damon; Script Recorder: Meri McDonald; Camera Operator: R.C. Reuben; Produced by AF Productions; Distributed by Danton Films; SCA Distributors, aka *Red, Hot and Sexy, Sun Bunnies*, 90 minutes, color

    Cast: Brenda Fogarty (Elaine Street), Linda Gildersleeve (Sheila), Mariwin Roberts (Laurie), Wendy Cavanaugh (Bonnie), Harvey Shain (Chris), John Aquaboy (Dennis), Rick Cassidy (Dave), Con Covert (Bruce Collins), Correy Brandon (J.B.), Richard Parnes (Bellboy), Forman Shane (Chris), Stephen Apostolof (Piano Player, uncredited)

Hot Ice (1978)

    Directed by Stephen Apostolof; Screenplay: Stephen Apostolof, Edward D. Wood, Jr.; Produced by Stephen Apostolof (as A.C. Stephen); Assistant Director: Edward D. Wood, Jr.; Distributed by Frontier Amusements, 94 minutes, color

    Cast: Stephen Apostolof, Patti Kelly, Teresa Parker, Forman Shane, Max Thayer, Edward D. Wood, Jr.

Additional credits:

    Director: *Crossroads of Laredo* (new compilation, 1995, also performer); *Hellborn* (1993) (segments *Hellborn* and *Home Movie*, also performer, editor)

    Performer: *The Baron of Arizona* (1950); *Meatcleaver Massacre* (1977); *Mrs. Stone's Thing* (aka *Love Making USA*) (1978)

    Story, Characters: *For Love and Money* (1969) (story, as Edward Davis); *The Lawless Rider* (1954) (story, uncredited); *The Astounding She-Monster* (1957) (creative consultant, uncredited)

    Documentaries and Related films: *On the Trail of Ed Wood* (1990); *Flying Saucers Over Hollywood: The* Plan 9 *Companion* (1992); *Plan 69 from Outer Space* (1993) (1958 screenplay *Plan 9 from Outer Space*); *Hellborn* (1993) (segment *Hellborn*); *Ed Wood: Look Back in Angora* (1994); *Glen & Glenda* (1994) (1953 screenplay); *Take It Out in Trade: The Outtakes* (1995); *The Haunted World of Edward D. Wood Jr.* (1996); *Hollywood Rated "R"* (1997); *I Woke Up Early the Day I Died* (1998); *The Erotic World of A.C. Stephen* (1999); *Devil Girls* (1999); *The Interplanetary Surplus Male and Amazon Women of Outer Space* (2003); *Night of the Fools* (2003); *Vampira: The Movie* (2007)

Chapter Notes

Introduction

1. Doyle Greene, *Mexploitation Cinema: A Critical History of Mexican Vampire, Wrestler, Ape-Man and Similar Films, 1957–1977* (Jefferson, NC: McFarland, 2005), 15.
2. Jeffrey Sconce, "Trashing the Academy: Taste, Excess, and an Emerging Politics of Cinematic Style," *Screen* 36.4 (Winter 1995), 371–93.
3. Greene, 13.
4. Greene, 13.
5. Rudolph Grey, *Nightmare of Ecstasy: The Life and Art of Edward D. Wood, Jr.* (Los Angeles: Feral House, 1992), 16.
6. Mic Hunter, *Abused Boys: The Neglected Victims of Sexual Abuse* (Lexington, MA, Lexington Books, 1990), 17.
7. Grey, 16.

Chapter 1

1. Rudolph Grey, *Nightmare of Ecstasy: The Life and Art of Edward D. Wood, Jr.* (Los Angeles: Feral House, 1992), 20.
2. Grey, 17.
3. Tom Keene (real name: George Duryea) made a name for himself primarily in low-budget RKO Westerns produced during the early 1930s, and later in Westerns from Monogram and Republic Pictures in the 1940s. By the time he appeared in *Crossroad Avenger*, Keene was reduced to playing infrequent, small roles in the lowest-budget productions.
4. Like co-star Keene, Tom Tyler had made a name for himself as a Western star many years prior to his *Crossroad Avenger* appearance. Tyler came into his own in the mid–1920s in a highly popular series of silent Westerns. The advent of sound dented Tyler's charisma, due in no small part to a thick foreign accent, and the cowboy star took smaller character roles throughout the 1930s. Tyler had a brief career peak in 1941 when he played the lead in the popular Republic serial *Adventures of Captain Marvel*. Failing health robbed Tyler of further successes, and he made infrequent appearances until his death in 1954. In the Rudolph Grey book, Wood's compatriot, actor John Andrews, tells a story wherein Wood, driving drunk through Los Angeles on a December day in the early 1950s, accidentally "met" down-and-out screen legend Tyler when he ran over him with his car! Grey, 36.
5. Supporting actors Lyle Talbot, Kenne Duncan, Harvey Dunn, Don Nagel and Bud Osborne appeared in numerous later Wood projects; one might even consider them, as a group, Wood's recurring "ensemble." Several, interestingly, were former "stars" in the B-movie universe. Talbot was a prolific actor who appeared in nearly 300 films and television programs. He got his show biz start as a magician before turning to theater. Movie-wise he started in the silents, then moved effortlessly into "talkies" due to his deep, booming *basso* voice. Talbot co-founded the Screen Actors Guild and continued to thrive on television well into the 1980s. He would work for Wood several more times after *Crossroad Avenger*. Kenne Duncan appeared in innumerable B-Westerns for Republic and other independent studios in a prolific career which spanned five decades, and continued well into the television era. Duncan, who often played clever and charismatic villains, was the "heavy" in several Wood film projects. Duncan killed himself in 1972 after a long, losing battle with alcohol. Bud Osborne was yet another ubiquitous face in B-Westerns, in an amazing six decades career (almost 600 performances). He began his screen career as a stuntman, but his rough good looks soon led to acting roles. In addition to acting, the adept Osborne was often called upon to drive stagecoaches and wagons in films, a talent he picked up while working for "Wild West" shows as a youth. Little is known about character actor Harvey Dunn (sometimes billed as Harvey B. Dunne) other than the fact that his distinctive visage and eccentric persona graced many of Wood's films. Dunn worked as a supporting player in both B-movies and television series for a span of about a decade starting in the early 1950s. He died in 1968 of cirrhosis of the liver, yet another victim of Wood's muse, "the demon rum." Don Nagel was primarily a stunt man, but he did play supporting characters in over a dozen films and TV shows.
6. Grey, 199.
7. Grey, 204.
8. Edward D. Wood, Jr., *Hollywood Rat Race* (New York: Four Walls Eight Windows Press, 1998), 32.
9. Wood, *Hollywood Rat Race*. 83.
10. Wood, *Hollywood Rat Race*. 125.
11. Edward D. Wood, Jr., *Suburban Orgy* (Shreveport, LA: Ramble House Press, 2001), 157–63.
12. Wood, *Suburban Orgy*, 138–42.
13. Grey, 214.

Chapter 2

1. Richard W. Haines, *The Moviegoing Experience, 1968–2001* (Jefferson, NC: McFarland, 2003), 5.
2. Felicia Feaster and Bret Wood, *Forbidden Fruit: The*

Golden Age of the Exploitation Film (Baltimore, MD: Midnight Marquee, 1999), 24.

3. Rudolph Grey, *Nightmare of Ecstasy: The Life and Art of Edward D. Wood, Jr.* (Los Angeles: Feral House, 1992), 39.

4. available at: http://www.christinejorgensen.com/MainPages/Home.html, accessed on 5/21/08.

5. Judith Butler, *Gender Trouble: Feminism and the Subversion of Identity* (New York: Routledge, 2006), xxiii.

6. Frank J. Dello Stritto, "The Road to Las Vegas: Bela Lugosi in American Theatre," *Cult Movies* #11, 1994, 64.

7. Fred Olen Ray, "(Interview with) Edward D. Wood, Jr.," *Cult Movies* #11, 1994, 30.

8. Grey, 39.

9. Richard Bojarski, *The Films of Bela Lugosi* (Secaucus, NJ: Citadel Press, 1080), 231.

10. Grey, 32.

11. Butler, 186.

12. Butler, 187.

13. Carl G. Jung, *Aspects of the Feminine* (New York: MFJ Books, 1996), 50.

14. Butler, 8.

15. Butler, 14.

16. Butler, 189.

17. Butler, 191.

18. Carl G. Jung, *Aspects of the Masculine* (New York: MFJ Books, 1996), 163.

19. Butler, 192.

20. Jung, *Aspects of the Masculine*, 136.

21. Jung, *Aspects of the Masculine*, 85.

22. Butler, 146.

23. Jung, *Aspects of the Masculine*, 39.

24. Jung, *Aspects of the Feminine*, 110.

25. Jung, *Aspects of the Masculine*, 112.

26. "The male-female syzygy is only one among the possible pairs of opposites, albeit the most important one in practice and the commonest. It has numerous connections with other pairs which do not display any sex differences at all and can therefore be put into the sexual category only by main force. These connections, with their manifold shades of meaning, are found more particularly in Kundalini yoga, in Gnosticism, and above all in alchemical philosophy, quite apart from the spontaneous fantasy-products in neurotic and psychotic case material." Jung, *Aspects of the Masculine*, 120.

27. Jung, *Aspects of the Masculine*, 85.

28. Jung, *Aspects of the Masculine*, 150.

29. Jung, *Aspects of the Masculine*, 82.

30. Jung, *Aspects of the Feminine*, 12.

31. Jung, *Aspects of the Feminine*, 89.

32. Jung, *Aspects of the Masculine*, 6.

33. Jung, *Aspects of the Masculine*, 16.

34. Jung, *Aspects of the Masculine*, 150.

35. Jung, *Aspects of the Masculine*, 154.

36. Jung, *Aspects of the Feminine*, 33.

37. Roland Barthes, "Striptease," in *Mythologies* (New York: Hill and Wang, 1991), 100.

38. Jung, *Aspects of the Masculine*, 8.

39. Jung, *Aspects of the Feminine*, 10.

40. Jung, *Aspects of the Feminine*, 160.

41. Jung, *Aspects of the Masculine*, 23.

42. Jung, *Aspects of the Masculine*, 63.

43. Jung, *Aspects of the Masculine*, 115.

44. Jung, *Aspects of the Masculine*, 143.

45. Jung, *Aspects of the Masculine*, 138.

46. Jung, *Aspects of the Masculine*, 109.

47. Butler, 175.

48. Jung, *Aspects of the Feminine*, 12.

49. Jung, *Aspects of the Feminine*, 60.

50. Butler, 189.

51. Jung, *Aspects of the Masculine*, 143.

52. Butler, 153.

53. Jung, *Aspects of the Feminine*, 170.

54. "The purpose of the dialectical process is to bring these contents into the light: and only when this task has been completed, and the conscious mind has become sufficiently familiar with the unconscious processes reflected in the anima. will the anima be felt simply as a function." Jung, *Aspects of the Feminine*, 99.

55. Jung, *Aspects of the Masculine*, 47.

56. Jung, *Aspects of the Masculine*, 105.

57. Butler, 189.

58. Jung, *Aspects of the Masculine*, 86.

59. Jung, *Aspects of the Masculine*, 17.

60. Jung, *Aspects of the Feminine*, 136.

61. Jung, *Aspects of the Masculine*, 18.

62. Butler, 187.

63. Jung, *Aspects of the Feminine*, 113.

64. Jung, *Aspects of the Masculine*, 117.

65. Jung, *Aspects of the Masculine*, 144.

66. Butler, 187.

67. Jung, *Aspects of the Feminine*, 94.

68. Jung, *Aspects of the Masculine*, 150.

69. Jung, *Aspects of the Masculine*, 65.

70. Jung, *Aspects of the Masculine*, 69.

71. "Unfortunately our Western mind, lacking all culture in this respect, has never yet devised a concept nor even a name, for the *union of opposites through the middle path*, that most fundamental item of inward experience, which could respectably be set against the Chinese concept of Tao. It is at once the most individual fact and the most universal, the most legitimate fulfillment of the meaning if the individual's life." Jung, *Aspects of the Feminine*, 94.

72. Jung, *Aspects of the Masculine*, 20.

73. Jung, *Aspects of the Feminine*, 41.

74. Jung, *Aspects of the Masculine*, 141.

75. Frank Henenlotter, "Rudolph Grey on Ed Wood," *Cult Movies* #11, 1994, 74.

76. Feaster, 120.

77. Butler, 189.

Chapter 3

1. James George Frazier, *The New Golden Bough* (New York: New American Library, 1964), 384–403.

2. Frazier, 415.

3. The Texas-based White and Houck co-produced many popular Westerns starring B-level cowboy star "Lash" LaRue in the late 1940s and early 1950s. Houck, also known as Joy M. Houck, hailed from New Orleans and owned a chain of successful movie theaters throughout Louisiana, Mississippi and Arkansas. In the early 1950s, Houck and White formed a distribution company named Howco Productions which began by releasing their own Westerns. Soon, Howco veered off into the more lucrative field of exploitation films such as the aforementioned *Mesa of Lost Women*, a bizarre, cheaply made science-fiction thriller starring Jackie Coogan as a mad scientist who creates spider-women hybrids in his mountain laboratory. Howco changed its corporate banner in 1957 to Howco International and became a successful independent film producer and distributor through the mid–1970s, releasing popular drive-in double-bills such as *The Brain From Planet Arous* and *Teenage Monster* (1957) and *Carnival Rock* and *Teenage Thunder* (1958). One of Howco's last double-bills was *Night of Bloody Horror* and *Women and Bloody Terror* (1970), both directed by Houck's son, Joy N. Houck, Jr., "Joy Theatre," archived at: http://cinematreasures.org/theatre/6327, accessed 12/8/07.

4. Rudolph Grey. *Nightmare of Ecstasy: The Life and Art of Edward D. Wood, Jr.* (Los Angeles: Feral House, 1992), 50.

5. As was his wont, Wood hired for the key role of the wise elder a seasoned actor who had passed his glory days. Herbert Rawlinson had been a prolific actor for over 40 years, appearing in over 300 films, having made a name for himself as a dashing leading man in silent films starting in 1915. More recently, Rawlinson had amassed an impressive body of radio voice work. *Jail Bait* would prove to be Rawlinson's final film role, as he died the day after shooting ended. Grey, 48.

6. Vincent F. Hopper, Gerald B. Lahey, editors. *Medieval Mysteries, Moralities, and Interludes* (Great Neck, NY: Barron's Educational Series, 1962), 33.

7. Hopper, Lahey, 31.

8. David C. Hayes, *Muddled Mind: The Complete Works of Edward D. Wood, Jr.* (Shreveport, LA: Ramble House Press, 2001), 143.

9. Hopper, Lahey, 30.

10. Grey, 50.

11. According to Lyle Talbot, this scene was quickly shot, "on the fly" as was most of Wood's cinema, at a motel on Sunset Boulevard in Los Angeles, until the unaware motel manager happened on the scene and shooed the crew away. Grey, 48, 50.

12. Hayes, 142.

13. Hopper, Lahey, 32, 34.

14. Hayes, 112.

Chapter 4

1. Herbert Marcuse, *Eros and Civilization: A Philosophical Inquiry into Freud* (New York: Vintage Press, 1955), 74.

2. Starting perhaps with the notoriously nihilistic crime thriller *Kiss Me Deadly* (1955, d: Robert Aldrich), the Cold War thriller genre had its heyday in the late 1950s with films like *The World, the Flesh and the Devil* (1959, d: Ranald MacDougall) and *On the Beach* (1959, d: Stanley Kramer). The genre struggled to maintain a presence through the early 1960s, when real-life events such as the Cuban Missile Crisis brought the specter of atomic holocaust into the living room of every man, woman and child, a bone-chilling terror no movie could attempt to equal; the sole exception may be the stunning *The Manchurian Candidate* (1962, d: John Frankenheimer), a film so boldly paranoid and viciously cynical, it boggled the popular mind at the time. Perhaps not coincidentally, the genre had its final statement in the troubled year of 1964, with three big-budget productions glorifying and mocking the genre to a point of exhaustion. *Dr. Strangelove; or How I Stopped Worrying and Learned How to Love the Bomb* (1964, d: Stanley Kubrick), rushed into theatres a mere eight weeks after the assassination of President John F. Kennedy, tackled Armageddon and, most significantly, evil right-wing conspiracy inside the U.S. government, in a vicious satire ostensibly reactionary, yet ultimately fatalistic. In the paranoid *Seven Days in May* (1964, d: John Frankenheimer), which followed a few weeks later, a speculated-about plot to kill JFK was effectively turned into a fictional conspiracy to take over the U.S. government. Later in the year, very near the one-year anniversary of JFK's assassination, the disturbing *Fail-Safe* (1964, d: Sidney Lumet) fantasized darkly about a government, and its flunky, the Military-Industrial Complex, automated and soulless and out of control in a world gone wholly insane. Yet perhaps the most stunning and indelible Cold War thriller was none of these, but an all-out war of man against his neighbors, cleverly disguised as an epic slapstick farce. *It's a Mad Mad Mad Mad World* (1963, d: Stanley Kramer), released a mere two weeks *before* JFK's murder, brilliantly reduced the Cold War thriller formula to its barbaric, comical essence, simultaneously punctuating and making obsolete a genre which had heretofore conceived of the bad guys as being "out there." *It's a Mad Mad Mad Mad World*'s gleeful cross-country apocalypse, wherein ordinary citizens were pitted against each other in a literal fight to the death over Big Money (read: Capitalism), was an eerie foreshadowing of an era of optimism about to end. Followed immediately by the barbaric crime of November 22, 1963, it signaled the end of the innocent notion of "us against them," as U.S. and world citizens came to realize with a shock that their real enemy was within the gates.

3. Rudolph Grey, *Nightmare of Ecstasy: The Life and Art of Edward D. Wood, Jr.* (Los Angeles: Feral House, 1992), 66.

4. Oscar Budel, "Contemporary Theater and Aesthetic Distance," in *Brecht: A Collection of Critical Essays* (Englewood Cliffs, NJ: Prentice-Hall, 1962), 59–85.

5. Much has been made about the apocryphal story that Wood and some of his cronies actually stole this movie prop, used previously in the John Wayne adventure film *Wake of the Red Witch* (1948), from the Republic Studios lot in the dead of night. Some parties insist the daring and highly symbolic theft occurred, which would make the prop's appearance and significance in *Bride of the Monster* all the more noteworthy; others maintain that Wood legally rented the prop and invented the robbery yarn later as one of the many "tall tales" he liked to tell friends and acquaintances. The truth likely remaining unknown, the legend of this prop, and which story is real or unreal, underscores perfectly Wood's intention to undermine cinema reality by undermining cinema history. Wood knew that making a film is, essentially, creating a historical event which will last into the future, so the history of that event is as important as the "product" itself. In the case of a movie, the product is the evidence of its history, of its genesis. An old movie is, at root, the best example of "living history," and Wood knew how to augment his creations' history admirably.

6. In true Brechtean form, Wood here has helpfully shown the audience his agenda by contrasting two versions of the same object (the octopus) and saying, "This one is *real*, and this one is *unreal*; please take care to note the difference." Wood is defining here the difference between representational and non-representational art, or theater, in a way that almost anyone could understand. These two diametrically opposed incarnations of the title monster could additionally be seen as yet another, quite abstract, example of *Bride of the Monster*'s recurring binary of passive vs. aggressive personalities, of "master" and "slave." Certainly the menacing "real" octopus is the "master" of the fictional construct dubbed "the Monster," whereas the dopey-looking "fake" prop is the "slave" to that notion. Furthermore, the "real" octopus, gifted with ambulatory movement, could not be more "aggressive," while the listless rubber "fake" is the very embodiment of "passivity."

7. Georg Wilhelm Friedrich Hegel, *Phenomenology of the Spirit* (New York: Harper & Row, 1967), 186.

8. The winsome water nymph, leaning over a body of water to test or protect its purity, was successfully incorporated into a familiar trademark for a beverage company in the late 1800s, inspired by a provocative painting of the goddess by Paul Thurman, which was to become the iconic "White Rock Girl." Archived at http://www.whiterocking.com/pcw.html, accessed: 1/3/08.

9. According to Dolores Fuller, Wood had originally intended her to be the *Bride of the Monster* lead, but relegated her to this perfunctory cameo after actress Loretta King

approached Wood with significant financing for the picture, under the condition that *she* be the star. Yet King refuted this claim categorically, so the truth remains, like so much of Wood mythos, unknown and perhaps unknowable. If the story is at least partially true, one can blame Wood for the cruel move towards his lover and muse, but can also understand the brutal necessity of accepting money from any and all sources in the desperate world of independent low-budget filmmaking. Regardless, the event did apparently accelerate the breakup of Wood and Fuller, which occurred shortly after, and the tension in the scene between Fuller and King may reflect harsh betrayal by Wood towards his loyal partner. Grey, 67, 68.

10. Barring some unrevealed personal prejudice, the reasons for Wood's disdain of Strasberg's "method" acting, in which repetitive practice of a part theoretically led to an actor's embodying his character, resulting in a realism which is in stark contrast to the dramatic theatrics of the day, may be clear in that they surely clashed with the melodramatic histrionics which Wood preferred. Truth be told, however, Wood's blasé directorial style, which purportedly left the actors to their own devices in developing character, combined with Wood's rushed, single-take approach to filming, could not be farther from Strasberg's patient, well-rehearsed and thoughtful approach to character development in stage acting. Grey, 55.

11. Marcuse, 216.

12. This infamous line, which has been distorted beyond recognition due to one misinterpreted screening, remains clear as a bell in the extant VHS and DVD releases. In Harry and Michael Medved's judgmental tome on obscure films, *The Golden Turkey Awards*, they proudly boasted that Lugosi states in this scene, "Don't be afraid of Lobo, he's harmless as *kitchen*!" (255). This wildly inaccurate claim, based likely on one viewing of the film in a theater setting with inferior sound quality, quickly became urban legend, as very few people at that time had access to the film in any format. Perhaps the Medveds, not caring one whit for accuracy, thought Lugosi used the word "kitchen" and didn't bother to confirm it by multiple viewings, or perhaps they were mesmerized by the giant refrigerator which stands behind Lugosi during this scene. When *Bride of the Monster* was released on home video, any interested viewer could hear that the line was spoken correctly. However, the cult of Ed Wood as "the worst director of all time" was already in full swing, and many people, including those with good intentions, bought into this myth and helped perpetuate it. This supposed gaffe was even embraced by a befuddled, elder Wood who, having likely not seen the film in years, told in an interview conducted mere months before his 1978 death a confusing anecdote about the line, which appeared without footnote in Rudolph Grey's *Nightmare of Ecstasy*. Grey, 63, 66.

13. Curt Pardee, personal correspondence, 9/10/08.

14. According to Wood, Lugosi was immensely proud of this speech, and in fact offered passersby on the corner of Hollywood Boulevard and Vine Street an impromptu performance of it shortly after shooting finished. Grey, 70.

15. Hegel, 187.

16. Marcuse, 11.

17. Marcuse, 203.

18. Hegel, 190.

19. Wood claimed that Lugosi did get into the freezing water to wrestle with the rubber octopus, but a viewing of the scene contradicts this fanciful claim. Grey, 67.

20. According to screenwriter Dennis Rodriguez, entrepreneur Donald McCoy, who financed much of *Bride of the Monster*, had two conditions attached to his financial contribution. Firstly, his son Tony would star in the film. Secondly, the film must end with an atomic explosion!

Whether McCoy was a closet nihilist, or had his tongue firmly in cheek with this bizarre request, cannot be known, but as Wood was a genius in incorporating disparate stock footage seamlessly into his bizarre patchwork scenarios, the result in this case was nothing short of extraordinary. Grey, 69–70.

21. The distributor listed at the end of *Bride*, Filmakers Releasing Organization (sic), was likely Arkoff's corporate name at the time. Filmakers Releasing Organization became American Releasing Corporation, which then became the legendary American International Pictures.

Chapter 5

1. David C. Hayes, *Muddled Mind: The Complete Works of Edward D. Wood, Jr.* (Shreveport, LA: Ramble House Press, 2001), 17.

2. Fred Olen Ray. "Edward D. Wood, Jr.," *Cult Movies* #11, 1994, 32.

3. Hayes, 17.

4. Rudolph Grey. *Nightmare of Ecstasy: The Life and Art of Edward D. Wood, Jr.* (Los Angeles: Feral House, 1992), 202.

5. Walter H. Sokel, "Brecht's Split Characters and His Sense of the Tragic," in *Brecht: A Collection of Critical Essays* (Englewood Cliffs, NJ: Prentice-Hall, 1962), 127.

6. Sokel, 136.

7. Sokel, 128.

8. Sokel, 129.

9. Charlotte Austin, an impressive actress who had several brushes with Hollywood fame, gives her role an authority which belies the film's preposterous premise and threadbare *mise-en-scène*. Specifically, her ability to connote thwarted, barely contained lust is positively brilliant.

10. Carol J. Adams, "Woman-Battering and Harm to Animals," *Animals & Women: Feminist Theoretical Explorations* (Durham: Duke University Press, 1995), 56.

11. Adams, 57.

12. Adams, 58.

13. Adams, 59.

14. In 1952, hypnotist Morey Bernstein claimed that he was able to "regress" a subject, Virginia Tighe, to reveal an alleged past life in which she was "Bridey Murphy," a young Irish woman of the 19th century. According to Bernstein, Tighe-as-"Murphy" was able to recall significant historical details of the period. Bernstein published his accounting of this unusual experiment in the 1956 book *The Search for Bridey Murphy*, which became an instant bestseller and started a controversial, if short-lived obsession with hypnotic regression. See Paul Edwards, *Reincarnation: A Critical Examination* (Amherst, NY: Prometheus Books, 1996), 72–74.

15. Marti Kheel, "License to Kill: An Ecofeminist Critique of Hunters' Discourse," in *Animals & Women: Feminist Theoretical Explorations,* 110.

16. Kheel, 106.

17. Kheel, 87, 93, 96–97.

18. Adams, 68.

19. Allen Edwardes and R.E.L. Masters, *The Cradle of Erotica* (New York: Lancer, 1962), 31.

20. Edwardes, 32–33.

21. Adams, 80.

22. Kheel, 89.

23. Adams, 79.

24. Adams, 80.

Chapter 6

1. Harry and Michael Medved, *The Golden Turkey Awards: The Worst Achievements in Hollywood History* (New York: Berkley Books, 1981), 252–61.

2. Medved, 308–16.

3. According to Gregory Walcott, producer J. Edward Reynolds took the workprint of *Plan 9* to New York City to seek distribution, but there were no takers, so he returned to California and made a deal with Hal Roach's tiny releasing arm, Distributors Corporation of America. Perhaps as few as 15 release prints were struck, so it appears that *Plan 9* was barely released theatrically. Gregory Walcott interview in the home video documentary *Flying Saucers Over Hollywood: The* Plan 9 *Companion* (Atomic Pictures, 1991).

4. Martin Esslin, *The Theatre of the Absurd, 3rd Edition* (New York: Penguin Books, 1985), 328.

5. Esslin, 416.

6. Esslin, 425–26.

7. Hal Erickson, *Syndicated Television: The First Forty Years, 1947–1987* (Jefferson, NC: McFarland, 1989), 80–83.

8. Various interviews in *Flying Saucers Over Hollywood: The* Plan 9 *Companion.*

9. Vincent F. Hopper, Gerald B. Lahey, editors, *Medieval Mysteries, Moralities, and Interludes* (Great Neck, NY: Barron's Educational Series, 1962), 6.

10. Hopper, Lahey, 1.

11. Hopper, Lahey, 9.

12. Hopper, Lahey, 48.

13. Martin E. Browne, editor, *Religious Drama 2: Mystery and Morality Plays* (Gloucester, MA: Peter Smith, 1977), 267.

14. Criswell, "Criswell Predicts on Outer Space." *Spaceway Science Fiction*, February 1954, 2.

15. The thunder-and-lightning cuts in *Plan 9* were all duly noted in Wood's original screenplay, with the note "Shock value cut" illustrating that Wood was well aware of their intrinsic narrative value. Edward D. Wood, Jr., Plan 9 from Outer Space: *The Original Uncensored and Uncut Screenplay* (Newbury Park CA: Malibu Graphics, 1990), 4.

16. According to Wood, the actual graveyard seen in *Plan 9* was an old Mexican one in Sacramento, in the process of being torn up and relocated. Ed Wood interview, *Nightmare of Ecstasy: The Life and Art of Edward D. Wood, Jr.,* 78.

17. Lyn Lemon interview, *Nightmare of Ecstasy,* 76.

18. Maila Nurmi interview, *Nightmare of Ecstasy,* 81.

19. Paul Marco interview, *Nightmare of Ecstasy,* 76.

20. Brad Linaweaver interview, *Flying Saucers Over Hollywood: The* Plan 9 *Companion.*

21. Paul Marco interview, *Nightmare of Ecstasy,* 76.

22. Kathy Wood interview, *Nightmare of Ecstasy,* 75.

23. Kathy Wood interview, *Nightmare of Ecstasy,* 85.

24. Robert R. Rees, "The Vampira Chronicles." *Cult Movies* #11, 1994, 35–36.

25. Maila Nurmi interview, *Vampira: The Movie,* Alpha New Cinema (DVD), 2007.

26. According to Maila Nurmi, Lugosi and Wood were watching Vampira introduce *White Zombie* one evening in 1954, and Lugosi commented, "I'd like to work with her." Nurmi interview in *Flying Saucers Over Hollywood: The* Plan 9 *Companion.*

27. David Skal interview, *Vampira: The Movie.*

28. Wood's initial description of the Vampire Girl in his screenplay is quite different from what eventually appeared on-screen: "The brush parts to reveal a hideous head of a once beautiful girl. The blonde hair straggling, teeth bared over bright red lips. One eye closed and scarred, the other wide and bright red with lust." Wood, Plan 9 from Outer Space: *The Original Uncensored and Uncut Screenplay.* 4.

29. Paul Marco interview, *Flying Saucers Over Hollywood: The Plan 9 Companion.*

30. Legendary genre film historian Forrest J Ackerman owns the cape used by Lugosi in *Plan 9*, which he claims was the cape originally worn by Lugosi in a 1932 stage production of *Dracula*, so it is in a very real sense the *original* Dracula who prowls the outdoor cemetery in *Plan 9*, raising his caped arms to the heavens. Ackerman interview, *Flying Saucers Over Hollywood: The* Plan 9 *Companion.*

31. James George Frazier. *The New Golden Bough* (New York: New American Library, 1964), 301.

32. Eugene Ionesco, as quoted in Esslin. 191.

33. In the original screenplay, the UFO is first noted thus: "A cigar-shaped light flashes across the sky." Wood, Plan 9 from Outer Space: *The Original Uncensored and Uncut Screenplay.* 5.

34. According to producer David Friedman, Don Davis played the drunk in the alley in this amazing montage sequence (and, ironically, later "drank himself to death"). Even more surprising is the claim that Davis also edited *Plan 9*, a statement which remains unverified. Friedman interview, *Nightmare of Ecstasy,* 85.

35. Both the interior sets and the miniatures sequences of the alien craft accurately reflect the somewhat minimalist ambience of science-fiction television programming (SF was a popular genre in the medium's early days). Specifically, *Plan 9*'s sets and costuming share a stagey, theatrical ambience with lower-budgeted TV series of the time period such as the Dumont network's popular *Captain Video* (1949–1957) and the syndicated series *Captain Z-Ro* (1955). David Weinstein, *The Forgotten Network: Dumont and the Birth of American Television* (Philadelphia: Temple University Press, 2004), 70.

36. Various interviews. *Nightmare of Ecstasy,* 76–81.

37. It might be rewarding to consider the numerological significance of Wood's choice of the number "9" for his iconic spiritual-alien intervention, as many mythologies consider "9" a sacred number in the delineation of creation, history and prophecy. Mesoamerican mythology speaks of Nine Underworlds which represent strictly hierarchical creation cycles, while Norse mythology claims that the universe consists of nine concentric worlds; Hopi Indian tradition also relegates the extant cosmos to Nine Worlds. This recurring chimerical motif was captured in literature by Dante Alighieri in *Divine Comedy*, the epic poem wherein the author traverses the nine circles of the Judeo-Christian Hell; the number "9" may thus have had an especial spiritual resonance which Wood, wittingly or unwittingly, tapped into. Carl Johan Calleman, "The Nine Underworlds," *The Mystery of 2012: Reflections, Prophecies & Possibilities* (Boulder, CO: Sounds True, 2007), 81–83.

38. Harry Thomas interview, *Flying Saucers Over Hollywood: The* Plan 9 *Companion.*

39. Gregory Walcott interview, *Flying Saucers Over Hollywood: The* Plan 9 *Companion.*

40. Makeup man Harry Thomas asked *not* to be listed in *Plan 9*'s credits because Wood wouldn't implement any of his imaginative suggestions for making the aliens look "alien." According to Thomas, Wood's stock answer was, "We don't have time." Thomas interview, *Nightmare of Ecstasy,* 84.

41. Esslin, 410.

42. Kathy Wood interview, *Nightmare of Ecstasy,* 80–81.

43. Dudley Manlove interview, *Nightmare of Ecstasy,* 80.

44. Phil Cambridge interview, *Nightmare of Ecstasy,* 86.

45. Ernest Becker, *Escape from Evil* (New York: Free Press, 1975), 77.

46. Browne, 304.

47. Frazier, 305–06.

48. Bob Burns interview, *Nightmare of Ecstasy*, 85.

49. Randall M. White. *Castle of Doom* (circa 1933), soundtrack of the English-language version of *Vampyr* (1932, d: Carl Dreyer). Sinister Cinema VHS release.

50. "*Plan 9* is an hour and a half magic act, and there was nothing up Ed Wood's sleeve." Brad Linaweaver interview, *Flying Saucers Over Hollywood: The* Plan 9 *Companion*.

51. Esslin, 424.

52. In *Nightmare of Ecstasy*, Phil Cambridge quotes Ed Wood: "If you want to know me, see *Glen or Glenda?*, that's me, that's my story. No question. But *Plan 9 from Outer Space* is my pride and joy…" Cambridge interview, *Nightmare of Ecstasy*, 86.

Chapter 7

1. Martin Esslin, *The Theatre of the Absurd, 3rd Edition* (New York: Penguin Books, 1985), 76.

2. Conrad Brooks, "Criswell Predicts," *Cult Movies* #11, 1994, 37.

3. Criswell, *Your Next Ten Years* (Anderson, SC: Droke House, 1969), 105.

4. Rudolph Grey. *Nightmare of Ecstasy: The Life and Art of Edward D. Wood, Jr.* (Los Angeles: Feral House, 1992), 207, 216.

5. Paul Marco interview. Tom Weaver, *Interviews with B Science Fiction and Horror Movie Makers* (Jefferson, NC: McFarland, 1988), 257.

6. I. Fradkin, "On the Artistic Originality of Bertolt Brecht's Drama," in *Brecht: A Collection of Critical Essays* (Englewood Cliffs: Prentice-Hall, 1962), 107.

7. Buddy Barnett and Michael Copner, "Valda Hansen: Farewell to the White Ghost," *Cult Movies* #11, 1994, 54–55.

8. Valda Hansen interview, *Nightmare of Ecstasy*, 1992, 90.

9. Don Fellman interview. *Nightmare of Ecstasy*, 126.

10. Edward D. Wood, Jr., *Hollywood Rat Race* (New York: Four Walls Eight Windows Press, 1998), 104.

11. Esslin, 76.

12. Edward D. Wood, Jr., "The Final Curtain," in *The Horrors of Sex* (Shreveport, LA: Ramble House Press, 2001), 13.

13. Wood, "The Final Curtain," 13.

14. Wood, "The Final Curtain," 15.

15. Wood, "The Final Curtain," 16.

16. Wood, "The Final Curtain," 16.

17. Wood, "The Final Curtain," 17.

18. Wood, "The Final Curtain," 18.

19. Wood, "The Final Curtain," 18.

20. *The Holy Bible*, revised standard version (New York: Thomas Nelson and Sons, 1946), 1 Corinthians 15, 51–52.

21. Valda Hansen interview, Buddy Barnett and Michael Copner, "Valda Hansen: Farewell to the White Ghost," *Cult Movies* #11, 1994, 55.

22. Esslin, 61.

23. Esslin, 84.

24. Esslin, 45.

25. Esslin, 88.

26. Paul Marco interview, *Nightmare of Ecstasy*, 94.

27. Maila Nurmi interview, *Vampira: The Movie*, Alpha New Cinema (DVD), 2007.

28. Valda Hansen interview, *Nightmare of Ecstasy*, 92.

Chapter 8

1. Rudolph Grey, *Nightmare of Ecstasy: The Life and Art of Edward D. Wood, Jr.* (Los Angeles: Feral House, 1992), 207.

2. Grey, 207.

3. Andrea Dworkin, *Pornography: Men Possessing Women* (New York: E.P. Dutton, 1989), 24.

4. Dworkin, xxxviii.

5. Dworkin, 15.

6. Dworkin, 53.

7. Dworkin, 53.

8. Dworkin, 15.

9. Grey, 207.

10. Conrad Brooks interview, *Nightmare of Ecstasy*, 97.

11. According to Roy Reid, Jean Fontaine had a nightclub act in Los Angeles, and used her own wardrobe for *The Sinister Urge*. Reid interview, *Nightmare of Ecstasy*. 98.

12. Dworkin, 64.

13. Dworkin, 55.

14. Dworkin, 29.

15. Dworkin, 138.

16. Dworkin, 138.

17. Dworkin, 53.

18. Dworkin, 56.

19. Dworkin, 29.

20. Dworkin, 47.

21. Dworkin, 85.

22. Dworkin, 201.

23. Dworkin, 27.

24. Dworkin, 200.

25. Grey, 98, 99, 100.

26. Reid, interview. *Nightmare of Ecstasy*, 97.

Chapter 9

1. Barbara G. Walker, *The Crone: Woman of Age, Wisdom, and Power* (San Francisco: HarperCollins, 1985), 80.

2. Pat Barringer was supposedly "discovered" by filmmaker William Rotsler after he perused *Orgy of the Dead* publicity material and subsequently appeared in several Rotsler films (as Pat Barrington), including *The Agony of Love* (1966). Barringer was prolific in men's magazine pictorials as well, often under her real name, but also as Vivian Greg(g) and Yajah. Barringer was also a headline dancer at the Colony Club in Gardena, California.

3. The dazzling Fawn Silver (aka Fawn Silverton) had an all-too-brief career as a leading lady in low-budget films; her two "biggest" films are probably *Terror in the Jungle* (1968) and *Legend of Horror* (1972).

4. Walker, 21.

5. Walker, 74.

6. Walker, 174.

7. Walker, 80.

8. Walker, 14.

9. Walker, 29.

10. Walker, 79.

11. Walker, 79.

12. Walker, 26.

13. Walker, 49.

14. Bunny Glaser also performed in Stephen Apostolof's *The Bachelor's Dreams* (1967).

15. Coleen O'Brien was a dancer and model who sometimes appeared in men's magazine pictorials as Colleen Murphy; she also appeared in *Mondo Freudo* (1966) and *The Bachelor's Dreams* (1967).

16. Walker, 100.

17. Walker, 100.

18. Texas Starr is the stage name of Lorali Hart, who became famous as a "mature" porn star in the 1980s and 1990s, and also made brief appearances in the *Naked Gun* film series.

19. Nadejda Dobrev has had a long career in stage, film and television, and is still working today.

20. Andrea Dworkin, *Pornography: Men Possessing Women* (New York: E.P. Dutton, 1989), 92.

21. Dworkin, 100.

22. Very little is known about Stephanie Jones; *Orgy of the Dead* appears to have been her only film. It is likely that she also worked as a nude model.

23. Mickey Jines was a favorite model with figure photographers; her pictorial career spanned the entire 1960s. Jines starred in a few other exploitation films, the most notable being *Secret Sex Lives of Romeo and Juliet* (1969).

24. Walker, 57.

25. Walker, 60.

26. James George Frazer, *The New Golden Bough* (New York: New American Library, 1964), 37.

27. Dworkin, 56.

28. Walker, 49.

29. Barbara Nordin was a popular dancer at the Lakewood Club, a Los Angeles night spot; she appeared in a few other exploitation films, including *Maidens of Fetish Street* (1966) and *My Tale Is Hot* (1964). She also did her share of pictorials in men's magazines.

30. Dene Starnes appeared in many men's magazines pictorials and nudist magazines (one of which claims a relative of hers founded a nudist club).

31. Rene de Beau appeared in men's magazine pictorials under her own name and also as Dorinda Davis and Liz Trainor (the latter due to her resemblance to "Liz" Taylor).

32. According to Rudolph Grey, the eclectic but stultifying music score is by an uncredited Jaime Mendoza-Nava. Grey, *Nightmare of Ecstasy: The Life and Art of Edward D. Wood, Jr.* (Los Angeles: Feral House, 1992), 209.

33. Frazer, 654.

34. Edward D. Wood, Jr., *Suburban Orgy* (Shreveport, LA: Ramble House Press, 2001), 122.

35. Wood, *Suburban Orgy,* 183.

36. Wood, *Suburban Orgy,* 148.

37. Wood, *Suburban Orgy,* 155.

38. Wood, *Suburban Orgy,* 155.

39. Wood, *Suburban Orgy,* 200.

40. Grey, 209.

41. Grey, 129.

42. Grey, 129.

Chapter 10

1. David C. Hayes, *Muddled Mind: The Complete Works of Edward D. Wood, Jr.* (Shreveport, LA: Ramble House Press, 2001), 144.

2. Edward D. Wood, Jr., *Wood on Screen* (Shreveport LA: Woodpile Press, 2007), 202.

3. Wood, *Wood on Screen,* 145.

4. Wood, *Wood on Screen,* 146.

5. Wood, *Wood on Screen,* 221–22.

6. Wood, *Wood on Screen,* 117.

7. Wood, *Wood on Screen,* 199.

8. Ted Gorley interview, *Nightmare of Ecstasy: The Life and Art of Edward D. Wood, Jr.* (Los Angeles: Feral House, 1992), 133.

9. Robert R. Rees, "The Vampira Chronicles," *Cult Movies* #11, 1994, 36.

10. Herbert Marcuse, *Eros and Civilization: A Philosophical Inquiry into Freud* (New York: Vintage Press, 1955), 21.

11. John d'Addario, DVD liner notes, *Necromania*. (Fleshbot Films, 2004), 6.

12. Marcuse, 27.

13. Charles Anderson interview, *Nightmare of Ecstasy,* 133.

14. Anderson interview, *Nightmare of Ecstasy*. 133.

15. Rudolph Grey, *Nightmare of Ecstasy,* 137.

16. Wood, *Wood on Screen,* 129.

17. Wood, *Wood on Screen,* 192.

18. Wood, *Wood on Screen,* 149.

19. Wood, *Wood on Screen,* 177.

20. Wood, *Wood on Screen,* 211.

21. Wood, *Wood on Screen,* 222.

22. Wood, *Wood on Screen,* 223.

Chapter 11

1. An interesting discussion of the "Pete LaRoche mystery" can be found online at "The Hunt for Edward D. Wood, Jr.": http: www.edwoodonline.com/thehunt/apocrypha.html. Accessed on 6/7/08.

2. Email message from Heather Tanchuck, available at http://www.angelfire.com/ca3/jerrywarren/edwood.html. Accessed on 5/10/08.

3. Ray, 32.

4. William Schallert, instantly familiar to Baby Boomers as Patty Lane's father on the popular television series *The Patty Duke Show*, plays the corrupt preacher in an effective comic turn which is a refreshing departure from his mostly villainous character roles throughout the 1950s. Ultimately, Schallert's preacher is a villain of sorts as well, as an exiled carnival worker and petty thug, not to mention a bogus "man of the cloth."

5. Rudolph Grey, *Nightmare of Ecstasy: The Life and Art of Edward D. Wood, Jr.* (Los Angeles: Feral House, 1992), 7.

6. Edward D. Wood, Jr., *Hollywood Rat Race* (New York: Four Walls Eight Windows, 1998), 138.

7. Nona Carver interview, Grey. 131–32.

8. Grey, 211.

9. Ray, 32.

10. According to Philip R. Frey, Wood's *Venus Flytrap* screenplay was "apparently" written in the 1950s. While Frey offers no source to verify this claim, if true, it goes some way in explaining the film's overarching melodramatics and stock 1950s "evil scientist" motif. It would also make the similarities to Roger Corman's 1960 *The Little Shop of Horrors* all the more remarkable, unless these scenes were added by Wood (or others) later. Available at "The Hunt for Edward D. Wood, Jr.," http://edwoodonline.com/thehunt/VENUS.html, accessed on 7/28/08.

11. Judging from some landmarks seen in the film, it would appear that this footage was shot in or around Hakone National Park, a popular vacation destination lying at the foot of Mt. Fuji.

12. Assuming he penned this portion of the script, Wood certainly knew his botany: There *is* an underwater plant, known as the *Aldrovanda vesiculosa* or "Waterwheel," which shares many properties with the Venus's-flytrap, looks much like the rubber prop used in the film, and flourishes off the coastal waters of Japan.

13. A typical example occurs in Wood's novel *The Only House*: "[A]nd you can only get stinkin' kids from a stinkin' cock." Edward D. Wood, Jr., *Wood On Screen* (Shreveport, LA: Woodpile Press, 2007), 195.

14. "Apes" was apparently one of Wood's favorite derogatory terms for youth, as witness this passage in *The Only House*, Wood's novelization of *Necromania*: "And she was knocked up ... pregnant ... with child ... going to lay another house ape, screaming brat, fuck-head, stinking ass kid on the doorstep of the world." Wood, *Wood On Screen,* 192.

15. Frank Henenlotter, "Rudolph Grey on Ed Wood," *Cult Movies* #11, 1994, 77.

16. Wood's third role in *Fugitive Girls* is a brief, faceless cameo at the film's start, wherein he stands over the comatose body of the protagonist, Paula, and shouts, "The guy

in there is bleeding to death. Somebody call an ambulance!" The viewer never sees Wood, as he is shot from the waist down, but the voice is clearly his.

Chapter 12

1. Edward D. Wood, Jr., *Hollywood Rat Race* (New York: Four Walls Eight Windows, 1998), 117.

2. Martin Esslin, *The Theatre of the Absurd, 3rd Edition* (New York: Penguin Books, 1985), 411.

3. Esslin, 427.

4. Rudolph Grey. *Nightmare of Ecstasy: The Life and Art of Edward D. Wood, Jr.* (Los Angeles: Feral House, 1992), 160.

5. Maila Nurmi interview, *Flying Saucers Over Hollywood: The* Plan 9 *Companion.*

6. Kalynn Campbell, personal correspondence, 8/25/08.

Bibliography

Adams, Carol J. "Woman-Battering and Harm to Animals." In *Animals & Women: Feminist Theoretical Explorations*. Edited by Carol J. Adams and Josephine Donovan. Durham: Duke University Press, 1995.

Adorno, Theodor. *The Culture Industry*. London: Routledge, 1999.

Arnason, H.H., Marla F. Prather and Daniel Wheeler. *History of Modern Art*, 4th Ed. New York: Harry N. Abrams, 1998.

Barthes, Roland. "Strip Tease." *Mythologies*. trans: Annette Lavers. New York: Hill and Wang, 1991.

Becker, Ernest. *Escape from Evil*. New York: Free Press, 1975.

Bojarski, Richard. *The Films of Bela Lugosi*. Secaucus, NJ: Citadel Press, 1980.

Browne, E. Martin, editor. *Religious Drama 2: Mystery and Morality Plays*. Gloucester, MA: Peter Smith, 1977.

Büdel, Oscar. "Contemporary Theater and Aesthetic Distance," in *Brecht: A Collection of Critical Essays*, edited by Peter Demetz. Englewood Cliffs, NJ: Prentice-Hall, 1962.

Bürger, Peter. *Theory of the Avant-Garde*, trans. Michael Shaw. Minneapolis: University of Minnesota Press, 2002.

Burton, Richard F., trans. *The Book of the Thousand Nights and a Night*. London: Burton Club, 1885–1888.

Butler, Judith. *Gender Trouble*, 2d Edition. New York: Routledge, 1990.

Calleman, Carl Johan. "The Nine Underworlds," in *The Mystery of 2012: Reflections, Prophecies & Possibilities*. Boulder, CO: Sounds True, 2007.

Criswell. *Your Next Ten Years*. Anderson, SC: Droke House, 1969.

Dello Stritto, Frank J. "The Road to Las Vegas: Bela Lugosi in American Theatre," *Cult Movies* #11, 1994.

_____, and Andi Brooks. *Vampire Over London: Bela Lugosi in Britain*. Los Angeles: Cult Movies Press, 2000.

Dworkin, Andrea. *Pornography: Men Possessing Women*. New York: E.P. Dutton, 1989.

Edwardes, Allen, and R.E.L. Masters. *The Cradle of Erotica*. New York: Lancer, 1962.

Erickson, Hal. *Syndicated Television: The First Forty Years, 1947–1987*. Jefferson, NC: McFarland, 1989.

Esslin, Martin. *The Theatre of the Absurd,* 3rd Edition New York: Penguin Books, 1985.

Feaster, Felicia, and Bret Wood. *Forbidden Fruit: The Golden Age of the Exploitation Film*. Baltimore, MD: Midnight Marquee, 1999.

Frazer, James George. *The New Golden Bough*. Edited by Dr. Theodor H. Gaster. New York: New American Library, 1964.

Greene, Doyle. *Mexploitation Cinema: A Critical History of Mexican Vampire, Wrestler, Ape-Man and Similar Films, 1957–1977*. Jefferson, NC: McFarland, 2005.

_____. *Politics and the American Television Comedy: A Critical Survey from* I Love Lucy *Through* South Park Jefferson, NC: McFarland, 2008.

Grey, Rudolph. *Nightmare of Ecstasy: The Life and Art of Edward D. Wood, Jr.* Los Angeles: Feral House, 1992.

Haines, Richard W. *The Moviegoing Experience, 1968– 2001*. Jefferson, NC: McFarland, 2003.

Hayes, David C. *Muddled Mind: The Complete Works of Edward D. Wood, Jr.* Shreveport, LA: Ramble House Press, 2001.

Heffernan, Kevin. *Ghouls, Gimmicks, and Gold: Horror Films and the American Movie Business, 1953–1968*. Durham, NC: Duke University Press, 2004.

Henenlotter, Frank. "Rudolph Grey on Ed Wood." *Cult Movies* #11, 1994.

Hopper, Vincent F., and Gerald B. Lahey, editors. *Medieval Mysteries, Moralities, and Interludes*. Great Neck, NY: Barron's Educational Series, 1962.

Hunter, Mic. *Abused Boys: The Neglected Victims of Sexual Abuse*. Lexington, MA, Lexington Books, 1990.

Jameson, Fredric. *Postmodernism, or the Cultural Logic of Late Capitalism*. Durham: Duke University Press, 1999.

Jung, Carl G. *Aspects of the Masculine/Aspects of the Feminine,* translated by R.F.C. Hull. New York: MJF Books, 1989.

Kheel, Marti. "License to Kill: An Ecofeminist Critique of Hunters' Discourse," in *Animals & Women: Feminist Theoretical Explorations,* edited by Carol J. Adams & Josephine Donovan. Durham: Duke University Press, 1995.

Kuenzli, Rudolf, ed. *Dada and Surrealist Films*. New York: Willis, Locker & Owens, 1987.

299

Mantegazza, Paolo. *L'Amour dans l'Humanité*. Paris: n.p., 1886.

Marcuse, Herbert. *Eros and Civilization: A Philosophical Inquiry into Freud*. New York: Vintage Press, 1955.

Medved, Harry, with Randy Dreyfuss. *The Fifty Worst Films of All Time (And How They Got That Way)*. New York: Popular Library, 1978.

Medved, Harry, and Michael Medved. *The Golden Turkey Awards: The Worst Achievements in Hollywood History*. New York: Berkley Books, 1981.

Peary, Danny, *Cult Movies: The Classics, the Sleepers, the Weird and the Wonderful*. New York: Gramercy Books, 1981.

Ray, Fred Olen. "Edward D. Wood, Jr." *Cult Movies* #11, 1994.

Sarris, Andrew. "Notes on the Auteur Theory in 1962." In *Film Theory and Criticism: Introductory Readings*, 2d Ed. Edited by Gerald Mast and Marshall Cohen. New York: Oxford, 1979.

Sconce, Jeffrey. "Trashing the Academy: Taste, Excess, and an Emerging Politics of Cinematic Style," in *Screen* 36.4 (Winter 1995).

Vogel, Amos. *Film as a Subversive Art*. New York: Random House, 1974.

Walker, Barbara G. *The Crone: Woman of Age, Wisdom, and Power*. San Francisco: HarperCollins, 1985.

Weinstein, David. *The Forgotten Network: Dumont and the Birth of American Television*. Philadelphia: Temple University Press, 2004.

Wood, Edward D., Jr. "Breasts of the Chicken." *Gold Diggers Magazine*, May-June, 1972.

_____. "Come Inn." *Young Beaver Magazine*, February 1971.

_____. *Hollywood Rat Race*. New York: Four Walls Eight Windows, 1998.

_____. *The Horrors of Sex*. Shreveport, LA: Ramble House Press, 2001.

_____. *Killer in Drag*. Angora Press, circa 1967.

_____. *Plan 9 from Outer Space: The Original Uncensored and Uncut Screenplay*. Newbury Park CA: Malibu Graphics, 1990.

_____. *Suburban Orgy*. Shreveport, LA: Ramble House Press, 2001).

_____. *Wood on Screen*. Shreveport, LA: Woodpile Press, 2007.

Index

References to pages with photographs are in **bold italic**.

301